CRIMINAL LAW

AUSTRALIA
Law Book Co.
Sydney

CANADA and USA
Carswell
Toronto

HONG KONG
Sweet & Maxwell Asia

NEW ZEALAND
Brookers
Wellington

SINGAPORE and MALAYSIA
Sweet & Maxwell Asia
Singapore and Kuala Lumpur

CRIMINAL LAW

Fourth Edition

Timothy H. Jones, LL.B., M.Phil., Ph.D.
Professor of Public Law, Swansea University

and

Michael G.A. Christie, M.A., LL.B.
Former Lecturer in Private Law, University of Aberdeen

THOMSON

™

W. GREEN

Published in 2008 by
W. Green & Son Ltd
21 Alva Street
Edinburgh EH2 4PS

www.wgreen.thomson.com

Typeset by J.P. Price, Chilcompton, Somerset
Printed by Ashford Colour Press, Gosport, Hants

No natural forests were destroyed to make this product;
only farmed timber was used and replanted

A CIP catalogue record of this book is available from the British
Library

ISBN 978–0–414–01683–5

PREFACE TO FOURTH EDITION

It is five years since the last edition. During this time, the criminal law of Scotland has continued to respond to its new, devolved and human rights influenced legal environment. Scottish judges and lawyers have accommodated this transformation without significant disruption to the legal system. No doubt the forthcoming period will see further changes, some of which cannot be anticipated at this date. It is encouraging, however, that the Scottish Law Commission has undertaken a thorough review of the law pertaining to sexual offences. It is anticipated that legislative activity will result.

Through all the editions of this book, we have endeavoured to present an account of Scottish criminal law which is sensitive to its traditions, since we value a body of law which has strong roots in the history of the country. At the same time, we have tried to take account of modern, theoretical work on the criminal law. We do not see a conflict between valuing tradition and being open to new ideas. We believe that in this way the criminal law of Scotland will continue to meet contemporary needs as successfully as in the past.

We have been pleased by the generally positive response to the approach that we have taken. This edition therefore adopts substantially the same format as previous editions. We have updated the text to take account of judicial and legislative developments up to March 1, 2008.

T.H.J.
M.G.A.C.

April, 2008

CONTENTS

CONTENTS

TABLE OF CASES

TABLE OF UNITED KINGDOM STATUTES

TABLE OF STATUTES OF THE SCOTTISH PARLIAMENT

Prospective legislation

TABLE OF UNITED KINGDOM STATUTORY INSTRUMENTS

TABLE OF STATUTORY INSTRUMENTS OF THE SCOTTISH PARLIAMENT

TABLE OF CONVENTIONS AND TREATIES

CHAPTER 1

INTRODUCTION TO CRIMINAL LAW

WHAT IS CRIMINAL LAW?

The criminal law consists of a series of rules. These rules define **1–01**
what is not permissible in social conduct according to certain moral
principles or political policies. An example of a moral principle is
that "injuring others in their persons or property is wrong".
Accordingly, the criminal law includes such well-known crimes as
theft, assault and rape. An example of a political policy which
forms the basis of a criminal offence is that a licence must be
purchased for a television receiver.

Public law

It is important to appreciate from the outset that criminal law **1–02**
forms part of "public law", rather than "private law".[1] Private law
(sometimes referred to as "civil law"[2]) is concerned with regulating
disputes which do not directly involve the state. This is not to say
that the state does not take an active interest in areas such as
company law or family law. What it does mean is that governmen-
tal agencies are not directly on the side of one of the litigants: the
state does not claim a direct interest in the outcome of a particular
court case.

The same cannot be said of public law, which relates directly to **1–03**
the state in a political and sovereign role. In a broad sense, public
law is concerned with the structure of government, and the powers,
duties and obligations of public officials and private citizens.
Criminal law has a public law character. A crime constitutes an
offence not just against an individual, but also against the state.
The state must take a direct interest in protecting persons within

---

[1] Erskine, IV, iv, 1, refers to "that part of our public law which relates to crimes".
[2] See, generally, P.H. Robinson, "The Criminal—Civil Distinction and the Utility of
Desert" (1996) 76 *BUL Rev.* 201.

its territory from conduct which has been declared to be, or accepted as, criminal. This feature is reflected in the fact that crimes are generally prosecuted in the name of the Crown on behalf of the community, rather than by privately retained lawyers, let alone aggrieved individuals (see below, para.2–55). Private prosecution indeed is highly exceptional in Scotland (see below, para.2–56). Thus it is that reports of serious criminal cases are cited as *"Her Majesty's Advocate v [name of the accused]"*. Her Majesty's Advocate refers to the chief Scottish law officer of the Crown (more commonly known as the "Lord Advocate"). In less serious cases, the prosecution will be recorded in the name of the local procurator fiscal, holding office under the Lord Advocate. It is these public officials and their deputes who are charged with the task of conducting criminal prosecutions on behalf of the state. Unlike private law litigation, furthermore, where the aggrieved party (the "pursuer" in Scottish terminology) must instigate legal action against the "defender", the Crown, through its appointed representatives, can undertake the prosecution of a person accused of committing a crime, even if this is against the wishes of the victim (or "complainer").

THE PROPER SCOPE OF THE CRIMINAL LAW

1–04 A question which has long been the subject of debate among both criminal lawyers and philosophers is that of the proper scope of the criminal law. In particular, this debate has been concerned with the extent to which the criminal law should be used to enforce moral standards. A number of scholars have argued that society is permitted, and sometimes obliged, to enforce morality by means of the criminal law. The legal philosopher H.L.A. Hart identified two versions of this argument: the "conservative thesis" and the "disintegration thesis".[3] According to Hart, the conservative thesis stands for,

> "the claim that society has the right to enforce its morality by law because the majority have the right to follow their own moral convictions that their moral environment is a thing of value to be defended from change."[4]

Proponents of the disintegration thesis value morality as, "the cement of society, the bond, or one of the bonds, without which men would not cohere in society".[5] It must be upheld in order to

---

[3] H.L.A. Hart, "Social Solidarity and the Enforcement of Morality" (1967) 35 *U Chi L Rev* 1, drawing upon R. Dworkin, "Lord Devlin and the Enforcement of Morals" (1966) 75 *Yale LJ* 986.
[4] H.L.A. Hart, "Social Solidarity and the Enforcement of Morality" (1967) 35 U *Chi L Rev.* 1, 2.
[5] H.L.A. Hart, "Social Solidarity and the Enforcement of Morality" (1967) 35 *U Chi L Rev.* 1, 1.

prevent social disintegration. In his book, *The Enforcement of Morals*, the principal advocate of the disintegration thesis, Lord Devlin, argued that,

> "the law must protect . . . the institutions and the community of ideas, political and moral, without which people cannot live together. Society cannot ignore the morality of the individual any more than it can his loyalty; it flourishes on both and without either it dies."[6]

Writing more than two centuries earlier, the institutional writer Erskine had similarly argued that crimes should be penalised because they threatened to "loosen the bonds of society".[7]

In common parlance, the criminal law tends to be discussed in **1–05** terms of serious crimes against the person (such as murder, rape and assault), and serious crimes against property (including theft, fire-raising and malicious mischief). Questions as to the proper scope of the criminal law do arise, even in relation to such long-recognised crimes. Recent issues before the Scottish courts have included the meaning of consent in the definition of rape,[8] the distinction between murder and culpable homicide where the issue of provocation arises[9] and whether it is competent to charge a company with culpable homicide.[10] However, the main focus of the "criminalisation" debate has tended to be elsewhere, involving those crimes intended to protect public morality, for example, "public indecency" (see below, Ch.12).[11]

Scotland would generally be regarded as having a highly moralis- **1–06** tic criminal law (at least in its origin[12]), but there are types of behaviour which, although generally regarded as immoral, have never been within its scope: for example, breach of contract. Thus, to say that the task of the criminal law is to uphold moral standards is not a sufficient answer to the question as to the proper scope of the criminal law. It merely raises the further issues of how much morality, and whose, the law should uphold. Lord Devlin appeared to concede as much, since he recognised the impossibility of setting theoretical limits on the power of the law to enforce morality. His solution was to apply the standard of the "reasonable" or "right-minded" person, "the man in the jury box", because,

---

[6] Lord Devlin, *The Enforcement of Morals* (London: Oxford University Press, 1965), p.22.
[7] Erskine, IV, iv, 2.
[8] *Lord Advocate's Reference (No.1 of 2001)*, 2002 S.L.T. 466.
[9] *Drury v HM Advocate*, 2001 S.L.T. 1013.
[10] *Transco Plc v HM Advocate (No.1)*, 2004 J.C. 29.
[11] See *Webster v Dominick*, 2003 S.C.C.R. 525.
[12] See, further, L. Farmer, "Narratives of Guilt and Innocence in Scottish Criminal Trials," 2000 J.R. 285, 294–295.

"the moral judgment of society must be something about which any 12 [presumably 15 in Scotland] men or women drawn at random might after discussion be expected to be unanimous."[13]

The harm principle

1–07   A very different approach from that of Lord Devlin can be found in the philosophy of liberalism. The most famous statement of the liberal approach to the role of the law in the maintenance of morality is that of the nineteenth-century philosopher, John Stuart Mill. He maintained,

> "the only purpose for which power can be rightfully exercised over any member of a civilized community, against his will, is to prevent harm to others. His own good, either physical or moral, is not a sufficient warrant."[14]

An individual is only answerable to society for conduct "which concerns others".[15] Under the harm principle, therefore, the individual should be granted the maximum degree of liberty consistent with the rights of others. Thus one might say that an individual should be permitted to behave in a shamelessly indecent fashion, perhaps by showing an obscene film to a number of willing viewers, if no "harm" is caused.[16]

1–08   The harm principle has been developed by Feinberg, who, as a further justification for criminalisation, puts forward an "offense principle". This is based upon the necessity "to prevent serious offense to persons other than the actor".[17] His preferred version of the harm principle is:

> "It is always a good reason in support of penal legislation that it would probably be effective in preventing (eliminating, reducing) harm to persons other than the actor (the one prohibited from acting) *and* there is probably no other means that is equally effective at no greater cost to other values."

This reformulation emphasises a concern with the efficacy of utilising the criminal law.

1–09   The harm principle has been very influential among writers on the criminal law. It captures the common feeling that the interests of the state should make accommodation for individual freedom. It

[13] Devlin, *The Enforcement of Morals* (1965), p.15.
[14] J.S. Mill, *On Liberty* (London: John W. Parker and Son, 1859), Ch.1, para.9.
[15] Mill, *On Liberty* (1859), Ch.1, para.9.
[16] See *Webster v Dominick*, 2003 S.C.C.R. 525, overruling *Watt v Annan*, 1978 J.C. 84.
[17] J. Feinberg, *Harm to Others* (New York: Oxford University Press, 1985), p.26.

also reflects the view that a primary function of the criminal law is the prevention of harm.[18] This approach is very different from that of the disintegration thesis, which asserts that the role of the law is to protect the moral and political institutions of society, and the "community of ideas" necessary for society to cohere (see above, para.1–04). From this perspective, it would be legitimate to criminalise indecent behaviour, even though no "harm" has been caused to anyone, because someone who acts in that fashion (for example, encouraging the patrons of a nightclub to expose their private parts in return for free drinks[19]) could be regarded by the members of a jury as posing a threat to society's moral fabric.

PUNISHMENT

The rules of the criminal law define crimes and can be dis- **1–10** tinguished from those found in other branches of the law by the way in which it is sought to make them effective. As is well understood, those who contravene the criminal law make themselves liable to *punishment.* Indeed, so varied are the moral principles and political policies (which inspire what is not permitted) that it is sometimes suggested that punishment is *the* distinctive characteristic which all crimes share. This, however, leads to the question: "What is punishment?" In times past, the answer would not have proved too difficult—at least in practical terms. When those found to be contraveners of the criminal law were regularly hanged, beheaded, mutilated, branded, whipped or otherwise corporally abused, then punishment clearly entailed the infliction of some kind of physical suffering.[20] But from the nineteenth century onwards, such physical suffering has increasingly come to be regarded as unsuitable in a developed western society. Today, therefore, the principal sanctions for criminal behaviour are expressed as terms of imprisonment or monetary penalties (fines). There are more anodyne alternatives available too—which include probation orders, community service orders and awards of compensation to victims. Since awards of compensation (damages) can also be made under quite different branches of the law (for example, for failing to honour an agreement under the law of contract, or injuring someone by carelessness under the law of delict), and civil penalties are not unknown either (see below, para.2–18), one must endeavour to be much more precise in order to appreciate why punishment is so closely associated with the criminal law.

---

[18] See, more generally, P.H. Robinson, "A Theory of Justification: Societal Harm as a Prerequisite for Criminal Liability" (1975) 23 *U.C.L.A. L Rev* 266, 266–271.
[19] Compare the facts at issue in *Geddes v Dickson,* 2001 J.C. 69, noting the impact of *Webster v Dominick*, 2003 S.C.C.R. 525.
[20] See Hume, *Commentaries*, ii, 488 *et seq.*

1-11   This point was taken up by the American scholar, Henry M. Hart. In a famous article,[21] he stated that the differentiating feature of the criminal law is that only criminal sanctions (that is, punishments) are both accompanied and justified by the condemnation of the community (that is, by a finding of guilt, which is referred to as "conviction"). Accordingly, one could say that it is this feature of the criminal law which distinguishes it from the civil law of contract and delict. The essential quality of punishment for a crime is to be found in the criminal conviction itself. In practice, a requirement to pay damages for breach of contract, or for the consequences of a negligent act, could have a punitive impact as great as the imposition of a fine in a criminal court. The distinctive character of the judgment of a criminal court is to be found in its informational and symbolic function: the formal declaration that the accused has done wrong.[22] Indeed, Hart's preferred definition of a crime was,

> "conduct which, if duly shown to have taken place, will incur a formal and solemn pronouncement of the moral condemnation of the community."[23]

1-12 This definition, however, is only really persuasive in relation to the more serious crimes long recognised by the common law. In modern times, the ambit of the criminal law has expanded enormously. Of course, Henry M. Hart was aware of this development. He remarked upon the unfortunate tendency of modern criminal statutes to punish individuals whose conduct is "morally neutral". Hart considered this to be an abuse, because "a criminal conviction carries with it an ineradicable connotation of moral condemnation and personal guilt."[24] Nevertheless, the problem with Hart's definition remains that it is difficult to maintain that public condemnation always inheres in a criminal conviction. For example, it would be unrealistic to suggest that every individual convicted of careless driving is subject to denunciation by his community. However, this problem is as much one of the adequacy or suitability of a particular sanction, or of the appropriateness of bringing the conduct in question within the scope of the criminal law.[25] The notion of punishment remains central to any plausible and self-

---

[21] H.M. Hart, "The Aims of the Criminal Law" (1958) 23 *Law and Contemp Probs* 401.
[22] See A.P. Simester and G.R. Sullivan, *Criminal Law: Theory and Doctrine*, 2nd edn (Oxford: Hart, 2003), pp. 4–5.
[23] Hart, "The Aims of the Criminal Law" (1958) 23 *Law and Contemp Probs* 401, 405.
[24] Hart, "The Aims of the Criminal Law" (1958) 23 *Law and Contemp Probs* 401, 424.
[25] There have been suggestions that minor violations of the criminal law should be dealt with separately; see, e.g. K. Mann, "Punitive Civil Sanctions: The Middle Ground Between Civil and Criminal Law" (1992) 101 *Yale LJ* 1795.

contained account of the criminal law; and punishment cannot be imposed without conviction by a competent court.

PRINCIPLES OF CRIMINAL RESPONSIBILITY

Conviction certainly entails more than a mere finding that, e.g. "A **1–13** killed B". This in itself is a legally neutral statement. To justify punishment, the stage has to be attained where it is possible to conclude, e.g. that "A is guilty of murdering B". Clearly that stage could not be reached in law if A was an armed police officer who had killed B, a suicide bomber, about to detonate the explosives he was carrying. The prime function of the criminal law is that of articulating the circumstances under which it is justifiable to hold a person punishable for his conduct. This is a two-stage process.

First, there must be examination of what in general will have to **1–14** be shown for conviction to be justified, no matter which particular crime is involved. This concerns what are known as the principles of criminal responsibility. Some basic principles of that sort are considered as part of Ch.2, while the better known and more traditional ones are dealt with in Ch.3 (*actus reus* and *mens rea*), Ch.4 (voluntariness) and Ch.5 (causation). These principles are regarded as essential moral and legal safeguards to ensure that only those who deserve it are in fact convicted and made liable to punishment. If occasionally adherence to these allows a few, possibly "guilty" persons to escape condemnation, this tends to be regarded as an acceptable price to pay. Different legal systems, however, display varied approaches to the acceptability of allowing such escapes from justice. Scottish criminal law, in particular, is currently in a phase of viewing with suspicion the suggestion that such principles should be weighted in favour of accused persons— as readers will doubtless conclude for themselves from their own studies and observations. But where derogations from, or adjustments to, these principles seem to have occurred, it will clearly be necessary to assert some cogent, countervailing justifications. That having been stated, it is also necessary to declare that some of the principles espoused by academic writers and others are controversial—in terms of their interpretation and scope, as well as their applicability (see, in particular, the discussion of the concept of voluntariness in Ch.4). A fair amount of space, therefore, has been reserved for their discussion. As has been aptly written: "We must not be naive about the subtlety with which the law is capable of reflecting fine moral judgments and distinctions."[26]

Secondly, there must be an examination of what precisely has **1–15** been made or declared punishable under Scots law. The principles referred to in the previous paragraph do not provide any guide to

---

[26] N. Lacey, *State Punishment: Political Principles and Community Values* (London: Routledge, 1988), p.71.

the individual acts and omissions that are not permitted under a particular system of law. Although there may be a basic core of crimes (nominally, at least) common to most legal systems, the totality of criminal acts and omissions is usually unique to a particular country or society. Chapters 9 to 12 are, therefore, devoted to a detailed study of selected acts and omissions proscribed under the law of Scotland. Unless plainly stated to the contrary, what is discussed there has no necessary application to the United Kingdom as a whole, or to any other jurisdiction.

AIMS OF THE CRIMINAL LAW

1–16 The aims of the criminal law are very much those of its central characteristic—namely, punishment. The prevailing theoretical approaches to the justification of punishment are retributivism and utilitarianism. Retributivism is founded on the idea that the criminal, because of the wrongdoing, deserves punishment. It is an approach which looks back in time to the commission of the crime in question. Utilitarianism, on the other hand, looks forward to the consequences of imposing punishment. The infliction of punishment upon the wrongdoer is justified because it serves a useful purpose: its imposition will result in benefits to society. In practice, the legal system tends to reflect aspects of both approaches. Criteria derived from both theories are to be found in the most commonly articulated reasons for the imposition of punishment.

Deterrence

1–17 The aim of punishment most closely associated with utilitarianism is deterrence. Unlike the branches of the civil law, which are expressed in terms of conditional causes and effects (for example, if one does not make a will, then one's property on death will devolve in certain predetermined ways), the intention of the criminal law is to *prevent* persons acting (or, sometimes, omitting to act) in particular ways. One could envisage this being promoted by a system of incentives and rewards, such as lower insurance premiums for drivers who avoid committing motoring offences. However, this would be regarded as too fragile a method of preventing harmful, injurious, destructive or antisocial behaviour; and, in practice, criminal justice systems rely on punishment. It would be naive indeed to imagine that the mere threat of punishment could entirely eradicate the sorts of behaviour which have been proscribed by the criminal law. The most that can be hoped for is that the threat will exercise sufficient psychological restraint over the *majority* of the population. The threat itself should be sufficient to deter. For those who were not in fact deterred, punishment within the parameters imposed by the law must actually be imposed with the object of personal deterrence for the future. Publicity for the punishments imposed might also be important in helping to restrain those still wavering on the brink of criminal conduct.

Retribution

Of course, if deterrence were the only aim, then the maximum 1–18 possible penalties would always seem justified, whenever there was an opportunity to impose punishment in fact.[27] This might well be effective in preventing the individuals who were sentenced from committing further crimes, particularly if life imprisonment or capital punishment were to be meted out to them. However, this policy would be counter-productive as far as the rest of society was concerned, if that punishment was not seen to be proportionate to what the individual had actually done. Not only, therefore, should a sentence after conviction aim to deter (both personally and generally); it should also aim to be "just desserts"[28] for what has been done, after all the circumstances have been taken into consideration. This principle of just desserts should not be confused with the biblical enjoinment of an eye for an eye and a tooth for a tooth. Although its advocates do sometimes use it to argue that more punishment than is applied currently can be justified, modern Scots law has departed from corporal punishments. Further, it is clearly impossible to order the rape of a convicted rapist, or take property from a convicted, but destitute thief.[29] Judges are simply required to do the best they can in the way of proportionality, given the circumstances of the offender, the nature of the crime, and what the law will allow. One might think that a victim's views would be relevant to consideration of sentence under this heading, but Scots law has not in the past favoured such an approach.[30]

Reformation

The modern criminal law may also aim to reform or rehabilitate. 1–19 It is unlikely that the primary punishments (prison or fines) will have any such effect. In particular, an enlightened prison regime is currently the exception rather than the rule in Scotland. However, alternative "punishments" (depending on the significance one cares

---

[27] Indeed, it is a familiar criticism of utilitarianism that the punishment of the innocent could be justified in the interests of deterrence. The retributivist has to recognise, however, that any system of criminal justice runs the risk of convicting the innocent. This is why appeals are allowed and there is the opportunity for reconsideration afforded by the Scottish Criminal Cases Review Commission. History shows that no system is foolproof.

[28] The classic account remains A. von Hirsch, *Doing Justice* (North Eastern University Press, 1976). The approach is developed in A. von Hirsch, *Past or Future Crimes. Deservedness and Dangerousness in the Sentencing of Criminals* (New Brunswick, N.J.: Rutgers University Press, 1985) and *Censure and Sanctions* (New York: Oxford University Press, 1991).

[29] This was an issue which taxed I. Kant, *The Philosophy of Law. An Exposition of the Fundamental Principles of Jurisprudence as the Science of Right*, translation by W. Hastie (Edinburgh: T. and T. Clark, 1887), pp.243–244.

[30] *HM Advocate v McKenzie*, 1990 J.C. 62; but note the impact of the Criminal Justice (Scotland) Act 2003, which makes provision for the use of "victim statements" in the sentencing process.

to give to that term), such as community service and probation, do seem to contemplate more than deterrence or retribution (often, one might add, to the dismay of the victims of the crimes in question).

Public protection

1–20   The notion of deterrence implies that an offender, or a potential offender, will be capable of exercising rational judgment and can be deterred by the threat of punishment from infringing the criminal law. Where this is clearly not so, then measures may have to be taken to protect others from the future conduct of that sort of convicted person—which may entail incarceration, or other restraint, far beyond the requirements of simple deterrence or retribution. When insanity is involved, then the same principle applies—although one might not wish (or indeed have) to register a conviction in such a case. Scots law certainly appears to adhere to these particular views (see Ch.4, following).

CRIMINAL PROCEDURE

1–21   The criminal law would be quite ineffective in pursuing its aims unless there were police to detect and deter the commission of crimes, prosecutors to conduct cases against suspected persons, courts to assess the evidence for and against such suspects, the whole panoply of prisons, social work agencies (for probation and community service schemes) and so on. In brief, criminal law requires complementary procedural devices. The law of criminal procedure is, however, generally beyond the scope of this book.[31]

CRIMINAL EVIDENCE

1–22   The success of criminal prosecutions (on which the efficiency of the law is often seen to depend) and the procurement of fair dealing for suspected persons are predicated on the sort of evidence that can be led before a court of law. Again, there are detailed rules, and principles, which operate here; but the law of criminal evidence is generally also beyond the scope of this book.[32]

---

[31] See Renton and Brown's *Criminal Procedure According to the Law of Scotland*, edited by Sir Gerald Gordon, assisted by C.H.W. Gane, 6th edn (Edinburgh: W. Green, 1996).

[32] See F. Raitt, *Evidence*, 3rd edn (Edinburgh: W. Green, 2001); *Walker & Walker on Evidence*, edited by Margaret L. Ross, assisted by James Chalmers, 2nd edn (LexisNexis UK, 2000).

CHAPTER 2

NATURE AND SOURCES OF
SCOTS CRIMINAL LAW

General

Unlike many European countries, e.g. France, Germany, and the **2–01**
USA (both at federal and individual state levels), there is no
criminal code in Scotland.[1] This means that there is no convenient
place where any *official* list or description of Scottish crimes can be
found. Equally there is no authorised account of the principles
which govern the operation of the criminal law. It follows that this
area of the law is less certain (but more flexible) in Scotland than
may be the case elsewhere. Whether this is an advantageous
situation will often depend on the perspective, i.e. whether one
views the matter from the point of view of the accused or the
prosecutor.

Of course, the absence of a code does not make it impossible to **2–02**
give a perfectly intelligible and pragmatic account of Scots criminal
law.[2] Both principles and crime descriptions appear, for example,
in modern textbooks (such as this one) and have been compiled
from authoritative sources. As textbooks themselves are not normally recognised as being in any way authoritative, it is necessary

---

[1] Dissatisfaction with this state of affairs has led a group of Scottish law professors
to draft an unofficial code. The text of that code ("A Draft Criminal Code for
Scotland") together with commentary was published under the auspices of the
Scottish Law Commission in September 2003. For an account by one of the code's
authors of some of the deficiencies she perceives in the existing Scots "common
law" (see below, paras 2–03 to 2–09), see Pamela R. Ferguson, "Codifying
Criminal Law (1): A Critique of Scots Common Law" [2004] Crim.L.R. 49. The
same author also compares the Draft Criminal Code for Scotland with its English
counterpart in "Codifying Criminal Law (2): The Scots and English Draft Codes
Compared" [2004] Crim.L.R. 105. For some critical analysis of a specific part of
the Scots Draft Criminal Code, see Jennifer Temkin, "A New Law on Sexual
Offences for Scotland: A Comment on the Draft Criminal Code", 2006 J.R. 29;
and for some acknowledgment of the usefulness of the draft code, see "Report on
Rape and Other Sexual Offences", Scot. Law Com. No.209 (December 2007),
para.1.9.

[2] See below, Ch.14.

to appreciate what are the true legal sources on which their authors have relied. These sources must invariably be checked too before any legal opinion based on textbook or periodical literature is ventured. Although legal sources may be described as a constant, interpretation of what they are found to contain is a very real variable of which careful account must be taken.

SOURCES—THE COMMON LAW

2–03 Traditionally, rules pertaining to the "common law" are said to be those of such long standing that their origins cannot be traced. Such rules are often described as "consuetudinary", i.e. customary. Alternatively, if a rule does in fact have a clear origin, it is still reckoned as a common law one if it has no *legislative* foundation. More practically, however, it is the criminal law expounded by judges of the superior criminal courts in actual proceedings before them which lawyers are wont to refer to as "common law". The superior criminal courts in Scotland for this purpose are the High Court of Justiciary as a trial court and the High Court of Justiciary as an appeal court (in the widest sense).[3] Since 1999, decisions of the Judicial Committee of the Privy Council[4] on "devolution issues"[5] referred or appealed to them[6] must be included[7] where such issues are concerned with matters affecting the common law—as, for example, where claims should be made that the Lord Advocate has undertaken (or proposes to undertake) the prosecution of a common law crime which allegedly does not conform to applicable rights under the European Convention on Human Rights.[8]

---

[3] See *Jessop v Stevenson*, 1988 J.C. 17 at 20, final paragraph; *Elliott v HM Advocate*, 1995 S.L.T. 612, Lord Justice-Clerk Ross at 615K–L.

[4] When the relevant provisions of the Constitutional Reform Act 2005 come into force, the jurisdiction of the Judicial Committee of the Privy Council in devolution issues will be transferred to the Supreme Court of the United Kingdom: see Pt 3, especially ss.23, 40(4)(b), and also Sch.9, especially paras 93, 103, 106.

[5] See below, para.2–13.

[6] See the Scotland Act 1998 Sch.6 paras 9, 11, 13, 33, 34: note that paras 11, 13, 33, 34 are prospectively amended by the Constitutional Reform Act 2005 Sch.9 paras 103(5), (8), 106(4), (5); see above, fn.4.

[7] Such decisions are binding on all courts, other than the Judicial Committee itself: see the Scotland Act 1998 s.103. When the Supreme Court of the United Kingdom assumes the jurisdiction of the Judicial Committee of the Privy Council in devolution issues, that court's decisions on such issues will not be binding on the court itself but will be binding "in all [other] legal proceedings": see the Constitutional Reform Act 2005 s.41(3); and see above, fn.4.

[8] *cf. Smith v Donnelly*, 2001 J.C. 65, where a devolution issue was raised on the basis that the common law offence of breach of the peace was too vaguely defined to conform with Art.7 of the European Convention on Human Rights. An appeal against the decision of the Scottish Appeal Court to the Judicial Committee of the Privy Council does not seem to have been attempted—although such an appeal would have been competent, with the appropriate leave.

The High Court of Justiciary was altered to more or less its **2–04** modern form in 1672,[9] but its authenticated history can be traced for many centuries prior to that. To establish any part of the common law through judicial decisions from earliest times down to the present would thus be a mammoth task involving (inter alia) painstaking research in the records of the court as these are preserved in the Scottish National Archives in Edinburgh. In practice then, a simpler route has evolved.

Professor (sometimes "Baron") David Hume made a study of **2–05** what might be gleaned from High Court decisions down to 1797. With some (minor) additions of his own, he was thus able to deduce and publish an account of the common law of Scotland pertaining to criminal matters. Two new editions were produced by him which updated the common law to 1819 and 1829. He died in 1838, but a prominent advocate (Benjamin R. Bell) republished the 1829 edition together with updating notes of his own (drawn from High Court decisions) in 1844. This is invariably, though not quite accurately, referred to as the fourth edition of Hume's *Commentaries*. This work has for many decades been accorded authoritative status. Whenever a question relating to the common law of crimes is at issue, the starting point for Scottish lawyers (and sometimes the end point too) is any statement Hume might have made on the matter. Occasionally, judges of the High Court have disagreed with his pronouncements,[10] but more often than not, they have treated his writings with the utmost deference.[11] Hume's *Commentaries* are, therefore, much more than a mere textbook. They are regarded as an important *source* of the common law of crimes at the time they were written, and indeed as the initial point for subsequent research into the present state of that common law.

It is necessary to establish an initial point for research since the **2–06** common law is constantly being developed by High Court judges in actual criminal proceedings before them. So long as there is a common law of crimes in Scotland, this evolutionary process will continue. That process applies to the definitions of existing crimes, defences to those crimes, evidential and procedural matters, and even to principles. The notion of flexible development is simply inseparable from the notion of common law, insofar as Scots criminal law is concerned. Nor is such development of the law necessarily incompatible with the European Convention on Human Rights (insofar as the Convention rights have been incorporated within domestic law by virtue of the Human Rights Act 1998)

---

[9] See the Scots Act c.40 in A.P.S. viii, 80, 87–88.
[10] See, e.g. *John Smith* (1838) 2 Swin. 28; *S v HM Advocate*, 1989 S.L.T. 469; *Lord Advocate's Reference (No.1 of 2001)*, 2002 S.L.T. 466.
[11] See, e.g. *Thomson v HM Advocate*, 1983 J.C. 69; *Khaliq v HM Advocate*, 1984 J.C. 23; *Drury v HM Advocate*, 2001 S.L.T. 1013.

provided that that development remains within reasonable and foreseeable bounds.[12]

2–07　　There are some other text-writings which judges of the High Court have looked upon with something of the same favour accorded to Hume. Foremost among these is Archibald Alison's *Principles of the Criminal Law of Scotland*, published in 1832. Although this work relies heavily on Hume's earlier text, it nevertheless, "draws freely on [Alison's] own experience as an advocate-depute [i.e. criminal prosecutor] and quotes over 1,000 cases in which he was personally engaged and of which there was and is no other published report".[13] It is also possible that J.H.A. Macdonald's *Practical Treatise on the Criminal Law of Scotland* (latest edition 1948) may continue to enjoy some particular authority over and above its status as an important textbook of the nineteenth and twentieth centuries.[14]

2–08　　No text-writings, other than those mentioned above, have been regarded as sources of criminal common law. For example, the outstanding work of scholarship written in the twentieth century on Scots criminal law, Gordon's *Criminal Law*,[15] contains much lucid, influential and persuasive writing on the subject; but the author's opinions and deductions have very rarely been preferred to those of Hume, Alison and Macdonald.[16]

2–09　　The present common law, then, consists of the deductions, conclusions and opinions of Hume, Alison and Macdonald together with such alterations, additions and amendments as have been made to date by appropriate courts[17] in particular criminal proceedings before them. Since the early nineteenth century, such proceedings have been published in a variety of different law reports (see Appendix B), and these provide the most important modern source of the common law.

---

[12] See, e.g. *SW v United Kingdom; CR v United Kingdom* (1996) 21 E.H.R.R. 363, especially at 398–399, paras 35/33, 36/34; see also *HM Advocate v H*, 2002 S.L.T. 1380, per Lord Maclean at 1381, para.5, and *Lucas v United Kingdom* (2003) 37 E.H.R.R. (CD) 86—the judgment in which being conveniently set out at 2004 S.C.C.R. at 377F-383C. Reference should also be made to Ch.14.

[13] Sheriff J. Irvine Smith at p.vii of his introduction to the 1989 reprint of Alison's *Principles* (Butterworth).

[14] *cf.* the opinion of Lord Cameron in *Watt v Annan*, 1978 J.C. 84 at 88 *et seq.*, and that of Lord Justice-Clerk Gill in *Webster v Dominick*, 2005 1 J.C. 65 at 78, para.44; *cf.* also *Drury v HM Advocate*, 2001 S.L.T. 1013, where Macdonald's account of murder was considered to be incomplete, if not erroneous.

[15] G.H. Gordon, *Criminal Law* (Edinburgh: SULI/W. Green, 1968). The current edition is the third, edited by Michael G.A. Christie, Vol.1 (2000), Vol.2 (2001), to which there is a supplement (2005).

[16] See, e.g. *Smart v HM Advocate*, 1975 J.C. 30; *Roberts v Hamilton*, 1989 J.C. 91; *Scott v HM Advocate*, 1995 S.C.C.R. 760. Although the trial judge, Lord Osborne, referred to academic writings as part of the reason for the directions he gave the jury in *Jamieson v HM Advocate (No.1)*, 1994 S.L.T. 537 at 539H, those writings were entirely ignored by the Appeal Court in deciding that what he had said amounted to a misdirection in law.

[17] See above, para.2–03.

SOURCES—LEGISLATION

Legislation refers to technically written rules promulgated in a **2–10** predefined way at a particular point in time by a person or body recognised as having the authority to do so. Such rules differ from those of the common law in that they are not subject to similar development, i.e. they cannot be added to or altered by judges in actual criminal proceedings before them. They may only be enlarged or amended by subsequent acts of legislation. Of course, judges can interpret the words of such rules. Indeed they must do this if the arid generalisations of legislation are to be made applicable to (and thus decisive of) actual criminal cases. If such interpretations are made by judges of the High Court of Justiciary, then such decisions make law in a very real sense. The interpretations then become part of the legislative rule itself. But it is not the case that such interpretations would ever be spoken of as forming part of the common law. Common law and legislation thus remain separate sources of the criminal law; but, although the common law can have no effect on existing legislation, the converse is not true. Legislative rules can radically alter portions of the common law (see, e.g. s.13[18] of the Criminal Law (Consolidation) (Scotland) Act 1995, which radically alters the common law prohibition against male homosexual practices).

Parliamentary Legislation

The supreme source of criminal legislation in Scotland is Parlia- **2–11** ment. Today, there are two parliaments to consider—the United Kingdom Parliament in London (hereafter referred to as "Parliament", for convenience), and the Scottish Parliament in Edinburgh[19]: the former of these enjoys absolute sovereignty over the whole of the United Kingdom, whilst the latter is able to legislate only for Scotland and within parameters set for it by Parliament under the Scotland Act 1998.[20] Parliament may enact what it pleases; and a great deal of criminal law for the United Kingdom, and for Scotland in particular, has been produced in this way.[21] Primary legislation[22] enacted by

---

[18] As amended by the Sexual Offences (Amendment) Act 2000 ss.1(3), 2(4), the Convention Rights (Compliance) (Scotland) Act 2001 (asp 7) s.10, and the Mental Health (Care and Treatment) (Scotland) Act 2003 (asp 13) Sch.5 Pt 1.

[19] The Scottish Parliament must not be confused with the old Scots Parliament which legislated for Scotland until disbanded under the terms of the Union with England Treaty in 1707: see A.P.S. xi, 406 *et seq.* Legislation of the old Scots Parliament was not set aside in 1707; but that legislation has gradually been removed or radically altered by various "Statute Law Revision" or "Statute Law Repeals" Acts of Parliament. Enactments of the old Scots Parliament are now of little importance to the criminal law.

[20] Hereafter, in this chapter, referred to as the "1998 Act".

[21] Thus, e.g. all the law on offences relating to road traffic matters and prohibited drugs has been enacted by Parliament.

[22] As opposed to "delegated or subordinate" legislation: see below, para.2–14.

Parliament is referred to as an "Act of Parliament" or a "statute". So absolute is Parliament's sovereignty that it is possible (although unlikely) for it to enact legislation which is not compatible with the rights and fundamental freedoms of the European Convention on Human Rights, as these rights and freedoms (known as "Convention rights") have been brought within the law of the United Kingdom by the Human Rights Act 1998[23]: should this happen, and the legislation cannot be interpreted so as to conform with Convention rights, the validity and enforceability of that legislation is unaffected—and the most which can be done by courts is to issue a "declaration of incompatibility".[24] The position of the Scottish Parliament is, however, somewhat different, in that its powers have been devolved from the sovereign United Kingdom Parliament.

The Scottish Parliament

2–12   The Scottish Parliament, which met for the first time in 1999, has the authority to make laws known as "Acts of the Scottish Parliament".[25] Such Acts must, however, conform to the "legislative competence" set for it under the 1998 Act: in particular, it must not enact laws which would apply outwith Scotland,[26] relate to reserved matters,[27] or be incompatible with any of the Convention rights (as set out in the Human Rights Act 1998) or with European Community law.[28] Any Act which exceeds the Scottish Parliament's legislative competence is simply not law.[29] Even where matters do fall within the legislative competence of the Scottish Parliament, the United Kingdom Parliament retains overall power of enactment, thus maintaining its absolute sovereignty.[30] Scottish criminal law is, however, devolved to the Scottish Parliament, and it may thus legislate for Scotland relative to criminal offences, jurisdiction, evidence, procedure, penalties and the treatment of offenders.[31] The offices of the chief Scottish prosecutors, i.e. the offices of the

---

[23] See s.1 and Sch.1 (both as amended by art.2 of the Human Rights Act 1998 (Amendment) Order 2004 (SI 2004/1574)) of the Human Rights Act 1998.

[24] See Human Rights Act 1998 ss.3, 4: not all courts have this power—see s.4(5) and *Smith v Scott*, 2007 S.L.T. 137 (a decision by three judges, of the Court of Session, constituting the Registration Appeal Court). See also s.10 of the 1998 Act. (It should be noted that s.4(5) is amended by the Mental Capacity Act 2005 Sch.6 para.43, and by the Armed Forces Act 2006 Sch.16 para.156; it is also prospectively amended by the Constitutional Reform Act 2005 Sch.9 para.66.)

[25] See the 1998 Act s.28(1).

[26] As defined in s.126(1) of the 1998 Act; and see s.29(2)(a).

[27] As set out in Sch.5 of the 1998 Act—which include matters and offences relating to misuse of drugs, firearms, official secrets, road traffic, and, abortion (see Sch.5 Pt II ss.B1, B4 and B8, E1 and J1: and see s.29(2)(b)).

[28] See s.29(2)(d) of the 1998 Act.

[29] 1998 Act s.29(1); *cf. Adams v The Scottish Ministers*, 2003 S.L.T. 366, OH.

[30] See s.28(7) of the 1998 Act.

[31] See s.126(5) of the 1998 Act: Sch.5 must be consulted, however, for specific matters which are reserved to Parliament.

Lord Advocate (sometimes referred to as "Her Majesty's Advocate") and Solicitor General for Scotland, are now offices within the "Scottish Executive" of the Scottish Parliament; and all members of the Scottish Executive are collectively known as the "Scottish Ministers".[32] It follows, therefore, that most functions to be performed in Scotland by Ministers of the Crown under United Kingdom Parliamentary legislation, i.e. legislation enacted prior to the commencement of the 1998 Act, will now be performed in Scotland by the Scottish Ministers.[33]

Devolution issues

Issues relating to the competence of the Scottish Parliament to **2–13** enact particular laws, or to the way in which members of the Scottish Executive (in particular, the chief prosecutors or law officers) carry out or propose to carry out their functions, may arise before or be referred to the courts. These are generally known as "devolution issues". For the purposes of this book, the most important of these issues concern the following: whether an Act of the Scottish Parliament falls within that Parliament's legislative competence[34]; whether the purported or proposed exercise of a function by a member of the Scottish Executive (in particular by the Lord Advocate[35] in undertaking criminal proceedings against a person for a particular crime) is incompatible with any of the relevant rights and fundamental freedoms of the European Convention on Human Rights[36]; and, whether the failure by a member of the Scottish Executive (in particular the Lord Advocate) to act is incompatible with any of these rights and freedoms.[37] Such issues may arise, of course, before any Scottish criminal court; but district

---

[32] See s.44(1), (2) of the 1998 Act; *cf.* the current *de facto* position—see 2007 S.L.T. (News) 116.

[33] See s.53 of the 1998 Act.

[34] This is important since if any provision of an Act is not within the Scottish Parliament's legislative competence, that Act cannot be treated as law: s.29(1) of the 1998 Act. See, e.g. *A. v The Scottish Ministers*, 2002 S.C. (P.C.) 63.

[35] This reference includes any person (such as a procurator fiscal) deriving authority from the Lord Advocate, but not (unusually) if such a person is at the relevant time performing a statutory duty *ex officio* where he neither acts on behalf nor comes within the responsibility of the Lord Advocate: see *Goatley v HM Advocate*, 2007 S.L.T. 14, opinion of the court at 19J–L, para.15 (relative to the Crown Agent).

[36] This refers to those rights and freedoms (the Convention rights) brought into United Kingdom law by the Human Rights Act 1998. It should also be noted that under s.57(2) of the Scotland Act 1998, members of the Scottish Executive (including, of course, the Lord Advocate and Solicitor General for Scotland) have no power to do any act insofar as that act is incompatible with any Convention right or with European Community Law: see, e.g. *Stevens v HM Advocate*, 2002 S.L.T. 1249, Lady Paton at 1252K–1253 B, paras 18–20; see also *HM Advocate v H*, 2002 S.L.T. 1380, and *cf. Dickson v HM Advocate*, 2008 S.L.T. 12 (court of five judges).

[37] See Sch.6 Pt I para.1(a), (d), (e) of the 1998 Act.

courts (or J.P. courts), sheriff courts and trial courts of the High Court[38] may refer such issues to the High Court of Justiciary (sitting as a non-trial court)[39] for resolution there: and, indeed, if such an issue arises in proceedings before a bench of two or more judges of the High Court, that court may choose to refer the determination of the issue to the Judicial Committee of the Privy Council,[40] which normally sits in London. The intention appears to be that disputes over devolution issues should be debated and settled at a high level of the court hierarchy; and, further, provision is made for appeals (with leave) from the decision on a devolution issue by a bench of two or more judges of the High Court to the Judicial Committee of the Privy Council.[41] Provision is also made for the Lord Advocate or the Advocate General[42] to require a Scottish court to refer a devolution issue which has arisen before it to the Judicial Committee of the Privy Council, provided that the Lord Advocate or Advocate General is a party to these proceedings.[43] Despite the fact, however, that many constitutional matters may fall to be decided ultimately by the Judicial Committee (because of that court's role in the determination of devolution issues), that committee is not as such a constitutional court[44]; and constitutional matters which are not also devolution issues cannot be heard by it.[45]

SUBORDINATE (OR DELEGATED) LEGISLATION

2–14   The United Kingdom Parliament, and now the Scottish Parliament, may permit other persons or bodies to create legislation. Thus, Acts of Parliament or Acts of the Scottish Parliament may delegate

---

[38] See Appendix D. "High Court" is an abbreviation for the "High Court of Justiciary".

[39] 1998 Act Sch.6 Pt II para.9. It is assumed that such a High Court will consist of a bench of at least three judges: but *cf. Stevens v HM Advocate*, 2002 S.L.T. 1249, where Lady Paton opined that it was not necessary under the terms of s.4 of the Human Rights Act 1998 for more than one judge of the High Court to determine the compatibility with Convention rights of a particular provision of a statute passed by the United Kingdom Parliament.

[40] For the prospective effect of the Constitutional Reform Act 2005 on the jurisdiction of the Judicial Committee of the Privy Council, see above, fn.4.

[41] 1998 Act Sch.6 Pt II para.13 (as amended prospectively by the Constitutional Reform Act 2005 Sch.9 para.103). See, e.g. *HM Advocate v R.*, 2003 S.L.T. 4.

[42] The Advocate General for Scotland is the law officer who advises the United Kingdom Government on Scottish legal matters: see s.87 of the 1998 Act.

[43] 1998 Act Sch.6 Pt V para.33; see, e.g. *Spiers v Ruddy*, 2008 S.C.C.R. 131: for the prospective effect of the Constitutional Reform Act 2005 (in terms of Sch.9 paras 93 and 106 thereof) on the jurisdiction of the Judicial Committee of the Privy Council, see generally, above, fn.4.

[44] Nor will the "Supreme Court of the United Kingdom" be such a court when (inter alia) it eventually displaces the jurisdiction of the Judicial Committee of the Privy Council in respect of devolution issues: see above, fn.4: *cf.* the role of the Supreme Court in the United States of America.

[45] See *Hoekstra v HM Advocate (No.5)*, 2001 S.C. (P.C.) 37; *cf. Mills v HM Advocate (No.2)*, 2001 S.L.T. 1359 at 1365B–C, where the court actually refers to the Judicial Committee of the Privy Council's role as "a constitutional court", in the context of the constitutional settlement effected by the 1998 Act.

the power to legislate—always making clear, of course, the parameters within which the person (typically a secretary of state) or body, e.g. the Scottish Ministers, in question must operate. As far as Scottish delegated (or subordinate) legislation is concerned, what is enacted will not be law if it would have been outwith the legislative competence of the Scottish Parliament were it to have been included in a statute[46]; and a member of the Scottish Executive has no power to make any subordinate legislation which would be incompatible with any of the Convention rights[47] or with European Community law.[48]

A great deal of the criminal law is now to be found in such delegated (or subordinate) legislation, especially, for example, much of the road traffic law; and many criminal procedure rules are to be found in law-making which has been delegated to the judges of the High Court of Justiciary.[49]

Types of subordinate legislation

Legislation, made by a Secretary of State, the Scottish Ministers, **2–15** or the High Court of Justiciary under the authority of a Parliamentary Act, always has the title and form of a "Statutory Instrument" or "Scottish Statutory Instrument",[50] and may be found in any well-stocked law library or by calling up the appropriate web sites.[51] "Byelaws", however, make up a separate form of delegated legislation. In particular, Scottish local authorities may make these, their powers to do so being apparently very wide:

> "A local authority may make byelaws for the good rule and government of the whole or any part of their area, and for the prevention and suppression of nuisances therein."[52]

Their discretion here, however, is contained by the requirement that any proposed byelaw should first have been confirmed by the Scottish Ministers[53] before it acquires the force of law. Byelaws

---

[46] 1998 Act s.54. See above, para.2–12.
[47] i.e. those parts of the European Convention on Human Rights taken into United Kingdom law by virtue of the Human Rights Act 1998.
[48] See s.57(2) of the 1998 Act.
[49] See the Criminal Procedure (Scotland) Act 1995 s.305. Rules of procedure enacted by the High Court are called "Acts of Adjournal".
[50] The standard abbreviation for a statutory instrument is "SI"; for a Scottish Statutory Instrument the abbreviation is "SSI". Acts of Adjournal enacted by the High Court are published as statutory instruments in terms of the Law Reform (Miscellaneous Provisions) (Scotland) Act 1966 s.10.
[51] For SIs, the address is: *http://www.opsi.gov.uk/stat.htm* [accessed February 29, 2008]; and for SSIs, one must envoke:
http://www.scotland-legislation.hmso.gov.uk/legislation/scotland/s-stat.htm [accessed February 29, 2008].
[52] Local Government (Scotland) Act 1973 s.201(1), (2), as amended by the Local Government etc. (Scotland) Act 1994 s.180(1), Sch.13 para.92(61).
[53] See s.53 of the Scotland Act 1998.

certainly form a source (although admittedly a minor source) of criminal law.[54]

In addition to byelaws, a Scottish local authority or National Park Authority can make "Management Rules" relating to the conduct of persons on property which the authority owns or manages. Whilst it is not a crime to contravene such rules, it is an offence to refuse to leave such property when an authorised officer requires one to do so on the grounds that a breach of the rules has taken place or is likely to happen.[55]

Extra-national legislation

2–16 Since the accession of the United Kingdom (and thus Scotland) to the European Community (known as the European Economic Community prior to the coming into force of the Treaty on European Union in November 1993),[56] certain Community legislation (in particular regulations) promulgated by the Council or the Commission is of direct effect within Scotland, and automatically supersedes any existing (and contrary) national law. Other Community legislation, e.g. Directives, requires express implementation in this country before the expiry of predetermined calendar dates.[57] Where implementation is required, however, this can be achieved by (for example) mere ministerial regulations or orders in council—although no really serious crimes can be created in Scotland in such ways.[58] Nevertheless, the importance of Community law as a source of criminal law is constantly increasing, especially in the areas of road traffic law and environmental protection. Where Community law is of relevance to the criminal law, questions of interpretation are bound to arise. Under Art.234 of the Treaty Establishing the European Community,[59] national courts may request preliminary rulings from the European Court of Justice as to the interpretation and validity of Community laws,

---

[54] See, e.g. *McCallum v Brown*, 2000 J.C. 6. See also Gordon Junor, "Byelaws—By Law", 2002 S.L.T. (News) 131.

[55] See the Civic Government (Scotland) Act 1982 ss.112–118, as extended and modified by the National Parks (Scotland) Act 2000 (asp 10) Sch.2 para.10.

[56] See the European Communities Act 1972, as amended.

[57] See the consolidated version of the Treaty Establishing the European Community 1957, as amended, Art.249 (originally Art.189); European Communities Act 1972 s.2, as amended in particular by the Legislative and Regulatory Reform Act 2006 s.27(1).

[58] See the European Communities Act 1972 s.2(2)(a) (amended as in fn.57, above, and as varied *quoad* the Scottish Ministers by art.3 of the Scotland Act 1998 (Transfer of Functions to the Scottish Ministers etc.) Order 2005 (SI 2005/849)) and Sch.2 para.1(1)(d), as amended by the 1998 Act Sch.8 para.15.

[59] Consolidated version: the Article was originally numbered 177.

and Scottish courts have made such requests on several occasions.[60] If the meaning of a particular piece of Community legislation is plain, however, Scottish courts may give it that meaning without resort to the European Court.[61] Equally, where there are previous rulings of the European Court which are applicable to the case on hand, Scottish courts are bound to take account of those rulings.[62]

Jurisprudence of the European Court of Human Rights

Under the provisions of the Human Rights Act 1998, parts of **2-17** the European Convention on Human Rights have been incorporated within Scots (and United Kingdom) law. Thus, persons charged with, and/or proceeded against, for offences have the benefit of the applicable rights and fundamental freedoms (the "Convention rights") set out in Sch.1 to the Act[63]; and the jurisprudence of the European Court of Human Rights (and other judicial organs at one time established under the terms of the Convention) must be taken into account by any court in Scotland (or indeed elsewhere in the United Kingdom) in determining any issue relative to Convention rights which has arisen in proceedings before it.[64] The Human Rights Act also makes it unlawful[65] for a public authority (which includes expressly any court and impliedly any public prosecutor[66]) to act (or fail to act) in any way which is incompatible with applicable Convention rights—as, presumably, these rights are understood in the jurisprudence of the European

---

[60] See, e.g. *Wither v Cowie*, 1994 S.L.T. 363 (where, inter alia, a Council regulation required Member States to notify the Commission of any change to their existing sea-fishing laws, and a sheriff court requested a preliminary ruling on the validity of UK fishing laws which had been implemented without such prior notification), and *Walkingshaw v Marshall*, 1992 S.L.T. 1167 (where certain UK legislation, prohibiting the carriage of particular types of nets by British registered fishing vessels in Scottish inshore waters, having been attacked as both discriminatory and contrary to the principle of proportionality and thus contrary to Community law, was referred by the High Court of Justiciary to the European Court for a preliminary ruling as to its validity).

[61] See, e.g. *Westwater v Thomson*, 1993 S.L.T. 703—although it was emphasised there that the principles to be employed in interpreting Community law are those of the European Community and not those of the domestic law of Scotland.

[62] See, e.g. *Baron Meats Ltd v Lockhart*, 1991 J.C. 129, where the High Court of Justiciary followed a prior decision of the European Court on the meaning of "door to door selling" as applicable to vehicles fitted out as mobile shops.

[63] See the Human Rights Act 1998 s.7(1).

[64] See the Human Rights Act 1998 s.2. Notice that the courts are not bound by such jurisprudence, but are simply required to take it into account. It is anticipated, however, that courts will be slow to depart from opinions cast by the European Court of Human Rights itself. Notice too that Convention rights issues will often coincide with devolution issues: see above, para.2-13.

[65] This does not mean that a criminal offence is thereby committed: see s.7(8), "Nothing in this Act creates a criminal offence."

[66] Under s.6(3) of the Human Rights Act 1998, a public authority includes a court and any person whose functions include functions of a public nature.

Court of Human Rights.[67] If a court finds that an act (or omission) by a public authority is thus unlawful, that court may grant such relief (within its powers) as it considers "just and appropriate".[68] In addition, the same Act preserves the right of an individual to petition the European Court of Human Rights directly—once all available avenues of relief under Scots law have been explored without success.[69]

THE DEFINITION OF CRIME

2–18 Among other things, the sources of the criminal law referred to above should reveal the current catalogue of crimes. A comprehensive yet succinct definition of what makes any particular act or omission or situation criminal rather than not is probably an impossibility, given the enormous range of matters which are definitely criminal.[70] There seems little to connect (morally or otherwise), e.g. the deliberate killing of another human being (intentional murder at common law) and trading as a window cleaner without having obtained a licence.[71] It is possible, of course, to refer to the threat of punishment which is often said uniquely to underlie any truly criminal proscription (see above, Ch.1). But this raises the problem of what content should be given to the term "punishment". Under the Local Government Finance Act 1992,[72] for example, a failure to supply particular information to a local authority in connection with council tax results in the imposition of a penalty of £50 (rising to £200 for subsequent failures). The imposition of such penalties might well be taken as punishment of a very real sort; but it is abundantly clear that no crime is intended or involved. It is equally possible to stress that crimes are uniquely the objects of a particular type of procedure—involving prosecutors, courts and proceedings which are very definitely different from anything encountered in the civil law field.[73] But such attempts at definition are problematic, often circular and perhaps unnecessary. Modern statutes invariably identify clearly what is intended to be criminal by employing the word "offence" (virtually a legal synonym for "crime") in the context of "summary" or "indictment", i.e. plainly criminal, procedure. The

---

[67] See s.6(1), (3), (6): under subs.(2), there is no unlawfulness if the public authority could not have acted differently due to the terms of applicable primary (and sometimes subordinate) legislation.

[68] See s.8 of the Human Rights Act 1998; *cf.* s.9.

[69] See s.11 of the Human Rights Act 1998.

[70] See Gordon, *Criminal Law*, 3rd edn, Ch.1; J.C. Smith and B. Hogan, *Criminal Law*, edited by Sir John Smith, 10th edn (LexisNexis UK, 2002), Ch.2.

[71] Civic Government (Scotland) Act 1982 ss.7 and 43.

[72] See s.97(4) and Sch.3 of the Local Government Finance Act 1992. The Treasury has the authority (under Sch.3 para.5) to alter the value of the penalties set out in the text.

[73] Gordon, *Criminal Law*, 3rd edn, para.1.04.

maximum fine or period of imprisonment will also clearly be stated. The identification of what is criminal under legislative provisions is, therefore, unlikely to present difficulties.

In the common law field, where inevitably matters are rather **2–19** more fluid, identification of particular acts or omissions as criminal or not may indeed pose occasional problems. But even here, resort is not had to any standard definition of the essence of "crime". Such issues of identification are resolved by the "inherent" power of the High Court of Justiciary to declare the common law, which it does from time to time in particular cases according to *ad hoc* criteria of its own choosing.

THE DECLARATORY POWER OF THE HIGH COURT

In "declaring the common law", the High Court may simply be **2–20** declaring the ambit of a known crime (a function usually accepted as necessary under any common law system),[74] or (more specifically) correcting errors into which previous courts had fallen[75]; or it might be purporting to exercise a distinct power to criminalise behaviour which was not previously known to be criminal. Any exercise of such a distinct power (usually referred to as the "declaratory power") would now be contrary to the principles of clarity, accessibility and non-retroactivity of criminal provisions— principles which are expressed in, or implied by Art.7(1) of the European Convention on Human Rights.[76] In more detail, the main principle here (sometimes expressed in Latin as *nullum crimen sine lege*) enjoins that no one should be convicted for an act or omission which was not clearly and knowably criminal at the time it was done. A corollary may also be stated—namely that no one should be denied a defence which was clearly relevant and available in law at the time of commission of some act or omission. Insofar, therefore, as it might purport to recognise a power of the courts to make new common law crimes or cancel common law

---

[74] See below, Ch.14, especially para.14–08 *et seq.*, for a discussion of the High Court's ability to develop the law in this way.

[75] See, e.g. *Brennan v HM Advocate*, 1977 J.C. 38, overruling *Kennedy v HM Advocate*, 1944 J.C. 171, in which the High Court had erroneously followed English law; *Galbraith v HM Advocate (No.2)*, 2001 S.C.C.R. 551, overruling *Connelly v HM Advocate*, 1990 S.C.C.R. 504, in which the High Court had interpreted the defence of diminished responsibility too restrictively; *Lord Advocate's Reference (No.1 of 2001)*, 2002 S.L.T. 466, overruling *HM Advocate v Sweenie* (1858) 3 Irv. 109, in which the High Court had misinterpreted the essential elements of rape; and *Webster v Dominick*, 2005 1 J.C. 65, overruling *Watt v Annan*, 1978 J.C. 84, in which the High Court had erroneously confirmed as criminal, conduct described as "shamelessly indecent".

[76] See above, para.2–17. See also Jacobs and White, *The European Convention on Human Rights*, edited by C. Ovey and R. White, 3rd edn (New York: Oxford University Press, 2002), p.187 *et seq.*

defences in actual cases, Scots criminal law would breach these principles.[77]

During the time when a "declaratory power" was believed to be possessed lawfully by the courts, however, the writers who espoused it and the judges who operated it might be thought to have given some useful guidance relative to the circumstances in which a new crime could legitimately be created, i.e. some useful guidance on what identifies particular behaviour as criminal. This matter is briefly considered in the paragraphs which follow.

Historical authority for the existence of the power

2–21   It appears that the first written notice of such a power was given by Hume in the 1797 edition of the *Commentaries*[78] although he gives few examples of its actual use. That might give rise to the charge that the declaratory power was something of a novelty—if not a product of the author's own imagination—but Alison[79] also refers to it, independently of any reference to Hume, and apparently quotes 16 different instances of its application. The judges of the High Court also endorsed the existence of the power in many cases.[80] There is also clear confirmation of this situation in Macdonald,[81] although his primary (footnote) authority is given as Hume. There can be little doubt, therefore, that the authoritative text-writers and the judges themselves asserted the right of the High Court of Justiciary to enlarge the contents of the common law; but what principles would have to be satisfied before particular behaviour could be criminalised, and how would the High Court have had to be constituted in order to make criminal what was not known to have been criminal before? Attempting to answer these questions posed certain difficulties.

---

[77] Adherence to such principles, and Convention rights generally in the matter of legislation is, of course, the responsibility of Parliament, although all criminal courts are obliged to interpret legislation so as to conform with Convention rights: see the Scotland Act 1998 s.101; the Human Rights Act 1998 s.3. In respect of the Scottish Parliament, any enactment which is not in conformity with Convention rights is not within its legislative competence, and, therefore, would not be law: Scotland Act 1998 s.29.

[78] Hume, *Commentaries*, i, 52; 1844 edn, i, 12.

[79] Alison, *Principles*, i, 624 *et seq.*

[80] See *Taylor,* October 19, 1808, Burnett App. no. x, per Lords Craig, Armadale, Meadowbank (by implication) and Lord Justice-Clerk Hope; *Bernard Greenhuff* (1838) 2 Swin. 236, per Lords Moncreiff (at 265) and Mackenzie (at 268–69), and Lord Justice-Clerk Boyle (at 259), who all make reference to Hume, and Lord Medwyn (at 270) who favoured Alison's analysis; *Sugden v HM Advocate*, 1934 J.C. 103, per Lord Justice-Clerk Aitchison (at 109) who refers to it as a "prerogative of the Justiciary derived from its history, and coming down from the days of the Justiciar"; and *Grant v Allan*, 1987 J.C. 71, per Lord Justice-Clerk Ross at 77 where he asserts that "there are circumstances where it will be appropriate for the court to exercise this power", whilst conceding that great care requires to be taken in its exercise.

[81] J.H.A. Macdonald, *A Practical Treatise on the Criminal Law of Scotland*, 5th edn (Edinburgh: W. Green, 1948), p.193.

Meaning of the "High Court" in the context of the power

It seems agreed that the declaratory power was only possessed by 2–22 the High Court of Justiciary[82] and not by any lesser court (see Appendix D). What is unclear, however, is what was here meant by the "High Court". According to the court itself in *Jessop v Stevenson*[83]: "A decision of a judge of the High Court of Justiciary is a decision of the High Court of Justiciary." That does not mean, however, that a single High Court judge could (or can)[84] necessarily exercise all the powers of that institution as a "Collegiate Court".[85] Gordon opined in 1978 that a "quorum" of the court had to be present,[86] but it is hard to know what that meant in the context of the declaratory power. Prior to the reforms of the late nineteenth century, when all judges of the Court of Session also became members of the supreme criminal court,[87] it was feasible, and not uncommon, for the whole court of six or seven judges— depending on whether the Lord Justice-General was present—to sit in relation to decisions on inter alia the exercise of the power.[88] A possible de facto exercise of the power by two judges on circuit at Aberdeen was clearly unusual and required explanation.[89] But the whole court now consists of at least 37[90] judges; and in modern times, therefore, it would not have been unreasonable to conclude that a minimum of three judges would have formed a "quorum" for the purposes of the declaratory power. That represents the minimum number for appeal proceedings,[91] and for matters certified to the High Court under the Criminal Procedure (Scotland) Act 1995 s.103(4); and it is by appeal or certification that issues concerning the exercise of the power would have come before that court.

---

[82] See Gordon, *Criminal Law*, 2nd edn (Edinburgh: W. Green, 1978), para.1–43.

[83] *Jessop v Stevenson*, 1988 J.C. 17 at 20.

[84] *cf. Stevens v HM Advocate*, 2002 S.L.T. 1249.

[85] See "Courts", *Stair Memorial Encyclopaedia*, 6, 859 and 904.

[86] Gordon, *Criminal Law*, 2nd edn, para.1–43; see also *Khaliq v HM Advocate*, 1984 J.C. 23, per Lord Avonside at 24.

[87] Criminal Procedure (Scotland) Act 1887 s.44.

[88] See *Rachel Wright* (1809) Burnett 134; App. No.vii; *Greenhuff* (1838) 2 Swin. 236; *William Fraser* (1847) Ark. 280; *John Ballantyne* (1859) 3 Irv. 352. In *Lord Advocate's Reference (No.1 of 2001)*, 2002 S.L.T. 466, the majority of the court took the view that a six judge court did not qualify as "the whole court", and that thus a six judge court, in *Charles Sweenie* (1858) 3 Irv. 109, could be overruled by a modern court of seven.

[89] *Margaret Irvine*, September (1784) Burnett 133, commented on in *Wright* (1809) Burnett 134; App. No.vii, per Lords Craig, Armadale, Meadowbank and Lord Justice-Clerk Hope.

[90] This number does not include temporary judges, nor those who have retired but sit in terms of s.22 (as amended prospectively by the Constitutional Reform Act 2005 Sch.9 para.43) of the Law Reform (Miscellaneous Provisions) (Scotland) Act 1985.

[91] Criminal Procedure (Scotland) Act 1995 ss.103(2), 173(1); but note that for appeals against (generally) sentence alone, the quorum of the court falls to two (unless the two are unable to agree)—see s.103(3) (as amended by the Crime and Punishment (Scotland) Act 1997 Sch.1 para.21(13)(a)) and s.173(2).

Rationale for the power

2–23   Both Hume[92] and Alison[93] assume that it will always be necessary to create new crimes; and in fact few would dispute that
assumption. They further assume, however, that both Parliaments
and the High Court are competent to create such new crimes. But
the rationale behind the court's entitlement to do so is simply not
revealed. Since Parliaments are constitutionally recognised as
having legislative functions, it is hardly surprising that they may
from time to time increase the stock of available crimes. Courts in
the modern world, however, are not generally recognised as having
legislative powers co-extensive with those of legislatures, and some
explanation for the High Court's one time ability to declare acts
(or omissions) to be criminal would seem to be called for. The best
explanation which the judiciary themselves have suggested is that
the High Court simply occupied a unique constitutional position
within the United Kingdom:

> "I hold it to be law, that the right of enquiring into all
> injuries to individuals by criminal acts, as well as of defining
> in such cases the nature and extent of the punishment, is
> constitutionally entrusted to this Court."[94]

2–24   It seems, therefore, not particularly clear why the High Court ever
had, or claimed to have, such a power—there having been competent legislatures for Scotland at all times during the existence of
that court; nor is it always clear what size of court was necessary to
operate the power: but that the power was used in the nineteenth
and twentieth centuries seems beyond doubt, and this would seem
to hold out the prospect of providing some answer to the troublesome question: "What are the essential characteristics of behaviour
deemed to be criminal?" If the court declared some act or
omission to be criminal, one would expect to obtain useful
information as to why it had done so.

Criteria for the power's exercise

2–25   Hume's somewhat unhelpful view[95] was that the power might be
exercised where the act (or omission) in question was, "obviously
of a criminal nature". In the case of *John Ballantyne*[96] Lord

---

[92] Hume, *Commentaries*, i, 12.
[93] Alison, *Principles*, i, 624.
[94] *Wright* (1809) Burnett, App. No.vii, per Lord Meadowbank; see also *Sugden v
HM Advocate*, 1934 J.C. 103 at 109, where Lord Justice-Clerk Alness asserted the
power to be a "prerogative right of the Justiciary derived from its history . . .".
[95] Hume, *Commentaries*, i, 12.
[96] *Ballantyne* (1859) 3 Irv. 352 at 359.

Justice-Clerk Inglis ventured the view that Hume meant by that acts which were *mala in se*, i.e. evils in themselves. This, if correct, connotes the criterion of "immorality", with all the vagueness that that implies. Nevertheless, some judges have clearly opined that the perceived (public) immorality of an act (or omission) will suffice to exercise the crime-making power,[97] especially if likely to corrupt the young,[98] or pose "danger" to society.[99] In more modern times, however, the High Court appears to have rejected such a criterion. More had to be shown than that the act (or omission) was "reprehensible and immoral"[100]; in particular, it might suffice if "injurious consequences to persons or property" could be demonstrated[101]—which itself shows a tendency towards the acceptance of Alison's less vague criterion (see below, para.2–26). The major problem with any appeal to immorality is, of course, that few people can be found to agree as to what is or is not immoral. And this problem is merely rephrased by opining that an act (or omission) must be "so grossly immoral and mischievous on the face of it that no man can fairly be ignorant of its nature" before the court could exercise its crime-making power.[102]

The other most often-quoted criterion is that proffered by **2–26** Alison.[103] His view was that the power might be exercised in respect of an act (or omission) which was both in itself wrong (*malum in se*) and hurtful to the persons or property of others. There is a pragmatic flavour to this which almost anticipates the development of the "harm" principle by John Stuart Mill and others[104]; and there was some judicial acceptance of it.[105] It also may underlie the decisions in *Strathern v Seaforth*[106]—a decision which definitely involved use of the power, according to *Sugden v HM Advocate*[107]—and *Khaliq v HM Advocate*,[108] where use of the power was less certain.

---

[97] See *Greenhuff* (1838) 2 Swin. 236, per Lord Justice-Clerk Boyle at 258; Lord Meadowbank at 264.

[98] *Greenhuff* (1838) 2 Swin. 236, per Lord Justice-Clerk Boyle at 258.

[99] *Greenhuff* (1838) 2 Swin. 236, per Lord Moncreiff at 266; *John Barr* (1839) 2 Swin. 282, per Lord Mackenzie at 310.

[100] *Grant v Allan*, 1987 J.C. 71, per Lord Justice-Clerk Ross at 77; *HM Advocate v Semple*, 1937 J.C. 41, per Lord Justice-Clerk Aitchison at 45–46 and Lord Fleming at 47.

[101] *Ballantyne* (1859) 3 Irv. 352, per Lord Justice-Clerk Inglis at 359–360.

[102] *Greenhuff* (1838) 2 Swin. 236, per Lord Mackenzie at 268, approved in *Ballantyne* (1859) 3 Irv. 352, by Lord Justice-Clerk Inglis at 360.

[103] Alison, *Principles*, i, 624.

[104] Mill, *On Liberty*, Chs I and IV. See above, paras 1–07 to 1–09.

[105] See *Kerr v Hill*, 1936 J.C. 71, per Lord Justice-General Normand at 75; *Ballantyne* (1859) 3 Irv. 352, per Lord Justice-Clerk Inglis at 359–360; *HM Advocate v Semple*, 1937 J.C. 41, per Lord Justice-Clerk Aitchison at 45–46 and Lord Moncrieff at 48; *John Barr* (1839) 2 Swin. 282, per Lord Medwyn at 315.

[106] *Strathern v Seatorth*, 1926 J.C. 100.

[107] *Sugden v HM Advocate*, 1934 J.C. 103, per Lord Justice-Clerk Alness at 109.

[108] *Khaliq v HM Advocate*, 1984 J.C. 23.

2–27   There are various other criteria which have been judicially mentioned as justifying the exercise of the power—for example, that the act was criminal under English common law,[109] that it would be absurd to take any other view,[110] and that there must be something akin to a "public nuisance".[111] None of these, however, really provided any sensible or practical test.

Lord Cockburn's views

2–28   Of the six judicial opinions cast in the case of *Bernard Green-huff*,[112] the only dissenting voice was that of Lord Cockburn. He rejected flatly any suggestion that the court might declare an act (or omission) to be criminal simply on the grounds of its immorality. If immoral acts were to be criminalised, then that was a matter for Parliament and not for the court.[113] But the High Court might, he thought, legitimately develop the common law in certain ways since:

> "An old crime may certainly be committed in a new way; and a case, though never occurring before in its facts, may fall within the *spirit* of a previous decision, or within an established *general principle* . . . There is no . . . exercise of any extraordinary power needed, in the Court's merely determining that an act that has never presented itself before, *comes within the range of a known term, case or principle*."[114]

2–29   Clearly, a crime can be committed in a new way.[115] Hume would no doubt have been surprised to learn that a person could be killed by exposure to a radioactive source; but the method employed is hardly of the essence of criminal forms of killing, and death occasioned by deliberate irradiation would hardly excite comment as an example of murder (all other things being equal).

2–30   Equally, it is always possible to argue that some act (or omission) falls within the spirit of a previous decision (meaning, no doubt, that one may extend by analogy the definition, as previously understood by the courts, of any common law crime) and that it ought, therefore, to be considered as an example of that crime. Lord Cockburn himself gave colour to such argument in the case of *John Barr*,[116] where falsely swearing that one was qualified to vote

---

[109] See *Greenhuff* (1838) 2 Swin. 236, per Lord Justice-Clerk Boyle at 258, Lord Moncreiff at 266 and Lord Mackenzie at 269; *Barr* (1839) 2 Swin. 282, per Lord Moncreiff at 314.

[110] See *Strathern v Seaforth*, 1926 J.C. 100, per Lord Justice-Clerk Alness at 102.

[111] *Greenhuff* (1838) 2 Swin. 236, per Lord Medwyn at 270.

[112] *Greenhuff* (1838) 2 Swin. 236.

[113] *Greenhuff* (1838) 2 Swin. 236 at 272.

[114] *Greenhuff* (1838) 2 Swin. 236 at 274 (italics as in the original report).

[115] See, e.g. Lord McCluskey's acknowledgment of this in *HM Advocate v Harris*, 1993 J.C. 150 at 159F.

[116] *Barr* (1839) 2 Swin. 282.

in an election was considered by him to be a species of fraud or of perjury,[117] since it shared the essential characteristics of those crimes. With respect to any common law crime, however, it can be a somewhat arbitrary process to identify what are its essential characteristics—as was amply demonstrated in the case of *William Fraser*.[118] There the accused had intercourse with a married woman by pretending to be her husband. He thus obtained her consent by a trick. Surely the essence of rape was thus satisfied, there being no true consent? Yet the majority of the court (including Lord Cockburn) held that consent had been obtained, and that, therefore, rape must be ruled out. It could not thus be extended. Quite apart from the arbitrary way in which these two cases (*Barr* and *Fraser*) were determined, it should be noted that extending crimes to novel situations by means of analogy is as much a breach of the principle *nullum crimen sine lege* (see above, para.2–20) and of Art.7 of the European Convention on Human Rights as declaring acts to be criminal simply because they offend against some supposed rule of morality or whatever.[119]

Lord Cockburn's third suggestion that a novel act, insofar as the **2–31** criminal law is concerned, may nevertheless fall within an established general principle is no less perplexing, since he did not explain what was meant by such a principle nor how such principles were to be established. As Gordon[120] has, surely correctly, pointed out, principles may be deduced, from existing known crimes, of such generality as to be capable of encompassing many different forms of behaviour. Thus, for example, from the known crimes of theft, fraud and embezzlement, it may be deduced that "dishonest conduct is criminal". If that deduction were then considered as some general principle supporting those known crimes, there could be no limit, on Cockburn's thesis, to the proscription of, say, many supposedly legitimate business activities simply on the basis that they smacked of "dishonesty". This would appear to be a highly questionable process, since it seems perfectly capable of upholding the declaratory power (so heavily criticised by Cockburn) in all but name.

Nevertheless, since Cockburn was apparently offering an alterna- **2–32** tive to the declaratory power, an alternative which was, therefore, not subject to the rules for the power's operation, e.g. only exercisable by a quorum of the High Court (see above, para.2–22), it became acceptable for even single judges of the court to "find" general principles in order to justify decisions which otherwise might have entailed the declaration of new crimes. Thus in *HM*

---

[117] *Barr* (1839) 2 Swin. 282 at 316–317.
[118] *Fraser* (1847) Ark. 280.
[119] See *Kokkinakis v Greece* (1993) 17 E.H.R.R. 397 at 423, para.52, which was affirmed in *SW v United Kingdom; CR v United Kingdom* (1996) 21 E.H.R.R. 363 at 398–399, paras 35–33 and 36–34.
[120] Gordon, *Criminal Law*, 3rd edn, para.1.22.

Advocate v Martin[121] Lord Cameron was able to invoke the "principle" that conduct which violated the order and course of justice was criminal. That then enabled him (at least in part) to find that helping a prisoner to escape from an extramural working party was indeed a crime, without any resort to the declaratory power. Similarly, in *Khaliq v HM Advocate*,[122] it was possible to determine that the supply of harmful substances to others was criminal, since it fell under the broad criminalising "principle" of "that which was capable of causing real injury". Again, in *Watt v Annan*,[123] showing an obscene or indecent film to consenting adults was found criminal since it lay within the general "principle" that "all shamelessly indecent conduct is criminal". Where it suited the High Court to do so, however, an "obvious" general "principle", e.g. that dishonest conduct is criminal, was ignored, and the alternative exercise of the declaratory power deliberately avoided.[124]

2–33   It is, therefore, uncertain whether Lord Cockburn was simply describing a legitimate developmental facility possessed (relative to the common law) by the High Court, or whether he was drawing attention to another *form* of the declaratory power he had been at such pains to discredit. Fortunately, the power is now relegated to the realm of "historical curiosity"; but unfortunately, it seems plain that former attempts by the High Court to formulate new types of criminal behaviour by exercise of the power do little to answer the general question why certain conduct deserves to be stigmatised as criminal at all.

CLASSIFICATIONS OF CRIMES

2–34   Scots law does not formally group crimes into classes. Thus, the classifying of crimes as "felonies, misdemeanours, or petty misdemeanours" as favoured in the American Law Institute's Model Penal Code,[125] is unknown in this country. Nor is any particular distinction made here between the terms "crime" and "offence". It

---

[121] *HM Advocate v Martin*, 1956 J.C. 1 at p.3.
[122] *Khaliq v HM Advocate*, 1984 J.C. 23.
[123] *Watt v Annan*, 1978 J.C. 84. This case was overruled by a court of five judges in *Webster v Dominick*, 2005 1 J.C. 65, where Lord Justice-Clerk Gill said at 75, para.28: "The decision in *Watt v Annan* was a direct consequence of *McLaughlan v Boyd* [1934 J.C. 19]. The excessive statement of Lord Justice General Clyde in *McLaughlan v Boyd* [at 23, lines 4–7] set no limit to the ambit of shameless indecency. The effect of the statement was to enable the court, by characterising any form of conduct as shamelessly indecent, *to exercise the declaratory power*. The result was the creation of a crime that had no basis in principle and was unconstrained by any clear or logical boundaries [emphasis added]."
[124] See *Grant v Allan*, 1987 J.C. 71. See also *HM Advocate v Forbes*, 1994 S.L.T. 861, where the Crown's argument, that "housebreaking with intent to commit any crime" was a general principle (see 863F), was rejected by the court (see 864J).
[125] American Law Institute, Model Penal Code Official Draft (1985), s.1.04(1).

thus makes equal legal sense in Scotland to speak of the "crime" or the "offence" of murder.

Of course, there are two distinct types of criminal procedure in **2–35** this country. "Summary" procedure is (supposedly, if not in fact) flexible, quick and relatively informal; involves a non-jury type trial (if a trial is held); and is normally reserved for the less serious type of crime. On the other hand, "solemn" procedure (or procedure "on indictment") is more lengthy and rule-bound; involves a judge and jury trial (if a trial is held); and is supposedly reserved for the more serious type of offence. It might appear, therefore, that a classification by way of procedure would be appropriate—crimes being divided into those which were "summary" and those which were "indictable". This is not possible, however. Most common law crimes may be processed by either form of procedure—depending upon the discretion of the prosecutor and the seriousness of the individual case. It is thus generally not the type of crime that is more or less serious, but individual examples of it. Whilst it is true that some statutory offences are designated as attracting only summary procedure, or triable only on indictment, it is equally true that many such offences may be processed in either way, thus equating them with common law offences, from the procedural point of view. There is no satisfactory way, therefore, of classifying crimes in Scotland according to the procedural regime which they attract.

It is traditional, however, and very convenient, particularly for **2–36** the purposes of textbook writing, to group crimes together according to some significant feature that they possess (or, more accurately, appear to possess) in common. Thus, later chapters in this book are headed, "Crimes Against the Person", "Crimes of Dishonesty", "Crimes Against Property", and so on: but these groupings have no official basis whatsoever. Gordon has stressed a similar (though more general) theme in his useful thesis that there are both conduct and result crimes.[126] His view is that in relation to some crimes, what is forbidden consists primarily of the "result" of conduct, the precise form of conduct employed to achieve that result being of minimal interest to the law. Murder is his stock example here. (One must pause, however, to observe that conduct is still involved in murder—and crucially so, if anyone is to be convicted of such a crime.) The alternative is a "conduct" crime, where the result, if any, of human conduct is in no sense required for conviction.[127] Although it is plain that not all offences can be neatly classified in such a way (see, for example, the offence of being "drunk and incapable of taking care" of oneself in a public place,[128] which seems to involve neither conduct nor result, and

---

[126] Gordon, *Criminal Law*, 3rd edn, para.3.05.
[127] Gordon's initial example being that of perjury—on which see *Lord Advocate's Reference (No.1 of 1985)*, 1986 J.C. 137.
[128] Civic Government (Scotland) Act 1982, s.50(1).

which Smith and Hogan[129] would refer to as a "state of affairs" crime), the identification of those crimes which require a result does highlight that area of the criminal law where issues of causation are at a premium (see below, Ch.5).

2–37   There is some judicial support for a classification of crimes based upon the Latin tags *mala in se* and *mala prohibita*. *Mala in se* refers to those crimes which are morally reprehensible—evils in themselves; and clearly murder, rape, assault and some other traditional common law crimes would answer to that sort of description. At the opposite end of the scale, *mala prohibita* are, "mere regulatory offences" or, "not criminal in any real sense"[130]—offences which have no perceptible moral content, and which may be described as administrative rules given the added efficacy that only criminal sanctions can command. Examples may be seen in the offences of installing or using a television receiver where the installation and use are not authorised by a licence,[131] and failing to exhibit in the prescribed manner a vehicle licence on a vehicle which is used or kept on a public road (and in respect of which excise duty is chargeable).[132] This sort of classification is often resorted to in relation to statutory offences—where criteria are being sought to identify offences of strict liability, i.e. those not requiring proof or inference of *mens rea* (see below, Chs 3 and 13). But there are many offences (even common law ones) where it cannot affirmatively be said that moral reprehensibility is always involved. Abortion, culpable homicide, carrying an offensive weapon, incest, having carnal knowledge of a girl under the age of 16, brothel keeping, and so on may or may not involve moral obloquy, depending upon the circumstances; but it is difficult to envisage any of them being described as a mere regulatory offence. Opinions on issues of morality are in any event so hopelessly diverse that this sort of classification is of very limited utility.

BASIC PRINCIPLES OF THE CRIMINAL JUSTICE SYSTEM[133]

Jurisdiction

2–38   No proceedings against a person for a crime can competently be commenced before a Scottish court (see Appendix D) unless that crime and the person alleged to have committed it are subject to

---

[129] Smith and Hogan, *Criminal Law*, 10th edn, pp.58–59.
[130] See *Sweet v Parsley* [1970] A.C. 132, per Lord Reid at 149F, quoting from Wright J. in *Sherras v De Rutzen* [1895] 1 Q.B. 918 at 922.
[131] See the Communications Act 2003 s.363.
[132] See the Vehicle Excise and Registration Act 1994 s.33 (as amended by the Finance Act 2002 Sch.5 para.10). See also *Strowger v John* [1974] R.T.R. 124.
[133] The paragraphs which follow are intended to provide no more than a basic sketch of the main features of the Scottish criminal justice system. For detailed discussion and commentary, the reader is referred to the standard works on procedure, e.g. *Renton and Brown's Criminal Procedure*, 6th edn, looseleaf with regular updating service, and evidence, e.g. Fraser P. Davidson, *Evidence* (Edinburgh: SULI/W. Green, 2007). For a modern guide to the European Convention on Human Rights, see Jacobs and White, *The European Convention on Human Rights*, 3rd edn.

the jurisdiction of that court. Diplomatic immunity apart, each "prosecutable person" (see below, para.2–43 *et seq.*), whatever his nationality, can be prosecuted before a court within whose territorial area he is alleged to have committed a crime. It is clearly important, therefore, to establish where an alleged crime was committed. If the place of the crime (usually referred to as the "*locus*") is outwith the United Kingdom, then generally there will be no jurisdiction possessed by any Scottish court in respect of that crime. But there are many exceptions, mostly statutory. Under s.11 of the Criminal Procedure (Scotland) Act 1995, for example, a British citizen or subject, who commits murder or culpable homicide (as these are understood in Scotland) in a country outwith the United Kingdom, may be prosecuted for what he did before a Scottish court. Other exceptions, such as piracy, may be within the jurisdiction of Scottish courts as a matter of international comity. If the *locus* is completely or partly outwith Scotland but within the United Kingdom, the issue of jurisdiction may depend on the nature of the crime itself and also whether that crime is of statutory or common law origin. In *Clements v HM Advocate*,[134] for example, the Scottish courts assumed jurisdiction over persons who were based in London and who had furnished their criminal activities only in that city. But the statutory crime in question[135] was one where criminal activities in one location vitally contributed to the end-result of the crime in another—and that other location was Edinburgh. Where, therefore, a crime is of such a nature that chains of interlocking activities in different parts of the United Kingdom are involved in its commission, the Scottish courts may have jurisdiction over persons who never visited Scotland at all (except to be prosecuted) and who were unaware that the end-*locus* was Scotland. The crime in that case was, however, of unusually wide scope.[136] As far as common law crimes are concerned, it seems that a similar rule will pertain where the crime in question involves a scheme of cross-border activities and where a material part of those activities takes place in Scotland.[137] In addition, of course, to a particular court having territorial jurisdiction in respect of the *locus*, it must also be competent to deal with the type of crime involved. Thus, e.g. only a High Court can competently try a person accused of murder or rape—even though the crime in question occurred within the territorial area of a sheriff, district or J.P. court.[138]

---

[134] *Clements v HM Advocate*, 1991 J.C. 62.
[135] A contravention of s.4(3)(b) of the Misuse of Drugs Act 1971, i.e. being concerned in the supplying of a controlled drug to another.
[136] See *Kerr v HM Advocate*, 1986 J.C. 41.
[137] See *Laird v HM Advocate*, 1985 J.C. 37. See also the provisions of the Criminal Procedure (Scotland) Act 1995 s.11(4) pertaining to theft and reset.
[138] For further details, discussion and authorities, see *Renton and Brown's Criminal Procedure*, 6th edn, under the title "Jurisdiction"; Gordon, *Criminal Law*, 3rd edn, para.3.41 *et seq.* For an account of the Scottish criminal courts, see below, Appendix D.

Prescription

2–39   A prosecution will be barred as incompetent if the time limit laid down by the law has prescribed before commencement of proceedings. There are two main aspects to this. First, in relation to common law crimes, there is no period of prescription at all.[139] Whatever may have been the position under Roman law or in Scotland during the eighteenth century, there is now no time bar on the prosecution of any common law offence (although the lack of availability of witnesses, and diminished powers of recollection by them may detrimentally affect proposed prosecutions relating to crimes allegedly committed many years in the past).

2–40   Secondly, in relation to statutory offences, each piece of relevant legislation must be consulted in order to determine if a specific time limit exists, and, if so, when the prescriptive period begins to run. The Road Traffic Offenders Act 1988 Sch.1, for example, identifies those offences to which the specific time limits contained in s.6 of that Act apply; and, as a more specific example, under s.44 of the Animal Health and Welfare (Scotland) Act 2006 (asp 11), proceedings for an offence under s.23 of that Act (e.g. causing or arranging an animal fight) cannot be brought more than three years after the commission of the offence (or, in the case of a continuous contravention, after the last date on which the offence was committed)—whereas the offence of abandoning an animal for which one is responsible (under s.29) appears to have no prescriptive period applied to it. Section 29 of that Act, however, furnishes a series of offences; and if no specific time limit is set in relation to a statutory offence which is triable summarily, then a general prescriptive period of six months (from the date of the alleged offence) applies.[140]

DELAY IN PROGRESSING PROCEEDINGS

2–41   There are statutory time limits applicable to prosecutions under either sort of procedure, i.e. summary or on indictment,[141] which are designed to ensure that accused persons will not remain in custody for too long before being brought to trial, or, in the case of solemn

---

[139] *Sugden v HM Advocate*, 1934 J.C. 103.
[140] Criminal Procedure (Scotland) Act 1995 s.136. The rule is a general one only, however, and may be excluded or varied by particularly statutory provisions: for example, under the Architects Act 1997 s.21(4)(c), and relative to an offence under s.20 of that Act, s.136 of the 1995 Act is to be read as if "two years" was substituted for the "six months" which generally applies. See also s.292 (as amended by the Criminal Proceedings etc. (Reform) (Scotland) Act 2007 (asp 6) Sch.1 para.24) of the 1995 Act for the meaning of an offence "triable only summarily".
[141] See above, para.2–35.

prosecutions alone, to ensure that accused persons who are not in custody will be brought to trial within a reasonable space of time.[142] In addition, delay in the progress of prosecutions is subject to **2–42** Art.6(1) of the European Convention on Human Rights,[143] which, insofar as relevant, states:

> "In the determination . . . of any criminal charge against him,[144] everyone is entitled to a fair and public hearing within a reasonable time by an independent and impartial tribunal[145] established by law."

What amounts to a "reasonable time" depends on the facts and circumstances of each case[146]; but the Convention right here extends to the whole proceedings, including any appeal.[147] If the delay is due to an act (or failure) of the Lord Advocate (or a prosecutor for whom he or she is responsible), then the matter will be a "devolution issue".[148]

PROSECUTABLE PERSONS

The range of persons who can be prosecuted for an alleged crime is **2–43** not confined to human beings, but, on the other hand, does not extend to all human beings. In particular, a "child" cannot be found guilty of any offence. Almost all legal systems have a similar rule, probably based on an assumed lack of capacity of young children for any true criminal appetite, or on some general notion that young children cannot be expected to exercise adult restraints. Whatever the basis for the rule, the great difficulty lies in determining an appropriate age when prosecution will be in order. In fact, all solutions to this problem involve the assigning of a totally arbitrary age limit. In England, this has been fixed at 10 years of age[149]; in

---

[142] Criminal Procedure (Scotland) Act 1995 s.65 (as amended by the Criminal Procedure and Investigations Act 1996 s.73(3); the Crime and Punishment (Scotland) Act 1997 Sch.1 para.21(9); the Criminal Procedure (Amendment) (Scotland) Act 2004 (asp 5) s.6; and the Criminal Proceedings etc. (Reform) (Scotland) Act 2007 (asp 6) Sch.1 para.12(1)) and s.147 (as amended by the said 2007 Act (asp 6) s.11).

[143] See the Human Rights Act 1998 Sch.1.

[144] For an account of the stage in criminal proceedings at which Art.6(1) may be engaged, see Jacobs and White, *The European Convention on Human Rights*, 3rd edn, pp.143–144. See also, e.g. *Dyer v Watson*, 2002 S.C.(P.C.) 89 and *Unterschutz v HM Advocate*, 2003 S.C.C.R. 287.

[145] cf. *Starrs v Ruxton; Ruxton v Starrs*, 1999 S.C.C.R. 1052; see also *Dickson v HM Advocate*, 2008 S.L.T. 12 (court of five judges).

[146] There are a considerable number of case decisions involving this aspect of Art.6, but see in particular *Gibson v HM Advocate*, 2001 S.L.T. 591.

[147] See, e.g. *Mills v HM Advocate (No.2)*, 2001 S.L.T. 1359; *Gillespie v HM Advocate (No.2)* , 2003 S.C.C.R. 82.

[148] See above, para.2–13 and *Mills v HM Advocate (No.2)*, 2001 S.L.T. 1359.

[149] Children and Young Persons Act 1933 s.50, as amended by the Children and Young Persons Act 1963 s.16(1).

Scotland, however, it is taken to be eight.[150] These age limits are clearly intended to refer to chronological and not mental age. A child under eight years of age cannot, therefore, be found guilty of any crime, no matter what he may apparently have done. Nor can this presumption be overcome by resort to "children's hearing" procedure.[151]

Older children

2–44   Children between the ages of eight and 16 can certainly be prosecuted before a criminal court, even though steps have to be taken to render the proceedings rather less public and awe-inspiring than where adult offenders alone are involved.[152] There is no equivalent in Scotland to the former English rule that a child between the ages of 10 and 14 must be shown to have had "mischievous discretion" before he can be convicted. The Scottish police, however, do not report most alleged child offenders to the public prosecutors. Instead, they resort to the Principal Reporter[153] to the Children's Panel. Under the Children (Scotland) Act 1995 Pt II Ch.3, the intention is that most (alleged) child offenders will appear before a body of three specially trained lay-adults, known collectively as a "children's hearing".[154] Such a hearing is arranged by the Principal Reporter, and, assuming that the child and any "relevant person"[155] (who must also attend) accept that the alleged crime was committed by that child, the only object is to secure that child's future welfare. The proceedings are not open to the public and may not be reported in the press. If it is not accepted that the

---

[150] Criminal Procedure (Scotland) Act 1995 s.41. The Scottish Law Commission, in their "Report on Age of Criminal Responsibility", Scot. Law Com. No.185 (2001), recommend at paras 3.2–3.5 that s.41 be repealed in favour of a rule that no child under the age of 12 can be prosecuted for any offence.

[151] See *Merrin v S*, 1987 S.L.T. 193, and see below, paras 2–44 to 2–45 for "children's hearings". (The Scottish Law Commission in their "Report on Age of Criminal Responsibility", recommend that the decision in *Merrin*'s case should be set aside by legislation: see the report at paras 3.21–3.26.)

[152] Criminal Procedure (Scotland) Act 1995 ss.42, 142. For the meaning of "child" relative to s.142, see s.307(1).

[153] See the Children (Scotland) Act 1995 ss.53(2), 93(1), and the Local Government etc. (Scotland) Act 1994 s.127.

[154] See Children (Scotland) Act 1995 Pt II Ch.2 and Sch.1. Notice that a child for the purposes of Pt II Chs 2 and 3 means a person who is under 16 years of age, or who is aged between 16 and 18 years if already subject to a supervision requirement: see s.93(2)(b) (as amended by the Criminal Justice (Scotland) Act 2003 (asp 7) s.52(b)(ii)) and s.70.

[155] Defined in the Children (Scotland) Act 1995 s.93(2)(b) to include any parent enjoying parental responsibilities or rights; any person who has parental responsibilities or rights vested in him; any person in whom parental responsibilities or rights are vested by, under or by virtue of a "permanence order" (on which see the Adoption and Children (Scotland) Act 2007 (asp 4) s.80(2) and Sch.2 para.9(8)); and any person who ordinarily has charge of, or control over, the child. Attendance by such a person is required under s.45(8). It is an offence not to attend, under s.45(9).

child in question committed the crime, then fact finding must be referred to a sheriff of the local sheriff court.[156] Appeal against his findings (or indeed the eventual decision of the hearing) lies ultimately to the Court of Session[157] rather than the Court of Criminal Appeal, since it is not intended that any of this process should be seen as a criminal proceeding and since the process indeed relates to all children thought to be in need of compulsory measures of supervision. That a child is thought to have committed a crime is, therefore, only one of a range of possible reasons for invoking this rather special (if not unique) procedure.[158]

The children's hearing process will probably not be used where a **2–45** child is alleged to have committed an offence which requires solemn procedure—either as a matter of law, i.e. in relation to murder or rape, or a select few statutory offences, or because the particular circumstances of the offence seem to necessitate it.[159] It should be noted that a children's hearing has no powers to impose fines, imprison, disqualify,[160] order forfeiture, or indeed to punish in any conventional sense.[161]

Non-human persons

A non-human, "legal" person can be prosecuted for an alleged **2–46** crime.[162] In Scotland, certain business organisations (or "corporations")—in particular companies formed and registered under the Companies Acts[163]—are treated in law as if they had an existence (a *persona*) separate from the human beings who direct them or are employed by them. But that existence, being the creation of statute law and thus a pure abstraction, is a peculiar one in that a company (or other corporation) cannot itself perform acts (or fail to perform them) and cannot itself possess any particular state of mind—although acts (or omissions) and states of mind are very generally required as essential components of criminal liability.[164] If, therefore, such an abstract "person" is to be

---

[156] Children (Scotland) Act 1995 ss.65(7), 68—s.68, being amended by the Antisocial Behaviour etc. (Scotland) Act 2004 (asp 8) Sch.4 para.4(4). The reference is to a sheriff even though the crime in question is not one, e.g. rape, within the ordinary jurisdiction of the sheriff court: see *Walker v C (No.2)*, 2003 S.L.T. 293.

[157] Children (Scotland) Act 1995 s.51.

[158] See Children (Scotland) Act 1995 s.52(2), as amended by the Criminal Procedure (Consequential Provisions) (Scotland) Act 1995 Sch.4 para.97(4), and the Antisocial Behaviour etc. (Scotland) Act 2004 (asp 8) s.12(3), for the complete range.

[159] See *Cairns v HM Advocate* (1973) S.C.C.R. Supp. 44.

[160] *cf. McCulloch v Murray*, 2005 S.C.C.R. 775.

[161] For comprehensive coverage of the matters briefly introduced above, paras 2–44 to 2–45, see Kenneth McK. Norrie, *Children's Hearings in Scotland*, 2nd edn (Edinburgh: W. Green, 2005).

[162] *Transco Plc v HM Advocate (No.1)*, 2004 J.C. 29.

[163] i.e. the Companies Act 2006, and its predecessors: see the 2006 Act s.1.

[164] See below, Ch.3. It now seems accepted that common law crimes in general require proof of *mens rea* for conviction: *Transco Plc v HM Advocate (No.1)*, 2004 J.C. 29, per Lord Hamilton (with whom Lord MacLean agreed) at 50–51, paras 42–43.

prosecuted, convicted and punished for crime, some rule will have to be formed which attributes the acts (or omissions) and mental states of human beings occupying posts within a company to that company itself: thus, such a human being who can be proved to have performed a criminal act (with the requisite state of mind) will himself bear criminal responsibility for it, and can be prosecuted accordingly—but so too will the company itself, by application of an accepted rule of attribution. Both "persons" will thus have liability.

Until the decision in the case of *Transco Plc v HM Advocate*,[165] it was not clear if Scots law had such a rule of attribution or whether companies (or other corporations) in Scotland might be prosecuted for all offences, irrespective of whether they were common law or statutory.[166] In *Transco Plc*,[167] however, an indictment was brought against a company for (inter alia) culpable homicide, in that the company had allegedly failed to obtemper its duties in providing safe regimes for the supply of gas to domestic premises and thus, in full knowledge of the risks, caused the deaths of four persons when an explosion occurred. The company, of course, was incapable itself of such failure or such knowledge; but the indictment alleged that the failure and knowledge had been attributed to the company over many years via committees and posts established within that company's organisation. The Appeal Court reviewed the authorities, and concluded that there was an accepted rule of attribution for corporate liability in English law,[168] that that rule was accepted also in Scots law,[169] and that the application of that rule was decisive of the company's objections to the competency and relevancy[170] of the charge of culpable homicide. The substance of the rule was (and is) that the company would itself be liable criminally if a named person (or group of persons acting collectively)[171] of sufficient status within that company[172] could be proved

---

[165] *Transco Plc v HM Advocate (No.1)*, 2004 J.C. 29.
[166] Under the Criminal Procedure (Scotland) Act 1995 ss.70, 143 (as amended, respectively, by the Criminal Proceedings etc. (Reform) (Scotland) Act 2007 (asp 6) ss.28, 17), it was (and is) simply assumed that prosecution of corporate bodies was (and is) generally possible: and many specific statutes made (and make) the assumption that corporate prosecution is to be expected: see the Adoption and Children (Scotland) Act 2007 (asp 4) s.115 for a typically worded modern example.
[167] *Transco Plc v HM Advocate (No.1)*, 2004 J.C. 29.
[168] Reference was made in particular to the opinions of Lord Reid in *Tesco Supermarkets Ltd v Nattrass* [1972] A.C. 153 HL at 170E–G, and Lord Hoffmann in *Meridian Global Funds Management Asia Ltd v Securities Commission* [1995] 2 A.C. 500 PC at 506 *et seq*.
[169] The court referred in particular to the opinion of the court in *Purcell Meats (Scotland) Ltd v McLeod*, 1987 S.L.T. 528.
[170] For an explanation of the significance of these objections, see the opinion of Lord Hamilton in *Transco Plc v HM Advocate (No.1)*, 2004 J.C. 29 at 46, para.31.
[171] See *Transco Plc v HM Advocate (No.1)*, 2004 J.C. 29, opinion of Lord Hamilton (with whom Lord MacLean agreed) at 58, para.62.
[172] i.e. sufficient status to be regarded, relative to the matter in question, as the directing (or controlling) mind and will of the company. In view of this, the rule is often referred to as the "directing mind and will" rule.

to have done a criminal act (or omission) with the required state of mind: in brief, the criminal responsibility of such a person (or group) would thus be attributed to the company itself. It is essential for the operation of the rule that some such person, or group, should be precisely identified[173]: and it was precisely because the Crown in *Transco Plc*[174] could not produce such identification that the charge of culpable homicide was held to be competent (since a company or other relevant corporation *can* be prosecuted for a common law crime)[175] but irrelevant (since the Crown were unable to show that the accepted rule of attribution could be satisfied in this case).[176]

Crimes committed by others

A person may be validly prosecuted for a crime he did not **2–47** personally commit. He may be liable for its commission "art and part", i.e. as an accessory (see below, Ch.7) or vicariously (usually by being the employer of the person actually responsible). Vicarious liability[177] seems to be confined, however, to statutory offences which make specific provision for it[178] and statutory offences where the courts have decided that it is appropriate.[179]

---

[173] Thus the rule is sometimes also referred to as the "identification" rule.

[174] *Transco Plc v HM Advocate (No.1)*, 2004 J.C. 29.

[175] This is in general true; but it may be a practical impossibility to indict a company for murder, since the only punishment available for a person convicted of that crime is life in prison: see the Criminal Procedure (Scotland) Act 1995 s.205.

[176] See *Transco Plc v HM Advocate (No.1)*, 2004 J.C. 29, opinion of Lord Hamilton at 58–59, para.63. The Crown had argued that the failures manifest, and knowledge of risks possessed, by many committees and (unnamed) persons within the company over many years might be attributed to the company on a cumulative basis; but the court rejected this contention, as resting on the application of a differently formed rule based on the principle of aggregation which was not accepted in either English or Scots law. (This case demonstrates the great difficulty of actually proving that the rule of attribution is satisfied, and thus that a corporate body such as a company is criminally liable for a common law offence: for that reason, the United Kingdom Government has created a discrete statutory offence known in Scotland as "corporate homicide". Briefly, this offence is committed by an organisation (which includes a corporation) if the way in which its activities are managed or organised causes a person's death and amounts to a gross breach of a relevant duty of care owed to that person: see the Corporate Manslaughter and Corporate Homicide Act 2007 s.1 and below, para.9–71, for a more detailed description of the offence.)

[177] See below, para.13–23.

[178] This is now very rare. For example, the express provision for such liability in the Licensing (Scotland) Act 1976 (see s.67(1), (2) and Sch.5 Table column 3) is not reflected in the Act which replaces it—viz the Licensing (Scotland) Act 2005 (asp 16) where the general approach to licensing offences is in any event different from that of its predecessor.

[179] It is now well accepted that vicarious liability does not apply to common law offences: see below, para.13–24, and *Transco Plc v HM Advocate (No.1)*, 2004 J.C. 29, per Lord Hamilton (with whom Lord MacLean agreed) at 54, para.53.

Insane persons

2–48   A prosecutable person must also be sufficiently sane to understand the proceedings against him, and to give instructions for (or be able to conduct personally) his defence. It is a plea "in bar of trial" that such a degree of sanity is lacking.[180] This plea should not be confused with the defence of insanity (see below, Ch.8).

RES JUDICATA

2–49   Once a person has been prosecuted for an offence and a verdict has been reached of either guilt or acquittal, it is not lawful for him to be re-prosecuted for that same offence. Again, a good plea "in bar of trial" would lie if such a re-prosecution were to be attempted. In Scotland, this plea is sometimes known as that of *res judicata* or "tholed assize", though no jury (assize) need have been involved at all. There is one exception to this in that the Appeal Court may give authority for a new prosecution after hearing an appeal.[181]

CHARGE MUST RELATE TO A KNOWN CRIME

2–50   The charging document in a solemn procedure case is known as an indictment. The equivalent in a summary procedure case is known as a complaint. These documents must allege that the accused committed a known crime. If they do not, then they may be attacked and disposed of as "irrelevant". There is really no problem in relation to statutory offences, since clearly an existing enactment either is or is not validly referred to. But common law offences do pose difficulties. Some of these offences are "innominate", i.e. having no short, recognisable name—or *nomen juris*—as opposed to the better known crimes with instantly recognisable titles, such as murder, theft and rape, and consequently must be charged by a more or less lengthy description.[182] It will often be a moot point whether the description given is adequate or whether it

---

[180] Criminal Procedure (Scotland) Act 1995 ss.54–57D, as amended and/or inserted by the Adults with Incapacity (Scotland) Act 2000 (asp 4) Sch.5 para.26(1), the Criminal Justice (Scotland) Act 2003 (asp 7) s.2, the Mental Health (Care and Treatment) (Scotland) Act 2003 (asp 13) s.133 and Sch.4 para.8(1)–(3), and the Criminal Procedure (Amendment) (Scotland) Act 2004 (asp 5) Sch.1 paras 13, 14. On the subject of "Insanity in Bar of Trial", see James Chalmers and Fiona Leverick, *Criminal Defences and Pleas in Bar of Trial* (Edinburgh: SULI/W. Green, 2006), Ch.14.

[181] See the Criminal Procedure (Scotland) Act 1995 ss.118(1)(c), 119 (as amended by the Criminal Procedure (Amendment) (Scotland) Act 2004 (asp 5) Sch.1 para.32, and the Criminal Proceedings etc. (Reform) (Scotland) Act 2007 (asp 6) Sch.1 para.16(6)) and ss.183(1)(d), 185. On the whole subject of "Res Judicata", see Chalmers and Leverick, *Criminal Defences and Pleas in Bar of Trial*, Ch.15.

[182] See, for example, charge (1) in *Khaliq v HM Advocate*, 1984 J.C. 23 at 24.

relates to something entirely novel.[183] It must also be borne in mind that conviction is possible in respect of any part of a charge, provided that part itself constitutes an identifiable crime,[184] and that specific statutes do allow "hidden" alternative charges to be considered by a judge (summary cases) or a jury (solemn cases).[185]

There is probably no *de minimis* principle[186] operated in Scots 2–51 criminal law. It is thus not a competent objection to any criminal charge that the matter is too trivial for consideration by a court. Scottish public prosecutors (see below, para.2–55) are deemed to have considered fully the matter of triviality at a stage prior to the drawing of a complaint or indictment.

ACCUSATORIAL FORM OF PROCEDURE

The principle followed by Scots criminal law is that the prosecutor, 2–52 public or private, must not only make the accusation against the person in question, but also prove the matter to the satisfaction of the judge (summary case) or jury (solemn case). On a charge being made by way of complaint or indictment, it is not for the accused to satisfy the judge or jury as to his innocence. To that extent at least, there is compliance with Art.6(2) of the European Convention on Human Rights[187] which states that: "Everyone charged with a criminal offence shall be presumed innocent until proved guilty according to law." The prosecutor must, therefore, provide the court with evidence. In Scotland, that generally entails the provision of two independent pieces of evidence in respect of every material issue in the case against the accused. The "evidential burden", therefore, lies on the prosecutor. But he also carries the "persuasive burden". He must persuade the judge (or the jury) that the case against the accused is true beyond reasonable doubt. If he fails on either of these burdens, the case will be lost (possibly at an early stage, on a plea from the accused that there is "no case to answer").[188] Precisely what the prosecutor must establish by way of evidence and persuasion depends upon the particular crime

---

[183] But compare the Criminal Procedure (Scotland) Act 1995 Sch 3 para.2, which requires only that the appropriate document sets forth facts relevant and sufficient to constitute a crime.

[184] Criminal Procedure (Scotland) Act 1995 Sch.3 para.9(2).

[185] See, e.g. the Criminal Law (Consolidation) (Scotland) Act 1995 s.14 (certain sexual offences—noting the interpretation in relation to statutory time bars made in *McNeil v HM Advocate*, 2006 J.C. 71); the Criminal Procedure (Scotland) Act 1995 Sch.3 para.8(2)–(4) (certain crimes of dishonesty) as also the general provision in para.14–where a statutory charge may contain a hidden common law one in respect of which conviction may follow (as, e.g. in *Horsburgh v Russell*, 1994 S.L.T. 942, *Anderson v Griffiths*, 2005 1 J.C. 169 and *Robertson v Klos*, 2006 S.C.C.R. 52).

[186] The complete Latin tag is *de minimis non curat lex*, i.e. the law does not concern itself with trivial matters.

[187] See the Human Rights Act 1998 Sch.1.

[188] See the Criminal Procedure (Scotland) Act 1995 ss.97, 160.

charged and its *actus reus* and *mens rea* requirements (see below, Ch.3). In a result crime (see above, para.2–36), the issue of causation (see below, Ch.5) will also have to be addressed.[189]

2–53   The Scottish prosecutor is regarded as being "the master of the instance". That means he has entire discretion as to whether the case should be prosecuted at all,[190] as to the way in which the case will be prosecuted (the accused, for example, having no right to demand jury trial), and as to the conduct of the case in court before a judge or a judge and jury.[191] He may in particular abandon the case, "desert the diet", either temporarily, *pro loco et tempore*, subject to any prescriptive time periods which apply (see above, paras 2–39 and 2–40) or permanently, *simpliciter*, or cause the proceedings to be adjourned, or even decline after a verdict of "guilty" to "move", i.e. ask, for sentence, in which event (or certainly in an indictment case) no sentence can be passed by the presiding judge.[192]

ADVERSARIAL FORM OF PROCEDURE

2–54   In Scotland, as in the Anglo-American family of legal systems, a trial is conducted by the opposing parties, i.e. the prosecutor and the accused—or more commonly, his lawyer or advocate,[193] before

---

[189] For detailed information on evidential matters, see Davidson, *Evidence*.

[190] Thus he may ignore the complainer's wish that the offender should not be prosecuted, see, e.g. *Sze v Wilson*, 1992 S.L.T. 569.

[191] Thus the Lord Advocate cannot be required to give reasons for any decisions taken which are entirely within the province of the Crown, see, e.g. *HM Advocate v O'Neill*, 1992 J.C. 22.

[192] For observations on the current practice, see *HM Advocate v McGee*, 2006 S.L.T. 818, Lord Hardie at 821E–L, para.9.

[193] Under the Criminal Procedure (Scotland) Act 1995 s.288C (as inserted by the Sexual Offences (Procedure and Evidence) (Scotland) Act 2002 (asp 9) s.1; and as amended by the Criminal Justice (Scotland) Act 2003 (asp 7) s.15(2), the Criminal Procedure (Amendment) (Scotland) Act 2004 (asp 5) s.4(1) and Sch.1 para.55(a),(b), and the Mental Health (Care and Treatment) (Scotland) Act 2003 (Modification of Enactments) Order 2005 (SSI 2005/465), Sch.1 para.27(5)), an accused is prohibited from conducting his defence in person at his trial for a listed sexual offence, or at any relevant preliminary hearing held in connection with proceedings for that offence; this also applies in the case of a non-listed offence where a court makes an order that it is satisfied that there is such a substantial sexual element in the alleged commission of the offence that that offence ought to be treated in the same way as one that is listed (s.288C(3), (4)). It is also now the case that an accused is not permitted to conduct his own defence in relation to any proof ordered in relation to a "victim statement" (as to the way in which a prescribed offence, or alleged offence, has affected a person, or persons, as identified by s.14 (as amended by the Civil Partnership Act 2004 Sch.28 para.67) of the Criminal Justice (Scotland) Act 2003 (asp 7)): see the Vulnerable Witnesses (Scotland) Act 2004 (asp 3) s.6—which adds ss.288E and 288F to the 1995 Act, and applies a similar restriction on the accused's conduct of his own defence in criminal proceedings relative to listed offences (see s.288E(3)) or other specified offences at the discretion of the court

a largely silent judge, or judge and jury. It is not for the judge (or the jury, if present) to question the witnesses. The judge (or jury) must simply follow the questioning and cross-questioning conducted by the two sides, then give a verdict according to what has been heard. It is also of the essence of this "adversarial" procedure that the accused (or his lawyer) is entitled to question the prosecutor's witnesses and introduce evidence of his own by way of defence.[194] General and special defences (see below, Ch.8) are regarded as the accused's responsibility—in the first instance, at least. He will have the "evidential burden" of placing some evidence favouring them before the court—but without assuming any responsibility for persuading the court of their truth. Insanity and diminished responsibility are well known exceptions to that principle, both of these defences requiring that the accused carries not only the usual evidential burden but also the persuasive burden since there is a presumption, which must be overcome, that he was sane (or, perhaps, not suffering from diminished responsibility) at the time of the offence.[195] The standard of proof required of him in such situations is "on the balance of probabilities", i.e. that it is more probable than not that he was insane or suffering from diminished responsibility at the material time. It is never for the accused to prove anything on the prosecutorial standard of "beyond reasonable doubt".

PUBLIC PROSECUTION

The norm, in Scotland, is for criminal prosecutions to be instituted 2–55 and conducted by the public prosecution service consisting of the Lord Advocate, the Solicitor General for Scotland, advocates-depute, and area and district procurators fiscal. The service

---

(s.288F) where a child under the age of 12 or a "vulnerable witness" (see s.271 of the 1995 Act, as substituted by the Vulnerable Witnesses (Scotland) Act 2004 (asp 3) s.1(1), and as modified by the above mentioned SSI 2005/465 Sch.1 para.27(3)) is to give evidence. When the accused is not permitted to conduct his own defence, he may engage a lawyer to act for him—which failing, the court will appoint one to so act: see s.288D of the 1995 Act (as inserted by the Sexual Offences (Procedure and Evidence) (Scotland) Act 2002 (asp 9) s.2(1), and as amended by the Criminal Justice (Scotland) Act 2003 (asp 7) s.15(3), the Criminal Procedure (Amendment) (Scotland) Act 2004 (asp 5) s.4(2) and Sch.1 para.56, and the Criminal Proceedings etc. (Reform) (Scotland) Act 2007 (asp 6) s.35(6)). It remains to be seen whether these provisions arc entirely compatible with Art.6(3)(c) of the European Convention on Human Rights (see the Human Rights Act 1998 Sch.1).

[194] See Art.6(3)(d) of the European Convention on Human Rights, as set out in the Human Rights Act 1998 Sch.1.

[195] The theoretical basis for placing such an onus on the accused in relation to diminished responsibility is, however, rather unclear: cf. Walker and Walker, *The Law of Evidence in Scotland*, 2nd edn, para.2.11.2; *Lindsay v HM Advocate*, 1996 S.C.C.R. 870; and *Galbraith v HM Advocate (No.2)*, 2001 S.C.C.R. 551.

operates from the Crown Office in Edinburgh and from area and district fiscals' offices throughout the country. Procurators fiscal normally deal with cases set for proceedings before sheriff and district (or J.P.) courts. In High Courts (as also before the Appeal Court), advocates-depute (or the Lord Advocate or the Solicitor General in person) normally present cases on behalf of the public.[196] It has become customary to designate public prosecutors as "the Crown".

Private prosecutors

2–56   Since considerable confidence is reposed in the public prosecution service, demand for private prosecution is low. It appears that a private party, wishing to prosecute under solemn procedure, must use the rather archaic and long-winded form of document called "criminal letters" rather than the more modern "indictment", and must apply (by "bill") to the High Court for the issue of such "letters". That court will not normally issue these unless the application for them is supported by the Lord Advocate, although it is possible in exceptional circumstances for the court to permit their issue without his concurrence.[197] It is essential, however, for the prospective private prosecutor to show that he has been personally wronged by the alleged offence. It is not possible in Scotland to prosecute in respect of a crime that is no more than a general public wrong.[198] It appears, too, that there are crimes which are always to be regarded as primarily public wrongs, in respect of which only public prosecutors can be permitted to take action.[199] Private prosecution under summary procedure is generally not competent.[200]

PUBLIC PROCEEDINGS

2–57   It is a principle of Scots criminal law (which thus far accords with Art.6 of the European Convention on Human Rights by which public authorities are now bound)[201] that criminal trials, though not necessarily preliminary proceedings, should take place in the presence of the accused[202] (so that he may participate, or, if legally

---

[196] Although solicitor-advocates may be permitted to do so, see the Criminal Procedure (Scotland) Act 1995 s.301.

[197] See *J & P Coats Ltd v Brown* (1909) 6 Adam 19; *X. v Sweeney*, 1982 J.C. 70.

[198] See *McBain v Crichton*, 1961 J.C. 25.

[199] See, e.g. *Meehan v Inglis*, 1975 J.C. 9.

[200] See s.138 of the Criminal Procedure (Scotland) Act 1995, and the now repealed s.63 of the Criminal Justice (Scotland) Act 1995.

[201] See above, para.2–17.

[202] Criminal Procedure (Scotland) Act 1995 s.92(1) (as amended by the Criminal Procedure (Amendment) (Scotland) Act 2004 (asp 5) s.10(1)) and s.153(1) (as amended by the Criminal Proceedings etc. (Reform) (Scotland) Act 2007 (asp 6) s.14(5)).

represented, instruct his lawyer) and in public (presumably so that justice can be seen to be done). To this principle, there are some exceptions. In particular, a summary trial may take place in the accused's absence if he fails to appear and the court is satisfied that it is in the interests of justice to do so[203]; also, the accused may be removed if he "misconducts himself"[204]; and, further, the public may be excluded when evidence is being tendered in a solemn trial for rape "or the like".[205] That justice must not only be done, but be seen to be done, is both proverbial and a ground of appeal. The test is not whether, for example, the trial judge was *in fact* impartial or in good faith, but whether any suspicion might linger in the mind of a reasonable person that there might have been a lack of impartial justice.[206] Curiously, there have been more reported cases on this matter since it was stated in *Bradford v McLeod* that the paucity of recorded examples was a tribute to Scots law.[207] Thus, imposing sentence without giving an opportunity for a plea in mitigation,[208] congratulating the mother of a young complainer who had just given evidence in court,[209] using intemperate language in court,[210] and falling asleep on the bench[211] have all fallen foul of the general principle.[212]

PROCEEDINGS CONDUCTED FAIRLY

It is axiomatic that all stages of criminal proceedings should be **2–58** conducted fairly and impartially according to predetermined rules of evidence and procedure. In particular, proceedings must not be conducted according to arbitrary and *ad hoc* rules. Scots law is also bound by Art.6 ("Right to a fair trial") of the European Convention on Human Rights,[213] whereunder not only does an accused

---

[203] See the Criminal Procedure (Scotland) Act 1995 s.150A, as inserted by the Criminal Proceedings etc. (Reform) (Scotland) Act 2007 (asp 6) s.14(4): note that this rule also applies to diets other than those of trial, and is subject to safeguards mentioned in s.150A.

[204] Criminal Procedure (Scotland) Act 1995 s.92(2)–(2F),(4) (as amended and/or inserted by the Criminal Procedure (Amendment) (Scotland) Act 2004 (asp 5) s.10(2)–(4)), and s.153(2).

[205] Criminal Procedure (Scotland) Act 1995 s.92(3): *cf.* Art.6(1) of the European Convention on Human Rights (see the Human Rights Act 1998 Sch.1).

[206] See *Hogg v Normand*, 1992 S.L.T. 736; *Starrs v Ruxton; Ruxton v Starrs*, 1999 S.C.C.R. 1052; *Rimmer, Petitioner*, 2002 S.C.C.R. 1.

[207] *Bradford v McLeod*, 1986 S.L.T. 244 at 248G.

[208] *Bassi v Normand*, 1992 S.L.T. 341.

[209] *Hogg v Normand*, 1992 S.L.T. 736.

[210] *Sneddon v Lees*, 1996 S.L.T. 294.

[211] *Frew v Brown*, 1996 S.L.T. 282. See also the following examples: *Faroux v Brown*, 1996 S.C.C.R. 891; *Lorimar v Normand*, 1997 S.C.C.R. 582 (and *Walls v Heywood*, 2000 S.C.C.R. 21); *Milton v McLeod*, 1999 S.C.C.R. 210; *Murray v Watt*, 2002 S.C.C.R. 122; *McDonald v Craigen*, 2002 S.C.C.R. 405.

[212] By way of contrast, what was alleged to have taken place in the privacy of the jury room was not considered to be covered by the principle—*Russell v HM Advocate*, 1991 J.C. 194.

[213] See the Human Rights Act 1998 Sch.1.

person have the right "to a fair and public hearing within a reasonable time by an independent and impartial tribunal established by law"[214] but also the following "minimum rights"[215]:

> "(a) to be informed promptly, in a language which he understands and in detail, of the nature and cause of the accusation against him;
> (b) to have adequate time and facilities for the preparation of his defence;
> (c) to defend himself in person or through legal assistance of his own choosing or, if he has not sufficient means to pay for legal assistance, to be given it free when the interests of justice so require;
> (d) to examine or have examined witnesses against him and to obtain the attendance and examination of witnesses on his behalf under the same conditions as witnesses against him;
> (e) to have the free assistance of an interpreter if he cannot understand or speak the language used in court".

In addition to these rights, under Scots law the accused or his legal representative always has the right to speak last in a criminal trial.[216]

NO RIGHT TO JURY TRIAL

2–59 Unlike the law of England and many states in the USA, Scots law does not permit accused persons to elect for a jury rather than a bench, i.e. judge alone, trial. They must simply accept what the prosecutor or, unusually, the law, e.g. in murder and rape cases, dictates. Scottish prosecutors' discretion is absolute in this matter, which explains why jury trials are much less common in this country than elsewhere. If jury trial is considered proper, the accused's case will be determined (unless foreclosed by, for example, a plea of guilty) by a jury of 15 persons, rather than the more usual six to 12 persons favoured elsewhere in the Anglo-American family of legal systems.[217] Scottish juries are selected almost totally

---

[214] See above, para.2–57.
[215] European Convention on Human Rights Art.6(3).
[216] Criminal Procedure (Scotland) Act 1995 ss.98, 161.
[217] But it is possible to proceed with a trial where a jury has been reduced to 12, although even then (as with a full jury) a guilty verdict can only be returned where a majority of eight favours it—Criminal Procedure (Scotland) Act 1995 s.90. Indeed, juries smaller than 15 are not unknown in Scotland. During the Second World War, and for a short time thereafter, trials were undertaken before juries of seven persons—see, e.g. *MacDermid v HM Advocate*, 1948 J.C. 12.

at random[218] with no recourse to the extensive *voir dire* processes found in so many American states.[219]

VERDICTS

In Scottish criminal trials, both judges (in bench trials) and juries **2-60** may consider three possible verdicts—guilty, not guilty, and not-proven. Although it is not easy to state or understand the circumstances under which a not-proven verdict will be appropriate,[220] there is no doubt that such a verdict effectively acts as one of acquittal.[221] It is also generally a misdirection in law for a judge to discourage a jury from returning a verdict of not-proven[222]; yet the view taken is that Scottish juries are so familiar with that "third verdict" that it is not generally a misdirection *not* to draw it specifically to their attention.[223] On the other hand, judges have been advised by the Appeal Court not to attempt to distinguish not-proven from not guilty.[224] Recent attempts to rid Scots law of the not-proven verdict have, however, been met by spirited professional opposition and the latest legislative reforms have left all three verdicts intact.

FAIR SENTENCING

It is also axiomatic that a person who pleads guilty to, or is found **2-61** guilty of, an offence should be sentenced fairly and impartially within the limits imposed by law. Criticisms of particular sentences as either too lenient or too severe are certainly as common in Scotland as elsewhere; but it is inevitable in any system which generally allows wide discretion to judges (the present norm in the United Kingdom) that not all sentencing exercises will meet with

---

[218] *cf. B v HM Advocate*, 2006 S.L.T. 143 (*sub nom, Brown v HM Advocate*, 2006 S.C.C.R. 80).

[219] All challenges to persons being sworn as jurors in Scotland require cause to be shown (unless both parties at the trial agree that a particular person should be "excused")—Criminal Procedure (Scotland) Act 1995 s.86. For an example of a case where undisclosed prior knowledge by a juror, as to the accused's criminal past, led to a conviction being quashed on the basis that the court had not been seen to be impartial (as is required under Art.6(1) of the European Convention on Human Rights), see *McLean v HM Advocate*, 2001 S.C.C.R. 526.

[220] *cf. McNicol v HM Advocate*, 1964 J.C. 25, observations of Lord Justice-General Clyde at 26–27.

[221] *McDonald v HM Advocate*, 1989 S.L.T. 298.

[222] *McNicol v HM Advocate*, 1964 J.C. 25.

[223] *Harkin v HM Advocate*, 1992 S.L.T. 785, following *MacDermid v HM Advocate*, 1948 J.C. 12.

[224] *Fay v HM Advocate*, 1989 J.C. 129; *Cussick v HM Advocate*, 2001 S.C.C.R. 683.

universal approval. Two provisions assist, however, in the attainment of greater consistency and fairness in sentencing. First, in the course of deciding appeals against sentence (in a broad sense), the Appeal Court may pronounce an opinion on the sentence or other disposal or order which is appropriate in any similar case[225]; and trial courts thereafter must consider any such opinion in the course of deciding upon appropriate sentences, or other disposals or orders, in individual cases.[226] Secondly, not only may the prosecutor appeal on a point of law against a sentence passed but he may also appeal on the ground that a sentence passed was unduly lenient.[227] There have been many reported decisions relative to sentences alleged to have been unduly lenient, and it has emerged that the proper test in such matters is not whether the Appeal Court itself would have imposed a heavier sentence but whether the trial judge's sentence was outwith the range of sentences which a judge at first instance, applying his mind to all the relevant factors, could reasonably have considered appropriate.[228] "Relevant factors" will obviously vary from case to case; but the gravity of the offence itself, the past criminal record of the accused, the effect of the crime on the victim (psychological as well as physical), and society's need for retribution and/or deterrence have all figured prominently in the Appeal Court's deliberations.[229]

---

[225] Criminal Procedure (Scotland) Act 1995 ss.118(7), 189(7), as these provisions are amended by the Protection of Children (Scotland) Act 2003 (asp 5) ss.16(4)(b), (10)(b) respectively, and re-amended (to restore them to much their original forms) by the Protection of Vulnerable Groups (Scotland) Act 2007 (asp 14) Sch.4 paras 18(c), 25.

[226] Criminal Procedure (Scotland) Act 1995 s.197.

[227] Criminal Procedure (Scotland) Act 1995 s.108 and s.175(4), (4A), both as substituted (or, in the case of s.175(4A) inserted) by the Crime and Punishment (Scotland) Act 1997 s.21(1), and as amended by (a) the Crime and Disorder Act 1998 Sch.6 paras 6, 7; and (b) the Proceeds of Crime Act 2002 s.115. Notice, however, that in terms of s.175(4), which relates to summary procedure, the prosecutor is restricted to such classes of case as may be specified by the Secretary of State. No such restriction applies to the Lord Advocate in solemn procedure cases.

[228] *HM Advocate v Bell*, 1995 S.L.T. 350.

[229] See, e.g. *HM Advocate v Callaghan*, 1996 S.C.C.R. 709; *HM Advocate v McC*, 1996 S.C.C.R. 842; *HM Advocate v Carpenter*, 1998 S.C.C.R. 706; *HM Advocate v Heron*, 1998 S.C.C.R. 449; *HM Advocate v Carnall*, 1999 S.C.C.R. 904; *HM Advocate v Allan*, 2000 S.C.C.R. 219; *HM Advocate v Paterson*, 2000 S.C.C.R. 309; *HM Advocate v Millbank*, 2002 S.C.C.R. 771; *HM Advocate v Hegarty* 2002 S.C.C.R. 1022; *HM Advocate v Metcalfe*, 2003 S.C.C.R. 499; *HM Advocate v Shearer*, 2003 S.C.C.R. 657; *HM Advocate v Stalker*, 2003 S.C.C.R. 734; *HM Advocate v Gilmour*, 2004 S.C.C.R. 117; *HM Advocate v Hercus*, 2004 S.C.C.R. 140; *Bott v Morton*, 2005 S.C.C.R. 311; *HM Advocate v Norris*, 2005 S.C.C.R. 482; *HM Advocate v Thomson*, 2006 S.C.C.R. 265; *HM Advocate v Kirk*, 2007 S.C.C.R. 44; *HM Advocate v Mullen*, 2007 S.C.C.R. 330; *Lord Advocate v Harrison*, 2008 S.L.T. 112.

RIGHT OF APPEAL

Scots law adheres to the principle that a convicted person should **2–62** have a right of appeal against his conviction, his sentence or both.[230] The single, broad ground is that there has been a miscarriage of justice. But leave of a single judge of the High Court of Justiciary is required.[231] Prosecutors in a summary case may appeal by stated case on a point of law against an acquittal, or against the sentence passed[232]—in addition to appealing against what they consider to have been an unduly lenient sentence.[233] The inviolability of jury acquittals, however, is jealously guarded, since prosecutors are not permitted to appeal against findings of "not guilty" (or "not proven"[234]) in solemn procedure cases. But it is possible for prosecutors to seek clarification of the law as pronounced by the judge in such a case where the accused has been acquitted (or convicted) by referring the legal issues involved to the Appeal Court for a ruling. This is known as a "Lord Advocate's Reference".[235] The outcome of such a reference has no effect on the original acquittal (or conviction).

LEGAL ASSISTANCE FOR THE ACCUSED

Given the ever-growing complexity of the criminal law and the **2–63** relative imbalance in resources between the State, in bringing prosecutions through its prosecution service, and the accused, in having to defend them, it is imperative that legal assistance should

---

[230] Criminal Procedure (Scotland) Act 1995 s.106 (as altered by (a) the Crime and Punishment (Scotland) Act 1997, ss.17(1),18(1), 23(b); (b) the Protection of Children (Scotland) Act 2003 (asp 5) s.16(2); (c) the Crime and Disorder Act 1998 Sch.8 para.119; and (d) the Protection of Vulnerable Groups (Scotland) Act 2007 (asp 14) Sch.4 para.14) and s.175 (as altered by (a) the 1997 Act, ss.17(2), 21(2), 23(c); (b) the 1998 Act Sch.8 para.123; (c) the Proceeds of Crime Act 2002 s.115(6)–(8); (d) the 2003 Act (asp 5) s.16(7); and (e) the 2007 Act (asp 14) Sch.4 para.21).

[231] Criminal Procedure (Scotland) Act 1995 s.107 (solemn case), as amended by the Crime and Punishment (Scotland) Act 1997 Sch.1 para.21(15), the Criminal Justice (Scotland) Act 2003 (asp 7) s.62, and the Criminal Proceedings etc. (Reform) (Scotland) Act 2007 (asp 6) Sch.1 para.16(1); and also (summary case) s.180 (as amended by the Bail, Judicial Appointments etc (Scotland) Act 2000 (asp 9) Sch.1 para.7(4), and the said 2007 Act (asp 6) s.25(1) and Sch.1 para.18(2)), and s.187 (as amended by the Protection of Children (Scotland) Act 2003 (asp 5) s.16(9); the Criminal Proceedings (Reform) (Scotland) Act 2007 (asp 6) s.25(3) and Sch.1 para.18(3); and the Protection of Vulnerable Groups (Scotland) Act 2007 (asp 14) Sch.4 para.24).

[232] Criminal Procedure (Scotland) Act 1995 s.175(3).

[233] Criminal Procedure (Scotland) Act 1995 s.175(4): see above, para.2–61.

[234] See above, para.2–60.

[235] Criminal Procedure (Scotland) Act 1995 s.123.

be provided for those who cannot afford to employ a lawyer.[236] Scots law prides itself in having made provision for legal aid since the early fifteenth century,[237] though it is doubtful that criminal cases were then catered for. Certainly the early, simple schemes have given way to much more complicated rules.[238]

PROVISION FOR EXTRAORDINARY CIRCUMSTANCES

The nobile officium

2–64 It is inevitable in any legal system that situations will arise which have not been foreseen and in respect of which the existing law consequently provides no answer or remedy. It would be possible, of course, for such matters to be resolved eventually by Parliament or the Scottish Parliament through legislation; but Scots law provides a quicker solution. Persons aggrieved by some issue, for which the law provides no relief, may apply by petition for the exercise of the *nobile officium* of the High Court of Justiciary. This refers to a broad, equitable power which that court traditionally possesses to effect relief in suitable cases, the suitability of a case being wholly within the discretion of the court. For example, under the extradition legislation in force in the 1970s, it was discovered that Parliament had provided only one way of challenging a person's detention where his extradition had been requested by a foreign state—namely by application for the English prerogative writ of *habeas corpus*. Since that writ was (and remains) unknown in Scotland, a person detained in this country successfully sought a Scottish way of challenging that detention by appropriately petitioning the High Court.[239]

2–65 Since the *nobile officium* power clearly represents an equitable jurisdiction, it would be wrong to regard cases where it had been exercised or denied as necessarily forming precedents for the future in like cases. But equitable decisions have always had a habit of crystallising into "hard" law, and it has become clear that the *nobile officium* power will not be exercised unless the matter in question is truly unforeseeable and extraordinary,[240] there is no

---

[236] And indeed this is a requirement under Art.6(3)(c) of the European Convention on Human Rights: see above, para.2–58, and *Vickers v Buchanan*, 2002 S.C.C.R. 637.

[237] A.P.S. ii, 1424, c.24, 8.

[238] See *The Parliament House Book* (Edinburgh: W. Green), Vol. 3, Division G "Legal Aid", for a detailed account of the relevant legislative rules.

[239] *Wan Ping Nam v Federal German Republic*, 1972 J.C. 43 (noting that the main legislative provisions relating to extradition are now to be found in the Extradition Act 2003, as amended). Resort to the *nobile officium* may be made by the Lord Advocate, as well as by some aggrieved private individual: see, e.g. *Lord Advocate, Petitioner*, 1998 J.C. 209 (noting that there is now no such offence as "shamelessly indecent conduct"—see *Webster v Dominick*, 2005 1 J.C. 65).

[240] Alison, *Principles*, ii, 23 (at para.13); *cf. La Torre v Lord Advocate*, 2007 S.L.T. 51.

other remedy available in law,[241] the petitioner is in good faith,[242] and there will be no conflict with statutory provisions to the contrary.[243] The decided cases certainly suggest that the High Court is reluctant to use this power save in the clearest instances of oppression or injustice.[244]

The Scottish Criminal Cases Review Commission

Since 1999, the Scottish Criminal Cases Review Commission has **2–66** been able to refer the case of any person convicted before a Scottish criminal court to the High Court, so that the case can be determined by that court as an appeal (in connection with conviction or sentence) under the Criminal Procedure (Scotland) Act 1995.[245] It does not matter whether that person in respect of that case had previously brought any appeal before the High Court or not; and it is within the commission's discretion to refer such a case to the High Court on the simple grounds that "a miscarriage of justice may have occurred" and "that it is in the interests of justice that a reference should be made".[246] The commission has wide powers of investigation relating to their functions,[247] and can seek the High Court's opinion on any matter germane to their task of "considering whether to make a reference".[248] Since no criminal justice system can ever guarantee the complete absence of miscarriages of justice, and since the *nobile officium* power of the High Court is in practice one of somewhat limited application,[249] the establishment of this commission is a matter of considerable importance.[250]

---

[241] See, e.g. *Wilson, Petitioner*, 1992 S.L.T. 145; *cf. Anderson v HM Advocate*, 1974 S.L.T. 239 (a person lodging a stated case is deemed to have abandoned any other mode of appeal: see now s.184 of the Criminal Procedure (Scotland) Act 1995).

[242] *Woods, Petitioner*, 1994 S.L.T. 197.

[243] See, e.g. *Young, Petitioner*, 1994 S.L.T. 269 (noting that the statutory provisions are now ss.116(1), 124(2) of the Criminal Procedure (Scotland) Act 1995); *McWilliam, Petitioner*, 2002 S.C.C.R. 656 (see also below, para.2–66).

[244] As, e.g. where the Appeal Court *per incuriam* exceeded its powers—*Allan, Petitioner*, 1993 J.C. 181 (noting that the statutory provision referred to is now s.189 (as amended) of the Criminal Procedure (Scotland) Act 1995). See also *Arthur, Petitioner*, 2003 S.C.C.R. 6, where the petitioner had been sentenced for murder prior to the prosecutor's having "moved for sentence", and the unusual case of *Cochrane, Petitioner*, 2006 S.L.T. 349; *cf. Granger, Petitioner*, 2001 S.C.C.R. 337.

[245] See ss.194B, 194E of the Criminal Procedure (Scotland) Act 1995, as inserted by the Crime and Punishment (Scotland) Act 1997 s.25.

[246] Criminal Procedure (Scotland) Act 1995 s.194C, inserted as above; *cf. Raza v Scottish Criminal Cases Review Commission*, 2007 S.C.C.R. 403 (petition to the Court of Session for judicial review of a decision by the Commission).

[247] See Criminal Procedure (Scotland) Act 1995 ss.194F–194I, inserted as above.

[248] Criminal Procedure (Scotland) Act 1995 s.194D(3), inserted as above: see, e.g. *Scottish Criminal Cases Review Commission, Petitioners*, 2001 S.C.C.R. 775.

[249] See above, para.2–65.

[250] *cf.* however, the unusual case of *Cochrane, Petitioner*, 2006 S.L.T. 349.

CHAPTER 3

ACTUS REUS AND MENS REA

BASIC CONCEPTS AND DEFINITIONS

3–01 The purpose of this chapter is to provide an introduction to the fundamental principles of criminal liability. The basic rule is commonly expressed in a Latin maxim: *actus non facit reum nisi mens sit rea*—conduct does not make a man guilty unless his mind is also guilty. Generally speaking, a crime will have these two features: the *actus reus*, the physical or external component; and *mens rea*, which is the mental element. *Actus reus* and *mens rea* constitute the essential ingredients of criminal liability at common law. There are, however, a large number of statutory offences which do not require proof of *mens rea*. These are the so-called crimes of "strict liability". Crimes of this type are discussed in Ch.13. For the time being, the focus will be on more traditional crimes which do require proof of both *mens rea* and *actus reus*.

3–02 An understanding of the terminology of *actus reus* and *mens rea* is essential to the student of criminal law. They constitute the fundamentals of the criminal lawyer's vocabulary. These terms do not, however, have a fixed meaning. The specific forms that *actus reus* and *mens rea* take differ from one crime to another. This point can be demonstrated in a straightforward way. The *actus reus* of common law rape is non-consensual sexual intercourse with a woman. In contrast, the *actus reus* of theft is the taking or appropriating, without lawful authority, of property which belongs to someone else. Similarly, the *mens rea* involved in murder is different from that involved in culpable homicide. In both crimes someone has been killed, but it is only by examining the accused's mental state that one can determine whether he is a murderer or not.

ACTUS REUS

CONDUCT REQUIRED

3–03 The *actus reus* of a crime is simply the harmful or blameworthy conduct which the law seeks to prevent. It is the "doing something wrong" ingredient of criminal liability. All crimes require conduct, or an overt act. Thought crimes are unknown in the Scottish legal system: "No one can be punished for merely what goes on in his own head."[1] The criminal law imposes punishment only for the actions which result from thoughts, not for "unfulfilled intents".[2] As Lord Justice-Clerk MacDonald emphasised in *HM Advocate v Mackenzie*,[3] a "mere expression of willingness" to do something "morally reprehensible" is insufficient. If the prosecution cannot prove the *actus reus* required by the definition of the crime charged, there cannot be a conviction for that crime. An accused has to have performed an, "act which falls within the category either of accomplished or attempted crime."[4] As is explained in detail in Ch.6, if the accused has advanced sufficiently far in his preparations, he can be convicted of an attempt to commit a crime.

It is also axiomatic that the accused must have actually done **3–04** something to bring about what the criminal law seeks to forbid. In *Hogg v Macpherson*[5] the appellant was the driver of a horse-drawn furniture van. While he was driving the van along a street on a very windy day, a "furious" gust of wind blew the van over. The van struck and broke a street lamp. Under legislation then in force, the appellant was liable to make recompense for the damage, whether it was caused by negligence or by accident. The offence of which the appellant had been convicted was that of failing to pay the sum demanded by the local authority.[6] It was accepted that the appellant could have done nothing to avoid causing the damage. Lord Justice-General Clyde observed:

> "All I can say is that it seems to me as plain as can be from the circumstances of the case that the breaking of the lamp was not the appellant's act at all, either negligent or accidental, and that, accordingly, upon the facts found proved, there was no justification for the award made."[7]

Consequently, the conviction could not stand.

CONDUCT CRIMES AND RESULT CRIMES

A distinction is sometimes drawn between "conduct crimes" and **3–05** "result crimes" (see above, para.2–36). On occasion, the law simply forbids a certain form of conduct. A straightforward example

---

[1] *Morton v Henderson*, 1956 J.C. 55, per Lord Justice-General Clyde at 57.
[2] *HM Advocate v Mackenzie*, 1913 S.C. (J.) 107, per Lord Justice-Clerk MacDonald at 111.
[3] *HM Advocate v Mackenzie*, 1913 S.C. (J.) 107 at 112.
[4] *HM Advocate v Mackenzie*, 1915 S.C. (J.) 107 at 112.
[5] *Hogg v Macpherson*, 1928 J.C. 15.
[6] General Police and Improvement (Scotland) Act 1862 s.128, as incorporated in the Edinburgh Municipal and Police Act 1879 s.93.
[7] *Hogg v Macpherson*, 1928 J.C. 15 at 17.

would be the possession of a controlled drug under the Misuse of Drugs Act 1971. It is simply the act of possessing the drug which constitutes the *actus reus*. More generally, however, the law requires some forbidden consequence to result from the conduct. Many common law crimes contain within their definition a requirement of resultant harm. The result of the crime of murder is obviously that someone is killed, but it is not really significant *how* the victim dies. The criminal law is concerned here only with penalising the result of the conduct. There are no separate laws governing, for example, murder by stabbing or murder by strangulation.

Causation

3–06 In a result crime, it is necessary to prove as part of the *actus reus* both conduct and consequences. The prosecution will also need to establish the existence of a sufficient causal link between the conduct of the accused and the result. In *Kimmins v Normand*,[8] the appellant had been convicted of the reckless injury of a police officer. Prior to commencing a search for controlled drugs, the officer had asked the appellant whether he was in possession of any needles. He denied that he was. In fact, there was an unguarded needle in the appellant's pocket, and an injury was caused to the police officer's hand. The Appeal Court held that there was a sufficient causal connection between the appellant's denial and the resulting injury. The reasoning was that it must have been obvious to the appellant that the explanation for the officer's question was that he was about to place his hand into the appellant's pocket. It was a reasonable inference that the denial would lead to the officer's doing so. The court's conclusion was that "there was a causal connection between the denial and the end result."[9] The issue of causation is examined in detail in Ch.5.

Types of Actus Reus

3–07 Regardless of whether a particular offence is classified as a conduct crime or a result crime, the *actus reus* will be one of three possible types: (1) an overt (or positive) act; (2) an omission—a failure to act where there is a legal duty to act; or (3) a state of affairs.

---

[8] *Kimmins v Normand*, 1993 S.L.T. 1260; distinguished in *Mallin v Clark*, 2002 S.L.T. 1202. For detailed discussion of the crime of reckless injury, see below, para.9–27.
[9] *Kimmins v Normand*, 1993 S.L.T. 1260 at 1261H. In the absence of injury, the appellant could have been charged with reckless endangerment; see *Normand v Morrison*, 1993 S.C.C.R. 207; *Donaldson v Normand*, 1997 S.L.T. 1303. In *Normand v Robinson*, 1994 S.L.T. 558, there was held to be a sufficient causal link between the organisation of a "rave" on derelict premises and the reckless endangerment of those in attendance.

1. Overt acts

What is meant by an "act" is simply a movement of a part of the **3–08**
body. The criminal law excludes consideration of the relevant
thought processes from the definition of the *actus reus* of a crime.
What the actor thought or intended will invariably be dealt with
under the head of *mens rea*. Generally the relevant act will have a
physical or external manifestation, but this need not necessarily
involve actual movement of the limbs. Merely speaking to another
person could constitute the *actus reus* of a crime (most notably
incitement and breach of the peace).

2. Omissions

The general rule of the common law is that there can be no **3–09**
criminal liability for an omission, unless at the time of the failure to
act there was a legal duty to act. It is only in limited circumstances
that the criminal law extends to acts of omission, as well as acts of
commission. There is, for example, no legal duty to prevent the
commission of a crime. But if the law *does* impose a duty to act,
then a failure to comply with that requirement can constitute
sufficient conduct for the *actus reus* of the crime.[10] There is no
exception for the accused who did not know that he was under a
legal duty. This legal duty to act can derive from a number of
sources. The obligation to act may be created by statute: there are
a number of statutory offences which are specifically defined in
terms of an omission to act. One straightforward example is failing
to provide a specimen of breath under the breathalyser legislation.[11] As well as conduct crimes of this kind deriving from statute,
it is possible to commit a result crime by means of omission. To
starve a child to death could be the result of an omission.[12] This
might be described as committing a crime of commission by
omission (assuming the presence of the requisite *mens rea* for
either culpable homicide or murder).

A duty to act?

There are also instances where the common law would probably **3–10**
impose a duty to act. This will be the case where, for example, an
individual has undertaken to do something upon which the health
and safety of others depends. Examples of this are the cases of
William Hardie,[13] where a charge of culpable homicide brought
against an Inspector of Poor who had ignored the deceased's
application for poor relief was held to be relevant; and an English

---

[10] See *Buchmann v Normand*, 1994 S.C.C.R. 929.
[11] Road Traffic Act 1988 s.8(9).
[12] See *George Fay* (1847) Ark. 397. For a rare modern example of homicide by
omission, see *Bone v HM Advocate*, 2005 S.C.C.R. 829.
[13] *William Hardie* (1847) Ark. 247.

case, *R. v Instan*,[14] where a fatal omission by a niece to provide food and medical attention for her invalid aunt resulted in a manslaughter (equivalent to culpable homicide) conviction. The crimes in these two examples were committed by failing to fulfil a legal duty. In *William Hardie* the legal duty was derived from a contract. The failure to act was not just a breach of contract with his employer, however, but provided the possible basis for a conviction[15]: the duty of care also extended to members of the public he was paid to protect. In *Instan* the duty had been assumed voluntarily. This would seem to imply that if someone agreed to look after a neighbour's child and the child drowned in the bath while that child-minder was watching television, then a conviction for culpable homicide could ensue. This scenario could be analysed either in terms of a voluntary assumption of a duty of care, or of a contractual obligation.[16]

The duty to limit the harm caused by a dangerous act

3–11   There may also be occasions where the accused has created a dangerous situation and is therefore under a legal duty to do what he can to remedy the situation. If he omits to do so, then this can constitute the *actus reus* of a crime. The accused in *HM Advocate v McPhee*[17] was charged with murder. He had committed a serious assault on a woman, and had left her injured and unconscious in an open field. Lord Mackay, the trial judge, upheld the relevancy of the indictment, stating that there could be a murder conviction,

> "if he is proved to have wickedly and feloniously exposed the unconscious woman regardless of consequences to the inclemency of the weather, and if she died in consequence . . . both of the beating and the exposure . . ."[18]

3–12   In *MacPhail v Clark*,[19] the accused was a farmer who was charged with culpable and reckless endangerment. He had set fire to some straw in a field near a public road, but neglected to ensure that no danger was caused. The fire spread to vegetation on the verge of the road with the result that there was a collision on the road. This resulted in injuries to people driving there at the time.[20] At no time

---

[14] *R. v Instan* [1893] 1 Q.B. 450.
[15] Although the charge was held to be a relevant one, it was not proceeded with.
[16] Failure to provide for a child in one's care also constitutes an offence in its own right: see the Children and Young Persons (Scotland) Act 1937.
[17] *HM Advocate v McPhee*, 1935 J.C. 46. See also *Miller and Denovan v HM Advocate*, 1960, noted at 1991 S.L.T. 211.
[18] *HM Advocate v McPhee*, 1935 J.C. 46 at 50. The accused was convicted of culpable homicide.
[19] *MacPhail v Clark*, 1983 S.L.T. (Sh. Ct.) 37.
[20] Since the crime charged seems to have been reckless endangerment, the injuries were not necessary to conviction, but acted by way of aggravation; see below, para.9–28.

did the accused make any attempt to remedy the dangerous situation which he had caused. The sheriff held that the accused, as a farmer, was aware of the dangers of straw burning and knew of the presence of the road. He had allowed the fire to spread and had thereby demonstrated a reckless indifference to the consequences of his actions. He was convicted. Where the farmer was at fault was in his omitting to take sufficient precautions to safeguard against the fire spreading. A somewhat different approach was taken in the more recent case of *McCue v Currie*,[21] where the court seemed reluctant to endorse the general proposition that there is a legal duty to act in a situation where a danger has been created. In this case, the accused had entered a caravan for the purpose of theft and was using a cigarette lighter to see his way around. He accidentally dropped the lighter. A fire was started. He was aware that this was the case, but did nothing to extinguish it or summon assistance. The caravan was destroyed. It was held that this could not amount to the crime of culpable and reckless fire-raising, since guilt must be determined by reference to the act of starting the fire (which was accidental) and not subsequent events (however reprehensible). What is surprising about this decision, perhaps, is the absence of recognition of a general proposition that an omission to do what there is a legal duty to do is the equivalent of an act. It may be that the "accidental" nature of the fire-raising had a particular influence on the decision of the court,

> "fire raising which is merely accidental . . . is not a crime, and cannot become so on account of subsequent behaviour on the part of the person concerned."[22]

No general duties to act

It has been stressed that, absent a legal duty to act, an omission **3–13** cannot constitute the *actus reus* of a crime. The corollary of this is that, if a court determines that the *actus reus* of a crime can be committed by omission, this is to impose a legal duty to act upon all citizens who find themselves in the same position. Naturally enough, the courts are somewhat reluctant to create new legal obligations of this kind, preferring to leave this activity to Parliament. This disinclination on the part of the judiciary can be seen clearly in the decision of the Appeal Court in *Paterson v Lees*.[23]

---

[21] *McCue v Currie*, 2004 S.C.C.R. 200.
[22] *McCue v Currie*, 2004 S.C.C.R. 200 at 207, para.25.
[23] *Paterson v Lees*, 1999 J.C. 159 (noting that the crime of shameless indecency no longer exists as a result of the decision in *Webster v Dominick*, 2003 S.L.T. 975). In *McCue v Currie*, 2004 S.C.C.R. 200 also it is stated that if there is a case for enacting a new crime of culpably failing to take appropriate steps after a situation of danger to persons or property has arisen as a result of a person's actions, that is a matter for legislative, rather than judicial, activity.

The charge here was of shameless indecency. The appellant had been acting as a babysitter, when one of the children put on a video containing indecent material. The appellant allowed the children to continue watching. In other words, he *omitted* to stop the children viewing the material in question. The Appeal Court was unanimous in deciding that the crime of shameless indecency could not be committed in this way: it was not a crime to permit children to view indecent material. Lord Justice-General Rodger stated[24]:

> "By holding that it was criminal for the appellant to do nothing and so to permit the children to view the film, the sheriff was in effect affirming that our criminal law imposes upon a person in the appellant's position a positive duty to act to prevent children from seeing obscene and indecent material."

His Lordship regarded this as "one giant leap for the law".[25] The decision as to whether this should be done was one for the legislature, and not for the court.

3–14   The criminal law has never imposed a general duty to assist another person who is in peril. The law does not maintain that everyone is obliged to be his brother's keeper.[26] There may be a moral duty to act, but this will not necessarily constitute a legal duty. The man who stands by and watches a small child drown in a swimming pool does not commit a crime, even though he might have saved the child with ease and at no risk to himself. The situation would, of course, be very different if the man was the child's father. There would then be a legal duty to act.[27] Similarly, a duty to intervene would arise if the bystander were an attendant employed to ensure the safety of swimmers. In some other jurisdictions, however, there exist specific offences of failing to assist a person who is in peril.[28] This is sometimes described as a duty of "easy rescue". It will be subject to some kind of proviso that the assistance can be rendered without danger. Although there may be strong moral arguments supporting the desirability of such an offence, the common law dictates otherwise.

---

[24] *Paterson v Lees*, 1999 J.C. 159 at 161F.

[25] *Paterson v Lees*, 1999 J.C. 159 at 161F.

[26] See J. Hall, *General Principle of Criminal Law*, 2nd edn (Indianapolis: Bobbs-Merrill Co. Inc., 1960), p.210.

[27] See the Australian case of *R. v Russell* [1933] V.L.R. 59. There is a possible analogy here with nineteenth century cases in which it was held to be homicide where a new-born baby died as a result of the mother's failure to summon help at the time of birth; see *Isabella Martin* (1877) 3 Coup. 379; *HM Advocate v Scott* (1892) 3 White 240. See also *Bone v HM Advocate*, 2005 S.C.C.R. 829, where the allegation against the appellant was that she had wilfully failed to protect and ensure the wellbeing of her child in the face of her co-accused's assaults, as a consequence of which the child had died.

[28] See, e.g. French Penal Code, Art.63(2).

3. A state of affairs

There are a number of statutory offences which are defined in **3–15** such a way that they can be committed when a certain state of affairs exists, or where the accused is in a particular situation. There is no express requirement of conduct. An example of this type of offence is s.4(1) of the Road Traffic Act 1988, which makes it an offence for a person to be unfit to drive through drink or drugs while in charge of a mechanically propelled vehicle on the road. The offence is a state of affairs: being in charge of a vehicle while unfit.[29]

MENS REA

THE MENTAL ELEMENT

As a general rule, the criminal law does not apply to an individual **3–16** who has acted without mental fault. The common law draws a general distinction between conduct which is meant and conduct which is not deliberate. This precondition for the establishment of criminal liability has long been part of the Scottish criminal legal heritage. The explanation for this requirement of a blameworthy state of mind is that it serves to justify the imposition of punishment. This mental element is generally referred to as the *mens rea*. It is a presumption of the common law that crimes require *mens rea*.[30] Statutory offences which impose strict liability are by way of an exception to the common law principle.

Mens rea and dole

Mens rea is not the easiest concept to grasp. In the simplest of **3–17** terms, it refers to the mental element required by the definition of a particular crime, as distinct from the *actus reus*. That is, the *mens rea* is the individual's state of mind at the time that the forbidden conduct took place. (Perversely and confusingly, some authorities refer to the *actus reus* as containing a form of *mens rea*. What is meant there is that the conduct, amounting to the *actus reus* of a particular crime, should be "voluntary" as a minimum requirement of liability. "True" *mens rea* would still have to be established over and above.) One can identify two distinct meanings attached to the concept of *mens rea* (treated quite separately from the *actus reus*). The first of these is that *mens rea* connotes a general notion of moral blameworthiness. This conception of *mens rea* correlates to the traditional Scottish term for the mental element of "dole",

---

[29] The question of whether an accused assumed charge of the vehicle is one of fact; see *Kelso v Brown*, 1998 S.L.T. 921.
[30] *Blane v HM Advocate*, 1991 S.C.C.R. 576, per Lord Justice-General Hope at 581D; *Paterson v Lees*, 1999 J.C. 159, per Lord Sutherland at 163E.

derived from the Latin *dolus* (the definition of which includes "evil intent, wrongdoing with a view to the consequences"[31]). It is the term dole which is to be found in many of the older cases. Hume defined dole as "that corrupt and evil intention, which is essential . . . to the guilt of any crime."[32] He stated that the requirement of dole did not mean that there had to be an intention to do the particular crime. Rather, the *actus reus* "must be attended with such circumstances as indicate a corrupt and malignant disposition, a heart contemptuous of order and social duty."[33] This conception of the mental element indicating an evil character might be appropriate to the most serious offences, such as murder or an aggravated assault, but it is plainly not applicable to the majority of crimes (which are far less serious). For most crimes, especially those created by statute, it is more helpful to think in terms of *mens rea* as a mental state specific to a particular crime.

3–18	This is the second meaning of *mens rea*, and is the conception which has gained prominence.[34] Nevertheless, the traditional approach to *mens rea* does persist. Although the term dole is not in common use today, the moralistic approach reflected in Hume still provides the background to the modern criminal law.[35] The concept of "wicked recklessness" has long been a significant aspect of the law of murder. More recently, it has been held that the epithet "wicked" should be applied to the intention to kill in murder.[36] The significance of this remains a matter for detailed discussion within the account of murder presented in Ch.9. In the context of intention, it may be that "wicked" is used as shorthand to refer to the absence of any applicable defence.

3–19	"Evil intent" features in the crime of assault. Again, it remains unclear whether the adjective "evil" has any particular legal significance. In the *Lord Advocates Reference (No.2 of 1992)*,[37] Lord Justice-Clerk Ross suggested that it means only "that assault cannot be committed accidentally or recklessly or negligently". If this is correct, the intention behind an assault would not have to accord with the dictionary definition of the word "evil" to attract criminal liability.[38] The desirability of a modern criminal law

---

[31] C.T. Lewis and C. Short, *A Latin Dictionary* (Oxford: Clarendon Press (1993 printing), 1879), p.607.

[32] Hume, *Commentaries*, i, 21.

[33] Hume, *Commentaries*, i, 22. The "character theory" of criminal responsibility is not, of course, unique to Hume. See, more generally, G. Mousourakis, "Character, Choice and Criminal Responsibility" (1998) 39 *Cashiers de Droit* 51.

[34] See, e.g. *Byrne v HM Advocate (No.2)*, 2000 S.L.T. 233.

[35] See *Transco Plc v HM Advocate (No.1)*, 2004 J.C. 29.

[36] *Drury v HM Advocate*, 2001 S.L.T. 1013.

[37] *Lord Advocate's Reference (No.2 of 1992)*, 1993 J.C. 43 at 48, relying upon Gordon, *Criminal Law*, 2nd edn, para.29.30; applied in *Quinn v Lees*, 1994 S.C.C.R. 159. For a fuller discussion of this issue, see below, paras 9–14 and 9–15.

[38] Support for this interpretation comes from the *Lord Advocates Reference No.1 of 2000*, 2001 J.C. 143 at 154D, where the opinion of the court was that the "malice" element of the common law crime of malicious mischief did "not require proof of spite or any other form of motive".

relying upon concepts of "evilness" and "wickedness", with the definition of crimes dependent upon the significance attributable to such notions, would no doubt be questioned by some. Certainly it reflects a perspective on the mental element in crime rather different from the more technical approach prevailing in Anglo-American criminal law. The debate between the two approaches is no doubt an interesting one, but rather misses the point. The Scottish approach is reflective of the historical background of the criminal law in the jurisdiction. The common law continues to rely upon moralistic concepts to describe the necessary mental element of crimes.[39]

There may indeed be some advantage to the "pre-modern" approach prevailing in Scots law. Some would see merit in its recognition "that what is ultimately in issue is the community's moral judgment on the accused's behaviour, and not the satisfaction of a legal formula."[40]

Subjectivity and objectivity

Criminal lawyers often refer to *mens rea* as being assessed either **3–20** subjectively or objectively. A subjective approach to *mens rea* requires that the accused had actually foreseen the consequences of his actions. Did he know that the particular result would ensue from his conduct? In contrast, if an objective approach to *mens rea* is adopted, the accused will be judged according to the standard of what he should have foreseen, or of what was foreseeable.[41] It will be permissible to conclude that he had the necessary *mens rea* because he really should have known what was going to happen. There will be less emphasis upon triers of fact putting themselves in the position of the accused and deciding what he actually thought at the time of the *actus reus*. It is easier for a prosecutor to prove beyond reasonable doubt the existence of *mens rea* if it is objectively, rather than subjectively, assessed; and in Scotland it is objectively assessed.[42]

Mens rea and motive

It is important at the outset to distinguish *mens rea* from motive, **3–21** since the two are not infrequently confused. Motive (sometimes called the ulterior intention) is concerned with the reason why an individual acted as he did. What caused him to act in the way in

---

[39] See *Transco Plc v HM Advocate (No.1)*, 2004 J.C. 29.
[40] G.H. Gordon, "Subjective and Objective *Mens Rea*" (1975) 17 *Criminal L.Q.* 355 at 390. The point is made of the role of wicked recklessness in murder.
[41] See, e.g. *Sutherland v HM Advocate*, 1994 S.C.C.R. 80, per Lord Justice-General Hope at 92C–D.
[42] Modern authorities for this proposition include *Jamieson v HM Advocate*, 1987 S.C.C.R. 484; *Blane v HM Advocate*, 1991 S.C.C.R. 576; *McIntosh v HM Advocate*, 1993 S.C.C.R. 464; *Transco Plc v HM Advocate (No.1)*, 2004 J.C. 29.

which the prosecution alleges? The substantive criminal law is generally unconcerned with motive in this sense. Lord Justice-Clerk Inglis observed in the case of *Alexander Milne*[43]: "The motive may remain a mystery, while the murder is an accomplished fact." That said, motive could be very significant in evidential terms.

3–22   Thus the criminal law is generally unconcerned with the reasons why the accused acted as is alleged. He may be a protester who believes himself to be acting for the best of reasons when breaking the law. This was the position in the *Lord Advocate's Reference (No.1 of 2000)*,[44] where protesters against nuclear weapons committed malicious mischief against property of the Royal Navy. The fact that they had not acted out of "spite" was regarded as irrelevant by the Appeal Court.[45] To similar effect is *Ralston v HM Advocate*,[46] which concerned a prisoner who had taken part in rooftop protest. He was convicted of committing a breach of the peace. He claimed that he had acted in order to protest against prison conditions. On appeal, the High Court upheld the sheriff's direction to the jury that, even if Ralston's motives had been blameless, they were irrelevant to determining whether his conduct constituted a breach of the peace. In the *Lord Advocates Reference (No.2 of 1992)*,[47] the accused contended that he had pointed a gun at the owner of a shop during an apparent armed robbery as part of a joke. It was held that this was a claim as to the motive or ulterior intention. This was irrelevant if he had been acting deliberately.

THE CATEGORIES OF MENS REA

3–23 The concept of *mens rea* embraces those who have made a decision and chosen to break the law. An example would be the person who drives his car towards another with the specific purpose of striking and killing him. *Mens rea*, however, is not limited to this one mental state. The criminal law distinguishes among a number of analytically distinct levels of *mens rea*. This reflects a recognition that some law-breakers act with a greater degree of "evil intent" or "wickedness" than others do, and can properly be held to a higher degree of culpability. Thus the individual who drives his car at such a speed that any reasonable person would foresee that someone might be killed, but does not aim the vehicle at anyone, would be held to be less culpable (subject to a less severe penalty) than the driver in the previous example.

3–24   This second example also illustrates the point that the *mens rea* of some crimes can extend to those who do not anticipate causing any harm, but really ought to have realised the risks involved in

---

[43] *Alexander Milne* (1863) 4 Irv. 301 at 345.
[44] *Lord Advocate's Reference (No.1 of 2000)*, 2001 J.C. 143.
[45] *Lord Advocate's Reference (No.1 of 2000)*, 2001 J.C. 143 at 154D–E.
[46] *Ralston v HM Advocate*, 1989 S.L.T. 474; followed in *HM Advocate v Forbes*, 1994 S.L.T. 861.
[47] *Lord Advocate's Reference (No.2 of 1992)*, 1993 J.C. 43.

their actions. *Mens rea* does not refer to any one mental state. It cannot be equated with intent. There are degrees of *mens rea*. In *Quinn v Cunningham*,[48] Lord Justice-General Clyde observed,

> "it is an essential element in the constitution of a crime at common law that there should be either an intention to commit a wrong or an utter disregard of what the consequences of the act in question may be . . .".

In relation to common law (and statutory) crimes, therefore, there are two core states of mind: (1) intention; and (2) recklessness. That said, Scottish practice recognises a wide variety of terms to indicate *mens rea* in common law crimes. These include, inter alia, knowledge, malice and wilfulness.

1. Intention

Some crimes, most notably assault,[49] theft[50] and wilful fire- **3–25** raising,[51] can only be committed intentionally.[52] This does not mean that there has to have been advance planning or prolonged deliberation. Intention involves no more than a resolve or purposive decision to act in a particular way. The Scottish courts have not progressed very far towards defining the concept of intention. Three reasons for this can be suggested. The first is that the generally objective approach to *mens rea* in Scots law makes it unnecessary to measure with precision the degree of intention present at the time of the *actus reus*. Whilst conceding that intention is a subjective state of mind,[53] it is accepted in Scots law that there can be objective proof (see below, paras 3–27 and 3–28).[54] The second reason is that there may have been a desire to avoid the difficulties in which the English courts have found themselves as the result of a series of cases on the concept of intention.[55] These problems have arisen as the result of judges attempting to give juries detailed guidance on how intention can be proved. Scottish courts have been more prepared to treat the concept of intention as an ordinary word, the meaning of which

---

[48] *Quinn v Cunningham*, 1956 J.C. 22 at 24.
[49] *Lord Advocates Reference (No.2 of 1992)*, 1993 J.C. 43; *HM Advocate v Harris*, 1993 J.C. 150.
[50] Hume, *Commentaries*, i, 73 ("felonious purpose" required).
[51] *Byrne v HM Advocate (No.2)*, 2000 S.L.T. 233.
[52] The common law presumption would be that intention is the requisite mental element, unless there is authority suggesting otherwise.
[53] See, e.g. *Boyle v Ritchie*, 1999 S.C.C.R. 278, per Lord Prosser at 281E–F.
[54] *Boyle v Ritchie*, 1999 S.C.C.R. 278; see also *Byrne v HM Advocate (No.2)*, 2000 S.L.T. 233 at 238G.
[55] See the decisions of the House of Lords in *Hyam v DPP* [1975] A.C. 55; *R. v Moloney* [1985] A.C. 905; *R. v Hancock and Shankland* [1986] A.C. 455; and *R. v Woollin* [1999] 1 A.C. 82.

will be apparent to juries. A third reason is that the English cases are concerned with intention in the law of murder. Since Scots law recognises the alternative *mens rea* of wicked recklessness, this means that intention is not necessarily the central issue in such cases.[56]

3-26   One useful definition of intention is that adopted by Lord Ross in his charge to the jury in *Sayers v HM Advocate*[57]:

> "An 'intention' to my mind connotes a state of affairs which the party 'intending' . . . does more than merely contemplate; it connotes a state of affairs which, on the contrary, he decides, so far as in him lies, to bring about, and which . . . he has a reasonable prospect of being able to bring about, by his act of volition."

Although helpful, this definition has to be read in the context of a conspiracy case. It is concerned with an intention to perform a future action.[58] The criminal law is generally concerned with determining what constitutes an intention to effect a result which has actually been brought about. Not all intended actions are preceded by an opportunity for reflection and conscious decision-making. This intuition sits well with the Scottish approach to *mens rea*, which tends not to see *mens rea* as a mental process which can be investigated separately from what the accused has actually done. As Lord Justice-Clerk Grant observed in *HM Advocate v Wilson, Latta and Rooney*[59]: "It is by their acts, as frequently happens in other spheres of life, that we know them."

Proving intention

3-27   Unless the accused has confessed to his state of mind, intention will have to be proved by inference from the evidence: "His intention must, in the absence of any admissions by him, be derived from the circumstances surrounding the incident."[60] In *Cawthorne v HM Advocate*,[61] Lord Avonside pointed out:

---

[56] See *Cawthorne v HM Advocate*, 1968 J.C. 32.
[57] *Sayers v HM Advocate*, 1981 S.C.C.R. 312 at 318. The source of this quotation is *Cunliffe v Goodman* [1950] 2 K.B. 237, per Lord Justice Asquith at 253.
[58] For discussion of this issue, see R.A. Duff, *Intention, Agency and Criminal Responsibility* (1990), pp.17 and 44–47.
[59] *HM Advocate v Wilson, Latta and Rooney*, 1968, unreported, but see C.H.W. Gane and C.N. Stoddart, *Casebook on Scottish Criminal Law*, 2nd edn (Edinburgh: W. Green, 1988), p.204.
[60] *Carr v HM Advocate*, 1995 S.L.T. 800 at 804B–C. See also Erskine, IV, 4, 8: "dole . . . can only be discovered from the outward circumstances from which it is presumed."
[61] *Cawthorne v Lord Advocate*, 1968 J.C. 32 at 33.

"It is impossible . . . to look into the mind of the man, and when, therefore, you are seeking to evaluate the effect of the evidence in regard to the nature and purposes of the act you can only do so by drawing an *inference* from what that man did in the background of all the facts of the case which you accept as proved."

This evidence will consist of the words and conduct of the **3–28** accused, and the circumstances surrounding the crime. Lord Justice-General Hope explained in *Hughes v Crowe*[62] that the actions of the accused have,

"to be of a sufficient quality to enable the inference to be drawn of *mens rea*. That is an inference to be drawn from the nature and quality of the acts complained of . . .".

In a case of assault, for example, the necessary intention could be inferred from the fact that a punch was thrown. The prosecution would not have to offer specific proof of the accused's intention. In an example such as this, the accused will need to raise a reasonable doubt about the presence of an intention to assault in order to secure an acquittal. He will bear the tactical burden of overcoming the inference that the assault was committed intentionally.[63] Sometimes, however, the conduct of the accused will be consistent with entirely innocent behaviour, and a simple inference of intention will be impossible. If this is the case, then some additional evidence will be required from the prosecution for the purpose of proving the presence of a criminal intent. An example might be a charge of theft by shoplifting, since it is possible to mistakenly leave a shop without paying. An intention to steal would also have to be shown to be present (see below, para.10–28). The prosecution might do so by producing evidence that the accused had acted furtively.[64]

Scottish criminal law recognises a distinction between an individ- **3–29** ual who has acted recklessly and one who has purposely brought about a particular result.[65] In practical terms, it is important to draw a boundary between recklessness and intention, because some crimes can only be committed intentionally. This point is

---

[62] *Hughes v Crowe*, 1993 S.C.C.R. 320 at 323. See also *MacDonald v Cardle*, 1985 S.C.C.R. 195 (a rather unusual case); *Mason v Jessop*, 1990 S.C.C.R. 387; *Carney v HM Advocate*, 1995 S.L.T. 1208; *McGill v HM Advocate*, 2000 S.C.C.R. 28.

[63] See F. Raitt, *Evidence*, 3rd edn, para.2.04.

[64] See Erskine, IV, 4, 8: "And in actions which are either innocent or criminal, according to the good or bad intention of the agent, dole must also in that case be presumed or not, from the circumstances previous to or concomitant with the crime." *Barr v O'Brien*, 1991 S.C.C.R. 67, provides an example of an intent to steal by shoplifting being proved by inference from the conduct of the accused.

[65] *HM Advocate v Harris*, 1993 J.C. 150, per Lord Justice-Clerk Ross at 154E, founding upon *HM Advocate v Phipps* (1905) 4 Adam 616.

emphasised in the opinion of the Appeal Court in *Byrne v HM Advocate (No.2)*.[66] This decision concerned the common law crime of wilful fire-raising, for which the requisite mental element is intention. The opinion emphasises that it is "vital for a judge to keep the concepts of intention and recklessness distinct . . . nor can any form of recklessness be treated as equivalent to intent."[67] It was therefore a misdirection to tell a jury that intention "could be implied from conduct indicating an utter disregard of the likelihood of the fire spreading to the subjects in question."[68] The court overruled (in part) an earlier decision, *Blane v HM Advocate*,[69] where it appeared to have been suggested that wilful fire-raising could be committed recklessly. In *Blane*, Lord Justice-General Hope had observed[70]:

> "since the matter must be approached objectively I think it is open to inference, where the accused is shown to have acted with a reckless disregard for the likely consequences of what he does, that he intended those consequences to occur."

This was to blur the distinction between the concepts of intention and recklessness; an approach rightly disapproved in *Byrne v HM Advocate*.[71] It is not possible to conclude that an individual intended a consequence as to which he was reckless. What a jury has to decide is whether the evidence is sufficient to permit an inference of intention to be drawn. This cannot be done "[i]f all that they infer from the evidence is that the accused was reckless, even to a very high degree".[72] However reckless an actor may have been as to the consequence of an action, this is quite different from having intended to bring it about.

2. Recklessness

3–30   The criminal law has long regarded the reckless law-breaker as culpable and deserving of punishment. What constitutes criminal recklessness is "a total indifference to and disregard for the safety of the public".[73] The standard applicable at common law is that articulated by Lord Justice-General Clyde in *Quinn v Cunningham*.[74] His opinion contains two definitions of recklessness as a mental element in crime: (i) "an utter disregard of what the consequences of the act in question may be so far as the public are

[66] *Byrne v HM Advocate (No.2)*, 2000 S.L.T. 233.
[67] *Byrne v HM Advocate (No.2)*, 2000 S.L.T. 233 at 238L and 239G.
[68] *Byrne v HM Advocate (No.2)*, 2000 S.L.T. 233 at 238J.
[69] *Blane v HM Advocate*, 1991 S.C.C.R. 576 at 582E. See below, para.11–32.
[70] *Blane v HM Advocate*, 1991 S.C.C.R. 576 at 582E.
[71] *Byrne v HM Advocate (No.2)*, 2000 S.L.T. 233.
[72] *Byrne v HM Advocate (No.2)*, 2000 S.L.T. 233 at 238L.
[73] *RHW v HM Advocate*, 1982 S.L.T. 420 at 420.
[74] *Quinn v Cunningham*, 1956 J.C. 22; applied in *Cameron v Maguire*, 1999 J.C. 63.

concerned"[75]; and (ii) "recklessness so high as to involve an indifference to the consequences for the public generally".[76] Although the wording is different, the legal principle is the same. The key notion is "disregard" or "indifference" to the risks attending the conduct in question. Examples of actions held to permit the requisite inference of criminal recklessness include:

1. test firing a high calibre rifle from the front of a house, in the vicinity of other properties and of areas to which the public had access[77];

2. chasing bullocks from a field, causing them to escape on to a railway line and then on to a public road[78];

3. driving at 156 mph on a road where the speed limit was 70 mph.[79]

The standard is an objective one. In none of these three examples had the accused given thought to the risk or danger involved in their actions. It was this very indifference which gave rise to culpability. The individual who chased the bullocks appears to have thought that he was involved in some kind of "game", being unaware of the seriousness of his actions.[80] The gentleman who was found to have discharged his firearm recklessly claimed to have thought that he was acting in a safe manner.[81] In respect of the speeding motorist, the risk to other road users was said to be obviously foreseeable and to drive at such an excessive speed could not be described as anything other than culpable and reckless.[82]

The decision in *Allan v Patterson*[83] concerned the interpretation **3–31** of the concept of recklessness in the context of the repealed statutory offence of reckless driving. Lord Justice-General Emslie stated that inquiry into the state of knowledge of the individual driver at the time of the offence was not required. In order to be able to "apply the adverb recklessly to the driving in question",[84] it had to be established,

"that it fell far below the standard of driving expected of the competent and careful driver and that it occurred either in the face of obvious and material dangers which were or

---

[75] *Quinn v Cunningham*, 1956 J.C. 22 at 24.
[76] *Quinn v Cunningham*, 1956 J.C. 22 at 25.
[77] *Cameron v Maguire*, 1999 J.C. 63.
[78] *Robson v Spiers*, 1999 S.L.T. 1141.
[79] *Robertson v Klos*, 2006 S.C.C.R. 52.
[80] *Robson v Spiers*, 1999 S.L.T. 1141 at 1143C.
[81] *Cameron v Maguire*, 1999 J.C. 63 at 64H, although he did concede: "On looking at it again now, I wouldn't do it again, no."
[82] *Robertson v Klos*, 2006 S.C.C.R. 52 at 60, para.[22].
[83] *Allan v Patterson*, 1980 J.C. 57; see also *Black v Allan*, 1985 S.C.C.R. 11, discussed below in para.11–26.
[84] *Allan v Patterson*, 1980 J.C. 57 at 60.

should have been observed, appreciated and guarded against, or in circumstances which showed a complete disregard for any potential dangers which might result from the way in which the vehicle was being driven."

This suggests that recklessness is a description of behaviour as much as a state of mind, although Lord Emslie did accept that,

"in reaching a decision upon the critical issue a Judge or jury will be entitled to have regard to any explanation offered by the accused driver designed to show that his driving in the particular circumstances did not possess the quality of recklessness at the material time."[85]

It is important, however, to read Lord Emslie's opinion in the context of a statute which made it an offence to drive recklessly. The offence was targeted at performing an otherwise lawful activity, but doing so in a way which could be described as reckless. But, as Lord Justice-General Hope explained in *Carr v HM Advocate*,[86] in relation to a common law crime (fire-raising in this instance),

"it is not the manner of doing an act which would otherwise be lawful which is in issue but the question whether the accused had the *mens rea* necessary for the commission of a crime."

The issue is "whether the accused's actions showed a complete disregard for any dangers which might result from what he was doing . . .". The decision in *Cameron v Maguire*[87] makes it clear that, at least in relation to common law crimes, the correct standard to apply is that laid down in *Quinn v Cunningham*,[88] and not that propounded in *Allan v Patterson*.

Objectivity and recklessness

3–32   As has been emphasised, the test for establishing recklessness is essentially an objective one. Scots law does not require that the accused has actually and subjectively realised the risk attendant upon his conduct before it can be categorised as criminally

[85] *Allan v Patterson*, 1980 J.C. 57 at 60.
[86] *Carr v HM Advocate*, 1995 S.L.T. 800 at 803K–L; applied in *Thomson v HM Advocate*, 1995 S.L.T. 827.
[87] *Cameron v Maguire*, 1999 J.C. 63, doubting *Gizzi v Tudhope*, 1983 S.L.T. 214, which had applied the *Allan v Paterson* test in the context of the common law crime of recklessly discharging a firearm. The approach in *Cameron v Maguire* was endorsed in *Transco Plc v HM Advocate (No.1)*, 2004 J.C. 29.
[88] *Quinn v Cunningham*, 1956 J.C. 22; see above, para.3–30.

reckless. An individual who has given no thought to a risk may be reckless. The argument would be that this very "thoughtlessness" is blameworthy: the accused really *ought* to have given thought to the risks. The two appellants in *Miller and Denovan v HM Advocate*[89] had been convicted of a murder in the course of a robbery. The deceased had been struck on the head with a large piece of wood. The intention of the appellants seems to have been to rob, not kill, and they were convicted on the basis of the alternative *mens rea* for murder of wicked recklessness. Lord Justice General Clyde observed[90]:

> "Both appellants displayed a callous disregard of whatever injuries they may have done him. They centred their whole attention upon snatching all they could from his pockets, rolling his body over . . . in order to get easier access to them. Once their purpose was achieved they fled into the night and left him to die."

The question which arises is how the appellants could be said to be reckless of their victim's life. They were so intent upon robbery that they did not notice the risk to life which their actions had brought about. Applying a subjective approach to recklessness, one would have to say that they had not been reckless as to the risk of death. Even though the appellants had perpetrated a vicious assault, there was no subjective appreciation or awareness of endangering life. In contrast, the objective approach taken in Scots law focuses upon the indifference to the victim's life demonstrated by the nature of the assault. Miller and Denovan's wicked recklessness was exhibited by what they did. The fact that they failed to appreciate the risk to the victim demonstrated their callous disregard for his life.

One issue which the Scottish courts have yet to address directly **3–33** is the position of the accused who would not have appreciated the risk attendant upon his action, even had he applied his mind to the issue. The "reasonable man" would have appreciated the risk, but the accused, perhaps because of immaturity or lack of understanding, could not. His action may have been the result of inadequacy (for which he cannot be blamed), rather than any sort of indifference or disregard on his part. In the context of intention, in *Petrovich v Jessop*,[91] the Appeal Court accepted that transient factors such as lack of sleep and stress could lead to a reasonable doubt as to the normal inference of *mens rea*. It may be that such

---

[89] *Miller and Denovan v HM Advocate*, 1960, noted in *Parr v HM Advocate*, 1991 S.L.T. 211. The ensuing discussion of this case has been influenced by A. Duff, *Intention, Agency and Criminal Liability* (Oxford: Basil Blackwell, 1990), pp.157–167.
[90] *Parr v HM Advocate*, 1991 S.L.T. 208 at 211K–L.
[91] *Petrovich v Jessop*, 1990 S.L.T. 594.

considerations could also refute an inference of recklessness. It remains to be seen what the position is as regards the permanent characteristics of the accused (but see below, para.4–45).

Negligence

3–34   Negligence is similar to recklessness in that it also requires an individual to have engaged in risk-creating conduct that deviates from the standards of the reasonably careful man. The difference lies in the degree of carelessness exhibited. The common law does not generally regard negligent conduct as sufficiently blameworthy to attract the sanction of the criminal law (rather than the law of delict). Although the notion of "gross negligence" has sometimes been used as an alternative for recklessness,[92] there is the potential for confusion with the civil law if the word "negligence" is used in this context.[93] There are many statutory offences which rely upon negligence.

CONCURRENCE OF ACTUS REUS AND MENS REA

3–35   If the definition of a crime requires both *actus reus* and *mens rea*, then there will need to be a concurrence or coincidence of these two elements in order for criminal liability to be established. If there is a *mens rea* without an *actus reus* or an *actus reus* without *mens rea* (unless the offence is one of strict liability), there is again no crime. This requirement of concurrence does not mean, however, that in a result crime the *mens rea* must continue until the result occurs. In a case of murder, for example, an error as to the method or time of death will not affect criminal liability. All that is necessary is that the *mens rea* actuates the conduct which causes the death. This point is illustrated by the decision of the Privy Council in *Thabo-Meli v R*.[94] The appellants had been convicted of murder before the High Court of Basutoland. They had struck the victim over the head and, believing him to be dead had thrown the "body" over a cliff. The evidence was that the victim in fact died from exposure from being left at the bottom of the cliff. The appellants argued that the elements of the crime were not satisfied as *mens rea* and *actus reus* did not coincide in time. At the time when the blow had been inflicted death had not occurred, even though *mens rea* was present, and at the time of death the appellants did not have *mens rea*. The Privy Council held that it was not possible to divide up what was in reality one series of acts

---

[92] *Paton v HM Advocate*, 1936 J.C. 19 at 22; see *McDowall v HM Advocate*, 1998 J.C. 194 at 198E–G, where Lord Justice-General Rodger applied to culpable homicide the common law test of recklessness described above.
[93] This point was made by Lord Osborne in *Transco Plc v HM Advocate (No.1)*, 2004 J.C. 29 at para.4.
[94] *Thabo-Meli v R.* [1954] 1 W.L.R. 228. See also *R. v Le Brun* [1992] 1 Q.B. 61.

in the way that the appellants had argued. Lord Reid observed that it would be,

> "too refined a ground of judgment to say that, because they were under a misapprehension at one stage and thought that their guilty purpose had been achieved before, in fact, it had been achieved, therefore they are to escape the penalties of the law."[95]

Generally the requirement of concurrence will mean that the **3–36** *mens rea* must either precede the forbidden conduct or exist contemporaneously with the *actus reus*, but it is possible that in an exceptional case *mens rea* could be superimposed upon it. A decision to this effect is the English one of *Fagan v Metropolitan Police Commissioner*.[96] The accused had driven his car on to a police officer's foot. The officer asked him to drive off his foot, but for a time the accused refused to do so. It could not be proved that the original driving on to the foot had been accompanied by the requisite *mens rea* for the crime of battery. Nevertheless, the majority of the Divisional Court took the view that the accused's conduct did constitute a battery. The reasoning was that the driving of the car on to the complainer's foot and allowing it to remain there could be treated as one continuing act of the application of force. On this analysis, the accused's act was not complete by the time his *mens rea* began (which would have been the case if the driving on to the complainer's foot had been treated as a single complete act). The accused's *mens rea* could therefore be superimposed on the existing continuing *actus reus* which he had caused. *Fagan* is thus persuasive authority for the view that, where an *actus reus* can be regarded as a continuing one, it is sufficient if *mens rea* is present at some stage during its continuance.

Transferred intent

The issue of concurrence can also arise where an individual acts **3–37** intending to harm or to kill one person, but in fact harms or kills someone other than the intended victim. The *actus reus* of assault or murder has been brought about, but in an unexpected way. This was the situation in *Roberts v Hamilton*.[97] A had aimed a blow at B, but struck C instead. One view would be that such an eventuality is irrelevant to the definition of the crime, and should have no effect upon the culpability of the accused.[98] In Anglo-American criminal law, this type of case is covered by the doctrine of transferred

---

[95] *Thabo-Meli v R.* [1954] 1 W.L.R. 228 at 230.
[96] *Fagan v Metropolitan Police Commissioner* [1969] 1 Q.B. 439.
[97] *Roberts v Hamilton*, 1989 J.C. 91.
[98] A.P. Simester and G.R. Sullivan, *Criminal Law: Theory and Doctrine*, 2nd edn, pp.159–160.

intent.[99] This operates to make the accused's criminal responsibility exactly the same as if the blow had landed upon the intended victim, rather than a bystander.[100] In *Roberts v Hamilton*, the accused was convicted of assault and this was upheld on appeal. One explanation offered for the decision was that the intention to assault the intended victim could be transferred to the actual victim.[101] Although Hume is supportive of the notion of transferred intent,[102] *Roberts v Hamilton* is rare as a modern Scottish authority recognising the doctrine. Indeed, whatever may be the position in Anglo-American criminal law, it is clear that there is no place in Scots law for a generalised doctrine of transferred intent, applicable to all crimes of intention. In relation to wilful fire-raising, the High Court has set its face against the doctrine. In *Blane v HM Advocate*,[103] it was held that an intention to set fire to moveable property could not be transferred to the heritable property destroyed by the resulting fire. This approach was endorsed in the full bench decision of *Byrne v HM Advocate*.[104] The explanation for the reluctance to transfer the intention in cases of wilful fire-raising is that the effect would be to penalise the accused for unintended consequences, in a crime where intention is required. Unlike the straightforward assault case, perhaps, the outcome of intentionally raising a fire is all too unpredictable. The intention may be to set fire to some old packing cases, but the warehouse can be destroyed. The appropriate charge in such a case is that of culpable and reckless fire-raising.[105]

---

[99] See, e.g. *People v Scott*, 14 Cal. 4th 544 (1996).

[100] For the doctrine of transferred intent to operate, the accused must have the requisite *mens rea* of the crime for which he is being prosecuted. That is, the doctrine will not operate where the accused has the *mens rea* for one crime, but in fact perpetrates the *actus reus* of a crime which requires a different *mens rea*.

[101] The additional explanation proffered was that what had happened was so unlikely under the circumstances that criminal liability could not be avoided (founding upon *Connor v Jessop*, 1988 S.C.C.R. 624, which followed Macdonald, p.2).

[102] Hume, *Commentaries*, I, 22–25; see also Erskine, IV, 4, 43. In *Roberts v Hamilton*, the Appeal Court rejected the appellant's contention that Hume's account of transferred intent was confined to murder.

[103] *Blane v HM Advocate*, 1991 S.C.C.R. 576; applied in *McKelvie v HM Advocate*, 1997 S.L.T. 758.

[104] *Byrne v HM Advocate (No.2)*, 2000 S.L.T. 233 at 239D.

[105] On fire-raising generally, see below, paras 11–28 *et seq*. It could equally be argued that the accused in *Roberts v Hamilton* could have been convicted of causing reckless injury. This crime is described in detail in Ch.9.

CHAPTER 4

VOLUNTARY ACTS AND AUTOMATISM

The Academic View

Textbooks and Others

"The foundation of criminal liability is conduct, for without **4–01** an act there can be no liability. But not any act will do. There are qualifications that an act must meet, and the first is that it be *voluntary*."[1]

This statement by an academic writer is echoed in major text books around the world. Thus, in Smith and Hogan's *Criminal Law*,[2] it is asserted that "the voluntariness of an act is a more fundamental element of criminal liability than . . . *mens rea*." Again, in Burchell and Milton's *Principles of Criminal Law* (South Africa), it is stated that,

"[t]o qualify as conduct of which the criminal law will take cognisance the conduct must be (*a*) that of a human being which was (*b*) voluntary."[3]

Gordon appears to take the same view, as the following quotation indicates: "the term 'act' is usually restricted to 'voluntary' acts, so that a man is responsible only for his voluntary acts."[4] Nor is that view confined to textbook writings. Many criminal codes in the United States, for example, have adopted the provision in the Model Penal Code[5] that:

"A person is not guilty of an offense unless his liability is based on conduct that includes a voluntary act or the

---

[1] H. Gross, *A Theory of Criminal Justice* (New York: Oxford University Press, 1979), p.67.

[2] Smith and Hogan, *Criminal Law*, 10th edn, pp. 38–39.

[3] Burchell and Milton, *Principles of Criminal Law*, 3rd edn, (Cape Town: Juta, 2005), p.178. See also Finbarr McAuley and J. Paul McCutcheon, *Criminal Liability* (Dublin: Round Hall Sweet & Maxwell, 2000), p.122; and Simister and Sullivan, *Criminal Law: Theory and Doctrine*, 2nd edn (2003), p.108.

[4] Gordon, *Criminal Law*, 3rd edn, para.3.08.

[5] American Law Institute, *Model Penal Code Official Draft* (1985), s.2.01.

omission to perform an act of which he is physically capable."[6]

In the United Kingdom, however, the proposed criminal code for England and Wales[7] makes no mention of the "voluntariness" of an act as an element (essential or otherwise) of criminal liability[8]; and the following judicial opinion is rather *un*-typical:

> "The requirement that [there] should be a voluntary act is essential, not only in a murder case, but also in every criminal case."[9]

Regrettably, it is not at all immediately apparent what is meant by these various views; and an illustration may help to clarify the issues involved.

Illustration

4–02   Suppose that John is seen at the wheel of his car, as it travels from Glasgow to Renfrew. On a perfectly straight piece of road, in good daylight conditions of visibility and weather, his vehicle is observed to swerve suddenly to the "wrong" side of the road and collide with an oncoming motorcycle. The motorcyclist is thrown into the air and his bike crushed. John's vehicle pauses for less than two seconds before speeding away from the scene of the incident. Some minutes later, his vehicle knocks down a police officer who had stepped into the road in order to signal him to stop. The police officer is seriously injured. On the face of things, John would seem to have committed a number of offences—since cars (at the time of writing, at least) are incapable of directing their own movements. The offences in question might include dangerous driving under s.2 of the Road Traffic Act 1988 (as substituted by s.1 of the Road Traffic Act 1991), or perhaps the lesser offence of careless or inconsiderate driving under s.3 of the Road Traffic Act 1988 (as substituted by s.2 of the Road Traffic Act 1991), and almost certainly failing to stop after an accident under s.170 of the Road Traffic Act 1988. Were the motorcyclist to die of his injuries, then even more serious charges might possibly apply, e.g. culpable homicide at common law; the offence of causing death by dangerous driving under s.1 of the Road Traffic Act 1988, as substituted by s.1 of the Road Traffic Act 1991; or the relatively new

---

[6] See, e.g. Joshua Dressler, *Understanding Criminal Law*, 2nd edn (New York: Matthew Bender, 1995), p.71.

[7] "Criminal Law: A Criminal Code", Law Com. No.177 (1989).

[8] The "Draft Criminal Code for Scotland with Commentary", published under the auspices of the Scottish Law Commission, also makes no mention of "voluntariness": see above, para.2.01 at fn.1.

[9] *Bratty v Att-Gen for Northern Ireland* [1963] A.C. 386, per Lord Denning at 409. What Lord Denning then went on to say is, however, quoted with apparent approval by the court in *Finegan v Heywood*, 2000 S.C.C.R. 460, at 463 D–E, para.6; see also 464A, para.7.

offence of causing death by careless, or inconsiderate, driving under s.2B of the Road Traffic Act 1988, as inserted by s.20(1) of the Road Safety Act 2006.[10] *A propos* the unfortunate police officer, charges of assault or even attempted murder at common law might easily be envisaged.

ACTS OF AN INNOCENT AGENT OR EVENTS BEYOND HUMAN CONTROL

If in the preceding example, John had been alert and apparently **4–03** in full control of his vehicle "at the relevant time," then one might assume that he had simply been travelling too fast for his own capabilities or the mechanical tolerances of his car (or that he had been paying scandalously little attention to his driving)—and that he had panicked when the "accidents" occurred. One would have little sympathy for his plight. But suppose that he had been driving competently enough at a wholly reasonable speed just before the first "accident", and that events thereafter were directed by a passenger who seized the steering wheel without prior warning and deliberately aimed the vehicle at the passing motorcyclist. The passenger also, one may conjecture (with some suspension of disbelief), caused the car to move off after the initial collision, and thereafter knock down the police officer, by physically forcing John's hands and feet to execute the required movements. If John had no reason to anticipate such behaviour on the part of his passenger, one would probably conclude that he had simply been an innocent agent (see below, para.7–33) in the execution of the real culprit's plan—no more responsible for the act or its result than a broken glass in the hands of a violent man.[11] John could not reasonably have been said to be "driving" or doing anything at all during the crucial time periods. If the question were to be posed: "Who was driving at the relevant moments?"—one would surely not answer that it was John. No part of the conduct or acts making up the *actus reus* of any of the crimes involved (see above, para.4–02) could be said to have been his; and the same conclusion would follow, at least in respect of the initial collision, if the car swerved because a sudden defect manifested itself in the steering, or a tyre burst without warning—assuming that either event placed the car beyond any reasonable human control.[12]

---

[10] For "culpable homicide", see below, paras 9–52 *et seq.*; for the statutory meaning of "dangerous driving", see s.2A of the Road Traffic Act 1988, as inserted by s.1 of the Road Traffic Act 1991; and for the statutory meaning of "careless or inconsiderate driving", see s.3ZA of the 1988 Act, as inserted by the Road Safety Act 2006 s.30.

[11] See, for instance, the contribution of Mr Smith to Mrs Craft's death in *R. v Mitchell* [1983] 2 W.L.R. 938.

[12] *cf. Attorney-General's Reference (No.4 of 2000)* [2001] 2 Cr.App.R. 417 CA, where

ACTING UNCONSCIOUSLY OR SEMI-CONSCIOUSLY

4–04 One might further suppose, however, again in relation to the above example (in para.4–02), that the car collided with the unfortunate victims because John was "unconscious" at the time, or, was "semi-conscious" or in a state of "impaired consciousness". Perhaps he had had an epileptic fit or a "heart attack" whilst at the wheel and was thus unaware of what he was doing for a particular period of time; or he might have become comatose or semi-conscious because he suffered from a condition (such as diabetes) where full consciousness depended upon a very fine balance being struck between the ingestion of prescribed drugs (such as insulin) and normal foodstuffs—and that balance had ceased to be maintained. Perhaps, again, he might have slept badly or not at all the night before and succumbed to tiredness whilst at the wheel (which might at least explain the initial collision under the postulated non-adverse road and weather conditions). Yet again John might have been drinking alcohol prior to setting out on his journey: he might have been plainly drunk. In all of these possible scenarios, John might nevertheless appear to be driving. It might appear that he was manipulating the controls and directing the movements of the vehicle—which is what "driving" amounts to in Scots law.[13] If one was now to ask: "Who was driving at the relevant moments?" it would be difficult to say it was anyone other than John himself—particularly since the vehicle was (apparently) purposefully driven off after the initial collision.

The problem

4–05 Where the only person (in retrospect, at least) who could have influenced the course of events apparently did things which had a major causal influence over that course of events (as in the illustration set out above at para.4–02), then a problem relating to his responsibility for the outcome exists if he "did" those things whilst he was unconscious or only semi-conscious (as in the various scenarios described above in para.4–04). If he apparently did those

---

the error of a driver in pressing the accelerator instead of the brake (which was proved against him) was contrasted with the situation where the engine of his vehicle might have suddenly surged due to mechanical defect (which he had claimed but was unable to establish). It might be noted here that "dangerous driving" extends to the case where "it would be obvious to a competent and careful driver that driving the vehicle in its current state would be dangerous": see s.2A of the Road Traffic Act 1988, as inserted by s.1 of the Road Traffic Act 1991. The situation postulated would be different, therefore, had John known of the defect, or the poor state of his tyres, prior to the commencement of his journey.

[13] See *Ames v MacLeod*, 1969 J.C. 1; *McArthur v Valentine*, 1990 J.C. 146; *Hoy v McFadyen*, 2000 S.C.C.R. 875; *cf. DPP v Alderton* [2004] R.T.R. 23 (an English case, the test for "driving" being slightly different there).

things, then it is very difficult to conclude that he did not do them at all. That does not lead to the conclusion, however, that he is necessarily criminally responsible for them. The first component of criminal liability, it will be remembered, is not just an "act", i.e. "doing something", but an *actus reus*. It can, therefore, be postulated that it is a "responsible" human act (and not a "bare" act) which the criminal law seeks. The law thus attempts, or should attempt, to give effect to the intuitive feeling that there is a significant difference in responsibility between a driver who collides with another vehicle because he has been wantonly driving too fast and one who (in fact) causes a similar "accident" because he has temporarily, through no fault of his own, lost the ability to comply with the dictates of the criminal law by making, or refraining from making, particular bodily movements. Of course, in many instances that difference in responsibility can be accounted for by the law's taking note that a person so incapacitated lacks *mens rea*. He may have "acted" after a fashion, but not so as to give rise to any inference that he intended the outcome, had knowledge of the criminative circumstances, or foresaw (objectively or subjectively) the risks, such was his lack of awareness of what was happening. To that extent, then, it would hardly be necessary to attempt to distinguish a "bare" act from a "responsible" one. The matter would simply be settled in terms of whether there was or was not *mens rea*—given his personal circumstances at the time.[14]

The need to distinguish different sorts of act

There are, however, some crimes (some statutory ones—see **4–06** below, Ch.13.) where liability is said to be "strict." That means in effect that there is no requirement that the prosecutor should show *mens rea* on the part of the accused, or bring forward evidence from which it might be inferred.[15] In bald terms, proof that the accused brought about the forbidden result or performed the forbidden conduct is quite sufficient for conviction.[16] To take effective cognizance of incapacitating defects (mental or physical) accompanying human conduct, it would be necessary, therefore, in such cases to distinguish between conduct amounting to a "bare"

---

[14] Of the crimes possibly committed in the scenario depicted above in para.4–02, failing to stop after an accident (see *Harding v Price* [1948] 1 K.B. 695), assault (see *Smart v HM Advocate*, 1975 J.C. 30), culpable homicide (see *Transco Plc v HM Advocate (No.1)*, 2004 J.C. 29; also see below, paras 9–52 *et seq.*), and attempted murder (see *Cawthorne v HM Advocate*, 1968 J.C. 32) all require some form of *mens rea*.

[15] *cf.* Chalmers and Leverick, *Criminal Defences and Pleas in Bar of Trial*, p.140, para.7–06; Smith and Hogan, *Criminal Law*, pp.38–39.

[16] Of the crimes possibly committed in the scenario depicted above in para.4–02, dangerous driving, careless (or inconsiderate) driving, and causing death by dangerous or careless (or inconsiderate) driving are probably all of this type.

act and that amounting to an *actus reus*.[17] Similarly, with respect to
any criminal justice system which pursues an objective method of
proving *mens rea* (as is believed to be the case in Scotland—see
above, Ch.3), it may be necessary to distinguish "responsible"
human conduct from "mere" human conduct, since proof of the
actus reus will very often imply the existence of the required *mens
rea*. In the illustration above (see para.4–02), for example, if John's
car was apparently driven *at* the unfortunate policeman, it would
be simple to infer from the facts that the driver intended to kill the
officer, or was completely indifferent whether he lived or died—
either (generally) sufficing for the crime of attempted murder.[18]
There is thus a case to be made for marking off "bare" human
conduct from the "responsible" sort.

What distinctions can be made?

4–07   With reference once again to the illustration (see above, paras
4–02 to 4–04), there is plainly a distinction to be made between
John's conduct where he willingly courts the risks of an "accident"
by wantonly driving too fast, and his conduct where he "drives" in
the throes of an epileptic fit or a heart attack. There is also perhaps
a further distinction to be made, for example, between his "driving" whilst experiencing such a fit or attack, and his doing so whilst
intoxicated—depending to a large extent on the way in which he
came to be intoxicated (though other factors are also involved, e.g.
the type and known effects of the intoxicant). These distinctions,
however, are exceedingly difficult to generalise. It is tempting to
conclude, for example, that the issue depends on whether or not
the apparent actor was conscious (in the sense of "being aware") of
what he was doing at the relevant time. But this is not an infallible
guide. A person afflicted by cerebral palsy will (usually) be fully
conscious of the random movements of his limbs; but it does not
follow that one should wish to label such movements as "responsible" acts, even though they might result in prima facie assaults
upon others unfortunate enough to be within range. The same
might be said of so called "reflex" movements where a human
physiological response is triggered automatically by the application
of external stimulus.[19]

4–08   It has become customary, at least in academic writings, to refer
to the primary distinction as that between a voluntary, i.e. responsible, act and an involuntary, i.e. bare, one. This, however, only
produces a terminological shift. Meaning must still be given to the

---

[17] *cf.* A. Ashworth, *Principles of Criminal Law*, 5th edn (Oxford: Oxford University
Press, 2006), p.98.
[18] *Cawthorne v HM Advocate*, 1968 J.C. 32; *cf. Drury v HM Advocate*, 2001 S.L.T.
1013.
[19] See *Jessop v Johnstone*, 1991 S.C.C.R. 238. For a more sophisticated analysis, see
Gross, *A Theory of Criminal Justice*, pp.67–73.

replacement terms. Equally, it has become customary to speak of a "voluntary" act as a "willed" bodily movement, or as conduct which flows from an exercise of "will"[20]—which suggests that the presence or absence of some mental process is the issue at stake. If this is correct, then a mental element must be involved in conduct truly amounting to an *actus reus*—although this disturbs the neat symmetry of criminal law theory, namely that the mental element of *mens rea* is separate from the *actus reus*.[21] It is, however, rather uncertain what can be meant by the "will" in such an analysis. Clearly it must be different from "wanting" or "desiring" what one does, since these terms normally connote the seeking of goals well beyond the actions themselves; nor can it be squared with more limited conceptions of "wanting" or "desiring", since one may in fact do something (e.g. visit a dentist) which is opposed to one's short term desires or wants (*cf.* the long term desire to have attractive and effectively-functioning teeth). The term "will", therefore, seems to be no less obscure than the terms "responsible" or "voluntary".

Legal effect of involuntariness

It is also uncertain what should be the result of making a **4–09** distinction between "bare" acts and "responsible" ones. For the authors of the American Model Penal Code, a person is to be held "not guilty of an offense" unless his conduct includes a voluntary act (see above, para.4–01). Fletcher,[22] on the other hand, remarks that "we intuitively recoil at the notion of punishing" persons in respect of acts where the "will" was not operative; and LaFave and Scott also suggest that it is punishment which cannot be justified for "involuntary" acts.[23] Obviously, punishment cannot be imposed unless there is a finding of guilt; but the converse is not necessarily true. A person may be convicted of an offence, but may thereafter be discharged without punishment at all (unless, of course, conviction itself is taken to be a form of punishment). As far as current Scots law is concerned, the criminal law does not always sanction acquittal in cases where there were "involuntary" acts[24]; but provided there are sound reasons for convicting in particular types of involuntariness, e.g. in cases of self-induced intoxication, and provided also that (save where there is a clear rule to the contrary)[25] the involuntariness of the acts is not to be totally

---

[20] See, for example, Smith and Hogan, *Criminal Law*, 10th edn, p.37; *cf.* Ashworth, *Principles of Criminal Law*, 5th edn, p.99.

[21] See G. Williams, *Criminal Law: The General Part*, 2nd edn (London: Stevens and Sons, 1961), p.12; G. Williams, *Textbook of Criminal Law*, 2nd edn (London: Stevens and Sons, 1983), p.147, para.7–2.

[22] G.P. Fletcher, *Rethinking Criminal Law* (Boston: Little, Brown, 1978), p.426.

[23] W.R. La Fave and W.A. Scott, *Criminal Law* [United States], 2nd edn, (St. Paul, Minnesota: West, 1986) pp.197–198.

[24] See below, para.4–35.

[25] As there is, e.g. in relation to self-induced intoxicaton.

disregarded at the point when an appropriate disposal of the case comes to be considered by the court, the law can still be regarded as both principled and fair.

Voluntariness as an essential element of liability

4–10   Regrettably, it is further uncertain whether the "voluntariness" of an act is indeed to be taken as an essential element of criminal liability. If it were to be accepted as an essential element[26] then one would expect "voluntariness" to be something which prosecutors were duty bound to establish at criminal trials. Neither academic writings nor judicial dicta, however, support such a proposition. At best, those who favour a requirement of "voluntariness" take the view that an act will be presumed to be "voluntary" until some evidence to the contrary is presented.[27] This has had the effect of highlighting the issue as one of "*in*voluntariness" and of shifting the emphasis from that of "fundamental element" to that of "defence". Smith and Hogan, for example, remark[28] that "[i]t is a defence known as 'automatism' that this element [that an act was voluntary] has not been proved by the Crown." Some text-writers, therefore, deal with the whole issue here under the heading of "Defences",[29] others tackle it almost exclusively under the title of "*Actus Reus*",[30] whilst others present it under both such headings.[31]

Involuntariness as a defence—automatism

4–11   In English and Scots criminal law, it is now clear that the whole issue has become one for the defence in the first instance. The accused must somehow place some evidence before the court or jury which will tend to displace the tacit presumption that his proven conduct was "voluntary." He must, therefore, discharge the initial evidential burden required by the defence of "automatism." He must show that his acts could be construed as "involuntary." If that construction finds favour, it may be that the reason for his

---

[26] See above, para.4–01, "a more fundamental element than . . . *mens rea*." See also Ashworth, *Principles of Criminal Law*, 5th edn, p.98.

[27] See *Bratty v Att-Gen for Northern Ireland* [1963] A.C. 386, per Lord Denning at 413; *Ryan v The Queen* (1967) 40 A.L.J.R. 488, per Barwick C.J. at 492, followed in *R. v Falconer* (1991) 65 A.L.J.R. 20; and Ashworth, *Principles of Criminal Law*, 5th edn, p.98.

[28] Somewhat oddly in its context at Smith and Hogan, *Criminal Law*, 10th edn, p.39.

[29] See Chalmers and Leverick, *Criminal Defences and Pleas in Bar of Trial*, Ch.7 (where the appropriate "defence" is examined along with "insanity"—these two defences being convincingly said there to be "two sides of the same coin": see in particular paras 7–01 and 7–26 *et seq*.); see also Williams, *Textbook of Criminal Law*, 2nd edn, Pt 4, Defences, Ch.29, pp.662–684.

[30] See Smith and Hogan, *Criminal Law*, 10th edn, pp.37–41, who nevertheless also treat it there as the defence of "Automatism."

[31] See, e.g. A.W. Mewett and M. Manning, *Criminal Law*, 2nd edn (Toronto: Butterworths, 1985), Ch.3, pp.73 *et seq*.; Ch.9, pp.279 *et seq*.

involuntariness falls within the definition of insanity accepted in law. In that event, "insane automatism" may be established,[32] although the conventional view in Scotland is that a burden of proof lies on the defence to satisfy the court of the accused's insanity on the balance of probabilities—a burden which exceeds a mere evidential one, and which may be more difficult to discharge. In English law, the scope of the independent defence has been narrowed to that of "non-insane automatism"; and that, as has repeatedly been said by English judges, is itself of very narrow scope.[33] The English judiciary, therefore, has taken every opportunity to make the defence difficult to establish; and in practice, pleas of non-insane automatism are seldom successful. The strange practice has also arisen in English law of permitting an accused to withdraw his defence of automatism in favour of a guilty plea where the trial judge has ruled that the defence truly amounts to one of insanity.[34] This seems to confound both principle and policy notions of public safety.

The scope of a legally relevant act

An added difficulty for those who favour an "involuntary act" **4–12** defence is that the judiciary has proved more than willing to enlarge the scope of the "acts" in question. In the illustration concerning John (see above, para.4–02), the incidents (possibly attracting criminal liability) are of fairly short duration. His car was "driven" into the path of a motorcycle, collided with that cycle, and then was "driven" away—all within the space of a few seconds, no doubt. Similarly, the knocking down of the police officer will have occupied a very short interval of time. If it was established that, during the relevant time periods, John was truly "unconscious", i.e. unaware of his surroundings and his obligations as a driver—even though his eyes may have been open and his behaviour apparently normal, and if his legally relevant acts were to be confined to only those narrow periods of time, then it is certainly possible to conclude that his actions were not "responsible" ones (with whatever effect that is deemed to have in law). He would not be responsible for what he did during those few seconds. It should not then matter what the reason for his unconsciousness was. In any event, if the reason was connected with something which was not his fault and which he could not have anticipated (a stroke or heart attack, for example), one would not wish to enlarge the field of view. But, if John (say) had known himself to be diabetic and had further known that failure to take insulin would lead to the rapid onset of unconsciousness, in his case due to hyperglycaemia,[35] then

---

[32] See, e.g. *R. v Burgess* [1991] 2 W.L.R. 1206, per Lord Lane C.J. at 1208E.

[33] See *Bratty v Att-Gen for Northern Ireland* [1963] A.C. 386; *R. v Quick* [1973] Q.B. 910; *R. v Sullivan* [1984] A.C. 156; *R. v Hennessy* [1989] 1 W.L.R. 287.

[34] See, e.g. *R. v Sullivan* [1984] A.C. 156; *R. v Hennessy* [1989] 1 W.L.R. 287.

[35] See *R. v Hennessy* [1989] 1 W.L.R. 287 and below, para.4–27; *cf. MacLeod v Mathieson*, 1993 S.C.C.R. 488 Sh.Ct.

one feels the need to inquire whether he had taken his medication at all that day. If he had not, then his "acts" may be seen as including the fault-ridden ones of failing to take insulin *and* then driving, all in the knowledge that unconsciousness might well intervene before his destination was reached. One would perhaps not then view the incidents as "involuntary" on his part at all— provided that a wide-angled view of his "actings" can legitimately be taken. Truly, he might have been unaware of what he was doing during an incident and its immediate aftermath; but he was certainly not unaware when he began to drive that his actions might pass beyond his control. This may be enough, therefore, to mark his acts as responsible ones after all (for the purposes of at least some crimes); but this will depend on how widely the law is prepared to look for relevant actings, and how concerned it is whether he should have been able to anticipate precisely what eventually happened. Enlarging the field of view, therefore, can turn unconscious or uncontrolled actions into responsible ones.[36]

Ryan v The Queen

4–13   A well known illustration here can be found in the Australian case of *Ryan v The Queen*[37] where the accused set out to rob a petrol filling-station. He carried a loaded, sawn-off rifle with him, and used it as a threat to subdue the person in charge of the cash-box there. The accused ordered that person to face a wall and hold his hands out behind him—so that these could then be tied securely with a piece of rope the accused thought he had in his pocket. Whilst he searched his pocket for that rope, two things happened. The person being coerced in that way suddenly crouched down and half turned round; and the accused "shot" him in the neck—killing him. The accused claimed that he had been holding the rifle (which did not have its safety catch set) with one hand, and that the act of pulling the trigger had been "involuntary." It was, he said, a reflex action "triggered" by the sudden movement on the part of the victim. Subsequent police tests suggested that there might be some basis for that possibility— which might have been decisive in the later proceedings for criminal homicide. In fact, he was convicted of murder; and his subsequent appeal was dismissed partly on the view that,

> "the jury, having concluded that the discharge of the gun was involuntary could have concluded that the act causing death was the presentation of the cocked, loaded gun with a safety

[36] cf. *Finegan v Heywood*, 2000 S.C.C.R. 460, where the appellant's condition of parasomnia—brought on (as he should have anticipated) by drinking some six pints of beer—was treated by the Appeal Court as one within the ratio of *Brennan v HM Advocate*, 1977 J.C. 38.
[37] *Ryan v The Queen* (1967) 40 A.L.J.R. 488.

catch unapplied and that its involuntary discharge was a likelihood which ought to have been in the contemplation of the applicant when presenting the gun in the circumstances."[38]

Where the focus was widened slightly beyond the mere pulling of the trigger, there was thus produced a voluntary act which the court could have accepted as *the* cause of the death in all the circumstances there.

Conclusion

It is *theoretically* satisfying to conclude that a person can only be **4–14** criminally liable for his "voluntary acts". But it is very difficult to give content to the word "voluntary"; and it is not always easy to identify what is *the* "act" for the purposes of a particular crime. It seems in general agreed, however, that a person should not be punished for his involuntary acts. Punishment after all cannot deter a person from repeating his conduct if he did not know or could not help what he was doing at the time.[39] Nor can it deter third parties successfully, since the imposition of punishment will be viewed as simply unfair in the circumstances. Still less would punishment be seen to be merited in such a case; and, therefore, its imposition could not be retributively justified.

The Position under Scots Law

Acts of an Innocent Agent or Events Beyond Human Control

Under Scots law, a person who is physically compelled by another **4–15** to be the innocent agent of a criminal act is not responsible for that act. Criminal liability clearly remains with the other person—since the act is truly his. It would be absurd and unjust to take any other view (see above, para.4–03), and the case of *Hugh Mitchell*[40] provides ample authority. There, Mitchell attacked his wife, kicking and punching her whilst she was holding their four-month old baby in her arms. In terms of the indictment, it was alleged that *he* caused his wife, by the assault he made upon her, to compress or squeeze the child so as to obstruct its respiration in some way—by all which, or part thereof, the child was mortally injured and thus culpably killed by *him*. This part of the charge was found relevant

---

[38] *Ryan v The Queen* (1967) 40 A.L.J.R. 488, per Barwick C.J. at 494.
[39] See, e.g. *Finegan v Heywood*, 2000 S.C.C.R. 460, where that part of the appropriate sentence which related to disqualification from driving was quashed on appeal.
[40] *Hugh Mitchell* (1856) 2 Irv. 488.

by the three-judge High Court; and the jury eventually convicted him of the culpable homicide of the child on the stated basis. There was no question of his wife's having had any liability at all for the child's death. Her contribution to the fatality was recognised as no greater than that of some inanimate object in the hands of her husband. It is equally apparent that Scots law would not hold a person criminally liable for an event which was beyond his power to control (although normally this would be treated as an event he had not *caused*). Reference may be made here to the decision in *Hogg v Macpherson*,[41] which is considered above at para.3–04. It will be seen that Lord Justice-General Clyde held there that "the breaking of the lamp was not the appellant's act at all, either negligent or accidental."[42] It seems that the same view could be taken of genuine reflex actions; but these are difficult to define, and there are few, reported Scottish cases which have featured them. In *Jessop v Johnstone*[43] Lord Justice-Clerk Ross did say:

> "We appreciate that there may be cases where a person instinctively reacts to violence in a reflex way, such as if a person is suddenly and without warning struck and turns round sharply so that he comes in contact with his assailant."

The appeal court held, however, that the facts of the case did not support a finding of "reflex response." Had the facts done so, presumably the court would have endorsed the sheriff's original decision to acquit—although that had been based by him on a consequent lack of *mens rea*.

Hypnotic or Similar Influences

4–16   If a person is forcibly or unwittingly hypnotised by another (assuming forcible or unwitting hypnotism of a person to be possible) and thus made to do that other's bidding, then that person surely becomes an innocent agent—just as much as if he had been physically compelled; and the same conclusion would seem to follow if drugs were to be administered to him by stealth or force, in order to make him comply with the administrator's criminal designs.[44]

ACTING UNCONSCIOUSLY OR SEMI-CONSCIOUSLY

4–17   Where a person has apparently acted purposively, and there was no question of physical compulsion by another or from natural phenomena (see above, para.4–15) and no question of hypnotic

---

[41] *Hogg v Macpherson*, 1928 J.C. 15.
[42] *Hogg v Macpherson*, 1928 J.C. 15 at 17.
[43] *Jessop v Johnstone*, 1991 S.C.C.R. 238 at 240E.
[44] See *HM Advocate v Raiker*, 1989 S.C.C.R. 149, per Lord McCluskey's charge to the jury at 154C—although his approach stressed the consequent lack of *mens rea* of the "innocent agent".

influence (see above, para.4–16) then it may be that he did so whilst unconscious, or whilst not fully conscious. He may have been observed in the act of assaulting another, driving a car, or taking things away from a store without paying for them; but it may also be the case that due to some mental dysfunction (going beyond mere inattention) he was not aware (or not fully aware) of what he was doing. His mental condition, then, may have been less than normal at the relevant time. Scots law does not ignore such a mental condition, but inquires into the cause producing it.

Causal factor—mental illness

If that cause is proved on the balance of probabilities to be a **4–18** "mental illness, mental disease or defect or unsoundness of mind"[45] then legal insanity is present, and the person concerned will be acquitted of the assault, the driving offence, the theft, or whatever. Of course, the acquittal will be on the ground of insanity; but that does not commit the court, in either a solemn or a summary case, to order the acquitted person's detention in a hospital. The court instead may make a guardianship order, a supervision and treatment order, or make no order at all.[46] The often expressed view, therefore, that an insanity plea holds severe consequences for an accused person,[47] is no longer as compelling as once was the case.

Causal factor—external to the accused—automatism

In *Ross v HM Advocate*[48] a full bench of five Appeal Court **4–19** judges decided, for the first time authoritatively,[49] that a straight-forward acquittal was competent where an accused person behaved in an apparently criminal fashion after drugs had been admin-istered to him without his knowledge or consent. Ross had been at a party where a can of lager from which he had been drinking was surreptitiously "laced" by others with LSD (lysergic acid diethylamide) and five or six "jellies" of temazepam. Unwitting as to its contents, Ross continued to imbibe from the same can, with

---

[45] *Brennan v HM Advocate*, 1977 J.C. 38, per Lord Justice-General Emslie at 45.
[46] Criminal Procedure (Scotland) Act 1995 s.57, as amended by the Adults with Incapacity (Scotland) Act 2000 (asp 4) Sch.5 para.26(1); the Criminal Justice (Scotland) Act 2003 (asp 7) s.2; and the Mental Health (Care and Treatment) (Scotland) Act 2003 (asp 13) Sch.4 para.8(3); see also s.57A–D (as inserted by the 2003 Act (asp 13) s.133), ss.58–61 (as amended by the 2003 Act (asp 13) Sch.4 para.8(4),(5),(6),(7),(10), and the Adult Support and Protection (Scotland) Act 2007 (asp 10) Sch.1 para.4), ss.62–63 and Sch.4 (as amended by the Mental Health (Care and Treatment) (Scotland) Act 2003 (Modification of Enactments) Order 2005 (SSI 2005/465) Sch.1 para.27).
[47] See, e.g. *Ross v HM Advocate*, 1991 J.C. 210, Lord Justice-General Hope at 213.
[48] *Ross v HM Advocate*, 1991 J.C. 210.
[49] See Lord Murray's direction to the jury in *HM Advocate v Ritchie*, 1926 J.C. 45, which was approved in *Ross*.

the result that his conduct became uncharacteristically bizarre and exceptionally violent. Amongst other things, he then stabbed several persons, inflicting upon them serious, life-threatening injuries. The case was, therefore, concerned with the criminal responsibility of one who knowingly consumes some alcohol whilst unknowingly ingesting hallucinogenic drugs, i.e. LSD—temazepam generally, and on its own at least, having a tranquillising effect. The Appeal Court, however, ignored the fact that Ross had knowingly taken drink, and instead was content to emphasise that proof of *mens rea* is essential for conviction,[50] that the burden of proving *mens rea* lies on the Crown throughout a trial,[51] and that some evidence introduced during the trial of an "external factor" operating on the accused's mental condition at the relevant time may prevent the Crown establishing that he had (or must have had) the necessary *mens rea*.[52] On the face of things then, the court treated the issue as one involving "lack of *mens rea*" rather than lack of voluntariness (or responsibility) in relation to the conduct itself. This approach leaves the issue of "strict liability" offences in limbo (see above, para.4–06); and indeed only Lord McCluskey[53] obliquely acknowledged that such offences might exist. Clearly if the only effect of an "external factor" is to negative *mens rea*, then persons (such as Ross) would have to be convicted of any strict liability offences of which they stood accused. Of course, the majority of the charges in Ross's case were common law ones; and the one statutory accusation (police assault under s.41(1)(a) of the Police (Scotland) Act 1967) did not involve strict liability and had, in any event, dropped from the picture at appellate level. It may well be, therefore, that the court did not address itself to the problem of "strict" statutory offences at all since these were simply not germane to the case on hand; and it remains just possible to read parts of the opinions as if something more fundamental than "lack of *mens rea*" was involved—in other words, as if a fundamental element was missing in a case such as that of *Ross* which rendered the *actus* not *reus* and which also had the effect of negativing *mens rea* where that was an essential requirement of the particular crime in question. This, however, is somewhat speculative,[54] and is not a view encouraged by later cases where reference

---

[50] *Ross v HM Advocate*, 1991 J.C. 210, per Lord Justice-General Hope at 217; per Lord McCluskey at 227–228.

[51] *Ross v HM Advocate*, 1991 J.C. 210, per Lord Justice-General Hope at 219; Lord Allanbridge at 223; Lord McCluskey at 228; and Lord Brand at 232.

[52] *Ross v HM Advocate*, 1991 J.C. 210, per Lord Justice-General Hope at 221; Lord McCluskey at 230.

[53] *Ross v HM Advocate*, 1991 J.C. 210, at 228.

[54] But see, for example, Lord Justice-General Hope's view at 222 that the external factor "must be one which resulted in a total loss of control of his actions in regard to the crime with which he is charged"; Lord Allanbridge's view at 223 that "an accused will not have the necessary *mens rea* if his mind is so affected by

is made to the "defence" of "automatism" consisting of an inability to form *mens rea*.[55] What is clear then is that an external factor affecting the normal mental condition of the accused can lead to an acquittal if certain qualifying conditions are met.

Automatism—qualifying conditions

As is so often the case with landmark decisions, the defence of **4–20** automatism created in *Ross v HM Advocate*[56] has been clarified in subsequent appeal court rulings. Perhaps the most important of these is *Sorley v HM Advocate*.[57] It is worth reproducing what was said by the Lord Justice-General there[58] in relation to the defence:

"As the law now stands on this matter, automatism consisting of an inability to form *mens rea*[59] which is due to an external factor,[60] and not to some disorder of the mind itself which is liable to recur,[61] is a defence so long as there is evidence that three requirements are satisfied. These are that the external factor must not be self-induced, that it must be one which the accused was not bound to foresee[62] and that it

---

[an external] factor that the result is a total loss of control over his actions which have led to the alleged crime charged being committed"; and Lord Weir's opinion at 232 that "the accused must have been suffering from a total alienation of reason rendering him incapable of controlling or appreciating what he was doing."

[55] See, e.g. *Sorley v HM Advocate*, 1992 J.C. 102, the opinion of the court at 105; *HM Advocate v Bennett*, 1996 S.C.C.R. 331, Lord Justice-General Hope at 336G–337A. See also the Criminal Procedure (Scotland) Act 1995 s.78(2), where "automatism" is treated as if it were a special defence. Chalmers and Leverick (*Criminal Defences and Pleas in Bar of Trial*, p.140, para.7–06) consider the problem in more detail and conclude either that it is incorrect to regard strict liability offences as being devoid of any element of *mens rea* or that automatism might "be regarded as a freestanding excuse defence so far as offences of strict liability are concerned."

[56] *Ross v HM Advocate*, 1991 J.C. 210.

[57] *Sorley v HM Advocate*, 1992 J.C. 102.

[58] *Sorley v HM Advocate*, 1992 J.C. 102 at 105.

[59] At least two of the charges in *Cardle v Mulrainey*, 1992 S.L.T. 1152 (driving without insurance, contrary to s.143(1)(a), (2), and, as the holder of a provisional driving licence, driving without a supervisor being present, contrary to s.97(3),(7) of the Road Traffic Act 1988) were probably of strict liability—a fact noted by the sheriff (see 1158I) but entirely ignored by the Appeal Court. The sheriff considered that, notwithstanding that *mens rea* did not have to be established by the Crown in respect of these offences, it would still on principle have to be shown that the accused's conduct was voluntary. Also, in *MacLeod v Mathieson*, 1993 S.C.C.R. 488 Sh.Ct, the sheriff assumed (but merely for the sake of dealing with and rejecting the defence arguments) that automatism applied to careless driving under s.3 of the Road Traffic Act 1988, although such an offence is not normally thought of as requiring *mens rea*.

[60] See below, paras 4–24 to 4–32.

[61] See below, paras 4–33 *et seq.*

[62] In *MacLeod v Mathieson*, 1993 S.C.C.R. 488 Sh.Ct, the sheriff decided that this

must have resulted in a total alienation of reason amounting
to a total loss of control of his actions in regard to the crime
with which he is charged . . .".

The first of these requirements seems to disqualify an accused
person from availing himself of the defence if, for example, he
voluntarily pours alcohol down his throat[63] or voluntarily ingests
some other substance which has the effect of producing a total
alienation of his reason.[64] It has been shown, however, that it is not
the voluntariness or deliberateness of the pouring or ingesting
which is crucial. In *Ebsworth v HM Advocate*,[65] the accused had
broken a bone in his leg. Since the fracture refused to heal, the
injury was extremely painful, and the accused's remedy was to take
large quantities of proprietary analgesics (on this occasion, 50
tablets of paracetamol) combined with prohibited drugs (on this
occasion, 10 tablets of diamorphine). He took these quite deliberately. He then suffered "a total alienation of reason", and committed various offences (including assault to severe injury and
permanent disfigurement) whilst in that mental state. The trial
sheriff withdrew Ebsworth's defence of automatism from the jury,
on the basis that his condition was self-induced and his motive
irrelevant. The Appeal Court, however, ruled that the first two of
the qualifying conditions for the defence should be seen as
together reaching out to meet the same goal. As Lord Justice-
General Hope put it:

> "The element of guilt or moral turpitude lies in the taking of
> drink or drugs voluntarily and reckless of their possible
> consequences."[66]

It is not so much, therefore, that the external factor itself must not
be self-induced; rather it is the "alienation of reason" produced by
that factor which must not have been deliberately or recklessly
effected by the accused. In *Ebsworth*, therefore, it was the grossly

---

requirement had not been met in relation to a charge under s.3 of the Road
Traffic Act 1988: the subsequent statutory definition of "careless, or inconsiderate driving" under s.3ZA of the 1988 Act (as inserted by the Road Safety Act
2006 s.30) would support his decision as also the conventional view that a s.3
offence is of strict liability: *cf.* Peter W. Ferguson, "Road Traffic Law Reform",
2007 S.L.T. (News) 27, at 28–29 (where, it seems, "2ZA" should be read as
"3ZA").
[63] In accordance with *Brennan v HM Advocate* 1977 J.C. 38. See in this context,
Finegan v Heywood, 2000 S.C.C.R. 460.
[64] If the accused's claim is that his drink was laced with drugs (of which he was
unaware and had no reason to suspect) by a third party, there must be evidence
to support that claim: see, e.g. *HM Advocate v Bennett*, 1996 S.C.C.R. 331.
[65] *Ebsworth v HM Advocate*, 1992 S.L.T. 1161.
[66] *Ebsworth v HM Advocate*, 1992 S.L.T. 1161 at 1166F. See *Finegan v Heywood*,
2000 S.C.C.R. 460.

excessive consumption of drugs—the purpose itself being not perhaps an illegitimate one—which ruled out the defence. Such excess simply courted totally unpredictable mental dysfunction (with concomitant effect on behaviour), and thus showed clear recklessness as to the consequences.

The third qualifying requirement insists that the external factor **4–21** should be shown to have caused the total alienation of reason, which should itself be characterised by a total loss of control over what one does.[67] If the alienation or loss of control is not total, this will rule out the defence and prevent acquittal on that ground[68]—although mitigation of punishment after conviction would remain possible. It is also highly desirable that medical evidence should be available to confirm that the alleged causal link between the external factor and the accused's state of mind (at the time of the offence) was a plausible one, and that that state of mind would reasonably have been describable in the circumstances as one of total alienation of reason.[69] For this purpose it seems that medical expert witnesses are permitted to sit in court during the leading of evidence[70] so that they may comment appropriately during their own evidence on what they have heard.[71]

EFFECT OF ROSS v HM ADVOCATE ON SCOTS LAW

Prior to the decision in *Ross*, the authoritative dictum in Scotland **4–22** was that of Lord Justice-General Clyde in his opinion in the certified case of *HM Advocate v Cunningham*[72] where he said that:

> "Any mental or pathological condition short of insanity — any question of diminished responsibility owing to any cause, *which does not involve insanity*—is relevant only to the question of mitigating circumstances and sentence."[73]

---

[67] In English law too, it has been held that the loss of control should be total—see, e.g. *Attorney General's Reference (No.2 of 1992)* [1994] Q.B. 91 CA, Lord Taylor of Gosforth, C.J. at 105C.

[68] See *Cardle v Mulrainey*, 1992 S.L.T. 1152, where the suggestion that this was too strict a standard was rejected. See also *HM Advocate v Bennett*, 1996 S.C.C.R. 331, Lord Justice-General Hope (opinion of the court) at 338A.

[69] *Sorley v HM Advocate*, 1992 J.C. 102. In *MacLeod v Napier*, 1993 S.C.C.R. 303, Lord Justice-Clerk Ross at 307C indicated that it might be possible to succeed without expert evidence, but considerable detailed evidence would then be essential to convince the court that there was a satisfactory basis for the defence. (According to *Sorley*, if there is no such satisfactory basis, the trial judge should withdraw the defence from the jury, in a solemn case.)

[70] i.e. evidence given by eyewitnesses who saw the accused's behaviour and can provide information sufficient to satisfy all the essential elements of the defence: *Sorley v HM Advocate*, 1992 J.C. 102, Lord Justice-General Hope at 107.

[71] See, e.g. *Cardle v Mulrainey*, 1992 S.L.T. 1152; *MacLeod v Mathieson*, 1993 S.C.C.R. 488 Sh.Ct.

[72] *HM Advocate v Cunningham*, 1963 J.C. 80 at 84.

[73] The phrase in italics reads "short of insanity" in the version given at 1963 S.L.T. 345 at 347.

Those, and there were many, who would then have liked Scots law to recognise acquittals in at least some cases of mental dysfunction not related to mental illness, suggested that Lord Clyde's opinion should be seen as advocating extension of the concept of legal insanity.[74] That would at least have secured an acquittal—although the then consequences (mandatory incarceration in a mental hospital, for an indictment case at least) were not to their liking and often absurd, e.g. that a person suffering from diabetic hypoglycaemia (see below, para.4–27) should be so incarcerated for wholly pointless psychiatric "treatment".[75] But contrary views, i.e. that *Cunningham* really required conviction in non mental illness cases, existed,[76] and prior to *Ross v HM Advocate* (see above, para.4–19), it seemed certain from cases subsequent to *Cunningham* that these contrary views prevailed. Whatever may have been the case in English law, where a very wide view was favoured, Scots law has so far not been prepared to extend its notion of legal insanity to mental dysfunctions not clearly related to recognised mental illnesses.[77] Prior to *Ross*, therefore, where an accused person was not fully aware of what he was doing owing to a mental dysfunction, the only question to be answered was whether that mental condition was due to genuine mental illness or not. If it was, then the test for legal insanity would probably have been met, and the accused would have been dealt with according to the law relating to offenders who committed their offences whilst insane (see Ch.8). If it was not, then conviction seemed inevitable (in the absence of any other line of defence); but the disposal of the convicted person would then have been at large—attracting such mitigation as the merits of the case seemed to require.

4–23   The full bench in *Ross v HM Advocate*,[78] however, decided that Lord Clyde's opinion, offering only insanity or conviction with mitigation of penalty in all cases of mental dysfunction, was over concerned with public policy or safety, and too little concerned with basic principle.[79] Lord Clyde's opinion was thus overruled to the extent that "it held that *any* mental or pathological condition short of insanity is relevant only to the question of mitigating circumstances and sentence."[80] Straightforward acquittal *was* possible if the accused's mental dysfunction was not due to insanity, but

---

[74] See Gordon, *Criminal Law*, 2nd edn, para.3–18; W.M. Reid, "Three Steps Back", 1963 S.L.T. (News) 166.
[75] Acquittal of an accused person on the ground of insanity no longer, of course, necessitates such incarceration: see above, para.4–18.
[76] See, e.g. J.W.R. Gray, "A Purely Temporary Disturbance", 1974 J.R. 227.
[77] See *Brennan v HM Advocate*, 1977 J.C. 38, opinion of the court at 46, where the charge to the jury in *HM Advocate v Aitken*, 1975 S.L.T. (Notes) 86, is strongly disapproved.
[78] *Ross v HM Advocate*, 1991 J.C. 210, and see above, para.4–19.
[79] See, e.g. *Ross v HM Advocate*, 1991 J.C. 210, Lord Justice-General Hope at 217–218.
[80] See *Ross v HM Advocate*, 1991 J.C. 210, Lord Justice-General Hope at 222.

rather to the effect of an "external factor"—provided certain safeguards were met (see above, paras 4–20 to 4–21).

External factors

The court in *Ross v HM Advocate* did not find it necessary to **4–24** explain what was meant by "external factor"; nor did it seek to provide illustrations of the concept. Lord Justice-General Hope did,[81] however, refer to the English case of *R. v Sullivan*[82] and, with apparent approval, to that part of Lord Diplock's opinion there where he said:

> "I do not regard that learned judge [Devlin J. in *R. v Kemp* [1957] 1 Q.B. 399 at 407] as excluding the possibility of non-insane automatism (for which the proper verdict would be a verdict of 'not guilty') in cases where temporary impairment (not being self-induced by consuming drink or drugs) results from some external physical factor such as a blow on the head causing concussion or the administration of an anaesthetic for therapeutic purposes."

It would appear, therefore, that the Scottish court had in mind external *physical* factors, such as those considered in the paragraphs which follow.

(1) Alcohol and non-prescribed drugs

Whether the effects on the mind of the voluntary ingestion or, as **4–25** the case may be, inhalation or injection, of alcohol or non-prescribed drugs can be taken into account for the purposes of criminal liability would seem to depend on the "knowledge" of the person concerned.[83] If he knew he was taking the substance in question, and willingly did so, and knew, or ought to have known, the effects it might have on him, then it has been recognised for some time that criminal liability is neither excluded nor diminished.[84] If the consumption or ingestion was not voluntary, then *Ross v HM Advocate* clearly allows acquittal—at least in respect of an offence requiring *mens rea*.[85] Of course, it would not be

---

[81] *Ross v HM Advocate*, 1991 J.C. 210 at 216.
[82] *R. v Sullivan* [1984] A.C. 156 at 172G–H.
[83] *cf.* the English case of *R. v Hardie* [1985] 1 W.L.R. 64, and below, paras 8–59 *et seq.*
[84] See *Brennan v HM Advocate*, 1977 J.C. 38, which dealt with gross, self-induced intoxication with alcohol and LSD—both substances popularly associated with violent and irrational behaviour. See also *Finegan v Heywood*, 2000 S.C.C.R. 460.
[85] *Ross v HM Advocate*, 1991 J.C. 210, per Lord McCluskey at 225–226; and see above, para.4–19. See also *Sorley v HM Advocate*, 1992 J.C. 102 (LSD and sleeping pills); *Cardle v Mulrainey*, 1992 S.L.T. 1152 (amphetamines); and *MacLeod v Napier*, 1993 S.C.C.R. 303 ("speed").

impossible for a long course of voluntary consumption of alcohol
or drugs to result in a condition of legal insanity (see above,
para.4–18) or "diminished responsibility"[86]; but occasional episodes of consumption and drunkenness cannot have such legal
results.[87]

(2A) Prescribed drugs—general

4–26   Where medically prescribed drugs are taken by the person for
whom they were intended (in accordance with medical advice as to
dose, contra-indications and circumstances), and have an unforeseen effect on that person's mental condition leading to the alleged
commission of a criminal act, then this ought to result in his
acquittal.[88] Anaesthetics administered as part of some proper
surgical, medical or dental treatment must follow the same rule—
as hinted at by Lord Fraser in his charge to the jury in *McGregor v
HM Advocate*[89]—a charge approved of generally by Lord Justice-
General Hope in *Ross v HM Advocate*.[90]

(2B) Prescribed drugs—diabetes—hypoglycaemia

4–27   Normally functioning bodily processes effect the production of
glucose which then enters the bloodstream. The pancreas detects
the rising levels of glucose in the blood and produces insulin—thus
enabling the cells of the human body to take up the glucose which
they require to perform their proper functions. In this way glucose
is consumed, the rising blood-glucose level is checked and reversed
and the production of insulin falls off—until the bodily processes
referred to above repeat themselves—in an automatic fashion. The
result is that blood-glucose concentrations are kept within normal
parameters. In simple terms, diabetes is an illness in which the
sufferer either produces no insulin (type 1 diabetes) or produces
insulin which is ineffective (type 2 diabetes). If that illness is
untreated, a very high blood-glucose level (sometimes referred to
as hyperglycaemia) can occur, and can result in drowsiness,
inability to concentrate, and perhaps even coma.[91] Treatment of
type 1 diabetes generally involves the taking of insulin by the
patient; type 2 diabetes can be treated by diet or by appropriate
drugs. It must be obvious that effective treatment by insulin or

---

[86] See *Galbraith v HM Advocate (No.2)*, 2002 J.C. 1; and see also below, paras 4–49
and 4–50.
[87] e.g. see the rejection of Lord Stewart's charge to the jury in *HM Advocate v
Aitken*, 1975 S.L.T. (Notes) 86 by the court in *Brennan v HM Advocate*, 1977 J.C.
38 at 46.
[88] See *Ebsworth v HM Advocate*, 1992 S.L.T. 1161, per Lord Justice-General Hope
at 1166 H—J; *cf. Carrington v HM Advocate*, 1994 S.C.C.R. 567.
[89] *McGregor v HM Advocate*, (1973) S.C.C.R. Supp. 54 at 57.
[90] *Ross v HM Advocate*, 1991 J.C. 210 at 217.
[91] See, e.g. *R. v Hennessy* [1989] 1 W.L.R. 287.

drugs requires care, so that normal blood-glucose levels can be maintained at any particular time. In particular, if too much insulin (or too much of the relevant drug) is injected or ingested, especially in the absence of adequate foodstuffs, blood-glucose levels may fall too rapidly for normal bodily processes to respond; the result may be a condition known as hypoglycaemia. Such a condition may occur very rapidly, and is characterised by drowsiness, inability to concentrate, growing unawareness of actions, and (finally) coma—if unchecked. Diabetics are, or should be, aware of the possibility of hypoglycaemia occurring during the management of their illness, and should, therefore, take appropriate precautions since persons experiencing such a condition have been known to act aggressively,[92] and will almost certainly be unable safely to operate machinery or drive motor vehicles.[93] A hypoglycaemic condition can, therefore, be of interest to the criminal law; and if such a condition occurs and appears to result in criminal conduct, it is of some importance to establish whether that condition was caused by the taking of medication (a plain external factor) or by the illness itself (a matter considered further below at para.4–42).

Where, for example, a crime is apparently committed by a **4–28** person experiencing an "attack" of hypoglycaemia due to his intake of prescribed medication, then he should be acquitted if a criminal charge is brought. He would clearly have been suffering from a sufficient mental dysfunction at the relevant time—a mental dysfunction due to an external factor. It does not matter here that the medication was voluntarily taken by that person. It is the mental dysfunction (and its sufficiency) which counts; and surely no diabetic could be assumed to have taken medication in order to induce a condition of hypoglycaemia. Of course, the other qualifying conditions for a "defence" based on an external factor still apply (see above, paras 4–20 to 4–21). In particular, the mental dysfunction and its effects must not be ones the accused had any reason to anticipate. If, for example, the accused had injected himself with the correct dose of insulin, but then neglected to eat food (contrary to medical advice), then normally he should be able to foresee that his motor skills might be adversely affected. It should be plain to him that he ought to avoid driving or operating machinery. If he does not refrain from such activities, then he should not be immune from criminal liability for the consequences.[94] On the other hand, if the accused is alleged to have committed crimes of violence in the course of (for example) an insulin-induced, hypoglycaemic episode, then the question arises whether it is common knowledge (and if so, whether apparent to the particular accused person) that failure to take food can have

---

[92] See, e.g. *R. v Bailey* [1983] 1 W.L.R. 760.
[93] See, e.g. *MacLeod v Mathieson*, 1993 S.C.C.R. 488 Sh. Ct.
[94] See, e.g. *Moses v Winder* [1981] R.T.R. 37.

such violent repercussions.[95] If it is common knowledge, and particularly where it was known to the accused, then he surely was bound to anticipate that violence would ensue. The opposite conclusion will obviously be reached if there was no such knowledge. From this point of view, the conviction ordered by the Appeal Court in the case of *Carmichael v Boyle*[96] must now be doubted.

4–29 *Carmichael v Boyle.* Boyle was charged with breach of the peace, assault and statutory assault under the Police (Scotland) Act 1967 s.41(1)(a). He was a doubly unfortunate individual, in that he suffered from both an abnormally low level of intelligence and an unstable form of diabetes. His form of that disease was particularly difficult to manage, the balance between intake of insulin and food being an extremely critical one. Boyle, in view of his limited intellect, found it very difficult to follow his medically prescribed regime. He frequently omitted to have regular meals, and thus had often become hypoglycaemic. He had also been violent when in such a condition. It was claimed on his behalf, nevertheless, that he should be acquitted of the charges brought against him since he had taken his prescribed insulin on the day in question, but, thereafter, having failed to take sufficient food, had exhibited the classic signs of hypoglycaemia at the time of the alleged offences. It was argued, therefore, that he would probably have been unaware of what he had been doing at the relevant times. There was no question of his mental condition at those relevant times being treated as insanity, of course. Medical evidence simply confirmed that there was no underlying mental illness. The sheriff, who dealt with this case, frankly admitted that he had no sympathy with the then Scots law rule (see above, para.4–22), and, therefore, sought to avoid it. He did so by holding (in terms which now seem wholly proper) that the charges against Boyle entailed crimes which required *mens rea* to be established. Since the accused had been seen kicking and punching other people by several witnesses, there was no doubt that there was sufficient evidence from which the *mens rea* of assault could be inferred. Persons who kick and punch can usually be taken to have intended those actions. But the sheriff also considered that the evidence of hypoglycaemia meant that the accused could not in fact have been capable of intending the actions which amounted to the assaults charged. He, therefore, acquitted him on that basis. On appeal by the prosecutor, the Appeal Court simply affirmed that the then existing rule had to be applied—namely, since Boyle had not been insane at the times in question, he had to be convicted. Standing the more modern decision in *Ross v HM Advocate*[97] Boyle was probably entitled to an

---

[95] See, e.g. *R. v Bailey* [1983] 1 W.L.R. 760, per Griffiths L.J. at 764H–765B.
[96] *Carmichael v Boyle*, 1985 S.L.T. 399.
[97] *Ross v HM Advocate*, 1991 J.C. 210 and above, para.4–19.

acquittal. His condition was brought about by the insulin he had legitimately taken—by an external factor. It was true, of course, that he had failed to take sufficient food and had been drinking; but such were his intellectual failings that it could hardly be said that he should have anticipated the consequent mental dysfunction and its violent effects.[98]

(3) Toxic fumes

Exposure to toxic fumes, which have a sufficient effect on the **4–30** mental condition of an accused person at the material time, must surely result in an acquittal on any relevant criminal charge— provided that the qualifying conditions set out in *Ross v HM Advocate*[99] are satisfied: toxic fumes in such a situation would clearly form an external factor. Such exposure was argued in *HM Advocate v Murray*[100] by way of defence to certain driving offences; but the decision in that case was made many years prior to the handing down of the opinions in *Ross*. If an identical case were to present today, however, it is doubtful if the qualifying conditions referred to above could be satisfied. In *Murray*, the accused was charged with serious offences—causing the death of three passengers in the car he was driving (when it collided with a parked van), and driving with more than the permitted level of alcohol in his blood (both statutory offences now contained in ss.1 and 5(1) of the Road Traffic Act 1988, as amended). At the trial, Murray attempted to lead evidence that just before he had left his work at a dry-cleaning establishment to drive home on the evening in question, he had been exposed to the toxic fumes of tetrachlorethylene (a chemical used in the dry-cleaning process). He had apparently hoped thereby to convince the jury that he had not been aware of what he was doing and that he was thus entitled to an acquittal. The trial judge ruled, however, that although the evidence could be heard, it could not lead to an acquittal on the first charge. At best, it could simply lead the jury to make a recommendation for leniency. Of course, the evidence of intoxication by a substance other than alcohol would have gone to the merits of the second charge since it clearly required the intoxicant to be alcohol—but that is a separate issue. The trial judge was no doubt influenced by the now-discredited rule laid down in *HM Advocate v Cunningham*.[101] But, as the accused worked in an establishment where toxic chemicals were admittedly used, should he not have been aware of the possibility of exposure to the fumes from those chemicals and of the likely effect on his driving skills?

---

[98] *cf. R. v Quick* [1973] Q.B. 910, per Lawton L.J. at 922E–G.
[99] *Ross v HM Advocate*, 1991 J.C. 210: see above, paras 4–20 to 4–21, for "qualifying conditions".
[100] *HM Advocate v Murray*, 1969 S.L.T. (Notes) 85.
[101] *HM Advocate v Cunningham*, 1963 J.C. 80; see above, paras 4–22 and 4–23.

Was what happened not something he was bound to foresee? Such matters would perforce require to be investigated before an acquittal under the post-*Ross* law could be sustained.

(4) Blows producing concussion

4–31   If a person were to be the victim of an assault which left him dazed and concussed, or if he were to be struck on the head in some accidental way which left him similarly (but temporarily) incapacitated, then an external factor would be present to avoid conviction for any crime apparently committed by him when he was so dazed and concussed. This must follow from the decision in *Ross v HM Advocate*.[102]

(5) Stress, anxiety and depression

4–32   An attempt was apparently made in the English case of *R. v Hennessy*[103] to argue that stress, anxiety and depression could be external factors if they resulted in some relevant mental dysfunction at the time the defendant was alleged to have committed a crime. It was claimed that the defendant in the case was diabetic, and that psychological stress on such a person could lead to a state of hyperglycaemia (see above, para.4–27). The defendant, however, had neglected to take any insulin for some days prior to his "committing" the alleged offences; and the Court of Appeal[104] pointed out that,

> "stress, anxiety and depression can no doubt be the result of the operation of external factors, but they are not, it seems to us, in themselves separately or together external factors of the kind capable in law of causing or contributing to a state of automatism."

Indeed, the Court of Appeal also pointed out that the accused's line of defence, if successful, would have amounted to legal insanity, as that concept is defined in England. Despite what is hinted at in *Hennessy*, it is suggested that Scots law would not and should not accept a stressful situation as a sufficient "external factor" since it lacks the direct quality of (apparently required) "physical contact" with the accused, and, in any event is hardly an unforeseeable occurrence with unforeseeable effects. Stress is a common human experience for which no particular provision

---

[102] *Ross v HM Advocate*, 1991 J.C. 210; see above, para.4–19; *cf. Stevenson v Beatson*, 1965 S.L.T. (Sh. Ct.) 11, noting that the sheriff there erroneously held that an "onus" lay on the accused; and *cf.* also the English case of *R. v Stripp* (1978) 69 Cr.App.R. 318.
[103] *R. v Hennessy* [1989] 1 W.L.R. 287.
[104] *R. v Hennessy* [1989] 1 W.L.R. 287, per Lord Lane C.J. at 294C.

should be made by the criminal law unless, of course, that sort of experience is so serious as to lead to diminished responsibility.[105]

Causal factor—internal

If the position of external factors which produce total alienation **4–33** of reason is reasonably clear, the same cannot be said of non-external, i.e. "internal", factors. Lord Justice-General Hope in *Ross*[106] stressed that the court was "not concerned in this case with a pathological condition such as epilepsy or with the questions of public policy which may affect how such cases should be approached." Accordingly, the opinions cast in that case provide no guidance as to the treatment of non-external factor situations, other than to indicate that a problem exists in respect of them. Lord McCluskey made this plain when he said[107]:

> "The policy of the law in relation to the criminal responsibility of persons who act under the influence of a continuing or recurrent mental or pathological condition short of insanity which derives from some disease or physical morbidity might have to be different."

But how different? If external factors, leading to temporary but total loss of control via total alienation of reason, can lead to straightforward acquittals where certain qualifying conditions are met (see above, paras 4–20 to 4–21), presumably internal factors leading to a similar loss of control may justifiably have a different outcome—and especially so if there was a risk of recurrence and a consequent issue of public safety. If, for example, such an internal factor were regarded as creating a situation of legal insanity at the time an alleged crime was committed, then the verdict would have to be one of acquittal on the ground of insanity (see above, para.4–18). This was certainly the favoured approach of Lord Denning in *Bratty v Att-Gen for Northern Ireland*[108] where he said,

> "any mental disorder [including epilepsy or cerebral tumour] which has manifested itself in violence and is prone to recur is a disease of the mind. At any rate it is the sort of disease for which a person should be detained in hospital rather than be given an unqualified acquittal."[109]

---

[105] See *Galbraith v HM Advocate (No.2)*, 2002 J.C. 1; and see below, paras 4–49 and 4–50.

[106] *Ross v HM Advocate*, 1991 J.C. 210 at 217.

[107] *Ross v HM Advocate*, 1991 J.C. 210 at 231.

[108] *Bratty v Att-Gen for Northern Ireland* [1963] A.C. 386 at 412.

[109] Echoes of this occur in *Ross v HM Advocate*, 1991 J.C. 210, opinion of Lord Justice-General Hope at 213: "We are concerned here only with a mental condition of a temporary nature which was the result of an external factor and not of some disorder of the mind itself which was liable to recur."

With the modification that genuine external causes of mental dysfunction are to be excluded from that dictum,[110] Lord Denning's formulation has repeatedly been endorsed in England.[111] The standard English approach, therefore, is to treat internal causes of mental dysfunction leading to total loss of control as examples of legal insanity, and especially so if such mental dysfunction is associated with violence and is likely to recur.[112] Is this, or should this also be the standard approach in Scotland?

4–34   It is suggested that this has not hitherto been, nor should be followed in Scotland. The English definition of insanity is very wide (or at least is very wide for the purposes of the defence of automatism)[113] whereas the Scottish definition is believed to be more restrained and better grounded in common sense.[114] The basis of the Scottish approach seems to be that insanity must relate to genuine mental illness; and from that basis, it would be exceedingly odd to have to regard persons suffering from the effects of a disease such as diabetes or epilepsy as insane. Such a standard rule would perforce possess a somewhat unreal, if not fictional quality. In any event, it appears to have been agreed in *Ross v HM Advocate*[115] that Lord Clyde's original dictum in *HM Advocate v Cunningham*[116] was defective rather because of its width than anything else. As Lord Justice-General Hope said:[117]

> "The conclusion which I invite your Lordships to reach in this case is that *Cunningham* was wrongly decided in so far as it held that *any* [Lord Hope's own emphasis] mental or patho-logical condition short of insanity is relevant only to the question of mitigating circumstances and sentence."

That conclusion (with which the remaining members of the Appeal Court agreed) suggests that there may be a class of mental dysfunction, caused by an internal factor not amounting to mental illness, where a special approach is called for. Although the court in *Ross* did not go on to specify what that special approach should be,[118] it must be plain that two considerations influence the solution. The first of these is that there may be a need to cater for future public safety where an internal factor produces a mental condition whereunder the accused is unable to prevent himself

---

[110] See *R. v Quick* [1973] Q.B. 910, per Lawton L.J. at 917F–918G and 922E–923C.
[111] See, e.g. *R. v Burgess* [1991] 2 W.L.R. 1206, per Lord Lane C.J. at 1211G–1212A.
[112] See Smith and Hogan, *Criminal Law*, 10th edn, p.39.
[113] See, e.g. *R. v Hennessy* [1989] 1 W.L.R. 287, per Lord Lane C.J. at 291C–293H; and *R. v Sullivan* [1984] A.C. 156, per Lord Diplock at 170–173.
[114] See below, Ch.8 at paras 8–14 *et seq.*
[115] *Ross v HM Advocate*, 1991 J.C. 210.
[116] *HM Advocate v Cunningham*, 1963 J.C. 80 at 84; see above, para.4–22.
[117] *Ross v HM Advocate*, 1991 J.C. 210.
[118] See, e.g. *Ross v HM Advocate*, 1991 J.C. 210, Lord McCluskey's opinion at 231, quoted above at para.4–33.

acting violently (or perhaps just "criminally"), and especially so where such a mental condition may occur again. Indeed, there is a feeling that internally generated mental dysfunctions are very likely to recur since there may be no obvious and understandable external cause for them: thus, the perceived need to consider future public safety in relation to "internal" rather than "external" factors. The second consideration concerns the frequent references in *Ross* and elsewhere to such mental conditions being "short of" or "not amounting to" insanity. These references emphasise clearly that acquittal on the ground of insanity cannot be a legitimate option in such cases unless resort is had to the grossest of fictions.

The preferred Scottish approach?

What then is the preferred Scottish solution to the problem **4–35** posed above in para.4–33? Decided cases from the late nineteenth century to the present day suggest that the preferred approach may involve conviction of such persons in respect of crimes factually proved against them, coupled to disposals which cater inter alia for future public safety. The emphasis, in other words, lies not so much on punishment, since in many such cases consideration of penalty would be quite unjust, but rather on a disposal which gives due consideration to the need to limit future danger to others. This approach can be seen in most of the Scottish cases considered in the paragraphs which follow. Whilst it is true that the persons concerned in many of these cases may have been more deserving of sympathy than prosecution and criminal conviction, public policy surely required a realistic solution to a difficult problem. After conviction, of course, a court will usually be able to consider a wider range of criteria as to the future dangerousness of such a person than would have been possible under the rules of evidence which pertain during a trial.[119] Conviction also opens up the widest possible range of disposals as the law presently stands.[120] Whilst fairly recent reforms have greatly enhanced what a court may do after an acquittal on the ground of insanity,[121] the arguments against returning an insanity verdict at all in respect of a person

---

[119] *cf.* however, the provision for risk assessment and lifelong restriction orders under ss.210B–210F of the Criminal Procedure (Scotland) Act 1995, as inserted by the Criminal Justice (Scotland) Act 2003 (asp 7) s.1, noting that s.210EA is added by the Management of Offenders etc. (Scotland) Act 2005 (asp 14) s.19, and that s.210F is amended by the 2005 Act (asp 14) s.14; *cf.* also diminished responsibility: see *Galbraith v HM Advocate (No.2)*, 2002 J.C. 1, and below, paras 4–49 and 4–50.

[120] *cf.* a straightforward acquittal, to which no conditions whatsoever can be attached.

[121] See above, para.4–18.

suffering from the disorders mentioned in the following paragraphs remain compelling.[122]

Non-insane internal factors

(1) "Naturally" induced sleep

4–36   Whilst it is unusual for "criminal" acts to be performed during natural sleep, it is not entirely unknown. In the case of *Simon Fraser*[123] the accused was asleep in bed together with his wife and 18 month old son (apparently a not-uncommon domestic arrangement in the nineteenth century). According to his own declaration,[124] he dreamt that a white beast flew through the floor and round the back of the bed where the child was lying. He further dreamt that he tried to catch it, and indeed caught something which he dashed against the floor and door of the room. He then came to his senses and found that it was his son he had caught and so treated. The child died shortly afterwards of its injuries. Fraser never denied that he had caused his son's death. In reply to a murder charge brought against him, however, he pled "not guilty" and advanced the defence that he was asleep at the time. At his trial, three medical experts testified that he was *not* insane but that he did suffer from an abnormal mental condition. According, again, to his own declaration, Fraser had strange dreams every night—usually between midnight and 1am—but was rarely "outrageous" except every six months or so. By being "outrageous", he apparently meant "violent", since about 18 months prior to the killing of his child, he dreamt that his wife was being attacked by a dog which led him to throw some pieces of furniture at it. In consequence, his wife had received bruising to her arm and eye. The trial judge, Lord Justice-Clerk Moncreiff, told the jury[125] that he supposed they would agree that Fraser was totally unconscious of what he had done to his son and he suggested that they return a finding, "that the pannel [a Scots law term for the accused] killed his child, but that he was in a state in which he was unconscious of the act which he was committing by reason of the condition of somnambulism, and that he was not responsible." The jury did so.

---

[122] Powerful arguments have been expressed, however, against this view, and it has been concluded that the English approach, i.e, acquittal on the ground of insanity, has, in terms of certain dicta in the case of *Ross*, already been adopted in Scotland. See in particular, Graeme T. Laurie, "Automatism and Insanity in the Law of England and Scotland", 1995 J.R. 253; *cf.* the approach adopted by Chalmers and Leverick in *Criminal Defences and Pleas in Bar of Trial*, Ch.7, especially at paras 7–26 *et seq.*

[123] *Simon Fraser* (1878) 4 Coup. 70.

[124] N.A.S., J.C. 26/1269.

[125] *Simon Fraser* (1878) 4 Coup. 70 at 75.

Opinions as to what that verdict meant have varied.[126] However, **4–37** the preponderance of the evidence points to conviction.[127] The Solicitor-General, for example, who was prosecuting the case in person, successfully requested an adjournment of two days following the jury's verdict—the pannel to be kept in custody during that time. The original court records[128] narrate the fact of the adjournment as follows:

> "The court delayed pronouncing sentence in the meantime: Continued the diet against the pannel till Wednesday first the seventeenth current at three o'clock, and ordained him in the meantime to be detained in the prison of Edinburgh."

At the resumed diet, the Solicitor-General deliberately refrained from "moving for sentence"—a privilege he has where a person has been found guilty of a crime. The reason in this case why the prosecutor so refrained was that the pannel and his father had signed an agreement as follows[129]:

> "I, Simon Fraser, having in view the nature of the attacks to which I am occasionally subject at night, do hereby solemnly promise and undertake that I shall always sleep alone; and I, Simon Fraser, Senior, father of the said Simon Fraser, do hereby solemnly promise and undertake, so far as in my power, to see and take care that my son fulfils the promise before written made by him."

Prevention of harm to others in the future was thus thought to have been secured; and the ultimate mitigation of punishment was achieved by the prosecutor's declining to move for sentence at all. It is true, of course, that the court attached no sanction if the undertaking were to be breached by Fraser in the future. But the

---

[126] See, e.g. Williams, *Criminal Law: The General Part*, 2nd edn, p.173—"he . . . was not convicted of murder, nor indeed of anything"; *cf.* N. Walker, *Crime and Insanity in England* (Edinburgh: Edinburgh University Press, 1968–1973),Vol.1, p.170, where he questions the "assumption which one finds in later writers, that the result of Fraser's case was an acquittal." James Chalmers and Fiona Leverick, in *Criminal Defences and Pleas in Bar of Trial*, at para.7–31, correctly point out that J.H.A. Macdonald (who, as Solicitor General, prosecuted in *Simon Fraser*) referred in his book to the case as having resulted in an acquittal (see Macdonald, *Criminal Law*, revised by the author and N.D. Macdonald, Advocate, 3rd edn (Edinburgh: 1894), p.510; edited by R. MacGregor Mitchell, 4th edn (Edinburgh: 1929), p.569; edited by by James Walker and D.J. Stevenson 5th edn (Edinburgh: W. Green. 1948), pp.347–348): but Chalmers and Leverick eventually conclude that the case is "authority for very little, if anything."

[127] As Lord Justice-General Hope concluded in *Ross v HM Advocate*, 1991 J.C. 210 at 217.

[128] N.A.S., J.C. 4/77.

[129] N.A.S., AD14/78/166.

trial was widely reported in the press[130] and the public thus placed on its guard. In *Ross v HM Advocate*[131] Lord Justice-General Hope opined that the approach taken in *Simon Fraser* was "a very special one."[132] Special approaches may well, however, be justified in such unusual situations.

4–38   *R. v Burgess.* The outcome in *Simon Fraser* can be contrasted with the attitude of the Court of Appeal in the English case of *R. v Burgess*.[133] There the accused attacked a woman, hitting her over the head with a bottle and a video-recorder. He submitted a defence of non-insane automatism, in that he had been asleep and sleep-walking at the time. The trial judge ruled that his defence amounted to insanity, since there was no external cause for his mental dysfunction at the time of the attack. The jury, therefore, acquitted him on the ground of insanity—thus (as the law then was) automatically securing his detention in a mental hospital. It is difficult to feel completely comfortable with such a decision; but the Court of Appeal endorsed it fully.

4–39   *Finegan v Heywood.* Nowadays, it seems reasonably clear that *Simon Fraser*[134] would be regarded as a case to which diminished responsibility was probably applicable[135]; Fraser would thus have been convicted of culpable homicide—although the problem of an adequate disposal would remain. A more modern case of parasomnia (as sleep walking tends now to be referred to) arose in *Finegan v Heywood*.[136] The accused was charged in the sheriff court with a variety of driving offences contrary to the Road Traffic Act 1988.[137] These offences were probably all of "strict liability"[138]; but there was a further charge of theft, in respect of which proof of *mens rea* would, of course, have been a necessary element. He was acquitted of that common law charge, however, and his plea of automatism on the basis of somnambulism was rejected. He appealed against conviction of the driving offences on the basis that his plea of automatism should not have been rejected. The Appeal Court, however, upheld the convictions on the grounds that although he probably had been in a state of somnambulism at the time of the offences, it had been found by the sheriff that that state

---

[130] See, e.g. *The Scotsman*, July 16 and 18, 1878.

[131] *Ross v HM Advocate*, 1991 J.C. 210 at 217.

[132] A similar view was expressed by the court in *Finegan v Heywood*, 2000 S.C.C.R. 460 at 463B, para.4. See below, para.4–39.

[133] *R. v Burgess* [1991] 2 W.L.R. 1206.

[134] See above, paras 4–36 to 4–37.

[135] See *Galbraith v HM Advocate (No.2)*, 2002 J.C. 1; and see below, paras 4–49 to 4–50.

[136] *Finegan v Heywood*, 2000 S.C.C.R. 460.

[137] Driving with more than the permitted level of alcohol in his breath; taking and driving away a motor vehicle without the consent of the owner or other lawful authority; and, using a motor vehicle without insurance: contrary to ss.5(1)(a), 178(1)(a) and 143(1) and (2), respectively.

[138] See above, para.4–06, and below, Ch.13.

had been triggered by the appellant's voluntary consumption of at least six pints of beer; that the appellant had been aware that such consumption of alcohol acted as such a trigger; and that, therefore, the case was to be treated as similar to one where there had been self-induced intoxication by voluntary consumption of alcohol.[139] As the court said[140]:

> "[T]he defence of automatism cannot . . . be established upon proof that the appellant was in a transitory state of parasomnia which was the result of, and indeed induced by, deliberate and self-induced intoxication."

It does not necessarily follow, of course, that, had there been no element of "fault" on the appellant's part in his lapsing into a state of parasomnia, the court in *Finegan v Heywood* would have been prepared to accept that automatism had been made out; but if the facts had revealed that a soft drink had been spiked with alcohol by a third party without Finegan's knowledge at all, then the effect of his imbibing that might have created a situation which prima facie involved automatism—unless his susceptibility to parasomnia were to be used to distinguish that situation from the legal position established in *Ross*.[141]

(2) Disease—certain types of epilepsy

Violent, unpredictable behaviour can follow certain types of **4–40** epileptic fit, although the sufferer will probably be totally unaware of what he does. In *HM Advocate v Mitchell*,[142] for example, the accused had savagely killed a woman with blows from a knife and a meat-chopper. His defence was "psychic epilepsy"—that he had experienced the sort of epileptic fit which is not accompanied by the usual outward signs of a grand mal seizure, e.g. convulsions, tongue-biting, and foam evident at the mouth. As this, therefore, was a wholly "internal" fit and was consistent with a wholly mental condition, he submitted a defence of legal insanity. This was accepted as such by both the judge and the jury. Of course, it does not follow from that case that all types of epilepsy are to be regarded as mental illnesses for the purposes of the criminal law in Scotland[143] and if particular types do not square with the definition of legal insanity, then the result should be conviction accompanied by whatever disposal seems appropriate in the circumstances to secure public safety. This was made quite plain in *HM Advocate v Cunningham*.[144] That case concerned not crimes of violence, but

---

[139] Thus following the *ratio* of *Brennan v HM Advocate*, 1977 J.C. 38.

[140] *Finegan v Heywood*, 2000 S.C.C.R. 460 at 464F, para.10.

[141] *Ross v HM Advocate*, 1991 J.C. 210.

[142] *HM Advocate v Mitchell*, 1951 J.C. 53.

[143] *cf.* the approach taken by the English courts in *R. v Sullivan* [1984] A.C. 156.

[144] *HM Advocate v Cunningham*, 1963 J.C. 80, as modified by *Ross v HM Advocate*, 1991 J.C. 210; see above, paras 4–22 and 4–23.

taking and driving away a van without the permission of the owner, causing death by dangerous driving—the van had mounted the pavement and knocked down four pedestrians—and being unfit to drive owing to the consumption of drink or drugs.[145] The accused had tendered a defence of "temporary dissociation", i.e. that he had not been aware of what he had been doing at the critical times, owing to "an epileptic fugue or other pathological condition." Since this had been tendered as a defence which, if established, would lead to the unconditional acquittal of the accused, the prosecutor sought a ruling from the trial judge that acquittal could not follow from it unless the mental condition it referred to was consistent with legal insanity. The trial judge, Lord Wheatley, certified this point to a larger court of three High Court judges who confirmed that the prosecutor's contention was correct. If an epileptic or similar mental condition was not such as to amount to legal insanity, then the result would be conviction (assuming that the Crown's case was otherwise established) tempered by such mitigation of the "normal" sentence as seemed appropriate. There was no suggestion in the court's decision that such an accused person would have to be punished in any usual sense of that word.

4–41   It had sometimes been hinted at[146] that the pre-*Ross*[147] decision in *Cunningham*[148] was in any event inconsistent with the result of the full bench ruling in *HM Advocate v Hayes*,[149] but this was and is not really so. Andrew Hayes had been driving a bus when he had some sort of epileptic seizure. The result was that the bus ceased to be under his complete control, collided with two parked lorries and overturned. Several persons were injured (including the drivers of the two parked vehicles) and four passengers in the bus lost their lives. The charge brought against Hayes was one of culpable homicide at common law together with, as an alternative, the less serious statutory offence of dangerous driving. He submitted a defence of "temporary dissociation" (see above, para.4–40) due to "masked epilepsy" or other pathological condition. After trial, the jury found him guilty of culpable homicide but also found his defence of "temporary dissociation" proved. There can be little doubt, therefore, that he had been found guilty of the more serious crime; but his counsel asked the trial judge, Lord Carmont, to inquire if the jury meant by this that they would have found him guilty "if he had been a normal man." When the question was put,

---

[145] All statutory offences, now to be found in ss.178, 1 and 4(1) respectively of the Road Traffic Act 1988, as amended where appropriate by the Road Traffic Act 1991.

[146] See Gane and Stoddart, *A Casebook on Scottish Criminal Law*, 1st edn, p.216; Gordon, *Criminal Law*, 2nd edn, para.3–20.

[147] *Ross v HM Advocate*, 1991 J.C. 210.

[148] See above, para.4–40.

[149] High Court at Edinburgh, November 1, 1949, unreported, but noted in Gane and Stoddart, *A Casebook on Scottish Criminal Law*, 3rd edn, p.232, note 2.

it appeared that the jury might have meant just that—and Lord Carmont went on to inquire if they therefore wished to reconsider their verdict. This resulted in the jury's apparently wishing to find him "not guilty", and some confusion as to what was then the proper verdict. The court records[150] clearly reveal that Lord Carmont reinstated the jury's original verdict—such that the accused stood convicted of culpable homicide. Of course, this left the problem of disposal since the conviction had been accompanied by a finding that the defence had also been established. His Lordship, therefore, certified the question of disposal to a full bench of the High Court at Edinburgh (the court consisting of Lord Justice-General Cooper, Lord Justice-Clerk Thomson, and Lords Mackay, Carmont, Jamieson, Russell and Keith). It is highly significant that Hayes had his bail continued during the intervening period. It is also highly significant that the Solicitor-General (who was appearing in person for the Crown) opened the proceedings at Edinburgh by "moving for sentence." These things would have been impossible had Hayes not been convicted. The outcome was that he was not to be punished in any conventional way. Instead, he was to be discharged provided he agreed to surrender his driving licences and promised never to drive vehicles again—undertakings which he found it prudent to make. The seven judges of the High Court seemed keen to stress that this was not to be taken as a precedent—suggesting that all such cases (as indeed all sentencing decisions) should be treated on an individual basis. No formal agreement (as in *Simon Fraser's* case, see above, para.4–37) was necessary since the licences were presumably at once handed to the court. The licensing authorities were also to be notified accordingly.

(3) Disease—diabetes

A brief description of diabetes has already been given (see **4–42** above, para.4–27). It is clearly not a mental illness. It would be absurd to attempt to treat it by psychiatric means. Where the disease itself (as opposed to some drug or similar preparation taken for its treatment) creates a mental dysfunction leading to total lack of control, then it seems plain in England that the resulting condition amounts to legal insanity.[151] In Scotland, it is thought that the result of disease-induced hypoglycaemia (see above, para.4–27) leading to total loss of control at the time of an alleged offence should be conviction together with such disposal as will take into account the likelihood of future public danger from the person concerned. If this is correct, then the correctness of the decision in *Farrell v Stirling*[152] must be doubted. There the sheriff

---

[150] N.A.S., J.C. 5/28, Appendix No. 40.
[151] See, e.g. *R. v Quick* [1973] Q.B. 910, per Lawton L.J. at 922H–23A; *R. v Hennessy* [1989] 1 W.L.R. 287, per Lord Lane C.J. at 293G.
[152] *Farrell v Stirling*, 1975 S.L.T. (Sh. Ct.) 71.

had fully accepted[153] that the accused, "carried out his normal regime as a diabetic so far as injection of insulin and diet were concerned", yet acquitted him of a statutory driving charge where the evidence suggested total lack of control at the time. Where the disease itself randomly creates a situation of total lack of control despite the best endeavours of medicine to stabilise the sufferer's condition, a clear concern for future public safety exists to which neither straightforward acquittal nor acquittal on the ground of insanity provides an adequate or realistic response.[154]

(4) Disease—spontaneous hypoglycaemia

4–43   What pertains to diabetes should also follow in relation to other diseases which produce (of their own accord) similar effects. Thus, in *Stirling v Annan*[155] the accused was said to suffer from a condition known as "spontaneous hypoglycaemia." That illness caused the sufferer to experience sudden and unexpected diminutions in the level of sugar in his blood from time to time. During such hypoglycaemic episodes, he was reckoned to be totally unaware of what he might in fact be doing—such as (in the case itself) removing and pocketing various items from the shelves of a self-service store, and thereafter walking from the store without attempting to pay for them. Stirling was in fact convicted of theft in respect of the items he had taken—a decision which, it is suggested, was probably correct. On appeal, however, the advocate-depute conceded that a miscarriage of justice might have occurred. The conviction was thus quashed. To date, it remains unclear why such a concession was made. There was certainly no suggestion that any external factor was involved which might have brought the case (prospectively, of course) within the ambit of *Ross v HM Advocate*.[156]

(5) Disease in general—HM Advocate v Ritchie

4–44   Many diseases, or sudden illnesses for that matter, can lead to total unconsciousness or to mental conditions where the patient is totally unable to control his actions. Heart attacks, strokes,[157] arteriosclerosis,[158] and brain tumours[159] may obviously all have such

---

[153] *Farrell v Stirling*, 1975 S.L.T. (Sh. Ct.) 71 at 73, column 2.
[154] In *MacLeod v Mathieson*, 1993 S.C.C.R. 488 Sh. Ct., the sheriff was prepared for the sake of argument to accept that hypoglycaemia was an external factor—possibly because of doubts as to whether it was caused by insulin or the disease. In rejecting the accused's defence of automatism, he distinguished *Farrell v Stirling*, 1975 S.L.T. (Sh. Ct.) 71, on the ground that there, the accused had had no prior warning that he was subject to such attacks.
[155] *Stirling v Annan*, 1984 S.L.T. 88.
[156] *Ross v HM Advocate*, 1991 J.C. 210; see above, para.4–19.
[157] See, e.g. the English civil case of *Roberts v Ramsbottom* [1980] 1 W.L.R. 823.
[158] See, e.g. the English case of *R. v Kemp* [1957] 1 Q.B. 399.
[159] See, e.g. the English case of *R. v Charlson* [1955] 1 W.L.R. 317.

effects. A related situation appears to have occurred in *HM Advocate v Ritchie*,[160] as that case is now properly to be understood.[161] The accused was charged with culpable homicide in that he, whilst driving a motor vehicle, had knocked down and killed a pedestrian; his defence (tendered as a "special defence") amounted to this—that, "by the incidence of temporary mental dissociation due to toxic exhaustive factors he was unaware of the presence of the deceased on the highway and of his injuries and death, and was incapable of appreciating his immediately previous and subsequent actions." It appears that the phrase "toxic exhaustive factors" referred to the absorption of toxins into the accused's blood from lung abscesses, from which he had suffered since being wounded during the "war". Thus, in post-*Ross*[162] terminology, his state of unawareness was actually due to disease—a non-external factor[163]—but fell "short of insanity". The case is reported in terms of Lord Murray's charge to the jury. His Lordship did not distinguish between internal and external factors; nor did he consider (it seems) insanity as a possible interpretation of the accused's "special defence". In fact, he presented the jury with a stark choice between (a) the accused's having overestimated his strength and capabilities in view of recent illness (this probably amounting to a "fault" element in itself) and thus having driven recklessly, and (b) his having become, while ordinarily quite justified in driving, "owing to a cause which he was not bound to foresee, and which was outwith his control—either gradually or suddenly not the master of his own action" such that "a question as to his responsibility or irresponsibility for the consequences of his action" arose "and may form the ground of a good special defence."[164] The jury returned a verdict of not guilty on the grounds that Ritchie was, at the relevant time, "suffering from abnormality, and was therefore not culpable . . .".[165]

The soundness of Lord Murray's direction to the jury was attacked by the court in *HM Advocate v Cunningham*[166]; but

---

[160] *HM Advocate v Ritchie*, 1926 J.C. 45.

[161] See Chalmers and Leverick, *Criminal Defences and Pleas in Bar of Trial*, para.7–34 (which draws upon the researches of Jenifer Ross in the N.A.S.).

[162] *Ross v HM Advocate*, 1991 J.C. 210.

[163] Unless the wound suffered in the war could be counted as "external"; but the application of ordinary principles of causation would surely end any such argument: see below, Ch.5 generally, and para.5–07 in particular.

[164] *HM Advocate v Ritchie*, 1926 J.C. 45, Lord Murray's charge to the jury at 49. The Crown's contention in the case was that the accused had caused the death by grossly negligent driving, and that any state of "mental dissociation" arose subsequently, and in direct response to, the accused's discovery of the "accident". The accused's contention was that he had been in a state of dissociation prior to the "accident"; accordingly no *culpa* or blame attached to him, and he was thus entitled to a verdict of not guilty. The Crown suggested that if the jury accepted the accused's version of the facts, the trial judge should advise them to return a special verdict similar to that in *Simon Fraser*'s case ((1878) 4 Coup. 70; see above, paras 4–36 to 4–37): this Lord Murray declined to do.

[165] *HM Advocate v Ritchie*, 1926 J.C. 45 at 51.

[166] *HM Advocate v Cunningham*, 1963 J.C. 80, Lord Justice General Clyde at 83.

Cunningham was overruled by the larger court in *Ross v HM Advocate*[167]—and the impression gained from the opinions cast in *Ross* is that Lord Murray was generally correct to advise the jury in the way that he had. Where he had been wrong was to direct them that the *onus* to prove a defence of "mental dissociation" lay on the accused. But he might also, of course, have been wrong to direct the jury that they might return an unqualified verdict of acquittal—depending on what verdict *should* follow on automatism consequent upon a non-external factor. It has been suggested above that conviction, with its myriad disposal possibilities, might be justified in such circumstances—actual disposal depending particularly on the possibility of recurrence and the issue of public safety. Other commentators tend, however, to favour a verdict of acquittal on the simple ground of automatism.[168] The problem may be capable of resolution, however, if "external factor" were to include the results of physical disease[169]; but until the Appeal Court has the opportunity of clarifying the terms used in *Ross*'s case,[170] the problem will remain.[171]

(6) Weak intellect

4–45   In *Clark v HM Advocate*[172] a married couple was charged with the wilful neglect of a young child in a manner likely to cause it unnecessary suffering and injury—contrary to the Children and Young Persons (Scotland) Act 1937 s.12(1).[173] The defence attempted at the trial to lead psychiatric evidence that both of the accused were "so feckless and incompetent that they did not appreciate what the result of their failure [to provide adequate food and medical aid for the child] would be."[174] In brief, the argument was that they were well aware of what they did or refrained from doing for the child, but were totally unaware of the

---

[167] *Ross v HM Advocate*, 1991 J.C. 210 (court of five judges).
[168] See, e.g. Chalmers and Leverick, *Criminal Defences and Pleas in Bar of Trial*, Ch.7, especially paras 7–28 *et seq.*, where (at para.7–34) the authors eventually conclude that, were a case similar to that of *Ritchie* to occur today, an unqualified acquittal on the ground of automatism would be justified on policy grounds.
[169] As opposed, perhaps, to "mental disease"; but that would present its own problems in relation to mental abnormalities consequent upon epilepsy or diabetes: *cf*. Chalmers and Leverick, *Criminal Defences and Pleas in Bar of Trial*, para.7–35.
[170] *Ross v HM Advocate*, 1991 J.C. 210.
[171] For a short critical appraisal of the "external factor doctrine", see R.D. MacKay and B.J. Mitchell, "Sleepwalking, Automatism and Insanity" [2006] Crim.L.R. 901, especially from p.903.
[172] *Clark v HM Advocate*, 1968 J.C. 53.
[173] Children and Young Persons (Scotland) Act 1937 s.12(1) is currently to be read as amended by the Children Act 1975 Sch.4 Pt III, the Children (Scotland) Act 1995 Sch.4 para.7(2)(a), and the Criminal Justice (Scotland) Act 2003 (asp 7) s.51(5)(a).
[174] *Clark v HM Advocate*, 1968 J.C. 53, per Lord Justice-Clerk Grant at 56.

effects which their conduct or omissions would have because of some congenital weakness of intellect from which they suffered. Whilst it is true that such weakness of intellect is an internal factor, it is also true that such weakness had no effect on the ability of the two accused to control their conduct. It is suggested, therefore, that there was no relevant internal factor in the case, and that the "normal" convictions affirmed by the appeal court were correct. Weakness of intellect has, therefore, little relevance in this part of the criminal law, unless it substantially impairs the ability of the accused to determine and control his actions, when it may amount to diminished responsibility.[175]

(7) Hysterical amnesia

Loss of memory (amnesia) is also a condition which should have **4–46** no bearing whatever on criminal liability—assuming that it occurred after the critical event(s) and is not symptomatic of some graver and more long-lasting mental condition. On that assumption, it can have no effect on a person's ability to control his conduct at the time of an alleged offence. There is a suggestion, however, that "hysterical amnesia" at the time of the alleged offence might be pled as at least a mitigatory matter in an appropriate case. In *Russell v HM Advocate*[176] a defence of that description (of which few further details are revealed) was not considered improper except insofar as it paralleled a plea in bar of trial which had already been rejected.[177]

CONCLUSION

If the approach of Scots law to the problem of non-insane internal **4–47** factors has been properly set out above in para.4–35, then Scotland deals with cases of total loss of control (following from total alienation of reason) in relation to proven criminal conduct according to the following categories: (1) where that total loss of control is caused by mental illness, then the accused will be acquitted on the ground of insanity, with the consequences which such a verdict has (see above, para.4–18); (2) where that total loss of control is caused by an external factor which meets the qualifying conditions, then the accused will be acquitted unconditionally on the ground of automatism; and (3) where that total loss of control is due to disease or illness not amounting to insanity and especially where it is likely to recur, then the accused should probably be convicted in order that measures of treatment or restraint may be considered for the purpose of future public safety,

---

[175] See below, paras 4–49 and 4–50. See also *John McLean* (1876) 3 Coup. 334, per Lord Deas at 337–340.
[176] *Russell v HM Advocate*, 1946 J.C. 37, per Lord Justice-Clerk Cooper at 45.
[177] See also the English case of *R. v Isitt* [1978] R.T.R. 211.

there being no such thing as "acquittal with conditions" in Scots law. Difficult issues appear to be raised, of course, where there are two or more causal factors at work. In diabetic automatism cases, for example, the effect of insulin (external) on the accused's mental state may have to be weighed against the causal factor of the disease itself (internal): and in the "lager can" type of case, where drugs are allegedly pushed into the accused's chosen alcoholic drink,[178] the effect of drink knowingly ingested (external, but generally not relevant to the defence of automatism) should strictly be weighed against the effect of the drugs (external, and possibly within the defence) on the accused's mental state. These are, however, issues of fact and degree—and will have to be solved in a common-sense way.

4-48 In the case of crimes which require *mens rea*, the method of dealing with accused persons who fall within category (3) above may seem unjustifiable—since such accused clearly possess no more subjective *mens rea* than those who fall within category (2). But unless *HM Advocate v Cunningham*[179] and leading decisions which followed it[180] are overturned completely,[181] the preferring of convictions is possibly the best way of reconciling the prior case-law with what was said by the Appeal Court in *Ross*. Of course, the opinions in *Ross* do not rule out straightforward acquittals for at least some persons who fall within category (3)—perhaps, for example, for those who suffer a wholly unforeseeable stroke or heart attack whilst driving a mechanically propelled vehicle.[182] And it may be that Scots law will eventually categorise such persons according to a more sophisticated classification. But it is certainly to be hoped, in accordance with a general approach which Scots law has long favoured, that all those—especially police, prosecutors and judges—who influence the practice of the law (and thus the law itself) will approach difficult cases in this area bearing in mind "in a common sense way their sense of fairness."[183]

A NOTE ON DIMINISHED RESPONSIBILITY[184]

4-49 It has been suggested above[185] that Scots criminal law envisages the conviction of those who were at the material time unconscious or semi-conscious due to "internal factors", but that their mental

---

[178] e.g. *Ross v HM Advocate,* 1991 J.C. 210; *Sorley v HM Advocate,* 1992 J.C. 102; *Cardle v Mulrainey,* 1992 S.L.T. 1152.
[179] *HM Advocate v Cunningham,* 1963 J.C. 80.
[180] In particular *Clark v HM Advocate,* 1968 J.C. 53 and *Carmichael v Boyle,* 1985 S.L.T. 399.
[181] *Ross v HM Advocate,* 1991 J.C. 210 did not go that far—see Lord Justice-General Hope's opinion at 222.
[182] See, however, below, paras 4–49 to 4–50.
[183] *R. v Quick* [1973] 1 Q.B. 910, per Lawton L.J. at 922C.
[184] For the most recent scholarly account of diminished responsibility, see Chalmers and Leverick, *Criminal Defences and Pleas in Bar of Trial,* Ch.11.
[185] See above, para.4–47.

abnormality (not amounting to insanity) should be taken into account in mitigation of punishment or (exceptionally perhaps) by substitution of some appropriate disposal which does not reflect the ordinary notion of punishment at all. This seems to be supported by the modern view of diminished responsibility.[186] Of course, it may be that diminished responsibility is strictly a concept or doctrine confined to homicide cases[187]: but in the leading case of *Galbraith v HM Advocate*,[188] although there are dicta which suggest that it is so confined,[189] there are also dicta which suggest that it is simply a general mitigatory concept to which, in the case of murder, effect cannot be given unless there is a conviction for culpable homicide.[190] It is submitted that the correct view is the latter, i.e. that diminished responsibility is a general mitigatory plea.[191] If that is correct, then what is said about that plea in *Galbraith* is of relevance to cases where crimes were committed when their alleged authors were not acting voluntarily due to mental abnormality caused by "internal factors" (or even by external ones, where not all of the criteria for automatism can be met[192]).

Following the decision of the Appeal Court in *Galbraith*,[193] an **4–50** accused person will be considered as having been of diminished responsibility if he suffered at the relevant time from a mental

---

[186] See *Galbraith v HM Advocate (No.2)*, 2002 J.C. 1, and the text below.

[187] As a "plea", diminished responsibility has been said to be confined to murder: see, e.g. *HM Advocate v Cunningham*, 1963 J.C. 80, per Lord Justice-General Clyde at 84; and as a "defence", in *Brennan v HM Advocate*, 1977 J.C. 38 at 47, the opinion of a court of seven judges was that it was "available only where the charge is murder and which, if ... established, [could] result only in the return of a verdict of guilt of the lesser crime of culpable homicide". The sense seems to be that in Scots law, "diminished responsibility applies in cases where, because the accused's ability to determine and control his actings is impaired as a result of some mental abnormality, his responsibility for any killing can properly be regarded as correspondingly reduced. The accused should, accordingly, be convicted of culpable homicide rather than of murder": *Galbraith v HM Advocate (No.2)*, 2002 J.C. 1, opinion of the court per Lord Justice General Rodger at 16, para.41. *cf. HM Advocate v Blake*, 1986 S.L.T. (Notes) 661 (in which, at 662K–663C, Lord Brand directed a jury that diminished responsibility may reduce a charge of attempted murder to one of assault: there appears to have been no appeal as to the correctness of that direction).

[188] *Galbraith v HM Advocate (No.2)*, 2002 J.C. 1.

[189] *Galbraith v HM Advocate (No.2)*, 2002 J.C. 1 at 16, para.41: see the quotation above set out towards the end of fn.187.

[190] *Galbraith v HM Advocate (No.2)*, 2002 J.C. 1 at 17–18, paras 44–45, opinion of the court per Lord Justice General Rodger. Murder, of course, carries a fixed penalty of life in prison (see the Criminal Procedure (Scotland) Act 1995 s.205(1), as amended by the Convention Rights (Compliance) (Scotland) Act 2001 (asp 7) s.2) whereas culpable homicide does not.

[191] *cf.* Chalmers and Leverick, *Criminal Defences and Pleas in Bar of Trial*, p.238, para.11–20, where they conclude that the "doctrine" of diminished responsibility is restricted to murder, in view of what was said in *Cunningham* and *Brennan* [see above, fn.187]."

[192] See, e.g. *HM Advocate v Bennett*, 1996 S.C.C.R. 331, especially at 338A.

[193] *Galbraith v HM Advocate (No.2)*, 2002 J.C. 1.

abnormality which substantially impaired his ability to determine and control his actings. The mental abnormality in question, which may be temporary or permanent, must be recognised by "the appropriate science" but may be caused in a wide variety of ways: thus, it may be congenital (such as weak intellect); it may have an organic basis (as in the case of a brain tumour, a stroke, a disorder of the thyroid, or certain forms of diabetes); it may be due to accident (for example, a head injury or shock) or illness (such as a fever); it may be due to a side effect of drugs administered or prescribed for therapeutic reasons; or it may be due to a mental illness (such as schizophrenia or depression) or to the psychological effects of exposure to sexual or other abuse.[194] As the court in *Galbraith* was at pains to point out that diminished responsibility is not dependent on there being an abnormality of mind which amounts to a mental disease or something bordering on insanity, the scope of the plea is sufficiently wide to extend to many of the states of mind considered in relation to the voluntariness of acts: but *Galbraith* reinforces the rule that diminished responsibility does not result in acquittal. Indeed, it ensures conviction; but the sort of conviction which should be followed by an appropriately mitigated sentence.

---

[194] See *Galbraith v HM Advocate (No.2)*, 2002 J.C. 1, especially at 19–21, paras 51–53. Only "psychopathic personality" and the effects of self-induced intoxication are, of this time, definitely ruled out by the courts: *Galbraith v HM Advocate (No.2)*, 2002 J.C. 1 at 21, para.54 at "6."

CHAPTER 5

CAUSATION

Introduction

The issue of causation is raised by the legal definitions of many **5–01** different crimes. For example, as is described in Ch.10, it is a requirement of the crime of fraud that there be a causal connection between the false pretence and the actions of the dupe. There are also many crimes which contain in their definitions an element of resultant harm. These include crimes against property, such as malicious mischief or fire-raising, and also crimes against the person. An example of the latter is the crime of aggravated assault. This might result in, for example, severe injury or permanent disfigurement to the victim of the attack. As previously noted, liability for a result crime, such as an aggravated assault, can only be imposed upon an individual if it was his conduct which *caused* the harm to the complainer (see above, para.3–06). If the prosecution cannot establish a causal link between the accused's conduct and the consequences of the assault, then liability for the aggravating features of the crime will not be imposed upon him.

In many cases causation can be determined without any great **5–02** difficulty. If A attacks B with a hatchet, there is no problem in attributing the resultant severe injury to the conduct of A. The facts speak for themselves. This is not to say, of course, that difficult factual issues cannot arise.[1] In particular, problems can arise when there are a number of factors contributing to the result and/or when other events intervene between the conduct of the accused and the consequential harm. Without doubt the most complex and difficult problems arise in the law relating to homicide. Most of the important authorities on causation concern either murder or culpable homicide. There may have been a considerable length of time elapsing between the infliction of the original injury and the death. The explanation for the importance attached to causation in the law of homicide is that the law strives to determine when a death is attributable to the conduct of the accused.[2]

---

[1] See, e.g. the facts at issue in *Garden v HM Advocate,* 1999 S.L.T. 1352.
[2] Fletcher, *Rethinking Criminal Law*, p.358.

CAUSATION IN FACT

THE "BUT FOR" TEST

5–03   The first issue to be considered in a result crime, such as homicide, is whether the accused did *in fact* cause the victim's death. The issue is frequently resolved by the application of the "but for", or *sine qua non,* test: but for the conduct of the accused, would the victim have died? It is not necessary that the conduct of the accused has been the only cause of the harm. Nor is it necessary that his conduct be a substantial cause, provided that it is a material, and more than a minimal, cause.[3]

NECESSITY FOR CAUSAL LINK

5–04   In most cases, proof of causation in fact will not present any major problem to the prosecution. As in the aggravated assault example outlined above, the issue will be self-evident. But the existence of a causal link will always need to be established: it should not be taken for granted.[4] On occasion, the evidential issues to be considered may be complex, perhaps with conflicting medical evidence.[5] In *Hendry v HM Advocate,*[6] a conviction for culpable homicide was upheld on appeal. The appellant had assaulted a 67 year old man, who died as a result of a heart attack a short while thereafter. Only minor injuries had been caused to the deceased, but he had a pre-existing heart condition which could have led to death after any degree of exertion or distress. There were further complicating factors, in that the deceased had angina, he had consumed a large amount of alcohol, he had eaten a large meal, and he had climbed a flight of stairs. All of these were stress factors which could have additionally contributed to the heart attack. The key issue for the prosecution was to prove beyond reasonable doubt the existence of a causal link between the assault and the heart attack.

5–05   In *Lourie v HM Advocate,*[7] the appellants' convictions for culpable homicide were quashed by the Appeal Court. Lourie and another youth had been charged on the basis that they had entered the house of an elderly woman uninvited and stolen a handbag in her presence. The appeal was allowed because there was insufficient evidence that the deceased had observed the theft and it was unclear whether or not the appellants had entered the house uninvited. The prosecution maintained that the woman had been

---

[3] See *Watson v HM Advocate* (1978) S.C.C.R. Supp. 192.
[4] See *Malone v HM Advocate,* 1988 S.C.C.R. 498.
[5] See, e.g. *Karling v HM Advocate,* 1999 S.C.C.R. 359.
[6] *Hendry v HM Advocate,* 1987 J.C. 63.
[7] *Lourie v HM Advocate,* 1988 S.C.C.R. 634.

put in a state of fear and alarm by the appellants' actions. It was argued that the deceased's fatal heart attack had been a direct consequence. The death had ensued soon after the visit by the appellants. An expert medical witness called by the prosecution testified that a heart attack could have been the result of an increase in strain. The defence argued either that the death could have been a complete coincidence, or that she had died as the result of exertion which may have accompanied the events which took place. It was argued that if the latter was indeed the case, the death was not the result of the illegal act in the sense that the act had caused the woman's death. The first point to note about a set of facts such as these is that any doubt would have to be resolved in favour of an accused. If a jury thought that the woman's death might have been coincidental, then there would have to be an acquittal. The defence's second argument is more problematic. Assuming that there had been sufficient evidence to support the prosecution case, the woman had only been required to exert herself because of the unlawful actions of the appellants. But for their actions, the woman would have lived longer. To anticipate the discussion in the rest of this chapter somewhat, there would not then appear to be any difficulty in establishing the necessary causal link between the conduct of the accused and the consequential death of the victim.

CAUSATION IN LAW

CAUSES AND CONDITIONS

Causation is not, however, simply a question of fact. It is necessary, **5–06** but not sufficient, that the accused's conduct be a factual cause of the death or other type of harm. Not every factor which meets the "but for" standard is sufficient for the imposition of criminal liability.[8] If a reckless motorist drives the wrong way down a motorway and collides with another vehicle, killing the occupant, the presence of the other vehicle is a "but for" cause of the crash. Common sense suggests that the presence of the victim on the road should not be regarded by the criminal law as the cause of his death. This could be described instead as a *condition,* rather than a cause, of the fatality. A condition is a normal event or circumstance which is necessary for the result to occur, but cannot be said positively to have caused it.

PROXIMITY REQUIREMENT

There must be causation *in law*. The law requires that a cause be **5–07** "proximate". This requirement of proximity reflects the law's concern only with those causal factors that are closely connected to

---

[8] See *McDonald v HM Advocate*, 2007 S.C.C.R. 10, at 16, para.11.

the result. In relation to homicide, the rules of law relating to proximate cause are intended to provide a safeguard against liability attaching to an individual whose acts are remote from the victim's death, or where his conduct contributes only minimally. Similar considerations apply in relation to those other crimes in which the issue of causation is implicit.

THE LEGAL PRINCIPLES OF CAUSATION

5–08 The legal principles governing causation in law take the form of guidelines rather than strict legal rules. The most significant of these are examined in the following sections. What follows is not a description of rules which will consistently determine questions of causation. Causal analysis relies much upon common sense and moral intuition.

The characteristics of the victim

5–09 It is commonly stated that the accused must "take his victim as he finds him".[9] This is sometimes referred to as the "thin skull" rule. The rule means that the accused will be criminally liable if death results from some pre-existing weakness in the victim. As Lord Jamieson said in *Bird v HM Advocate*,[10] it is not a "defence that the victim was an old person, an infirm person, or a person that suffered from a bad heart, and that if he had been young and healthy the consequences would not have happened." The type of situation covered by the rule is where A strikes B on the head in a way that would normally cause only bruising, but, because B has an unusually thin skull, the blow fractures B's skull and he dies. A cannot then claim that B's unusual physique breaks the chain of causation between his conduct and the death. The basis for this rule is a consideration of public policy: the accused should not have injured the victim in the first place. On a strict analysis, however, it could not really be said that the accused had "voluntarily" caused the death of the victim, since he believed, perhaps quite reasonably, that the victim had a normal skull. It could even be argued that the death was accidental. Nevertheless, the criminal law obliges him to take responsibility for the consequences of his actions.

Psychological characteristics

5–10 This rule operates reasonably enough (if harshly on occasion) in relation to the' physical characteristics of the victim, but how far can it be taken? Should it extend to the psychological characteristics or religious beliefs of the victim? The English case of *R. v*

---

[9] See, e.g. *HM Advocate v Rutherford,* 1947 J.C. 1.
[10] *Bird v HM Advocate,* 1952 J.C. 23 at p.25.

Blaue[11] indicates that the courts would be unlikely to make any distinction between physical and psychological characteristics. The appellant in this case had stabbed the victim numerous times and pierced her lung, after she had rejected his sexual advances. The victim was a Jehovah's Witness. At the hospital to which she had been taken, the victim refused the immediate blood transfusion necessary to save her life. The refusal was based on her religious belief that it would be a sin to accept the transfusion. She died from her wounds shortly afterwards. The appellant contended that the deceased's refusal to have the blood transfusion was unreasonable and, as such, had broken the chain of causation. The Court of Appeal rejected this argument. Lord Justice Lawton stated:

> "[T]hose who use violence on other people must take their victims as they find them. This in our judgment means the whole man, not just the physical man. It does not lie in the mouth of the assailant to say that his victim's religious beliefs ... were unreasonable. The question for decision is what caused her death. The answer is the stab wound. The fact that the victim refused to stop this end coming about did not break the causal connection between the act and the death."[12]

Blaue is a persuasive authority for the view that an assailant must take his victim as he finds him, both physically and psychologically. One view would be that there are dangers in expressing the principle too widely. It would be asked whether psychological characteristics (including religious beliefs, however far removed from the mainstream) should be treated in the same way as the physical weaknesses of a victim. An alternative approach could be to focus less upon the reasonableness or otherwise of the victim's beliefs, and more upon the unreasonableness of expecting a person in a life-threatening situation to abandon her religious conviction.[13]

The conduct of the victim

It thus appears that even an "unreasonable" refusal of medical **5–11** treatment by a victim will not break the chain of causation. There are, however, a number of different ways in which a victim could contribute to his own demise. The question then arises: are there any circumstances in which the conduct of the victim will be held to have broken the causal link? In the case of *Joseph and Mary Norris*[14] the original wound inflicted by the accused was trivial. The

---

[11] *R. v Blaue* [1975] 1 W.L.R. 1411.
[12] *R. v Blaue* [1975] 1 W.L.R. 1411 at 1415.
[13] See H.L.A. Hart and T. Honoré, *Causation in the Law*, 2nd edn (Oxford: Clarendon, 1985), p.361.
[14] *Joseph and Mary Norris* (1886) 1 White 292.

victim went drinking, removed his bandages and went out late at night in poor weather. He contracted tetanus and died. Lord Craighill directed the jury that the question for them to answer was whether the tetanus would have developed whether or not the victim had acted in the way he did. If the tetanus was the consequence of the conduct of the accused, then they were liable for the result. If, however, the disease had been brought on by the imprudence of the victim, then there should be a verdict of not guilty.

No duty on complainer to mitigate harm

5–12   This charge to the jury is unusual in that, perhaps because of the trivial nature of the original wound,[15] considerable emphasis was placed on the conduct of the deceased. The more commonly expressed view is that a victim is not under any legal duty to mitigate the effects of the injuries inflicted upon him. The central issue is whether the injuries inflicted by the assailant are an operating and substantial cause of death. It would appear that the victim is quite at liberty to neglect his own well being and the assailant must take the consequences of his actions. This basic principle is restated in many of the relevant authorities.[16] For example, in *James Williamson*,[17] Lord Justice-Clerk Inglis said that the fact that a victim "is weaker than his neighbours, either from natural constitution or bad habit, can never make the slightest difference in the question of guilt or innocence."

5–13   Similarly, the accused has to take responsibility for any harm occurring to the victim during an escape. If he causes so much fear in the victim that he dies in the course of a desperate escape attempt, then the accused will be held to have caused the death of the victim. In *McDonald v HM Advocate*[18] the appellant and another were charged with culpable homicide by assaulting the deceased in his third-floor flat and causing him to fall from a window. His death had occurred after he had fallen to the ground while trying to escape shortly after the attack. Under these circumstances, the High Court took the view that a causal relationship between the assault and the subsequent death could be established.

---

[15] See also Hume, *Commentaries*, i, 182.

[16] See, e.g. *R v Dear* [1996] Crim.L.R. 595.

[17] *James Williamson* (1866) 5 Irv. 326 at 328.

[18] *McDonald v HM Advocate*, 2007 S.C.C.R. 10. See also the case of *Patrick Slaven* (1885) 5 Coup. 694, where the accused had assaulted a woman with intent to ravish her. They pursued her as she tried to escape, and she fell over a cliff and died. It was held that the conduct of the accused had caused the death.

The daft complainer?

In the English case of *R. v Roberts*,[19] the complainer was a young **5–14** lady to whom the appellant had given a lift. During the journey he made a number of improper suggestions to her and touched her breasts. The complainer jumped from the car, which was travelling at a speed between 20 and 40 mph, suffering grazing and concussion in the escape. The appellant claimed that the complainer's action in jumping out of the car had broken the chain of causation and thereby relieved him of liability for her injuries. The Court of Appeal was not impressed by this argument. Lord Justice Stephenson was of the opinion that only if the actions of the complainer had been "daft" would the chain of causation have been broken. In *R. v Williams and Davis*,[20] the deceased was a hitchhiker who had jumped from a moving car in order to escape an attempted robbery. The Court of Appeal set out two questions which should be addressed in such a case,

> "first, whether it was reasonably foreseeable that some harm . . . was likely to result from the threat itself; and, secondly, whether the deceased's reaction . . . was within the range of responses which might be expected from a victim placed in the situation which he was."[21]

What had to be considered was,

> "whether the deceased's conduct was proportionate to the threat; that is to say that it was within the ambit of reasonableness and not so daft as to make it his own voluntary act which amounted to a *novus actus interveniens* and consequently broke the chain of causation."[22]

These two English decisions lend support the view that, if the **5–15** victim acts unreasonably, the accused should not be held liable for the harm. The unreasonable behaviour becomes the cause. There is also a suggestion to this effect in *McDonald v HM Advocate*,[23] where it is said that if the victim of an assault,

> "reacted in a wholly unforeseeable or unreasonable way that would mean that the attack would cease to be a direct cause of the death and thus the requisite causal link would not be established."

---

[19] *R. v Roberts* (1971) 56 Cr.App.Rep. 95.
[20] *R. v Williams and Davis* [1992] 1 W.L.R. 380.
[21] *R. v Williams and Davis* [1992] 1 W.L.R. 380 at 389D.
[22] *R. v Williams and Davis* [1992] 1 W.L.R. 380 at 388H.
[23] *McDonald v HM Advocate*, 2007 S.C.C.R. 10 at 16, para.11, endorsing the approach of the trial judge.

Induced suicide

5–16   A not unrealistic scenario would have a rapist infecting his victim with AIDS. She decides to commit suicide rather than suffer a lingering death. Should the rapist be held to have caused the death? There are American cases, such as *People v Lewis*,[24] and *Commonwealth v Wright*,[25] which suggest that where the victim has, as a result of the egregious conduct of the accused, become so disturbed as to commit suicide, the accused will be held to have caused the death of the victim. The point has yet to be resolved in a Scottish case. In *John Robertson*,[26] Lord Handyside reserved his opinion on the question of whether an induced suicide would break the chain of causation:

> "If the act of suicide was the immediate consequence of the violence, I am not prepared to say what such a state of facts might warrant. I do not say that it would amount to culpable homicide, although it would certainly come very near to it."

Whether as a matter of principle, or through an application of the "thin skull" rule, it is possible that a court would determine that the rapist should be held to have caused the death of the victim.

The concept of a novus actus interveniens

5–17   It is a fundamental requirement of causation in law that the conduct of the accused be a sufficiently direct cause of the consequential harm to the victim. It is quite possible that a number of other "but for" causes will contribute to the eventual result. Some will be more significant than others, but very few will be of sufficient significance to break the causal chain. The legal term for an event which does break the chain of causation is a *novus actus interveniens*. The example which is frequently given is that of an assault victim left in a field who is subsequently struck by lightning and dies. The initial assault would not then be seen as the proximate cause of that result. In order to break the chain of causation between the assailant and the consequential harm in this way, the *novus actus* must supersede the original conduct. The law takes a very restrictive view of what can constitute a superseding cause significant enough to break the causal link. An individual can even be held responsible for the harms which result from the intervening conduct of his victim (see above, paras 5–12 and 5–13).

5–18   An informative authority in this regard is *Khaliq v HM Advocate*,[27] the celebrated decision concerning "glue sniffing kits". Here the High Court held that the subsequent voluntary acts of the purchaser of such a kit could not constitute a *novus actus interveniens* relieving the sellers of responsibility for the "real injury"

---

[24] *People v Lewis*, 124 Cal. 551 (1899).
[25] *Commonwealth v Wright*, 455 Pa. 480 (1974).
[26] *John Robertson* (1854) 1 Irv. 469 at 470.
[27] *Khaliq v HM Advocate*, 1984 J.C. 23; applied in *Ulhaq v HM Advocate*, 1991 S.L.T. 614; *Borwick v Urquhart*, 2003 S.C.C.R. 243.

caused. The causal link was not broken merely because a voluntary act on the part of the recipient of the intoxicant was required in order to bring about the harmful consequences. In the *Lord Advocate's Reference (No.1 of 1994)*,[28] this principle was applied in the context of culpable homicide. The fact that the deceased had voluntarily ingested the amphetamine supplied by the accused did not relieve him of criminal responsibility for the death.

Assault and subsequent infection

It is not difficult to envisage many natural events which could **5-19** intervene between the conduct of the accused and a resulting harm. A straightforward example would be the non-fatal wound which becomes infected and the victim dies as a result of the infection. There is no difficulty in saying that the individual who inflicted the wound is liable for the death. The immediate cause of death may have been the infection, but the original wound will be cognised by the law to be the proximate cause of death. This situation can be distinguished from that where the victim is exposed to some other, entirely unpredictable, cause of death. It is possible that the victim of an assault might coincidentally contract a fatal disease while lying in hospital. In the American case of *Bush v Commonwealth*,[29] the victim caught a fatal dose of scarlet fever from the hospital physician who treated him. It was held that it was the disease, not the original assault, which had caused the death.

In the case of *James Wilson*,[30] a wound inflicted on the victim **5-20** developed into erysipelas while he was being treated in hospital. There was a dispute as to whether another patient had infected the victim, or whether it was a direct complication of the original injury. Lord Cockburn charged the jury that the original wound should be regarded as the cause of death provided that the disease was "not altogether new, but a natural consequence of the injury."[31] If, on the other hand, "the disease was . . . entirely new— not produced by the wounds, but by infection, or some other external cause" death was caused by the coincidental infection and not by the wound. The *caveat* entered to this principle by Lord Cockburn is most important:

> "Suppose a man to die of apoplexy, but that apoplexy to have been caused by a blow. It will not . . . do for the prisoner to say . . . I gave you a blow, but I did not give you apoplexy. He must stand the peril of the consequences of his act."[32]

---

[28] *Lord Advocate's Reference (No.1 of 1994)*, 1995 S.L.T. 248; see also *Paxton v HM Advocate*, 2000 S.L.T. 771.
[29] *Bush v Commonwealth*, 78 Ky. 268 (1880).
[30] *James Wilson*, (1838) 2 Swin. 16.
[31] *James Wilson*, (1838) 2 Swin. 16 at 19.
[32] *James Wilson*, (1838) 2 Swin. 16 at 18. *cf. J. Campbell* (1819) Alison, *Principles*, i, 147.

This passage reiterates the basic principle of causation already referred to. It is clear that in order for a subsequent infection to constitute a *novus actus interveniens* it will need to be quite independent of the original wound. As it was put by the Courts-Martial Appeal Court in *R. v Smith*,[33]

> "only if the second cause is so overwhelming as to make the original wound merely part of the history can it be said that the death does not flow from the wound."

In a homicide case, the focus will be placed on the original wound. The subsequent aggravation will generally be disregarded, unless it has clearly arisen from an independent cause.

Medical treatment

5–21   In fact, *Smith* concerned poor medical treatment rather than a subsequent infection. The general principle in relation to *malregimen,* as it is sometimes called, is that negligent medical treatment is irrelevant since the accused must stand the consequences of his unlawful conduct. As was stated in the case of *James Williamson*,[34]

> "it will never do . . . if a wound calculated to prove mortal in itself is afterwards followed by death, to say that every criticism that can be made of the treatment of the patient after the wound is received is to furnish a ground for acquitting the person who inflicted the wound of either murder or culpable homicide."

The situation is essentially the same as when the victim unreasonably refuses medical treatment. The conduct of the accused will still be held to be the proximate cause of death. The only distinction which might be drawn is between negligent medical treatment which merely serves to aggravate the original wound and treatment which is so grossly negligent as to constitute an independent cause of death. "Ordinary" negligence would not appear to be sufficient. There would need to be something approaching criminal recklessness on the part of the doctor. As a matter of policy, a court would be most unwilling to regard anything done by a doctor in the ordinary course of medical treatment as constituting a *novus actus interveniens*,

> "it will only be in the most extraordinary and unusual case that [medical] treatment can be said to be so independent of the acts of the defendant that it could be regarded in law as

---

[33] *R. v Smith* [1959] 2 Q.B. 35 at 43.
[34] *James Williamson* (1866) 5 Irv. 326 at 328.

the cause of the victim's death to the exclusion of the defendant's acts."[35]

In *R. v Smith*[36] the appellant had been convicted of the murder of a **5–22** fellow soldier. The two had been involved in a fight, during the course of which the victim was stabbed a number of times with a bayonet. On the way to a medical station the victim was twice dropped from a stretcher and there was a considerable delay before he received treatment. The appellant contended that these subsequent events had broken the chain of causation. The court rejected this argument. It held that his conduct would be regarded as the cause in law, since it had been shown that it was the operating and substantial cause of death. In this case the victim had clearly died because of the stab wounds. Only if the original wounds could be said to have merely provided the setting in which some other causes of death operated would the court have been prepared to say that the chain of causation had been broken.

Discontinuing life support

In *Finlayson v HM Advocate*[37] it was held that switching off a life **5–23** support machine did not break the chain of causation. Here an injection of a controlled drug had caused brain death in the victim. The High Court determined that the effects of the injection constituted the substantial and continuing cause of death. This causative link had not been affected by the decision to switch off the life support machine, which was a reasonable one in the circumstances. The court decided, in effect, that the life support machine had merely held the consequences of the injection in abeyance. When the machine was switched off, the injection continued to be the cause of death. The court adopted the dictum of Lord Wright in *The Oropesa*[38]:

> "To break the chain of causation it must be shown that there is something which I will call ultroneous, something unwarrantable, a new cause which disturbs the sequence of events, something which can be described as either unreasonable or extraneous or extrinsic."

The finding of the court was that switching off the life support machine did not pass this test. A further observation made by the court was that switching off the machine was *foreseeable*.

---

[35] *R. v Cheshire* [1991] 1 W.L.R. 844, per Beldam L.J. at 851G.
[36] *R. v Smith* [1959] 2 Q.B. 35.
[37] *Finlayson v HM Advocate*, 1979 J.C. 33.
[38] *The Oropesa* [1943] P. 32 at 39.

The test of foreseeability

5–24   This concept of foreseeability is prayed in aid in many of the authorities concerning causation. For example, in *R. v Roberts*[39] the Court of Appeal relied upon the fact that the complainer's attempt to escape was a reasonably foreseeable consequence of what the appellant had done. The basic notion is that whether or not an intervening cause will be held to have broken the chain of causation depends upon its foreseeability. The test is whether the harm was due to an intervening event that a reasonable person could have foreseen. If not, then the superseding cause will be regarded in law as the proximate one. For example, A assaults B and leaves him unconscious on the seashore, below the high-water mark. B drowns when the tide comes in. It is plain that A cannot escape liability on the basis that he did not cause the death, but the sea did. The likelihood of B drowning was eminently foreseeable.[40] A possible limit to the test is that identified by Lord Reid in the civil case of *McKew v Holland and Hannen and Cubitts (Scotland) Ltd*[41]:

> "it does not follow that [an accused] is liable for every consequence which a reasonable man could foresee. What can be foreseen depends almost entirely on the facts of the case, and it is often easy to foresee [a] *novus actus interveniens* as being quite likely."

This is why the test is better seen as one of *reasonable* foreseeability, rather than one of foreseeability per se. The test is an objective one.

Foreseeability and malregimen

5–25   The foreseeability test could be applied to the *malregimen* cases. One application of the test would be that if the original assault is foreseeably fatal, then subsequent medical maltreatment could not break the chain of causation. An alternative application might be to say that "ordinary" negligence on the part of a doctor is foreseeable: everyone knows that doctors make mistakes.[42] The implication would be that grossly negligent or reckless treatment could break the chain of causation, since that would be unforeseeable.

5–26   In the English case of *R. v Jordan*[43] it was held that "palpably wrong" medical treatment had broken the chain of causation. As stressed earlier, however, it would be the truly exceptional case

---

[39] *R. v Roberts* (1972) 56 Cr.App.Rep. 95; see above, para.5–14.
[40] Compare the facts at issue in the New Zealand case of *R. v Hart* [1986] 2 N.Z.L.R. 408.
[41] *McKew v Holland and Hannen and Cubitts (Scotland) Ltd*, 1970 S.C.(HL) 20 at 25.
[42] See *R. v Cheshire* [1991] 1 W.L.R. 844, per Beldam L.J. at 849D–F.
[43] *R. v Jordan* (1956) 40 Cr.App.Rep. 152.

where such a conclusion could be reached. In *Jordan* the original wound inflicted on the victim had nearly healed at the time of death. The proximate cause of death was the injection of a drug to which the victim was allergic. The court held that the original injury was merely the setting within which another cause of death operated. In this case the court reached the conclusion described by Lord Justice-Clerk Inglis in the case of *James Williamson*[44]:

> "If a person receives a wound . . . which is not fatal in itself . . . and then afterwards by unskilful and injudicious treatment this wound assumes a more serious aspect, and finally terminates in death, it is possible to say . . . that the wound inflicted by the prisoner is not the cause of death, because it would not by itself have produced death but for the bad treatment which followed on it."

This passage needs to be treated with considerable caution. The deceased only received the poor medical treatment because he had been the victim of a life-threatening assault. Why should the assailant not be regarded as having caused the death?

Fatality and foreseeability

The argument is sometimes made that it is possible to draw a **5–27** distinction between an injury which is foreseeably fatal and one which is not. There is no guarantee, however, that a court would consider the foreseeability test as applicable in such a case. It may prefer a simple application of the "but for" or "thin skull" rules. Much may come to depend on the nature of the original assault. Which test a court decides to apply may well depend upon an assessment of the accused's "blameworthiness" (see below, para.5–33). In *R. v Blaue*[45] the English Court of Appeal did not apply the principle of foreseeability to the rule that the victim had to be taken as she was found. It will be recalled that there was a refusal to draw any distinction between physical characteristics which, even if unusual, can be argued to be foreseeable, and unusual psychological characteristics. It is surely not reasonably foreseeable that a victim will hold religious beliefs which preclude her accepting life-saving medical treatment (see above, para.5–10).

FACT, LAW AND POLICY

THE PROBLEM OF CAUSATION

The task which confronts the criminal lawyer in relation to **5–28** causation is that of defining the necessary circumstances for its establishment. Causation is important because, without this

---

[44] *James Williamson* (1866) 5 Irv. 326 at p.328; see above, para.5–15.
[45] *R. v Blaue* [1975] 1 W.L.R. 1411.

requirement, an individual with a negligible or non-existent connection to a crime could be punished. The criminal law does not
engage in a wide-ranging philosophical inquiry about the concept
of causation. The practical aim of the law is to identify those causes
for which the accused can be held responsible. This involves a
normative, as well as a factual judgment. In the simplest of terms,
these causes will be those that make some noteworthy contribution
to the circumstances surrounding the forbidden harm. Every cause
must meet the "but for" test. A helpful definition of what
constitutes a cause is that of Fletcher: "Among all the necessary
conditions for a particular event, the 'causes' are those conditions
that make the difference under the circumstances."[46] It should be
recognised that the criminal law does adopt an individualist
ideology in matters of causation.[47] The law does tend to locate
responsibility in individuals for their actions, in isolation from
societal factors. It is almost trite to say the legal analysis of
causation will be different from the psychological or sociological.
The criminal law does not, for example, accept unemployment or
upbringing as causal factors. The focus is necessarily much nar-
rower than this.

The legal context

5–29   The principle of proximate cause requires that the conduct of
the accused must have been the legal cause, as well as the factual
cause, of the *actus reus* in order for him to be criminally liable. This
concept of a proximate cause is a somewhat obscure one. There is
no precise method for identifying whether a cause is proximate or
not. A court will not discover the proximate cause purely by
applying a method derived from logic. It will be faced with two
major legal issues of causation to resolve. First, under what
circumstances can one say that there is a causal link between the
accused's conduct and the consequent harm? Secondly, what can
constitute a *novus actus interveniens* breaking the chain of causation? A number of the different tests employed by the courts to
resolve these questions have been outlined in this chapter. These
tend to take the form of guidelines, rather than strict rules.

The factual context

5–30   It should also be emphasised that, because causation is a mixed
question of law and fact, it is dangerous to reach dogmatic
conclusions independently of the facts of a case. The particular
constellation of facts confronting a court may be of primary
significance. A judge will be very wary of trespassing on the

---

[46] Fletcher, *Rethinking Criminal Law,* p.595.
[47] For a critical account, see A. Norrie, *Crime, Reason and History,* 2nd edn
(London: Butterworths, 2001), Ch.7.

territory of the jury.[48] In *Finlayson v HM Advocate,* Lord Justice-General Emslie said that,

> "it was not in any event a matter for the Judge to determine *ab ante* whether, as a matter of fact, it could be said that the chain of causation had been broken. That was a matter inextricably bound up with the other facts in the case which were for determination by the jury."[49]

It would, of course, be quite legitimate for a judge to point out **5–31** that a subsequent event could not in law constitute a *novus actus interveniens*. This might be the case if the victim had refused medical treatment because of his religious beliefs.[50] A judge would be at liberty to direct a jury that the refusal was, as a matter of law, not to be regarded as a superseding cause which had broken the chain of causation.

The policy context

One view of the issue of causation is that the courts do not in **5–32** fact rely upon generally applicable principles of the kind described in this chapter. Gordon's view is that:

> "What often happens in practice is that courts discuss causal theories learnedly and at length, and purport to reach a conclusion by reference to a logical appraisal of these theories; but in fact the causal criterion applied to the case is chosen, not because of its intrinsic logic and correctness, but because it is the one which leads most easily to the same answer as would be given the question: 'Should A bear the blame for this?'"[51]

The argument seems to be that courts resort to considerations of policy when determining whether the accused has caused a particular harm. (A more limited version of this argument is that a court will utilise a moral judgment in deciding whether or not causation is established.) There are difficulties with this interpretation. It is

---

[48] This concern also finds reflection in the treatment of expert (medical) evidence. It is not necessary for there to be such evidence expressed in a particular way before the jury is entitled to conclude that the causal link has been proved. It is for the jury, and not any expert witness, to determine whether a cause of death has been established beyond reasonable doubt. See *Hendry v HM Advocate,* 1987 J.C. 63; *Fyfe v HM Advocate,* 1998 S.L.T. 195; *Paxton v HM Advocate,* 2000 S.L.T. 771.

[49] *Finlayson v HM Advocate,* 1979 J.C. 33 at 36.

[50] See *R. v Blaue* [1975] 1 W.L.R. 1411; see above, para.5–10.

[51] Gordon, *Criminal Law,* 3rd edn, para.4.01. Having made this statement, Gordon does proceed to discuss the legal principles in detail. The law, it seems, is not so easily escaped.

always dangerous to claim that a court is doing something other than what it says it is. Perhaps a better view would be that the principles in this area of law are both flexible and overlapping. As a consequence, a court will have a choice over which principle or test to apply. For example, the doctrine of reasonable foreseeability can lead to a different conclusion from an application of the "thin skull" rule (see above, para.5–27). A further problem with the policy approach is that, even as a purported explanation of what the courts do in practice, it offers precious little guidance for future cases.

Causation and responsibility

5–33   Causation cannot simply be judged objectively in terms of physical acts. As Gordon recognises in the passage quoted above, some element of responsibility or blameworthiness must come into the equation. The legal analysis of causation is closely linked to the process of allocating responsibility for the criminal act. Indeed, one influential view is that an analysis of causation is dependent upon the criterion of blameworthiness.[52] The principle informing this approach is that if blame can be attributed to an accused, the result is proximate and the causal link will be established. This means that if an accused has *mens rea,* one can conclude that he expected, or should have expected, the harm resulting from his unlawful conduct. He is blameworthy and causation will be established. (This is not to say that the presence of *mens rea* can create a causal link which is not already there. Causation in fact would have to be established.) In contrast to the pure policy approach, there is here at least some guidance for resolving future cases. If the accused had the necessary *mens rea,* and contributed causally to bringing about the *actus reus,* he should be held responsible. On this analysis, it is defensible to maintain that the person who supplies potentially dangerous drugs to a victim, in the knowledge that the latter intends to consume them, is responsible for the harm suffered.[53] The voluntary action of the victim in taking the drugs is also a cause, but does not prevent the supply of the drugs also being regarded by the criminal law as a cause (rather than a condition) of the *actus reus.*

---

[52] Gross, *A Theory of Criminal Justice,* pp.232–254.
[53] See the *Lord Advocates Reference (No.1 of 1994),* 1995 S.L.T. 248; *Paxton v HM Advocate,* 2000 S.L.T. 771; contrast *R. v Kennedy (No.2)* [2007] UKHL 38.

CHAPTER 6

ATTEMPT

Introduction

The question to be addressed in this chapter can be stated quite **6–01** simply: under what circumstances does the criminal law impose responsibility for an endeavour to commit a crime? The key to understanding the law in this area is to appreciate that conduct prior to the successful completion of a criminal end can itself constitute a crime. Conduct which is criminalised at this preliminary stage is known as an "inchoate", or incomplete, crime. There are three principal inchoate crimes recognised in Scots law: *attempt*; *conspiracy*; and *incitement* (sometimes known as *instigation*). Conspiracy and incitement are discussed in the next Chapter. This Chapter is concerned solely with the law of attempt.

Attempted crimes fall into two common categories. The first is **6–02** where there has been an act designed to bring about a substantive crime, and which would have brought it about under normal circumstances. The expected chain of events is then interrupted by an unforeseen event. For example, a fire is raised in order to destroy a building, but is extinguished before it takes hold. A charge of attempted wilful fire-raising, with the building as its object, would be appropriate. The second type of attempted crime occurs where there has also been an act designed to bring about a substantive crime, but the expected result does not occur because of a misjudgment or mistake on the part of the perpetrator. Thus one could expect a charge of attempted murder in the typical examples where a weapon has misfired, or the bullet missed its target.

An attempt to commit any crime is criminal.[1] As the preceding **6–03** examples demonstrate, the basic notion of an attempted crime is easy to grasp. The difficulty is that the legal definition of attempt tends towards vagueness; different interpretations of the relevant

---

[1] Criminal Procedure (Scotland) Act 1995 s.294.

principles are to be found in the authorities. It is also true to say that some of the concepts underlying the crime of attempt are somewhat elusive and even counter-intuitive; this is particularly true in relation to so-called "impossible" attempts.

Why attempts are penalised

6–04   The clearest rationale for punishing attempts is that summarised by Hart: "The criminal had gone so far as to do his best to execute a wicked intention."[2] In particular, the individual who has attempted to commit a crime may well be equally as dangerous as the one who has succeeded in his criminal enterprise. The difference between the two attempts in terms of success or failure could simply be attributable to chance or luck. A further argument is that the individual who attempts to commit a crime causes harm worthy of punishment through the creation of public anxiety.

6–05   There is also the issue of deterrence to consider. Hart makes the point that,

> "the accused has manifested a dangerous disposition to do all he can to commit a crime, and the experience of punishment may check him in the future, since it may cause him to attach more weight to the law's threats."[3]

As far as more general deterrence is concerned, the same considerations which apply to a completed crime would appear to apply equally in the case of an attempt.

6–06   The criminalisation of attempts is also justifiable as a preventive measure. Without the recognition of inchoate crimes, the police would have no legal basis for intervening at a preliminary stage. After all, one fundamental aim of the criminal law must be to try to prevent would-be criminals from succeeding in their aims. This would become much more difficult if the criminal law was concerned only with completed crimes.

Disguised attempts

6–07   There are a number of substantive crimes which can be seen as "disguised" attempts. There exists a range of statutory offences which are targeted at preventing crimes, and which prohibit preparations to commit crimes. For example, the law restricts the carrying of weapons[4] and, in certain circumstances, equipment

---

[2] H.L.A. Hart, *Punishment and Responsibility* (Oxford: Clarendon Press, 1968), p.128.
[3] Hart, *Punishment and Responsibility*, p.129. See also W. Ullmann, "The Reasons for Punishing Attempted Crimes" (1939) 51 J.R. 353; R.A. Duff, *Criminal Attempts* (Oxford: Clarendon Press, 1996), Ch.5.
[4] See, e.g. the Carrying of Knives etc. (Scotland) Act 1993.

which could be of use in committing theft.[5] There are also common law crimes which serve a preventive purpose. Housebreaking with intent to steal[6] functions as an inchoate offence which penalises conduct in a similar way to the law of attempt, but at an even earlier stage in the criminal endeavour. An example should help to clarify the point: A breaks into a house in order to steal an item of property. He may not, however, have proceeded sufficiently far to be guilty of attempting to commit the intended crime (theft). As Lord Justice-General Normand observed in *Coventry v Douglas*[7]:

> "The mere presence of a person in a particular place may be only preparatory to the execution of the criminal intent, and not itself an overt criminal act."

The independent crime of housebreaking with intent to steal allows A to be apprehended at the time of gaining entry (or even attempted entry[8]). There is no need to wait on A beginning to perpetrate whatever crime he has in mind.

The common law crime of assault with intent to rape or ravish is by definition closely related to attempted rape. It can be utilised where there is a clear inference of the accused's intent, but the jury is not satisfied that he proceeded sufficiently far towards perpetration to be convicted of attempted rape.[9]

Assault itself is a crime which can encompass an incomplete **6–08** result. As is described in greater detail in Ch.9, although the attack on the complainer must be physical in character to constitute an assault, there need not be a physical result. In *Stewart v Procurator Fiscal of Forfarshire*,[10] the accused was convicted of assault after he had aimed a blow at the complainer, but had missed; and in *Gilmour v McGlennan*,[11] it was held that to point a toy gun at someone could constitute assault. Thus the definition of assault appears to include within its definition an attempt. It might be thought that the charge of attempted assault is redundant, since it could involve libelling that an accused had attempted to attempt to

---

[5] Civic Government (Scotland) Act 1982 s.58 (applicable where the accused has two or more convictions for theft).
[6] See *Charles Macqueen and Alex Baillie* (1810) Hume, *Commentaries*, i, 102.
[7] *Coventry v Douglas*, 1944 J.C. 13 at 20. In *HM Advocate v Forbes*, 1994 S.L.T. 861, the Appeal Court left open the question of whether it constituted attempted assault and rape to enter premises, strip down and prowl around with intent to assault and rape.
[8] See *Burns v Allan*, 1987 S.C.C.R. 449; *Heywood v Reid*, 1996 S.L.T. 378. For an account of the elements of this crime, see below, para.10–35.
[9] *Robertson v HM Advocate*, 1998 J.C. 213 (assault with intent to ravish); *McGill v HM Advocate*, 2000 S.C.C.R. 28 (assault with intent to rape). The alternatives of rape, attempted rape and assault with intent to ravish are implied in any charge of rape: Criminal Procedure (Scotland) Act 1995 Sch.3 para.10.
[10] *Stewart v Procurator Fiscal of Forfarshire* (1829) 2 S.J. 32.
[11] *Gilmour v McGlennan*, 1993 S.C.C.R. 837.

attack the complainer. The charge of attempted assault does, however, sometimes occur in practice.[12]

MENS REA

6–09 Just as in relation to a completed crime, the two elements of *mens rea* and *actus reus* are present in an attempted crime. As far as *mens rea* is concerned, the basic rule appears to be quite simple: the *mens rea* of an attempted crime is the same as that of the relevant substantive crime. Where the crime is one of intention, few problems are caused. For example, the requisite *mens rea* for the crime of attempted theft is the same as that for the substantive crime: the "essence" is "an intention to commit the crime of theft."[13]

RECKLESSNESS

6–10 The conceptual problems arise in relation to those crimes which can be perpetrated recklessly. If the *mens rea* of an attempted crime is the same as that of the substantive crime, does this mean that one can attempt to commit a crime of recklessness? Does the law recognise the possibility of a reckless attempt? The difficulty raised by this question is whether it should be possible to "blunder" into an attempt.[14] In other jurisdictions,[15] and perhaps in earlier times in Scotland,[16] the answer to these two questions would have been in the negative. It is a commonly expressed view that there must be an intention to commit the crime of which an attempt is libelled.[17] That is, an essential element of an attempt is that the result required by the definition of the substantive crime should have been intended. The very notion of an attempt appears to necessitate that the accused has "tried" to do something, and that there is an intended consequence. In murder, for example, this would be the death of the intended victim.

---

[12] See below, para.9–11. It also has distinguished academic support; see R.M. Perkins, "An Analysis of Assault and Attempts to Assault" (1962) 47 *Minn. L.Rev.* 71, 81–82.

[13] *Coventry v Douglas,* 1944 J.C. 13, per Lord Fleming at 19. See also *Johnstone v Lees,* 1995 S.L.T. 1174 (conviction for attempting to pervert the course of justice dependent upon intention).

[14] F. Sayre, "Criminal Attempts" (1928) 41 *Harv. L.Rev.* 821, 843; T. Arnold, "Criminal Attempts—The Rise and Fall of an Abstraction" (1930) 40 *Yale L.J.* 53, 68.

[15] See *Knight v The Queen* (1992) 175 C.L.R. 496 (Australia); *R. v Ancio* (1984) 6 D.L.R. (4th) 577 (Canada); Criminal Attempts Act 1981 s.1(1); and *R. v Whybrow* (1951) 35 Cr.App.R. 141 (England and Wales).

[16] See the references in Hume, *Commentaries*, i, 27–28, to "criminal purpose" and "criminal resolution".

[17] See R.M. Perkins, "Criminal Attempt and Related Problems" (1955) 2 *U.C.L.A. L.Rev.* 319, 340–341.

Scots law appears to take a rather different approach to the **6–11** *mens rea* of an attempted crime. There is an objective focus upon what the accused actually did, rather than what he intended at the time. Particular regard must be paid to the decision in *Cawthorne v HM Advocate*.[18] This case determined that the *mens rea* for attempted murder is the same as that for murder[19]; the only difference being that in attempted murder the victim does not actually die. As Lord Brand explained in the course of his charge to jury in *HM Advocate v Blake*[20]:

> " 'Attempt to murder' is the charge brought against a man who is alleged to have made an attack on another in circumstances in which, had his victim died as a result of his attack, the crime would have been murder."

Murder can be committed "unintentionally", in the sense that the accused need not foresee the death of the victim as a consequence of his conduct if he demonstrates wicked recklessness.[21] Following *Cawthorne*, one can say that wicked recklessness is sufficient *mens rea* for attempted murder; there need not be an actual intention to kill. An illustration of this approach to the *mens rea* of attempted murder is provided by Lord Keith's charge to the jury in *McGregor v HM Advocate*[22]:

> "If you go out and recklessly fire off a firearm or wave a knife or dagger about and kill somebody, that may be murder. The test of attempted murder is whether, if the actions of the accused had resulted in the death of one of the [victims] you would have said that was murder or not. If a man drives along with a policeman on his bonnet in such a way that the policeman falls off and is killed . . .—if you would have said that was murder, then you would be entitled to convict him [of attempted murder]."

The approach outlined above, which recognises that one can **6–12** attempt to commit a crime of recklessness, is at variance with the ordinary concept of an attempt. It is an unnatural use of language

---

[18] *Cawthrone v HM Advocate*, 1968 J.C. 32. Alison, *Principles*, i, 163, appears to endorse this approach, but this is because wicked recklessness is there treated as equivalent to an intention to kill. There is no authoritative judicial decision clarifying to which crimes of recklessness, other than murder, the *Cawthorne* principle applies.

[19] Lord Justice-Clerk Ross described this principle as "well settled" in *Brady v HM Advocate*, 1986 J.C. 68 at 76. See also *Strachan v HM Advocate*, 1994 S.C.C.R. 341.

[20] *HM Advocate v Blake*, 1986 S.L.T. 661 at 662H.

[21] See, e.g. *Miller and Denovan v HM Advocate*, 1960, noted in *Parr v HM Advocate*, 1991 S.L.T. 208 at 211 (discussed above in para.3–32).

[22] *McGregor v HM Advocate* (1973) S.C.C.R. Supp. 54 at 56.

to say that A, who is reckless as to the result of his assault upon B, and without intending to kill him, attempts to murder B.[23] The *Cawthorne* approach can, however, be seen as consistent with the prevailing objective approach to the establishment of criminal liability. In Scotland, the accused is to be sanctioned because he nearly committed a crime, that is, came close to perpetrating the *actus reus*. His blameworthy mental state is reflected in this fact.[24]

ACTUS REUS

POLICY ISSUES

6–13   The greater difficulties in the law of attempt relate to the *actus reus*. The primary issue is that of determining the point at which it can be said that the accused's conduct has proceeded sufficiently far towards the commission of a completed crime, so that it can be classified as a criminal attempt. Where can the line be drawn between a criminal attempt and a non-criminal preparation? There are two fundamental policy concerns which weigh upon this issue. The first is that of facilitating the police in the tasks of crime prevention and law enforcement. The test adopted for establishing the *actus reus* must offer a reasonable chance for intervention before the criminal endeavour reaches its proposed end. One decision which appears to conflict with this requirement is *Guthrie v Friel*.[25] The Appeal Court held that an appellant who had been apprehended sitting in his car, with the seat belt fastened, having started the engine, and with the headlights turned on, could not be said to be attempting to drive. It was stated that the position might have been different had the handbrake been released.

6–14   Of equal significance, perhaps, should be a concern for civil liberties and the rights of the individual. The criminal law should not seek to penalise conduct which is extremely preparatory to the commission of a crime. The law must avoid punishing an individual merely for having undesirable thoughts.[26] Given the inevitable tension between these two concerns, it is not surprising that Scots law does not provide a clear guide to the *actus reus* of attempted crimes. Although it is clear which is the prevailing test, no single approach to the question has received unequivocal support. The

---

[23] Not that this alone can be dispositive of the issue; see, further, T.H. Jones, "Attempted Murder", 1992 S.L.T. (News) 341.

[24] The Scottish approach appears consistent with that of O.W. Holmes, *The Common Law* (Boston: Little Brown and Co., 1881), p.66: "It may be true that in the region of attempts . . . the law began with cases of actual intent, as those cases are the most obvious ones. But it cannot stop with them, unless it attaches more importance to the etymological meaning of the word *attempt* than to the general principles of punishment."

[25] *Guthrie v Friel*, 1993 S.L.T. 899.

[26] *Morton v Henderson*, 1956 J.C. 55, per Lord Justice-General Clyde at 57.

relevant authorities are inconsistent as to what *actus reus* is necessary before preparatory actions by an accused constitute an attempt to commit a crime. It is only on rare occasions that the courts have articulated explicitly a test or theory to identify when a criminal attempt occurs. Nevertheless, it is possible to identify three significant theories by inference from the facts of different cases and the observations of judges. The three theories or tests are (1) irrevocability, (2) last act and (3) perpetration. A further problem is that these tests have a tendency to overlap one another; nor have the courts always sought to clarify which approach is being adopted.

IRREVOCABILITY THEORY

There are authorities which appear to suggest that a criminal **6–15** attempt cannot be committed at a stage before the final chain of events is irrecoverable by the actions of the accused. In *HM Advocate v Mackenzie*,[27] Lord Justice-Clerk Macdonald referred to the,

> "well-established and most just rule of law, which does not allow of punishment for unfulfilled intents and preparations which have not culminated in an irrevocable act of commission or attempt."

In *HM Advocate v Tannahill and Neilson*,[28] Lord Wark stated that in order to constitute a criminal attempt there had to be, "some overt act, the consequences of which cannot be recalled by the accused." This approach to the *actus reus* was endorsed by Lord Justice-General Clyde in *Morton v Henderson*.[29] In neither of these latter two cases, however, was there evidence of anything more than a mere suggestion that a crime (fraud in both instances) might be perpetrated. The judicial opinions expressed on both occasions went beyond what was immediately necessary to dispose of the cases, and are inconsistent with the views expressed elsewhere. That said, Lord Justice-Clerk Ross appeared to accept the applicability of the irrevocability test in *McKenzie v HM Advocate*.[30]

What appears to lie behind this approach to criminal attempts is **6–16** a feeling of disquiet about the very notion of criminalising behaviour prior to the commission of a crime. This general attitude

---

[27] *HM Advocate v Mackenzie*, 1913 S.C.(J.) 107 at 111. In *Burns v Allan*, 1987 S.C.C.R. 449, this case was cited as authority for the perpetration test (see below, para.6–19). The judgments in *Mackenzie* do say that the accused must have moved beyond the stage of preparation, but this is in the context of his having performed an irrevocable act.
[28] *HM Advocate v Tannahill and Neilson*, 1943 J.C. 150 at p.153.
[29] *Morton v Henderson*, 1956 J.C. 55.
[30] *McKenzie v HM Advocate*, 1988 S.L.T. 487.

is well summarised in the reported observations of the defence counsel in the case of *Samuel Tumbleson:*[31]

> "Attempts to commit crimes want that character of completeness, of finality, which would make it proper to prosecute them criminally. In many such cases it can hardly be said that the individual has proceeded beyond intention,—that he has done anything partaking, in strictness, of the character of an overt act; and it is of overt acts alone that the law can take cognizance."

One continues to find echoes of this language, even in contemporary decisions.[32]

LAST ACT THEORY

6–17 There are authorities which suggest that a criminal attempt occurs when an accused has done all that he believes is necessary to commit the proposed crime. In the case of *Janet Ramage*,[33] the accused had placed some poison in a teapot from which the intended victim was expected to take a drink. A charge of attempted murder was held to be relevant. Similarly, it was emphasised in *Samuel Tumbleson*[34] that, in order to constitute attempted murder by poisoning, it was not necessary that the intended victim should actually take the poison. An application of what has been described as the "irrevocability" test could not support these conclusions. In *Janet Ramage*, for example, the consequences of the accused's act were not incapable of recall: she could have removed the teapot before the victim drank any of the tea. What the accused had performed was the *last act* required to bring about the murder.

6–18 There is little to commend either the "last act" or "irrevocability" theories of criminal attempts. The conduct of an accused will commonly provide an adequate foundation for an inference of *mens rea* at a stage prior to the reaching of an irrevocable, or the last, act. There is also the practical point that an application of either test would severely hamper the police in seeking to prevent crime. It would become well nigh impossible to effect an arrest during an attempt in order to prevent the commission of the proposed crime.

---

[31] *Samuel v Tumbleson* (1863) 4 Irv. 426 at 428.
[32] See, e.g. *McKenzie v HM Advocate*, 1988 S.L.T. 487; *Guthrie v Friel*, 1993 S.L.T. 899.
[33] *Janet Ramage*, Hume, *Commentaries*, i, 28.
[34] *Samuel Tumbleson* (1863) 4 Irv. 426.

PERPETRATION THEORY

It is for these reasons that a more flexible approach to the *actus* **6–19** *reus* is generally thought to be preferable. An application of the "perpetration" theory simply involves asking whether or not the accused has committed an act which is sufficiently proximate to the commission of the completed crime. That is, an attempt involves perpetration rather than preparation. This is the prevailing approach to the *actus reus* of attempts in Scots law, "before a charge of attempting to do something can be established, the individual must have passed from mere preparation to perpetration."[35] The leading authority for this flexible approach to the *actus reus* of criminal attempts is *HM Advocate v Camerons*,[36] where Lord Justice-General Dunedin charged the jury that the fundamental issue was "to discover where preparation ends and where perpetration begins . . . [I]t is a question of degree, and . . . it is a jury question."

In this case the accused were convicted of attempting to defraud **6–20** an insurance company. The evidence produced at the trial was that the accused had staged a fake robbery, but that no formal insurance claim had been submitted. Clearly, therefore, the accused had not performed the last act necessary for the commission of the fraud. It would also have been possible for the accused to change their minds and to decide to proceed no further with the proposed fraudulent scheme. This case serves to illustrate the weaknesses of both the last act and irrevocability tests. Their application to the facts in this case could not have led to a conviction.

Examples of conduct which have been held to be more than **6–21** merely preparatory include:

1. Joining a queue at a turnstile: statutory offence of attempting to enter a football ground while drunk[37];

2. Menacing a police officer with a machete, without striking him, at the same time as threatening to kill him: attempted murder[38];

---

[35] *Guthrie v Friel*, 1993 S.L.T. 899, per Lord Justice-Clerk Ross at 901C. The judicial support is distinguished: *HM Advocate v Innes* (1915) 7 Adam 596, per Lord Justice-General Strathclyde at 601; *Docherty v Brown*, 1996 J.C. 48, per Lord Justice-General Hope at 50, and Lord Justice-Clerk Ross at 57 and 60.

[36] *HM Advocate v Camerons* (1911) 6 Adam 456 at 485. The Lord Justice-General was adopting this language from Hume, *Commentaries*, i, 29 (although Hume, *Commentaries*, i, 27, supports the last act doctrine).

[37] *Barrett v Allan*, 1986 S.C.C.R. 479 (the statutory offence is now contained in the Criminal Law (Consolidation) (Scotland) Act 1995 s.20(7)(b)).

[38] *Strachan v HM Advocate*, 1994 S.C.C.R. 341.

3. Disconnecting an external burglar alarm: attempted house-breaking with intent to steal[39];

4. Inserting a hand into a till: attempted theft[40];

5. Throwing a spade through the window of a post office: attempted robbery.[41]

6–22   One possible criticism of the perpetration theory is its vagueness. Not all of the examples listed above appear equally proximate to the perpetration of the substantive crime in question. The great difficulty is that of identifying the point at which an accused has moved from mere preparation towards the commission of a crime.[42] Is it the case that, as one trial judge observed,[43] "the answer to that question can only be intuitive and a matter of impression and degree"? It would be difficult for a workable law of criminal attempts to be very precise. Hume recognised that there is, "a great variety of ambiguous cases, with respect to which it is very difficult to say where preparation ends and perpetration begins."[44] In *Coventry v Douglas*,[45] Lord Justice-General Clyde likewise accepted that, "the line of demarcation between preparation and perpetration cannot be defined in any general proposition".

6–23   The perpetration theory approach does, nevertheless, possess the inestimable advantages of practicality and workability. Nor should it be thought that Scots law is alone in applying a flexible approach in determining what constitutes a criminal attempt. English law defines the *actus reus* of an attempt as "an act which is more than merely preparatory to the commission of the offence."[46] Other jurisdictions appear to apply equally vague tests.

IMPOSSIBILITY

6–24 It would be fair to suggest that no aspect of the criminal law has generated more confusion than the law relating to impossible attempts. Throughout the common law world much academic and

---

[39] *Burns v Allan*, 1987 S.C.C.R. 449. See also *Heywood v Reid*, 1996 S.L.T. 378: smashing a security light sufficiently proximate to constitute attempted house-breaking with intent to steal.

[40] *Coventry v Douglas*, 1944 J.C. 13.

[41] *Andrew v HM Advocate*, 2000 S.L.T. 402;

[42] A court in the United States referred to it as "a murky 'twilight zone'": *United States v Williamson*, 42 M.J. 613 (1995) at 617, fn.2.

[43] *Barrett v Allan*, 1986 S.C.C.R. 479, per Sheriff Hyslop at 480.

[44] Hume, *Commentaries*, i, 29.

[45] *Coventry v Douglas*, 1944 J.C. 13 at 20. See also Lord Walker, "The Growth of the Criminal Law", 1958 J.R. 230, 237: "it is needless to say the point when preparation ends and perpetration begins raises a problem of some nicety."

[46] Criminal Attempts Act 1981 s.1(1). It should not be thought that the application of this test in English law has been without difficulty. For discussion, see Simester and Sullivan, *Criminal Law: Theory and Doctrine*, 2nd edn, pp.295–297.

judicial energy has been expended in efforts to determine in what circumstances an accused can be convicted for an impossible attempt: that is, for an attempt to commit a crime which cannot for some reason succeed. The kind of situation at issue is where the accused has the requisite *mens rea* for the proposed crime and has moved from the stage of preparation to that of perpetration. The only defensive avenue open to him is that of the impossibility of perpetrating the intended crime. The classic question in this context is whether it could constitute attempted murder to shoot at a corpse, thinking that it was a live body.[47] More likely examples would be where the pocket which the accused intends to pick is empty, or where goods which the accused intends to reset are not in fact stolen. In *Docherty v Brown*,[48] Lord Justice-Clerk Ross suggested that the writing on this topic was out of proportion to its practical significance. It is not proposed to add greatly to that body of literature here.

In any event, the position in Scots law is clear. Following the **6–25** full-bench decision in *Docherty v Brown*,[49] it is settled as a general principle that the impossibility of completing the intended result does not act as a general defence to a charge of an attempted crime. It was recognised there that it is a basic characteristic of any attempted crime that the result has not been brought about. The reason for this lack of success would not appear to possess any legal significance. In *Docherty v Brown*, the accused had been charged with attempting to possess drugs with intention to supply, contrary to the Misuse of Drugs Act 1971.[50] The appellant had taken possession of some tablets in the mistaken belief that they contained a controlled drug, when they did not in fact do so. It was held that in such circumstances an attempt charge was relevant. All five judges were satisfied on this point. Lord Justice-Clerk Ross stated:

> "The fact that something is physically impossible will prevent an accused from being convicted of the complete crime, but it does not prevent him being relevantly charged with attempt to commit that crime provided that he has the necessary *mens rea*, and does some positive step towards executing his purpose."[51]

---

[47] This situation arose on the facts of *Collins v HM Advocate*, 1991 S.C.C.R. 898, but did not fall to be determined by the court.

[48] *Docherty v Brown*, 1996 J.C. 48 at 50.

[49] *Docherty v Brown*, 1996 J.C. 48. For analysis of this decision, see D. Sheldon, "Impossible Attempts and Other Oxymorons: *Docherty v Brown*", (1997) 1 *Edin. L.R.* 250.

[50] Misuse of Drugs Act 1971 ss.5(3) and 19.

[51] *Docherty v Brown*, 1996 J.C. 48 at 57.

An older authority is *Lamont v Strathern*.[52] In this case, the High Court held it was attempted theft where the accused had placed his hand in an empty pocket with the intent to steal. Lord Sands stated that he was unimpressed, "by the metaphysical argument that, whereas one cannot take what is not there, therefore one cannot attempt to take what is not there."[53]

6–26   In *Docherty v Brown*,[54] the Appeal Court disapproved two earlier cases which had suggested that where there was an attempt to procure a criminal abortion, but the prosecution was unable to prove that the woman was pregnant, no criminal liability attached to the attempt. The principal authority for this rule was *HM Advocate v Anderson*,[55] a decision which was followed in *HM Advocate v Semple*.[56] This rule had long appeared to be anomalous and inconsistent with the decision in *Lamont v Strathern*.[57] There had been attempts to reconcile the two, most recently in *Maxwell v HM Advocate*,[58] but these had not been convincing. It is unrealistic to try and differentiate a case of attempted abortion from one of attempted theft. In *Lamont v Strathern*, Lord Sands distinguished the rule in *Anderson* by stating that in the case of an attempted abortion "a pregnant woman is the condition of the offence", whereas, in the case of an attempted theft from the complainer's pocket, "a pocket which may contain something of value is the only condition."[59] This attempted distinction was ingenious, but unconvincing. The presence in the pocket of property to steal could equally be regarded as a condition of an attempted theft, something which the law does not require.[60]

6–27   The feature which is common to all these cases is that, had the facts been as the accused believed them to be, he would have perpetrated the intended crime. The conduct falls squarely within attempted crime. The accused had gone well beyond the stage of preparation. The requisite inference of *mens rea* could be drawn. The accused failed to perpetrate a crime because of a circumstance which was unknown to him and outwith his control. There is no convincing reason why there should be a defence available to the accused simply because he did not utilise the proper means to accomplish the crime, or because he was for some reason unable to commit the crime on the instant occasion. The lack of success is not related in any way to his intention to perpetrate the crime. The apparent "impossibility" of the result is irrelevant.[61]

---

[52] *Lamont v Strathern*, 1933 J.C. 33
[53] *Lamont v Strathern*, 1933 J.C. 33 at 36.
[54] *Docherty v Brown*, 1996 J.C. 48.
[55] *HM Advocate v Anderson*, 1928 J.C. 1.
[56] *HM Advocate v Semple*, 1937 J.C. 41.
[57] *Lamont v Strathern*, 1933 J.C. 33.
[58] *Maxwell v HM Advocate*, 1980 J.C. 40.
[59] *Lamont v Strathern*, 1933 J.C. 33 at 38.
[60] See *Docherty v Brown*, 1996 J.C. 48, per Lord Sutherland at 63.
[61] *Docherty v Brown*, 1996 J.C. 48, per Lord Justice-Clerk Ross at 60.

Nevertheless, there will no doubt continue to be disquiet about **6–28** attributing criminal liability to an accused who has attempted to do the impossible. There are two principal concerns. The first is that the conduct in impossible attempts cannot always be said to demonstrate criminality as serious as that which a prosecution for an attempted crime might suggest. For example, A is under the misapprehension that B has a weak heart and that, if subjected to a violent shock, will die. He is desirous of causing B's death. To this end, he suddenly jumps out in front of B, shouting loudly. When viewed objectively, this incident could not be described as an attempt to murder B. In subjective terms, of course, A has the *mens rea* of murder and he has clearly tried at least to begin to perpetrate the intended crime. The reason why the accused failed to commit the intended murder was due to a circumstance for which he was not responsible (that is, the fact that B has a strong constitution). There is, however, an alternative interpretation: A's criminal liability should relate to what he actually did. Adopting this perspective, his conduct would appear to constitute a simple assault or a breach of the peace. There was no outward manifestation of a criminal intention to kill B. A could be punished for attempted murder only on the basis of his thoughts.

The second concern is that many impossible attempts involve **6–29** conduct which appears innocuous when viewed objectively. In a case of attempted reset, for example, the retention of property which has not been stolen is objectively innocent. This may increase the risk of convicting those who are innocent. Where the conduct of an accused is objectively innocent, it is much more difficult to infer the presence of the necessary *mens rea*. The prosecution case will be based primarily on evidence of the accused's internal thought processes and subjective purpose. In endeavouring to prove the accused's guilt, the prosecution will be unusually dependent upon whether there has been a confession.[62] There may also be reliance upon hearsay testimony as to what the defendant said about his purpose to others, and upon other circumstantial evidence. This could mean that there would be a heightened danger of convicting an innocent person, or of attributing too much criminal liability to an accused. As in the scenario described in the previous paragraph, this could lead to a conviction for attempting a serious offence (murder), when a conviction for a completed less serious offence (assault or breach of the peace) might be more appropriate.

INHERENT IMPOSSIBILITY

Accepting that impossibility should not ordinarily afford a defence, **6–30** there remains to be considered the accused who fails to commit the intended crime because he has chosen an "inherently" impossible

---

[62] Compare the facts of *Anderton v Ryan* [1985] A.C. 560 (but note that the account of English law given there was overruled in *R. v Shivpuri* [1987] 1 A.C. 1).

or unreasonable method of attempting the crime. The example which is generally quoted is that of an attempt to murder by voodoo or witchcraft. Should the accused in such a case be held to be guilty of attempted murder, if it is proved that he believed that the invocation of a spell could kill? Should a case of this kind be treated differently from that where the accused tried to shoot the victim with an empty revolver? The difficulty is in being able to say that the accused is sufficiently dangerous to merit a conviction for attempted murder. In *Docherty v Brown*[63] Lord Justice-General Hope recognised that,

> "where on the true facts the notion that a crime could have been committed was fanciful . . . no good purpose would be served in prosecuting a person who acted in this way, because his actings were so wholly misconceived as to cause no risk of harm to anyone."

ABSOLUTE IMPOSSIBILITY

6–31 An issue of absolute impossibility would arise in a case where the crime which the accused thinks he is perpetrating is not recognised as such by the criminal law. The accused may think it a crime to hunt rabbits, but the criminal law prohibits neither the conduct of the accused nor the result which he intends to bring about. The accused cannot be prosecuted because he believed his conduct to be criminal. Regardless of his intention, an accused cannot be convicted of attempting to commit a non-existent crime. This doctrine of absolute impossibility can be seen as one aspect of the principle of prospectivity (see below, para.14–09). The conduct in question is not a crime either at common law or under statute; it cannot be criminalised retrospectively as a result of the accused's blameworthy mental state. If the intention of the accused does not correlate to a recognised crime, his desire to do something criminal is not sufficient for the imposition of criminal liability. It is not for the accused to extend the boundaries of criminal liability in this manner.

---

[63] *Docherty v Brown*, 1996 J.C. 48 at 51.

CHAPTER 7

COMPLICITY AND CONSPIRACY

Introduction

This Chapter is concerned with criminal acts that involve more **7–01** than one individual. It describes both the characteristics of multi-party criminal conduct and "the doctrine of law which ascribes to associates in crime in certain cases responsibility for the criminal acts of their associate."[1] There is an account of how the accused who associates himself with a criminal actor can be held liable, even though he does not personally bring about (that is to say, *cause*) the *actus reus*. The Scottish courts traditionally have adopted a rather robust attitude towards the collectivisation of criminal responsibility.[2]

In the ensuing discussion three types of criminal liability are **7–02** described. First, the law of complicity penalises all those who participate in the commission of a crime. Liability of this character is known in Scots law as *art and part* guilt. Secondly, there is the crime of *conspiracy*, which penalises all those who merely agree to commit a crime. Conspiracy is a crime in its own right, but can also form the basis of art and part guilt. That is, where the conspiracy is put into effect and the crime committed, liability for complicity can be founded on the accused's conspiratorial relationship with others. Thirdly, there is the crime of *incitement* (sometimes known as *instigation*), which is committed where the accused solicits another to perpetrate a crime.

ART AND PART GUILT

The basic principle

Art and part guilt, sometimes described as "acting in concert", **7–03** has long formed part of the common law. The fundamental principle is that where two or more people engage together in

---

[1] *Docherty v HM Advocate*, 1945 J.C. 89, per Lord Moncrieff at 94.
[2] See *McKinnon v HM Advocate (No.2)*, 2003 S.L.T. 281; *Vogan v HM Advocate*, 2003 S.C.C.R. 564.

committing a crime, each actor is equally guilty of the whole crime irrespective of the particular role played by each individual. The law recognises that, to be found guilty of a crime, the accused need not have participated in every act necessary to constitute that crime. The example that is commonly given by way of illustration is that the man who keeps watch during a robbery by standing at the door of a bank is as guilty of the crime of robbery as the man who actually takes the money from the safe.

7–04   Naturally, there are certain restrictions to the broad principle of art and part guilt. More is required than proof that two or more people were involved.[3] The law does not recognise guilt by association.[4] The accused must have been aware of what the others involved in the criminal enterprise were doing. Further, in that knowledge, he must have assisted the others to some extent. That is, he must have participated in some way in the acts involved. Both of these requirements are described in this chapter.

PARTIES TO CRIME

7–05 There is not, in Scots law, a separate offence of "aiding and abetting" someone in the commission of a crime. The general rule is that no distinction is drawn between the different parties involved on the basis of their degree of involvement. This means that anyone who involves himself in even a minor way in a criminal enterprise may be unsure when he is criminally liable and when he is not. This uncertainty is the price to be paid for his immoral actions.[5] It can, nevertheless, sometimes be helpful to visualise a number of different roles where several individuals participate in the commission of a crime: (1) the *instigator*, who intends that the crime be committed and persuades someone else to do so; (2) the *aider*, who assists in the commission of the crime; and (3) the *principal*, who is the "actual" perpetrator of the crime.

DIRECT AND DERIVATIVE LIABILITY

7–06 In art and part guilt these different degrees of participation merge into joint liability for the commission of the crime, but it is only the principal who is directly liable; it is only he who is guilty of the whole crime in his own right. The art and part guilt of the instigator and the aider must derive from the commission of the crime (and be dependent upon it), since they only participate in the circumstances surrounding the criminal enterprise. In terms of

---

[3] See *Hobbins v HM Advocate*, 1997 S.L.T. 428, per Lord Justice-General Hope at 431B–C; *Rooney v HM Advocate*, 2007 S.C.C.R. 49.

[4] See *Khalid v HM Advocate*, 1990 J.C. 37.

[5] L. Katz, *Bad Acts and Guilty Minds* (Chicago: University of Chicago Press, 1987), p.260.

the example above, one can say that the lookout derives his criminal liability from the commission of the robbery. He is guilty art and part because he has assisted in the commission of the crime, not because he directly stole anything from the bank.

It is important to appreciate that art and part guilt does not **7–07** impose criminal liability for the actions of another simply because of a relationship between the parties. As will be more fully described in succeeding paragraphs, there must be some behaviour on the part of the instigator or aider designed to persuade or assist before the law imposes liability on him for the actions of the actual offender. What this notion of derivative liability does signify is that the art and part guilt of the instigator or aider (but not that of a joint principal) is dependent upon the crime having been perpetrated.[6] If the crime is not committed, or if the accused cannot properly be said to have participated in its commission, the question of art and part guilt does not arise, although that of conspiracy or incitement may do. Art and part guilt is not a form of inchoate liability.

COMMON PURPOSE

The starting place for any discussion of the concept of art and part **7–08** guilt must be to consider how an individual who is not directly engaged in the conduct that constitutes the *actus reus* of the crime can be held liable for the actions of others. The criminal law generally recognises only personal liability: the derivative liability inherent in art and part guilt appears to be inconsistent with this fundamental principle. An individual may become art and part guilty of the crime as the result of personal conduct, but once he is subsumed into the legal category of art and part guilt his criminal liability becomes dependent upon the actions of another person. The justification for this type of derivative liability is that the person involved art and part intends to assist, or participate in, the commission of the crime. In the terminology of art and part guilt, there must be a "common purpose". This requires actual knowledge, or at least "reasonable expectation",[7] on the part of the aider. A common purpose cannot be established by evidence that the accused "'*may* have known what the other . . . *might* have been doing'".[8] If the common purpose or plan cannot be established, then the principle of art and part guilt cannot be invoked. Each accused would have to be judged on the basis of his own actions, and not those of his co-accused or of anyone else.

---

[6] See, further, S. Kadish, "Complicity, Cause and Blame: A Study in the Interpretation of Doctrine" (1985) 73 *Cal. Law Rev.* 323, 337–342.
[7] *Docherty v HM Advocate*, 1945 J.C. 89, per Lord Moncrieff at 96; *Hobbins v HM Advocate*, 1997 S.L.T. 428, per Lord Justice-General Hope at 431B. The test is an objective one; see *McKinnon v HM Advocate (No.2)*, 2003 S.L.T. 281 at 286F.
[8] *Khalid v HM Advocate*, 1990 J.C. 37, per Lord Justice-General Hope at 39 (disapproving sheriff's charge).

7–09   If there is a common purpose, the particular accused, by providing voluntary and intentional or reckless assistance, identifies himself with the conduct of the co-accused whom he has assisted (and who may be the "actual" perpetrator of the *actus reus*). He thereby becomes art and part guilty of the crime. The criminal actions of the co-accused can then be imputed to him. The *mens rea* required for the crime in question will be inferred upon proof of the intentional or reckless assistance in the commission of the crime. It would, of course, be open to an accused to rebut this inference by pointing to evidence suggestive of a reasonable doubt. Art and part guilt is not based on innocent assistance.

DEGREES OF INVOLVEMENT

7–10   Art and part guilt covers a wide range of degrees of involvement in the commission of crimes. It can extend from the offering of relatively minor assistance or advice, to full participation in the *actus reus* of the crime. The criminal law regards all conduct within these extremes as constituting art and part guilt. In terms of the example outlined above (see above, para.7–03), art and part guilt would include the individual who, with knowledge of the plan, supplied the robber with some piece of information or equipment which was utilised to facilitate entry to the bank. This would still be the case even if the counsellor or supplier were nowhere near the bank at the time of the robbery. Indeed, his physical presence or absence is irrelevant to the question of art and part guilt. The person who supplies a necessary piece of equipment may in fact be of more assistance to the actual perpetrator of the crime than the lookout.

7–11   It is possible, of course, to draw a distinction between the individual who provides some minor assistance or counsel and the individual who fully participates in the commission of the crime itself. Indeed, the criminal law would tend to see the latter as simply a joint criminal enterprise, with more than one primary or principal offender, rather than as an example of art and part guilt. In terms of the bank robbery example: if two or more people were involved in entering and stealing from the safe in the bank, it would not be strictly necessary to analyse the situation in terms of art and part guilt. Both can be regarded as joint principal offenders. Nevertheless, it is clear that the principle of art and part guilt extends to this situation just as much as when there has been something less than full participation in the crime by an aider or instigator. In practice, however, the criminal law would draw a distinction between these two situations—if only in terms of sentencing.

Assistance and participation

7–12   It bears repeating that, before art and part guilt can be established, the prosecution have to prove that the accused assisted the principal offender to commit the crime. Once assistance has been established, however, the precise extent of it is not really significant. Depending upon the precise facts at issue, almost any type of assistance can suffice. This requirement of assistance is generally described as one of participation. This does not mean, of course, that the accused has to have participated in the perpetration of the *actus reus* of the crime before art and part guilt can be attributed to him. Rather, what is meant is participation in the criminal enterprise which results in the commission of the crime.

Further, it is not necessary for the prosecution to prove that the **7–13** crime would not have been committed without the accused's participation. In art and part guilt there is no "but for" requirement: an accused will still be regarded as guilty art and part even if his participation was causally unnecessary to the commission of the crime. That is, it is no defence for the lookout and the supplier of the getaway vehicle to state that the principal offender would have perpetrated the bank robbery regardless of their assistance. This absence of a causation requirement is reflected in the fact that any degree of assistance or participation suffices.

Psychological assistance

The requisite assistance or participation required to establish art **7–14** and part guilt could come in the form of psychological influence. This would occur when the accused has counselled or instigated the commission of the crime. The legal terminology for this state of affairs is "antecedent (or prior) concert". If the accused cannot be proven to have actually participated in the *actus reus* of the crime, he can only be guilty art and part if there is evidence of prior concert.[9]

In a case where antecedent concert is libelled, it is necessary for **7–15** the prosecution to establish that the commission of the crime was a likely result of the psychological assistance rendered by the accused. The instigation would have to be such as to induce the criminal conduct. Advice of a very general character would not be sufficient to establish guilt.[10] There would have to be a connection between the instigation and a specific crime. *HM Advocate v Johnstone and Stewart*[11] illustrates this requirement. The alleged crime here was that of being art and part guilty in an illegal abortion. The first accused had given the name of an abortionist (the second accused) to another woman. The accused had no connection with the abortionist, whom she knew only by name. Because of this tenuous link, she was acquitted. Lord Moncrieff charged the jury that the mere giving of a name in these circumstances could not constitute participation in the subsequent crime.

---

[9] *Spiers v HM Advocate*, 1980 J.C. 36. See *Little v HM Advocate*, 1983 J.C. 16, for an example of instigation as the basis for art and part guilt.
[10] Hume, *Commentaries*, i, 278–279.
[11] *HM Advocate v Johnstone*, 1926 J.C. 89.

In order to establish antecedent concert there would have had to be some communication between the two accused.

Physical assistance

7–16   Physical assistance can take a variety of forms. For example, it could entail supplying a weapon to be utilised during a bank robbery. As such, it would constitute antecedent concert. Alternatively, art and part guilt could involve participating more directly in the crime by acting as the lookout or by driving the getaway vehicle.

Prior agreement

7–17   Art and part guilt can most easily be proved where there is actual participation in the crime itself. In many such cases there will have been a prior agreement to participate in the commission of the crime. A straightforward example is provided by the facts in the case of *HM Advocate v Fraser and Rollins*.[12] In accordance with a pre-arranged plan, a woman lured the victim to a park where two men were waiting to rob him. The victim was assaulted and died of his injuries. All three were equally liable for the man's death and equally guilty of murder.

Spontaneous assistance

7–18   The concert necessary to art and part guilt can also arise from a spontaneous coming together at the time of the offence. The traditional approach can be seen in the case of *HM Advocate v Gallacher*.[13] This case arose out of a feud between the members of a travelling circus and some of the inhabitants of Hamilton. As is often the case the precise facts are not too clear, but it appears that one of the local men started a fight with the deceased victim, who had been mistaken for one of the circus staff. A number of other men joined in and stood around the victim who was kicked to death. Three members of the crowd were convicted of murder. There was no evidence of antecedent concert. The conviction was based on the fact that they "were in a kicking crowd animated by a common purpose, joining in the attack, assisting and encouraging". It is important to recognise, however, that the accused who joins in an assault which has already commenced does not in any way become responsible by adoption for what has gone on before his intervention.[14] Accession after the fact is not a doctrine which is

---

[12] *HM Advocate v Fraser and Rollins*, 1920 J.C. 60.
[13] *HM Advocate v Gallacher*, 1951 J.C. 38, unreported on this point; discussed by Gordon, *Criminal Law*, 3rd edn, para.5–55.
[14] *McLaughlan v HM Advocate*, 1991 S.L.T. 660; *Kabalu v HM Advocate (No.1)*, 1999 S.C.C.R. 348.

recognised in Scots law.[15] Equally, it is possible for there to be an initial common purpose (perhaps to assault the victim), which changes (perhaps to a murderous one).[16] In order to establish art and part guilt, it would have to be proved that the accused was still a participant at this later stage. Even in the circumstances of a group assault, the modern tendency is to recognise the desirability of discriminating among the accused by reference to the degree of participation and *mens rea*.[17] The prosecution has to prove that an accused was a participant rather than a bystander.

Participation by omission?

The first principle to note is that, "mere presence at the scene of **7–19** a crime is insufficient of itself to constitute art and part guilt."[18] Evidence of active encouragement or assistance is required.[19] In *HM Advocate v Kerr*[20] the three accused were charged with assault with intent to ravish. One of the accused did not actually participate in the attack, but had stood nearby watching. He did not speak to either his co-accused or to the complainer during the attack. His conduct was held not to attract art and part guilt. In such a case, however, the outcome would be different if there was sufficient evidence that the accused had been present as part of a common plan and in order to assist the actual perpetrator(s).[21]

The corollary of this principle is that neither does failure to **7–20** prevent the commission of a crime impose art and part guilt. The fact that this makes the commission of the crime easier would appear to be irrelevant. However, if it could be established that the reason for the "omission" was a desire to assist or encourage the commission of the crime, there would not then appear to be any barrier to art and part guilt. There would then be the necessary common purpose. Similarly, if there is a legal duty to intervene, art and part guilt can arise out of a failure to act. In *Bonar and Hogg v*

---

[15] Hume, *Commentaries*, i, 281; *Collins v HM Advocate*, 1991 S.C.C.R. 898, per Lord Allanbridge at 903E (although noting that, "a jury in Scotland can consider anything which an accused does after the victim dies to see if such evidence assists them as a jury to determine whether or not that accused was acting in previous concert with the killer or killers as the time of the death"). See also *Martin v Hamilton*, 1989 J.C. 101.

[16] See *Mowat v HM Advocate*, 1999 S.C.C.R. 688.

[17] The same approach has been applied to the issue of an individual's liability for specific crimes alleged to have been committed by a mob; see *Coleman v HM Advocate*, 1999 S.L.T. 1261. The crime of mobbing is discussed in Ch.12.

[18] *Quinn v HM Advocate*, 1990 S.C.C.R. 254, per Lord Justice-Clerk Ross at 260G. See also *Lawler v Neizer*, 1993 S.C.C.R. 299; *Mowat v HM Advocate*, 1999 S.C.C.R. 688.

[19] *Jamieson v Guild*, 1989 S.C.C.R. 583.

[20] *HM Advocate v Kerr* (1871) 2 Coup. 334; see also *Mowat v HM Advocate*, 1999 S.L.T. 688.

[21] *Stillie v HM Advocate*, 1992 S.L.T. 279. See also *White v MacPhail*, 1990 S.C.C.R. 578.

McLeod[22] a senior police officer was held to be guilty art and part in an assault on a prisoner by a junior officer which he had done nothing to prevent and from which he had failed to disassociate himself. The position of the senior officer was stated to have been that of an official standing by and allowing a breach of the law.

LIABILITY FOR THE OUTCOME

7–21 The essence of art and part guilt is that the accused either execute a common plan, or demonstrate a spontaneous common purpose. It is necessary to establish the presence of concert, either prior to the commission of the crime, or through a coming together at the time of the *actus reus*. If the prosecution cannot prove concert, then each individual will be liable only to the extent that his own actions can be proved to the satisfaction of the court.[23] This may even result in the acquittal of both. As Lord Justice-General Emslie observed in *Morton v HM Advocate*[24]:

> "It is undoubtedly true that where two people are charged with a crime and there is no concert and there is no evidence as to which of the two committed the critical act then neither can be convicted."

HM Advocate v Welsh and McLachlan[25] provides an example. The two accused were alleged to have broken into a house where one of them (it was not known which) had killed the owner. There was no evidence of a common plan between the accused to use violence, and the violence was both sudden and unexpected. Lord Young charged the jury that each accused could only be held culpable for his own actions. Since it was not known who had killed the victim, both accused were acquitted of homicide.

7–22 The basic problem facing the prosecution in a case such as *Welsh and McLachlan* is an evidential one. There are difficulties when the circumstances are suggestive of death as the result of a single blow.[26] Can it be proved that the accused was at least complicit in the death, rather than a bystander? The result in *Welsh and McLachlan* would have been very different had the prosecution been able to prove a common purpose or plan. In that case one could then apply the basic doctrine of art and part guilt that all the accused are regarded as equally liable for the outcome of the criminal conduct. The particular outcome does not have to be

---

[22] *Bonar and Hogg v McLeod*, 1983 S.C.C.R. 161.
[23] *Humphries v HM Advocate*, 1994 S.C.C.R. 205.
[24] *Morton v HM Advocate*, 1986 S.L.T. 622 at 623C.
[25] *HM Advocate v Welsh and McLachlan* (1897) 5 S.L.T. 137. See also *HM Advocate v Robertson* (1896) 2 Adam 92; *Alexander v Adair*, 1938 J.C. 28; *Docherty v HM Advocate*, 1945 J.C. 89.
[26] *Docherty v HM Advocate*, 1945 J.C. 89, per Lord Carmont at 101.

intended by the accused before he can be found guilty art and part. Rather, he will be held responsible for any *foreseeable* consequence. For example, if during the course of an armed robbery of a bank one accused shot and killed an assistant for refusing to hand over any money, on a strict application of art and part guilt the co-accused would be equally guilty of murder. Although the specific killing may not have been planned, it is a foreseeable consequence of an armed robbery. This rule can operate harshly on occasion. The accused can still be convicted as guilty art and part even though he lacks the *mens rea* of the specific crime of murder. This would particularly be the case if he had played only a small part in the criminal enterprise.

Distinguishing between co-accused

Perhaps it is in order to alleviate the harshness of the doctrine **7–23** that the courts are sometimes prepared to distinguish between co-accused in apportioning culpability. In fact, it is conceivable that the minor participant in the bank robbery scenario would be convicted of culpable homicide and the actual killer of murder. Both are guilty of homicide, but their culpability could be assessed separately by reference to their respective *mentes reae* at the time of the offence. *Melvin v HM Advocate*[27] provides authority for this proposition. The two accused had been charged with robbery and murder, but there was no evidence of antecedent concert. One accused was convicted of murder and the other of culpable homicide. It was held that it was legitimate to assess the degree of recklessness displayed by each of the accused in this way. In *Malone v HM Advocate*[28] this issue arose in the context of a fatal assault committed jointly by the two accused. It was stressed that only striking differences in the conduct of each assailant could justify convicting one accused of culpable homicide and the other of murder.[29] It is thus not necessary in every case where there are two or more accused of murder art and part to charge the jury that it is possible to find one accused guilty of murder and another guilty of culpable homicide.[30]

Foreseeability and the common purpose

An accused will not be held responsible for any conduct on the **7–24** part of a co-accused which goes unforeseeably outwith the common plan or purpose. In *Welsh and McLachlan*[31] Lord Young made the

---

[27] *Melvin v HM Advocate*, 1984 S.L.T. 365; distinguished in *McKinnon v HM Advocate (No.2)*, 2003 S.L.T. 281.

[28] *Malone v HM Advocate*, 1988 S.C.C.R. 498.

[29] It is possible that one accused might be able to avail himself of a defence of provocation (or diminished responsibility) which would warrant a verdict of culpable homicide, despite an equal participation in the attack: *Gray v HM Advocate*, 1994 S.L.T. 1237.

[30] *Moir v HM Advocate*, 1993 S.L.T. 1191.

[31] *HM Advocate v Welsh and McLachlan* (1897) 5 S.L.T. 137; see above, para.7–22.

point that an unexpected attack need not be foreseeable to anyone other than the actual assailant. Thus, if the reason for the shooting in the bank robbery example had been that the assistant was having an affair with the killer's wife, the homicide would then be unrelated to the planned crime and there would be no art and part guilt for the death.

7–25   This issue, as to whether the use of a weapon by a co-accused was foreseeable, is not uncommon in cases of alleged art and part guilt in murder.[32] Lord Justice-Clerk Wheatley identified the essential question in *Walker and Raiker v HM Advocate*[33]: did the accused know, or should he have known, that use of a weapon was involved in the planned crime? Was it within the scope of the common purpose? If the use of a weapon by one accused is sudden and unexpected, liability for the consequences of its use will not be imposed on a co-accused.[34] In *Boyne v HM Advocate*[35] the Appeal Court reiterated the basic principle that, to be found guilty art and part, the accused would have to know or, "have reasonable cause to anticipate" that a weapon might be used on the victim. This issue had to be addressed, "from the appellant's state of knowledge about what was going on."[36] In *Brown v HM Advocate*[37] it was stated that a jury was not bound to convict of murder where two accused had been involved art and part in a knife attack on the deceased. In a case where "the murderous act went beyond the joint common purpose and there was no evidence to show which of the two assailants had used the knife", one could not exclude the possibility that, "all that was in contemplation was to use weapons to inflict serious injury", and that the appropriate verdict was culpable homicide.[38] To secure a verdict of guilty of murder art and

---

[32] See, for example, *Kiely v HM Advocate*, 1988 S.C.C.R. 120. A related question which can arise is whether the weapon used by the actual perpetrator is of a similar type to that which the accused had contemplated. In *O'Connell v HM Advocate*, 1987 S.C.C.R. 459, the issue was whether a metre long piece of wood was a lethal weapon of a similar nature to a hammer. It was held that this was a question of fact for the jury to determine.

[33] *Walker and Raiker v HM Advocate*, 1985 J.C. 53; distinguished (on its factual application) in *Mathieson v HM Advocate*, 1996 S.C.C.R. 388. See also *Carrick v HM Advocate*, 1990 S.C.C.R. 286; *Robertson v HM Advocate*, 1990 S.C.C.R. 345.

[34] *Docherty v HM Advocate*, 1945 J.C. 89, per Lord Moncrieff at 95–96.

[35] *Boyne v HM Advocate*, 1980 S.L.T. 56. In *Docherty v HM Advocate*, 1945 J.C. 89 at 96, Lord Moncrieff alluded to "the doctrine that secondary responsibility for a criminal act arises only in cases of reasonable expectation." See also *Hobbins v HM Advocate*, 1997 S.L.T. 428, per Lord Justice-General Hope at 431B.

[36] *Boyne v HM Advocate*, 1980 S.L.T 56, per Lord Justice-Clerk Wheatley at 59. Lord Wheatley also gave the example of an accused who, as a member of a gang, was involved in an attack on a victim. He sees another member of the gang unexpectedly take out a knife and deliver a fatal blow. If the accused then carried on with the attack on the victim that would constitute art and part guilt of murder.

[37] *Brown v HM Advocate*, 1993 S.C.C.R. 382.

[38] *Brown v HM Advocate*, 1993 S.C.C.R. 382, per Lord Justice-General Hope at 392A.

part, therefore, the prosecution would have had to prove either that the accused (wickedly)[39] intended the death of the victim or had contemplated, as part of the common purpose, an act of the necessary degree of wicked recklessness (such as that the deceased would be stabbed by plunging a knife into his heart).[40] The change in emphasis in *Brown* was that it suggested that the prosecution had to prove, not only that the accused contemplated the use of a weapon by the principal offender, but also that its use would be accompanied with the requisite *mens rea* of murder (either a (wicked)[41] intention to kill or, more usually in such cases, wicked recklessness). This test was rejected as too individualistic in *McKinnon v HM Advocate (No.2)*,[42] where the court took a more traditional approach. The emphasis should be placed on what was foreseeable given the nature and scope of the criminal purpose. The *Brown* approach was, of course, premised upon the idea that to associate oneself with a knife attack can give rise to an inference of something less than wicked recklessness. This is not an approach commanding universal support. Some doubt has been expressed about the appropriateness of a verdict of culpable homicide, rather than murder, in the circumstances of an assault with a murderous weapon, such as a knife.[43] On the other hand, it is possible for an accused not to appreciate the full significance of the attack in which he participated. As Lord Sutherland noted in his charge to the jury in *Mathieson v HM Advocate*, the accused might have thought that the knife "was only going to be used to inflict the odd cut or slash or something of that kind".[44]

Distributing liability between the parties

Thus it is possible for a co-accused to be guilty of a lesser **7–26** offence than the actual perpetrator of the crime. Does this mean, conversely, that someone who assists in the commission of a crime can be guilty art and part of a more serious offence than the actual offender can, or that he can be convicted if the actual offender is acquitted? The answer to both these questions is a qualified affirmative. It is arguable whether or not there is a conceptual barrier to a conviction for a more serious offence than that of the actual offender. One difficulty can be mentioned at the outset. Art

---

[39] See *Drury v HM Advocate*, 2001 S.L.T. 1013.
[40] *Brown v HM Advocate*, 1993 S.C.C.R. 382 at 391E–F. See also *Codona v HM Advocate*, 1996 S.L.T. 1100.
[41] See *Drury v HM Advocate*, 2001 S.L.T. 1013.
[42] *McKinnon v HM Advocate (No.2)*, 2003 S.L.T. 281. This much is clear in relation to cases of antecedent concert; the possibility remains that a different (*Brown*-type) approach could be taken in respect of spontaneous concert.
[43] See *Coleman v HM Advocate*, 1999 S.L.T. 1261, per Lord Coulsfield at 1269G–1270D; *Barrie v HM Advocate*, 2002 S.L.T. 1053 (referring the issue to a larger court). See, further, the account of murder in Ch.9.
[44] *Mathieson v HM Advocate*, 1996 S.C.C.R. 388 at 393F

and part guilt can be derived from the commission of a crime, without "direct" involvement in its perpetration. How can it then be possible to be more guilty art and part than the "actual" offender? How can the person who merely assisted him acquire guilt beyond that of the actual perpetrator? One view would be that once it has been established that the actual offender caused the *actus reus*, the liability of any other particular accused should be assessed according to his own *mens rea*. Such an approach would appear to be in accord with the decision in *Melvin v HM Advocate*.[45]

7-27   It is debatable how far outside the law of homicide the approach should be taken—given that it does appear to represent a departure from the traditional rule of equality of liability for the outcome among the participants. Further, there are obvious limitations to the *Melvin* doctrine. If A instigates B to commit an aggravated assault on C, but B perpetrates a simple assault only, then it would not be possible to convict A of an aggravated assault. This crime has not been committed. A has the appropriate *mens rea*, but there is no *actus reus*. He can only be guilty art and part of the assault which B actually commits. (He would also be guilty of inciting B to commit an aggravated assault.) In the context of homicide, however, it is submitted that the flexible approach does make sense. If unlawful homicide is regarded as a single crime which has two levels of culpability (murder and culpable homicide), then there is no objection in principle to saying that the liability of the aider or instigator should be founded on his own *mens rea*. For example, the accused, assuming that he has the requisite *mens rea* for murder, could instigate a homicide in circumstances where the actual killer is guilty of culpable homicide only. An example would be where the instigator informs the killer that if he returns home he will find his wife committing adultery. As is detailed in Ch.9, it is likely that the husband will have available the partial defence of provocation. This could result in a conviction for culpable homicide, instead of murder. The instigator, however, acted with deliberation and premeditation. He cannot claim to have been provoked. He would be convicted of murder.

Acquittal of the actual offender

7-28   Do the same considerations apply where the actual offender is acquitted? Does the acquittal mean that there is no crime of which to be art and part guilty? The fact that the principal offender was acquitted does not necessarily mean that the crime in question has not been committed, or that the accused did not participate. The actual offender may have been acquitted because he was, for

[45] *Melvin v HM Advocate*, 1984 S.L.T. 365; see above, para.7–23. The absence of antecedent consent is crucial, see *McKinnon v HM Advocate (No.2)*, 2003 S.L.T. 281 at 288F.

example, insane or coerced. In these two instances a crime would have been committed of which one could still be guilty art and part. There are cases, however, where acquittal of the actual offender would be inconsistent with the establishment of art and part guilt. If in a case of a planned rape the accused who actually had sexual intercourse with the complainer was acquitted of rape because the woman had in fact consented, the co-accused who assisted would also be entitled to an acquittal. There would not have been a crime of which to be guilty art and part.

It appears that the mere fact that it would have been legally **7–29** impossible for a particular accused to have committed the crime in his own right is no bar to a conviction on the basis of art and part guilt. Hume gives the example of an unmarried man or woman who goes through a marriage ceremony knowing that the other party is already married. Art and part guilt would attach to this assistance to commit bigamy.[46] *Vaughan v HM Advocate*[47] illustrates the point. Vaughan had been accused of acting in concert with the mother of a small boy, in forcing the child to have intercourse with the mother contrary to the Incest Act 1567.[48] The accused was not related to either the mother or the boy. This meant, of course, that he could not himself have committed incest in this instance. The High Court held that he could still be guilty art and part for acting in concert with the co-accused mother in the commission of the offence. Similarly, in *Reid v HM Advocate*,[49] it was held that a woman could be guilty art and part of the statutory offence of living off the earnings of prostitution, even though the relevant provision applies only to a "male person".[50]

Acquittal of joint principal

The doctrine of art and part guilt is apt to cover the situation **7–30** where it would perhaps be more accurate to speak in terms of there being more than one principal offender, rather than a single principal offender and a number of lesser participants in the commission of the crime (see above, para.7–11). In such a case there is no difficulty in convicting one accused while another is acquitted.[51] The explanation might simply be that there is more probative evidence against one party to the joint enterprise than against the other.[52] *Capuano v HM Advocate*[53] illustrates this situation. The appellant had been charged with assault through

---

[46] Hume, *Commentaries*, i, 462.
[47] *Vaughan v HM Advocate*, 1979 S.L.T. 49.
[48] See now Criminal Law (Consolidation) (Scotland) Act 1995 s.1.
[49] *Reid v HM Advocate*, 1999 J.C. 54.
[50] Criminal Law (Consolidation) Scotland Act 1995 s.11(1).
[51] See *Johnston v HM Advocate*, 1998 S.L.T. 788 at 790G.
[52] *Low v HM Advocate*, 1994 S.L.T. 227.
[53] *Capuano v HM Advocate*, 1985 S.L.T. 196. See also *HM Advocate v Camerons* (1911) 6 Adam 456; *Tobin v HM Advocate*, 1934 J.C. 60.

acting along with others. His two co-accused had been acquitted. The appellant's argument was that, since he was charged with being involved as an accessory, he could not be convicted when the others were acquitted. The Appeal Court stated that there was ample evidence of the appellant's participation in the crime, and that this was not a case where the conviction depended upon that of the co-accused principal offenders.[54] Lord Justice-General Emslie gave the example of four robbers libelled to have acted in concert, three of who entered the premises and one who remained outside in order to drive them away from the location. If the only positive evidence of identification were of the driver, it would be appropriate for him alone to be convicted.[55] It has also been held that the acquittal of an alleged accomplice at an earlier trial is not a bar to a subsequent conviction of an accused libelled to have acted in concert with him.[56] An acquittal in a criminal trial does not, of course, amount to a positive finding of innocence. It indicates, rather, that the prosecution was unable to prove its case beyond a reasonable doubt.

Actual offender acquitted because mens rea absent

7–31   The more difficult case arises where the accused is alleged to have participated in some capacity other than that of a joint principal, but the actual offender is acquitted because he lacks the *mens rea* necessary for the crime. Since Scots law purports to draw no distinction between the parties to a crime this point might seem to be irrelevant. It is sometimes argued, however, that in cases of this nature there is no crime of which to be guilty art and part.

7–32   A case at point here is the much-discussed decision of the English Court of Appeal in *R. v Cogan and Leak*.[57] Cogan was acquitted of the rape of Leak's wife on the basis that he lacked the necessary *mens rea*. The "crime" had been instigated by Leak, who compelled his wife to have sexual intercourse with Cogan. Leak falsely told Cogan that his wife would agree to the intercourse. Cogan's "mistake" as to the wife's consent negated his *mens rea*. The question arose as to whether Leak could be convicted as an accessory. The court held that he could and offered two explanations why this was so. The first was that Cogan could perhaps be regarded as Leak's innocent agent. Since Leak caused Cogan to misunderstand the situation, he had used Cogan's "body as the instrument for the necessary physical act."[58]

---

[54] Although the accused was in fact libelled to have acted in concert with unnamed others, in addition to the co-accused; see the discussion in *Howitt v HM Advocate*, 2000 J.C. 284 at 287H–I.

[55] *Capuano v HM Advocate*, 1985 S.L.T. 196 at 196.

[56] *Howitt v HM Advocate*, 2000 J.C. 284 (opinion of the full bench, overruling *McAuley v HM Advocate*, 1946 J.C. 8).

[57] *R. v Cogan and Leak* [1976] 1 Q.B. 217.

[58] *R. v Cogan and Leak* [1976] 1 Q.B. 217 at 223.

The concept of innocent agency or instrumentality is an accepted **7–33** principle of criminal law (see above, para.4–03). The doctrine can be invoked where the accused has, with the requisite *mens rea*, manipulated an insane person or a child below the age of criminal responsibility to commit a crime. It would not be necessary to have resort to the doctrine of art and part guilt. His guilt does not owe anything to the conduct of a co-accused. He will be convicted because he is regarded as directly liable for committing the crime. In crimes such as theft or housebreaking with intent to steal, the acquittal of an innocent agent does not present a barrier to establishing liability.

The difficulty in applying this doctrine to Leak was the then **7–34** existence in English law of the marital rape exemption.[59] Similar conceptual difficulties would arise where it was a woman who utilised an innocent agent to have non-consensual sexual intercourse with the complainer. She could not commit the crime of rape herself, so how can the existence of an innocent agent make her directly liable?

The court's second explanation was that there was no reason why **7–35** Leak could not be viewed as Cogan's accomplice. The fact that Cogan was innocent was held not to alter the fact that the complainer was raped.[60] That is, the *actus reus* of rape was committed when Leak's wife was forced to have non-consensual sexual intercourse. The argument would appear to be that Cogan committed the crime of rape at Leak's instigation and that this crime could then be imputed to Leak. The difficulty with this approach is in being able to say that the crime of rape was committed where the *mens rea* was absent. One of the constituent elements of the crime of rape was lacking. Cogan's behaviour was immoral and reprehensible, but English law did not regard it as a crime. If Cogan did not commit a crime, then how could one say that Leak was engaged in a criminal act with him? How could there be liability as an accomplice if there was no crime?

Dissociation

One final issue to consider in relation to art and part guilt is **7–36** whether it is ever possible to assist in a criminal endeavour, but then escape liability through abandoning the enterprise and withdrawing. An instigator could, perhaps, avoid art and part guilt if he terminated his relationship with the other participants and communicated this fact to them.[61] More generally, if an accused can bring

---

[59] Now no longer accepted in either Scotland (see *S v HM Advocate*, 1989 S.L.T. 469) or England (see *R. v R* [1992] 1 A.C. 599).

[60] Likewise, the fact that Leak himself could not rape his wife would not be a barrier to accomplice liability; see above, para.7–30.

[61] *HM Advocate v Baxter* (1908) 5 Adam 609, per Lord Macdonald at 615. It is suggested there that it might be necessary to communicate with the police.

forward evidence of dissociation, this will go to the issue of whether he was in fact acting in concert. Lord Justice-General Emslie said in *MacNeil v HM Advocate*,[62]

> "evidence of 'dissociation' by a participant in the preparation of a crime or offence in contemplation will be highly relevant in any decision as to whether he can be held to be in concert with those who proceed to commit it."

To accord some legal recognition to the existence of dissociation is only sensible. To hold otherwise might deter people from withdrawing from a criminal enterprise and be taken to indicate that there was no point in doing so.

CONSPIRACY

Legal definition

7–37   Conspiracy is "constituted by the agreement of two or more persons to further or achieve a criminal purpose".[63] A definition which continues to have some attraction for the Scottish courts is that of the Lord Chancellor, Viscount Simon, in the *civil* case of *Crofter Hand-Woven Harris Tweed Co v Veitch*[64]:

> "Conspiracy, when regarded as a crime, is the agreement of two or more persons to effect any unlawful purpose, whether as their ultimate aim, or only as a means to it, and the crime is complete if there is such agreement even though nothing is done in pursuance of it."

Amendment to this definition is necessary: the word "unlawful" has to read as "criminal", to make it consistent with what Lord Cameron said in *Maxwell v HM Advocate*.[65] Lord Cameron there defined a criminal purpose as "one which if attempted or achieved by action on the part of an individual would itself constitute a crime by the law of Scotland."[66] This means that, before a conspiracy can be classified as criminal, its purpose necessarily would have had to be criminal if done by one person.

7–38   It should be stressed that, unless the prosecution can prove the existence of an agreement, there cannot be a conviction for conspiracy. Under no circumstances, of course, could the mere

---

[62] *MacNeil v HM Advocate*, 1986 J.C. 146 at 159.
[63] *Maxwell v HM Advocate*, 1980 J.C. 40, per Lord Cameron at 43; adopted in *Howitt v HM Advocate*, 2000 J.C. 284 at 287C.
[64] *Crofter Hand-Woven Harris Tweed Co v Veitch*, 1942 S.C. (HL) 1 at 5; quoted in *Maxwell v HM Advocate*, 1980 J.C. 40, per Lord Cameron at 43; and in *HM Advocate v Megrahi (No.1)*, 2000 S.L.T. 1393, per Lord Sutherland at 1395F.
[65] *Maxwell v HM Advocate*, 1980 J.C. 40.
[66] *Maxwell v HM Advocate*, 1980 J.C. 40 at 43. This too is the import of *Cochrane v HM Advocate*, 2002 S.L.T. 1424 at 1426.

presence of the accused be sufficient.[67] There must be *actual* agreement between the parties to a conspiracy. As is the case with instigation as a basis for art and part guilt, matters must go beyond simply putting a suggestion to someone with a view to further discussing the issue, and maybe reaching agreement in the future. That would not constitute a conspiracy, there being no "meeting of minds". Rather, it might be an attempted conspiracy or incitement (see below, para.7–57).

FORMS OF CONSPIRACY

It is possible that the members of an alleged conspiracy actually **7–39** might have met together to agree their plan, but this is not essential to the establishment of conspiratorial liability. Conspiracies can take a variety of other forms. In particular, it is not necessary for every member of a conspiracy to be aware of the existence of every other member.

Chain conspiracies

A "chain" conspiracy can arise where A agrees with B who **7–40** agrees with C, and so on. The fact that A is unaware of C's involvement is no bar to saying that they, along with B, are parties to the same conspiracy. The difficulty raised for the prosecution by this type of conspiracy is as to how the individuals in the chain can properly be linked together, particularly where there is a large number of links.

Wheel conspiracies

A conspiracy can also take the form of a wheel. This occurs **7–41** where there are a number of parties who each agree with one central ringleader, who forms the "hub" of the wheel. Each agreement between the hub and a party to the conspiracy forms a "spoke". For the wheel conspiracy fully to take shape, however, the prosecution would need to be able to establish the existence of a "rim" around the wheel. This is essential to proving the existence of one large, single conspiracy. If there is no rim, then there are simply a number of conspiracies to which the hub is a party: there are as many conspiracies as there are spokes in the wheel.

CONTROVERSIAL NATURE OF CONSPIRACY

From a prosecution perspective, conspiracy can be a useful way of **7–42** dealing with behaviour considered to be dangerous or undesirable, but which does not constitute a complete or attempted crime.

---

[67] *Coleman v HM Advocate*, 1999 S.L.T. 1261, per Lord Justice-Clerk Cullen at 1264L–1265A, 1269A, 1273D.

Despite this apparent utility to prosecutors, the crime of conspiracy remains controversial. From a defence perspective, the crime of conspiracy is problematic. It can be used to penalise conduct which is extremely precursory to the perpetration of the *actus reus* of a substantive crime. Further, the crime lays stress upon the mental state of the accused, since the crucial issue is whether there was an agreement between the parties to the alleged conspiracy. There may be less emphasis upon the conduct of an accused. This heightens the danger that an accused will be penalised not for what he himself did, but for consorting with other people who are much more intimately involved in the "conspiracy". The criminal law should be scrupulous in seeking to avoid guilt by association or guilt by confusion; a zealous prosecutor could use conspiracy as a catchall charge.

PROVING THE CONSPIRATORIAL AGREEMENT

7–43   Proof of the agreement essential to a criminal conspiracy will generally be inferential. Sometimes overt acts will have been committed by some or all of the accused, but this will not always be the case. But even if there have been some such overt acts, the existence of *mens rea*, in the form of an agreement and commitment to the criminal purpose of the conspiracy, will have to be proved by inference. For example, if a group of men is apprehended wearing masks and carrying weapons, while sitting in a car outside a bank, there is a clear inference to be drawn that there is an agreement to rob the bank. The group is unlikely to be there for any other purpose.[68]

7–44   Lord Justice-Clerk Grant pointed out to the jury in *HM Advocate v Wilson, Latta and Rooney*[69]:

> "[Y]ou won't often get eye-witnesses of the agreement being made or eavesdroppers who actually heard it being made. Accordingly, in many cases it is a question of judging from the acts of the alleged conspirators whether in fact there was a conspiracy between them in pursuance of which they are acting."

The evidence derived from such a decisional process will not always be as unambiguous as the example in the previous paragraph. An individual who may appear at an early stage of the conspiracy to be involved might not be firmly committed and could have ceased to play any part before the complete crime had been

---

[68] Compare the facts of *West v HM Advocate*, 1985 S.C.C.R. 248; see also *Coleman v HM Advocate*, 1999 S.L.T. 1261, per Lord Justice-Clerk Cullen at 1264L–1265A.
[69] 1968, unreported, but see Gane and Stoddart, *Casebook on Scottish Criminal Law*, 2nd edn, p.203.

committed. This problem is raised in a crucial form by the absence of any requirement of proximity, such as is to be found in the law of attempt.

A RATIONALE FOR THE CRIME OF CONSPIRACY?

It is possible to identify two main justifications for criminalising **7–45** conspiracies. The first is that recognition of the crime of conspiracy can serve as an instrument to prevent the commission of crimes. Conspiracy, like attempt, is an inchoate crime. All that is required to constitute a conspiracy is an agreement. It is not necessary to have done anything in pursuance of it. This means that the law relating to conspiracy becomes operative at an earlier stage than the law of attempt. The agencies of law enforcement are thereby given the opportunity to intervene at an earlier stage than would otherwise be the case. In this sense, conspiracy is a useful adjunct to the law of attempt. The intervention of the criminal law is justified by the fact of the agreement to commit a crime. This agreement and consequent commitment to the criminal enterprise is regarded as sufficient evidence of the threat posed by the accused.

The second justification is concerned with the special dangers **7–46** which are perceived to attend criminal conduct by a group. The rationale here is similar to that underlying art and part guilt. The premise is that a conspiracy poses a greater threat to law and order than a number of individuals working alone. If there is a conspiracy, it may be more likely that the proposed crime will be committed. Even if one individual reneges on the agreement, his co-conspirators can still continue. Psychological factors relating to the nature of groups may make it more likely that the criminal purpose will be achieved. The co-conspirators will provide one another with mutual support and loyalty. Most conspiracies do lead to the commission of the planned crime.

RELATIONSHIP WITH ART AND PART GUILT

In addition to constituting a crime in its own right, conspiracy can **7–47** provide a method of holding one member of a criminal group accountable for the actions of his co-accused. As Lord Justice-Clerk Grant expressed it in *Wilson, Latta and Rooney*[70]:

> "Normally a man is responsible only for what he himself does, but if he is involved in a conspiracy he may be responsible not only for what he himself does but for what his fellow-conspirators do."

---

[70] 1968, unreported, but see Gane and Stoddart, *Casebook on Scottish Criminal Law*, 2nd edn, p.203.

That is, a conspiracy can provide the basis for establishing art and part guilt. To give an example: two accused agree together that a particular individual should be murdered. This agreement in itself makes them guilty of conspiracy. If one accused then goes on to perpetrate the killing, the conspiratorial agreement can form the basis for holding the other accused guilty art and part of the murder.

7–48 However, art and part guilt can arise without there being a conspiracy. If during a bank robbery a customer were spontaneously to come to the assistance of the robber, there would be art and part guilt. There would not be a conspiracy, of course, because there was no agreement between the two individuals. In many instances of art and part guilt, however, there will be sufficient evidence from which to infer the existence of a conspiratorial agreement. An example would be the supplier of a weapon used in the course of the robbery.

CONSPIRACY IN PRACTICE

7–49 The basic legal concept underlying a criminal conspiracy is straightforward, but this does not mean that there are no difficulties in practice. In practical terms, an obvious problem is that caused by a trial involving a potentially large number of accused, each with individual legal representation. The most significant difficulty, however, is caused by the tendency to have over-long and complex indictments. Even a cursory examination of the reported cases in this area of law will show this.

Agreement pursued by specic crimes

7–50 One category of conspiracy is where specific crimes have been carried out in pursuance of the agreement.[71] The case of *Wilson, Latta and Rooney*[72] provides an example. The indictment contained libels of a conspiracy to pervert the course of justice and the commission of subornation and attempted subornation in pursuance of the conspiracy. The jury was informed that it was still possible to convict of subornation, even if there was an acquittal in relation to the conspiracy.

Agreement pursued by criminal means

7–51 Conspiracy indictments sometimes do not set out any specific crime by means of which the agreement was to be carried out. The indictment will state instead that the conspiracy was to be effected by "criminal" or "violent" means. An example is provided in the

---

[71] See, e.g. *HM Advocate v Megrahi (No.1)*, 2000 S.L.T. 1393.
[72] 1968, unreported, but see Gane and Stoddart, *Casebook on Scottish Criminal Law*, 2nd edn, p.203.

unreported case of *HM Advocate v Walsh*.[73] The charge here was of conspiring to further the purposes of the IRA, "by the unlawful use of force and violence . . . for the purpose of endangering . . . lives . . . and destroying property."

If the indictment libels a conspiracy to achieve some purpose by **7–52** criminal means, then the prosecution will have to prove the existence of these. This point was made clear in *Sayers v HM Advocate*.[74] The indictment libelled a conspiracy to further the purposes of the Ulster Volunteer Force by criminal means. Sayers was found guilty by the jury, but under deletion of the criminal means detailed in the indictment. On appeal, it was held that there was inadequate specification and that the charge of which Sayers had been found guilty was therefore irrelevant. The crime of conspiracy could not be established in the absence of specification of the alleged criminal means.

Conspiracy and non-proximate preparations

A charge of conspiracy can be utilised as a substitute for one of **7–53** attempt. There has been an agreement to commit the crime, but the accused has not moved sufficiently far towards perpetration to constitute an attempt. *West v HM Advocate*,[75] which concerned a conspiracy to assault and rob people employed in particular premises, provides an example of this type of conspiracy. The libel was that in furtherance of a conspiracy the accused,

> "did loiter in the vicinity of said premises . . . and thereafter enter said premises while . . . in possession of a blade from a pair of scissors, and . . . in possession of an open razor, all with intent to assault said employees with said weapons and rob them of money."

On appeal, it was held that there was sufficient evidence from which the existence of a conspiracy could be inferred.

Impossibility

If the factory outside which the appellant in *West v HM Advocate* **7–54** was apprehended had in fact been deserted, would the "impossibility" of carrying out the agreed crime have afforded a defence? This issue of impossibility in relation to inchoate crimes was addressed in detail in the previous chapter on attempt. It is not proposed to repeat in substance what was said there. The same conceptual problems which arise in relation to attempting to do the impossible appear also in conspiracy.

---

[73] 1921, unreported. Discussed by Gordon, *Criminal Law*, 3rd edn, paras 6.64 to 6.65.
[74] *Sayers v HM Advocate*, 1982 J.C. 17.
[75] *West v HM Advocate*, 1985 S.C.C.R. 248.

7–55   In conspiracy, as in attempt, it is difficult to see why mere impossibility should afford a defence. It should not be relevant to the question of conspiratorial liability that the agreement to carry out the robbery could not be fulfilled because of a mistake in the planning. This appears to have been the approach taken in *Maxwell v HM Advocate*.[76] Here Lord Cameron stressed that since a conspiracy is an agreement to achieve a criminal purpose, it is the criminality of the purpose and not the result which makes the agreement criminal.

Withdrawal as a defence?

7–56   The crime of conspiracy is committed the moment that the agreement is made. This means that there is no such thing in legal terms as "withdrawal" from a conspiracy. But if an accused had signalled his dissociation from the purpose of the conspiracy, this could serve to relieve him of art and part guilt for the subsequent commission of the completed crime by his co-conspirators (see above, para.7–36).

INCITEMENT

ATTEMPTED CONSPIRACY

7–57   It is a crime to attempt to form a conspiracy. The crime is known as incitement. It is committed where the accused has approached another person and invited him to participate in the perpetration of a crime.[77] There is no requirement that the accused actually instruct the other person to commit the crime in question.[78] An example of an appropriate libel in an indictment might be that of an "attempt by A to induce B to enter the conspiracy and incite him to assist in carrying out a robbery." The crime is complete as soon as the incitement occurs. The law does not insist upon any further action towards committing the *actus reus*. The requisite *mens rea* is that of a serious intention that the party incited commit the relevant crime.[79]

RELATIONSHIP WITH ART AND PART GUILT AND CONSPIRACY

7–58   As in the case of conspiracy, incitement is not only a crime in its own right, but can provide a foundation for art and part guilt. Incitement is one of the ways in which an individual can participate in and assist the commission of a crime. Thereafter he can be

[76] *Maxwell v HM Advocate*, 1980 J.C. 40.
[77] See *HM Advocate v Tannahill and Neilson*, 1943 J.C. 50; *Morton v Henderson*, 1956 J.C. 55.
[78] *Baxter v HM Advocate*, 1998 J.C. 219 at 221E.
[79] *Baxter v HM Advocate*, 1998 J.C. 219 at 222B, 223A.

called to account for the criminal act (see above, para.7–14). To give an example: A incites B to murder C. At this stage A is guilty of the crime of incitement. If B does kill C, then A is guilty art and part of the murder. A will not be convicted of incitement, because this crime merges with his art and part guilt for murder. If the murder bid failed, then the incitement would similarly merge with the attempted murder.

In this example, of course, there is an intermediate stage of **7–59** conspiracy when B agrees to A's suggestion. Again, if the murder were perpetrated, this would be treated as a basis for establishing art and part guilt, rather than a crime in its own right. A conspiracy charge would only become appropriate if B agreed to the proposal, but failed to carry it into effect.

POLICY ARGUMENTS

The crime of incitement permits the application of criminal liability **7–60** at a much earlier stage than the law of attempt, or even the crime of conspiracy. If the accused has invited another to commit a crime, that is sufficient in itself. There is no requirement of agreement, and none of moving towards the perpetration of the proposed crime. In *Baxter v HM Advocate*,[80] for example, the accused's conviction for incitement to murder was upheld in circumstances where he had done little more than discuss with the incitee the possible ways to kill the intended victim and the fee payable. One argument would be that the crime of incitement is directed at behaviour too remote from the actual commission of the *actus reus*. If A incites B to commit a particular crime, he hopes that B will enter a conspiratorial agreement to commit the crime. Assuming that B agrees, the crime of conspiracy is committed. However, there is no requirement that the proposed conspiracy be proximate even to an attempt to commit the crime which the inciter originally had in mind. Thus one view could be that incitement is an excessively inchoate crime and penalises behaviour which is too preparatory to the commission of the intended crime.

The justification for criminalising the act of incitement is largely **7–61** the same as that for a completed conspiracy. Incitement is regarded as worthy of punishment because it is an attempt to form a conspiracy. This is conduct which is regarded as sufficiently dangerous in itself to justify the intervention of the criminal law. Particular dangers are seen to flow from the agreement of a number of individuals to commit a crime (see above, para.7–46). A further rationale is that of protecting the individual who is incited from corruption.

---

[80] *Baxter v HM Advocate*, 1998 J.C. 219.

CHAPTER 8

DEFENCES

INTRODUCTION

8–01 This chapter discusses a wide range of defences[1] which an accused can plead in a criminal case. The accused's interest in raising a legally recognised defence is that it can serve either to elide criminal liability altogether or to diminish the seriousness of the crime for which he is convicted. The most significant of this latter category of "partial" defences are diminished responsibility and provocation, which do not lead to acquittal, but to conviction for culpable homicide rather than murder.

DEFENCES IN PRACTICE

8–02 It is possible to identify two principal ways in which defences can operate. First, some defences represent an effort by the accused to raise a reasonable doubt concerning a material element of the prosecution's case. Examples would include the defence of mistake of fact, which negates the *mens rea* of the crime, and the defence of alibi, which establishes that the accused could not have perpetrated the *actus reus*. These can be described as "failure of proof" defences. They do not provide a ground of defence independent of the definition of the crime. A failure of proof defence is the absence of one or more of the requisite elements of the crime in question. Secondly, there are those defences (including self-defence, coercion and necessity) which result in the acquittal of the accused even though the prosecution has proved each element in the definition of the crime. This means that, as Lord Justice-General Rodger observed in *Drury v HM Advocate*,[2] "a person who intentionally kills in self-defence is not guilty of murder or indeed of any other crime."

---

[1] See Chalmers and Leverick, *Criminal Defences and Pleas in Bar of Trial* for a modern, analytical study of defences in Scotland.
[2] *Drury v HM Advocate*, 2001 S.L.T. 1013 at 1016I, para.10.

Justifications

Some defences—notably self-defence—amount to a justification **8–03** for the accused's conduct. The essence of a justification defence is that it renders a notional infringement of the criminal law lawful. According to Hart,[3] a justified act is one that, "the law does not condemn, or even welcomes". The accused who raises a justification defence asserts that he has done nothing wrongful for which he should be punished. For example, if A kills B in self-defence, this act is justified. A may have perpetrated the *actus reus* of unlawful homicide, but, because of the fact that A acted to counter unjustified and life-threatening aggression from B, his use of fatal force becomes justified. The act of killing B is permitted by the criminal law.

Excuses

An excuse defence exculpates the accused who has satisfied all **8–04** the elements of a crime but who, because of some excusing condition, cannot be regarded as responsible for his actions. The basic distinction between a justification and an excuse is that the former focuses upon the conduct of the accused, whereas the latter concentrates upon his responsibility. Unlike a justification, an excuse does not render conduct lawful and proper. An excuse negates the accused's personal responsibility for violating the criminal law. Excuses are recognised by the criminal law in circumstances where an accused has perpetrated an unjustifiable act, but cannot be regarded as morally blameworthy. The accused who pleads the defence of involuntary intoxication to a charge of murder does not claim that the killing was justifiable. His contention is that he should not be regarded as morally blameworthy, and should therefore be excused from criminal responsibility.

MITIGATING CIRCUMSTANCES

Plea in mitigation

Even if an accused cannot avail himself of a legally recognised **8–05** defence, he can always ask a court to take what he claims to be mitigating circumstances into account. The fact that he does not fulfil the legal requirements of a defence does not mean that the accused will not be able to persuade a court to impose a lesser punishment upon conviction than would normally be the case. As was stressed in *Falconer v Jessop*,[4] "one of the rights which an accused person has is to speak in mitigation before sentence is passed."

---

[3] Hart, *Punishment and Responsibility*, p.13.
[4] *Falconer v Jessop*, 1975 S.L.T. (Notes) 78.

Evidence of mitigating circumstances

8–06   Further, an accused is entitled to introduce evidence of mitigating circumstances in the course of his trial. This is the case irrespective of the irrelevance of the evidence as a defence. In *Clark v HM Advocate*[5] Lord Walker noted that,

> "an accused person is entitled as of right to lay before the jury all evidence which might properly induce them to commend him to leniency in the event of his being held guilty."

Thus, an accused who wishes to argue that his conduct was not wholly voluntary, but is unable to meet the strict legal test of involuntariness, might be able to lead the self-same evidence at his trial by way of mitigation.[6] Likewise, an accused who is unable to establish a defence of coercion or necessity may be able to persuade a court that the special circumstances which led to the commission of the crime indicate that a less severe sentence would be appropriate.[7]

SPECIAL DEFENCES

Procedure

8–07   "Special defence" is a procedural term of art in Scots law. It refers to certain defences which an accused is not allowed to state unless a written plea has been lodged at least seven clear days before the preliminary hearing (where his case is to be heard in a High Court) or at, or before, the first diet (where he is to be tried before a sheriff-and-jury court), except where he is able to satisfy the court that there was cause for his not having done so.[8] The

---

[5] *Clark v HM Advocate*, 1968 J.C. 53 at 58.
[6] See above, paras 4–19 to 4–21; *HM Advocate v Murray*, 1969 S.L.T. (Notes) 85.
[7] See *Graham v Annan*, 1980 S.L.T. 28; *Morrison v Valentine*, 1990 S.C.C.R. 692; *Cochrane v HM Advocate*, 2001 S.C.C.R. 655.
[8] Criminal Procedure (Scotland) Act 1995 s.78(1),(3) (as amended by the Criminal Procedure (Amendment) (Scotland) Act 2004 (asp 5) Sch.1 para.25(a),(b)). "Preliminary hearings" apply to High Court proceedings (see the 1995 Act, ss.72–72D–as substituted/inserted by the 2004 Act s.1(3)), and "first diets" are procedural steps in indictment cases before the sheriff court (see the 1995 Act s.71, as amended by the Sexual Offences (Procedure and Evidence) (Scotland) Act 2002 (asp 9) s.8(2) and Sch.1 para.5; the Vulnerable Witnesses (Scotland) Act 2004 (asp 3) ss.2(1), 7(1); the Criminal Procedure (Amendment) (Scotland) Act 2004 (asp 5) ss.14(1), 19 and Sch.1 para.20; the Criminal Procedure (Amendment) (Scotland) Act 2004 (Incidental, Supplemental and Consequential Provisions) Order 2005 (SSI 2005/40) art.4; and the Criminal Proceedings etc. (Reform) (Scotland) Act 2007 (asp 6) Sch.1 para.12(2): see also the 1995 Act s.66(6), as amended by the Criminal Justice (Scotland) Act 2003 (asp 7) s.61(1)(b), and the 2004 Act (asp 5) s.1(1).

position is similar (*mutatis mutandis*) in summary prosecutions.[9] There is no definitive list of special defences, but one can identify four generally accepted ones[10]: (1) alibi; (2) incrimination; (3) insanity; and (4) self-defence.

The features common to these special defences are those **8–08** described by Lord Walker in *Adam v MacNeill*[11]:

> "Generally speaking, a special defence is one which puts in issue a fact (1) which is not referred to in the libel, and (2) which, if established, necessarily results in acquittal of the accused."

Notice need not be given in respect of any defence other than the four recognised special defences and the three (coercion, automatism and consent in sexual offences)[12] treated as if they were special.[13] The category of special defences is not an exclusive one; the statutory list is not exhaustive of potential defences. It is a concept of procedural, rather than substantive, law.

ALIBI

The defence of alibi is quite simply that, at the time when the **8–09** crime is alleged to have been committed, the accused was not at the place libelled.[14] In order to be relevant, the special defence lodged as the foundation for the plea of alibi must be definite.[15] It must specify the place where the accused alleges that he was, and at what time.

---

[9] See the Criminal Procedure (Scotland) Act 1995 s.149B, as inserted (in substitution for original ss.149, 149A) by the Criminal Proceedings etc. (Reform) (Scotland) Act 2007 (asp 6) s.19.

[10] *cf.* Chalmers and Leverick, *Criminal Defences and Pleas in Bar of Trial*, para.2–03.

[11] *Adam v MacNeill*, 1972 J.C. 1 at 5.

[12] Consent is defined to include a defence both of actual consent on the part of the complainer and of the accused's belief that such consent existed: Criminal Procedure (Scotland) Act 1995 s.78(2A) (inserted by the Sexual Offences (Procedure and Evidence) (Scotland) Act 2002 (asp 9) ss.6(1)(b)), 149B(3)–s.149B having been substituted for the original ss.149 and 149A by the Criminal Proceedings etc. (Reform) (Scotland) Act 2007 (asp 6) s.19. The relevant sexual offences are listed in s.288C of the 1995 Act (inserted by s.1 of the 2002 Act, and as amended by the Mental Health (Care and Treatment) (Scotland) Act 2003 (Modification of Enactments) Order 2005 (SSI 2005/465) Sch.1 para.27(5)).

[13] Criminal Procedure (Scotland) Act 1995, s.78(2), (2A), (2B)—as amended and/or inserted by the Sexual Offences (Procedure and Evidence) (Scotland) Act 2002 (asp 9) s.6(1)—and s.149B(2), s.149B having been substituted for the original ss.149 and 149A by the Criminal Proceedings etc. (Reform) (Scotland) Act 2007 (asp 6) s.19.

[14] For discussion of the scope of the defence, see *Balsillie v HM Advocate*, 1993 J.C. 233.

[15] See *HM Advocate v Laing* (1871) 2 Coup. 23.

INCRIMINATION

8–10 The defence of incrimination (otherwise known as impeachment) is that the crime was not committed by the accused, but by another person, named if known. It is not a special defence where the accused utilises a "cut-throat" defence and incriminates his co-accused, but the same statutory requirement that notice of intention to lead such evidence be lodged is applicable.

INSANITY

8–11 If the accused was insane at the time of committing the crime charged, he is entitled to an acquittal upon that basis.[16] The effect of this defence is that, even if the accused did commit the crime, his insanity relieves him of responsibility for his actions and he cannot be convicted. In effect, the *actus reus* is admitted, but *mens rea* is denied. The fact that an accused is found not guilty by reason of insanity does not mean, however, that he has to be released. An accused who pleads successfully the special defence of insanity will have his case disposed of in terms of statutory provisions under which (by virtue of the imposition of a compulsion order and restriction order) he can be detained in a hospital without limit of time.[17] Indeed, it is possible for an accused who has been acquitted on the grounds of insanity to lose his liberty for as long as, or even longer than, if he had been convicted and sentenced to imprisonment. In this context insanity would not be operating as a defence in the traditional sense; rather, it would serve as a mechanism for activating the (potentially indefinite) confinement of a person who is considered to be a danger to society.

8–12   Attitudes to the insanity defence tend to be ambivalent. The Scottish legal system attaches great significance to the principle that an accused should only be regarded as criminally liable when his conduct can be regarded as that of a responsible actor. If an

---

[16] Continued use of the term "insanity" for, or as part of, this defence is controversial; indeed the Scottish Law Commission has recommended a statutory replacement for the common law defence, that replacement utilising the concept of "Mental Disorder": see "Report on Insanity and Diminished Responsibility", Scot. Law Com. No.195 (July 2004), paras 2–19 to 2–24. It is to be noted that the Commission do not wish the replacement defence to be known simply as "mental disorder".

[17] Criminal Procedure (Scotland) Act 1995, s.54(6); s.57(1)(a), (2)(a) and (b) (as amended by the Criminal Justice (Scotland) Act 2003 (asp 7) s.2(a), and the Mental Health (Care and Treatment) (Scotland) Act 2003 (asp 13) Sch.4 para.8(3)(a)), s.57(4) (as substituted by the 2003 Act (asp 13) Sch.4 para.8(3)(d)); s.57A(7) (inserted by the 2003 Act (asp 13) s.133); and s.59 [as amended by the 2003 Act (asp 13) Sch.4 para.8(5)). Notice that under s.57(2), as amended, a court has a range of disposals which are open to it in such a case; see also s.57(3), as substituted by the Criminal Justice (Scotland) Act 2003 (asp 7) s.2, and as amended by the 2003 Act (asp 13), Sch.4 para.8(3)(b).

accused can establish that this necessary element of rationality did not characterise his conduct at the time of committing the crime, then he should not be regarded as blameworthy. On the other hand, were the insanity defence to be raised, it could well be in a highly publicised and serious case. It is possible that the desire to punish a wrongdoer may take precedence over the view that punishment of the mentally ill is inappropriate.

Legal and clinical insanity

It is important to emphasise at the outset that insanity is a purely **8–13** legal concept. It is not a clinical term derived from psychiatry or psychology. Insanity is not synonymous with any medical conception of mental disorder. In *Brennan v HM Advocate*[18] Lord Justice-General Emslie stated that the legal meaning to be attributed to the concept of insanity for the purposes of the special defence was not, "to be resolved upon medical opinion for the time being." His Lordship's view was:

> "It is, on the contrary, a question which has been resolved by the law itself as a matter of legal policy in order to set, in the public interest, acceptable limits upon the circumstances in which any person may be able to relieve himself of criminal responsibility."[19]

This quotation identifies the practical, as well as legal, problem in cases where the special defence of insanity is raised. Should the conduct of the accused be excused because of his mental state at the time of an otherwise criminal act? How is the availability of such a defence to be evaluated?

The alienation of reason test

There are few modern decisions which offer guidance as to the **8–14** appropriate legal standard to be applied. There is no fully developed modern discussion in a criminal appeal.[20] What has been said tends to be brief and obiter.[21] The starting place has to be the test articulated by Hume, who set the threshold of what can amount to insanity at a high level. The modern approach of the Scottish courts appears to be derived from this. Hume[22] stated that

---

[18] *Brennan v HM Advocate*, 1977 J.C. 38 at 42.
[19] *Brennan v HM Advocate*, 1977 J.C. 38 at 42–43.
[20] Lord Strachan's charge to the jury in *HM Advocate v Kidd*, 1960 J.C. 61, forms the basis of the account in Gordon, *Criminal Law*, 3rd edn, para.10–40, apparently because it can be read as giving a broader test than Hume. Lord Strachan further developed his account in the civil case of *Breen v Breen*, 1961 S.C. 158 at 196–197.
[21] See, in particular, *Cardle v Mulrainey*, 1992 S.L.T. 1152.
[22] Hume, *Commentaries*, i, 37; see also Hume, *Commentaries*, i, 39: "the distemper must . . . be absolute in degree".

what was required for insanity to act as "a defence in law" was a disorder which,

> "must . . . amount to an absolute alienation of reason, . . . such a disease as deprives the patient of the knowledge of the true aspect and position of things about him,—hinders him from distinguishing friend or foe,—and gives him up to the impulse of his own distempered fancy."

This approach to insanity was endorsed by the Appeal Court in *Brennan v HM Advocate*,[23] and in *Cardle v Mulrainey*.[24] In *Brennan*, Lord Emslie restated the import of Hume's definition in the following terms:

> "In short, insanity in our law requires proof of total aliena-tion of reason in relation to the act charged as the result of mental illness, mental disease or defect or unsoundness of mind."[25]

Lord Justice-General Hope in *Cardle v Mulrainey* reiterated this requirement of, "a total alienation of the accused's mental faculties of reasoning and of understanding what he is doing".[26] His Lordship explained that if, "the accused knew what he was doing and was aware of the nature and quality of his acts and that what he was doing was wrong",[27] the requisite degree of alienation of reason had not been present. There is an argument that Lord Hope's account may set too strict a standard. It appears incon-sistent with Alison, who stated that an alienation of reason did not require that the accused, "was altogether furious, or did not understand the distinction of right or wrong."[28] Alison further noted:

> "Cases of that extreme kind very seldom occur, and certainly much more unfrequently than the instances in which the

---

[23] *Brennan v HM Advocate*, 1977 J.C. 38 at 43.

[24] *Cardle v Mulrainey*, 1992 S.L.T. 1152 at 1160F–K.

[25] *Brennan v HM Advocate*, 1977 J.C. 38 at 45.

[26] *Cardle v Mulrainey*, 1992 S.L.T. 1152 at 1160E, doubting the approach taken by Lord Strachan in *HM Advocate v Kidd*, 1960 J.C. 61. See also *HM Advocate v Blake*, 1986 SLT 661, per Lord Brand at 661L, "there must have been some mental defect by which his reason was overpowered, and he was thereby rendered incapable of exerting his reason to control his conduct and reactions."

[27] *Cardle v Mulrainey*, 1992 S.L.T. 1152 at 1160D. This clarification was made in the context of the defence of non-insane automatism, but it seems clear that the Lord Justice-General saw it as equally applicable to insanity. The phraseology is reminiscent of the English law, founded upon *M'Naghten's Case* (1843) 10 C. & F. 200, although the rules derived from that case do not form part of the law of Scotland: *McKenzie v McKenzie*, 1960 S.C. 322, per Lord Walker at 326–327; *Breen v Breen*, 1961 S.C. 158, per Lord Cameron at 176 and Lord Strachan at 196.

[28] Alison, *Princples*, i, 645.

pannel's state of mind has been such as to render him not a
fit object of punishment."[29]

The issue of whether the accused's reason was alienated in **8–15**
relation to the crime in question is one for the jury to determine, in
the light of the evidence and their common sense. In the terms
utilised by Lord Strachan in his charge to the jury in *HM
Advocate v Kidd*, "it is to be judged on the ordinary rules on which
men act in daily life."[30] The jurors are the arbiters of insanity. They
can take account of any medical evidence given by expert witnesses, but such evidence is not conclusive. The significance of
medical evidence is severely limited by the fact that insanity is a
legal, rather than medical, concept. Further, medical witnesses can
only speculate as to the accused's state of mind at the time of the
actus reus, since the information upon which their judgment is
based will have been obtained subsequent to the crime being
committed.

Temporary insanity

The very notion of temporary insanity is something of a mis- **8–16**
nomer. In the context of insanity as a special defence, the issue is
the capacity of the accused at the time of the *actus reus*. Was it the
insanity which led to its commission?[31] The accused's "insanity"
need not be permanent. Hume concedes that the accused's condition need not be a continuous one[32]:

> "whether his malady is constant and unremitting, or only
> returns at intervals, still his defence shall be equally available,
> if he was then . . . void of reason."

Indeed, if the accused's mental incapacity were a continuing one,
he might well be found unfit to plead. This would occur where the
accused's mental condition meant that he was unable to instruct his
legal representatives in a rational and comprehensible way, or to
follow what went on at the trial.[33] Insanity would then operate as a
plea in bar of trial.[34] If, however, the accused were to regain his
fitness to plead, he could be put on trial.

---

[29] Alison, *Princples*, i, 645.
[30] *HM Advocate v Kidd*, 1960 J.C. 61 at 70; see also *HM Advocate v Blake*, 1986
S.L.T. 661, per Lord Brand at 662A.
[31] See *Eugene Whelps* (1842) 1 Broun 378, per Lord Justice-Clerk Hope at 381.
[32] Hume, *Commentaries*, i, 39. Voluntary intoxication can never amount to "temporary madness" (Hume, i, 45) sufficient to found the special defence of insanity
(see below, para.8–67).
[33] *HM Advocate v Wilson*, 1942 J.C. 75; *Stewart v HM Advocate*, 1997 J.C. 183;
McLachlan v Brown, 1997 J.C. 222; *Hughes v HM Advocate*, 2002 J.C. 23.
[34] Criminal Procedure (Scotland) Act 1995 s.54, as amended by the Mental Health
(Care and Treatment) (Scotland) Act 2003 (asp 13) Sch.4 para.8(2), and by the
Criminal Procedure (Scotland) Act 2004 (asp 5) Sch.1 para.13.

8–17 If an action is done in self-defence it is not criminal. A special defence is available to an accused whose otherwise criminal use of physical force against the complainer (or deceased) is justifiable[35] because it was necessary to protect himself (or a third party) from an attack, or threat of attack, by the complainer. The defence is premised on the fact that the accused did commit the actions libelled by the prosecution. To be relevantly pled as a special defence, therefore, the accused will have to admit that he perpetrated the acts libelled, albeit that he claims to have been justified in so acting.[36]

8–18   It is possible to identify two principal situations where a plea of self-defence can arise. The first is where it is pled by an accused charged with either murder or a crime related to it (for example, attempted murder or assault to the danger of life). Secondly, the accused charged with a non-aggravated assault may claim to have been justified in utilising a lesser, non-fatal degree of force. As might be expected, most of the relevant authorities concern the application of the defence in homicide prosecutions. The ensuing discussion reflects this emphasis and is concerned principally with the use of a fatal degree of force in self-defence. The problem which the law has to confront is that of drawing an appropriate line between the State's obligation to protect its citizens and the individual's right to use deadly force to repel an aggressor.[37]

The rules of self-defence

8–19   Since a killing perpetrated in self-defence is not criminal, the parameters of this special defence are severely restricted. There are three conditions which have to be met before the defence is available. The classic formulation of these requirements is to be found in Lord Keith's charge to the jury in *HM Advocate v Doherty*[38]: (i) "there must be imminent danger to the life or limb of the accused"; (ii) "the retaliation that he uses in the face of this danger must be necessary for his own safety"; and (iii) "if the person assaulted has means of escape or retreat, he is bound to use

---

[35] In some cases, the person utilising self-defence will be *excusable* rather than have had his actions considered as justifiable, e.g. where he has made a reasonable, but erroneous, assumption as to the need for defensive measures of force: see below, para.8–26 and Chalmers and Leverick, *Criminal Defences and Pleas in Bar of Trial*, para.3–04.

[36] See *HM Advocate v McGlone*, 1955 J.C. 14.

[37] G.P. Fletcher, *A Crime of Self-Defense* (New York: Free Press; London: Collier, Macmillan, 1988), p.18. Article 2 of the European Convention on Human Rights, which protects the right to life, allows for deprivation of life "when it results from the use of force which is no more than absolutely necessary . . . in defence of any person from unlawful violence".

[38] *HM Advocate v Doherty*, 1954 J.C. 1 at 4–5.

them." These three prerequisites are cumulative. If any one of the three is insupportable on the evidence, the trial judge is under a duty to withdraw the issue from the jury.[39] But if there is even slight evidence to support the accused's claim to have been acting in self-defence, the matter should be left to the jury to consider.[40]

Imminence requirement

Unless the threat is imminent, self-defence does not act as a **8–20** justification.[41] This notion of imminence connotes that, unless the accused had acted against his assailant, the assault would have occurred immediately. The conduct of the accused would not fulfil the legal requirement if the assailant had threatened to put his life at risk on some subsequent occasion.

Necessity and proportionality

The second rule of self-defence has two elements to it: the force **8–21** must be both necessary in the circumstances and proportional to the threat which is being combated. The moral basis of the common law's approach to self-defence is that human life, including that of an assailant, should not be taken unnecessarily. This means that an accused is not justified in killing an assailant where a non-fatal response would be sufficient to counter the attack. One might say, for example, that, if there were an attempt to stab the accused by an elderly and infirm assailant, it would not be justifiable for the accused to kill in self-defence, if he knows that he can avoid his own death by disarming the assailant.

This example illustrates the requirement that the degree of force **8–22** used in retaliation by the accused must not be disproportional[42]: it must not exceed what is reasonably necessary in the circumstances. This rule is subject to the clarification which follows, since the courts do not weigh the matter too finely. In *Doherty*, Lord Keith told the jury:

> "You do not need an exact proportion of injury and retaliation; it is not a matter that you weigh in too fine scales . . . Some allowance must be made for the excitement or the state of fear or the heat of blood at the moment of the man who is attacked . . .".[43]

---

[39] *Pollock v HM Advocate*, 1998 S.L.T. 880 at 883B–C.
[40] *Crawford v HM Advocate*, 1950 J.C. 67 at 69; applied in *Whyte v HM Advocate*, 1997 S.L.T. 24 at 25J. See also the non-homicide case of *Croly v HM Advocate*, 2004 S.C.C.R. 389.
[41] Hume, *Commentaries*, i, 224.
[42] *Pollock v HM Advocate*, 1998 S.L.T. 880 at 883A.
[43] *HM Advocate v Doherty*, 1954 J.C. 1 at 4–5. See also *Whyte v HM Advocate*, 1997 S.L.T. 24.

The same point is made in Hume[44]:

> "In deciding on pleas of this sort, the Judge will not insist on
> an exact proportion of injury and retaliation, but rather be
> disposed to sustain the defence unless the [accused] has been
> transported to acts of great cruelty or great excess."

8–23   What is necessary in any particular case is a matter for the jury
to decide on the evidence, but it will be directed that the benefit of
the defence is lost where the force used to counter the attack is
excessive. As Lord Cameron observed in *Fenning v HM Advocate*[45]:

> "[T]he protection which the law affords to the victim of an
> attack is not a licence to use force grossly in excess of that
> necessary to defend himself. . . . That is the foundation upon
> which the plea itself is based."

In *Doherty* Lord Keith emphasised that the jury had "to consider
[the] question of proportion between the attack made and the
retaliation offered."[46] The nature of the attack which is being
countered is of particular relevance in determining the proportionality or otherwise of the degree of retaliatory force used by the
accused. The law appears to be that an accused can never be
justified in using fatal force to combat what he knows to be a non-
fatal attack, even if the only means of countering the attack is to
kill the assailant.[47] In *McCluskey v HM Advocate*,[48] Lord Strachan
stated:

> "Speaking generally, homicide will not be justified by self-
> defence unless it is committed of necessity in the just
> apprehension on the part of the killer that he cannot
> otherwise save his own life."

In *Doherty* Lord Keith gave the following example:

> "[I]f a man was struck a blow by another man with the fist,
> that could not justify retaliation by the use of a knife, because
> there is no real proportion at all between a blow with a fist
> and retaliation by a knife . . .".[49]

---

[44] Hume, *Commentaries*, i, 335.
[45] *Fenning v HM Advocate*, 1985 J.C. 76 at 81.
[46] *HM Advocate v Doherty*, 1954 J.C. 1 at 5.
[47] The one exception to this strict rule appears to be in the case of common law
rape; see below, para.8–35.
[48] *McCluskey v HM Advocate*, 1959 J.C. 39 at 40.
[49] *HM Advocate v Doherty*, 1954 J.C. 1 at 5. See also *Moore v MacDougall*, 1989
S.C.C.R. 659.

Indeed, if it were clear that the accused had acted "with an intensity and savagery which went far beyond any measures reasonably required"[50] in self-defence, the trial judge would have a duty to withdraw the issue from the jury.

In *McCluskey* the accused was charged with murder. He claimed **8–24** that the killing arose out of his defending himself from an attempt by the deceased to commit sodomy upon him. Lord Strachan, the trial judge, refused to charge the jury that, if they believed the accused's story, they could acquit on the basis of self-defence. In the event, he was convicted of culpable homicide. On appeal, danger to life was stressed as a necessary condition to a successful plea. Lord-Justice General Clyde was firmly of the opinion that there could be "no justification at all for extending this defence to a case where there is no apprehension of danger to the accused's life ... but merely a threat ... of an attack on the appellant's virtue."[51] *McCluskey* was followed in *Elliott v HM Advocate*,[52] where the evidence was that the accused had killed not in fear of his life, but in fear that he would be subjected to homosexual assaults. The trial judge's withdrawal of the plea of self-defence from the jury was upheld on appeal.

The duty to retreat

If reasonable means of escape from the attack are available, then **8–25** there is an obligation to use them.[53] There is a duty to retreat, rather than use fatal force against the assailant. The proviso to this rule is that it should be a safe avenue of retreat. Hume[54] points out that,

> "though the party ought to retire from the assault, yet this is always said under provision, that he can do so without materially increasing his own danger, or putting himself to an evident disadvantage with respect to his defence".

The rationale for this rule lies in its consistency with the general principle that, out of proper respect for the value of human life, fatal force should not be inflicted other than when absolutely necessary. Imposing a duty to withdraw does not increase the risk of harm to the victim of an attack, because, as Hume suggests, retreat is not insisted upon where it might place the would-be self-defender in danger.

---

[50] *Pollock v HM Advocate*, 1998 S.L.T. 880 at 883D.
[51] *McCluskey v HM Advocate*, 1959 J.C. 39 at 42.
[52] *Elliott v HM Advocate*, 1987 S.C.C.R. 278.
[53] See, e.g. *McBrearty v HM Advocate*, 1999 S.L.T. 1333. See also the non-homicide case of *McInally v HM Advocate*, 2006 S.C.C.R. 391: the rule also, of course, applies to such cases.
[54] Hume, *Commentaries*, i, 229.

The self-defender's belief

8–26   Where there has been an apprehension of danger by an accused, a plea of self-defence is not necessarily defeated by the fact that he was in error. The availability of the special defence is based on reasonable appearances, rather than objective reality. An accused is excusable for having used fatal force in self-defence where he reasonably believes that his assailant poses an imminent danger to his life, and that fatal force is necessary to protect himself. Self-defence is permissible where the accused makes a reasonable error of fact regarding the material conditions of the defence. In *Owens v HM Advocate*[55] Lord Justice-General Normand stated:

> "[S]elf-defence is made out when it is established to the satisfaction of the jury that the [accused] believed that he was in imminent danger and that he held that belief on reasonable grounds. Grounds for such belief may exist though they are founded on a genuine mistake of fact."

This statement of law was affirmed in *Jones v HM Advocate*.[56] Lord Justice-Clerk Ross observed:

> "The question is whether the assault by the appellant was justified, and whether the evidence discloses that what he did was for his own safety in order to ward off danger actually threatened or which he reasonably apprehended was threatened."[57]

8–27   In *Crawford v HM Advocate*[58] Lord Justice-General Cooper emphasised that,

> "when self-defence is supported by a mistaken belief rested on reasonable grounds, that mistaken belief must have an objective background and must not be purely subjective or of the nature of a hallucination."

This issue as to the reasonableness, or otherwise, of a would-be self-defender's error is discussed further in the subsequent account of error of fact (see below, paras 8–54 to 8–56).

---

[55] *Owens v HM Advocate*, 1946 J.C. 119 at 125.
[56] *Jones v HM Advocate*, 1990 J.C. 160.
[57] *Jones v HM Advocate*, 1990 J.C. 160 at 172, emphasis added.
[58] *Crawford v HM Advocate*, 1950 J.C. 67 at 71.

Defence of others

The special defence extends to the use of reasonable force to **8–28** protect another person from an unjustified attack.[59] Lord Wheatley stated in *HM Advocate v Carson*[60]: "If a man sees another man being unlawfully attacked, he is entitled to stop that unlawful attack." Where the accused has come to the assistance of a third party, the defence will be available even though he need not have become involved, and could have retreated from the situation.[61] The "duty to retreat" necessarily has a different application when the action in question was undertaken to defend another.

Self-generated self-defence

It may be counter-intuitive to suggest that a self-generated **8–29** necessity to kill could support a claim of self-defence.[62] If A picks a fight with B, threatening to kill him, he is not justified in killing B if the latter responds to A's original threat by attacking him. One cannot say, however, that a person who starts a fight can never plead self-defence,

> "in a case in which there is a struggle, the right of self-defence may be invoked by the original assailant as well as by a man who was at the outset his victim."[63]

It is possible to conceive of circumstances where A could be justified in using a fatal degree of force against B, even though he perpetrated some wrongful act which initiated the chain of events leading to the fatal outcome for which he is being prosecuted. If A perpetrated a minor assault upon B, causing the latter to become unreasonably provoked and to attempt to kill A, the original assailant would appear to be justified in killing B, even though he is not free from fault. In *HM Advocate v Robertson and Donoghue*,[64] Lord-Justice General Normand observed that if,

> "the victim, in protecting himself or his property, uses violence altogether disproportionate to the need, and employs savage excess, then the assailant is in his turn entitled to defend himself against this assault by his victim."

---

[59] See *Moss v Howdle*, 1997 S.L.T. 782 at 786C–D; *Barrie v HM Advocate*, 2002 S.L.T. 1053 at 1055H, para.4.

[60] *HM Advocate v Carson*, 1964 S.L.T. 21.

[61] *Fitzpatrick v HM Advocate*, 1992 S.L.T. 796.

[62] See Hume, *Commentaries*, i, 223.

[63] *HM Advocate v Robertson and Donoghue*, 1945, unreported, per Lord-Justice General Normand, quoted in *Boyle v HM Advocate*, 1993 S.L.T. 577 at 587D.

[64] *HM Advocate v Robertson and Donoghue*, 1945, unreported, per Lord-Justice General Normand, quoted in *Boyle v HM Advocate*, 1993 S.L.T. 577 at 587D. See also *HM Advocate v Kizileviczius*, 1938 J.C. 60.

8–30   In *Boyle v HM Advocate*,[65] the accused admitted committing a breach of the peace through being part of a mob which had threatened another group of people. He had joined in the subsequent fight, armed with a knife, and had killed a member of the opposing mob. He pled self-defence, claiming that he had acted to protect a third party. The Appeal Court regarded it as,

> "a misdirection for the trial judge to tell the jury that the appellant could not plead self defence if he was a willing participant in the sense that he joined in the fight willingly. Even if he was a participant in the sense that he stepped forward into the fight, it would all depend . . . upon the circumstances whether self defence could be pleaded."[66]

This approach to the issue was followed in *Burns v HM Advocate*.[67] The important issue is whether the victim's retaliation to the accused's initial assault is such that the latter is entitled to defend himself. This,

> "depends upon whether the violence offered by the victim was so out of proportion to the accused's own actings as to give rise to the reasonable apprehension that he was in an immediate danger from which he had no other means of escape, and whether the violence which he then used was no more than was necessary to preserve his own life or protect himself from serious injury."[68]

Self-defence and provocation

8–31   Provocation is discussed in detail in the next chapter, but it bears stressing at this juncture that the issues of self-defence and provocation are quite different in substance and effect.[69] They are conditional upon distinct factual circumstances. It is not uncommon for an accused in a murder trial to plead both, but they are not matters of concurrent consideration: the issue of provocation only comes into play once the jury has rejected the claim of self-defence.

8–32   Self-defence is a special defence which, if successfully pled, results in an acquittal. A killing in self-defence is justified. Provocation does not lead to an acquittal. If established, it will result in a verdict of guilty of culpable homicide. It is not a justification for the killing; it is an excuse which affects the accused's culpability

---

[65] *Boyle v HM Advocate*, 1993 S.L.T. 577.
[66] *Boyle v HM Advocate*, 1993 S.L.T. 577 at 588A.
[67] *Burns v HM Advocate*, 1995 S.L.T. 1090.
[68] *Burns v HM Advocate*, 1995 S.L.T. 1090, per Lord Justice-General Hope at 1093I.
[69] Although, as noted in *Drury v HM Advocate*, 2001 S.L.T. 1013, both can impact upon the otherwise "evil" character of an intent to kill.

(culpable homicide, instead of murder).[70] The rationale is that an accused who has been provoked into losing his self-control should not be judged by the same standards as the person who kills "in cold blood".

Women and self-defence

An all too common scenario in self-defence cases is that of a woman who has killed her male partner, who has physically and sexually abused her over a long period of time. Many such homicides will be "confrontational".[71] These occur where the woman has killed her abusive partner when he was posing an immediate danger to her life. There is no difficulty in accommodating such a case within the rules of conventional self-defence described above. A second category of case can be described as "non-confrontational". These occur where the abuser has been killed either while asleep, or during some other lull in the violence. Can the woman be said to have acted in self-defence, when the man is not about to attack her on the occasion in question? If the homicide were a pre-emptive move on the part of the woman, it would be difficult for her to satisfy the rules of self-defence, particularly the imminence requirement. As a matter of principle, it would be difficult to justify such a killing. The abuser has not lost his right to life through being violent on other occasions. He is still entitled to the same legal protection as any other victim of a would-be self-defender. In the event that self-defence is not available, there may be the possibility of a verdict of culpable homicide rather than murder, on the basis of "cumulative" provocation.[72] **8–33**

A further possibility is that the woman may misinterpret an innocent movement on the part of the man as an attack to the danger of her life. She will want to rely upon the fact that she had been "battered" on previous occasions to support the reasonableness of her erroneous view that she was about to be attacked. This is an evidential problem.[73] The general rule is that while an accused can lead evidence concerning the victim's general character, it is not competent to lead evidence of specific acts of violence alleged to have been committed by the deceased upon the accused some time previously.[74] The difficulty posed by this evidential rule concerns how the accused can establish that the deceased was a violent person unless she is permitted to cite specific actions on the **8–34**

---

[70] *Drury v HM Advocate*, 2001 S.L.T. 1013, per Lord Justice-General Rodger at 1017I, para.16.
[71] The terminology is adapted from H. Maguigan, "Battered Women and Self-Defense: Myths and Misconceptions in Current Reform Proposals" (1991) 140 *U. Pa. L. Rev.* 379 at 382 fn.2.
[72] See below, para.9–61.
[73] Raitt, *Evidence*, 3rd ed, para.13–08.
[74] See *HM Advocate v Fletcher* (1846) Ark. 171; *Brady v HM Advocate*, 1986 J.C. 68.

part of the man. There have been occasions, however, when courts have been prepared to depart from a strict application of this doctrine. In *HM Advocate v Kay*[75] the accused had killed her husband and pled self-defence. Lord Wheatley admitted evidence of assaults upon her by the deceased on five previous occasions as relevant to her claim that she reasonably believed her life to be in danger on the instant occasion. The basis for this decision was that the indictment libelled that the accused had herself demonstrated malice towards the deceased on previous occasions. In the interests of fairness, therefore, the accused was allowed the opportunity to prove in turn by detailed evidence that she had reason to apprehend danger from the deceased.

8–35   The one exception to the danger to life requirement for killing in self-defence is in the case of rape. In his opinion in *McCluskey v HM Advocate*,[76] Lord Justice-General Clyde specifically makes allowance for the availability of the plea to a woman who has killed in the course of resisting an attempt to rape her. This privilege was not extended to the male victim of a homosexual attack. Lord Clyde's reasoning was based on the fact that rape, unlike sodomy, required a complete absence of consent on the part of the complainer.[77] It may be doubted whether this accords with the modern view of rape, which no longer holds that there is any requirement of overcoming the complainer's will by force.[78] If rape is non-consensual sexual intercourse, this need not entail a danger to life. This at least raises a question over the appropriateness of an exemption from the normal rules of self-defence.

OTHER DEFENCES

ACCIDENT

8–36 One can envisage many different circumstances where an accused could be responsible for accidentally bringing about the *actus reus* of a crime. If a result has been brought about accidentally, that would be inconsistent with the existence of *mens rea*. No criminal responsibility can rest upon an accused for an accident.[79] In *Mackenzie v HM Advocate*,[80] Lord Avonside pointed out that the

---

[75] *HM Advocate v Kay*, 1970 J.C. 68; described as "a very special case" by Lord Justice-Clerk Ross in *Brady v HM Advocate*, 1986 J.C. 68 at 74.
[76] *McCluskey v HM Advocate*, 1959 J.C. 39.
[77] *McCluskey v HM Advocate*, 1959 J.C. 39 at 42–43.
[78] See the *Lord Advocate's Reference (No.1 of 2001)*, 2002 S.L.T. 466.
[79] See *McCue v Currie*, 2004 S.C.C.R. 200, at 207D, para.25 In that case, it was held that accidentally setting fire to property did not amount to culpable and reckless fire-raising, and could not become so by the subsequent failure of the accused to attempt to extinguish the flames or summon appropriate assistance.
[80] *Mackenzie v HM Advocate*, 1983 S.L.T. 220 at 223–224.

defence of accident is always open and that, "however tenuous the evidence may have been, 'accident' is a question of fact and must be left to the decision of a jury."

Objective test

It bears pointing out that the fact that a result was accidental **8–37** from the accused's perspective does not mean that the criminal law will regard it as such. In *McGregor v HM Advocate*[81] Lord Keith gave the example of an accused who had driven his car along with a policeman on the bonnet in such a way that the policeman had fallen off and was killed. He pointed out that "it is a matter of more or less accident whether he is killed or not, whether he happens to land on his head or some other part of his body." Nevertheless, the motorist would still be regarded as criminally responsible for causing this "accidental" death. It is necessarily an objective test and a court will take cognisance of the principle, outlined by Macdonald, "that where the result . . . was likely to occur, the perpetrator is answerable."[82] Likewise, the doctrine of transferred intent operates in a limited way to penalise a result of the accused's conduct which he might regard as accidental (see above, para.3–37).

Crimes of recklessness

Crimes of recklessness and negligence can function in a similar **8–38** manner. The fact that an accused has been involved in a road traffic "accident" does not mean that he will not be convicted of dangerous or careless driving. Worthy of note is *HM Advocate v Pearson*,[83] where the accused was charged with the murder of one woman and the assault of another. He claimed that he had "accidentally" stabbed the two women while swinging a knife about recklessly. In the course of his charge to the jury, Lord Cameron stated:

> "If you on the evidence came to the conclusion that . . . the accused . . . whilst recklessly swinging that knife about stabbed this unfortunate woman, that would not in law be accident entitling him to an acquittal . . .".[84]

Accident and self-defence

It is not unknown for an accused to lodge a special defence of **8–39** self-defence and then to introduce evidence supportive of a claim of accident at his trial. The relationship between these two

---

[81] *McGregor v HM Advocate*, (1973) S.C.C.R. Supp. 54 at 56.
[82] Macdonald, *Criminal Law*, 5th edn, p.2; see also *Roberts v Hamilton*, 1989 J.C. 91.
[83] *HM Advocate v Pearson* (1967) S.C.C.R. Supp. 20.
[84] *HM Advocate v Pearson* (1967) S.C.C.R. Supp. 20 at 21.

defences is a complex one. It has been held by the Appeal Court that the two pleas will not always be mutually exclusive.[85] But, in order to succeed in the plea of self-defence, it is necessary for an accused to admit bringing about the *actus reus* of the alleged crime (see above, para.8—17). This will ordinarily give rise to an inference of *mens rea* and may be difficult to reconcile with a claim that the *actus reus* was brought about accidentally. This might seem to suggest that an accused should have to make a choice between the defences of accident and self-defence. However, in practice, accused persons can be inclined to make claims such as: "I was acting in self-defence when I killed him, but it was an accident anyway"; or "I killed him accidentally, but I acted in self-defence." If the accused adduces any evidence, however improbable, his claim will go to the jury. Nevertheless, it is arguable that the issues of accident and self-defence should be regarded as distinct in conceptual terms. It is submitted that the proper basis of self-defence is that the crime may have been committed with *mens rea*, but that the accused was justified in acting as he did. The fact that he was acting in self-defence may preclude the characterisation of his intent as "evil" or "wicked", but it does not mean that his action was unintended. If the accused lacks *mens rea* because it was an accident, he is not guilty, irrespective of circumstances suggestive of self-defence. That is, the defence operates even though the prosecution can prove all the elements of the crime. As Lord Morison stated in his charge to the jury in *Surman*[86]:

> "Self-defence is a *deliberate act intended by the victim of an attack* for his own protection and an act which has been reasonably committed for . . . the protection of the person who is accused."

Lord Morison went on to say that a person who kills in self-defence lacks "wicked intent."[87] In this second quotation the judge is using the notion of intent in a broad sense to indicate that there is a difference in moral terms between a "wicked" killer and one who kills in self-defence. That there is such a moral difference is unarguable, but the criminal law caters for this difference through the existence of the doctrine of self-defence. It seems to be an unnecessary complication or qualification to merge the concepts of self-defence and *mens rea* in the way Lord Morison indicates. It is certainly not the case that an accused's plea of self-defence will be defeated because he possessed *mens rea*.[88] Self-defence, unlike

---

[85] See *Surman v HM Advocate*, 1988 S.L.T. 371, per Lord Justice-Clerk Ross at 374L; *HM Advocate v Woods*, 1972 S.L.T. (Notes) 77.

[86] *Surman v HM Advocate*, 1988 S.L.T. 371 at 372K (emphasis added).

[87] *Surman v HM Advocate*, 1988 S.L.T. 371 at 372L. Although not referred to in *Drury v HM Advocate*, 2001 S.L.T. 1013, this is consistent with the view expressed there that murder requires a wicked intent to kill.

[88] See *Drury v HM Advocate*, 2001 S.L.T. 1013, per Lord Justice-General Rodger at 1016I, para.10.

accident, is not a failure of proof defence. By way of contrast, reference can be made to Lord Cameron's charge to the jury in *HM Advocate v Brogan*,[89] where he simply observes that an act done in self-defence lacks a "criminal quality". That is to do no more than to restate the basic principle that otherwise criminal conduct will not be regarded as such if perpetrated in self-defence, and is consistent with the approach adopted here. If the plea of self-defence is applicable, it is difficult to see how the *actus reus* can have been brought about accidentally. If it was brought about accidentally, the accused lacks the requisite *mens rea* and should be acquitted.[90] The issue of self-defence is pre-empted by the defence of accident and, it is argued here, is superfluous, since it has no effect upon the accused's intention to bring about the *actus reus* (intention here being used in a narrow sense, specific to a particular crime, in contrast to Lord Morison's view in *Surman*).

ERROR

Error of law

It is not a requirement of *mens rea* that the accused should have **8–40** been aware of the illegality of his behaviour. Subject to very limited exceptions, ignorance or error of law is no defence.[91] This doctrine is deeply embedded in Scottish criminal jurisprudence. According to Hume,[92] even though the accused "thought that it was a lawful act, and liable to no punishment, . . . he still has no defence in this sort of imperfect and corrupt belief." In *Clark v Syme*[93] the accused was charged with malicious mischief after he had killed his neighbour's sheep. His defence was that he believed that he had a legal right to do so after giving due warning to the neighbour about sheep damaging his crops. Lord Justice-General Clyde was unequivocal in rejecting this defence of error of law[94]:

> "The mere fact that his criminal act was performed under a misconception of what legal remedies he might otherwise have had, does not make it any the less criminal."

---

[89] *HM Advocate v Brogan*, 1964 S.L.T. 204.

[90] See *HM Advocate v Woods*, 1972 S.L.T. (Notes) 77, per Lord Justice-Clerk Grant at 78.

[91] See, e.g. *HM Advocate v H*, 2002 S.L.T. 1380, per Lord Maclean at 1381J, para.5. Some other jurisdictions do have a less restrictive approach. In South African criminal law, in particular, error or ignorance of law can be a defence to a crime which relies upon intention. See, generally, K. Amirthalingam, "Mens Rea and Mistake of Law in Criminal Cases: A Lesson from South Africa" (1995) 18 *U. N.S.W. Law Jnl* 428.

[92] Hume, *Commentaries*, i, 26. In *Tennant v Gilmour*, 1923 J.C. 19, Lord Justice-General Clyde held that misconstruing a statutory regulation could not afford a defence.

[93] *Clark v Syme*, 1957 J.C. 1.

[94] *Clark v Syme*, 1957 J.C. 1 at 5; applied in the *Lord Advocate's Reference (No.1 of 2000)*, 2001 J.C. 143 at 181F, para.109. See also below, paras 11–15 to 11–17.

The rationale for the rule

8–41 Various reasons have been given for the rule that error of law does not affect criminal responsibility. Sometimes it is said that there is a powerful presumption that citizens have knowledge of the criminal law, but there can be little justification for this view. There may be a distinction to be drawn between the traditional common law of crimes and the modern statutory offences. Common law crimes tend to be in accord with widely held moral values; a claim to be ignorant of the criminal character of appropriating someone else's property may scarcely be credible.[95] On occasion, however, the common law may develop in an unexpected way.[96] It might be argued that some recognition of error of law is therefore appropriate. In Scotland, however, this would be regarded as a question of judicial restraint in the development of the law, rather than the occasion for the application of a defence. In respect of statutory offences, most people have only a vague idea of the detailed content of the modern criminal law. It contains a myriad of regulatory and technical offences. The rule that dictates the irrelevancy of error of law, however, is premised upon the notion that the law is both settled and readily comprehensible. Anyone who purports to have made an error of law is blameworthy for not having made the effort to become acquainted with the law's prohibitions.[97] Whether this is a defensible approach might be doubted. The criminal law is not always accessible to the ordinary citizen. Even to the legally trained, the law can be complex.

8–42 A pragmatic justification for the rule is that accused persons would raise fraudulent claims of error of law which the prosecution would find difficult to disprove.[98] But is an error of law claim any more difficult to judge than any other matter (such as whether the accused in a common law rape case honestly believed that the complainer was consenting) with which the criminal courts deal on a regular basis? The more plausible justification for the general rule of law is a broader utilitarian one. It is in the interests of society for citizens to educate themselves regarding the criminal law so that they will obey it. The best way to achieve this end is to apply a strict rule that errors of law will not be excused.[99] There

---

[95] See *Dewar v HM Advocate*, 1945 J.C. 5; followed in *Herron v Diack*, 1973 S.L.T. (Sh. Ct.) 27.

[96] L. Hall and S.J. Seligman, "Mistake of Law and Mens Rea" (1940–41) 8 *U. Chi. L. Rev.* 641, 675, refer aptly to "the indefiniteness of the premises from which the common law may deduce criminality" (footnote omitted). In respect of modern Scots law, human rights law acts as an external restraint upon judicial creativity; see below, Ch.14.

[97] See H.M. Hart, "The Aims of the Criminal Law" (1958) 23 *Law and Contemp Probs* 401, 412–415.

[98] J. Austin, *Lectures on Jurisprudence or The Philosophy of Positive Law*, abridged by R. Campbell (J. Murray, 1880), p.239.

[99] O.W. Holmes, *The Common Law*, p.48. For criticism of this thesis, see L.D. Houlgate, "*Ignorantia Juris*: A Plea for Justice" (1967) 78 *Ethics* 32, 38.

could otherwise be the risk that citizens would be encouraged to be ignorant of the standards of behaviour mandated by the criminal law.

Error of law and mens rea

The typical error of law case is that exemplified by *Clark v* **8–43** *Syme*[100]: the accused claims that he made an error regarding the criminal law under which he is being prosecuted. The law's analysis of this situation is that if the accused, with *mens rea*, brings about the *actus reus* of a crime, he is criminally liable. It is no defence for him to say that he did not know that the *actus reus* was proscribed by the criminal law. A far less common alternative is that an accused will admit awareness of the criminal law for which he is being prosecuted, but will instead claim to have been in error about the civil law. It is arguable that in some circumstances a mistake regarding the civil law could operate to negative the *mens rea* in the definition of the crime. For example, if A is charged with malicious mischief arising out of an incident where he has intentionally damaged property belonging to B, an error of the civil law which led him to believe that the property was his own should be a defence.[101]

The limitation to this principle is that it could not apply where **8–44** the criminal law sets a standard which is not the same as that by which the accused chooses to abide. The principle must be confined to the civil law, and to concepts such as the ownership of property. It was no defence for the accused in *Clark v Syme*[102] to assert that he believed the law permitted him to kill his neighbour's sheep. In *Andrew Ewart*,[103] the accused, together with his victim, had been guarding a churchyard. The accused mistook his colleague for a "body-snatcher" and shot and killed him. He was held guilty of murder, since it would have been murder to kill someone who had in fact come to remove dead bodies. His error was as to the criminal law. (The error of fact as to the victim's identity was similarly irrelevant.)

Erroneous claims of right

The defence of claim of right in crimes of dishonesty is said to **8–45** be a recognised exception to the general rule as to the irrelevancy of error of law.[104] If that is so, then an error as to a belief in a legal right to appropriate will exclude the *mens rea* of theft, as it eliminates the requisite element of "dishonest" appropriation. If A

---

[100] *Clark v Syme*, 1957 J.C. 1.
[101] A persuasive authority to this effect is the English case of *R. v Smith* [1974] Q.B. 354.
[102] *Clark v Syme*, 1957 J.C. 1.
[103] *Andrew Ewart* (1828) Syme 315.
[104] Gordon, *Criminal Law*, 3rd edn, para.14.55. See, further below, para.10–17.

appropriates B's property under the misconception that it is lawfully his, A's action is not theft. This conclusion would be in accord with the general principle described above, under which an error of civil law can operate as a defence by preventing the accused from having *mens rea* in acting as he did. Again, however, the accused's error would have had to be one which led him to believe that he had a right to act as he did. It could not be sufficient that he simply believed that his act of appropriation did not constitute a crime. The distinction between an error of civil law (the law of property) and criminal law (the law of theft) is fundamental. An error as to the former might give rise to the defence of claim of right; an error as to the latter never could.

Dewar v HM Advocate

8–46   Dewar, the manager of a crematorium, had been convicted of the theft of a large quantity of coffin lids and a number of coffins.[105] His defence was that he believed that the coffin lids were his to keep or use as he saw fit: to treat as scrap. His belief was that he was merely following the general and accepted practice in crematoria. It was conceded that this belief was unfounded in fact. The jury was charged in terms of the law of erroneous claim of right. On appeal, however, the view was taken that the law of error was inapplicable. The basis for this opinion was that the accused claimed an error of law which was supported only by his belief that his actions were merely in accord with common practice. The court accepted that a defence of claim of right could succeed where it was based on an error of fact, but stressed that the error must be "founded on rational grounds", and could not be based on the "singular" idea of the accused himself.[106] (For discussion as to whether the accused's belief need be reasonable, see below, paras 8–50 *et seq.*)

8–47   An alternative approach to that of the Appeal Court in *Dewar* would be to concede that the accused may have been making an error about the law of property, in which case it could have constituted a relevant error of law (serving to negative the *mens rea* of theft). On this view, the issue would become whether Dewar had acted as he did because of a belief that it was not contrary to the criminal law to appropriate the coffin lids; or whether his behaviour had been actuated by an error as to the law of property. One imagines that it would have proved difficult for Dewar to satisfy a court that the latter had been the case. Nevertheless, it is difficult to agree with the conclusion of Lord Justice-General Normand that the answer to the question was so obvious that there was no need for Dewar's claim to be put before the jury.

---

[105] *Dewar v HM Advocate*, 1945 J.C. 5.
[106] See also Hume, *Commentaries*, i, 78.

Error of fact

The criminal law takes a more charitable view of errors of fact **8–48** than errors of law. There are two principal ways in which error of fact can affect criminal responsibility. First, the accused may claim to have been in error about a fact that would make his conduct justifiable or excusable. For example, A erroneously believes that he is about to be subjected to a fatal attack by B, so he kills him in self-defence (see above, paras 8–26 and 8–27). Secondly, the accused may claim to have been in error about a fact relevant to an ingredient of the definition of the crime for which he is being prosecuted. The present discussion is concerned mainly with this second category of error.

A shoots and kills B because of his mistaken belief that he is **8–49** shooting at a deer. A has perpetrated the *actus reus* of the crime of murder. Applying an objective test, one can draw an evidential inference of the presence of the requisite *mens rea*. The accused was in error about the fact that he was shooting at a human being: a fundamental element of the law of murder. He is, of course, not guilty of murder. His error of fact will operate to negative the constituent of *mens rea* included in the crime of murder (an intention to kill, or wicked recklessness as to the death of, a human being). A will be found not guilty of murder because the prosecution will be unable to prove one of the prerequisites of the crime; the *mens rea* of murder cannot be satisfied by an intention to kill a deer. It should be stressed that error of fact operates as a defence in this manner only to the extent that it can be demonstrated to have affected A's *mens rea*.[107] Indeed, it might be thought misleading to utilise the term "defence" in this context. The issue could be interpreted as simply whether or not the accused had the *mens rea* required by the definition of the crime concerned.[108]

Need A's error of fact as to his target's identity be a reasonable **8–50** one, in order to provide an answer to a criminal charge? At one time an unequivocally affirmative response would have been given to this question. By analogy from the law of erroneous self-defence, the conclusion would have been drawn that the accused's erroneous belief must be subjected to a reasonableness test (see above, paras 8–26 and 8–27). Authority would also have been derived from *Dewar v HM Advocate*,[109] where Lord Justice-Clerk Cooper charged the jury that the accused's error as to a claim of right had to be a "reasonable belief, based on colourable grounds."

---

[107] See *McIver v HM Advocate*, 1991 S.L.T. 81.
[108] In this case, murder; a conviction for culpable homicide, however, would not be precluded.
[109] *Dewar v HM Advocate*, 1945 J.C. 5 at 8; see above, para.8–46, and below, para.10–17.

Honest error in rape

8–51   The decisions in *Meek v HM Advocate*[110] and *Jamieson v HM Advocate*[111] appear to represent a new common law approach to the issue. It was held that an erroneous belief in the complainer's consent need not be reasonable in order to constitute a defence to a charge of rape.[112] The reasoning behind this approach seems to be that where an error as to the complainer's consent exists, even if 1it is unreasonable, it prevents the formation of the requisite *mens rea*. This leads to the conclusion that an accused acting under such a misconception cannot be guilty. The import of *Meek* and *Jamieson* may thus be that where an error of fact relates to a definitional element of a crime, it need not be held on reasonable grounds before it constitutes a defence.[113]

8–52   In terms of the error of fact doctrine, *Meek* is then an explicable decision: an accused either possesses the *mens rea* required by the definition of a crime or he does not. Nevertheless, *Meek* has proved to be a controversial decision. The burden of risk of the "error" made by the male accused seems to be placed upon the female complainer. The *actus reus* of rape was reviewed by a full court in the *Lord Advocate's Reference (No.1 of 2001)*.[114] There is at least a suggestion that the subjective approach to *mens rea* reflected in *Meek* and *Jamieson* may be revisited.[115] For the present, however, these latter two decisions reflect the law. But even if a subjective approach to the issue is adopted, it may be unlikely that an accused would be acquitted where the woman had clearly indicated that she was not consenting; indeed, the appeal in *Meek* was not allowed. It seems doubtful whether a jury would conclude that the accused in such a case had been genuinely, as opposed to recklessly, in error about the complainer's lack of consent. Lord Justice-General Emslie pointed out in *Meek*[116]:

---

[110] *Meek v HM Advocate*, 1983 S.L.T. 280.

[111] *Jamieson v HM Advocate (No.1)*, 1994 J.C. 88. See also *McPhelim v HM Advocate (No.1)*, 1996 S.C.C.R. 647; *Marr v HM Advocate (No.1)*, 1996 S.L.T. 1035 (applying the "honest error" doctrine to "indecent" assault).

[112] According to the *Lord Advocate's Reference (No.1 of 2001)*, 2002 S.L.T. 466, per Lord Justice-General Cullen at 476A–B, para.44, the definition of the crime of rape is intentionally or recklessly having sexual intercourse without consent. See the account of rape given in Ch.9.

[113] In its "Report on Rape and Other Sexual Offences", Scot Law Com. No.209 (2007), the Scottish Law Commission recommends that the law should provide a definition of consent for sexual offences. This definition would have two elements: first, a general definition of consent as meaning "free agreement"; secondly, a non-exhaustive list of factual situations which define when a person has not consented to sexual activity. As is discussed further in Ch.9, this proposal—if implemented—would have major implications for the role of consent in the law of rape. For the present, however, the discussion in the text reflects the authors' understanding of the current (unreformed) law.

[114] *Lord Advocate's Reference (No.1 of 2001)*, 2002 S.L.T. 466.

[115] *Lord Advocate's Reference (No.1 of 2001)*, 2002 S.L.T. 466, per Lord Justice-General Cullen at 473G–H, paras 28–29, 476B, para.44.

[116] *Meek v HM Advocate*, 1983 S.L.T. 280 at 281.

"The absence of reasonable grounds for such an alleged belief will . . . have a considerable bearing upon whether any jury will accept that such an 'honest belief' was held."

It is unnecessary for a trial judge to give a full *Meek/Jamieson* direction in every rape case. If the evidence presents the jury with a "simple choice" between violence and consent, with "no room for any halfway house", the honest belief of the accused does not arise as an issue[117]: unless the issue of honest belief has been raised in the evidence, the jury does not need to be directed on the matter.[118] But,

"in any rape case in which there is no evidence of the use or threat of force at the time of, or immediately preceding, the sexual penetration, and the evidence provides some proper basis upon which the jury might hold that the man believed that the woman was consenting to intercourse, specific directions on mens rea, including direction about actual, honest belief, will be required."[119]

Thus far, it does not appear that these decisions concerned with **8–53** the law of rape portend a new trend. The Appeal Court has hinted that they may not lay down a general principle applicable in contexts other than the law of rape.[120] For them to do so, of course, the observations of Lords Normand and Cooper in *Dewar v HM Advocate*[121] would have to fall by the wayside. One application of the approach in the rape decisions would be that it signifies that an erroneous belief in a claim of right need not be held on reasonable grounds in order to provide a defence. The issue is simply as to the presence or otherwise of the *mens rea* of theft.

Self-defence

The question arises whether it is logical to say that the accused's **8–54** belief need not be reasonable in cases of rape where consent is erroneously believed to exist, but must be in cases of self-defence

---

[117] *Quinn v HM Advocate*, 1990 S.C.C.R. 254, per Lord Justice-Clerk Ross at 263D.
[118] *Doris v HM Advocate*, 1996 S.L.T. 995, per Lord Justice-General Hope at 997G. See also *Robertson v HM Advocate*, 1998 S.C.C.R. 390 at 393E–G; *Blyth v HM Advocate*, 2005 S.C.C.R. 710, opinion of the court at 714B–F, para.10; *A v HM Advocate*, 2007 S.C.C.R. 85, opinion of the court at 89F–90B, paras 14–15; and *Wiles v HM Advocate*, 2007 S.C.C.R. 191.
[119] See *McKearney v HM Advocate*, 2004 S.C.C.R. 251, per Lord McCluskey at 265D, para.35; *cf.* Lord Justice-Clerk Gill at 254D–F, paras 11–12. See also *Cinci v HM Advocate*, 2004 S.C.C.R. 267.
[120] See *Jamieson v HM Advocate (No.1)*, 1994 J.C. 88, per Lord Justice-General Hope at 93D–E. Even within the context of rape, some doubt has been expressed; see the *Lord Advocate's Reference (No.1 of 2001)*, 2002 S.L.T. 466, per Lord Justice-General Cullen at 473G–H, paras 28–29, 476B, para.44.
[121] *Dewar v HM Advocate*, 1945 J.C. 5.

where a danger to life is erroneously believed to exist. A theoretical distinction can be drawn between an error as to a definitional element in a crime and an error as to a fresh issue, such as the necessity of self-defence. It appears that the courts would wish to maintain this distinction. This is the clear implication of the decision in *Jones v HM Advocate*.[122] On the question of a plea of self-defence founded on an error of fact, the opinions of Lord Justice-Clerk Ross and Lord Wylie both included a requirement that the danger to life should be "reasonably apprehended."[123] There is no reference to *Meek*. In *Jamieson v HM Advocate*,[124] the Appeal Court expressly stated, in reaffirming *Meek*, that it should not be taken "as casting any doubt on the soundness of the *dicta*" in *Owens v HM Advocate*[125] and *Crawford v HM Advocate*.[126] The court did not suggest, "that in any other case, where a substantive defence is based on a belief which is mistaken, there need not be reasonable grounds for that belief."[127]

8–55   In *Drury v HM Advocate*,[128] a decision concerned with provocation, a full bench restated the *mens rea* of murder in terms either of a wicked intention to kill or wicked recklessness. In relation to intention, "wickedness" refers to the absence of an excuse or justification, such as provocation or self-defence. Lord Justice-General Rodger explained that,

> "the person who kills under provocation is to be convicted of culpable homicide rather than of murder because, even if he intentionally kills his victim, he does not have the wicked intention which is required for murder."[129]

The same analysis is applied to self-defence.[130] This seems to raise an issue in relation to error in self-defence. *Drury* suggests that the "wicked intention" in murder excludes actions taken in self-defence. This must also apply to erroneous self-defence. It has been argued that this may have implications for the reasonableness requirement, which could be seen as inconsistent with the *Drury* approach of self-defence affecting directly the "wicked" nature of the intention.[131] If an accused honestly believes himself to be acting

---

[122] *Jones v HM Advocate*, 1990 J.C. 160.
[123] *Jones v HM Advocate*, 1990 J.C. 160 at 172, 174.
[124] *Jamieson v HM Advocate (No.1)*, 1994 J.C. 88 at 93D–E.
[125] *Owens v HM Advocate*, 1946 J.C. 119.
[126] *Crawford v HM Advocate*, 1950 J.C. 67.
[127] *Jamieson v HM Advocate (No.1)*, 1994 J.C. 88 at 93D–E.
[128] *Drury v HM Advocate*, 2001 S.L.T. 1013.
[129] *Drury v HM Advocate*, 2001 S.L.T. 1013 at 1019I–J, para.20.
[130] *Drury v HM Advocate*, 2001 S.L.T. 1013 at 1016I–J, para.16. See also Lord Johnston at 1029F, para.18, and Lord Nimmo Smith at 1030I, para.2.
[131] See James Chalmers, "Collapsing the Structure of Criminal Law," 2001 S.L.T. (News) 241; Fiona Leverick, "Mistake in Self-Defence after Drury," 2002 J.R. 35.

in self-defence, his intention could hardly be described as "wicked". There is, however, no suggestion in *Drury* that the court wished to overturn the established authorities, which impose a "reasonableness" requirement in respect of erroneous self-defence. What may be envisaged is that, in order to negate "wickedness", an error must meet a minimum standard of reasonableness. If an error is quite unreasonable, it cannot counter the "wicked" character of the accused's intention.[132] This interpretation reconciles *Drury* with the traditionally objective approach to issues of *mens rea* employed by the Scottish courts. Admittedly, the effect of *Drury* is far from a simplifying one. There is much to be said for an analysis which separates the operation of defences from the definition of crimes. This was the method adopted in *Jamieson v HM Advocate*,[133] where the court distinguished those errors which affect *mens rea* from those which affect "substantive defences". It is also the approach taken in the post-*Drury* case of the *Lord Advocate's Reference (No.1 of 2000)*,[134] where it was stressed that the defence of necessity could have no effect upon the *mens rea* of malicious mischief, and the requirement of a reasonable belief in the necessitous circumstances was confirmed.

One final point is that, even if it were thought desirable to admit **8-56** of honest, but unreasonable, errors in self-defence, it would not be possible to concede to an accused the privilege of using an unreasonable degree of force in self-defence. That is, even if the accused's unreasonable belief in the necessity for self-defence were thought not to affect the availability of the special defence, it would be excessively subjectivist to say that an accused could be allowed to judge for himself what amounted to a reasonable degree of force in those imagined circumstances. A standard of reasonableness would have to be maintained in this regard at least.

Reliance on erroneous advice

Where a person in fact commits an offence, this may arise **8-57** because she relied on the erroneous advice of another. Does she, therefore, have a defence based on this type of error? If that advice came from a source on whom, or in which, it would have been reasonable to rely, it would seem harsh indeed to hold her criminally liable for the offence: surely there is a strong case to be made out for an acquittal in such circumstances? The fault, if any, will lie with the person tendering the advice. But if there is a defence of "reliance on erroneous advice" in Scots criminal law, it rests on two cases which are somewhat special, in that both were

---

[132] *Drury* does not hold that anything which the accused thinks provocative will meet the legal standard. The law lays down requirements which must be satisfied before the defence is available.

[133] *Jamieson v HM Advocate (No.1)*, 1994 J.C. 88.

[134] *Lord Advocate's Reference (No.1 of 2000)*, 2001 J.C. 143.

concerned with statutory offences. The first of these is *Roberts v The Local Authority of Burgh of Inverness*.[135] There, it was an offence under s.61 of the Contagious Diseases (Animals) Act 1878[136] to do anything, without lawful authority or excuse, in contravention of (inter alia) relevant regulations of a local authority. Under such regulations, it was permitted to move a "milch" cow from the County of Inverness to the Burgh of Inverness provided that a particular declaration and licence accompanied the beast. Roberts was accordingly charged as being a person who had moved such a cow without declaration or licence. He had, however, applied for the appropriate documents to the only person who could grant them; and that person had told Roberts that they were no longer required. This information was erroneous; but it was information on which Roberts relied. At his appeal against conviction, the question at issue was whether, in the circumstances, he had had "lawful excuse". Lord Justice-Clerk Macdonald held that he had, opining[137]:

> "It is monstrous to suppose that a man who acts on the advice of the authorised servant of the Local Authority, who declines to give him a certificate because it is unnecessary, is to be found guilty of an offence . . .".[138]

8–58   The other, more modern, case is that of *Dyer v Gallacher*.[139] Here the accused was charged with having in his possession, with a view to their sale, a collection of hats and scarves which apparently bore the registered trade marks of Rangers Football Club, Plc—all contrary to s.92(1)(c) of the Trade Marks Act 1994. There was a defence to such an offence if the accused showed on reasonable grounds that he believed that no infringement of the trade marks in question had been involved.[140] After trial, the sheriff acquitted the accused for reasons which the Appeal Court eventually rejected: this meant that a conviction would have to be substituted for the original verdict, unless the statutory defence could be made out. The court held that the respondent (the Crown having brought the appeal), although wrong in his view of the law, had had reasonable grounds for his erroneous belief: it seems that he had been acquitted on similar charges on a previous occasion, and that the head of the appropriate department entrusted with enforcement of the legislation had publicly described the state of the law

---

[135] *Roberts v The Local Authority of Burgh of Inverness* (1889) 2 White 385.
[136] This Act was repealed (for Scotland) in 1914.
[137] *Roberts v The Local Authority of Burgh of Inverness* (1889) 2 White 385 at 392.
[138] It may be significant that the Lord Justice-Clerk also emphasised that both parties—the appellant and his adviser—had been in good faith: *Roberts v The Local Authority of Burgh of Inverness* (1889) 2 White 385 at 391.
[139] *Dyer v Gallacher*, 2007 S.C.C.R. 152.
[140] See s.92(5) of the Trade Marks Act 1994.

as "muddied". The respondent thus fell to have his acquittal sustained.[141] It will be appreciated that the cases outlined in this, and the immediately preceding, paragraph are hardly conclusive as to the existence of any general defence of "reliance on erroneous advice".[142]

INTOXICATION

The ensuing discussion is concerned with examining whether, and **8–59** in what circumstances, an accused can avoid the imposition of criminal liability for his wrongdoing as a result of his intoxication from either drink or drugs. The law relating to intoxication can be divided into two general categories: voluntary and involuntary. Different considerations apply according to which classification of intoxication is under discussion.

Voluntary intoxication

Intoxication can be said to be voluntary where the accused is **8–60** blameworthy in becoming intoxicated. This fault element will exist where he has voluntarily consumed a substance, which he either knew, or should have known, would cause him to become intoxicated. (An exception to this rule is necessary for the circumstance where the intoxicant has been medically prescribed, or is taken for a medicinal purpose.)[143] The general rule is that voluntary intoxication is not an excuse for a criminal act. As Hume describes,[144] if Scots law,

> "does not consider the man's intemperance as an aggravation, [it] at least sees very good reasons why it should not be allowed as an excuse, to save him from the ordinary pains of his transgression."

The rationale underlying this approach is one of public policy: it arises from recognition of the potential for harm which can follow from the ingestion of alcohol or drugs.[145] A further policy consideration is that alcohol is a factor in the commission of many crimes. The implications of accepting voluntary intoxication would be open-ended.[146]

---

[141] The following passage from the Appeal Court's opinion (2007 S.C.C.R. 152 at 158D, para.18) is perhaps worthy of note: "The sheriff . . . accepted that reasonable ground for belief could not be founded on error of law. Even if that is correct (as to which we reserve our opinion), it does not preclude the section 92(5) defence in the present case . . .".

[142] For general discussion of this matter, see Chalmers and Leverick, *Criminal Defences and Pleas in Bar of Trial*, paras 13–25 to 13–36.

[143] See *Ebsworth v HM Advocate*, 1992 S.C.C.R. 671, per Lord Justice-General Hope at 680B–D.

[144] Hume, *Commentaries*, i, 45.

[145] See *DPP v Majewski* [1977] A.C. 443, per Lord Elwyn-Jones at 469F.

[146] See Alison, *Principles*, i, 661.

Voluntary intoxication and mens rea

8–61   There have been attempts in the past to raise a defence based upon the argument that intoxication can negative the mental element in crime. The contention has been that an accused's mind can be so affected by alcohol or drugs that he is incapable of forming the requisite *mens rea*. Scots law does not recognise any such defence, "where the absence or apparent absence of *mens rea* is attributable to self-induced intoxication, that cannot produce any kind of defence."[147] As exemplified by the decision in *Brennan v HM Advocate*,[148] the High Court takes the view that a voluntarily intoxicated accused is responsible for the consequences of his actions. He can be held responsible for anything that happens while he is intoxicated. The potential consequences of becoming intoxicated are widely known; an accused can be blamed for taking the risks which everyone knows to be involved in becoming intoxicated.

8–62   In *Brennan* the court was facilitated in adopting this approach by the fact it was a crime of recklessness which was at issue. Murder need not be committed intentionally; wicked recklessness suffices. Even if intoxication could negative the presence of an intention to kill, it was of no avail unless it could also negative wicked recklessness. The crucial question in *Brennan* was whether his conduct displayed wicked recklessness. The court's view was that voluntary intoxication was sufficiently reckless in itself:

> "[I]t is extremely difficult to understand how actings may lose the quality of . . . recklessness because the actor was in an intoxicated state brought about by his own deliberate and conscious purpose."[149]

8–63   Did Brennan know what he was doing? He had ingested between 20 and 25 pints of beer, a glass of sherry and a quantity of LSD. His claim that he did not know what he was doing when he stabbed his father to death is not implausible. It is possible to become so intoxicated as to lose appreciation of what one is doing. But this is somewhat beside the point in a crime which can be committed recklessly. The act of getting intoxicated is culpable in itself. As *Brennan* indicates, if the crime is one of recklessness the accused's attempt to use intoxication as an excuse to negative his *mens rea* will necessarily fail.[150]

---

147 *Donaldson v Normand*, 1997 S.L.T. 1303 at 1304J. For the differing ways in which voluntary intoxication is treated in other jurisdictions, see Chalmers and Leverick, *Criminal Defences and Pleas in Bar of Trial*, paras 8–14 and 8–15. Although Scots law adopts a robust approach, it would not be alone in refusing to admit evidence of intoxication as a defence to any crime. See M. Keiter, "Just Say No Excuse: The Rise and Fall of the Intoxication Defense" (1997) 87 *J. Crim. L. & Criminology* 482 (describing developments in the United States).

148 *Brennan v HM Advocate*, 1977 J.C. 38.

149 *Brennan v HM Advocate*, 1977 J.C. 38 at 50.

150 See, for example, *Donaldson v Normand*, 1997 S.L.T. 1303, where the *Brennan* doctrine is applied to the crime of culpable and reckless conduct.

The extent of the no-excuse rule

The issue remains whether the rule that voluntary intoxication **8–64** does not negative *mens rea* applies to all crimes, or only to those which can be committed recklessly. There are some crimes, including assault and theft, which can only be committed intentionally. Does this mean that it is a defence for the accused to show that he was so drunk as to be unable to form the requisite intention to assault or steal? It seems not. The no-excuse rule appears to apply to all crimes, irrespective of the particular *mens rea* required by any definition of the crime. In *Brennan*, the court took a robust view of the purported excuse of intoxication, concluding:

> "There is nothing unethical or unfair or contrary to the general principle of our law that self-induced intoxication is not by itself a defence to any criminal charge, including in particular the charge of murder."[151]

This approach was re-affirmed in *Ross v HM Advocate*.[152] Lord Justice-General Hope explained that, "where the condition which has resulted in an absence of *mens rea* is self induced . . . the accused must be assumed to have intended the natural consequences of his act."[153] This "exception" to the normal rule of criminal responsibility requiring *mens rea* is justified on "grounds of public policy."[154]

A possible conceptual difficulty with this no-excuse rule is that it **8–65** equates the wrongful act of becoming intoxicated with the degree of culpability required by the definition of the crime. In *Brennan*[155] voluntary intoxication was equated with wicked recklessness. Getting intoxicated may be reckless, but is it "wickedly" so? The problem becomes more acute in crimes with a special degree of intention, such as theft. When the courts insist upon a particular *mens rea* in the definition of a common law crime, they do so because it is that particular mental element which renders the accused more blameworthy than when that element is absent. A refusal to regard as relevant any claim that the accused lacked the requisite *mens rea* might be seen as defeating the purpose of including the specific mental element in the definition of the crime.

A plea in mitigation?

It is clear that voluntary intoxication is not a defence to a **8–66** criminal charge. It is not uncommon, however, for it to be led by way of a plea in mitigation, particularly in cases of minor breaches

---

[151] *Brennan v HM Advocate*, 1977 J.C. 38 at 51.
[152] *Ross v HM Advocate*, 1991 J.C. 210.
[153] *Ross v HM Advocate*, 1991 J.C. 210 at 214.
[154] *Ross v HM Advocate*, 1991 J.C. 210 at 214.
[155] *Brennan v HM Advocate*, 1977 J.C. 38.

of the peace and similar offences. Hume himself observes[156] that intoxication might be used in mitigation of sentence in relation to crimes,

> "which are neither attended with any profit to the delinquent, nor any necessary or immediate damage to one's neighbour, or to society; and which are chiefly reputed criminal, on account of the violation of order and decency, and the possible evil influence on the minds of others."

If A has been shouting and bawling in the street in a way which would otherwise satisfy the definition of breach of the peace, intoxication offers at least some explanation as to his conduct. It may allay the fear that he is a dangerous individual, rather than simply an annoying drunk. (This is not to suggest, of course, that drunks cannot sometimes be dangerous; the line between drunkenness as an explanatory or mitigating factor and as an aggravating factor is a fine one.)

Insanity

8–67   The law does not recognise a defence of (temporary) insanity resulting from the voluntary ingestion of alcohol or drugs. In *HM Advocate v McDonald*,[157] Lord Justice-Clerk Macdonald pointed out that, although,

> "we talk of a man being mad with drink because at the time when he has got . . . drink in him he acts like a madman . . . he is not in these circumstances a madman recognised by the law as irresponsible for his actions."

In *Brennan* it was stressed that the transitory effects of the alcohol and LSD were not sufficient in law to amount to insanity. (This has also been held for diminished responsibility.)[158] Even if the accused's mental faculties had been substantially impaired, that could not amount to insanity and he had to be regarded as legally responsible for his actions. Similarly, in *Finegan v Heywood*,[159] it was held that the defence of automatism (parasomnia, in this instance) could not be established where it "was the result of, and indeed induced by, deliberate and self-induced intoxication."

"Real" insanity

8–68   In *McDonald*, Lord Justice-Clerk Macdonald drew a distinction between an isolated act of drinking, which might cause an individual to act like a "madman", and the prolonged imbibing of excessive drink which had caused actual brain disease. He regarded

---

[156] Hume, *Commentaries*, i, 46.
[157] *HM Advocate v McDonald* (1890) 2 White 517 at 519.
[158] See *Galbraith v HM Advocate (No.2)*, 2002 J.C. 1 at 21G.
[159] *Finegan v Heywood*, 2000 S.L.T. 905 at 908H.

the latter as exculpatory. He spoke of a defence of insanity caused by alcohol as applying when a "man's reason is overthrown, either permanently or for a course of time." In such a case the accused does not know "the 'quality of what he is doing', and he is not responsible."[160]

As Lord Justice-Clerk Macdonald realised, habitual and exces-   **8–69** sive indulgence in alcohol or drugs can result in permanent brain damage and a mental disorder sufficient to amount to insanity. (In *Brennan* there was no evidence of brain damage.) Insanity caused by alcohol or drugs is not regarded as different to any other kind of insanity. In the case of *Alexander Milne*, Lord Justice-Clerk Inglis observed[161]:

> "[I]f the mind is diseased . . . then that is insanity, which will take away criminal responsibility. If there be such insanity, it matters not . . . what was the exciting cause of that insanity. It may be drunkenness . . . it is of no consequence [what] it is, if insanity is actually produced and is present at the time."

Thus a mental disorder caused by the long-term use of intoxicants is not inconsistent with an insanity defence. If the accused does meet the requirements of the insanity defence, he is entitled to an acquittal upon that basis.

Involuntary intoxication

Intoxication might be said to be involuntary where the alcohol or   **8–70** drug has been consumed as the result of an honest error, or another person has used fraud or coercion to cause the accused to consume it (see above, paras 4–16 and 4–25). In *McGregor v HM Advocate*[162] Lord Keith's charge to the jury suggested that involuntary intoxication could result in incapacity to form the *mens rea* and could therefore be a defence. He drew an analogy between involuntary intoxication and somnambulism. On appeal, however, the view was expressed that this direction had been too favourable to the accused. In *HM Advocate v Raiker*[163] Lord McCluskey suggested that an accused would lack, "the criminal state of mind that is a necessary ingredient of any crime" where he had acted, "wholly and completely under the influence of some drug which was administered by force or by stealth without his consent." This view would appear to be correct, but for coerced intoxication to afford a defence it would be necessary to show that the acts were the product of the involuntary intoxication and that, "it was a drug which like hypnosis put his will as it were under the control of another."[164]

---

[160] *HM Advocate v McDonald*, (1890) 2 White 517 at 521.
[161] *Alexander Milne* (1863) 4 Irv. 301 at 344.
[162] *McGregor v HM Advocate* (1973) S.C.C.R. Supp. 54.
[163] *HM Advocate v Raiker*, 1989 S.C.C.R. 149 at 154B–C.
[164] *HM Advocate v Raiker*, 1989 S.C.C.R. 149 at 154B–C.

8–71   Following the decision in *Ross v HM Advocate*,[165] it is clear that involuntary intoxication can operate as a defence where it constitutes non-insane automatism (see above, paras 4–19 *et seq.*). The preconditions for the availability of the defence, as described by Lord Justice-General Hope,[166] are,

> "that the external factor [the intoxication] . . . must not be self-induced, that it must be one which the accused was not bound to foresee and that it must be one which resulted in a total loss of control of his actions in regard to the crime with which he is charged."

In *Sorley v HM Advocate*[167] it was stressed that there are strict limits to the availability of the defence. There is a requirement of clear evidence of the accused's state of mind and also of the "causative link" between the involuntarily consumed intoxicant and his behaviour.[168] The presence of self-induction will be fatal to any claim of involuntariness.[169]

COERCION

The character of the defence

8–72   To establish the defence of coercion in relation to a serious crime, an accused must show that he violated the criminal law in order to avoid imminent death or serious injury at the hands of a coercer.[170] A classic example for an application of the defence would be the motorist who is forced at gunpoint to transport an armed robber away from the scene of the crime. He is subsequently charged with being art and part of the robbery. In a situation such as this, the doctrine of coercion recognises that for the driver to violate the law is less serious than to adhere to the letter of the law, thereby risking death or serious injury.

8–73   If the accused has been coerced into committing a crime, he avoids the harm which has been threatened to him, but does so at the expense of contravening the law and possibly injuring an innocent third party. Unlike the person who has acted in justifiable self-defence, he does not promote a value supported by the law.

---

[165] *Ross v HM Advocate*, 1991 J.C. 210.
[166] *Ross v HM Advocate*, 1991 J.C. 210 at 222.
[167] *Sorley v HM Advocate*, 1992 J.C. 102.
[168] *Sorley v HM Advocate*, 1992 J.C. 102, per Lord Justice-General Hope at 107; see also *Ebsworth v HM Advocate*, 1992 S.L.T. 1161; *MacLeod v Napier*, 1993 S.C.C.R. 303.
[169] See *Finegan v Heywood*, 2000 S.L.T. 905.
[170] See, generally, *Moss v Howdle*, 1997 J.C. 123; *Cochrane v HM Advocate*, 2001 S.C.C.R. 655.

The common law imposes strict limits upon the availability of coercion as a defence. In *HM Advocate v McCallum*[171] Lord Allanbridge pointed out to the jury:

> "When you come to consider this defence [coercion], I think it is right—as I am sure you will appreciate—that it would make life very easy for criminals and very difficult for law enforcement if, whenever a criminal was actually caught, he could turn round and say, 'I admit I committed the crime but I was coerced into doing it by someone else.' That being so, any such defence must be very carefully considered indeed."

The rationale of the defence

The basis of the defence of coercion in Scots law is that **8–74** identified by Lord Hunter in *Thomson v HM Advocate*,[172] where he said,

> "that the will and the resolution of the accused must have been overborne by threats which he believed would be carried out so that he was not at the material time acting of his own free will."

Similarly, in *HM Advocate v Docherty*,[173] Lord Keith told the jury that, "[t]he essence of the matter is that the will of the accused should be overborne by threats which he believed would be carried out." Statements such as these can be misleading. A coerced individual retains free will in the sense that he can choose how to conduct himself. If he decides to break the criminal law in order to avoid death or serious injury, then he makes a choice. The law's emphasis on this purported lack of free will is more a reflection of the fact that the accused's opportunity to exercise his capacity to choose will have been substantially undermined by the coercer's threats. The reason for not imposing criminal liability on the coercee is the recognition that it is unfair to punish the blameless person whose only choice was the morally unacceptable one between self-sacrifice and breaking the law.

Coercion and mens rea

It is sometimes suggested that a coerced accused should be **8–75** found not guilty on the basis that he lacked *mens rea* at the time of committing the crime. An observation to this effect can be found in Lord McCluskey's charge to the jury in *HM Advocate v Raiker*,[174]

---

[171] *HM Advocate v McCallum* (1977) S.C.C.R. Supp. 169.
[172] *Thomson v HM Advocate*, 1983 J.C. 69 at 74.
[173] *HM Advocate v Docherty* (1976) S.C.C.R. Supp. 146.
[174] *HM Advocate v Raiker*, 1989 S.C.C.R. 149 at 154B.

where it is suggested that a person who acts under coercion, "lacks the criminal state of mind that is a necessary ingredient of any crime." This view of the effect of coercion can be questioned.[175] If B threatens A that he (A) will be killed unless he assaults C, A has the requisite intent for the crime of assault against C when he hits him. A may be excused for having *mens rea* because he was coerced, but the intention to assault is present. If A does not have the requisite *mens rea*, he is not guilty of assault, irrespective of whether he was subjected to coercion. Conversely, even if A does possess the requisite *mens rea*, his conduct can be excused by operation of the defence of coercion.[176]

The rules of coercion

8–76   The rules governing the availability of the defence of coercion are still largely those outlined by Hume.[177] He identifies four "qualifications": (1) "an immediate danger of death or great bodily harm"; (2) "an inability to resist the violence"; (3) "a backward and an inferior part in the perpetration"; and (4) "a disclosure of the fact, as well as restitution of the spoil, on the first safe and convenient occasion." According to the decision of the High Court in *Thomson v HM Advocate*,[178] it appears that the first two remain preconditions for the availability of the defence, but that the extent of participation in the crime and/or restoration of the spoils go only to the credibility of the accused's plea. As regards the nature of the coercer's threat, it is thought that something less than one of death or serious injury would be insisted upon by a court where the crime committed by the coercee was not a particularly serious one: the rule laid down in *Thomson* should be read in the context of a case of armed robbery.

Threats of present and future violence

8–77   In his initial opinion in *Thomson*, Lord Hunter states that, "all the Scottish authorities are based on the principle that a defence of coercion, in order to be successful, requires that the danger must be immediate."[179] This requirement that the threat be imminent will be familiar from the discussion of self-defence (see above, para.8–20). It was explained in the following terms by Lord Justice-Clerk Wheatley in the same case[180]:

---

[175] *Lord Advocate's Reference (No.1 of 2000)*, 2001 J.C. 143, held that the closely related defence of necessity could have no impact upon *mens rea*.
[176] For a useful discussion of the relationship between coercion and *mens rea*, see the Canadian case of *Hibbert v The Queen* (1995) 99 C.C.C.3d 193.
[177] Hume, *Commentaries*, i, 53.
[178] *Thomson v HM Advocate*, 1983 J.C. 69.
[179] *Thomson v HM Advocate*, 1983 J.C. 69 at 74.
[180] *Thomson v HM Advocate*, 1983 J.C. 69 at 77.

"[I]t is only where, following threats, there is an immediate danger of violence, in whatever form it takes, that the defence of coercion can be entertained, and even then only if there is an inability to resist or avoid that immediate danger."

One question which arises is whether the defence can ever be **8–78** founded on present threats of future harm. In general terms the answer has to be in the negative, because of the immediacy requirement. In Lord Wheatley's terms, there must be an "immediate danger of the threat being implemented in the event of non-compliance at the point of time when the decision had to be made."[181] Lord Allanbridge charged the jury in *HM Advocate v McCallum*[182]:

"It is one thing to force a man to commit a crime by actually holding a pistol to his head . . . —that is an immediate threat. It is another thing to threaten a man that if he does not commit a crime he . . . can be killed or injured in the future—that is a future threat. . . . [W]hen you are considering in law the question of the defence of coercion it is to immediate and not to future threats that you look."

The reason for discounting threats pertaining to the future is that the individual threatened is expected to seek the protection of the police.[183] In *Thomson*, however, Lord Wheatley does concede that,

"even in the ordinary condition of a well-regulated society there may be circumstances where a person is exposed to a threat of violence . . . from which he cannot be protected by the forces of law and order and which he is not in a position to resist."[184]

Lord Wheatley appears to be suggesting that there could be an exceptional case where threats of future danger could be admitted as evidence of coercion, if recourse to the police would be ineffective. His Lordship goes on to say that:

"If such a situation arose it would have to be determined on its facts, and no profit can be gained from an exercise in hypothetical cases."[185]

Objective standard

The law applies an objective test when considering the impact of **8–79** the threats upon the coercee. Only limited account is taken of the personal characteristics of the accused, even though these may

---

[181] *Thomson v HM Advocate*, 1983 J.C. 69 at 80.
[182] *HM Advocate v McCallum* (1977) S.C.C.R. Supp. 169.
[183] See *Trotter v HM Advocate*, 2001 S.L.T. 296.
[184] *Thomson v HM Advocate*, 1983 J.C. 69 at 78.
[185] *Thomson v HM Advocate*, 1983 J.C. 69 at 78.

have affected the way in which the accused reacted to the threats made to him. As stated in *Cochrane v HM Advocate*,[186] the jury is required to, "consider whether an ordinary sober person of reasonable firmness, sharing the characteristics of the accused, would have responded as the accused did." If the accused does not possess, "reasonable firmness", the jury must disregard this fact, and take account only of his other characteristics.[187] Thus, in *Cochrane*, no account could be taken of the fact that the appellant was unusually compliant (in the top 10 per cent of the population, according to expert evidence). Lord Justice-General Rodger explained that the logic of the objective test requires the jury to disregard the fact that the accused is more susceptible to threats than the norm, unless some kind of recognised psychiatric condition is involved. This is a hard rule, but is explicable in terms of the law's caution in admitting coercion as a defence. The intention is to keep the operation of the defence within strict limits.[188]

A defence to murder?

8-80   In his charge to the jury in *Collins v HM Advocate*,[189] Lord Allanbridge stated that "as a matter of law coercion is not a defence in Scotland to the crime of murder". His explanation was:

> "It is because of the supreme importance that the law affords to the protection of human life. It is repugnant that the law should recognise in any individual in any circumstances however extreme the right to choose that one innocent person should be killed rather than any other person including himself."

It should not be thought, of course, that the unavailability of the defence of coercion is likely to act as a deterrent to an individual who has to choose between death and killing an innocent. Kant made the point that the possibility of subsequent punishment could not overcome the certainty of being killed.[190]

NECESSITY

8-81   To the extent that Scots law recognises a defence of necessity, it is a limited and residual one. It exculpates conduct contrary to the criminal law that the dictates of common sense and moral fairness

---

[186] *Cochrane v HM Advocate*, 2001 S.C.C.R. 655, per Lord Justice-General Rodger at 670F–G, para.29; see also 667C–G, paras 21–22. (There are parallels with the law of provocation, described in Ch.9.)

[187] *Cochrane v HM Advocate*, 2001 S.C.C.R. 655 at 671A, para.29.

[188] *Cochrane v HM Advocate*, 2001 S.C.C.R. 655 at 666E–F, para.20.

[189] *Collins v HM Advocate*, 1991 S.C.C.R. 898 at 902C. See to like effect *HM Advocate v Peters* (1969) 33 J.C.L. 209. For a detailed discussion of this issue, see Chalmers and Leverick, *Criminal Defences and Pleas in Bar of Trial*, paras 5–27 to 5–31.

[190] Kant, *The Philosophy of Law*, p.53. The point is made of necessity, but is applicable to coercion.

suggest is excusable or justifiable, but which does not fall within the categories of a traditionally recognised defence (for example, self-defence or coercion). Necessity has long been problematic, partly due to Hume's evident disapproval of the plea,[191] and because of a lack of direct High Court authority. Hume appears to reject necessity even as a mitigating factor. In the case of stealing food because of hunger, for instance, he rejects a defence of, "compulsion by want".[192] Hume notes the difficulty of distinguishing genuine cases from those of, "pretended necessity". He fears that everyone could become the judge of, "his own wants and distresses". Nevertheless, the High Court in modern times had not been prepared to say that a defence of necessity did not exist, despite having had opportunities so to do.[193] It is only recently, however, that the High Court has acknowledged formally that there is a defence of necessity, if in a limited way.[194] The particular form of necessity which has been recognised as a defence is coercion by force of circumstances.[195] The theoretical basis of the defence is that coercion itself is but a, "species of the genus necessity".[196] It is founded upon the notion that,

> "there is so pressing a need for action that the actor has no alternative but to do what would otherwise be a criminal act under the compulsion of the circumstances in which he finds himself."[197]

This coercion or compulsion must dominate the mind of the accused at the time of the otherwise criminal act; there must be a causal relationship. If the accused has not made a choice between saving life and limb or contravening the criminal law, and has acted without thinking, the defence will not be available.[198]

The facts of *Moss v Howdle*[199] appear exemplary for an examination of necessity as a defence. The appellant had been convicted of a speeding offence on a motorway. He had been driving, when his passenger suddenly shouted out in pain. Thinking that the passenger was severely ill, the appellant had driven at high speed to **8–82**

[191] Hume, *Commentaries*, i, 55; see also Alison, *Principles*, i, 675.
[192] Hume, *Commentaries*, i, 55.
[193] See, e.g. *Morrison v Valentine*, 1991 S.L.T. 413; *McLeod v MacDougall*, 1989 S.L.T. 151.
[194] See *Moss v Howdle*, 1997 J.C. 123 (where the opinion of the court emphasises the coercive character of the defence); *Lord Advocate's Reference (No.1 of 2000)*, 2001 J.C. 143 (where the term necessity is used).
[195] It is evident that the development in English law of a defence of duress of circumstances has had some influence upon the Scottish courts. For discussion of the English case law, see Simester and Sullivan, *Criminal Law: Theory and Doctrine*, 2nd edn, pp.597–599, and Chalmers and Leverick, *Criminal Defences and Pleas in Bar of Trial*, para.4–07.
[196] *R. v Howe* [1987] A.C. 417, per Lord Hailsham at 429C–D; adopted in *Moss v Howdle*, 1997 J.C. 123 at 127H–128B.
[197] *Lord Advocate's Reference (No.1 of 2000)*, 2001 J.C. 143 at 157G, para.39.
[198] See *Dawson v McKay*, 1999 S.L.T. 1328 at 1332B–G.
[199] *Moss v Howdle*, 1997 J.C. 123. For analysis of this decision, see M.G.A. Christie, "The Mother of Invention? Moss v Howdle" (1997) *Edin. L.R.* 479.

the nearest service station. In fact, the passenger was merely suffering from cramp, but it was accepted that the accused had reasonably believed him to be seriously ill. The first matter to be considered is whether there is any general defence applicable to circumstances such as these. The Appeal Court accepted that there was, drawing the parallel with coercion. The latter defence is available where the accused has committed a crime in order to escape from a threat of death or serious injury made by a third party. The court could,

> "see no reason why it should be excluded simply because the immediate threat of death or great bodily harm which the accused is trying to evade arises . . . from illness, rather than from the actings of a third party."[200]

The defence recognised by the court is one of necessity, in the form of coercion by the circumstances in which the accused finds himself. It is clear that the defence can be based upon a medical emergency.[201] Other relevant circumstances could include natural disasters and the actions of third parties. The argument for the defence is at its strongest in a case such as *Moss v Howdle*, where the accused was not acting out of self-interest, but (as he thought) in order to secure the health of his passenger. Not all potential cases of necessity will be so suggestive of altruism. Reference can be made to the sheriff court decision in *Tudhope v Grubb*.[202] The accused was charged with an offence of attempting to drive with an excess of alcohol in his blood. He had attempted to drive in order to escape further injury after he had been assaulted by a number of men. The sheriff decided that in these circumstances a defence of necessity was available and the accused was acquitted.

8–83   There are a number of limitations to the availability of the defence of necessity. As summarised in the *Lord Advocate's Reference (No.1 of 2000)*,[203] these include: (i) "good cause to fear that death or serious injury would result unless he acted"; (ii) "that cause for fear must have resulted from a reasonable belief as to the circumstances"; (iii) "the actor must have been impelled to act as he did by those considerations"; and (iv) "the defence will only be available if a sober person of reasonable firmness, sharing the characteristics of the actor, would have responded as he did." These requirements are familiar from coercion.[204] As in that

---

[200] *Moss v Howdle*, 1997 J.C. 123 at 127H.
[201] *Moss v Howdle*, 1997 J.C. 123 at 128E–F.
[202] *Tudhope v Grubb*, 1983 S.C.C.R. 350 Sh. Ct.; apparently approved in *Moss v Howdle*, 1997 J.C. 123 at 127D–G.
[203] *Lord Advocate's Reference (No.1 of 2000)*, 2001 J.C. 143 at 158H–I, para.42.
[204] As in relation to coercion, it is most unlikely that necessity could ever afford a defence to a murder charge. See above, para.8–80; *R. v Dudley and Stephens* (1884) 14 Q.B.D. 273; *cf.* Chalmers and Leverick, *Criminal Defences and Pleas in Bar of Trial*, paras 4–23 to 431.

defence, the fundamental condition is an immediate danger to life or of serious injury.[205] The court observed in *Moss v Howdle*[206] that this "requirement is apt to delimit the scope of the defence and to keep it within narrow bounds." The requirement of immediacy is a significant one. If the danger is other than immediate, there will be time to take an alternative course of action. Thus, in the *Lord Advocate's Reference (No.1 of 2000)*,[207] there was no question of a defence of necessity being available to the respondent anti-nuclear protesters, who over several months had planned their activities, which included malicious mischief against naval property. Their actions were not committed as a response to any immediate perception of danger; there was no indication that the damage done by the protesters could have had any conceivable impact upon the supposed risk posed by nuclear weapons.[208]

It is fundamental that there be no alternative means of prevent- **8–84** ing the threatened harm. If there is a non-criminal course open, this must be taken. This is where the appellant in *Moss v Howdle*[209] fell short of qualifying for the defence. The Appeal Court adopted the sheriff's finding, which was that the appellant had not asked his passenger what was wrong with him. The correct thing for the appellant to do would have been to stop at the side of the motorway, inquire what was wrong, and then decide upon an appropriate course of action. The appellant did have a choice about what to do. The Appeal Court concluded[210]:

> "Since the sheriff has found that the appellant could have prudently followed an alternative course of action which would not have involved committing the offence in question or any offence at all, we too must proceed on the basis that he had a real choice and was not constrained to commit the offence. That being so, the defence of coercion . . . is not available to him."

---

[205] *McNab v Guild*, 1989 S.C.C.R. 138 at 141D–142A; *Moss v Howdle*, 1997 J.C. 123 at 126E.

[206] *Moss v Howdle*, 1997 J.C. 123.

[207] *Lord Advocate's Reference (No.1 of 2000)*, 2001 J.C. 143.

[208] *Lord Advocate's Reference (No.1 of 2000)*, 2001 J.C. 143 at 178H–179D, para.100.

[209] *Moss v Howdle*, 1997 J.C. 123.

[210] *Moss v Howdle*, 1997 J.C. 123 at 130E–F. See also *Ruxton v Lang*, 1998 S.C.C.R. 1, which suggests that even where there is no alternative to a course of action which contravenes the criminal law, this must be brought to an end as soon as the relevant coercive circumstances have ceased.

CHAPTER 9

CRIMES AGAINST THE PERSON

Introduction

9–01 The crimes considered in this chapter all deal with readily identifiable harms caused to particular victims. They all thus fall within John Stuart Mill's "harm principle" (see above, para.1–07), and require no further justification. "Harm" here means physical injury (including death) as well as the fear and alarm caused by the threat of such injury.

1. ABDUCTION

9–02 Hume[1] discusses abduction under the description: "Of forcible abduction and marriage." This suggests that the crime might be rather limited both as to victim and purpose; but this is not the modern approach. A charge of abduction of a child of six has been received without objection,[2] as has such a charge relating to an adult male.[3] Burnett's remark would, therefore, seem to have been accepted, namely:

> "When the abduction is neither with a view to marriage, nor rape, it is punishable *tanquam* [sic] *crimen in suo genere* [i.e. as a crime in its own right] as an unjust oppression, and restraint."[4]

It is thus thought that Sheriff Mitchell correctly stated the law when he said,

---

[1] Hume, *Commentaries*, i, 310.
[2] *M v HM Advocate* (1980) S.C.C.R. Supp. 250. See also the first charge in *Anderson v HM Advocate*, 2001 S.C.C.R. 738 (abduction of nine year old boy).
[3] *Elliot v Tudhope*, 1987 S.C.C.R. 85. For a modern example of a charge of abduction see *Bashir v HM Advocate*, 2006 S.C.C.R. 99.
[4] J. Burnett, *A Treatise on Various Branches of the Criminal Law of Scotland* (Edinburgh: printed by George Ramsay & Co for Archibald Constable & Co, 1811), 109.

"the essence of abduction [is] to carry off a person against his or her will without lawful authority. It humbly [seems] to me that abduction for any purpose is criminal. I refer to Macdonald and to the 5th edn, at p.124."[5]

Thus, a man wrongfully arrested by a police officer on a wholly spurious charge of breach of the peace was criminally abducted by that officer, according to the decision in *Elliot v Tudhope*, where it was also accepted by Sheriff Mitchell[6] that, "unlawful detention was a recognised crime at common law." It has been held, however, that a charge of abduction, which specified that a child below the age of puberty was confined, "against his will", required the Crown to show that the child was unwilling to go with his alleged abductor, and that such a charge could not be established solely on proof that the "carrying off" had been without "parental authority".[7] The *mens rea* element of abduction is uncertain, but probably amounts to intention to carry off (or, possibly, just detain) a person knowing that it is against that person's will; the causing of actual fear and alarm seems to be unnecessary here.[8]

2. ASSAULT

Introduction

The crime of assault covers a very wide spectrum of harmful or alarm-producing behaviour. As was said by Lord Justice-Clerk Hope in *Kennedy v Young*[9]: "The word assault is one of the most flexible terms." In Hume's time, however, it seems that "assault" was just one of a number of expressions used to denote criminal forms of "real injury." As he puts the matter[10]: **9–03**

---

[5] *Elliot v Tudhope*, 1987 S.C.C.R. 85 at 93.
[6] *Elliot v Tudhope*, 1987 S.C.C.R. 85 at 93.
[7] *Brouillard v HM Advocate*, 2004 J.C. 176, opinion of the court at 183–184, paras 22–23. The court observed in that case that where the victim was, e.g. too young to give a valid consent, then it had not been authoritatively settled whether, or under what circumstances, a charge of abduction could validly be brought; and that it had not been settled whether such a charge could be brought where a child was enticed or induced to go away with his alleged abductor (see 183, para.20, where reference is made to Alison's *Principles*, p.630—and to his statement that the latter was "a crime at common law" (under reference to the case of *Richard Smith*, July 16, 1829, where a teacher of elocution had enticed a girl of nine years to come with him to recite poetry to an audience; *cf. Margaret Macmillan or Branughan* (1839) Bell's Notes, 26)—and to Lord Kincraig's view, in *M v HM Advocate* (1980) S.C.C.R. Supp. 250 at 250, that evidence of a child's being led away or induced to follow "would be sufficient proof that she was taken away against her will"); *cf.* the crime of "Plagium", which is dealt with below at para.10–15.
[8] See *Brouillard v HM Advocate*, 2004 J.C. 176, opinion of the court at 181, para.15—the sheriff's view on this point being unchallenged.
[9] *Kennedy v Young* (1854) 1 Irv. 533 at 539.
[10] Hume, *Commentaries*, i, 327–328.

"the law is provided with sundry . . . terms . . . such as assault, invasion, beating and bruising, blooding and wounding, stabbing, mutilation, demembration, and some others. But although the injury do not come under any of those terms of style, nor be such as can be announced in a single phrase . . . [l]et the libel . . . give an intelligible account of it in terms at large; and, if it amount to a real injury, it shall be sustained to infer punishment . . .".

Despite its undoubted width, assault in modern Scots law is a more specific crime than the foregoing quotation would tend to imply, and, in particular, can be distinguished from other forms of "real injury."

DEFINITION OF ASSAULT

9–04 Until fairly recently, criminal courts in Scotland have tended to favour the account of assault given by Macdonald at pp.115–119.[11] The following working definition is, therefore, based on Macdonald's central concept of an "attack": thus, an assault is committed when one person makes an attack upon another with the intention of effecting the immediate bodily injury of that other person or producing the fear of immediate bodily injury in his mind. The details of this definition will be explained in the following paragraphs.

The actus reus: an attack

9–05 Use of the term "attack" may seem strange in view of the great variety of conduct which the common law has accepted as sufficient for assault (see below, paras 9–06 to 9–11). But it is submitted that the sense of an unjustified, hostile, direct approach to the victim, which the word carries, is apt to describe the vast majority of assault situations encountered in practice. Whilst it is true that spitting on someone has been described as an assault,[12] as has the cutting-off of a woman's hair whilst she was asleep,[13] and the forcible stopping of a man's horse,[14] and that arguably some of these situations may not amount to "attacks" in any usual sense of that term, it is also clear that the law's acceptance of them as criminal assaults is highly exceptional, if not remarkable. It is also

---

[11] See, e.g. *Smart v HM Advocate*, 1975 J.C. 30 at 33; *cf. Lord Advocate's Reference (No.2 of 1992)*, 1993 J.C. 43.

[12] *James Cairns* (1837) 1 Swin. 597, per Lord Justice-Clerk Boyle at 610.

[13] *Charles Sweenie* (1858) 3 Irv. 109, per Lord Cowan at 145. (It should be noted that the ratio of this case was overruled by a majority of the seven judges who sat in *Lord Advocate's Reference (No.1 of 2001)*, 2002 S.L.T. 466.) *cf. DPP v Smith* [2006] 1 W.L.R. 1571 (interpreting the words "actual bodily harm" in English legislation).

[14] *Kennedy v Young* (1854) 1 Irv. 533.

remarkable that a "verbal attack" on another seems not to amount to an assault. "[M]ere words cannot constitute an assault", says Macdonald at p.115; and this seems to be tacitly accepted. There is, however, no authority to vouch that rule, other than a passage in Alison[15] where that author appears to be expounding English rather than Scots law.

Attacks producing injury

　　Although Macdonald[16] emphasises that the conduct sufficient for **9–06** an assault need not injure the victim at all, bodily harm is very often the result of an attack. Such harm may be slight or serious. Examples of the former have included the marks produced by compressing the victim's arm[17] or seizing him by the throat in order to march him rapidly to a police interview-room,[18] or even the disfigurement effected by cutting off some of his hair.[19] But examples of trivial injuries are seldom included in the law reports, which tend to feature more serious matters. Thus, at the other end of the scale, are found the results of holding someone's head under water,[20] blocking the air supply to a critically-ill patient in intensive care,[21] and pouring petrol over someone whose clothing then caught fire.[22] It will be plain, therefore, that it matters not whether an injury is serious or utterly trivial, so long as it was produced by a deliberate attack upon the victim; and it will also be plain that it matters not whether the victim was conscious or not at the time of the attack made upon him. Thus, it made no difference at all that a man, who had part of his nose bitten off, had been insensible through drink at the time[23] or that a person had been asleep when paper was stuffed into his hand and ignited.[24]

Those entitled to use reasonable force

　　"It happens from time to time that charges of assault are **9–07** made against officials and others who are entitled, in virtue of their office, to exercise in certain circumstances physical force. I may cite as examples police officers, prison warders, asylum attendants, railway servants and ships' officers."[25]

---

[15] Alison, *Principles*, i, 176.
[16] Macdonald, *Criminal Law*, 5th edn, p.115.
[17] *Aitken v Wood*, 1921 J.C. 84.
[18] *Bonar v McLeod*, 1983 S.C.C.R. 161.
[19] See above, para.9–05.
[20] *Kepple v HM Advocate*, 1936 S.L.T. 294.
[21] *Atkins v London Weekend Television Ltd*, 1978 J.C. 48.
[22] *Williamson v HM Advocate*, 1984 S.L.T. 200.
[23] *Charles McEwan* (1824) in Hume, *Commentaries*, i, 331 fn.a.
[24] *Lachlan Brown* (1842) 1 Broun 230.
[25] *Brown v Hilson*, 1924 J.C. 1, per Lord Sands at 6. The list may now include stewards or "bouncers" whose responsibilities extend to the maintaining of order at events attended by large numbers of people—see, e.g. *HM Advocate v Harris*, 1993 J.C. 150.

This is undoubtedly true; but such persons will not be seen as carrying out attacks, provided the force they use is no more than is necessary, for example, to arrest a suspect.[26] They will thus escape conviction for assault since there is no hostile use of force, although it can also be said, of course, that they lack the necessary *mens rea* for the crime (see below, paras 9–12 to 9–16).[27] In a similar way, parents (or those *in loco parentis*)[28] might at common law have disciplined their young children by slapping or smacking, and would not have been seen to be "attacking" them unless tempers were lost and reasonable chastisement became excessive punishment. That, of course, would have been a matter of degree in all the circumstances of each case.[29] Under statute, however, those who physically punish a child, i.e. a person under the age of 16, and who claim in answer to a charge of assault to have been justified in so doing (on the basis of the exercise of a parental right or a right derived from their having charge of that child) will have the grounds of that claim particularly scrutinised according to (a) the nature of what was done, the reason for it and the circumstances in which it took place; (b) the duration and frequency of what was done; (c) any mental or physical effect on the child; (d) the child's age; and (e) the child's personal characteristics—including (but not limited to) the child's sex and state of health at the time, and such other factors as the court in question considers appropriate: further, it is now the law that if the punishment included or consisted of a blow to the head, shaking or the use of an implement, a court must find that such an assault was *not* justifiable.[30]

Members of staff at Scottish schools (whether public or private) were at common law permitted to keep discipline by imposing reasonable corporal punishment on pupils[31]; but their power to do so has been abrogated by statute.[32]

Those who play sports, such as rugby or ice-hockey, which allow physical tackling of opponents in the course of play, will, however, escape conviction for criminal assault, provided that they confine themselves to what the rules of the game allow by way of physical

---

[26] *cf. Marchbank v Annan*, 1987 S.C.C.R. 718; *Codona v Cardle*, 1989 S.L.T. 791; *Norman v Smith*, 1983 S.C.C.R. 100.

[27] See, e.g. *HM Advocate v Harris*, 1993 J.C. 150, Lord McCluskey (dissenting) at 161B–C.

[28] See, e.g. *Stewart v Thain*, 1981 J.C. 13.

[29] Contrast *Guest v Annan*, 1988 S.C.C.R. 275, and *Peebles v MacPhail*, 1990 S.L.T. 245. See also *Kennedy v A*, 1993 S.L.T. 1134 Ex.Div., Court of Session.

[30] See the Criminal Justice (Scotland) Act 2003 (asp 7) s.51.

[31] See, e.g. *McShane v Paton*, 1922 J.C. 26; *cf. Gray v Hawthorn*, 1964 J.C. 69.

[32] See Standards in Scotland's Schools, etc. Act 2000 (asp 6), s.16. "Pupil" and "school" for the purposes of the 2000 Act (see s.58(2)) have the same meanings as they have in the Education (Scotland) Act 1980 s.135 (as amended, *quoad* relevant, by the Registered Establishments (Scotland) Act 1987 s.2(2); the 2000 Act (asp 6) Sch.2 para.3, Sch.3; the Education (Additional Support for Learning) (Scotland) Act 2004 (asp 4) Sch.3 para.3; and the School Education (Ministerial Powers and Independent Schools) (Scotland) Act 2004 (asp 12) s.3).

contact with members of the opposing team. There will then be no question of there being any "attack".[33]

Attacks producing fear

"Gestures threatening violence so great as to put another in **9–08** bodily fear, whether accompanied by words of menace or not, constitute assault."[34] This statement was impliedly approved by Lord Justice-Clerk Ross in *Atkinson v HM Advocate*[35] where the masked accused burst into a shop and vaulted a counter, thus placing a cashier in a state of fear and alarm for his safety. This was considered quite sufficient by itself for conviction, and confirms the conclusion derivable from earlier authorities that actual injury is not required. All that is necessary is that the accused should have made some unjustified, hostile, direct approach to the victim which led him to fear that he was about to be injured. Thus, if a weapon such as a firearm is directed threateningly towards another, that will be enough, even if the accused himself knows that no injury can actually be caused by it.[36] Similarly, where the victim is menaced with a cutting, striking or stabbing instrument, assault may well be made out at that stage.[37] It would be a mistake, however, to imagine that presenting a weapon at another is always sufficient for assault; it has been held, for example, that producing a knife during an interlude in a fight, and holding it out towards one's opponent whilst saying "fuck off", could be a legitimate method of trying to avoid the resumption of hostilities rather than a hostile act itself.[38] No weapons, however, are necessarily required for this form of assault. In *John Irving*,[39] for example, the accused had repeatedly shaken his fist in the face of his victim; and that, accompanied by threatening words, was clearly sufficient.

The question arises in relation to attacks which produce fear **9–09** rather than actual injury whether the victim has to be conscious of the attack made upon him. Must he have been personally aware of

---

[33] See, e.g. *Lord Advocate's Reference (No.2 of 1992)*, 1993 J.C. 43, per Lord Justice-Clerk Ross at 48E; *cf. Dobbs and Macdonald v Neilson* (1899) 3 Adam 10, where an inferior criminal court quite unaccountably convicted two professional boxers for what they did to each other during the course of a friendly contest, fought according to that sport's normal rules.

[34] Macdonald, *Criminal Law*, 5th edn, p.115.

[35] *Atkinson v HM Advocate*, 1987 S.C.C.R. 534 at 535.

[36] *Gilmour v McGlennan*, 1993 S.C.C.R. 837; *Lord Advocate's Reference (No.2 of 1992)*, 1993 J.C. 43.

[37] See *Norval v HM Advocate*, 1978 J.C. 70, where a sword, hammer and knife were presented; *Bryson v HM Advocate*, 1961 S.L.T. 289, where a candlestick was brandished at a policeman and a threat made to strike him with it. See also *Strachan v HM Advocate*, 1995 S.L.T. 178 (where the charge was actually one of attempted murder).

[38] *Mackenzie v HM Advocate*, 1983 S.L.T. 220, per Lord Justice-Clerk Wheatley at 223.

[39] *John Irving* (1833) Bell's Notes 88.

the menaces and threats to his safety? Although the matter is not free from difficulty, it is suggested that it should be unnecessary to show that he was so aware. On any other view, it would be no assault to brandish an axe in anger at a person who was asleep or intoxicated, which surely cannot be right. There is no authority on the point, however. Where the victim has actually been alarmed, it is equally unclear whether his alarm must be considered reasonable in the circumstances. The point was raised, but not decided, in *Gilmour v McGlennan*.[40]

Indirect attacks

9–10		The classic example of an indirect attack is the setting of some animal upon one's victim. Naturally, the animal would have to be one generally regarded as amenable to human control, such as a dog. In *Kay v Allan*[41] it was indeed said that encouraging a boxer-dog to attack two young boys trespassing in the accused's garden was an assault; but the decision of the Appeal Court proceeded on a concession by the Crown to the effect that it had to be shown in such a case,

> "that the person accused caused the dog in some way to move at the alleged victim with the intention that the dog in so moving would at least frighten him."[42]

It appears, then, that it is not necessary for the dog (or similar animal) to attack and injure the victim. An unusual instance of an indirect attack occurred in *David Keay*,[43] where the accused, who was riding in a carriage, whipped a pony as he overtook it. This caused the frightened animal to bolt and throw its young rider, who was seriously injured. The court seemed to entertain no doubt that this was an assault on the person who was hurt. It has been held to be no answer to a charge relating to an instruction to a dog that it should "fetch" another person that the instruction was intended as a joke, since a dog cannot distinguish between a jocular command and a hostile one.[44]

The immediacy of the attack

9–11		It would seem that an attack, as described above, should be followed, or be capable of being followed, by immediate injury if assault is to be made out. If a significant temporal gap exists between the conduct of the accused and some resultant injury, then the crime (if any) is probably not one of assault. So, in *Charles*

---

[40] *Gilmour v McGlennan*, 1993 S.C.C.R. 837.
[41] *Kay v Allan* (1978) S.C.C.R. Supp. 188.
[42] *Kay v Allan* (1978) S.C.C.R. Supp. 188 at 190.
[43] *David Keay* (1837) 1 Swin. 543.
[44] *Quinn v Lees*, 1994 S.C.C.R. 159.

Costello[45] a separate, innominate offence was significantly charged (and upheld) where the accused had sent the victim a box of gunpowder, so ordered as to explode in his face when the package was delivered and opened. On the other hand, in *Smith v Paton*[46] the accused was charged with attempted assault, in that he had sent to his victim a postal packet so designed that concealed razor blades would lacerate the fingers of anyone opening it. He pled guilty, however, and thus no matter of principle was discussed.[47]

The mens rea of assault

The overwhelming preponderance of authority points to assault **9–12** being a crime of intention.[48] Although Hume's treatment of assault is somewhat superficial, he does refer to intent being required—in particular the intent to hurt and wound[49]; and in the case of *John Roy*[50] it is plain that the prosecutor gave up the case because he could not show any intention to injure. It had been suggested by him that assault covered all injuries causally connected to a criminal act of the accused (in this case, the kicking-in of a house window—malicious mischief) but the court would have none of that. Again, in the later case of *HM Advocate v Phipps*[51] Lord Ardwall told the jury that they could not convict of assault unless they found that the accused had had evil intent or an intention to do bodily injury. This was a curious way to present the matter in the context of that case, since the accused (the two sons of the shooting tenant on a Scottish estate) conceded that they intended to frighten the victims by the device of firing off loaded shotguns. They had heard voices from the far banks of a river, and had assumed that they were having to contend with poachers. At the pitch-black of midnight, therefore, they fired off their weapons in the direction of the voices they had heard, their object being to scare off the men in question and secure their poaching gear. It did not occur to them that anyone on the far bank would be within range; but such was the case. Two of the "poachers" were injured.

---

[45] *Charles Costello* (1882) 4 Coup. 602.
[46] *Smith v Paton*, unreported, June, 1986, Dundee Sheriff Court.
[47] *Paton's* case is doubly curious in that it is often stated that in view of the width of the concept of "attack", there is no such thing in practice as attempted assault—see P.W. Ferguson, *Crimes Against the Person*, 2nd edn (Edinburgh: Butterworths, 1998), para.1–03; Gordon, *Criminal Law*, 3rd edn, para.29.02. See also above, para.6–08.
[48] See *Lord Advocate's Reference (No.2 of 1992)*, 1993 J.C. 43, per Lord Justice-Clerk Ross at 48C–D, Lord Cowie at 51B–C, and Lord Sutherland at 52I–53A; *Harris*, 1993 J.C. 150, per Lord Justice-Clerk Ross at 154D–E (quoting Gordon, *Criminal Law*, 2nd edn, at para.29–30), and Lord Murray 156C; *Drury v HM Advocate*, 2001 S.L.T. 1013, Lord Mackay of Drumadoon at 1033I–J, para.10, where his Lordship refers inter alia to the "standard definition of assault".
[49] Hume, *Commentaries*, i, 328.
[50] *John Roy* (1839) Bell's Notes 88.
[51] *HM Advocate v Phipps* (1905) 4 Adam 616 at 630.

Clearly the accused had no intention of injuring anyone but they did intend to frighten off the men concerned, by causing them to be alarmed for their personal safety. As actions on the part of one person which cause another to feel alarm for his safety are undoubtedly sufficient for the *actus reus* of assault, an intention to produce such alarm must certainly form the correlative *mens rea*. Lord Ardwall's virtual direction to the jury to acquit the accused must, therefore, be based on his belief that it was lawful to frighten off persons supposed to be engaged in poaching.[52]

9–13 It must follow, therefore, that two forms of *mens rea* are sufficient for assault. The first relates to an intention to do bodily harm,[53] and the second to an intention to place someone in a state of fear and alarm for his personal safety.

Must the intent be evil?

9–14 According to Macdonald[54]: "Evil intention [is] of the essence of assault." A similar remark was made by Lord Ardwall in the case of *HM Advocate v Phipps*,[55] although he seemed to explain there that "evil" intent meant, "an intention to do bodily injury." In the leading case of *Smart v HM Advocate*[56] the Appeal Court said:

> "If there is an *attack* on the other person *and it is done with evil intent*, that is, intent to injure and do bodily harm, then . . . the fact that the person attacked was willing to undergo the risk of that attack does not prevent it from being the crime of assault."[57]

Discounting for the present what the court said about the role of consent (see below, para.9–18), it seems that the relevant form of the *mens rea* here is really a straightforward "intent to do bodily injury" rather than an "evil intent" to do so. And this, with some degree of hesitation, appears to be the present law. In the leading modern authority on this precise issue,[58] the trial judge directed the jury that whether or not there was evil intent was at the heart of the case.[59] The accused had burst into a shop, held out a handgun

---

[52] *HM Advocate v Phipps* (1905) 4 Adam 616 at 634.
[53] The court in *McDonald v HM Advocate*, 2004 S.C.C.R. 161 at 170E–F, para.23, reserved its opinion, "as to whether . . . notwithstanding consent to the infliction of pain in a sexual context, an intention to cause pain could justify a conviction for assault in the absence of an intention to cause actual physical injury."
[54] Macdonald, *Criminal Law*, 5th edn, p.115.
[55] *HM Advocate v Phipps* (1905) 4 Adam 616 at 630.
[56] *Smart v HM Advocate*, 1975 J.C. 30 at 33.
[57] This passage was quoted, with evident approval, in the homicide case of *McDonald v HM Advocate*, 2004 S.C.C.R. 161; see the opinion of the court at 170D–E, para.23.
[58] *Lord Advocate's Reference (No.2 of 1992)*, 1993 J.C. 43.
[59] *Lord Advocate's Reference (No.2 of 1992)*, 1993 J.C. 43, quoted by Lord Justice-Clerk Ross at 46D.

in front of him, and given the startled assistants a command to hand over the contents of the till. The assistants were alarmed for their own safety. The accused's story was, however, that he had then begun laughing, announced it was all a joke, and left the premises. At his trial for (inter alia) assault, he submitted that he had had no evil intent, the whole episode having been an essay in the art of the practical joke. The trial judge told the jury that if they believed the accused's story, they should acquit since there would indeed be no *evil* intent. The accused was duly acquitted (on a not proven verdict) and in the course of a subsequent Lord Advocate's reference, Lord Justice-Clerk Ross opined as follows:

> "It has often been said that evil intention is of the essence of assault (Macdonald's *Criminal Law*, p. 115). But what that means is that assault cannot be committed accidentally or recklessly or negligently (Gordon's *Criminal Law* (2nd ed.), para. 29–30). In the present case, it is plain that when the accused entered the shop, presented the handgun at Mrs Daly and uttered the words which he did, he was acting deliberately. That being so, in my opinion, he had the necessary intent for his actions to amount to assault . . .".[60]

It appears to follow, therefore, that the epithet "evil" is an unnecessary, if not misleading, one, and that the proper recension of the *mens rea* is indeed what is stated above at para.9–13. A difficulty with this view, however, is that it was not necessarily shared by the other two judges in the case. Lord Cowie, for example, was of the opinion that "evil intent" *was* an essential element in the crime,[61] and that it was necessary to establish that the act of the accused had indeed been evil. As he put it:

> "Having established that the act is an evil one [based on its quality], all that is then required to constitute the crime of assault is that that act was done deliberately and not carelessly, recklessly or negligently."[62]

Equally, Lord Sutherland in his opinion indicated that, "[t]he words "evil intent" have an eminently respectable pedigree."[63] It is true too in other modern cases that some judges continue to favour "evil intention" as the proper description of the *mens rea* of assault.[64] The conclusion is that one cannot entirely be certain

---

[60] *Lord Advocate's Reference (No.2 of 1992)*, 1993 J.C. 43 at 48C–D.
[61] *Lord Advocate's Reference (No.2 of 1992)*, 1993 J.C. 43 at 51B.
[62] *Lord Advocate's Reference (No.2 of 1992)*, 1993 J.C. 43 at 51C–D.
[63] *Lord Advocate's Reference (No.2 of 1992)*, 1993 J.C. 43 at 52H.
[64] See, e.g. *Boyle v HM Advocate*, 1993 S.L.T. 577, Lord McCluskey's charge to the jury at 579K–580C; *Harris*, 1993 J.C. 150, Lord Justice-Clerk Ross at 154D–E

whether "evil intent" is simply an outmoded way of referring to "intent" or whether (for some judges at least) "evil intent" has a meaning distinct from simple intent. It is suggested that the former is the better view.

9–15   There may be some advantage, nevertheless, in requiring an intention to be "evil". Sportsmen playing a physical contact sport where heavy tackling, or even punching is permitted within the rules; police arresting unwilling suspects; nurses subduing violent patients; and parents and others disciplining unruly children (on all which, see above, para.9–07), may all be said in a quite literal sense to intend the force they use. But, provided that the force used is no more than permitted within the rules of the sport or than necessary for the legitimate aim pursued, there is no evil intention in respect of it. If only bare intent is required for the crime, rather than evil intent, then a game of, say, rugby must inevitably be analysed as a continuous sequence of assaults, which will then require justification or excuse. Even more telling is the effect upon surgical or dental treatment. It is very odd somehow to have to regard a surgical operation, say, for the amputation of a limb, as a theoretical assault requiring justification by way of "necessity" or "the ultimate good of the patient"; and yet it is certainly arguable that the surgeon involved intends to do what he does, and that that involves bodily harm. But a surgeon (or indeed any other professionally trained medical operative) will not lightly be assumed to have any *evil* intent. Insistence on an *evil* intention will thus avoid the awkward notion of a prima facie, but justifiable assault in relation to medical treatment. As against all this, of course, is the inherent vagueness of the moral concept "evil". Vague concepts within a criminal justice system are perfectly capable of giving rise to unexpected, and even unwanted submissions—such as, that practical joke scenarios do not qualify as assaults since they cannot be thought of as "evil". There may, however, be *something* to be said in favour of terms which allow discretion to the court to deal with awkward situations sensibly. It cannot always be wise to rely solely on the exercise of restraint on the part of the prosecutor.[65]

Is recklessness sufficient for assault?

9–16   There is no evidence in favour of recklessness, still less negligence, being a sufficient form of *mens rea* for assault, and indeed a considerable body of evidence against. Quite apart from the authorities referred to above at para.9–12, the court in *David*

(quoting directly from Macdonald, *Criminal Law*, 5th edn, p.115), Lord McCluskey (dissenting) at 158I–159A, 159B; *Kennedy v A*, 1993 S.L.T. 1134, opinion of the court at 1137A: *Drury*, 2001 S.L.T. 1013, Lord Mackay of Drumadoon at 1033I, para.10, where his Lordship states: "The standard direction on assault refers to the fact that 'evil intention' is of the essence of the crime"; *McDonald v HM Advocate*, 2004 S.C.C.R. 161, opinion of the court at 170D, para.23.
[65] See *Lord Advocate's Reference (No.2 of 1992)*, 1993 J.C. 43, Lord Justice-Clerk Ross at 48E–F.

Keay[66] was at some pains to avoid concluding that an assault might have been recklessly committed. Where the accused had whipped a pony because it was apparently in the path of his carriage, thus causing it to throw and injure its rider, Lord Moncreiff said: "I cannot see what purpose the pannel could have, except either to do him a direct injury, or to put him in alarm."[67] His Lordship also remarked there that it would not amount to an assault if a person were to throw a stone heedlessly out of a window and thus injure some innocent passer-by.[68] Further evidence is provided by the decision of the Appeal Court in *Roberts v Hamilton*.[69] There, the accused was charged with assault in that she had aimed a blow with a stout pole at A but had in fact missed and hit B, who happened to be within range. The accused had had no intention to injure B at all; and, in fact, it would seem to have been an act of recklessness or carelessness that had resulted in the injury. But the court held[70] that as long as there was intent to hit someone, then that intent was transferred to the person actually struck. Thus assault has been zealously preserved as a crime of intention in Scots law.[71]

AGGRAVATED ASSAULTS

An assault charge may be aggravated, or made more serious in various ways. Prime amongst these are statements in the indictment of ultimate intentions which the accused is alleged to have had. Hume[72] mentions particularly in this context the intent to kill,[73] the intent to ravish,[74] and the intent to rob. The mode of perpetration of the assault is also often encountered as an aggravation, particularly if a weapon such as a firearm was used.[75] It is also common, even up to the present day, to find the results of the **9–17**

---

[66] *David Keay* (1837) 1 Swin. 543.

[67] *David Keay* (1837) 1 Swin. 543 at 545.

[68] It could, however, amount to some crime involving culpable and reckless behaviour—as in *W v HM Advocate*, 1982 S.L.T. 420 (*sub nom. RHW v HM Advocate*, 1982 S.C.C.R. 152). Such crimes are dealt with separately in this chapter (see below, paras 9–24 to 9–33); and their very existence underlines the fact that recklessly caused injuries are not assaults.

[69] *Roberts v Hamilton*, 1989 S.L.T. 399.

[70] *Roberts v Hamilton*, 1989 S.L.T. 399 at 401F–H.

[71] Compare the position in England, as shown in *R. v Venna* [1976] Q.B. 421.

[72] Hume, *Commentaries*, i, 328–329.

[73] See, e.g. *Mysie or Marion Brown or Graham* (1827) Syme 152; *cf.* Ferguson, *Crimes Against the Person*, 2nd edn, para.1–17.

[74] See, e.g. *James Gibbs* (1836) 1 Swin. 263; *HM Advocate v Stopper*, 2002 S.C.C.R. 668; *cf. Rodgers v Hamilton*, 1994 S.L.T. 822, where the outcome of the appeal would now have been different, *stante* the decision in *Lord Advocate's Reference (No.1 of 2001)*, 2002 S.L.T. 466: see below, paras 9–75 and 9–82; *cf. Spendiff v HM Advocate*, 2005 S.C.C.R. 522.

[75] Macdonald, Criminal Law, 5th edn, p.118. Assault, and other offences may also be aggravated by racism or religious prejudice: see the Crime and Disorder Act 1998 s.96, and the Criminal Justice (Scotland) Act 2003 (asp 7) s.74.

attack specified as aggravations—e.g. that they were "to the danger of life",[76] "to severe injury, permanent disability and permanent disfigurement",[77] or even "to severe internal injury".[78] The place of the assault may be taken as an aggravation. It has always been regarded as more heinous, for example, to attack a person violently in his own home—and especially so if his home had been entered by the accused for that very purpose. (This used to be regarded as the separate offence known as "hamesucken"[79]; but that is not the present practice.)[80] An assault may also be aggravated by indecencies[81]: thus, punching (or threatening) a woman and then fondling her breasts is clearly an aggravated assault[82]; but such fondling unaccompanied by such violence or intimidation[83] seems to be either an "indecent" assault[84] or no crime at all, depending upon whether such familiarities are consented to (see below, para.9–19).

CONSENT AS A DEFENCE

9–18 No current version of the definition of assault in Scotland includes the phrase "without his consent" among its terms.[85] "Lack of consent" is not, therefore, a definitional element. "Consent of the victim" might nevertheless be considered as a defence to an assault charge. But in the few cases where consent has been tendered as a defence, the courts have generally reacted unenthusiastically. Where, for example, what is involved is the deliberate physical injury of another, in pursuance of a quarrel at least, it is no defence that that other person agreed to accept the risk of injury, as in *Smart v HM Advocate*[86] where both parties to a consensual, "no holds barred" fight stood to be successfully prosecuted for assault.

---

[76] Which can be added whether or not there were actual injuries. See *Peter Leys* (1839) 2 Swin. 337; *cf. Jane Smith or Thom* (1876) 3 Coup. 332; *Kerr v HM Advocate*, 1986 S.C.C.R. 81; *cf.* also *Gaffney v HM Advocate*, 2007 S.C.C.R. 296 (not possible to dispose of a case on the basis that it had been "to the danger of life" when such an aggravation had not been included in the indictment).

[77] Which may appear separately, or together as in *Williamson v HM Advocate*, 1984 S.L.T. 200.

[78] As in *Kirkwood v HM Advocate*, 1939 J.C. 36, where the shaft of a hammer was thrust into the victim's private parts.

[79] See Hume, *Commentaries*, i, pp.312 *et seq.*; Alison, *Principles*, pp.199 *et seq.*; *cf.* Macdonald, *Criminal Law*, 5th edn, p.118.

[80] See *HM Advocate v Forbes*, 1994 S.L.T. 861, per Lord Justice-General Hope at 862J–L.

[81] Macdonald, *Criminal Law*, 5th edn, p.119.

[82] *cf.* charge (2) in *Grainger v HM Advocate*, 2005 S.C.C.R. 175, quoted in the opinion of the court at 177B–C, para.1.

[83] *cf.* the charges in, e.g. *Turner v Scott*, 1996 S.L.T. 200.

[84] In *Grainger v HM Advocate*, 2005 S.C.C.R. 175 at 179F–180A, para.17, the Appeal Court rejected the submission that "indecent assault" was an offence separate from assault: it was "essentially an assault aggravated by indecency in the manner of its commission."

[85] *cf.* the definition of theft below at para.10–02.

[86] *Smart v HM Advocate*, 1975 J.C. 30 at 33.

It may be too that where a person agrees to be injured for his own (perhaps sexual) gratification, his consent will not prevent his injurer's conviction for assault. If that is so, then Scots and English law would be at one in this matter, namely, that for reasons of public policy, persons cannot be permitted to consent to their own injury.[87] It remains uncertain whether or not consent would be a defence where the victim agreed to be placed in a state of fear and alarm for his personal safety.

Consent and indecent assault

"If A touches B in a sexual manner and B consents to him doing **9–19** so (and there is nothing else involved which would constitute a crime under statute or at common law) there is no assault because there is no evil intention to attack the person of B."[88] But perhaps what truly elides assault in that sort of situation is the consent of the person being touched, or rather, A's knowledge of that. Indeed, if that person consents to straightforward fondlings, touchings, embracings and the like, there is probably no need to consider the intent of the other person at all. If there was in fact no consent on the part of the victim, an honest belief in consent on the part of the accused should be sufficient to secure his acquittal of a "pure" indecent assault, on analogy with the decision in *Meek v HM Advocate*[89] relating to rape. But in one case which raised this issue,[90] the advocate-depute maintained that such a belief might secure an acquittal if based on reasonable grounds.[91] At the end of the day, however, the Appeal Court was content to declare that the victim had not consented, that the appellant had gone further than had been justified by the general conviviality of the occasion, and that he had taken advantage of the victim by, "touching her in a sexual manner deliberately and without her consent . . .".[92] Whether an honest belief *not* based on reasonable grounds would

---

[87] *R. v Brown* [1994] 1 A.C. 212 HL; *Laskey, Jaggard and Brown v United Kingdom* (1997) 24 E.H.R.R. 39: *cf. Attorney-General's Reference (No.6 of 1980)* [1981] Q.B. 715, which appears to preserve consent as a "defence" in relation to minor injuries—a distinction which the court in *Smart v HM Advocate*, 1975 J.C. 30, considered wrong. (The Scottish Law Commission has, however, recently recommended amendment of the common-law position here: see below, para.9–92.)

[88] *Smart v HM Advocate*, 1975 J.C. 30 at 33. For proposed reforms to this aspect of assault, see the Scottish Law Commission's "Report on Rape and Other Sexual Offences", Scot. Law Com. No.209 (December 2007): see the brief account of some of these proposals below at paras 9–90 to 9–93.

[89] *Meek v HM Advocate*, 1983 S.L.T. 280, confirmed in *Jamieson v HM Advocate (No.1)*, 1994 S.L.T. 537; see also *Lord Advocate's Reference (No.1 of 2001)*, 2002 S.L.T. 466, Lord Justice-General Cullen at 473C–H, paras 28–29.

[90] *Young v McGlennan*, 1990 S.C.C.R. 373; *cf. Peace v HM Advocate*, 2003 S.L.T. 419, where the existence of a "genuine belief in consent" defence was simply assumed.

[91] *Young v McGlennan*, 1990 S.C.C.R. 373 at 742F (as précised by Lord Justice-General Hope).

[92] *Young v McGlennan*, 1990 S.C.C.R. 373 at 743F.

have been sufficient was not commented upon. If consent is obtained by fraud, then that probably precludes conviction for indecent assault[93]; but a medical practitioner cannot claim that a patient's consent to medical examination for a specific complaint permits him to explore the patient's body entirely as he wishes until the patient expressly demurs.[94] For their greater protection, it appears to be accepted that girls under the age of 12 can give no valid consent to sexual "indecencies".[95] That safeguard for girls under puberty is presumably derived from the correlative common law offence of "lewd, indecent and libidinous practices and behaviour", a protection which has been extended by statute to girls under 16.[96]

LEWD, INDECENT AND LIBIDINOUS PRACTICES

9–20 "In the modern law, where indecent conduct is directed against a specific victim who is within the class of persons whom the law protects, the crime is that of lewd, indecent and libidinous practices."[97] Children under the age of puberty (that is, under 14 for boys, and under 12 for girls) are certainly within that class, and may be exclusively so. In *McLaughlan v Boyd*,[98] it was decided that the common law did not support the contention that such lewd practices could be committed only where the victim had been proved to be below the age of puberty at the time; and in *Bratty v HM Advocate*,[99] an appeal against conviction on charges of lewd practices, on the ground that each of the female victims had been over the age 12 at the relevant time, was refused: but much of the former decision has subsequently been disapproved,[100] whilst much of the latter has been described as "confused".[101] In any event, the

---

[93] See the civil case of *Gray v Criminal Injuries Compensation Board*, 1993 S.L.T. 28, where the "victim" was the innocent partner in a bigamous marriage. Fraud itself would remain a legitimate charge, however.

[94] *Hussain v Houston*, 1995 S.L.T. 1060.

[95] See *C v HM Advocate*, 1987 S.C.C.R. 104, where the point was strongly urged by the Crown and conceded by the appellant.

[96] Criminal Law (Consolidation) (Scotland) Act 1995 s.6, as amended by the Crime and Punishment (Scotland) Act 1997 s.14.

[97] *Webster v Dominick*, 2005 J.C. 65, per Lord Justice-Clerk Gill at 79, para.49. The Scottish Law Commission, in a recent report, proposes the abolition of this crime and its replacement by a series of more detailed and directed statutory offences: see below, para.9–90.

[98] *McLaughlan v Boyd*, 1934 J.C. 19.

[99] *Batty v HM Advocate*, 1995 J.C. 160, as properly understood: see *Webster v Dominick*, 2005 J.C. 65, opinion of Lord Justice-Clerk Gill at 76–77, paras 35–36.

[100] *Webster v Dominick*, 2005 J.C. 65, opinion of Lord Justice-Clerk Gill at 78, para.46.

[101] *Webster v Dominick*, 2005 J.C. 65 at 76, para.35. Both cases mentioned in the text were contaminated by the discussion they contain of the now discredited offence of "shamelessly indecent conduct". See also *Sneddon v HM Advocate*, 2005 S.L.T. 651, where in charge (1), concerning the appellant "P", although the victim had been aged 15 at the relevant time, it was not suggested that a verdict of lewd practices could be substituted for that of the now discredited offence mentioned above.

protection of this offence has been extended by statute to girls under the age of 16.[102] Consent of the child in these offences is irrelevant. It seems that the essence of the crime lies in, "the tendency of the conduct to corrupt the innocence"[103] of the victim; and the conduct thus may take many forms, as, e.g. indecent exposure,[104] indecent contact,[105] the taking of indecent photographs,[106] the showing of indecent materials,[107] sending sexually suggestive text messages,[108] and "other forms of indecent conduct carried out in the presence of the victim."[109]

PROVOCATION

The treatment of provocation by both Hume[110] and Macdonald[111] **9–21** strongly suggests that it is available as a complete defence. This may be correct relative to intentional murder,[112] due to the way in which that crime has been redefined[113]; but, unless the "wicked intent" of murder is to be equated with assault's "evil intent",[114] it seems reasonable to endorse the accepted view[115] that the function

---

[102] Criminal Law (Consolidation) (Scotland) Act 1995 s.6, as amended by the Crime and Punishment (Scotland) Act 1997 s.14(2). There is no general extension for boys of 14 years or over, but male persons under 16 are protected by statute from acts of sodomy or gross indecency: Criminal Law (Consolidation) (Scotland) Act 1995 s.13, as amended by the Sexual Offences (Amendment) Act 2000 ss.1(3), 2(4); the Convention Rights (Compliance) (Scotland) Act 2001 (asp 7) s.10; and, the Mental Health (Care and Treatment) (Scotland) Act 2003 (asp 13) Sch.5 Pt 1.

[103] *Webster v Dominick*, 2005 J.C. 65, per Lord Justice-Clerk Gill at 79, para.49; *Moynagh v Spiers*, 2003 S.L.T. 1377, opinion of the court at 1378I–J, para.2.

[104] See, e.g. the charge in *Hogg v Normand*, 1992 S.LT. 736; *cf. Anderson v HM Advocate*, 2001 S.C.C.R. 738.

[105] See, e.g. the charges in *RL v HM Advocate*, 1969 J.C. 40; *Moynagh v Spiers*, 2003 S.L.T. 1377; *NKS v HM Advocate*, 2006 S.C.C.R. 70; *Dunnigan v HM Advocate*, 2006 S.C.C.R. 398.

[106] *cf.* the charges in *HM Advocate v Millbank*, 2002 S.L.T. 1116.

[107] *cf.* the charge, framed as one of "shameless indecency", in *Webster v Dominick*, 2005 J.C. 65, and the Lord Justice-Clerk's comments upon it as possibly being one of lewd practices, at 81, para.61.

[108] See, e.g. the sending of same, charged as part of a course of indecent conduct, in *Stephen v HM Advocate*, 2006 S.C.C.R. 667; and *cf.* Lord Justice-Clerk Gill's opinion in *Webster v Dominick*, 2005 J.C. 65 at 79, para.49, that the crime may be committed "by means of a lewd conversation with the victim, whether face to face or by a telephone call or through an internet chat room."

[109] *Webster v Dominick*, 2005 J.C. 65, per Lord Justice-Clerk Gill at 79, para.49.

[110] Hume, *Commentaries*, i, 333–337.

[111] Macdonald, *Criminal Law*, 5th edn, pp.116–117.

[112] But not to culpable homicide: see below, paras 9–44 and 9–59.

[113] See *Drury v HM Advocate*, 2001 S.L.T. 1013, and below, para.9–42.

[114] See above, paras 9–14 to 9–16, as to the meaning of "evil intent" in assault; and see *Drury v HM Advocate*, 2001 S.L.T. 1013, Lord Mackay of Drumadoon at 1033I, para.10, where it is opined that the wickedness which murder requires is different from "evil intent" in assault.

[115] See Gordon, *Criminal Law*, 3rd edn, para.29.44; *Lennon v HM Advocate*, 1991 S.C.C.R. 611, opinion of the court at 614F.

of provocation in assault[116] is to, "have a very considerable bearing upon the penalty which ought to be imposed in respect of [a] finding of guilt."[117] In short, the expectation is that it will lessen the sentence which might otherwise be imposed.

9–22 It seems that a wide variety of matters may be raised as provocation at a trial for assault. These obviously include a violent attack made on the accused to which he responds there and then in the heat of the moment[118]; but there the response must keep some sort of proportion to the original violence offered. As Hume put it:

> "The general rule being once announced, that the person assaulted must keep within the bounds of an allowable resentment, the application is matter of common sense; and little aid is to be derived from any thing that books can teach on the subject."[119]

But finding one's spouse in the throes of homosexual passion has also been considered sufficiently provoking,[120] as have insulting words and behaviour. Thus, in the old case of *Ensign Andrew Monro*[121] the accused was understandably moved to violence on being called a "bougar" and "son of a whore"; and in *James McEwen*[122] provocation was found in a newspaper article which was libellous of the accused's mother. In cases such as these, however, where there is no physical assault on the accused, it is unrealistic to require some degree of proportion to be shown between the provoking event and the accused's reaction to it, and it would be better to follow the lead set by the full bench in the homicide case of *Drury v HM Advocate*[123]: there the test laid down for cases of

---

[116] As also in appropriate cases of breach of the peace: *MacNeill v McTaggart* (1976) S.C.C.R. Supp. 150 at 151.

[117] *MacNeill v McTaggart*, (1976) S.C.C.R. Supp. 150 at 151.

[118] See Hume, *Commentaries*, i, 334–335.

[119] Hume, *Commentaries*, i, 335; and see *Lennon v HM Advocate*, 1991 S.C.C.R. 611, although what was said there relative to homicide must now be read subject to the opinions of the court in *Drury v HM Advocate*, 2001 S.L.T. 1013. It should be noted that in *Gillon v HM Advocate*, 2006 S.L.T. 799 (court of five judges), at 806D, para.19, the court upheld the proportionality test, where the provocation consists of violence, "as expounded particularly by Lord Justice Clerk Ross in *Robertson v HM Advocate*", 1994 J.C. 245, at 249E–F, viz: ". . . the principle has been expressed in different ways but it has been made clear that the retaliation used by the accused must not be grossly disproportionate to the violence which has constituted the provocation." Thus the phrase "no gross disproportion" has been authoritatively preferred to the alternative "no cruel excess" (*cf. Lennon v HM Advocate*, 1991 S.C.C.R. 611).

[120] *HM Advocate v Callander*, 1958 S.L.T. 24.

[121] *Ensign Andrew Monro* (1700) Hume, *Commentaries*, i, 334, fn.2.

[122] *James McEwen* (1838) Bell's Notes 91; *cf.* the case of *Patrick Murray Kay* (same citation) decided on the same day, where the article in question was directed against the accused's father—but in respect of his "public character as provost of Dundee."

[123] *Drury v HM Advocate*, 2001 S.L.T. 1013.

provocation by discovery of sexual infidelity was one of loss of self-control on the part of the accused, provided that an ordinary man or woman (as the case may be) would have reacted in a similar way to the accused in the same circumstances.[124]

In all cases, however, the assault must follow soon after the provocation, whatever it be. The intention is to make suitable allowance for incidents and events which excite the accused to a state of retaliatory passion, and not to cater in any way for a long-nurtured thirst for vengeance. Hume[125] mentions the 1746 case of *Alexander Lockhart* who was permitted to adduce evidence of provocation by insulting words given him by the victim in the morning of May 4, in alleviation of an assault perpetrated by him on the evening of the same day; but that must surely be the limit of the law's toleration. It is probable, however, that this rule and other rules for provocation are less strictly applied in assault than they are in homicide cases.[126]

DIMINISHED RESPONSIBILITY

This matter was clarified in the homicide case of *Galbraith v HM* **9–23** *Advocate (No.2)*.[127] Indeed, what is now known as diminished responsibility was probably first used at some stage in the second half of the nineteenth century, as a palliative to a conviction for murder with its then mandatory capital punishment consequence.[128] *Galbraith* makes it quite plain that,

> "diminished responsibility applies in cases where, because the accused's ability to determine and control his actings is

---

[124] See, in particular, the opinion of Lord Justice-General Rodger in *Drury*, 2001 S.L.T. 1013 at 1021I–1022F, paras 27–30. This means that there are two types of rule—depending on the nature of the provocation: in the homicide case of *Gillon v HM Advocate*, 2006 S.L.T. 799, it was argued (inter alia) that there should be but one type—viz the one currently employed in cases of sexual infidelity—irrespective of the provocation; but the court (of five judges) affirmed that there should be no change (other than by legislation) to the present law: *cf.* Chalmers and Leverick, *Criminal Defences and Pleas in Bar of Trial*, Ch.10, especially para.10–09 (written prior to the decision in *Gillon*). (It should be noted that of the two English cases (*R. v Smith (Morgan)* [2001] 1 A.C. 146 HL, and *Attorney General for Jersey v Holley* [2005] 2 A.C. 580 PC) particularly referred to in *Gillon*, the English Court of Appeal has subsequently preferred the approach adopted in *Attorney General for Jersey v Holley*: see *R. v James* [2006] 2 W.L.R. 887.)

[125] Hume, *Commentaries*, i, 334, 336, 337.

[126] See below, paras 9–60 *et seq.*

[127] *Galbraith v HM Advocate (No.2)*, 2002 J.C. 1, court of five judges: this case overrules the previous account of diminished responsibility given in *Connelly v HM Advocate*, 1990 JC 349; prior statements of the law here (particularly in *Williamson v HM Advocate*, 1994 S.C.C.R. 358 and in *Martindale v HM Advocate*, 1994 S.L.T. 1093) are thus impliedly disapproved.

[128] See *Galbraith v HM Advocate (No.2)*, 2002 J.C. 1, Lord Justice-General Rodger (giving the opinion of the court) at 11D–13C, paras 25–29.

impaired[129] as a result of some mental abnormality, his responsibility for any killing can properly be regarded as correspondingly reduced",

and that, "[t]he accused should, accordingly, be convicted of culpable homicide rather than of murder."[130] This suggests that diminished responsibility is a plea peculiar to murder indictments, and indeed there have been opinions from the bench to that effect.[131] But *Galbraith* also states that, "[b]ecause the individual is not fully responsible in law for what he does when his mental state is substantially impaired, the law mitigates the punishment which it deems appropriate for his criminal acts"; and, thus, in a murder case, adequate scope for mitigation cannot be achieved unless a conviction for culpable homicide (which has no fixed penalty) is returned by the jury.[132] There is no reason, therefore, why diminished responsibility should not be applicable to offences other than murder, and, in particular, to assault;[133] the rules for its operation, however, may not perhaps require to be as strict as those laid down (albeit tentatively)[134] in *Galbraith* for cases of homicide.[135] Perhaps all that need be emphasised here is that the mental abnormality, which substantially impairs the ability of the accused to determine and control his acts and omissions, must not (as a result of legal policy) be one which is produced by self-induced intoxication[136] or which amounts to "psychopathic personality"[137]: the mental abnormality should probably, however, be one "recognised by the appropriate sciences."[138]

---

[129] It should be noted that the court emphasises that the impairment has to be substantial: *Galbraith v HM Advocate (No.2)*, 2002 J.C. 1, opinion of the court at 17H–18A, para.44, 18E, para.46.

[130] *Galbraith v HM Advocate (No.2)*, 2002 J.C. 1, opinion of the court, at 16E, para.41.

[131] *HM Advocate v Cunningham*, 1963 J.C. 80, per Lord Justice-General Clyde at 84; *Brennan v HM Advocate*, 1977 J.C. 38 at 47.

[132] *Galbraith v HM Advocate (No.2)*, 2002 J.C. 1, opinion of the court at 18B–D, para.45.

[133] And see Macdonald, *Criminal Law*, 5th edn, p.117; *cf*. Chalmers and Leverick, *Criminal Defences and Pleas in Bar of Trial*, Ch.6, and in particular paras 11–19 and 11–20. The Scottish Law Commission, in its "Report on Insanity and Diminished Responsibility", Scot. Law Com. No.195 (July 2004), does not accept that diminished responsibility applies outwith murder, and recommends that the plea should not be extended to offences other than murder (para.3–50); the Commission does state, however, that: "[W]here in a non-murder case there are mitigating circumstances which in a murder case would constitute diminished responsibility, these can be the subject of a plea in mitigation and be reflected in the actual sentence handed down by the court" (para.3–46).

[134] See *Galbraith v HM Advocate (No.2)*, 2002 J.C. 1, opinion of the court at 16D, para.40.

[135] See below, paras 9–66 to 9–68.

[136] *Brennan v HM Advocate*, 1977 J.C. 38; see *Galbraith*, 2002 J.C. 1, opinion of the court at 17B–C, para.43.

[137] *Carraher v HM Advocate*, 1946 J.C. 108; see *Galbraith*, 2002 J.C. 1, opinion of the court at 17C, para.43.

[138] *Galbraith v HM Advocate (No.2)*, 2002 J.C. 1, opinion of the court at 21F, para.54, at "4".

3. NON-INTENTIONAL INJURY

Introduction

Using Hume's concept of "real injury" (see above, para.9–03) as **9–24** an established general principle[139] the Scottish courts have developed a series of related crimes. These differ from assault in that injuries suffered by the victim are not caused intentionally by the accused. Rather they are the product of recklessness on his behalf. It has been said frequently by the judiciary that non-intentionally caused injuries are not criminal at common law unless the conduct of the accused went well beyond carelessness. A very significant derogation from the standard of care expected of a person of ordinary understanding and competence has to be shown. In the leading case of *HM Advocate v Harris*,[140] three of the five judges emphasised this point,[141] and indeed considered that the standard referred to in *Quinn v Cunningham*[142] was essentially correct. That standard was itself derived from an earlier culpable homicide case[143] where the requirement was stated to be "gross, or wicked, or criminal negligence, something amounting, or at any rate analogous, to a criminal indifference to consequences . . .". A high standard of recklessness[144] of this nature is, therefore, essential, and forms the *mens rea* of each such crime. It was also held to be correct in *Harris* that actual injury was not always necessary—that there was a crime, or class of crimes, of which the essence was causing danger to the "lieges" by the recklessness of one's conduct.[145] Although criticised by Lord McCluskey,[146] Lord Prosser

---

[139] See *Khaliq v HM Advocate*, 1984 J.C. 23, per Lord Justice-General Emslie at 31–32.

[140] *HM Advocate v Harris*, 1993 J.C. 150.

[141] *HM Advocate v Harris*, 1993 J.C. 150, Lord Murray at 155H–I, Lord Morison at 162A–C, and Lord Prosser at 168E, 169B (where he sought to distinguish between recklessness of the required high standard, and "mere" recklessness).

[142] *Quinn v Cunningham*, 1956 J.C. 22—overruled in other respects by *HM Advocate v Harris*, 1993 J.C. 150. See also *Cameron v Maguire*, 1999 S.C.C.R. 44, opinion of the court at 46F–47A.

[143] *Paton v HM Advocate*, 1936 J.C. 19, Lord Justice-Clerk Aitchison at 22.

[144] It has to be noted, however, that in some cases, the Appeal Court has criticised judges who directed juries that a *high degree* of recklessness was required. The criticism was based on the view that such directions introduced unnecessary complications where the simple distinction to be made was between negligent or accidental conduct (which was not criminal) and reckless behaviour (which was): see, e.g. *Carr v HM Advocate*, 1995 S.L.T. 800, Lord Justice-General Hope at 803K–L and 804A (a case involving reckless fire-raising).

[145] This was conceded by counsel for the respondent in the case, a concession which all five judges considered to have been correctly made. Notice that Lord Prosser sensibly objected to the use of the archaic expression "lieges": as he put it, at 166C, ". . . danger to others can be referred to as danger to others without obsolete terms which need explaining." Evidence of actual danger to others is not always necessary, since the quality of the conduct may be sufficient to "satisfy the test of being described as culpable and reckless": *Robertson v Klos*,

was surely correct when he opined that recklessness (in this context at least) consists of a failure in one's duty to so conduct oneself that foreseeable danger of significant injury to others as a consequence of one's actions is set at an absolute minimum.[147] Clearly the nature of the activity and the degree of risk involved are important considerations in the assessment of conduct as "reckless"; but Lord Prosser appears to emphasise that recklessness and danger to others are interdependent in crimes of this nature—and that it makes sense to consider whether there had been danger to others even where injury *is* actually caused.[148] Certainly, where unintentional injury does result from the conduct of the accused, it is plainly necessary to categorise that injury as accidentally, negligently or recklessly caused—only the last of the three being relevant from the point of view of the criminal law. Equally, if significant unintentional injury has been caused by one's conduct, a strong inference arises that one's conduct probably was dangerous to others. It may be sufficient in fact that the conduct was dangerous in respect of the victim alone. The existence of danger to others, due to one's conduct, is thus a useful (if not essential) guide to separating the relevant from the irrelevant in crimes of this sort. Of course, "conduct" in this context will generally be something positive on the part of the accused—including, for example, the denial of the existence of some factor which creates danger for the potential victim[149]; where the conduct is said to be a mere failure to declare the existence of such a factor, the sufficiency of such conduct will depend on the exact circumstances of each case.[150] The essential elements of the best known of these offences are discussed in the paragraphs which follow.

OFFENCES INVOLVING A RELATIONSHIP
BETWEEN ACCUSED AND VICTIM

Cruel and barbarous treatment

9–25   Indictments for offences of this description were found frequently in the nineteenth century. Very often such a charge would be combined with an allegation of "Wilful and Culpable

---

2006 S.C.C.R. 52, opinion of the court at 60D, para.21; see also 61B, para.24.

[146] *HM Advocate v Harris*, 1993 J.C. 150 at 159H–I. The basis of his criticism was that complex accounts of the *mentes reae* appropriate to particular crimes will simply create difficulties for judges and confusion for juries.

[147] *HM Advocate v Harris*, 1993 J.C. 150 at 165C–D.

[148] *HM Advocate v Harris*, 1993 J.C. 150 at 165E–F.

[149] See, e.g. *Kimmins v Normand*, 1993 S.L.T. 1260 (false denial by a man about to be searched under s.23 of the Misuse of Drugs Act 1971 that he had an unguarded hypodermic needle about his person).

[150] *Mallin v Clark*, 2002 S.L.T. 1202, opinion of the court at 1205F–G, para.10, and J–K, para.12: in this case, *Kimmins v Normand*, 1993 S.L.T. 1260, was distinguished—see opinion of the court at 1205H, para.11.

Neglect"[151]; but a composite charge of that nature was regarded as containing one offence only.[152] It seems, since it is difficult to be certain about this, that the offence is aimed at those who are close relatives or guardians of the victim, or at any person who can be said to have undertaken his care and custody.[153] Thus, in *John McRae*, the accused was alleged to have confined his weak-minded wife in a space no longer than three and a half feet, and no higher than two and a half feet for almost four months. This was further alleged to have caused the unfortunate woman serious injury to her mind and body. He was convicted—as was his co-accused, a female servant within the household. It is to be noted that a close, personal relationship existed between victim and accused, and that the injurious consequences of their actions featured prominently in the charge. Where these features were found to be absent from an apparently similar indictment, the High Court found the charge to be irrelevant.[154]

Cruel and unnatural treatment

Nineteenth-century indictments[155] often alleged cruel and **9–26** unnatural, or just cruel treatment; but it is difficult to see how that varied (if at all) from the "cruel and barbarous" variety. In *William Fairweather*,[156] for example, a father was accused of confining his weak-minded daughter in a small hutch in an outhouse for about a month, whereby her life was endangered and she was reduced to a state of almost total idiocy. He pled guilty to the charge, which factually looked identical to that in *John McRae* (see above, para.9–25). In both cases, it is very likely that the accused meant the victims no harm. They probably thought, given nineteenth-century standards, that what they did was as good a method as any of coping with mental illness. But they all exhibited utter disregard for the health and safety of the persons concerned. Very much the same might be said of the inn-keeper and his assistant in *McManimy and Higgans*.[157] Those two accused evicted a man suspected of typhoid from an inn in Stirling, and carried him by rail (on the outside part of a carriage) to a Glasgow station where he was abandoned for the police to discover. Although the unfortunate victim died shortly thereafter in hospital, the accused pled

---

[151] The epithets "culpable" and "wilful" although often found in indictments and complaints for these offences are possibly mere surplusage—see, e.g. *Harris*, 1993 J.C. 150, Lord Justice-Clerk Ross at 154C–D, Lord McCluskey (dissenting) at 158A–C, Lord Prosser at 165H to 166A–B.

[152] *John McRae* (1842) 1 Broun 395, pcr Lord Cockburn at 399.

[153] See the form of indictment in *John McRae* (1842) 1 Broun 395.

[154] See *Robert Watt and James Kerr* (1868) 1 Coup. 123, where the accused was alleged to have forced young, ill-clad stowaways to leave his ship and find their way as best they could across ice floes towards land, which was many miles distant.

[155] For a more modern example, see *Lambert v HM Advocate*, 1993 S.L.T. 339.

[156] *William Fairweather* (1842) 1 Broun 309.

[157] *McManimy and Higgans* (1847) Ark. 321, which also involved homicide.

guilty to reckless, cruel and culpable removal of a sick person from his bed whilst he was helpless, to his injury and the danger of his life, and to reckless and cruel treatment involving desertion of a sick person. Their pleas were accepted; and it is to be noted that they were designed as persons *entrusted* with the care of a sick person, or who had *assumed custody and charge* of him. Such ascriptions would be unnecessary, of course, where the accused was a parent of the victim. Thus, in *Rachel Gibson*[158] a mother was alleged, amongst other things, to have treated her new born child cruelly and unnaturally by putting it in a basket and sending it, suitably labelled, by rail as an ordinary parcel. It was her clear intention to desert the child in that somewhat novel way, by which it, "was seriously injured in its health." (She pled guilty after the indictment had been held relevant.)

OFFENCES INVOLVING INJURY, OR DANGER OF INJURY
TO ONE OR MORE OF THE LIEGES

Reckless injury

9–27   It has fairly recently been made clear that there is a discrete offence of unintentionally but recklessly causing injury to another. In *HM Advocate v Harris*,[159] a steward at a night club was charged with recklessly seizing hold of the victim, pushing her on the body and causing her to fall down a flight of steps on to the roadway outside the premises, where she was run over by a vehicle to her severe injury and permanent disfigurement. This was one of two alternative charges in the indictment, the other being one of assault. It was objected, first, that the non-assault charge was not a crime known to the law of Scotland since it had not been specifically stated that what the steward had done was also "to the danger of the lieges". It was held on this point that such an addendum was unnecessary, and, insofar as prior authority[160] had required such an additional formula, that prior authority would be overruled. Secondly, it was claimed that since the facts were identically stated in both alternative charges, there was no difference between those charges, and that both, therefore, amounted to assault. (No doubt since it was possible that the accused had not intended to do more than carry out his duty of ejecting the complainer from the premises, using no more than reasonable force, it was also possible that the prosecutor would not succeed in proving that the accused had intended to injure her. It was thus to the accused's possible advantage to have the "recklessness" charge removed, since he might remain vulnerable to that.) Four of the

---

[158] *Rachel Gibson* (1845) 2 Broun 366.
[159] *HM Advocate v Harris*, 1993 J.C. 150.
[160] *Quinn v Cunningham*, 1956 J.C. 22.

five judges supported the prosecution's view that recklessly causing injury was a distinct type of crime, and that it was properly posited here as an alternative to assault.[161] It was emphasised that although a steward may be entitled intentionally to manhandle persons attending a night club and to eject them using reasonable force without being criminally liable for assault, yet "if reasonable force is not exceeded, ejection may ... be culpably reckless ... if insisted upon in face of danger to the person being ejected or to that person's actual severe injury."[162] As a result of the clarification of the law in *Harris*, this particular crime probably now embraces former cases relating to injuries caused by the reckless driving of a horse and cart[163] or a locomotive,[164] the reckless navigation of a ship,[165] the reckless disposal of a glass bottle,[166] and the like. There must, of course, be a causal link established between the accused's reckless conduct and the injury to the complainer, but that link seems easily drawn. In *Kimmins v Normand*,[167] for example, a person being legitimately searched for drugs by the police was asked if he had about his person any needles or similar sharp instruments. It was held on appeal that his denial of having any such object, when he well knew that he had an unprotected hypodermic needle in his pocket, provided the necessary causal link to the injury of a policeman who subsequently placed his hand in that pocket in the course of the search.[168] The charge was thus fully relevant as one of "recklessly causing injury". (That charge also alleged that the unfortunate policeman had been "exposed to the risk of infection" when the needle entered his hand; but this is probably a matter of aggravation rather than any necessary element in the description of the crime.)[169]

Reckless endangerment of the lieges

Where no injury is caused by reckless behaviour, but that **9–28** behaviour is objectively dangerous to others, a distinct offence of recklessly causing such danger is available.[170] Modern examples may be seen in *Normand v Robinson*,[171] where the accused

---

[161] See *HM Advocate v Harris*, 1993 J.C. 150, Lord Justice-Clerk Ross at 154D–E, Lord Murray at 156E, Lord Morison at 162G, and Lord Prosser at 167H–I. (Lord McCluskey dissented on this point.)

[162] *HM Advocate v Harris*, 1993 J.C. 150, Lord Murray at 156E.

[163] *Alexander Lawson* (1829) Bell's Notes 76.

[164] *Thomas Smith* (1853) 1 Irv. 271.

[165] *Archibald Grassom* (1884) 5 Coup. 483.

[166] *W v HM Advocate*, 1982 S.L.T. 420 (*sub nom. RHW v HM Advocate*, 1982 S.C.C.R. 152).

[167] *Kimmins v Normand*, 1993 S.L.T. 1260.

[168] *Kimmins v Normand*, 1993 S.L.T. 1260, per Lord Justice-General Hope at 1261H.

[169] *cf.* the charge in *Mallin v Clark*, 2002 S.L.T. 1202.

[170] *HM Advocate v Harris*, 1993 J.C. 150.

[171] *Normand v Robinson*, 1994 S.L.T. 558.

organised a mass entertainment known as "a rave" in derelict premises which were completely unsafe for the holding of such an event, and in *Normand v Morrison*,[172] where the accused allegedly denied to police officers who were about to search her that she had an unprotected hypodermic needle in her handbag—thus exposing those officers (or any one of them who undertook the search) to the risk of infection. It does not seem essential to the relevancy of such a charge that the words, "to the danger of the lieges [or others]" should actually appear on it, provided that such danger can readily be inferred[173]: and it does not seem to be (nor could be) an objection to such a charge that injuries were actually caused. In *MacPhail v Clark*,[174] for example, the accused set fire to stubble in a field in such a reckless manner that smoke in great quantity drifted over the carriageway of a nearby road thus causing acute problems of visibility for drivers of vehicles there. Whilst the accused unconcernedly continued with other tasks in the same field, road accidents occurred because of the smoke. There were injuries as a result of those accidents; but the charge appears to have been one of reckless endangerment to which the accounts of accident and injury were added by way of aggravation. In a case where the causal link between the accused's reckless conduct and actual injury to another is weak or difficult to prove, treating the injury as an aggravation is obviously a sensible course of action for the Crown to adopt.

Administration of noxious substances

9–29   It has been clear since the early nineteenth century that the deliberate and reckless (in the sense of having complete disregard for the consequences) administration of deleterious substances to anyone, to his injury, is criminal.[175] Thus Hume makes mention that the administration of a powerful aphrodisiac (cantharides) to three women, such that they were injured in their health, was considered a relevant crime.[176] Nor did it matter that the motive was merely one of sport or jest. In *Henry Inglis, Andrew and Robert Colvilles*,[177] for example, the administration of snuff in a draught of liquor to the victim as something of a joke was clearly criminal (although charged as culpable homicide, since the person who drank it died in consequence). It will be plain, therefore, that it is not necessary to show that the accused forced the noxious substance into the mouth or body of the victim. It is quite enough that

---

[172] *Normand v Morrison*, 1993 S.C.C.R. 207 Sh. Ct.
[173] See the complaint in *Normand v Morrison*, 1993 S.C.C.R. 207. See also *Donaldson v Normand*, 1997 S.C.C.R. 351, and *Robertson v Klos*, 2006 S.C.C.R. 52.
[174] *MacPhail v Clark*, 1983 S.L.T. (Sh. Ct.) 37.
[175] *Alexander Mitchell* (1833) Bell's Notes 90.
[176] Hume, *Commentaries*, i, 237 at note "b"—the case of *John Ferguson and John Eadie* (1822).
[177] *Henry Inglis, Andrew and Robert Colvilles* (1784) Hume, *Commentaries*, i, 237.

he caused the victim to take it, the self-administration, so to speak, not representing any *novus actus interveniens* (see above, paras 5–17 *et seq.*). In *Robert Brown and John Lawson*[178] it seems to have been quite sufficient that the accused gave a quarter of a pint of whisky to a seven year old child, who then, as far as one can determine, proceeded to drink it off by himself. (The child suffered from epileptic fits thereafter.) Naturally, whether a substance is truly noxious or not will depend on the age and disposition of the victim[179]; but substances prescribed by a doctor, or having apparent medicinal properties, are unlikely to be regarded as "deleterious", unless the circumstances are special.[180] It is possible too that consent might be a defence to a charge of administration of things having such medicinal properties.[181]

Supplying of potentially noxious substances

A state of intoxication has always held a considerable fascination **9–30** for human beings of all ages, and the obtaining of substances which will effect such a state has been seen at all times as a desirable goal. Those who are excluded by virtue of youth or lack of means from having ready access to "normal" and reasonably safe intoxicants have proved peculiarly inventive in exploiting substances really intended for some harmless, household purpose. Boot-polish, lighter fuel, paint thinners, and various glues, for example, can be turned to use as highly dangerous intoxicants when inhaled or ingested instead of being utilised for their intended purposes. It was indeed the desire to control abuse of such substances which led the Appeal Court in *Khaliq v HM Advocate*[182] to invent or perhaps "discover" the crime referred to here as "supplying potentially noxious substances." The offence itself is rather more complex, however, than that somewhat simple title would suggest.

The charge in *Khaliq*[183] contained at least five elements: (1) that **9–31** the accused shopkeepers wilfully and recklessly supplied, i.e. sold, or perhaps bartered, substances capable of giving off toxic fumes, e.g. "Evo-stik" glue; (2) that they did so to customers who were children, aged between eight and 15 years; (3) that the substances were specially supplied in, or with, containers, e.g. otherwise empty plastic bags, to facilitate the inhalation of those toxic fumes; (4)

---

[178] *Robert Brown and John Lawson* (1842) 1 Broun 415.
[179] cf. *Borwick v Urquhart*, 2003 S.C.C.R. 243, where the accused supplied the complainer (a 13 year old girl) with a half-bottle of vodka for which she provided the purchase price; she then proceeded to consume the contents at a rapid rate, with the inevitable consequence of acute intoxication: the complaint, however, followed the type of charge favoured in *Khaliq v HM Advocate*, 1984 J.C. 23 (see below paras 9–30 *et seq.*).
[180] *Peter Milne and John Barry* (1868) 1 Coup. 28, per Lord Cowan at 31.
[181] *Peter Milne and John Barry* (1868) 1 Coup. 28.
[182] *Khaliq v HM Advocate*, 1984 J.C. 23.
[183] *Khaliq v HM Advocate*, 1984 J.C. 23, quoted at 24 (charge (1)).

that the accused did so, well knowing that those customers intended to inhale the fumes and that such inhalation would or could be injurious to their health and a threat to their lives; and (5) that by virtue of their conduct, the accused caused those customers to inhale the fumes to the danger of their health and lives (on which, see above, para.5–18). That complex indictment was found relevant before the trial court, and the accused were convicted. Both findings were upheld on appeal. Although Lord Justice-General Emslie said[184]: "That the persons supplied were children is not . . . essential to the relevancy of the charge", it was widely felt that his remarks were mere *obiter*, since public concern at the time had centred on glue-sniffing *by children*. Indeed, when Parliament eventually placed a virtual embargo on sales of such substances to children[185] it did not extend the legislation to Scotland, since it apparently was of the persuasion that that was already the law in this country due to the decision in *Khaliq*. It was also widely felt that it had been very significant that the substances had been supplied in "user-friendly" kits. These "feelings" thus enabled the decision in *Khaliq* to be limited in a sensible way, so that it would not be seen as extending to the supply of whisky to a known alcoholic or cigarettes to a known sufferer from lung cancer.[186] But the subsequent decision in *Ulhaq*[187] (see below, para.9–32) has demonstrated that such perceived limitations were wrong.

9–32   In *Ulhaq v HM Advocate*[188] a shopkeeper was again charged with the same type of offence first seen in *Khaliq*. Significant differences existed, however, between the two fact situations. In *Ulhaq*, the customers were not children. They were all between 20 and 29 years of age, and could thus be described accurately as adults. What they had bought from the store in question were vast quantities of lighter fuel and glue—but all in their original cartons, tins and tubes. No inhalation-assisting "kits" were supplied at all. It was argued in vain, however, that those issues made any significant difference. It was enough that the storekeeper knew that his customers intended to use the substances for no proper purposes, that he supplied them on that basis, and that he thus caused them to abuse the substances in question to their injury and danger. This decision then resurrects the spectre of criminality surrounding, for example, the sale of significant quantities of alcohol to a known alcoholic. It may be that the case depends solely on its own facts, and is confined to volatile substances such as lighter fuel and glues. If that, however, is felt to be an essentially naive view, then the

---

[184] *Khaliq v HM Advocate*, 1984 J.C. 23 at 33.
[185] See the Intoxicating Substances (Supply) Act 1985. See also the indictments in *Khalid v HM Advocate*, 1990 J.C. 37, and *Borwick v Urquhart*, 2003 S.C.C.R. 243.
[186] See *Skeen v Malik*, unreported, 1977, in Gane and Stoddart, *Casebook on Criminal Law*, 2nd edn, p.453 at pp.456–457.
[187] *Ulhaq v HM Advocate*, 1991 S.L.T. 614.
[188] *Ulhaq v HM Advocate*, 1991 S.L.T. 614.

decision may only be rescued from uncontrolled expansion by reference to this: that the crime ought to be limited to the kind of substances which are potentially noxious if used in a way that their manufacturers never intended as proper, e.g. by being inhaled or swallowed, and which are not otherwise regulated in terms of sale, purchase or possession by Parliament.[189] (The signs are, however, that the courts are not persuaded that such limitations upon the offence would be justified.)[190] It might be thought, of course, that there is a problem with establishing a causal link in such cases since the person supplied must choose to use the substance in a way that its manufacturer did not intend. It might be thought, therefore, that the exercise of such choice amounts to a *novus actus interveniens*[191] which thus breaks the chain of interlinking events between the supplying and the abuse. In *Khaliq*,[192] however, such an argument was dismissed by the Appeal Court. The view was taken that the abuse of the substances was the "known, intended and expected purpose"[193] of their being supplied at all, and that there was such a close connection between supplying and administration in such circumstances that it was legitimate to treat the supply as

---

[189] *cf.* cigarettes and ethyl alcohols. See, e.g. in relation to tobacco, the Children and Young Persons (Scotland) Act 1937 s.18, as amended by the Protection of Children (Tobacco) Act 1986, the Children and Young Persons (Protection from Tobacco) Act 1991, and the Smoking, Health and Social Care (Scotland) Act 2005 (Variation of Age Limit for Sale of Tobacco etc. and Consequential Modifications) Order 2007 (SSI 2007/437) art.2.

[190] See *Lord Advocate's Reference (No.1 of 1994)*, 1995 S.L.T. 248, where the "supplying" of drugs (controlled under the Misuse of Drugs Act 1971) was considered equivalent to the offence fashioned in *Khaliq* and *Ulhaq* for the purposes of culpable homicide where the person supplied died after ingesting those drugs. The "rules" pertaining to the "reckless supply of potentially noxious substances" were thus made available against the supplier in a culpable homicide prosecution, and enabled objections to the establishing of a causal link there to be swept aside: *cf. HM Advocate v C*, 2007 S.L.T. 963 (opinion of Lord McEwan on a preliminary plea). See also *Borwick v Urquhart*, 2003 S.C.C.R. 243, where the court held (at 247C–D, para.7) that the circumstances fell "very directly within the decision in *Khaliq*", in that the appellant had (at his suggestion) bought alcohol (a half-bottle of vodka) for a 13 year old female complainer, who had supplied the money for same and who had proceeded to drink all of the bottle's contents "very quickly": she became very drunk, if not unconscious, as a result. It was argued that Borwick's conviction of the relevant offence had represented an extension of the crime set out in *Khaliq*; but the appeal court rejected that submission and declined to refer in any detail to the "crime of culpable and reckless conduct in *Khaliq*, or [any] other case" (opinion of the court at 247C, para.7); *cf.* the House of Lords' decision in *R. v Kennedy* [2007] 3 W.L.R. 612, where it appears that English law differs from the law in Scotland.

[191] See above, paras 5–17 *et seq.*

[192] *Khaliq v HM Advocate*, 1984 J.C. 23.

[193] *Khaliq v HM Advocate*, 1984 J.C. 23, per Lord Justice-General Emslie at 33.

analogous to administration (and thus criminal), "even in the absence of words of instigation on the part of the suppliers."[194]

Discharge of firearms

9–33 It is certainly criminal to discharge firearms recklessly to the danger or actual injury of the lieges.[195] That no one need actually be injured is understandable given the lethal nature of such weapons; but in the absence of real injury, it seems necessary that there were likely to be people within range at the time, as in *David Smith and William McNeil*[196] where much emphasis was placed on the fact that the accused shot through the glass window of an inhabited house, to the imminent danger of those living there. There seems little to be gained by treating this as an offence separate from "reckless injury" (see above, para.9–27) or "reckless endangerment of the lieges" (see above, para.9–28), although an especially dangerous *modus*, of course, is involved in this instance of those crimes.

4.(A) COMMON LAW HOMICIDES

Introduction

9–34 There are two forms of criminal homicide recognised by Scots common law—murder and culpable homicide. The *actus reus* of both of those crimes is identical. It consists of positive conduct by the accused, or a failure by him to act where he had a legal duty to do so, which causes the death of another human being.[197] "Failures to act" have already been explored in Ch.3,[198] and "causation" issues in Ch.5. But the question of when a person is dead raises some nice issues of its own. Before a "person" can be killed, he must have been alive. In a sense (and for some, a very real sense), a human foetus is alive from the moment of its conception onwards. If that were so for the purposes of the criminal law, then it would be homicide to end a foetus's "life" by destroying it in its

---

[194] *Khaliq v HM Advocate*, 1984 J.C. 23. This method of establishing a causal connection was used a fortiori in *Lord Advocate's Reference (No.1 of 1994)*, 1995 S.L.T. 248 (see above, fn.190) where prohibited (and thus dangerous per se) drugs were supplied to a person who had voluntarily sought them, voluntarily selected a particular dose of them, voluntarily taken that dose, and then died from the effects.

[195] See, e.g. *Robert Anderson* (1832) Bell's Notes 73; *Gizzi v Tudhope*, 1983 S.L.T. 214; *Cameron v Maguire*, 1999 S.C.C.R. 44.

[196] *David Smith and William McNeil* (1842) 1 Broun 240.

[197] Gordon, *Criminal Law*, 3rd edn, paras 23.04 to 23.08. If, of course, there is sufficient evidence that the deceased was seen alive after the date and time when he is alleged to have been killed by the accused, it may be impossible to sustain a conviction for homicide: see *Johnston v HM Advocate*, 2006 S.C.C.R. 236.

[198] See above, paras 3–09 *et seq*.

mother's womb. That is not, however, the approach taken. Hume makes it plain that the destruction of life in the womb is not homicide but the separate crime of abortion.[199] The criterion for homicide thus appears to be that the victim had been a "self-existent human life."[200] At the very least, the victim must have been born alive at one point in time, and killed at another, because of some action or inaction on the accused's part. As Hume colourfully indicates,[201] until a foetus is born alive, it is merely "pars viscerum matris", i.e. part of its mother's viscera.[202] It seems, however, that the Appeal Court has accepted that a child born alive can be subsequently killed by some injury which was caused to it in the womb.[203]

Abortion

The crime of abortion at common law consists of intentionally **9–35** causing or procuring the termination of pregnancy and consequently the destruction of a developing foetus.[204] The method of achieving such an end is probably of little moment, but the cases on the subject generally refer to the use of instruments or the administration of drugs.[205] It is also essential that there had been a criminal purpose, since it may have been necessary to cause the abortion[206]—to save the life of the mother, for example. Since the Abortion Act 1967, however, the common law crime has ceased to be of any real significance. The import of the Act[207] is that an abortion carried out by a qualified doctor will not be criminal, provided that two independent doctors certify that there would be greater risk to the physical or mental health of the mother or any of her existing children in carrying the foetus to term than in terminating the pregnancy (which may be done on these grounds until the end of the 24th week of the pregnancy only), or (and the following are without time limit) that there would be grave permanent injury (mental or physical) to the mother (or risk to her life) if the pregnancy were allowed to continue, or that there would

---

[199] Hume, *Commentaries*, i, 186; see below, para.9–35.
[200] As Macdonald puts it, *Criminal Law*, 5th edn, p.87, although this has to be seen simply as a useful way of referring to the demarcation line between a foetus and a child born alive. A newly born infant, and indeed a person in a coma or persistent vegetative state (see below, para.9–70) can hardly be said to be "self-existent", yet are clearly not beyond the protection of the law of homicide.
[201] Hume, *Commentaries*, i, 186.
[202] cf. the view in English law: see *Attorney General's Reference (No.3 of 1994)* [1998] A.C. 245 HL, especially the opinion of Lord Hope of Craighead at 267 D-G. See also Smith and Hogan, *Criminal Law*, 10th edn, pp.354–355.
[203] *McCluskey v HM Advocate*, 1988 S.C.C.R. 629 at 632.
[204] Macdonald, *Criminal Law*, 5th edn, p.114.
[205] See *Minnie Graham* (1897) 2 Adam 412.
[206] Macdonald, *Criminal Law*, 5th edn, p.114.
[207] See Abortion Act 1967 s.1(1), as amended by the Human Fertilisation and Embryology Act 1990 s.37.

be substantial risk of serious handicap to the child if the foetus were allowed to be born.

Death

9–36   There is no particular legal definition of death. In modern times, it is clear that the cessation of breathing or heart-beat does not conclusively show that a person is dead. Medical science has in any event invented the technological means of sustaining breath and pulse in situations where a person has lost the means of sustaining them for himself.[208] It is thought, therefore, that an appropriate legal test for death must now involve the permanent cessation of brain activity. But the courts have not commented on the matter, although at least one reported case presented the opportunity for them to do so.[209]

Res judicata

9–37   Homicides are often caused by actions which are crimes in their own right, e.g. by assaults or by administration of noxious substances such as active poisons. Since Scots law never had any rule equivalent to that of the now repealed English "year and a day" rule[210] it can happen that an accused is convicted and sentenced for an assault upon a person who later, much later, dies of his injuries. The view taken, however, is that the original conviction for any such crime less than homicide does not prevent a new trial for homicide, if the victim subsequently dies.[211] From this point of view, homicide is not just an aggravated form of assault or other offence of real injury, but a separate class of crime.

Casual Homicide

9–38   The older text-writers[212] emphasise that some killings are not criminal, and that in particular some may be described as "casual". Hume indicates that such a killing occurs,

> "when a person kills unintentionally, who is lawfully employed, and neither means bodily harm to any one, nor has failed in the due degree of care for preventing danger to his neighbour."

What he seems to mean by this is simply that accidental homicides are not criminal (as in the case of *John Leper*,[213] where a prisoner

---

[208] See below, e.g. para.9–70 (persistent vegetative state).
[209] See *Finlayson v HM Advocate*, 1979 J.C. 33; see above, para.5–23.
[210] See *R. v Dyson* [1908] 2 K.B. 454; Law Reform (Year and a Day Rule) Act 1996.
[211] *Tees v HM Advocate*, 1994 S.L.T. 701.
[212] e.g. Hume, *Commentaries*, i, 194.
[213] *John Leper* (1682) Hume, *Commentaries*, i, 194.

insisted on running ahead of his guard, despite warnings that the castle which they were traversing was in part ruinous and dangerous; the prisoner having become lost and fallen 20 feet to his death, it was held that no blame for the death could be attached to his escort).

Justifiable homicide

Other killings which are not criminal are those which are **9–39** justifiable. Hume,[214] for example, mentions homicides effected by soldiers with good cause (in war, perhaps, or in the quelling of a riot), or police officers. It is thought, however, that police officers would only be justified in killing where it was necessary to do so in self-defence—a broad category open to anyone (see above, paras 8–17 *et seq.*), and also, it seems, to women in particular in avoidance of rape (see above, para.8–35). Despite some dicta to the contrary,[215] it is not thought that homicide in defence of property alone can ever be justifiable.

Excusable homicide

It is not clear whether there is any such class as that of **9–40** "excusable homicide"[216] but it remains possible that the Scottish courts will not follow English authority, and will not rule out a defence of coercion to a homicide charge (see above, para.8–80).[217] If that happens then, as coercion is an excuse personal to the accused, this class would have at least one member.

Penalties for homicide

The two forms of criminal homicide are distinguishable from **9–41** one another by reference to their *mens rea* requirements and also according to the penalty which follows conviction. For murder there is a mandatory life sentence, with appropriate provision for those who are under 18 and those who are under 21.[218] The trial judge must, however, state the length of the "punishment part" of the sentence which he thinks appropriate to be served in order to "satisfy the requirements for retribution and deterrence".[219] Culpable homicide, on the other hand, has no mandatory penalty, and

---

[214] See Hume, *Commentaries*, i, 195–222, especially from 205 at "5".

[215] *Edward Lane* (1830) Bell's Notes 77, per Lord Moncreiff, that a servant might be justified in killing an intruder found in his master's house "[if he] had reasonable grounds to think . . . that he could not otherwise protect his master's property."

[216] See above, paras 8–03 and 8–04, for the difference between an excuse and a justification.

[217] Which refers to Lord Allanbridge's direction to the jury in *Collins v HM Advocate*, 1991 S.C.C.R. 898 at 902C. See the detailed consideration given to this matter in Chalmers and Leverick, *Criminal Defences and Pleas in Bar of Trial*, pp.113–118, paras 5–27 to 5–31.

[218] Criminal Procedure (Scotland) Act 1995 s.205, as amended by the Convention Rights (Compliance) (Scotland) Act 2001 (asp 7) s.2.

[219] Custodial Sentences and Weapons (Scotland) Act 2007 (asp 17) s.20. For further details, see *Sentencing Practice* (Edinburgh: W. Green, 2002), paras C10.0001 *et seq*. See also *Stewart v HM Advocate*, 2002 S.C.C.R. 915; *Walker v HM Advocate*, 2002 S.C.C.R. 1036.

carries a sentencing range no different from that which a trial court has for any common law crime (see Appendix D). It follows then that wide sentencing options exist for those convicted of culpable homicide, and instances can easily be found of very lenient disposals which reflect the circumstances involved. In *Robert Bruce*,[220] for example, where the death was something of a mischance occasioned during the course of a consensual fight, the accused was convicted and fined one shilling (although he was also required to find caution to keep the peace for one year); and in the controversial case of *HM Advocate v Sherman*[221] the accused was admonished after having been convicted of the culpable homicide of his wife and child by shooting. The implication of the penalty differences between the two crimes is that in essence all murders are taken to be equally morally bad,[222] whereas culpable homicide cases vary enormously in moral culpability. It is also implied, of course, by reference to sentence that only a High Court can deal with a case of murder; and it is a matter of law that a district or J.P. court can never deal with a case of murder or culpable homicide.[223]

MURDER

Definition of murder

9–42   In the homicide case of *Drury v HM Advocate*,[224] the majority of the five-judge Appeal Court was of the view that Macdonald's oft-quoted account of murder was incomplete.[225] In terms of that account, murder was,

> "constituted by any wilful act causing the destruction of life, whether intended to kill, or displaying such wicked recklessness as to imply a disposition depraved enough to be regardless of consequences."[226]

The case was chiefly concerned with the plea of provocation; but the majority of the court was of the view that Macdonald's account did not explain why, for example, a person who killed intentionally

[220] *Robert Bruce* (1855) 2 Irv. 65.
[221] *HM Advocate v Sherman*, unreported, February 27, 1990, High Court at Aberdeen.
[222] It should be noted that this proposition is tempered by the concept of the "punishment part" referred to in the text above.
[223] Criminal Procedure (Scotland) Act 1995 s.7(8)(b), as amended by the Criminal Proceedings etc. (Reform) (Scotland) Act 2007 (asp 6) Sch.1 para.9(4).
[224] *Drury v HM Advocate*, 2001 S.L.T. 1013.
[225] *Drury v HM Advocate*, 2001 S.L.T. 1013, Lord Justice-General Rodger at 1016H–I, para.10; Lord Johnston at 1029F–G, para.18; Lord Nimmo Smith at 1030I–K, para.2; and Lord Mackay of Drumadoon at 1033F, para.8.
[226] Macdonald, *Criminal Law*, 5th edn, p.89.

while defending himself or while responding to provocation was either not guilty of anything (in the case of self-defence) or guilty only of culpable homicide (in the case of provocation): if he intended to kill, why was he not guilty of murder, since he appeared to fall within the first limb of Macdonald's account of that crime? The court's answer was that although the Macdonald account would suffice "in many cases—as, for instance, where the only real issue in dispute is the identity of the killer . . .",[227] that account was not an appropriate jury direction where provocation or self-defence was in issue, since (in the words of the Lord Justice-General) "it does not describe the relevant intention."[228] To remedy this defect, the Lord Justice-General stated:

> "In truth, just as the recklessness has to be wicked so also must the intention be wicked. Therefore, perhaps the most obvious way of completing the definition is by saying that murder is constituted by any wilful act causing the destruction of life, by which the perpetrator either wickedly intends to kill or displays wicked recklessness as to whether the victim lives or dies. Saying that the perpetrator 'wickedly' intends to kill is just a shorthand way of referring to what Hume (vol. i, p. 254) describes as the murderer's 'wicked and mischievous purpose' in contradistinction to 'those motives of necessity, duty, or allowable infirmity, which may serve to justify or excuse' the deliberate taking of life".[229]

In consequence, the definition of murder has become a little uncertain—given that the court in *Drury* seems to consider Macdonald's account of the crime to be satisfactory where, for example, self-defence or provocation is not in issue at a trial. Also it is a little uncertain what the term "wickedly" should mean when allied to Macdonald's "intention to kill", since Lord Justice-General Rodger's opinion in particular can be read restrictively[230] (in the sense that "wickedly" is but an abbreviation for the absence of a

---

[227] *Drury v HM Advocate*, 2001 S.L.T. 1013, Lord Justice-General Rodger at 1016I, para.10; *cf.*, Lord Nimmo Smith at 1030I–J, para.2.
[228] *Drury v HM Advocate*, 2001 S.L.T. 1013, Lord Justice-General Rodger at 1016J, para.11.
[229] *Drury v HM Advocate*, 2001 S.L.T. 1013, Lord Justice-General Rodger at 1016J–K, para.11. See also Lord Johnston at 1029E–F, para.18, Lord Nimmo Smith at 1030L–1031A, para.3; Lord Mackay of Drumadoon at 1033G–H, para.9. For criticism of this "completion" of Macdonald's account of murder, see James Chalmers, "Collapsing the Structure of Criminal Law", 2001 S.L.T. (News) 241; Fiona Leverick, "Mistake in Self-defence after *Drury*", 2002 J.R. 35. That the intention to kill is usually now qualified by "wickedness" is referred to by the court in *HM Advocate v Purcell*, 2007 S.C.C.R. 520 at 526, para.9.
[230] See *Drury v HM Advocate*, 2001 S.LT. 1013 at 1018F–H, para.18, 1019I–J, para.20.

limited range of applicable "defences" such as self-defence, provocation and diminished responsibility)[231] or rather more widely (in
the sense that "wickedly" refers to the absence of any acceptable
factor which can excuse, justify or provide mitigation for the
killing).[232] Further uncertainty too is created in that the opinions in
Drury can be read as if the element of wickedness now carries the
same meaning across both branches of the *mens rea* of the crime.[233]
It would be awkward, however, to have to conclude that there were
two different definitions of murder depending upon the circumstances of an individual trial; it would also place too much
discretion in the hands of a jury if a wide interpretation of
"wickedly" were to be preferred in relation to intentional killings;
and, it would perhaps be too bold to conclude that in *Drury's* case
the Appeal Court had swept away the accepted view of the
meaning of "wicked recklessness" without detailed consideration of
the relevant cases and text-writings.[234]

It is suggested, therefore, that, following the decision in *Drury*,
the modification of Macdonald's account of the crime provides the
following definition: "murder is constituted by any wilful act
causing the destruction of life, whether wickedly intended to kill (in
the sense that a deliberate killing was not done by the accused in
self-defence, or in response to provocation, or whilst he was
suffering from diminished responsibility)[235] or displaying such
wicked recklessness as to imply a disposition depraved enough to
be regardless of consequences." In other words, it consists of the
actus reus proffered generally above at para.9–34, together with
two alternative forms of *mens rea*.

Actus reus

9–43   Murder is a result crime (see above, para.2–36). From this point
of view, it is certainly correct to say that the type of conduct which
causes death is of little consequence (see above, para.3–05). But

---

[231] See Chalmers, "Collapsing the Structure of Criminal Law", 2001 S.L.T. (News)
241, 242; Leverick, "Mistake in Self-Defence after *Drury*", 2002 J.R. 35, 41; Sir
Gerald H. Gordon, "Commentary" to *Drury v HM Advocate*, 2001 S.C.C.R. 583
at 618G–619A, 619F.

[232] *cf.* Gordon, "Commentary" to *Drury v HM Advocate*, 2001 S.C.C.R. 583 at
619G–620C.

[233] See *Drury v HM Advocate*, 2001 S.L.T. 1013, Lord Justice-General Rodger at
1016J, para.11: "In truth, just as the recklessness has to be wicked so also must
the intention be wicked."

[234] It is also the express or implied view of the commentators mentioned above in
fn.20, that the re-definition of murder undertaken in *Drury* applies only to
intentional killings; and indeed the judge's direction at Drury's first trial was
considered by the Appeal Court to have been defective in relation to intentional
rather than "wickedly reckless" killings.

[235] Diminished responsibility is mentioned by Lord Justice-General Rodger in *Drury
v HM Advocate*, 2001 S.L.T. 1013 at 1017B, para.13, in the same context as
provocation. In the later case of *Galbraith v HM Advocate (No.2)*, 2002 J.C. 1,
however, diminished responsibility was said to reduce murder to culpable
homicide (rather than, as one might have anticipated, to negate such wickedness
as constitutes an essential part of the *mens rea* of murder).

the conduct in question must be capable of raising an inference that *mens rea* of either type existed. What might reasonably be said at present, therefore, is that the range of conduct capable of raising such an inference is vast. It extends, for example, to the use of severe physical violence, as in *Charles McDonald*[236]—fists, stones and bottles; the employment of weapons, as in *Cawthorne v HM Advocate*[237]—rifle firing high-velocity bullets; the administration of poisons, as in *Christian Gilmour*[238] and *Madeleine Smith*[239]; setting fire to the victim's clothing, as in *HM Advocate v Kennedy*[240]; boring holes in a ship's bottom, as in *HM Advocate v Monson*[241]; throwing the victim twice from a fourth floor window, as in *McGuire v HM Advocate*[242]; and deserting a young child as in *Elizabeth Kerr*[243] or a seriously injured adult, as in *HM Advocate v McPhee*.[244]

Mens rea: wicked intent

As discussed above (see para.9–42), a "wicked" intent to kill is a **9–44** sufficient form of *mens rea* for murder, provided it is understood that "wicked" stands as an abbreviation for the absence of a limited range of pleas.[245] These pleas certainly extend to self-defence[246] and provocation,[247] and most likely to diminished responsibility too[248]; and the effect of these pleas is to prevent the Crown establishing the *mens rea* of intentional murder.[249] In relation to a deliberate killing, therefore, such pleas are part of the *mens rea* of the crime, in the sense that it is their absence which makes the killing "wicked".[250] Thus, where no such plea arises in any particular case, it is probably unnecessary to direct a jury of the need to prove "wicked intent" as opposed to intent, since it seems

---

[236] *Charles McDonald* (1867) 5 Irv. 525.
[237] *Cawthorne v HM Advocate*, 1968 J.C. 32.
[238] *Christian Gilmour* (1844) 2 Broun 23.
[239] *Madeleine Smith* (1857) 2 Irv. 641.
[240] *HM Advocate v Kennedy* (1907) 5 Adam 347.
[241] *HM Advocate v Monson* (1893) 1 Adam 114.
[242] *McGuire v HM Advocate*, 1995 S.C.C.R. 776.
[243] *Elizabeth Kerr* (1860) 3 Irv. 645, though she pled guilty to culpable homicide.
[244] *HM Advocate v McPhee*, 1935 J.C. 46.
[245] See *Drury v HM Advocate*, 2001 S.L.T. 1013. Although the term "plea" has been used here, in other contexts the term "defence" would be more appropriate.
[246] See above, paras 8–17 *et seq.*
[247] See below, paras 9–59 *et seq.*
[248] *cf. Galbraith v HM Advocate (No.2)*, 2002 J.C. 1; see below, paras 9–66 to 9–67.
[249] That does not imply, of course, that the *mens rea* of any other crime is necessarily excluded: where, for example, the plea was one of provocation or diminished responsibility, the accused will be convicted of culpable homicide—see *Drury v HM Advocate*, 2001 S.L.T. 1013; *Galbraith v HM Advocate (No.2)*, 2002 J.C. 1.
[250] Some would argue that this has the effect of allowing an honest but unreasonably erroneous belief (in the need for self-defence or in the provocative nature of a situation) to defeat the establishment of *mens rea* in an intentional killing: see Leverick, "Mistake in Self-defence after *Drury*", 2002 J.R. 35.

that no general notion of wickedness is in fact involved.[251] If that is correct, then intentional killings (where no such plea arises) based on "good" ulterior motives, such as mercy killings, are prima facie murders.[252] How prosecutors in the exercise of their discretion deal with such "good motive" intentional killings is, of course, beside the point, as far as the *mens rea* of murder is concerned.

It seems, however, that the notion of "wicked" in "wicked intent" is not of the same order as the "wickedness" in relation to that recklessness which is sufficient as the alternative *mens rea* for murder[253]: and, insofar as self-defence, provocation and diminished responsibility are applicable to murders based on "wicked reckless- ness" rather than "wicked intent", it seems that these pleas stand as defences which will be brought into play only after the necessary *mens rea* has been established.[254] This does not make for very consistent theory; but this seems to be an inevitable consequence of the way in which the decision in *Drury v HM Advocate*[255] has come to be understood.

Mens rea: wicked recklessness

9–45   The alternative form of *mens rea* is "wicked recklessness", and it is thought that this means a form of recklessness which transcends "simple" recklessness. More is required than the usual, "utter disregard of what the consequences of the act in question may be, so far as the public are concerned." That may be enough for some instances of culpable homicide; but it clearly cannot also be sufficient for murder, if the two crimes are to be distinguished successfully. The difference, of course, may simply be one of degree; that recklessness for murder is morally a more reprehens- ible form than normal. It is thought, however, that it is possible to be more specific than that. In particular, from the accounts of this alternative form of *mens rea* given by Hume,[256] three issues seem to be involved: first, that the accused should have meant to perpetrate some great and outrageous bodily harm; secondly, that that harm was such as might well have resulted in death; and thirdly, that that

---

[251] See, e.g. *Arthur v HM Advocate (No.1)*, 2002 S.C.C.R. 796, Lord Hamilton at 800E, para.12: "The trial judge directed the jury on the alternative bases on which a verdict of murder might be returned. No issue arises about the terms in which he directed them on the first of these alternatives (intention to kill)."

[252] This would simply confirm the view of most commentators: see Gordon, *Criminal Law*, 3rd edn, paras 25.02 and 25.03 (although provision is made there for a possible alternative reading of *Drury*); Ferguson, *Crimes Against the Person*, 2nd edn, para. 3.02.

[253] *cf. Scott v HM Advocate*, 1995 S.C.C.R. 760—a case decided, of course, prior to (but not mentioned in) *Drury v HM Advocate*, 2001 S.L.T. 1013.

[254] Thus, it may still be possible vis a vis "wicked recklessness" to support a rule that erroneous beliefs (relative to the need for self-defence or the provocative nature of a situation) require to be based on reasonable grounds.

[255] *Drury v HM Advocate*, 2001 S.L.T. 1013.

[256] Hume, *Commentaries*, i, 191, 238, 256.

harm showed an absolute or utter indifference as to whether the victim lived or died. Hume requires, then, an assault (or something close to it) of such seriousness that it might easily have resulted in death and which shows in the circumstances a complete indifference to the life of the victim. That sort of approach will certainly suit most of the reported cases,[257] though not all of the judicial dicta on the matter.

Intent to do outrageous or excessive bodily harm

It must be remembered, of course, that "wicked recklessness" is **9–46** an alternative form of *mens rea*, and that it applies where the accused is assumed not to have had an intent to kill. Hume's initial requirement of an intent to "do him an excessive and outrageous bodily harm"[258] will itself, however, be objectively assessed, such that it can be deduced not only from actual physical violence[259] but also, for example, from setting fire to a house, *known to be inhabited*, in the early hours of the morning.[260] It is more difficult to make such a deduction in some cases, such as that of *Cawthorne v HM Advocate*.[261] There, the accused fired several rounds of high-velocity bullets into a room where, as he well knew, a number of people had taken refuge from him. No attempt was made to avoid hitting anyone there by, for example, firing towards the ceiling. On the assumption that this intent was merely to frighten those people and not to injure or kill them at all, the Appeal Court still determined that he had shown the wicked recklessness necessary for murder. It may be that this is a maverick decision; or it may be that Hume's initial requirement would be better phrased as "an intent to do the victim any great and outrageous *harm*", so as to accommodate frightening persons in such a way. It is difficult, however, to see that *Cawthorne's* case was one of wicked recklessness at all. Anyone doing what he did might reasonably be supposed to have ("wickedly") intended to kill.

Hume, of course, made an intent to do outrageous bodily harm **9–47** only one of three necessary requirements if murder was to be brought home to a person who did not have an intent to kill. An

---

[257] See, in particular, *Arthur v HM Advocate (No.1)*, 2002 S.C.C.R. 796. It probably also suits the opinion of the court (on a certified issue) in *HM Advocate v Purcell*, 2007 S.C.C.R. 520: see in particular 526E–527D, paras 10–11. (Commentators differ on the significance of *Purcell*: *cf.* Michael Plaxton, "Foreseeing the Consequences of Purcell", 2008 S.L.T. (News) 21, and Gordon's Commentary to the case, at 2007 S.C.C.R. 520 at 530–531.)

[258] Hume, *Commentaries*, i, 238.

[259] As in *HM Advocate v Fraser and Rollins*, 1920 J.C. 60, or *Brennan v HM Advocate*, 1977 J.C. 38.

[260] See the facts in the English cases of *R. v Nedrick* [1986] 1 W.L.R. 1025; *Hyam v DPP* [1975] A.C. 55; *cf.* the opinion of the court in *HM Advocate v Purcell*, 2007 S.C.C.R. 520 at 528D–529E, paras 14–17, although there the court was concerned with the (now) discredited "doctrine of constructive malice".

[261] *Cawthorne v HM Advocate*, 1968 J.C. 32.

intent to do serious bodily harm is not by itself, therefore, a sufficient form of *mens rea* for murder. Unfortunately, it is clear that some judges have taken the view that it was. This must be a clear misreading of what Hume intended. Certainly Hume did write the following: "[O]ur practice ... does not distinguish between an absolute purpose to kill, and a purpose to do any excessive and grievous injury to the person."[262] But, after quoting some illustrations, he continued:

> "Because in committing any such desperate outrage on the body [i.e. any one of the examples he had just quoted], the pannel shows an utter contempt of the safety and the life of his neighbour, and if not a determination to kill him, at least an absolute indifference whether he live or die."[263]

His illustrations (hamstringing the victim, cutting out his tongue, beating him to within an inch of his life) clearly support the three-fold approach detailed above (see para.9–45), and thus give no support for the view that death following *any* deliberate infliction of grievous bodily harm is automatically murder.

9–48   In any event, a *mens rea* for murder in terms of "an intent to do serious bodily injury" is part of the English account of this crime[264]; and the Appeal Court has soundly rejected the view that the Scots and English definitions of murder are the same.[265] Beyond that, the vagueness of the phrase "serious bodily injury" makes for uncertain and possibly unfair decisions. In the event of someone dying, for example, after having had his arm deliberately broken by the accused, it would have to follow that the crime was murder,[266] notwithstanding that death was not reasonably to be anticipated from such an injury, and that the actions of the accused might not have shown utter indifference whether the victim lived or died. It is submitted, therefore, that Scots cases, where judges have opined that an intent to do serious injury is an independent form of *mens rea* for murder, are wrong.[267] Such a submission can be supported

---

[262] Hume, *Commentaries*, i, 256.

[263] Hume, *Commentaries*, i, 257.

[264] See, e.g. *R. v Moloney* [1985] A.C. 905, per Lord Bridge of Harwich at 927H; *Attorney General's Reference (No.3 of 1994)*, [1998] A.C. 245, Lord Mustill at 250D–F.

[265] *Brennan v HM Advocate*, 1977 J.C. 38.

[266] *R. v Cunningham* [1982] A.C. 566, per Lord Edmund Davies at 582H–583A.

[267] See, e.g. *Margaret Robertson or Brown* (1886) 1 White 93, per Lord McLaren at 104; *William Marshall* (1897) 4 S.L.T. 217, per Lord Young at 217; *George Paterson* (1897) 5 S.L.T. 13, per Lord Young at 13; *Kennedy v HM Advocate*, 1944 J.C. 171, per Lord Justice-General Normand at 177; *Lord Advocate v Kidd*, 1960 J.C. 61, per Lord Strachan at 74; *Cawthorne v HM Advocate*, 1968 S.L.T. 330, per Lord Avonside at 330 and Lord Guthrie at 332; *Brennan v HM Advocate*, 1977 J.C. 38 at 47; and *HM Advocate v Hartley*, 1989 S.L.T. 135, per Lord Sutherland at 135.

by reference to the House of Lords Select Committee on Murder and Life Imprisonment.[268] Not only did many prestigious contributions from advocates, solicitors and academics in Scotland deny the existence of such a form of *mens rea*, but so also did evidence from the Lord Justice-Clerk, Lord Ross and the then Lord Justice-General, Lord Emslie. Lord Emslie in particular[269] implied that Lord Sutherland in *HM Advocate v Hartley*[270] had been incorrect to tell the jury that an intent to do serious bodily harm was enough by itself to constitute the *mens rea* of murder; and he also said[271] in relation to the opinion of the court in *Brennan v HM Advocate*, which was apparently compiled by him, that he had merely been careless in expressing himself there, when he had written:

> "Our definition of murder includes the taking of human life by a person who has an intent to kill or to do serious injury or whose act is shown to have been wickedly reckless as to the consequences."[272]

Alternatively, he thought that perhaps the second "or" in the quotation should have appeared as "and."

Lethal weapons and particular crimes

Some judicial dicta, and Hume,[273] appear to support the view **9–49** that death causally connected to the use of certain weapons or the perpetration of certain crimes, will automatically be classed as murder. The authority for this is sparse, however. Lord Sands in *HM Advocate v Fraser and Rollins*[274] certainly told the jury that if there was an attempt at a crime of serious violence, then any resultant death of the victim was murder. He further gave as examples an abortion involving the use of instruments which ended with the death of the woman concerned,[275] and any rape or robbery in which the victim was killed.[276] His conclusion then followed,

> "if a man uses reckless violence that may cause death, and uses that violence in perpetrating a crime, it is murder. You do not require the deliberate intention to kill, but you must have reckless use of force without any consideration of what the result of that use of force may be."[277]

---

[268] H.L. 78-I to III, session 1988–89.
[269] I.L.L. 78-III, Q. 2017.
[270] *HM Advocate v Hartley*, 1989 S.L.T. 135 at 135.
[271] H.L. 78-III, Q. 2020.
[272] *Brennan v HM Advocate*, 1977 J.C. 38 at 47.
[273] Hume, *Commentaries*, i, 24, 25.
[274] *HM Advocate v Fraser and Rollins*, 1920 J.C. 60 at 62.
[275] *HM Advocate v Fraser and Rollins*, 1920 J.C. 60 at 62.
[276] *HM Advocate v Fraser and Rollins*, 1920 J.C. 60 at 62–63.
[277] *HM Advocate v Fraser and Rollins*, 1920 J.C. 60 at 63.

It is submitted that this is either a rather loose form of Hume's tripartite requirement (see above, para.9–45) or is simply wrong.[278] Similarly, it would be wrong to imagine that murder is automatically relevant if death follows upon a crime in which a certain type of weapon was employed. In *HM Advocate v McGuinness*,[279] for example, Lord Justice-Clerk Aitchison told the jury:

> "If people resort to the use of deadly weapons of this kind [knives, pokers, hatchets], they are guilty of murder whether or not they intended to kill."

That, however, is not really the point. The true issue is that the more dangerous to life a particular weapon is, the more likely its deployment will show that the accused meant to perpetrate some outrageous bodily harm, that his actions were very likely to result in death, and that those actions showed an absolute indifference as to whether his victim lived or died. In other words, dangerous or lethal weapons will often make it simpler to fulfil Hume's requirements for non-intentional murder.[280]

Examples of "wicked recklessness"

9–50   Cases of murder founded on "wicked recklessness" are easily found amongst the law reports. Amongst the clearest of these must figure the ancient case of *Patrick Stewart*.[281] In the belief that the victim had had sexual intercourse with his daughter, the accused had him bound with cords, his penis cut off, his scrotum filled with ashes, his leg broken with a blow from an axe, and his person then carried off to a close confinement—where death ensued. An equally clear application of the "wicked recklessness" test can be found in *George Paterson*[282] where the drunken accused not only violently struck the unfortunate female victim, but also thrust a red-hot poker into her rectum and private parts. The test was also considered to be fulfilled in the case of *John McCallum and William Corner*.[283] These two accused partially severed the cable which lowered men in a bucket to the bottom of a pit. Their intention was to cause some injury to the victim, who they knew

---

[278] *cf.* Gordon, *Criminal Law*, 3rd edn, paras 23.26 to 23.28; Ferguson, *Crimes Against the Person*, paras 2–18, 2–19.

[279] *HM Advocate v McGuinness*, 1937 J.C. 37 at 40.

[280] See above, para. 9–45; *Parr v HM Advocate*, 1991 J.C. 39, Lord Justice-General Hope at 47; *Broadley v HM Advocate*, 1991 J.C. 108; *Arthur v HM Advocate (No.1)*, 2002 S.C.C.R. 796; *cf.*, Gordon, *Criminal Law*, 3rd edn, paras 23.26 to 23.28, for the support which exists for the view that a death caused in the course of a robbery is always to be treated as murder.

[281] *Patrick Stewart* (1602) Hume, *Commentaries*, i, 260; R. Pitcairn, *Ancient Criminal Trials in Scotland* (Edinburgh: 1833), Vol.II, p.392.

[282] *George Paterson* (1897) 5 S.L.T. 13.

[283] *John McCallum and William Corner* (1853) 1 Irv. 259.

would be next to be lowered on that particular cable. He fell violently to the bottom of the mine shaft when the cable broke under the strain—just as the accused had intended. They had not intended his death, however. On their own admissions, they had simply intended to injure him to a certain degree, to the extent of a broken leg, for example. In the whole circumstances of the case, there could be little doubt that wicked recklessness was displayed there.[284] It has been held too that, in an appropriate case, evidence of the accused's utter indifference as to whether his victim lived or died may be sought from his conduct during, before and after the fatal attack.[285]

Consent and murder

In *HM Advocate v Rutherford*,[286] where the accused had strangled **9–51** a woman, part of the defence case involved the plea that the victim had desired him to do so—that she had wanted to be killed. Lord Justice-Clerk Cooper simply told the jury that consent was not a defence to murder, apparently as a matter of law. He made no attempt to justify his ruling, although the accused in that case would have faced almost insuperable difficulties in establishing that the woman had indeed consented. Even if cast-iron proof had been available, however, it seems unlikely in the extreme that it would have been treated as having any relevance to the outcome of the trial.

CULPABLE HOMICIDE

Definition of culpable homicide

There is no single, simple definition of culpable homicide. **9–52** Essentially (and admittedly unhelpfully) it covers any killing of a human being brought about by another in circumstances where that other should be accounted criminally responsible for it.[287] It clearly excludes murder, and both casual and justifiable homicides (see above, paras 9–38, 9–39 and 9–42 *et seq*.); and it is common enough for juries to be told that culpable homicide "means

---

[284] See also *Andrew Ewart* (1828) Syme 315, and *Miller and Denovan v HM Advocate*, 1960, noted in *Parr v HM Advocate*, 1991 S.L.T. 208 at 211; *cf.* the fact situation in *John Campbell* (1836) 1 Swin. 309, where at the end of the day the jury convicted of culpable homicide.
[285] *Halliday v HM Advocate*, 1998 S.C.C.R. 509.
[286] *HM Advocate v Rutherford*, 1947 J.C. 1 at 5–6; *cf. McDonald v HM Advocate*, 2004 S.C.C.R. 161, where the accused was convicted of culpable homicide on a charge of murder.
[287] In *Drury v HM Advocate*, 2001 S.L.T. 1013, Lord Justice-General Rodger said at 1017B, para.13: "[Culpable homicide] covers the killing of human beings in all circumstances, short of murder, where the criminal law attaches a relevant measure of blame to the person who kills."

unlawful killing of a human being in circumstances which don't amount to murder."[288] The *actus reus* of the crime is plainly the same as that for murder, although the conduct would presumably be less than that capable of raising an inference of murderous *mens rea*, except perhaps where there is virtually murder (in the sense that wicked recklessness has been established) but for the existence of provocation or diminished responsibility (see below, paras 9–59 *et seq.* and 9–66 *et seq.*). The *mens rea* of culpable homicide depends on the category of the crime.

9–53   Hume deals with four categories of culpable homicide. The first of these clearly relates to an assault which results in death, yet does not display either an intent to kill or the excessive violence, the great likelihood of death, and the utter indifference to the life of the victim that are the hallmarks of murder (see above, paras 9–44 and 9–45). As he puts it:

> "[W]here there is a wrongful purpose to do any bodily harm, though not outrageous or excessive, yet still if death unfortunately ensue, the invader is not free of guilt . . . He is so far blameable, as he did a thing which was wrong and unlawful in itself, and which might [in the sense of 'did'(?)] end in the death of his neighbour."[289]

The second covers a situation "where the homicide is done in prosecution, generally, of any wrong and unlawful act, though without malice to any individual",[290] and seems to involve offences of recklessly caused real injury. Thirdly, Hume mentions that,

> "some punishment is due, though the slaughter happen in the performance even of a lawful act, if there be great heedlessness and indiscretion, or a want of due caution and circumspection, in the way of doing the thing."[291]

This may be termed "recklessly-performed, lawful-act" culpable homicide. Fourthly, and finally, Hume considers cases where the killing is preceded by provocation[292] to be culpable homicide. To that fourth category must now be added killings where the accused was suffering from diminished responsibility at the time.[293] All these categories are illustrated in the paragraphs which follow.

---

[288] *Berry v HM Advocate* (1976) S.C.C.R. Supp. 156, per Lord Keith at 156.

[289] Hume, *Commentaries*, i, 191; see also i, 234 at "3".

[290] Hume, *Commentaries*, i, 192; see also i, 234 at "2".

[291] Hume, *Commentaries*, i, 192; see also i, 233 at "1".

[292] Hume, *Commentaries*, i, 239 *et seq.*

[293] It is also possible for the Crown to take the view that killings which fulfil the requirements for murder, e.g. mercy killings, should be indicted *ab initio* as cases of culpable homicide: but that is a matter of prosecutorial policy and not of law: see Gordon, *Criminal Law*, 3rd edn, paras 25.02 to 25.07: the last of these paragraphs concerns death caused by omission—in respect of which see *Bone v HM Advocate*, 2005 S.C.C.R. 829, where the appellant appears initially to have been charged with murder.

Assault type

Where death is causally related to an assault, but is not the **9–54** readily foreseeable result of it, it will not generally be possible to infer the *mens rea* for murder; but the perpetrator of the assault is not guiltless, nor is he guilty only of assault. He is taken as a matter of law to be guilty of culpable homicide, irrespective of how trivial the assault may have been.[294] Of course, the more serious the assault is in real terms, the more likely that the *mens rea* for murder may be inferred, as in the borderline case of *Patrick Slaven*,[295] where the victim was twice assaulted by men who were intent on ravishing her, and, having made her escape, was chased by them until she fell over a precipice to her death. As it was put in *John McCallum and William Corner*[296]:

> "If one purposes to inflict a very slight injury, which he has no right to inflict, and death unexpectedly and out of all reasonable calculation ensues, that is culpable homicide; if a more serious injury was intended, the case may be one of murder."

This is clearly capable of being a very harsh rule, bearing in mind the great width of the crime of assault (see above, paras 9–03 *et seq.*). In *Robert Vance*,[297] for example, the accused who was fighting another, threw back his arm and struck the victim, causing him to fall over and hit his head. The victim died from the resultant injury. It was not even clear from the facts that the accused knew the victim had been standing behind him; but as Lord Moncreiff[298] was reported to have said,

> "in so far as the misfortune which befell Deans [the victim] was concerned, it was clear that it was undesigned on the part

---

[294] See, e.g. *HM Advocate v Delaney*, 1945 J.C. 138; *Bird v HM Advocate*, 1952 J.C. 23; *McDermott v HM Advocate*, 1973 J.C. 8; *Gardiner v HM Advocate*, 2007 S.C.C.R. 379; *cf. HM Advocate v McGinlay*, 1983 S.L.T. 562; *Drury v HM Advocate*, 2001 S.L.T. 1013, Lord Cameron of Lochbroom at 1025I, para.6.

[295] *Patrick Slaven* (1885) 5 Coup. 694; *cf.* the unusual situation in *McDonald v HM Advocate*, 2007 S.C.C.R. 10, where culpable homicide was charged *ab initio*, and the main issue concerned the causal link between the assault and the death. See also the case of *McDonald v HM Advocate*, 2004 S.C.C.R. 161, where it was accepted by the Crown that an intention to cause pain (in the context of an allegedly consensual sexual encounter) would have been insufficient to justify a conviction for culpable homicide (see the opinion of the court at 167D, para.15, and 168B, para.18): the court, however, reserved its opinion as to whether in an appropriate case such an intention, in such a context, would be insufficient to meet the requirements of assault (opinion of the court at 170F, para.23).

[296] *John McCallum and William Corner* (1853) 1 Irv. 259, per Lord Justice-General McNeill at 270–271.

[297] *Robert Vance* (1849) J. Shaw 211.

[298] *Robert Vance* (1849) J. Shaw 211 at 214.

of the pannel, yet . . . it could not be said that the pannel was free from blame, inasmuch as he was engaged in an illegal act at the time, and the blow was given in the course of the fight . . . [and] it must be held to be culpable homicide."

The jury, however, found the accused not guilty (as is always their privilege).

Unlawful act type

9–55   What is thought to be involved here is the perpetration of a crime other than assault which might reasonably involve personal injury, and in fact ends in death. Crimes of real injury, where the *mens rea* requirement is recklessness, are prime candidates.[299] The causal connection between the crime itself and the death must, of course, be established; but once it is established, the result is culpable homicide, even though there was no question of there being any intent to kill. There are many reported cases which support this type. For example, in *James Niven*[300] the accused discharged a firearm in a public street. An innocent passer-by was killed due to, according to the accused's story, a piece of metal having by accident been included with the gunpowder. The court had no doubt that this was culpable homicide (although the jury acquitted Niven of the charge). The offence involved there was clearly the reckless discharge of firearms to the danger of the lieges (see above, para.9–33). A very similar offence is involved in the hypothetical situation spoken of by Lord Moncreiff in *David Keay*.[301] There, his Lordship said that if a person threw a stone out of a window, and the stone happened to hit someone causing his death, then that would be culpable homicide. Similarly again, in *Mathieson v HM Advocate*[302] the accused committed the crime of reckless fire-raising by setting some cans of paint alight. The paint was stored at the rear entrance of a building which itself caught fire, thus resulting in the deaths of four persons. And in *Sutherland v HM Advocate*,[303] even wilful fire-raising of the accused's own property with intent to defraud insurers was considered appropriate since the way in which the operation had been carried out exhibited the necessary recklessness in relation to the death which occurred. There have also been cases of culpable homicide where the unlawful activity consisted of the administration of noxious substances to the victim in a reckless fashion. Thus, in *Elizabeth Hamilton*[304] the accused nursery maid gave 10 drops of

---

[299] See in particular the opinion of the court in *HM Advocate v Purcell*, 2007 S.C.C.R. 520 at 527A–D, para.11.
[300] *James Niven* (1795) Hume, *Commentaries*, i, 192.
[301] *David Keay* (1837) 1 Swin. 543 at 545.
[302] *Mathieson v HM Advocate*, 1981 S.C.C.R. 196.
[303] *Sutherland v HM Advocate*, 1994 S.L.T. 634.
[304] *Elizabeth Hamilton* (1857) 2 Irv. 738.

laudanum to her 10 month-old charge to quieten him, even though she had been distinctly told by the child's mother to administer nothing of that nature to him at all; and again in *Adam Philip*[305] the accused gave 10 full glasses of whisky to a 10 year-old boy, thus occasioning his death. It has also been held that supplying a controlled drug (amphetamine) to a person who died after ingesting it provided a proper basis for culpable homicide.[306] Equally, therefore, the reckless supply of potentially noxious substances (see above, paras 9–30 *et seq.*) should merit a charge of culpable homicide, where death resulted.

The *mens rea* element for culpable homicide of this sort is **9–56** presumably the recklessness generated by, or associated with, the primary crime, which recklessness is carried forward as it were to the death itself. If that is so, then it may be possible to charge culpable homicide in relation to primary crimes (unlawful acts) which would not normally be expected to cause personal injuries at all, but where the crime itself was carried through in such a reckless manner as to make a resulting death not entirely unforeseeable. An example of such a crime would be theft. Unlike robbery (for which see Ch.10), theft would seldom be linked with injury, let alone death; but Gordon refers to the unreported case of *Finnigan*[307] where the accused was convicted of culpable homicide for having stolen a gas meter by wrenching it away from its supply pipe, thus causing the death of a person who occupied another part of the same building. A more modern version of the same thinking may be found in *Lourie v HM Advocate*[308] where two youths, who were alleged to have pushed their way into an elderly woman's house and there stolen her handbag in her presence, were convicted of culpable homicide, on the basis that their behaviour had caused her fatal shock. (Their convictions were quashed on appeal on the ground of insufficiency of evidence.)

Recklessly-performed, lawful-act type

The essence of this form of culpable homicide is that the accused **9–57** in fact caused the death of another because of the grossly careless way in which he performed some otherwise not unlawful, i.e. not criminal at common law, activity. Hume[309] gives the example of building work being carried out in such a fashion that debris is carelessly cast into the street below, to the fatal injury of some passer-by. He also mentions the careless felling of a tree,[310] the

---

[305] *Adam Philip* (1818) Hume, *Commentaries*, i, 237, fn.a.
[306] *Lord Advocate's Reference (No.1 of 1994)*, 1995 S.L.T. 248. See also *HM Advocate v C*, 2007 S.L.T. 963.
[307] *Finnigan*, unreported, 1958, High Court at Glasgow, at Gordon, *Criminal Law*, 3rd edn, para.26.27.
[308] *Lourie v HM Advocate*, 1988 S.C.C.R. 634.
[309] Hume, *Commentaries*, i, 192–193.
[310] *Mathew Graham* (1813) Hume, *Commentaries*, i, 192, fn.2.

careless driving of a coach[311] and also the presenting of a gun at another, not knowing it was loaded[312]: in each case a fatality had resulted. The lack of care which must be shown, however, is high. In the "driving" case of *Paton v HM Advocate*[313] Lord Justice-Clerk Aitchison remarked:

> "[I]t is now necessary to show gross, or wicked, or criminal negligence, something amounting, or at any rate analogous, to a criminal indifference to consequences."

It used to be assumed that gross negligence or simple recklessness[314] (as opposed to the "wicked" variety which suffices for murder) was all that was required for conviction of this type of culpable homicide[315]: indeed in *Transco Plc v HM Advocate*,[316] the Crown argued at the trial stage, "that *mens rea* played no part in culpable homicide of the kind with which the present case is concerned."[317] It is now clear from *Transco Plc*, however, that *mens rea* or dole is an essential element in all common law offences,[318] although the nature of it varies "as between one crime and another."[319] What is not particularly clear is the form which *mens rea* takes in this type of culpable homicide, save that it is, "the state of mind of the particular accused",[320] and that, "the state of knowledge of the accused is clearly critical."[321] Inferences may be drawn from the lack of care exhibited by the accused—in the sense of setting what he did, "against standards of conduct to be expected of persons carrying on operations of the relevant kind"[322]:

---

[311] *Thomas Clerk* (1805) Hume, *Commentaries*, i, 192, fn.2.
[312] *David Buchanan* (1817) Hume, *Commentaries*, i, 192, fn.2.
[313] *Paton v HM Advocate*, 1936 J.C. 19 at 22.
[314] As described in *Allan v Patterson*, 1980 J.C. 57: and indeed the test there was applied in *Sutherland v HM Advocate*, 1994 S.L.T. 634, and also in effect by the trial judge in *McDowall v HM Advocate*, 1998 S.C.C.R. 343, although that test was not considered appropriate for all crimes where recklessness was sufficient as the *mens rea*—see, e.g. *Thomson v HM Advocate*, 1995 S.L.T. 827 (involving reckless fire-raising).
[315] See para.9–45, above. It seems that "gross negligence" is all that is required in English law for "lawful act" type manslaughter: see *R. v Adomako* [1995] 1 A.C. 171 HL.
[316] *Transco Plc v HM Advocate (No.1)*, 2004 J.C. 29.
[317] *Transco Plc v HM Advocate (No.1)*, 2004 J.C. 29, Lord Hamilton (with whose opinion Lord MacLean agreed) at 50, para.41.
[318] *Transco Plc v HM Advocate (No.1)*, 2004 J.C. 29 at 50–51, para.42.
[319] *Transco Plc v HM Advocate (No.1)*, 2004 J.C. 29 at 51, para.43.
[320] *Transco Plc v HM Advocate (No.1)*, 2004 J.C. 29 at 51, para.44.
[321] *Transco Plc v HM Advocate (No.1)*, 2004 J.C. 29 at 51, para.45.
[322] *Transco Plc v HM Advocate (No.1)*, 2004 J.C. 29 at 51, para.44.

but such inferences may be offset, it seems, by explanations offered by the accused.[323]

Reported cases involving this form of culpable homicide are **9–58** legion. They include deaths caused by the grossly careless navigation of a boat,[324] dangerous driving of a motor vehicle,[325] folding up of a bed which had a child in it at the time,[326] and preparation of a headache remedy.[327] The unreported case of *Ross Fontana*[328] is also not without interest. He was convicted of culpable homicide because of the grossly improper way in which he had installed a gas fire. He had recklessly failed to provide flues for the removal of fumes, with the result that two people were poisoned by carbon monoxide when the fire was turned on.

Killings following upon provocation

It is a common human failing to lose one's self-control if one is **9–59** suddenly attacked or insulted or taunted by another; and that loss of control often manifests itself in violence, sometimes with fatal consequences for the victim. Such a victim is hardly blameless himself, of course, and may be said to have played some part in his own demise. For that reason, it may be thought that the law should make some concession to "human infirmity in those difficult and agitating situations, which require a more than ordinary strength of mind, and command of temper to withstand them."[329]

Indeed as Lord Cowie once put it to a jury:

> "If . . . you find that all the factors were present for a verdict of murder, but . . . you take the view . . . that he was

---

[323] This follows from Macdonald, *Criminal Law*, 5th edn, p.1—to which Lord Hamilton makes reference in *Transco Plc v HM Advocate (No.1)*, 2004 J.C.29 at 51, para.42: see also the opinion of Lord Osborne there at 31, para.3 (where he quotes from Macdonald), and at 34, para.4, where his Lordship seems to identify (by quoting from prior authorities) the mental element in this type of culpable homicide as, "a complete disregard of potential dangers", or as, "an utter disregard of what the consequences of the act in question may be so far as the public are concerned . . . [or as] recklessness so high as to involve an indifference to the consequences for the public generally." Lord Osborne's remarks probably do not form part of the ratio of the case—although both he and Lord Hamilton (with whom Lord MacLean agreed) criticise the circularity of Lord Justice-Clerk Aitchison's remarks (quoted in the text, above) as well as his use of the term "negligence": see *Transco Plc* at 33, para.4, 48–49, para.37.

[324] *Angus MacPherson and John Stewart* (1861) 4 Irv. 85.

[325] See, e.g. *McDowall v HM Advocate*, 1998 S.C.C.R. 343; also see *HM Advocate v Purcell*, 2007 S.C.C.R. 520.

[326] *Williamina Sutherland* (1856) 2 Irv. 455.

[327] *Edmund Wheatley* (1853) 1 Irv. 225, where a medical student who was learning the art of dispensing medicines in a chemist's shop, and who had no authority to do what he did, prepared a potion for a friend, thus causing his death. His actions were treated as having gone well beyond a mere careless error in dispensing; *cf. George Armitage* (1885) 5 Coup. 675 and *HM Advocate v Wood* (1903) 4 Adam 150.

[328] *Ross Fontana*, unreported, March 1990, High Court at Kirkcaldy.

[329] Hume, *Commentaries*, i, 249.

provoked . . . then for that reason . . . you could reduce the offence of murder to culpable homicide."[330]

Much the same was said by Lord Cullen to a jury in *Graham v HM Advocate*.[331] This commonly expressed view, however, that provocation reduces murder to culpable homicide, was considered to be unsound (or at least in relation to intentional killings) in *Drury v HM Advocate*.[332] As Lord Justice-General Rodger said of the trial judge's directions to the jury in that case:

> "By saying that, if provocation were established, this would reduce the crime from murder to culpable homicide, the judge could be thought to give the impression that provocation acts as some kind of laissez-passer by virtue of which an accused, who displays the hallmarks of a murderer and would otherwise find himself convicted of murder, is entitled to escape from that predicament to the somewhat less serious predicament of a conviction of culpable homicide. While the terminology of 'reducing murder to culpable homicide' is frequently encountered, it is essentially misleading . . . [since] it suggests that the jury would first conclude that, absent provocation, the accused would have been guilty of murder, and only at that stage would they consider provocation. In reality, however, evidence relating to provocation is simply one of the factors which the jury should take into account in performing their general task of determining the accused's state of mind at the time when he killed his victim."[333]

The tenor of the decision in *Drury* seems to be that a person who intentionally kills another because he was provoked into doing so lacks murderous intent: he does not have "wicked" intent, and thus cannot be shown to have had the necessary *mens rea* for murder. He will, however, be convicted of culpable homicide. (The same reasoning should probably apply in relation to diminished responsibility,[334] although in *Galbraith v HM Advocate (No.2)*,[335] which was decided after *Drury*, the Appeal Court appear to favour the formerly held view that that plea is a mitigatory one, in which murder gives way to culpable homicide in order to reflect the lower level of responsibility involved.)[336] This leaves unclear how provocation operates when the evidence in a homicide case reveals

---

[330] *Stobbs v HM Advocate*, 1983 S.C.C.R. 190 at 199.
[331] *Graham v HM Advocate*, 1987 S.C.C.R. 20 at 22.
[332] *Drury v HM Advocate*, 2001 S.L.T. 1013.
[333] *Drury v HM Advocate*, 2001 S.L.T. 1013 at 1018D–F, para.17.
[334] On which, see below, paras 9–66 *et seq*.
[335] *Galbraith v HM Advocate (No.2)*, 2002 J.C. 1.
[336] *Galbraith v HM Advocate (No.2)*, 2002 J.C. 1, opinion of the court at 18A–B, para.45; *cf*. Gordon's "Commentary" to the case, at 2001 S.C.C.R. 551 at 575, at "1" and "2".

wicked recklessness on the part of the accused[337]: it seems that there, the *mens rea* for murder will have been established, and that the former theory—that provocation reduces murder to culpable homicide—will probably continue to apply. If this is so, there then arises a theoretical awkwardness which is not easy to defend. Irrespective of whether this is truly the theoretical position, and, if so, what further implications it may have, no one doubts that the outcome of a successful plea of provocation will be a conviction for culpable homicide and not one for murder.[338] There are, however, various criteria to be met if a plea of provocation is to be attended with success.

Immediacy of retaliation

Hume[339] requires there to be a, "sudden impulse of resentment" **9–60** in retaliation of provocation, "suffered upon the spot." Macdonald puts the same point even more forcefully: "Provocation, although great, will not palliate [sic] guilt if any interval have elapsed between the provocation and the retaliation."[340] The point is that provocation is still at basis a concession to human infirmity and not an excuse for cold-blooded vengeance-taking. Once passions have been allowed to cool, provocation no longer applies.[341] Thus, in *Walter Redpath*[342] the accused was attacked by his eventual victim, and made efforts there and then to lift a stone in order to retaliate. He thought better of it, however, and instead went indoors to look out a firearm. Not long after, he returned to the scene of the initial attack with a gun and shot the victim. Although afterwards convicted of culpable homicide only, he should have been convicted of murder, according to Hume, since an interval for "cooling-off" had been allowed to elapse prior to the fatal conduct. It seems, then, that instant retaliation to a provoking incident is to be taken quite literally. Although the courts have not been quite as strict as Hume might have wanted them to be, any significant gap between provocation and retaliation is certainly such as to elide the plea.[343]

Cumulative provocation

Linked to the requirement of immediacy of retaliation is the rule **9–61** that there must be a specific, provoking incident. There must be such an incident, sufficiently provoking in itself in the eyes of the

---

[337] *Pace*, Lord Justice-General Rodger in *Drury v HM Advocate*, 2001 S.L.T. 1013, at 1018F–G, para.18, since what is said there appears to ignore what has come to be understood as "wicked recklessness".

[338] *Drury v HM Advocate*, 2001 S.L.T. 1013, Lord Justice-General Rodger at 1017I, para.16.

[339] Hume, *Commentaries*, i, 239.

[340] Macdonald, *Criminal Law*, 5th edn, p.94.

[341] See *Drury v HM Advocate*, 2001 S.L.T. 1013, Lord Justice-General Rodger at 1019L, para.21.

[342] *Walter Redpath* (1810) Hume, *Commentaries*, i, 252, fn.1.

[343] See *Parr v HM Advocate*, 1991 J.C. 39.

law, just before the fatal violence was delivered by the accused. If there had been a course of incidents of a provocative nature over a series of days, weeks or even years, but no final incident to which the accused responded then no provocation exists in law, and the crime will be murder. This has consistently been upheld by the courts.[344] In particular, this means that a woman, who for years has been subjected to violence by her partner, and who one day "snaps" at the end of her tether and kills him as he lies sleeping in a chair, must be convicted of murder, although she may be able to show that she was acting under diminished responsibility: see below, para.9–67. In practice, of course, it may be possible for particular judges to direct juries in appropriate cases involving provocation to ignore this rather harsh rule,[345] or for the Crown to accept a plea of guilty to culpable homicide.[346]

Recognised provocation

9–62   *Violence.* According to Macdonald,[347] the usual form of acceptable provocation is violence:

> "The defence of provocation is of this sort—'Being agitated and excited, and alarmed by violence, I lost control over myself, and took life, when my presence of mind had left me, and without thought of what I was doing'."

This statement has been specifically approved on several occasions.[348] However, the degree of violence visited upon the accused is of considerable importance. As Lord Cooper once said:

> "It takes a tremendous amount of provocation to palliate stabbing a man to death ... A blow with the fist is no justification for the use of a lethal weapon. Provocation, in short, must bear a reasonable retaliation to the resentment which it excites."[349]

---

[344] See *Thomson v HM Advocate*, 1986 S.L.T. 281; *Graham v HM Advocate*, 1987 S.C.C.R. 20; *Parr v HM Advocate*, 1991 J.C. 39.

[345] See, e.g. *Crawford v HM Advocate*, 1950 J.C. 67; but *cf. HM Advocate v Greig*, 1979, noted in Gane and Stoddart, *Casebook on Scottish Criminal Law*, 3rd edn, pp.423–424.

[346] See, e.g. *Walker v HM Advocate*, 1996 S.C.C.R. 818 at 822A, where in an appeal against sentence for culpable homicide, the court opined: "Considerable leniency was shown already to the appellant in the decision to reduce the charge from one of murder to culpable homicide . . .". See also Clare Connelly, "Women who kill violent men", 1996 J.R. 215 ("Cases and Comment").

[347] Macdonald, *Criminal Law*, 5th edn, p.94.

[348] See, e.g. *Cosgrove v HM Advocate*, 1990 J.C. 333, at 339; *Low v HM Advocate*, 1994 S.L.T. 277, Lord Justice-Clerk Ross at 285L.

[349] *Smith v HM Advocate*, unreported, 1952, High Court at Glasgow, at Gordon, *Criminal Law*, 3rd edn, para.25.19. Notice that in *Robertson v HM Advocate*, 1994 J.C. 245, Lord Justice-Clerk Ross (at 247F) thought that "retaliation" in the quotation should read "relation".

It is now clear that there must indeed be a reasonable or proportionate relationship between the accused's reaction and the victim's provocative attack.[350] There must not be a gross disproportion between that reaction and the attack,[351] for it is accepted that an equality or fine balance between the two cannot be looked for in such situations where there is loss of control.[352] Thus, in *Thomson v HM Advocate*[353] the accused stabbed his victim repeatedly with a knife (which he had taken the precaution of bringing with him to a meeting) after a trivial assault, which consisted in no more than the victim's physically attempting to stop him leaving the room where they both were. There was a gross disproportion between the violence and the retaliation, and the plea of provocation was ruled out. In the same way, it was ruled out in *Fenning v HM Advocate*[354] since it was a gross over-reaction to counter a drunken man's random gesticulations with a knife by beating his brains out with a stone or rifle butt. *Ensign Hardie*[355] was on firmer ground, however, since he had been struck with a "tree", i.e. a baulk of wood, and beaten by the eventual victim, who had been on horseback at the time.

Sexual infidelity. Since well before the time of Hume, it has been **9–63** recognised that a man who found his wife in the very act of adultery with another man might be convicted of culpable homicide rather than murder if he killed him, her or them on the spot.[356] Presumably, this would apply to a wife who had found her husband in similar adulterous circumstances. The basis was (and is) that such a spouse had been sorely provoked. The issue has not

---

[350] *Gillon v HM* Advocate, 2006 S.L.T. 799, opinion of the court (of five judges) at 811C–D, para.39; *McCormack v HM Advocate*, 1993 J.C. 170; *Robertson v HM Advocate*, 1994 S.L.T. 1004. The decision in *Gillon* brings to an end the suggestion that the "ordinary person" test, adopted by the Appeal Court in relation to "sexual infidelity" type provocation (see below, para.9–63), might be applied to provocation by violence too: see Chalmers and Leverick, *Criminal Defences and Pleas in Bar of Trial*, paras 10–09 and 10–18 to 10–20 (written prior to the decision in *Gillon*). There are thus two separate conditions to be met for the plea of provocation to succeed, the one to be used depending upon the nature of the provocation itself.

[351] *Gillon v H.M. Advocate*, 2006 S.L.T. 799, opinion of the court (of five judges) at 811C–D, para.39, where the formulation of the proportionality test favoured by Lord Justice-Clerk Ross in *Robertson v HM Advocate*, 1994 J.C. 245 at 249E–G, is preferred. See also *Low v HM Advocate*, 1994 S.L.T. 277, per Lord Justice-Clerk Ross at 286D–G (where it is stated that the self-defence threshold of "no cruel excess" should be confined to that defence, and not applied also to provocation).

[352] *Robertson v HM Advocate*, 1994 J.C. 245. See also *Gillon v HM Advocate*, 2006 S.L.T. 799, opinion of the court (of five judges) at 807B–D, para.22, where the fallacy of arguing that there never can be a reasonably proportionate retaliation, where death is caused by that retaliation, is exposed.

[353] *Thomson v HM Advocate*, 1986 S.L.T. 281.

[354] *Fenning v HM Advocate*, 1985 S.C.C.R. 219.

[355] *Ensign Hardie* (1701) Hume, *Commentaries*, i, 244, fn.2.

[356] *James Christie* (1731) Hume, *Commentaries*, i, 245–246.

been confined, however, to cases where the adultery was discovered as it actually took place. In *HM Advocate v Gilmour*[357] Lord Justice-Clerk Aitchison told the jury:

> "If you are satisfied that the accused found his wife in the act of adultery, or in circumstances that reasonably conveyed to his mind that his wife had just committed adultery, or was just about to commit adultery when discovered, you are entitled . . . to acquit the accused of murder and to find him guilty of culpable homicide only."

And further, in *HM Advocate v Hill*[358] it was accepted that provocation could be made out where a man's wife and her lover confessed to having committed adultery. This was all the more surprising since "words" are not generally accepted as sufficient for the plea of provocation to be upheld; and, of course, a confession refers to some incident which has taken place in the past. Still further, however, it has been decided that this form of provocation is open to a person merely cohabiting with another, provided that there can be shown to have been a bond of sexual fidelity between them at the material time.[359] There is no requirement, therefore, that sexual infidelity should be confined to those who are married or are civil partners.[360] But the Appeal Court has made very plain that the words used must go beyond mere insults in the course of a quarrel: they must "disclose in clear and unequivocal terms that the deceased had been committing adultery . . .".[361] Immediacy of reaction to the disclosure or discovery is, of course, crucial; but it has been held that a subsequent disclosure (to which the accused immediately reacted) was sufficient since it had been substantially different from a previous disclosure (to which the accused had not reacted).[362]

There is not, nor could be, any requirement in law for a degree of proportionality between the discovery (or disclosure) of the infidelity and the accused's violent reaction to it,[363] since the two are plainly not commensurable. It is not, however, sufficient

---

[357] *HM Advocate v Gilmour*, 1938 J.C. 1 at 2–3.

[358] *HM Advocate v Hill*, 1941 J.C. 59.

[359] See *McKay v HM Advocate*, 1991 J.C. 91; *Rutherford v HM Advocate*, 1997 S.C.C.R. 711.

[360] See the Civil Partnership Act 2004. In *HM Advocate v McKean*, 1996 S.C.C.R. 402, the trial judge, Lord MacLean, directed the jury (at 403A) that he saw "no reason why, in the modern context, the plea should not also be available to homosexual couples who live together and are regarded in the community as partners bound together by ties of love, affection and faithfulness . . .".

[361] *McKay v HM Advocate*, 1991 J.C. 91, per Lord Justice-General Hope at 96; see also *McCormack v HM Advocate*, 1993 J.C. 170, Lord Justice-General Hope at 179G–I.

[362] *Rutherford v HM Advocate*, 1997 S.C.C.R. 711.

[363] *Drury v HM Advocate*, 2001 S.L.T. 1013 (court of five judges).

(although necessary) for provocation to exist in law that the accused should have lost his self-control immediately on making the discovery or receiving the disclosure, unless an ordinary man (or woman) "having been thus provoked, would have been liable to react as he [or she] did."[364] The test relates to whether the ordinary man or woman's response would have been as extreme as that of the accused; and thus the jury in question will have to consider the "nature and degree"[365] of the accused's actual response and relate that to the presumed response of an ordinary individual in the same circumstances. It is not clear whether, or to what extent, the individual characteristics of the accused are relevant to the jury's determination[366]; but the opinion of the court (of five judges) in *Gillon v HM Advocate*[367] suggests that Scots law should be slow to saddle itself with the difficulties evident in other jurisdictions which have adopted an "individual characteristics" approach to provocation.

Words not sufficient

The general consensus has always been that words however, **9–64** "foul or abusive or . . . signs or gestures, how contemptuous or derisive so ever" cannot operate as provocation in relation to a murder charge.[368] This represents a conspicuous difference between the application of provocation in homicide and in assault (see above, para.9–22). In *William Aird*[369] the accused was denied provocation in relation to his killing of a woman who had thrown the contents of a chamber pot in his face; and that being so, abusive words and taunts could scarcely hope to fare any better. The Appeal Court, therefore, continues to uphold the orthodox view,[370] whilst recognising that there may be occasions when that view should yield.[371] It is not clear when that might legitimately happen, however, since each case appears to turn on its own facts and circumstances; but sexual insults and taunts were left to the

---

[364] *Drury v HM Advocate*, 2001 S.L.T. 1013, Lord Justice-General Rodger at 1023F, para.34.

[365] *Drury v HM Advocate*, 2001 S.L.T. 1013.

[366] The court in *Drury v HM Advocate*, 2001 S.L.T. 1013, reserved its opinion on this matter: see Lord Justice-General Rodger's opinion at 1022D–E, para.29; *cf.* the law in England, as set out in *R. v James* [2006] 2 W.L.R. 887 CA, upholding the decision in *Attorney General for Jersey v Holley* [2005] 2 A.C. 280 PC rather than that of the House of Lords in *R. v Smith (Morgan)* [2001] A.C.146.

[367] *Gillon v HM Advocate*, 2006 S.L.T. 799, see especially the opinion of the court at 809D–811C, paras 31–38.

[368] Hume, *Commentaries*, i, 247; Macdonald, *Criminal Law*, 5th edn, p.93.

[369] *William Aird* (1693) Hume, *Commentaries*, i, 248.

[370] See *Thomson v HM Advocate*, 1986 S.L.T. 281; *Cosgrove v HM Advocate*, 1990 J.C. 333; *McCormack v HM Advocate*, 1993 J.C. 170, Lord Justice-General Hope at 179D–E.

[371] See *Thomson v HM Advocate*, 1986 S.L.T. 281, per Lord Hunter at 286D; *Cosgrove v HM Advocate*, 1990 J.C. 333, per Lord Cowie at 339.

jury as provocation in *Berry v HM Advocate*,[372] as were (alleged) threats to tell the accused's wife of an adulterous association clandestinely enjoyed by the accused in *Stobbs v HM Advocate*.[373]

Effect on attempted murder

9–65   If a successful plea of provocation on a murder charge results in a conviction for culpable homicide, then provocation relative to a charge of attempted murder should logically result in a conviction for attempted culpable homicide. But the courts appear to have taken the view that attempted culpable homicide does not exist. The appropriate verdict, therefore, appears to be assault to severe injury under provocation.[374]

Diminished responsibility

9–66   The modern law on diminished responsibility is found in the full bench decision of *Galbraith v HM Advocate (No.2)*.[375] Although the concept of diminished responsibility had been recognised in Scots law since the second-half of the nineteenth century as a means of reducing murder to culpable homicide,[376] the opinion of the court in *Galbraith* shows that both the terminology by which it was known and the content of that concept remained largely unsettled and confused.[377] The prior jurisprudence, for example, had insisted that a plea of diminished responsibility could not succeed unless there was "mental disease" or a state of mind virtually "bordering on insanity".[378]

It is now clear that diminished responsibility refers to substantial mental impairment of an accused's ability to determine and control his acts and omissions due to mental abnormality. "Because the individual is [thus] not fully responsible in law for what he does when his mental state is substantially impaired, the law mitigates the punishment which it deems appropriate for his criminal acts"[379]; it follows that to give effect to whatever mitigation is

---

[372] *Berry v HM Advocate* (1976) S.C.C.R. Supp. 156.

[373] *Stobbs v HM Advocate*, 1983 S.C.C.R. 190.

[374] *Brady v HM Advocate*, 1986 S.L.T. 686; *Salmond v HM Advocate*, 1992 S.L.T. 156; *Drury v HM Advocate*, 2001 S.L.T. 1013, Lord Cameron of Lochbroom at 1025H, para.6. See also the remarks of Lord McEwan in *HM Advocate v C*, 2007 S.L.T. 963 at 965D, para.14.

[375] *Galbraith v HM Advocate (No.2)*, 2002 J.C. 1.

[376] See, e.g. *Alexander Dingwall* (1867) 5 Irv. 466.

[377] See *Galbraith v HM Advocate (No.2)*, 2002 J.C. 1, opinion of the court at 10I–16D, paras 23–40.

[378] See, e.g. *HM Advocate v Savage*, 1923 J.C. 49; *Connelly v HM Advocate*, 1991 S.L.T. 397; *Williamson v HM Advocate*, 1994 S.L.T. 1000; *Martindale v HM Advocate*, 1994 S.L.T. 1093. *Galbraith* re-interprets *Savage*, overrules *Connelly*, and, by implication, disapproves of much of what was said by the courts in *Williamson* and *Martindale*.

[379] *Galbraith v HM Advocate (No.2)*, 2002 J.C. 1, opinion of the court at 18A, para.45.

appropriate in an individual case, the accused must be convicted
not of murder (which carries a mandatory life sentence) but of
culpable homicide (where the sentence is generally at the discretion of the trial judge).[380]

Mental abnormality

Diminished responsibility entails a recognised mental abnor- **9-67**
mality which impairs to a substantial degree a person's ability to
control and determine his acts and omissions when he kills another
human being.[381] The mental abnormality has to be recognised by
the appropriate science,[382] but it is a legal decision whether what is
so recognised can be received as suitable for the plea. Thus,
although psychopathic personality may be so recognised, the law is
not prepared to include it within the plea; nor is the law prepared
to accept abnormal mental conditions (short of insanity) brought
about by self-induced intoxication with alcohol or drugs.[383] The
court in *Galbraith* expressly said, however, that it could see no
reason in principle why a recognised abnormality caused by sexual
or other abuse inflicted on the accused could not be relevant for
the purposes of the plea.[384] Indeed, the effects on the mind of self-

---

[380] The decision of the court in *Galbraith v HM Advocate (No.2)*, 2002 J.C. 1 makes
no mention of *Drury v HM Advocate*, 2001 S.L.T. 1013, although *Drury* was
decided several months prior to it: this is in some respects curious since
provocation and diminished responsibility are usually regarded as pleas similar
in their effect upon a charge of murder. But in *Drury*, the court was adamant
that provocation was not to be thought of as reducing or mitigating murder to
culpable homicide—or, at least, not in intentional murder—since provocation
was to be considered as a factor inconsistent with the "wickedness" which the
mens rea of such murder required. In *Galbraith*, although diminished responsibility is seen as a matter of responsibility, the operation of the concept on
murder is considered to be mitigatory and hence reductive. There is an
"awkwardness" about this which suggests that the theoretical position has yet to
be fully worked out by the courts.; *cf. Gillon v HM Advocate*, 2006 S.L.T. 799,
opinion of the court (of five judges) at 807K, para.24 (final sentence), and at
808L–809C, para.30, where it is agreed that the Lord Justice General's analysis
of the *mens rea* of murder (and culpable homicide) in *Drury*, whilst involving "a
departure from the more traditional formulation of the nature of provocation",
is independent of the criterion that should be adopted for use in the assessment
of a plea of provocation, either in the context of sexual infidelity or violence as
the basis of the plea.
[381] *Galbraith v HM Advocate (No.2)*, 2002 J.C. 1.
[382] *Galbraith v HM Advocate (No.2)*, 2002 J.C. 1, opinion of the court at 21E–F,
para.54 at "4". The effect of anger or jealousy would not be included since these
are normal rather than abnormal conditions: see the opinion of the court at 19I,
para.51.
[383] *Galbraith v HM Advocate (No.2)*, 2002 J.C. 1, opinion of the court at 17B–E,
para.43, upholding prior decisions to those effects in *Carraher v HM Advocate*,
1946 J.C. 108 and *Brennan v HM Advocate*, 1977 J.C. 38.
[384] *Galbraith v HM Advocate (No.2)*, 2002 J.C. 1, opinion of the court at 20I–21B,
para.53. This may have considerable bearing on the plight of women suffering
from "battered wife syndrome" or similar conditions caused by lengthy exposure
to physical and sexual abuse, since such women are often unable to fulfil the
requirements of provocation should they kill their abusers: see above, para.9–61.
Galbraith itself was such a case.

induced intoxication or of psychopathic personality apart,[385] the court in *Galbraith* has envisaged a wide category of "recognised mental abnormalities" caused in a wide variety of ways, such that diminished responsibility is now a plea of considerable scope. As the court stated:

> "Abnormality of mind can spring from a variety of causes. Again, we can see this in the cases on diminished responsibility which we have examined. Suggested causes for the accused's abnormality of mind include, for instance, sunstroke, chronic drinking bringing on *delirium tremens*, low intelligence and depression. But these are merely examples and it is not difficult to give others which might be relevant."[386]

And the court then referred to the results of head injuries, brain tumours, strokes, disorders of the thyroid, hypoglycaemia, drugs administered for therapeutic purposes—a nice mix of external and internal causes—in order to demonstrate that it was not necessary for the law to insist on conditions bordering upon insanity or to restrict the concept of diminished responsibility to "mental disease".[387]

Onus

9–68   The accused who wishes to submit a plea of diminished responsibility must show on a balance of probabilities that he was suffering from an appropriate condition of mental abnormality relevant to that plea. This aligns diminished responsibility with insanity[388] rather than, e.g. with provocation which places no such *onus* of proof on the accused. Nevertheless, the position relative to diminished responsibility was confirmed in *Lindsay v HM Advocate*,[389] where the court declined to submit the question for reconsideration by a full bench on the basis that the law on this

---

[385] It should be noted that in *Galbraith v HM Advocate (No.2)*, 2002 J.C. 1 at 16H–17B, para.42, the court held out the possibility that further exceptions may be recognised in the future: indeed at 16D, para.40, the court emphasised that the observations on diminished responsibility it was about to make were "somewhat tentative . . . [and] may have to be modified or refined in the light of experience in subsequent cases."

[386] *Galbraith v HM Advocate (No.2)*, 2002 J.C. 1 at 20B–C, para.52. The court then proceeded to quote from Lord Murray's charge to the jury in *HM Advocate v Ritchie*, 1926 J.C. 45 at 49, where his Lordship stated that relevant mental conditions might be congenital or not, permanent or temporary, and might "be induced by illness, fever, palsy, accident, injury or shock . . .".

[387] *Galbraith v HM Advocate (No.2)*, 2002 J.C. 1 at 20G, para.52. Thus, the prior law had been over-restrictive of the plea, and *Connelly v HM Advocate*, 1991 S.L.T. 397, was specifically overruled.

[388] See above, paras 8–11 *et seq*.

[389] *Lindsay v HM Advocate*, 1996 S.C.C.R. 870.

issue had been settled for a very long time.[390] If the accused succeeds in discharging the burden which lies on him, the result will be a conviction for culpable homicide rather than of murder; but his diminished responsibility should still be taken into account when the judge sentences him for the lesser crime.[391]

Effect on attempted murder

In a similar way to provocation (see above, para.9–65), dimin- **9–69** ished responsibility does not effect a conviction for attempted culpable homicide on an attempted murder charge. The appropriate verdict in such a case is one of assault.[392]

Persistent vegetative state

It has been declared by the Lord Advocate[393] that doctors who **9–70** withdraw life-sustaining "treatment" (in its widest sense, to include feeding and hydration) from patients who are in a "persistent vegetative state" will be immune from prosecution for homicide (murder or culpable homicide) in respect of such a patient provided that the Court of Session has first agreed to such withdrawal. The procedure to be employed before that court was laid down in *Law Hospital NHS Trust v Lord Advocate*,[394] where Lord President Hope described such a state as follows:

> "This is the result of irreversible damage to the cerebral cortex. The function of consciousness has been lost completely and for ever. The patient is wholly unaware of her surroundings. She cannot see, hear, feel pain or pleasure, communicate by words or movement or make voluntary movements of any kind. The brain stem structures are preserved, and so long as this continues she remains clinically alive. The vegetative reflexes which control such functions as breathing, cardiac action and digestion are maintained. Involuntary movements of the eyes and the ability to make sounds give the impression of apparent wakefulness ... [S]he remains alive only because feeding and hydration are provided to her artificially and because of the nursing care which she continues to receive in the hospital."[395]

---

[390] *cf.* the Appeal Court's view of the definition of rape in *Lord Advocate's Reference (No.1 of 2001)*, 2002 S.L.T. 466, where the law was changed notwithstanding that it had stood unchallenged for a considerable period of time: see Chalmers, "How (Not) to Reform the Law of Rape" (2002) 6 *Edin. L.R.* 388.

[391] *Strathern v HM Advocate*, 1996 S.C.C.R. 100.

[392] *HM Advocate v Blake*, 1986 S.L.T. 661, per Lord Brand at 663. In *Galbraith*, 2002 J.C. 1 at 18C, para.45, the court reserved its opinion on this issue.

[393] Policy statement, made on April 11, 1996.

[394] *Law Hospital N.H.S. Trust v Lord Advocate*, 1996 S.C. 301.

[395] *Law Hospital N.H.S. Trust v Lord Advocate*, 1996 S.C. 301 at 305.

4.(B) CORPORATE HOMICIDE

9–71 There is a statutory offence known in Scotland as "Corporate Homicide".[396] This offence is complex, and reference must be made to the appropriate legislation (the Corporate Manslaughter and Corporate Homicide Act 2007) for a detailed account of it.[397] In general, an organisation[398] commits this offence if the way in which its activities are managed or organised causes a person's death and amounts to a gross breach[399] of a relevant duty of care owed by it to that person. (An individual cannot be prosecuted for this offence by, for example, being allegedly art and part in its commission.)[400] An organisation is not liable unless the way in which its activities are managed or organised *by its senior management* is a substantial element in the breach of the relevant duty of care[401]: and a "relevant duty of care" means any of the duties, owed under the law of negligence,[402] as these are set out in s.2 of the Act.[403] These duties are qualified, however, by the exceptions detailed in ss.3–7, which cover certain issues relating, for example, to public policy decisions, military activities, policing and law enforcement, emergencies, and child protection.[404] The offence can

---

[396] See the Corporate Manslaughter and Corporate Homicide Act 2007 s.1(5)(b).

[397] See also Peter Ferguson, Q.C., "Corporate Manslaughter and Corporate Homicide Act 2007", 2007 S.L.T. (News) 251, for a detailed and helpful critique of the Act.

[398] "Organisation" means a corporation, a police force, a partnership (see s.25 of the Corporate Manslaughter and Corporate Homicide Act 2007), certain trade unions or employers' associations, and the government departments and other bodies set out in Sch.1 (which inter alia lists the Crown Office, the Procurator Fiscal Service, the National Archives of Scotland, and the Scottish Executive): see s.1(2), and note that Sch.1 is amended by the Serious Crime Act 2007 Sch.8 para.178, in a way reinforced by Sch.14.

[399] A breach is "gross" if the conduct in question "falls far below what can reasonably be expected of the organisation in the circumstances": see s.1(4)(b) of the Corporate Manslaughter and Corporate Homicide Act 2007.

[400] See s.18(2) of the Corporate Manslaughter and Corporate Homicide Act 2007.

[401] See s.1(3) of the Corporate Manslaughter and Corporate Homicide Act 2007. "Senior management" is defined in s.1(4)(c).

[402] Certain rules of the common law of negligence, which would have defeated a relevant duty of care from being owed by an organisation, are to be disregarded in the context of this offence: see s.2(6) of the Corporate Manslaughter and Corporate Homicide Act 2007.

[403] These duties include those owed to employees or other persons working for the organisation or performing services for it, those owed by it as an occupier of premises (or as a supplier of goods or services, as a "person" carrying on construction or maintenance operations, or as a user or keeper of plant, vehicles or "other thing"), or those owed to anyone held in custody: see Corporate Manslaughter and Corporate Homicide Act 2007 s.2(1)–(3), (7). Whether an organisation owes such a duty of care to any particular individual is a question of law: see s.2(5); but whether or not a breach of a duty is sufficiently "gross" for conviction is a matter for a jury to consider: see s.8.

[404] See also ss.11–14 of the Corporate Manslaughter and Corporate Homicide Act 2007.

be tried only on indictment and only in a High Court.[405] If an organisation is convicted of such an offence, the maximum penalty is "a fine"[406]; but the court can also make a "remedial order", under which that organisation must remedy the breach of duty (as also any identified health and safety deficiency) which led to the death, and/or a "publicity order", under which that organisation must publicise the fact and detail of the conviction, the amount of the fine imposed, and the terms of any remedial order passed.[407]

5. RAPE

DEFINITION OF RAPE

The current *actus reus* of rape[408] consists of a male person having **9–72** vaginal sexual intercourse with a female person[409] without the "active" consent of that female person.[410] The *mens rea* of the crime "includes the intention to have intercourse with the woman without her consent"[411] or recklessness as to the matter of consent.[412] The elements of the offence are considered in the paragraphs which follow.

Gender-specific

Rape is a gender-specific crime. In Scotland, it can only be **9–73** committed by males upon females, which appears to mean by persons biologically male at birth upon persons born biologically

---

[405] See s.1(7) of the Corporate Manslaughter and Corporate Homicide Act 2007. Under s.19, an organisation can also be charged, cumulatively or sequentially, with an appropriate "health and safety" offence.

[406] See s.1(6) of the Corporate Manslaughter and Corporate Homicide Act 2007.

[407] See ss.9 and 10 of the Corporate Manslaughter and Corporate Homicide Act 2007.

[408] Settled as recently as March, 2002: see *Lord Advocate's Reference (No.1 of 2001)*, 2002 S.L.T. 466. The Scottish Law Commission, in a recent report, proposes the abolition of this offence as it presently stands at common law: it is proposed that it be given a statutory definition which would elide its gender and orifice specificity; "consent" would remain, but be given a statutory significance; the appropriate *mens rea* would be altered: see "Report on Rape and Other Sexual Offences", Scot. Law Com. No.209 (December 2007); and see below, para.9–90, for a brief synopsis of the Commission's proposals.

[409] Sometimes referred to archaically as having "carnal knowledge" of her.

[410] *Lord Advocate's Reference (No.1 of 2001)*, 2002 S.L.T. 466, Lord Justice-General Cullen at 475F, para.39; *cf.* his Lordship's opinion at 476A, para.44.

[411] *Jamieson v HM Advocate (No.1)*, 1994 S.L.T. 537, per Lord Justice-General Hope at 541C (presumably now meaning knowledge on the male's part that the female had not given her consent): see *Lord Advocate's Reference (No.1 of 2001)*, 2002 S.L.T. 466, Lord Justice-General Cullen at 476B, para.44, where this interpretation is accepted without discussion.

[412] *Jamieson v HM Advocate (No.1)*, 1994 S.L.T. 537 at 541K (presumably meaning utter indifference on the part of the accused whether the female had consented or not). The account of the *mens rea* (*mutatis mutandis*) given in *Jamieson* was accepted by the majority of the court in *Lord Advocate's Reference (No.1 of 2001)*, 2002 S.L.T. 466—see in particular the opinion of Lord Justice-General Cullen at 473B–H, paras 28–29, and at 476B, para.44.

female[413]; but this is not necessarily so in modern times. Under the Gender Recognition Act 2004, a person who fulfils the statutory requirements may be issued with a "full gender recognition certificate", under which a person who had been male acquires "for all purposes"[414] the female gender, or a person who had been female, the male gender. If such a person acquires such a gender, and has also had full gender reassignment surgery, the law of rape operates as expected—as a gender specific crime. Since the issue of a full gender recognition certificate is not, however, dependent upon the completion of such surgery,[415] the 2004 Act makes provision for those in possession of such certificates (but who have not had such surgery) to be treated for the purposes of any gender specific offence as if they had not acquired their new gender.[416]

In historical times, the crime was thought to be an off-shoot of abduction.[417] The view then taken was that the carrying off and defiling of a female was of greater offence to her husband or father than to the female herself, a view which would now be regarded as outrageous. Echoes of it could still be heard in the nineteenth century, however, as in the case of *Charles Sweenie*[418] where Lord Ivory listed the evil consequences of rape as: "the danger of impregnation - the loss of status, - the taint to her family."

Vaginal sexual intercourse

9–74   Abduction is now totally unnecessary in relation to rape; and the old rule that the victim must register her complaint within 24 hours of the act has long ceased to apply.[419] Long delay in making a complaint is, however, unlikely to be propitious for a successful prosecution. But the act must consist of penetration of the victim's vagina by the accused's penis. Penetration need not be more than slight[420] but it must occur. Most authorities correctly say that ejaculation is unnecessary[421] but prosecutions are likely to be difficult without ejaculate to examine and submit to DNA profiling. Unlike the previous law in England, in this country there has never been any set age below which male sexual potency is presumed impossible. If a youngster in fact proves himself capable of penile

---

[413] *cf.* current English law, as contained in the Sexual Offences Act 2003 s.1 (with which must be read in particular ss.74–76); *cf.* s.2.

[414] See s.9 of the Gender Recognition Act 2004.

[415] See s.1 of the Gender Recognition Act 2004.

[416] See s.20 of the Gender Recognition Act 2004.

[417] See above, para.9–02; Sir George Mackenzie, *The Laws and Customs of Scotland in Matters Criminal*, 2nd edn (Edinburgh: 1699), I, 16.

[418] *Charles Sweenie* (1853) 3 Irv. 109 at 142: the decision in *Sweenie* was overruled by a seven judge court in *Lord Advocate's Reference (No.1 of 2001)*, 2002 S.L.T. 466.

[419] *Captain Charles Douglas* (1697) Maclaurin's Cases 13, No.12.

[420] *Alexander Macra or Macrae* (1841) Bell's Notes 83.

[421] *Duncan Macmillan* (1833) Bell's Notes 82; *Archibald Robertson* (1836) Bell's Notes 82–83.

penetration, then he can be prosecuted (all other things being equal).[422] What have come to be known graphically as "oral-sex" and "anal-sex" do not qualify as rape, however astonishing this may appear.[423] The essence of rape may well be considered popularly as the unwanted, violent invasion of any body orifice by any means, but law reform would be required to make that a reality in Scotland. At present, nothing short of, or different from, penile penetration of the vagina will suffice. Sexual activity short of, or different from, that amounts to indecent assault.[424]

Without her consent

The Appeal Court (organised as a court of seven judges) has **9–75** fairly recently determined by a majority of five to two that the essence of the *actus reus* of rape consists in the accused male's having vaginal intercourse with a female without that female's consent.[425] Consequently, the former requirement espoused by Hume,[426] in terms that there had to be evidence of resistance on the part of the female and corresponding force on the part of the male, was considered to be incorrect.

Hume was an avid reader of contemporary English legal works, and was especially impressed it seems by the writings of William Blackstone. Blackstone's *Commentaries on the Laws of England* were first published in 1769, and rape is described therein as: "the carnal knowledge of a woman forcibly and against her will."[427] Unsurprisingly, Hume uses much the same description,[428] Alison follows suit[429] and Burnett treads the same well-worn path.[430] Macdonald, whether he realised it or not, reproduced Blackstone's words exactly.[431] The courts too had been unusually conservative in their description of rape, mainly, it appears, preferring a definition which featured the formula "forcibly and against her will."[432]

---

[422] See *Robert Fulton Jnr* (1841) 2 Swin. 564.
[423] *Barbour v HM Advocate*, 1982 S.C.C.R. 195.
[424] *Barbour v HM Advocate*, 1982 S.C.C.R. 195.
[425] *Lord Advocate's Reference (No.1 of 2001)*, 2002 S.L.T. 466.
[426] See below; *cf.* Chalmers, "How (Not) to Reform the Law of Rape", (2002) 6 *Edin. L.R.* 388, 391–392, where the author argues that Hume had been misconstrued.
[427] William Blackstone, *Commentaries on the Laws of England* (Oxford: Clarendon Press, 1769), Vol.IV, Ch.15, p.210.
[428] Hume, *Commentaries*, i, 302.
[429] Alison, *Principles*, i, 209.
[430] Burnett, *Treatise*, 101.
[431] Macdonald, *Criminal Law*, 5th edn, p.119.
[432] See, e.g. amongst the more modern cases, *Stobbs v HM Advocate*, 1983 S.C.C.R. 190, per Lord Cowie at 200; *C v HM Advocate*, 1987 S.C.C.R. 104, per Lord Mayfield at 105; and *S v HM Advocate*, 1989 S.L.T. 469 at 471L–472E; *Jamieson v HM Advocate (No.1)*, 1994 S.L.T. 537, per Lord Justice-General Hope at 541C; *cf. W v HM Advocate*, 1995 S.L.T. 685, Lord Penrose's charge to the jury at 686B–C.

9–76   But in *Lord Advocate's Reference (No.1 of 2001)*,[433] the Appeal
Court by a majority declined to follow Hume, declared that an
earlier court in *Charles Sweenie*[434] had been in error in following
Hume, and corrected that error by laying down that neither
resistance nor force is an essential requirement of rape. Hence-
forth, therefore, any male who, with the required *mens rea*, has
vaginal intercourse with a female without her consent will prima
facie be guilty of rape. It is highly possible that "without her
consent" means here "without her *active* consent"[435]: and this will
mean that a female who is asleep or intoxicated or unconscious at
the time of the act may well be in a state of neutrality in relation to
consent, but plainly is not in any condition in which she can *actively*
give consent, and thus may be a victim of rape if taken advantage
of whilst she is so asleep, intoxicated or unconscious.[436] It must also
be the case that the intercourse must be without her *valid*[437]
consent, in the sense at least that a female under the age of 12 and
(perhaps) a female who is suffering from a sufficient degree of
mental abnormality are considered not to have consented as a
matter of law[438]; and this may be extended to the victim who is
coerced by violence or threats into permitting the intercourse to

---

[433] *Lord Advocate's Reference (No.1 of 2001)*, 2002 S.L.T. 466.

[434] *Charles Sweenie* (1858) 3 Irv. 109. The decision in *Sweenie* was overruled.

[435] See *Lord Advocate's Reference (No.1 of 2001)*, 2002 S.L.T. 466, Lord
Justice-General Cullen at 475F, para.39. Alternatively, the position may be
closer to that of current English statutory law: *cf.* the Sexual Offences Act 2003
s.74, which reads: ". . . a person consents if he agrees by choice, and has the
freedom and capacity to make that choice"; the English law, however, tempers
the foregoing definition by a series of rebuttable (s.75) and irrebuttable (s.76)
presumptions—see, e.g. *R. v Bree* [2007] 3 W.L.R. 600 CA.

[436] The court in *Charles Sweenie* (1858) 3 Irv. 109, where the victim was alleged to
have been asleep when she was violated, decided that she had not been raped,
either because no force had had to be used or because it could not be
determined that she had been "unwilling" in the sense of having withheld her
consent: but *Sweenie* is overruled by *Lord Advocate's Reference (No.1 of 2001)*,
2002 S.L.T. 466, and such a victim may now be viewed as having given no
consent to the act of intercourse. Similarly, where the female has been
intoxicated to the point of insensibility prior to the intercourse, there may have
been no consent on her part: *cf.* e.g. *HM Advocate v Logan*, 1936 J.C. 100, in
which Lord Justice-Clerk Aitchison's charge to the jury, insofar as inconsistent
with the decision in *Lord Advocate's Reference (No.1 of 2001)*, must be
considered as wrong; *cf.* also *HM Advocate v Grainger and Rae*, 1932 J.C. 40,
where Lord Anderson's opinion on the relevancy of the indictment is also now
impliedly overruled.

[437] But see below, para.9–79, on the matter of consent obtained by fraud.

[438] See *Lord Advocate's Reference (No.1 of 2001)*, 2002 S.L.T. 466, Lord
Justice-General Cullen at 473J, para.31, and again at 476A, para.44 where he
states: ". . . in the case of females who are under the age of 12 or who for any
other reason are incapable of giving . . . consent, the absence of consent should,
as at present, be presumed." See also Hume, *Commentaries*, i, 303, and below,
para.9–81.

take place—for there, there is no valid consent, but mere submission.[439] Although resistance and force are not now required elements of the *actus reus* of rape, evidence of such things will continue to be important, of course, in supporting the Crown's contention that the act of intercourse was without the victim's consent.[440]

The mens rea of rape

The *mens rea* of rape was effectively settled in *Jamieson v HM* **9–77** *Advocate*,[441] where the trial judge told the jury that the accused's "defence" of error as to the victim's consent was not sustainable unless based on reasonable grounds. The Appeal Court held that this was a clear misdirection, since the trial judge had been wrong not to follow a prior ruling by the court in 1982.[442] But the court also took the opportunity of explaining why reasonable grounds were *not* required in such cases. This was due to the form of the *mens rea* in rape. As Lord Justice-General Hope put it:

"[T]he *mens rea* of this crime includes the intention to have intercourse with the woman without her consent. The absence of a belief that she was consenting is an essential element in it. If a man has intercourse with a woman in the belief that she is consenting to this he cannot be guilty of rape."[443]

It is to be noted that the Lord Justice-General referred to the *mens rea* of rape as *including* such intention. There is, therefore, an alternative form, viz: where there is recklessness on the part of the male as to the female's consent.[444] If a man had intercourse with a woman who in fact had not consented, but he had failed to think about whether she was consenting or was utterly indifferent as to whether she consented or not, then he could be said to have a sufficient form of *mens rea* for the crime of rape. The two

---

[439] See *Lord Advocate's Reference (No.1 of 2001)*, 2002 S.L.T. 466, Lord Justice-General Cullen at 475F, para.39; see also, e.g. the situation in *Barbour v HM Advocate*, 1982 S.C.C.R. 195.

[440] They would also help to establish that the accused had the requisite *mens rea*: see *Lord Advocate's Reference (No.1 of 2001)*, 2002 S.L.T. 466, Lord Justice-General Cullen at 474K–L, para.35: *mens rea* is considered below at para.9–77.

[441] *Jamieson v HM Advocate (No.1)*, 1994 J.C. 88; what is stated there about rape in general is now modified, however, by the decision of the court in *Lord Advocate's Reference (No.1 of 2001)*, 2002 S.L.T. 466.

[442] *Meek v HM Advocate*, 1983 S.L.T. 280, which had apparently been followed in many similar (unreported) cases, such as that of *HM Advocate v Stevenson*, unreported, July 5, 1985, Appeal Court.

[443] *Jamieson v HM Advocate (No.1)*, 1994 J.C. 88 at 92E.

[444] *Jamieson v HM Advocate (No.1)*, 1994 J.C. 88 at 93F–G.

(known)[445] alternate forms of *mens rea* are thus intention (involving knowledge of her lack of consent) or recklessness (involving failure to think about, or complete indifference as to the issue of, her consent).[446] It had to follow, then, that an honest belief in the consent of the victim would, if believed by the jury, be sufficient to acquit, since it would negative both recognised forms of the *mens rea* of the crime.[447]

Marital rape

9–78   Hume hinted, rather than advanced as a definite rule, that a married man could not be convicted of raping his wife, if he had sexual intercourse with her without her consent.[448] What this was based on is hard to imagine, other than totally unacceptable views such as that a man had some "right" of property in his wife's body, or a "right" to expect that she would not deny him the means of acquiring legitimate heirs. In any event, if there ever was a soundly based "rule" of that nature in Scots law, it was laid to rest in *S v HM Advocate*.[449] The Appeal Court decided there that a married man was in no better position than any other man vis-à-vis the rape of his wife, thus culminating a process of attrition in respect of the "rule" begun by *HM Advocate v Duffy*[450] and *HM Advocate v*

---

[445] Since it seems that the *Jamieson* account of the *mens rea* of rape was simply adopted without discussion in the leading case of *Lord Advocate's Reference (No. 1 of 2001)*, 2002 S.L.T. 466—see the opinion of Lord Justice-General Cullen at 473B–H, 28–29, and his conclusion at 476B, para.44. All subsequent reported rape cases have accepted these two alternative forms of the applicable *mens rea*: see, e.g. *Gordon v HM Advocate*, 2004 S.C.C.R. 641, opinion of the court at 645B, para.6; *Blyth v HM Advocate*, 2005 S.C.C.R. 710, opinion of the court at 714C, para.10. Where there is no evidence of force having been used by the accused, a jury must be told of the need for sufficient evidence not only that the victim did not consent, but also that the accused knew of her lack of consent or was reckless as to whether she consented or not: see, e.g. *Cinci v HM Advocate*, 2004 S.C.C.R. 267 (where the trial judge's general account of the *mens rea* for rape is considered to have been correct—see opinion of Lord McCluskey at 273G–274C, para.18); *McKearney v HM Advocate*, 2004 S.C.C.R. 251, Lord Justice Clerk Gill at 254A–C, paras 8–9, and Lord McCluskey at 256C–F, para.23, 263E–264A, para.34.

[446] In *Lord Advocate's Reference (No.1 of 2001)*, 2002 S.L.T. 466, Lord Justice-General Cullen referred to recklessness as thus being understood in its subjective form: see 476B, para.44, which refers to what his Lordship had said earlier, at 473G–H, para.29.

[447] In so laying down the *mens rea* of rape, the court in *Jamieson* (as in *Meek*) followed the earlier English decision of the House of Lords in *DPP v Morgan* [1976] A.C. 182—even though the account of rape given by English law was not then identical to that accepted in Scotland. It is perhaps ironic, therefore, that the law in England was changed under the Sexual Offences Act 2003, such that the equivalent statutory offence there (under s.1) requires the accused to have had no reasonable belief in the consent of the victim.

[448] Hume, *Commentaries*, i, 306.

[449] *S v HM Advocate*, 1989 S.L.T. 469.

[450] *HM Advocate v Duffy*, 1983 S.L.T. 7.

Paxton.[451] English common law soon followed the Scottish lead here.[452]

Fraud and rape

Since consent to sexual intercourse now clearly elides rape, the **9–79** question arises: "What is the law if consent is obtained by deception?" Relevant pretences here might include promises of marriage, promotion or other reward. If these promises were never intended to be fulfilled, then fraud could certainly be made out.[453] In a slightly different way, fraud would also be relevant if a man deceived a woman into thinking that he was someone with whom she would have been happy to have intercourse, as where he pretended to be her husband[454] or lover. Such a case of "husband impersonation" arose in *William Fraser*.[455] Fraser was alleged to have inserted himself into the bed of a married woman, and there, by behaving familiarly with her, made her believe that he was her husband. It was on that basis that she allowed him to have intercourse with her. Three offences were charged as alternatives in the indictment against him, namely: rape; assault with intent to ravish; and the innominate crime of "fraudulently obtaining access to a married woman." The main debate centred on whether rape or the innominate offence was relevant in the circumstances. Four of the six judges observed that the proper definition of rape was the having of sexual intercourse without the woman's consent (see the opinions of Lord Justice-Clerk Hope, and Lords Mackenzie, Moncreiff and Cockburn). If that observation was correct (and later authorities did not accept that it was correct until the decision in *Lord Advocate's Reference (No.1 of 2001)*).[456] It seemed irrefutable that the victim had consented. Therefore, there could be no rape. Only Lord Cockburn, however, accepted the logic of that. The other three all maintained that Fraser was guilty of rape, apparently since the victim's consent had not been a proper one. There was no "informed" consent on her part owing to the element of deception. This interesting, if not bold, view was regrettably not shared by the remaining three judges, who sided with Lord Cockburn in deciding that consent obtained by fraud was nevertheless consent. In the final analysis, then, there was no rape here.

Disquiet over the decision in *William Fraser's* case (and similar **9–80** cases in England)[457] led in 1885 to a change in the law. Under the Criminal Law Amendment Act of that year, it was declared to be

---

[451] *HM Advocate v Paxton*, 1984 J.C. 105.
[452] See *R. v R* [1991] 3 W.L.R. 767. The alteration of the law achieved in *R. v R* was considered not to be in breach of Art.7(1) of the European Convention on Human Rights: *SW v United Kingdom* (1996) 21 E.H.R.R. 363.
[453] See below, paras 10–68 *et seq.*
[454] *cf. Gray v Criminal Injuries Compensation Board*, 1993 S.L.T. 28 (Court of Session, Lord Weir).
[455] *William Fraser* (1847) Ark. 280.
[456] *Lord Advocate's Reference (No.1 of 2001)*, 2002 S.L.T. 466.
[457] *R. v Clarke* (1854) 6 Cox C.C. 412; *R. v Barrow* (1868) 11 Cox C.C. 191.

common law rape in both Scotland and England to pretend to be a married woman's husband and thus obtain intercourse with her. The rule is now contained in s.7(3)[458] of the Criminal Law (Consolidation) (Scotland) Act 1995. It has no application, however, to any case of deception other than that relating to a married woman's husband. Now that it cannot be presumed that such a woman would have consented had the rogue really been her husband this specific statutory exception probably has little to justify it.[459]

Mentally ill victims

9–81   It is possible to argue that females suffering from certain mental illnesses or defects should be treated in the same way as young children. It would then be the case that intercourse with them could be assumed to be rape. Any consent apparently given could be ignored (although this could be harsh indeed where the victim exhibited no outward signs of mental illness). Despite some isolated dicta, however, such as that by Lord Cockburn in *William Fraser*,[460] there is no firm authority for treating mentally ill females any differently from females of normal mental capacities and abilities.[461] There are, however, statutory offences which might be used as alternatives to rape where the victim is mentally disordered.[462]

Clandestine injury to women

9–82   In *Charles Sweenie*,[463] as an alternative to rape, the indictment contained the innominate offence of "wickedly and feloniously having carnal knowledge of a woman whilst asleep, and without her consent." Four of the six judges eventually decided that the accused was guilty of the innominate offence, in that he had climbed into bed with a sleeping woman and had intercourse with her. She did not wake until he was withdrawing, it appears. Rape

---

[458] As amended by the Crime and Punishment (Scotland) Act 1997 Sch.1 para.18(3).
[459] Opinion was reserved on the matter of consent obtained by fraud in *Lord Advocate's Reference (No.1 of 2001)*, 2002 S.L.T. 466: see the opinion of Lord Justice-General Cullen at 475A–B, para.36.
[460] *William Fraser* (1847) Ark. 280 at 308.
[461] See Gordon, *Criminal Law*, 3rd edn, paras 33.09 to 33.11 (as substituted by the *Supplement* of 2005).
[462] See the Mental Health (Care and Treatment) (Scotland) Act 2003 (asp 13) s.311 (which creates a crime wider than common law rape) and s.313 (as amended by the Civil Partnership Act 2004, Sch.28 para.70—where the reference should be to s.313(3)(a)(ii) rather than the non-existent s.313(5)(a)(ii)), if the accused comes within the range of persons covered by that section: for the meaning of "mental disorder", see s.328.
[463] *Charles Sweenie* (1858) 3 Irv. 109: any authority which *Sweenie* represented (as to the requirements of rape) has been set aside by *Lord Advocate's Reference (No.1 of 2001)*, 2002 S.L.T. 466.

was out of the question in terms of the law at that time, since a sleeping victim could not be shown to have been "actively" unwilling.[464] Gordon, following Macdonald, referred to that innominate offence as "clandestine injury to women"[465]; but the changes effected to the definition of rape by the majority decision in *Lord Advocate's Reference (No.1 of 2001)*[466] make it difficult to understand what future the offence of "clandestine injury" can now have. The circumstances which led to its recognition as an independent offence, i.e. the vaginal penetration of a female when she is unconscious and unable to show her unwillingness, would not now be inconsistent with rape.[467] Yet, the offence is not condemned as obsolete in *Lord Advocate's Reference (No.1 of 2001).*[468] It would, therefore, remain possible for the Crown to choose to indict for "clandestine injury" rather than rape—perhaps, relative to a particular case, in the hope of more easily securing a conviction.[469]

Alternative verdicts

A case of rape must be tried in a High Court[470] but under s.14 of **9–83** the Criminal Law (Consolidation) (Scotland) Act 1995, a jury may convict of something other than rape, where that alone has been charged but the essentials of rape have not been established. The jury may instead convict of the statutory offences of procuring a woman or girl to have intercourse with a man by threats, false pretences or drugging,[471] of attempting to have intercourse with a girl under the age of 13,[472] or of having (or attempting to have) intercourse with a girl who is older than 13 but under 16 years of

---

[464] The then law required "resistance" on the part of the victim, that resistance having to be overcome by force on the part of the accused: see now *Lord Advocate's Reference (No.1 of 2001)*, 2002 S.L.T. 466

[465] Gordon, *Criminal Law*, 3rd edn, para.33.19, following Macdonald, *Criminal Law*, 5th edn, p.120. The *Supplement* to Gordon, of 2005, replaces the whole of the original Ch.33, and downgrades "clandestine injury" in view of the decision in *Lord Advocate's Reference (No.1 of 2001)*, 2002 S.L.T. 466; see the *Supplement* at p.146.

[466] *Lord Advocate's Reference (No.1 of 2001)*, 2002 S.L.T. 466.

[467] See, e.g. *Wiles v HM Advocate*, 2007 S.C.C.R. 191; *HM Advocate v L*, 2008 S.C.C.R. 51.

[468] *Lord Advocate's Reference (No.1 of 2001)*, 2002 S.L.T. 466; see Lord Justice-General Cullen's opinion at 474C–D, para.32.

[469] See *Spendiff v HM Advocate*, 2005 S.C.C.R. 522, where it was stated that the Lord Advocate, as master of the instance, might continue to "libel clandestine penetration of an unconscious female as indecent assault" should he wish to do so, notwithstanding that rape could now be charged in such circumstances: opinion of the court at 525G–526A, paras 5–6.

[470] See Criminal Procedure (Scotland) Act 1995 s.3(6).

[471] Criminal Law (Consolidation) (Scotland) Act 1995 s.7(2).

[472] Criminal Law (Consolidation) (Scotland) Act 1995 s.5(2), as amended by the Crime and Punishment (Scotland) Act 1997 s.14(1)(a).

age.[473] They may also convict of the common law offence of indecent assault.

6. THREATS AND EXTORTION

Introduction

9–84   Since it is accepted that words cannot amount to an assault (see above, para.9–05), it still seems necessary to deter in some other way the using of words in such a manner as to cause fear and alarm. The method adopted by the common law is to recognise that it is sometimes criminal to threaten to do things to the detriment of the person threatened. Depending on what is said, some threats are criminal as soon as they are communicated, irrespective of why they were said, as long as the accused meant to communicate them to the victim. With respect to other threats, they are not reckoned as criminal at all, unless they are made with the object of forcing the victim to do something he otherwise would not have been willing to do. In both cases, the *mens rea* element appears to be intention.

Threats criminal by themselves

9–85   Hume[474] made a distinction between verbal threats and written ones. On the apparent view that what is said is usually as transient as hot-air, verbal threats were only criminal if they related to burning down the victim's house or the like.[475] If they related only to "personal mischief", then the most that could be hoped for was an action for caution to keep the peace. This was apparently so even where there had been a threat to kill.[476] Written threats, however, were more serious—possibly since they could be read and re-read. If they related to personal violence or property damage, *and* demanded something as the price of non-implementation of the threat, then there was proper criminality.[477] As can be seen, however, all Hume's authorities are old and the law on this matter did not fully develop until much later in the nineteenth century.

---

[473] Criminal Law (Consolidation) (Scotland) Act 1995 s.5(3), as amended by the Crime and Punishment (Scotland) Act 1997 s.14(1)(b). Note that the time limit on commencing a prosecution for a s.5(3) offence no longer applies: see the Protection of Children etc. (Scotland) Act 2005 (asp 9) s.15, which repeals s.5(4) and (7) of the Criminal Law Consolidation (Scotland) Act 1995. Consequently, no problem, such as was principally involved in *McNeil v HM Advocate*, 2006 J.C. 71, would now arise.

[474] Hume, *Commentaries*, i, 135, 442.

[475] *Grizzel Sommerville* (1686) Hume, *Commentaries*, i, 135; *Laird and Lady Grant* (1712) Hume, *Commentaries*, i, 135.

[476] *Captain Andrew Nairne* (1712) Hume, *Commentaries*, i, 442.

[477] See *John Fraser* (1759) Hume, *Commentaries*, i, 439; *James Gray* (1737) Hume, *Commentaries*, i, 441.

The leading case on criminal threats is still that of *James* **9–86**
Miller.[478] It is important not for its facts, but for the light thrown on
the whole subject by Lord Justice-Clerk Inglis.[479] His view was that
it was wrong to make any distinction between what had been
spoken and what had been written. (This is clearly correct. The
effect on the victim is what really matters, rather than the method
of communication.) He also opined that certain threats, however
made, were criminal by themselves. He listed those as threats to
burn down a house, to put someone to death, to do someone
serious bodily harm, and (perhaps less understandably) to do
someone serious injury as to his property, fortune, or reputation.
With all of those, it did not matter whether the accused ever
intended to carry out what he threatened; nor did it matter that he
had no particular purpose to serve in making the threat at all.
Thus, in the later case of *Elizabeth Edmiston*[480] the accused tried in
vain to show that written threats to blow out the victim's brains and
burn his house about his ears were at worst a thoughtless frolic.
The court, following *James Miller*, ruled that it was of no consequence whether or not the accused really intended to cause serious
alarm. It was enough that threats of that description had been
communicated at all. Also in the still later case of *Margaret
McDaniel*[481] there was a verbal threat to tear the victim in pieces
and "do for her". Although there was an ulterior purpose of
discouraging the victim from giving evidence at a criminal trial, it is
significant that that purpose was libelled as an aggravation of the
threat—strongly suggesting that the threat was criminal by itself. A
less usual, but still criminal, threat consisted of part words, part
conduct in *HM Advocate v Hayes*.[482] There, the accused sent a
package containing explosives to the victim along with a letter. The
note indicated that an electric detonator would be sent next time,
thus threatening that the next package would blow up as soon as it
was opened. Lord Cameron had no doubt at all that a threat
criminal by itself was there involved, and that such a threat
constituted a crime as soon as it was uttered, or placed with the
postal authorities for onward transmission to the victim. There can
be little doubt then that *James Miller* has been followed in
subsequent cases, and must be taken to represent the modern law.

Extortion

Also in *James Miller*,[483] Lord Justice-Clerk Inglis intimated that **9–87**
threats, insufficient to be thought criminal by themselves, could
become criminal if "used for an unlawful purpose such as extorting

---

[478] *James Miller* (1862) 4 Irv. 238.
[479] *James Miller* (1862) 4 Irv. 238 at 244–245.
[480] *Elizabeth Edmiston* (1866) 5 Irv. 219, approved (*quoad* the principle it espouses)
in *Lord Advocate's Reference (No.2 of 1992)*, 1993 J.C. 43.
[481] *Margaret McDaniel* (1876) 3 Coup. 271.
[482] *HM Advocate v Hayes*, 1973 S.L.T. 202.
[483] *James Miller* (1862) 4 Irv. 238.

money."[484] Here, both the nature of the threat and the demand must be considered. In *Marion Macdonald*,[485] for example, the accused undertook to expose the alleged sexual improprieties of the victim upon her to his whole family, unless he agreed to pay her £10. The court had no doubt that a relevant charge had been made out when that sort of threat was allied to that sort of demand; and it was also opined that any offer by such an accused to show the truth of what she threatened to expose would be entirely irrelevant.[486] A similar type of decision can also be seen in *Hogg v HM Advocate*.[487]

9–88   There must, of course, be an actual threat—express or implied— for extortion to be made out. In *HM Advocate v Donoghue*[488] the accused told an agent for the owner of five stolen paintings that for £1,200 he would probably be in a position to secure their return. This was charged as attempted extortion; but clearly it could not succeed, since no threat (such as to destroy the paintings) had been made. It did constitute a suitable threat, however, for the accused to affix a notice to a car which had been parked on private property without permission, where that notice indicated that a wheel clamp had been secured to the vehicle, and that it would not be removed until a "levy on trespass parking" of £45 had been paid.[489] The threat, of course, must be accompanied by a demand. That demand generally is for the payment of money[490] but it is not necessarily restricted to that. Thus, in *George Jeffrey*,[491] the demands made were sometimes for goods; and in *Rae v Donnelly*[492] the price demanded for silence as to alleged sexual impropriety was the giving up of a claim for unfair dismissal on the part of one victim, and the tendering of his resignation on the part of the other.

Status of the threat and the demand

9–89   The crime of extortion must obviously not be so widely drawn that it prevents, say, a creditor from threatening to sue his debtor as a means of obtaining repayment of what is lawfully due. There, the demand for money would be quite legitimate, assuming that the due date for payment had come, as would the threat employed to pressurise the debtor. In the same way, it might be thought wrong for the law to penalise as extortion some matter which was ultimately for the victim's own benefit. If, for example, an

---

[484] *James Miller* (1862) 4 Irv. 238 at 246.
[485] *Marion Macdonald* (1879) 4 Coup. 268.
[486] *Marion Macdonald* (1879) 4 Coup. 268, per Lord Deas at 273.
[487] *Hogg v HM Advocate*, 1954 S.L.T. (Notes) 82.
[488] *HM Advocate v Donoghue*, 1971 S.L.T. 2.
[489] *Carmichael v Black; Black v Carmichael*, 1992 S.L.T. 897.
[490] See *Priteca v HM Advocate* (1906) 5 Adam 79; *Carmichael v Black; Black v Carmichael*, 1992 S.L.T. 897.
[491] *George Jeffrey* (1840) 2 Swin. 479.
[492] *Rae v Donnelly*, 1982 S.C.C.R. 148.

employee had been "caught with his hand in the till", it would clearly be to his benefit to take advantage of an offer from his employer to accept his resignation, even if pressurised into that by the threat of bringing in the police.[493] It was possibly to cater for situations such as these that Lord Justice-Clerk Thomson said of the type of threat made:

> "When the pressure consists in creating in the victim fear that, unless he yields, his position will be altered for the worse, it is criminal unless the pressure sought to be exerted is regarded by the law as legitimate."[494]

He then continued:

> "Legal process is such a form of pressure. So too . . . is the pressure exerted by one contracting party on another contracting party. I need not consider whether these are exhaustive of legitimate forms of pressure."

But more modern authority has emphasised that to enforce payment of a debt by any means other than those the law regards as legitimate is extortion, and that the only legally acceptable methods of enforcement are due process in a court of law, or lien (or retention) in relation to specific contracts.[495] Thus, irrespective of whether what is demanded is lawfully due or not (and that, of course, may be a matter which can only be resolved in court), a threat (for example) to detain (or injure) the "debtor's" person or property[496] would lead to a relevant charge of extortion.

7. PROPOSED REFORM OF SEXUAL OFFENCES

In a far reaching and detailed report,[497] the Scottish Law Commission has proposed that there should be what is virtually a statutory code of sexual offences. If the Commission's recommendations are accepted in full by the Scottish Parliament,[498] then most of the existing common law offences which apply to sexual matters (and many of the relevant statutory ones too) will be replaced (or, in some cases, consolidated). In particular, it is intended that common law rape should be abolished[499]: it would then be replaced **9–90**

---

[493] See *Hill v McGrogan*, 1945 S.L.T. (Sh. Ct.) 18.

[494] *Silverstein v HM Advocate*, 1949 J.C. 160 at 163.

[495] *Carmichael v Black; Black v Carmichael*, 1992 S.L.T. 897, per Lord Justice-General Hope at 900D–E.

[496] *Carmichael v Black; Black v Carmichael*, 1992 S.L.T. 897 at 900E.

[497] "Report on Rape and Other Sexual Offences", Scot. Law Com. No.209 (December, 2007) (hereafter "the Report").

[498] This is virtually certain, since the majority of the Report is unlikely to be politically (or otherwise) contentious.

[499] It is also proposed to abolish the offence of "clandestine injury to women", since it will be rendered truly unnecessary by the new scheme.

with a new statutory offence to be known as "rape".[500] This new
offence would be committed if a person ("A") penetrated with A's
penis[501] to any extent the vagina,[502] anus or mouth of another
person ("B"), without B's "consent" to that penetration and where
A had no reasonable belief[503] that B "consented" to it. "Penetration" relative to the offence would be construed as a continuing act
from entry until withdrawal[504]; however, if "consent" was initially
present, but withdrawn during penetration, it would only be from
the moment of determination of such "consent" that continued
penetration would count against A. "Consent" has been placed in
parenthesis thus far since a special meaning would be attributed to
it: consent would mean "free agreement".[505] That expression would
not, however, be assigned any fixed definition: instead, the Commission proposes that, "without prejudice to [its] generality", "free
agreement" should be taken as definitely absent in particular
circumstances.[506] The *mens rea* of the offence would be intention
on the part of A, or A's recklessness[507] as to whether there might
be penetration. This new offence of rape would be indictable only
in a High Court, and carry a maximum sentence of a fine and life
imprisonment.[508] There would be special provision (as now) for
persons suffering from "mental disorder",[509] in that such persons
would be considered incapable of "consenting" if unable to
understand what the "conduct"[510] was, to form a decision as to
whether to participate, etc. in that conduct, or to communicate any
such decision.[511] Children under the age of 13 ("young children")

---

[500] See the "Sexual Offences (Scotland) Bill", cll 40 and 1(1): this Bill (hereafter
"the Bill") appears as Appendix A to the Commission's Report.

[501] "Penis" includes an artificial one, formed by surgical treatment: see cl.1(4) of the
Bill.

[502] "Vagina" includes a surgically formed artificial vagina, the vulva and surgically
formed artificial vulva: see cl.1(4) of the Bill.

[503] On "reasonable belief", see cl.12 of the Bill.

[504] See cl.1(2) of the Bill.

[505] See the Bill, cl.9; see also cl.10: further, the word "consent" carries this meaning
in respect of other relevant offences in Pts 1 and 3 of the Bill.

[506] See cl.10 of the Bill for circumstances (a) through (g). These include: where the
person "B" was incapable of "consenting" due to the effect of, e.g. alcohol; where
B was asleep or unconscious and had not given any prior, relevant "consent";
where there had been agreement (or submission) due to violence (or threats of
such) against B or any other person, or due to B's having been unlawfully
detained by A; where A had deceived B as to the nature or purpose of the
conduct in question; where A had induced B to "agree" by impersonating a third
party personally known to B; or, where the only expression of "agreement" had
been made by a person other than B: see further cl.11.

[507] No other definition of "recklessness" is offered in the Bill. The Commission
assumes that the court would thus construe the concept in terms of the common
law.

[508] See the Bill Sch.3 para.5(1)–(3); cl.36 and Sch.1.

[509] As set out in s.328 of the Mental Health (Care and Treatment) (Scotland) Act
2003 (asp 13): see cl.13(3) of the Bill.

[510] "Conduct" since the provisions apply to offences under cll 1–6: see cl.13(1) of the
Bill.

[511] See cl.13(2) of the Bill.

also would receive special consideration,[512] as would children who have attained the age of 13 but who are under 16 years of age ("older children").[513]

A new offence of "sexual assault" is also proposed.[514] This would **9–91** replace (in general) those instances of assault which are aggravated by indecency.[515] The offence would be committed if a person ("A") intentionally or recklessly did, without another person ("B") having consented and without any reasonable belief that B had consented,[516] one or more of a number of specific things "sexually" to B[517]: whether conduct is "sexual" in a particular case would be determined by asking whether, "a reasonable person would, in all the circumstances of the case, consider [that conduct] to be sexual."[518]

One important proposed reform to the existing law of assault **9–92** should, however, be noticed: under cl.37 of the Scottish Law Commission's Draft Bill, it would no longer be assault for a person "A" (aged 16 or over) to attack another "B" (also aged 16 or over) where the primary purpose was the sexual gratification of at least one of them, they both agreed as to the purpose, and B consented[519] to the attack. It would be essential, however, that the attack should have been that which was unlikely to result in serious injury to B (even if, in the event, such injury should be caused).[520]

The Scottish Law Commission also proposes a considerable **9–93** number of new offences which vary in complexity.[521] These include "sexual coercion" (intentionally causing another person—who does

---

[512] In the current context, see in particular cll 14–17 of the Bill: see also cl.39 (exceptions to inciting or being art and part involved in such offences).

[513] In the current context, see in particular cll 21–24 of the Bill: it should be noticed that cl.27 would create defences for the "older children" offences; see also cl.39 (exceptions to inciting or being art and part involved in such offences). It might also be noticed that the existing common law offence of "lewd, indecent and libidinous practices or behaviour" (to be abolished in terms of cl.40(a)(iii)) would be subsumed by these new offences relative to younger and older children.

[514] See cl.2 of the Bill: *cf.* cll 15 and 22 for analogous offences where the victims are young.

[515] *cf.* cl.40(b) of the Bill.

[516] "Consent" would be interpreted as in the new offence of "rape"; see above, para.9–90.

[517] Under cl.2(2)(a)–(d) of the Bill, these things include: penetrating sexually (by any means) B's vagina, anus or mouth; touching B sexually; engaging in any other form of sexual activity in which A has physical contact with B; ejaculating semen on to B. There would be (deliberately) some overlap with the new offence of "rape": see, e.g. cl.2(6).

[518] See cl.2(3) of the Bill.

[519] "Consent" here, however, is intended to carry its ordinary common law meaning: see, e.g. the second paragraph of the Commission's "Note" to cl.9 of the Bill.

[520] See the Bill, cl.37(1)(a)–(d). Under cl.37(2), "an attack is unlikely to result in serious injury in any case if a reasonable person would, in all the circumstances of the case, consider that the attack would be unlikely to result in serious injury." As the "Note" to this clause indicates, it would have the effect of allowing certain activities of a sado-masochistic nature to be exempt from common law assault.

[521] Complexity is, however, sometimes inevitable in the process of translating relatively simple recommendations into workable statutory provisions.

not consent to it—to participate in a "sexual activity"),[522] and, "Coercing a person into being present during a sexual activity" (intentionally engaging in a sexual activity (for the purpose of obtaining sexual gratification or humiliating, distressing or alarming another person "B") in B's presence).[523] Of more relevance, however, to the present chapter of this book is perhaps the proposed new offence of: "Administering a substance for sexual purposes."[524] This has affinities with "rape" (both at common law and as redefined by the Commission) and with assault; but it is now proposed that there should be a discrete offence of intentionally administering a substance to, or causing a substance to be taken by, another without that other person's knowledge (or without any reasonable belief on the part of the accused that that other person knows), for the purpose of stupefying or overpowering that other person "so as to enable [the accused] to engage in a sexual activity which involves" that person.[525] If the accused were to induce in the other person a reasonable belief that the substance in question was of a substantially lesser strength and/or quantity than it actually was, then any knowledge (or belief as to knowledge) that the substance was being administered or taken is to be disregarded.[526]

---

[522] See cl.3 of the Bill: only a brief synopsis of the offence is attempted here.
[523] See cl.4 of the Bill: only a brief synopsis of the offence is attempted here.
[524] See cl.8 of the Bill.
[525] An activity is sexual if a reasonable person, in all the circumstances, would consider it to be so: see cl.8(2)(a) of the Bill.
[526] See cl.8(2)(b) of the Bill.

CHAPTER 10

CRIMES OF DISHONESTY

1. THEFT

Introduction

Scots law recognises a right of property or ownership in many **10–01** different things. It subsists, for example, in relation to land, buildings, jewellery, farm and domestic animals, vehicles, foodstuffs, crops, money, debts, stocks and shares, copyright, patents and so on. A right of property is a complex one, under which owners, depending on the precise nature of what they own, may normally use, consume, destroy, keep, conceal from public gaze, transfer to another (for a price or by way of gift), pawn, mortgage or otherwise deal with the subject of the right. At any one time, owners may or may not have possession; they may indeed be temporarily debarred from possession, as where, for example, they have pawned or hired out the thing that is owned. Ownership, however, will normally continue to exist notwithstanding the loss of possession. Theft is designed to help protect the right of property in things. It protects more than the mere possession, but less than the whole gamut of things in which ownership is legally recognised.

GENERAL DEFINITION OF THEFT

In the modern law, it is theft to appropriate moveable, corporeal **10–02** things belonging to another person, without the consent of that person, where the accused knows that those things belong to another and intends to deprive the owner of them or their use permanently, indefinitely, or (in certain circumstances) temporarily. No Scottish authority conclusively shows that any additional requirement of "dishonesty" (despite the title of this chapter) has to be shown or inferred[1]—unlike the situation in current English law under the Theft Act 1968 s.1(1)—but honesty, or rather the lack of it, cannot entirely be divorced from any meaningful discussion of theft. It is unnecessary to show that the accused made any material gain from the appropriation: "[I]t is the owner's loss and not the other's gain which is important."[2]

THE ACTUS REUS OF THEFT

Appropriation

10–03   It is thought[3] that this term now more accurately represents the essential element in the *actus reus* than the "taking" referred to by Hume. His views[4] were somewhat eccentric and can be seen clearly in the following extract:

> "All the necessary characters seem to be set forth in that short description of it, given in the civil law [i.e. Roman law], . . . the felonious taking and carrying away of the property of another, for lucre.
> I. The fundamental circumstance here . . . is this of the *taking* . . . In which it is implied, that the thing has not been previously in the possession of the thief, but in that of the owner, or some person for him, out of which the thief, without the consent of the owner, removes it."

For Hume, then, it was necessary to show that the accused had deprived the owner of the possession of the thing, provided that the accused had the necessary *mens rea* at the very moment of deprivation. If the accused had been given possession of the thing with the consent of the owner, and only later formed the intention of keeping it for himself and treating himself as if he were its owner, that was not theft. If a person hired a horse, took a watch on loan, or agreed to carry goods to a certain destination, then as a matter of fact he would have had possession with the owner's consent and it would be assumed that he had originally meant to act honestly, unless the contrary was clearly proved. If that was not

---

[1] *cf. Kane v Friel*, 1997 S.C.C.R. 207, a case of alleged theft by finding where the Appeal Court proceeded on the basis of the advocate-depute's concession that the Crown had to prove that any appropriation by the appellant of the goods in question had been dishonest: see 209G. See also *Mackenzie v MacLean*, 1981 S.L.T. (Sh. Ct.) 40, Sheriff Scott Robinson at 41, final text paragraph.
[2] *Carmichael v Black; Black v Carmichael*, 1992 S.L.T. 897, per Lord Justice-General Hope at 902F, quoting with approval from Gordon, *Criminal Law*, 2nd edn, para.14–63.
[3] *Carmichael v Black; Black v Carmichael*, 1992 S.L.T. 897 at 901H.
[4] Hume, *Commentaries*, i, 57.

proved and he subsequently converted the horse, watch or goods to his own purpose (e.g. by selling it or them), "he only breaks his contract, and abuses his powers as possessor."[5] In brief, a person already in possession of the thing with the consent of the owner would (somewhat generously) be presumed to be in honest possession of it. A later manifestation of dishonest intention might result in a wrong being committed, but it did not amount to theft.[6]

That Hume was strongly of the persuasion that theft protected **10–04** the owner's possession is further illustrated by his treatment of a finder of things which had been lost.[7] The person who lifts a wallet from the street where its owner has accidentally dropped it is plainly from that moment onwards in possession of it. In Hume's estimation, it could not be theft for him subsequently to, "keep it to himself" since,

> "there is no felonious intention, nor even a *trespass* in the first occupying of the thing, which is lying vacant, and inaccessible to the owner, and may lawfully be taken possession of for the sake of custody, or till offer of a reward. So much is this the case, that though caught in the very act of laying hold of the thing, the man could not be punished or found fault with."[8]

The assumption of initial honesty in such a case[9] seemed, indeed, to be decisive; on the premise that theft required a dishonest taking of possession, no subsequent dishonesty could count since no-one could again take what he had already taken.

Attractively logical though Hume's views were, the premise on **10–05** which they were founded was openly doubted by the judiciary even before his death on August 30, 1838. The leading reported case in this respect is that of *John Smith*,[10] although earlier cases in which Hume was not followed are referred to in the pleadings and opinions. Smith was alleged to have found a pocket book, £112 in bank notes and a bill of exchange—all of which having been accidentally dropped by the owner on or near a public road. The name of the owner appears to have been contained in the pocket book, and thus Smith could have had no doubt to whom the items belonged. He was charged with theft since, having found these

---

[5] Hume, *Commentaries*, i, 58–59.
[6] Hume, *Commentaries*, i, 58 at "2".
[7] Hume, *Commentaries*, i, 62.
[8] Hume, *Commentaries*, i, 62.
[9] *cf.* Burnett, *Treatise*, 123, where the assumption is put the other way.
[10] *John Smith* (1838) 2 Swin. 28, decided on March 12, 1838. For a modern example of a charge of theft by finding, see *MacMillan v Lowe*, 1991 J.C. 13, where in the special circumstances of the case, possession of the goods a mere four hours after they were found was sufficient to justify the conclusion that the finder had appropriated them.

things, he, "did then and there, or at some other time and place ... appropriate the same to his own uses and purposes." The words, "at some other time and place" plainly covered a situation which Hume would not have counted as theft; but the court of six judges unanimously found the whole indictment relevant. As Lord Meadowbank trenchantly remarked[11]:

> "It is of no consequence of what character the original possession of the property is. The moment the intention of appropriating the property of another is formed, then the theft is committed."

Lord Mackenzie was equally forthright in that he stated[12]:

> "We have determined that in the case of carriers, servants, clerks, shopmen, the appropriation of goods held on a limited title for behoof of the owner is theft; and of course all these decisions apply with greater force to the case of a finder, who took the goods honestly, and subsequently formed the felonious intention of appropriating them."

The words of Lord Cockburn[13] are also worthy of notice:

> "The definition which our law gives of theft, is, that it is ... fraudulent taking of the property of another for the sake of lucre. Now what is meant by this word *taking*? I know no authority, and no principle, for confining it to the act of first possessing ... I don't conceive that there can be any taking, in the sense of this definition, without an intention to take. It means appropriation."

10–06   If "appropriation" is what is required, and it is submitted that it is, then it covers a number of different situations. Certainly it includes Hume's dishonest taking possession of a thing and carrying it away. It has also been held to apply where a car found on private land without permission to be parked there was "wheel-clamped", thus immobilising it and depriving the owner of its use and enjoyment as a vehicle.[14] This would not be the case, however, if property had been incidentally (as opposed to deliberately) immobilised, e.g. "as a result of some legitimate act such as the

---

[11] *John Smith* (1838) 2 Swin. 28 at 52.

[12] *John Smith* (1838) 2 Swin. 28 at 53–54.

[13] *John Smith* (1838) 2 Swin. 28 at 56.

[14] *Carmichael v Black; Black v Carmichael*, 1992 S.L.T. 897, per Lord Justice-General Hope at 902B–C. Notice, however, that Lord Allanbridge considered that the facts amounted to a case of theft by finding (at 903B–C). (For wider discussion of the issues raised by this case, see Robin M. White, "Parking Fine: The Enforceability of 'Private' Parking Schemes", 2007 J.R. 1.)

closing or locking of a gate for security."[15] Appropriation also extends more widely to a manifest change in attitude towards things that the thief originally possessed lawfully and honestly, as where he subsequently applies or converts those things to his own use,[16] or claims them as his own.[17] That "appropriation" is indeed what is required is the only plausible explanation of the judiciary's rejection of Hume's view that a footman could not steal his livery[18] in cases such as *Elizabeth Anderson*,[19] where a discharged poorhouse inmate committed theft by purporting to sell the petticoat, shawl and shift given into her temporary possession by the relevant parochial board, and *John Martin*,[20] where again an inmate committed theft by purportedly selling his poorhouse "uniform". It also explains Lord Mackenzie's remarks in *George Brown*[21] that,

> "in the case of a horse hired without any felonious purpose, and afterwards carried off by the hirer, we have decided that a theft is committed [see Alison, *Principles*, i, 259–260 for possible authorities]. But that decision is contrary to the opinion of Baron Hume."

Thus Hume had become, "greatly qualified"[22] or, "seriously modified."[23] No doubt, the courts felt less need than usual to follow that authoritative writer since he himself had admitted[24]:

> "Thus much of the taking which is essential to the crime of theft. Upon the whole of which inquiry . . . it may be proper to remark, that our practice has not yet attained to sufficient maturity in these matters."

Moveable, corporeal things

Things can be stolen if they can be physically possessed and can **10–07** be moved from place to place. As Alison[25] narrates:

> "Theft may be committed of every inanimate thing, which is either moveable or capable of being severed from that which is naturally or artificially attached to it."

---

[15] *Carmichael v Black; Black v Carmichael*, 1992 S.L.T. 897, per Lord Justice-General Hope at 902D.
[16] *John Smith* (1838) 2 Swin. 28, per Lord Cockburn at 56–57.
[17] *John Waugh* (1873) 2 Coup. 424, per Lord Ardmillan at 427.
[18] Hume, *Commentaries*, i, 60.
[19] *Elizabeth Anderson* (1858) 3 Irv. 65.
[20] *John Martin* (1873) 2 Coup. 501.
[21] *George Brown* (1839) 2 Swin. 394 at 428.
[22] *John Smith* (1838) 2 Swin. 28, per Lord Moncreiff at 54.
[23] *Elizabeth Anderson* (1858) 3 Irv. 65, per Lord Ardmillan at 68.
[24] Hume, *Commentaries*, i, 69–70.
[25] Alison, *Principles*, i, 278.

It follows then that a growing crop becomes moveable property when cut from the field or dug up from the earth, and thus at that stage can be possessed and stolen.[26] Even a piece of land might gradually be stolen (all things being equal) by excavating its substance[27]; that could not, however, exhaust the right of property involved in land ownership, since that is a metaphysical entity said to extend *a coelo usque ad centrum*.[28] Such a right of property in land is, of course, created and evidenced by title deeds or land certificates. Once again, whilst it is possible to steal such deeds or certificates,[29] what is stolen is not the right of property in the land itself but the documents themselves, considered as miscellaneous collections of paper and parchment. The right to the land cannot in fact be stolen because it is the incorporeal, i.e. intangible, non-possessable, property of a particular individual.

10–08   Corporeal moveables are referred to by Bell[30] as including,

> "all things which, being themselves capable of motion or of being moved, may be perceived by the senses—seen, touched, taken possession of: as ships, household furniture; goods and effects of all kinds; farm stock and implements; horses, cattle and other animals; corn, money, jewels, wearing apparel."

Such moveables, it is said,[31] are the only things which can be stolen, since they are the only things capable of being physically possessed and carried away in accordance with Hume's account of theft (see above, para.10–03). Since his account has been departed from somewhat in modern law,[32] the need to confine theft to moveable, corporeal property is questionable. An extension of the crime to cover the appropriation of at least some types of incorporeal, i.e. intangible, property would, therefore, seem worth considering. No reported case has endorsed such an extension, however, and so called "intellectual property", e.g. copyrights, patents and designs, is protected either by civil law remedies or by particular statutory offences.[33] On the other hand, no reported case has ruled out such an extension, such authorities as there are having been concerned with innominate offences rather than theft.[34]

---

[26] See, e.g. *James Miln* (1758) Hume, *Commentaries*, i, 79—grain; and *Andrew Young* (1800) Hume, *Commentaries*, i, 79–80—potatoes.

[27] Hume, *Commentaries*, i, 80.

[28] i.e. "from the heavens right to the centre of the earth", see Bell, *Principles*, 10th edn, s.940.

[29] See *Patrick Eviot* (1614) Hume, *Commentaries*, i, 80.

[30] Bell, *Principles*, s.1285.

[31] Gordon, *Criminal Law*, 3rd edn, para.14–20.

[32] See above, paras 10–05 *et seq*.

[33] See, e.g. the Copyright, Designs and Patents Act 1988 s.107 (as amended by the Copyright, etc. and Trade Marks (Offences etc.) Act 2002 s.1(2), and by the Copyright and Related Rights Regulations 2003 (SI 2003/2498) reg.26(1) and Sch.1 para.9(2)).

[34] See *John Dewar*, Burnett, 115; N.A.S., J.C.13/21, October 3, 1777 (erroneously, it seems, referred to as a case of theft in Macdonald, *Criminal Law*, 5th edn, p.20); *HM Advocate v Mackenzie*, 1913 S.C. (J.) 107; *Grant v Allan*, 1988 S.L.T. 11.

As is obvious from the passage quoted from Bell, animate things **10–09** can also meet the test of being moveable and corporeal. Thus animals may be stolen,[35] as also "infant" children.[36] The conventional view is that an "infant" child is one below the age of puberty,[37] which means a boy under 14 or a girl under 12,[38] and the authorities certainly support the view that a young child must be involved.[39] The Scottish Law Commission, however, has recommended that such children should cease to be considered as "stealable", and that an appropriate statutory offence should be substituted.[40] Adults, i.e. apparently anyone beyond the age of pupillarity, cannot be stolen; but the crime of abduction substitutes for theft where such persons are forcibly taken away.[41]

Some things are difficult to perceive as moveable and corporeal **10–10** in the required sense. Currency, for example, in the form of banknotes can certainly be stolen, although the notes themselves appear to represent some ill defined, intangible right. Prosecutions for thefts of money assume, however, that the face value of what has been appropriated is involved, and not just such value as mere pieces of paper attract.[42] The reason for this is that such promise (an incorporeal matter) as is contained in a banknote is made to the bearer, and not to any particular person. Electricity is also thought to pose conceptual difficulties,[43] but it is clearly moveable and corporeal. The fact that it cannot as easily be possessed and taken away as many other forms of stealable property is probably not of great importance once it is recalled that appropriation is what is required in the modern law.

Belonging to another person

Since theft protects an owner's right of property, stealable things **10–11** must be owned—and owned by someone other than the accused. As Macdonald puts the matter[44]:

> "[A] person is not guilty of theft for irregularly taking that which is his own, although he may thereby commit some offence other than theft."

---

[35] Hume, *Commentaries*, i, 81.
[36] Hume, *Commentaries*, i, 84. See below, para.10–15.
[37] Macdonald, *Criminal Law*, 5th edn, p.21; Gordon, *Criminal Law*, 3rd edn, para.14.26.
[38] See "Child Abduction", Scot. Law Com. No.102 (1987), Pt III para.3–3.
[39] *Rachel Wright* (1808–09), Hume, *Commentaries*, i, 84, fn.2—child aged between two and three; *Mary Millar or Oates* (1861) 4 Irv. 74—child aged nine years nine months.
[40] "Child Abduction", Scot. Law Com. No.102 (1987), Pts III, IV.
[41] *Barbour v HM Advocate*, 1982 S.C.C.R. 195.
[42] *John Mooney* (1851) J. Shaw 496.
[43] Gordon, *Criminal Law*, 3rd edn, para.14.16.
[44] Macdonald, *Criminal Law*, 5th edn, p.16.

It is not possible in Scotland, therefore, for a person to steal his own car, by driving it off clandestinely from a repair-garage in order to avoid paying for work done on it.[45] Although the garage proprietor would have had a lien over such a car until the work had been paid for, such a lien, i.e. a right to retain possession, does not amount to any right of ownership. It has been declared that a pawnbroker has some form of ownership in relation to things which are pawned—certainly a form sufficient to save him from conviction for theft if he disposes of such things before the conclusion of the redemption period[46]—but this is at odds with the tenor of the present legislation[47] and Gordon[48] is surely correct to say that the view taken in the case must be wrong.

10–12   In contracts of sale involving "stealable property", ownership passes to the buyer according to the rules contained in the Sale of Goods Act 1979[49] ss.17, 18, 19, 20A and 21; but in lesser contracts than sale, such as loan, where the subject of the loan is money, or anything else which is consumed by use and is intended to be so consumed, e.g. a jar of coffee, ownership must pass on delivery by the lender. As Bell remarks[50]: "Possession in this, as in the case of ordinary moveables, presumes property." The obligation of the recipient is thus to return an equivalent sum of money, together with any interest charged, or an equivalent amount of the thing consumed. It is difficult to see that failure to do so could be more than a breach of contract. Theft must be negatived by his owner-ship of the thing lent. In a similar way, if a banknote is tendered for change into coin or notes of smaller denomination, or is tendered in payment for a purchased item, it seems that ownership of the note must pass on delivery. Failure either to give change at all or to give the correct change would, therefore, seem to be a breach of contract rather than theft. The original note and the pool of cash from which change might be had are both in the possession, and thus ownership of the defaulting party. Yet in *John Mooney*,[51] where a banknote was indeed tendered in payment for goods of considerably less value, and no change given, Lord Justice-Clerk Hope directed the jury that: "If there was theft at all, it was theft of the one-pound note." Although that direction might have had the merit of granting relief to the "innocent" party from having to pursue a claim according to the vagaries and expense of the civil law, his Lordship advanced no justification for considering that

---

[45] *cf. R. v Turner (No.2)* [1971] 1 W.L.R. 901, which depended on the extended meaning given to "belonging to another" by the (English) Theft Act 1968 s.5(1).
[46] *Catherine Crossgrove or Bradley* (1850) J. Shaw 301, per Lord Moncreiff at 305.
[47] Consumer Credit Act 1974, especially ss.116(3), 117(2), 118(1), 119(2) (though not applicable to Scotland), 120, 121, 122.
[48] Gordon, *Criminal Law*, 3rd edn, para.14.30.
[49] As amended by the Sale of Goods (Amendment) Act 1995 s.1.
[50] Bell, *Principles*, s.1333.
[51] *John Mooney* (1851) J. Shaw 496 at 497.

theft could be relevant there at all. Nevertheless, Mooney was convicted of the theft of the banknote and transported for seven years. If that was a "just" result, it was certainly not arrived at by any principled argument.

Almost all moveable, corporeal property in Scotland is owned by **10–13** someone—either by a particular person or, by way of fiction, by the Crown. If such property is truly abandoned by its modern-day owner, then the Crown fills any hiatus in ownership between abandonment and, say, its collection as waste by a local authority.[52] It thus remains theoretically stealable at every step.[53] It is also the case under feudal theory that treasure hidden or abandoned in antiquity belongs to the Crown[54] and can, therefore, be stolen by its finder. As Bell puts it[55]: "The rule is, 'Quod nullius est fit domini regis'." No doubt, neither that maxim nor its import is widely known to the general public, and it may be that a non-lawyer accused of stealing abandoned property could not be shown to have had sufficient dishonesty for an inference of theftuous intent to be drawn[56]; but where a crematorium manager espoused an honest belief that coffins delivered to his premises to be burnt were ownerless scrap, lawfully able to be appropriated by anyone including himself, the Appeal Court rejected his defence of error on the grounds that it did not rest on reasonable grounds.[57] Temporarily-lost property is, of course, not abandoned by its owner; and its finder is not even entitled to claim ownership where the original owner remains untraced.[58]

The case of indigenous animals living naturally in the wild is **10–14** special, although the rule is one of considerable antiquity. They form a conspicuous exception to what was stated at the beginning of the preceding paragraph. According to Hume[59]:

> "Our practice acknowledges, of course, the exception of those animals which are wild, and in no degree *sub domino* [i.e.

---

[52] *Mackenzie v Maclean*, 1981 S.L.T. (Sh. Ct.) 40; see also Environmental Protection Act 1990 s.45(9), noting that "waste" is defined by s.75(2) as substituted by the Environment Act 1995 Sch.22 para.88, and as amended by the Waste (Scotland) Regulations 2005 (SSI 2005/22) reg.3(4), and by the Manufacture and Storage of Explosives Regulations 2005 (SI 2005/1082) Sch.5 para.19(2); *cf.* the offence under s.60(1).

[53] In *Kane v Friel*, 1997 S.C.C.R. 207 at 209A, Lord Justice-General Rodger (giving the opinion of the court) said: "It is true that at common law most abandoned moveable property belongs to the Crown. The Advocate-depute did not seek, however, to found on that somewhat technical doctrine when arguing that the appellant had had the necessary *mens rea* for conviction of [theft]."

[54] *Lord Advocate v University of Aberdeen and Budge*, 1963 S.C. 533.

[55] Bell, *Principles*, s.1291.

[56] See *Kane v Friel*, 1997 S.C.C.R. 207.

[57] *Dewar v HM Advocate*, 1945 J.C. 5; see above, paras 8–46 and 8–47. There is, however, a considerable difference between sinks and metal *abandoned* as scrap (see *Kane v Friel*, 1997 S.C.C.R. 207), and a coffin (containing a human corpse) *delivered* to a crematorium for reduction to ashes.

[58] See the Civic Government (Scotland) Act 1982 s.73.

[59] Hume, *Commentaries*, i, 81.

within anyone's ownership], such as game in the fields, or fish in a lake or river: There may be a trespass in taking these without leave of the owner of the grounds, but they are not his property, to be stolen."

In fact they are no one's property until killed or taken into captivity. Then ownership follows possession[60] and they may then be stolen. The Theft Act 1607,[61] as it has come to be known,[62] is the sole survivor of a number of pieces of legislation passed by the Scots Parliament to clarify doubtful cases relating to wild animals.[63] It states (as amended[64] and using modern orthography): "Whosoever steals bees shall be called and convened therefor as a breaker of the law." Since the penalty was (and is) a small fine, it is difficult to be confident that this offence is, "raised to the rank of theft."[65]

10–15 Since "infant" children are stealable property (see above, para.10–09), they would apparently require to be owned by their parent(s) or guardian, if the usual rules for theft are applicable. This would involve a very odd conception of ownership since it clearly could not involve the usual property rights of, for example, destruction or sale. The essence of this sort of theft has, however, been described as the,

> "deliberate taking of a child from the custody of a parent or other person who has for the time being the parental right of custody in terms of the statute[66] or under an order made by the court. The matter does not depend on the natural relationship which exists between a father and his child. It depends entirely upon interference with the parental right of custody, by virtue of which the child is in the care and possession of the person from whom it has been taken."[67]

---

[60] Bell, *Principles*, s.1290.
[61] A.P.S. iv, c.6, 373.
[62] Statute Law Revision (Scotland) Act 1964 Sch.2.
[63] Hume, *Commentaries*, i, 82.
[64] See the Salmon and Freshwater Fisheries (Consolidation) (Scotland) Act 2003 (asp 15) Sch.4 Pt 2
[65] Hume, *Commentaries*, i, 82. There is also a modern statutory offence (based on repealed parts of the 1607 Act) under which a person is guilty if, without legal right or without permission, he fishes "in a proper stank or loch". See the Salmon and Freshwater Fisheries (Consolidation) (Scotland) Act 2003 (asp 15) s.11(1): "stank" and "proper stank or loch" are defined in s.11(2).
[66] See now the Children (Scotland) Act 1995 ss.1–4, 11 (noting that ss.3 and 11 are amended by the Family Law (Scotland) Act 2006 (asp 2) ss.23, 24, and that s.11 is further amended by the Adoption and Children (Scotland) Act 2007 (asp 4) s.107, Sch.2 para.9(2), Sch.3): under these provisions, the appropriate right would now be one of regulating the child's residence; *cf. Orr v K*, 2003 S.L.T. (Sh. Ct.) 70.
[67] *Hamilton v Wilson*, 1994 S.L.T. 431 (father of illegitimate child convicted of theft of the child from its mother), per Lord Justice-General Hope, at 433E.

Consequently, a parent may be excluded from having lawful custody, and may be able to steal his own child simply because he is excluded from possession.[68] It might be advantageous, therefore, to treat child stealing as a special crime of its own kind—as is more or less admitted by the authoritative writers in their description of it as "plagium".[69] A similar problem is encountered with the "theft" of human corpses. This is partly solved by the existence of the special crime of violation of sepulchres. It is committed by raising the body of a deceased person from its grave; but ceases to apply once the process of dissolution of the corpse has reached a rather ill defined stage.[70] That crime does not depend, however, on the recognition of any person's ownership of the remains. Between death and burial (or cremation), it is presumed that theft may still apply to the corpse[71]; but the early case of *Mackenzie* (1733), mentioned in the report of *HM Advocate v Coutts*,[72] does not seem to provide authority for this, since the charge was not one of theft.[73] In the case of *Dewar v HM Advocate*[74] a conviction for stealing coffins (or at least their lids), which had been delivered to a crematorium to be burnt, was upheld on appeal. There was no discussion which addressed the question of who owned these items at the time. But ownership here may be clearer than in the other situations outlined above. For the executors in each case must have authorised payment for the coffin and lid out of funds in respect to which they stood as trustees.[75] They were, therefore, the true owners[76] until such time as the whole coffin (along with its contents) was reduced to ashes in the crematorium's furnace.[77]

"[T]he charge of theft is competent . . . though the case should **10–16** be such in which it is difficult precisely to describe the owner, or the quality of the immediate interest in the thing . . . We are . . . content with such a description of the thing, as makes the title of possession or management clear, and excludes all pretence of right in the pannel."[78] It is, thus, sufficient in a charge of theft to allege

---

[68] *Hamilton v Wilson*, 1994 S.L.T. 431. See also *Downie v HM Advocate*, 1984 S.C.C.R. 365 Sh. Ct.; *Hamilton v Mooney*, 1990 S.L.T. (Sh. Ct.) 105.

[69] Hume, *Commentaries*, i, 82; Alison, *Principles*, i, 280—and see *Brouillard v HM Advocate*, 2004 S.C.C.R. 410, opinion of the court at 416B, para.19; J.M. Fotheringham, "Plagium: The Sins of the Father v. The Rights of the Parent", 1990 J.L.S.S. 506.

[70] *HM Advocate v Coutts* (1899) 3 Adam 50.

[71] Hume, *Commentaries*, i, 85, fn.1.

[72] *HM Advocate v Coutts* (1899) 3 Adam 50 at 57, fn.1.

[73] Gordon, *Criminal Law*, 3rd edn, para.14.27.

[74] *Dewar v HM Advocate*, 1945 J.C. 5.

[75] See Gordon, *Criminal Law*, 3rd edn, para.14.33, for authority that trustees own trust property.

[76] See the Succession (Scotland) Act 1964 s.14(1).

[77] See also *Herron v Diack and Newlands*, 1973 S.L.T. (Sh. Ct.) 27, a macabre case where it was assumed that an American funeral casket was stealable until committed with its contents to the waters of the River Clyde.

[78] Hume, *Commentaries*, i, 78.

that the property is owned by someone unknown, as long as it is made clear that that someone could not have been the accused.[79]

10–17   Where the alleged thief asserts a belief that the property in question was his own, or at least was available for him to deal with as he pleased, this is an admissible defence[80]:

> "[T]he person must however be excusable for believing, that the thing which he has taken is his own. For as to that sort of belief . . . which is directly in the face of law, and is grounded only in the violent passions of the man, or his blind prejudices in his own favour, it is what the Judge can have no regard to, and what none of the lieges can be allowed to entertain."[81]

Such a belief must, therefore, be more than honestly held; it must be based on reasonable grounds, as in *Dewar v HM Advocate*,[82] and the evidential burden of establishing that appears to lie with the accused.[83] This may or may not amount to what Gordon refers to as a "Claim of Right"[84] or the defence of "Entitlement".[85]

Without the consent of the owner

10–18   What was done must have been done without the consent of the owner or his authorised agent or representative. This is usually obvious from the facts and circumstances. Plainly there is appropriation without the owner's consent if foodstuffs or beverages given to the accused for safekeeping are consumed or destroyed by him. Similarly, a person entrusted with valuables whilst the owner travels abroad has no authority to sell or pawn them, or indeed to devote them to some worthy charity. To do so is to arrogate to himself the rights of the owner and that amounts to appropriation in the absence of error as to consent or a contract allowing him such rights, e.g. sale or gift. It probably also amounts to appropriation to sell such a valuable opportunistically for a far greater price than would normally have been commanded, even if the accused believed in good faith that he was thus benefiting the owner.[86] Retrospective consent might, of course, be given in such a case.

10–19   Whether appropriation within Hume's category of "taking and carrying away" is without the owner's consent is also usually obvious from the facts. Indeed, very little is required to satisfy the

---

[79] See the statutory styles in the Criminal Procedure (Scotland) Act 1995 Schs 2 and 5.
[80] Hume, *Commentaries*, i, 73.
[81] Hume, *Commentaries*, i, 74.
[82] *Dewar v HM Advocate*, 1945 J.C. 5, per Lord Justice-Clerk Cooper at 9.
[83] *Dewar v HM Advocate*, 1945 J.C. 5, per Lord Justice-General Normand at 12.
[84] Gordon, *Criminal Law*, 3rd edn, para.14.55; see also above, para.8–45.
[85] Gordon, *Criminal Law*, 3rd edn, para.14.57.
[86] Gordon, *Criminal Law*, 2nd edn, para.14–64.

notion of "taking and carrying away"[87] and thus it may be crucial to discover what consent, if any, the owner actually gave. According to Hume[88]: "In general, the law intends that the thing must be removed from the place and state of keeping in which it had been," but that slight removal will suffice if the owner must then search to find it. An illustration he gives (translated into modern terms) concerns a hotel guest who places an item of hotel property in his own case. Plainly, hotel managements intend that towels, televisions, kettles and the like should be used by guests; but they give no consent to their being removed from their possession and control in such a manner. In a similar way, there is probably appropriation where a person removes goods from a supermarket shelf (to which the management does presumably consent) but places them at once in his own bag or coat-pocket instead of the receptacle provided by the store.[89] Whether such appropriations amount to theft will, of course, depend on whether the *mens rea* element is satisfied (see below, paras 10–21 to 10–28).

Error as to consent

According to Alison[90]:   **10–20**

> "If the taker believed on rational grounds, that the owner would not object to his taking the goods, the crime will not be theft. This presumed consent may be inferred from the near relationship of the parties, or their intimate connexion, in the way of friendship, partnership, or business."

Although Alison provides no examples, it must be plain that a house guest might well consider that he would have the consent of his host to assuage nocturnal pangs of hunger or thirst by visiting the larder, fridge or wine cellar. It is to be noted that Alison requires such a belief to be based on reasonable grounds; and it may be thought that an honest but unreasonable belief would not be sufficient here (despite the decision to the contrary effect, so far as rape is concerned, in *Jamieson v HM Advocate (No.1)*).[91] But it is highly possible that the law on rape may soon be changed—from

---

[87] See, e.g. *John Paterson and Alexander Glasgow* (1827) Syme 174—bed clothes removed from beds and rolled in a counterpane to await later collection; *Cornelius O'Neill* (1845) 2 Broun 394—accused arrested as he drew a pile of clothes with a stick towards an open window outside which he was standing.
[88] Hume, *Commentaries*, i, 70 and 71.
[89] See *R. v McPherson* [1973] Crim.L.R. 191—a case under the (English) Theft Act 1968, wherein "appropriation" is given an interpretation at s.3(1) probably similar to that now favoured in Scotland; see also *Barr v O'Brien*, 1991 S.C.C.R. 67.
[90] Alison, *Principles*, i, 273.
[91] *Jamieson v HM Advocate (No.1)*, 1994 S.L.T. 537, following *Meek v HM Advocate* 1983 S.L.T. 280.

a common law based definition to one dictated by statute; and in that event, it seems that the "contrary decision" in *Jamieson* will be set aside.[92]

THE MENS REA OF THEFT

Knowledge and intention

10–21　Hume's view of the *mens rea* of theft is encapsulated in the following quotation[93]: "[The appropriation] must be with a felonious purpose; by one who knows that the thing belongs to another, and who means to deprive him of his property." It follows that if the accused does not know that the property is owned by another, then he ought to be acquitted provided (most probably) that the court takes the view that his lack of knowledge is reasonably understandable.[94] Thus in *Fraser v Anderson*,[95] by a majority of two to one, the High Court decided that where a person who had sold cattle to another, on a promise to pay at a fixed future date (a promise that appeared not to have been honoured), he might well not have understood that a breach of contract did not retransfer the right of property in them to himself. Consequently, where he had retained possession of the animals throughout, it was not theft for him to have purported to resell them to a third party.

10–22　Hume did not expressly say whether an intent to deprive the owner of his property *permanently* was required, but since he gave examples where only temporary deprivation was involved and plainly stated that these did not suffice for theft, it is highly probable that permanency was indeed what he had in mind.[96] Even as late as 1976, the conventional view remained that,

> "the essential feature of the *mens rea* of theft is an intention to appropriate and that appropriation involves an intention to deprive the owner permanently of his goods."[97]

10–23　That view had been given added veracity by the decision in *Strathern v Seaforth*.[98] In that case, the accused had taken a car from where it had been parked in a Glasgow street in order to have

---

[92] See the Scottish Law Commission's "Report on Rape and Other Sexual Offences", Scot. Law Com. No.209 (December, 2007).
[93] Hume, *Commentaries*, i, 73.
[94] cf. *Kane v Friel*, 1997 S.C.C.R. 207.
[95] *Fraser v Anderson* (1899) 2 Adam 705.
[96] His examples, at Hume, *Commentaries*, i, 73, include a servant riding his master's horse at night without permission, and a farmer finding his neighbour's plough and putting it to his own, unauthorised, temporary use.
[97] *Herron v Best*, 1976 S.L.T. (Sh. Ct.) 80, per Sheriff Macphail at 81.
[98] *Strathern v Seaforth*, 1926 J.C. 100.

the pleasure of driving it for a limited period. He was charged with clandestinely taking the vehicle where he knew that he did not have, nor could have expected to have the permission of the owner. The charge did not libel theft; nor did the court consider it as a case of stealing. It was a separate crime of its own kind. Macdonald[99] considers the case to illustrate that a kind of theft—*furtum usus*—had been accepted in Scotland. But *furtum usus* (theft of use) involves unauthorised use of what one possesses by consent of the owner,[100] which is clearly rather different from the true situation in the case. In the following year, the same crime featured in the case of *Murray v Robertson*,[101] where an acquittal was entered on appeal since the taking of fish boxes for unauthorised use had been openly rather than clandestinely done. A description of the essentials of the offence, therefore, in terms of clandestine "taking and using" (for a limited period) seems peculiarly apt[102]—and distances the crime from the conventional view of theft that there must be intent to deprive permanently.

Of course, at the precise moment when a car is taken away **10–24** without authority, it is impossible to say what the exact intention of the taker is. Indeed, it might well be inferred from his actions that his intent was to deprive the owner of it permanently. In any event, where any "taking and carrying away" is involved it is sufficient for inferring the *mens rea* of theft if the thing is left in a place where the owner would not be liable to find it by his own investigative efforts. For these reasons, then, in *Kivlin v Milne*[103] it was decided that theft was legitimately charged where a "joy-rider" of a motor vehicle had abandoned it in such a place that the owner would not have found it. As "joy-riders" may be assumed seldom to return the vehicle to the precise spot from which it was taken, *Kivlin v Milne*[104] substantially undermines the need for a separate crime of "taking and using" in such cases. In any event, such cases now fall under the terms of the statutory offence presently contained in s.178 of the Road Traffic Act 1988. More recently, the Appeal Court has decided that an intention to deprive someone of his property "indefinitely" would be sufficient in an appropriate case. In *Fowler v O'Brien*,[105] the accused had been refused permission to have a "shot" of the victim's bicycle, but decided to take the bike away in any event. This was *not* done clandestinely but quite openly. The accused gave no indication when it would be returned,

---

[99] Macdonald, *Criminal Law*, 5th edn, pp.19–20.
[100] See D. Matthaes, *De Criminibus: Text and Translations*, edited by M.L. Hewett and B.C. Stoop (Cape Town: Juta, 1987), i, i, 6.
[101] *Murray v Robertson*, 1927 J.C. 1.
[102] *cf.* Gordon, *Criminal Law*, 3rd edn, paras 15.29 to 15.32.
[103] *Kivlin v Milne*, 1979 S.L.T. (Notes) 2.
[104] *Kivlin v Milne*, 1979 S.L.T. (Notes) 2, in which no formal opinion was delivered by the Appeal Court.
[105] *Fowler v O'Brien*, 1994 S.C.C.R. 112.

nor did he state any conditions which would have to be fulfilled before its return. The victim did eventually recover his cycle—several days later. In upholding the conviction for theft, Lord Justice-General Hope concluded that this was not a case where an intent to deprive permanently might be inferred, since the victim had been able to recover the bike through his own efforts. Equally, however, it was not one of those cases where an intent to deprive temporarily might be sufficient—since the accused had not laid down any conditions relative to the return of the goods. There was thus no clear "nefarious purpose".[106] Instead he said this:

> "It appears to us that it would be more accurate to say that the owner was deprived of his bicycle indefinitely, since it was not made clear to him whether and, if so, when it would ever be returned to him."[107]

On the assumption then that an intent to deprive indefinitely can be distinguished from an intent to do so permanently, and can be applied generally, there must be at least two forms of the *mens rea* for theft.

10–25   There is, however, yet another possibility for the *mens rea* of theft. This was pointed out by Lord Justice-Clerk Macdonald, but lay dormant for many decades. In *HM Advocate v Mackenzie*[108] the male accused was charged with the theft of a book of secret chemical formulae. He had apparently "borrowed" the book just for the limited purpose of making copies of its contents. Was this truly theft? Lord Justice-Clerk Macdonald had no doubt that it was.

> "That such a taking, although there is no intention to retain the article, may be theft is, I think, clear. The article is taken from its owner for the serious purpose of obtaining something of value through the possession of it . . . In this case . . . if he [the prosecutor] can make out by his evidence that the book was taken, and taken for a nefarious purpose, he may be able to obtain a direction in law from the Judge at the trial that what was done constituted a theft of the book."[109]

In the current edition of Macdonald it is declared that temporary deprivation for an "illegitimate" purpose can constitute theft.[110] It seemed, therefore, that the intent required for this crime might be either an intention to deprive the owner permanently or an

---

[106] See below, paras 10–25 to 10–27.
[107] *Fowler v O'Brien*, 1994 S.C.C.R. 112 at 115B.
[108] *HM Advocate v Mackenzie*, 1913 S.C.(J.) 107.
[109] *HM Advocate v Mackenzie*, 1913 S.C.(J.) 107 at 110—a view in which Lord Dundas concurred.
[110] Macdonald, *Criminal Law*, 5th edn, p.20.

intention to deprive him temporarily provided that a nefarious or illegitimate purpose lay behind it.

But what was a nefarious or illegitimate purpose? The temporary **10–26** removal of a car to drive around in it did not seem to qualify[111]; nor did the unauthorised but temporary taking and using of fish boxes.[112] Removal of a book to copy out its secret and valuable contents was, however, sufficient, provided that the thief had no authority to have the book in his possession.[113]

The Appeal Court eventually seems to have endorsed Mac- **10–27** donald's view. In *Milne v Tudhope*[114] the accused had been paid in advance for certain house improvements. When these were completed, the owner of the house expressed dissatisfaction, and required further work to be done. The accused was unwilling to do so unless he obtained a promise of further payment. In the absence of such a promise, he removed a significant number of fittings from the house in order to force the owner to allow him to carry out the further work and to agree to pay him for it. The fittings were thus taken and held hostage temporarily to force the owner's hand. At the appeal against conviction for theft, counsel for the appellant seems to have conceded that intent to deprive temporarily for a nefarious purpose was sufficient. The main part of the debate thus focused on whether there had been a nefarious purpose in this case. The court held that there had been:

> "The appellant was trying to achieve something by a scheme which he must have known was unlawful. Whether 'nefarious' means 'criminal' in this context or unlawful does not matter for present purposes."[115]

Additionally, in *Kidston v Annan*[116] the Appeal Court determined that where the accused was in possession of a television set with the consent of the owner, it was "nefarious" for him to refuse to return it until an unagreed-to repair was paid for. Once again, there was no argument as to whether this alternative form of intent was valid or not; in the absence of contrary authority, therefore, its validity must be accepted. In *Sandlan v HM Advocate*[117] Lord Stewart seems to have accepted just that, in that he informed the jury that there were now two types of theft—the ordinary sort where there was intention to acquire things for personal benefit or profit, and the more unusual sort where things were taken,

> "not for the enjoyment or profit of the accused, but [as in this case] simply taken to give verisimilitude to the pretence of a

[111] *Strathearn v Seaforth*, 1926 J.C. 100.
[112] *Murray v Robertson*, 1927 J.C. 1.
[113] *HM Advocate v Mackenzie*, 1913 S.C.(J.) 107, per Lord Salvesen at 113.
[114] *Milne v Tudhope*, 1981 J.C. 53.
[115] *Milne v Tudhope*, 1981 J.C. 53 at 57. This point remains unsettled.
[116] *Kidston v Annan*, 1984 S.L.T. 279.
[117] *Sandlan v HM Advocate*, 1983 S.C.C.R. 71 at 82–83.

robbery. The intention would not be to deprive Hamilton Laidlaw permanently of their property in the jewellery, but simply to take it for a time as a manoeuvre to save Sandlan's face so that the true stock position could be concealed . . . The law is that such a taking of the goods of another, aimed at achieving a nefarious purpose, constitutes theft even if the taker intends all along to return the thing taken when his purpose has been achieved."

Intention may be inferred

10–28   Two fairly modern cases of theft have emphasised that although theftuous intent will normally be inferred from the facts and circumstances (in the usual Scottish manner, see above, paras 3–27 and 3–28), such an inference need not always be drawn, and sometimes is not to be drawn where evidence to the contrary is believed; as in *Petrovich v Jessop*[118] where a law student and alleged shoplifter had maintained that he had simply forgotten to pay for two books, on the basis that he had not slept for two nights and had been under examination and business stress; and, *Mason v Jessop*[119] where it was held that an intent to steal could not be inferred from the mere breaking of panes of glass in a church window by a drunken person looking for a place to consume a can of beer.

For lucre

10–29   Despite the inclusion of these words in Hume's definition of theft it is obviously unnecessary for the thief to make any economic gain from his crime. What matters is the owner's loss. Indeed, Hume concedes as much when he states that the phrase "for lucre" simply implies detention from its owner, or destruction of the thing taken.[120] For this reason, it cannot matter what actual value the thing appropriated has[121]; and prosecutions for thefts of items of minimal value are not uncommon.[122] It might be noted, however, that the value of items stolen does have a bearing on the jurisdiction of the J.P. Courts.[123] The fact that the *de minimis* rule (see above, para.2–51) plays an especially small part in this crime may reflect the lasting feeling that theft is a peculiarly heinous

---

[118] *Petrovich v Jessop*, 1990 S.L.T. 594, as explained in *Ivers v Normand*, 1994 S.L.T. 317.

[119] *Mason v Jessop*, 1990 S.C.C.R. 387.

[120] Hume, *Commentaries*, i, 75. See above, para.10–03.

[121] Hume, *Commentaries*, i, 76.

[122] See, e.g. *Walker v MacGillivray* (1980) S.C.C.R. Supp. 244, where newspapers valued at 38p were allegedly stolen.

[123] Criminal Procedure (Scotland) Act 1995 s.7(4), as amended by the Criminal Proceedings etc. (Reform) (Scotland) Act 2007 (asp 6) Sch.1 para.9(4).

offence—having once, of course, been punished by hanging.[124] It is also obviously of no benefit to the thief for him to change his mind and return what he had taken. Provided that he had at one time appropriated the property with the required sort of *mens rea*, the crime has been committed and cannot thereafter be uncommitted. In this connection, Hume quotes the case of *Finlay Macgibbon*,[125] where the accused stole six horses, and was prosecuted for their theft notwithstanding that he ultimately had returned them to their owner along with 200 merks by way of "compensation".

AGGRAVATIONS

Since theft ceased to be in any way a capital crime,[126] aggravations **10–30** have ceased to be of great importance; but two still figure prominently in charges, namely "housebreaking" and "opening lockfast places". According to Lord Justice-General Hope in *Peter Alston and Alexander Forrest*,[127] the old custom was to charge housebreaking as a separate crime. If that was ever so, however, it had certainly been abandoned by the time of Hume.[128]

Housebreaking

This aggravation applies where a theft was committed after the **10–31** thief entered any "shut and fast building,"[129] provided he effected entry by forcing a way past some obstacle placed there by the owner or occupier to deny access to those not entitled or invited to enter.[130] Despite its title, "housebreaking" is applicable to any building, whether a dwelling-house (occupied or not) or a commercial establishment (such as an office or shop). In the case of *John Fraser*[131] it was held that a hen house was a sufficient building for this purpose; and the statutory styles for theft mirror that exactly.[132] Of course, the most obvious instance of housebreaking occurs where a door or window has been broken or smashed by the prospective thief. The concept extends, however, rather more widely than that.

It seems to be well established that the security of a building can **10–32** be overcome in a variety of ways which do not involve destructive measures at all. Thus, if a key to a door is stolen, or a skeleton key

---

[124] See *James Joss* (1821) Shaw 29; *cf.* the Criminal Procedure (Scotland) Act 1887 s.56 (now repealed).
[125] *Finlay Macgibbon* (1669) Hume, *Commentaries*, i, 79.
[126] Criminal Procedure (Scotland) Act 1887 s.56 (now repealed).
[127] *Peter Alston and Alexander Forrest* (1837) 1 Swin. 433 at 473.
[128] Hume, *Commentaries*, i, 98 *et seq*. That there is no separate crime of housebreaking is well established: see, e.g. *Cochrane v HM Advocate*, 2002 S.C.C.R. 1051.
[129] Hume, *Commentaries*, i, 103.
[130] Hume, *Commentaries*, i, 98.
[131] *John Fraser* (1831) Bell's Notes 41.
[132] See the Criminal Procedure (Scotland) Act 1995 Sch.5—"You did break into a poultry house and steal three fowls."

carried and used to obtain unauthorised entry, that will be quite sufficient.[133] There is a suggestion in some cases that such house-breakings can be taken to the ultimate degree. So in *John Maclean*,[134] and also in *Crown v Devin and Polin*,[135] placing one's hand through a hole in a door and sliding back a bolt on the other side was considered sufficient; and in *John Dewar*[136] it seems that the court was prepared to accept that pressing a key out of a lock and winkling it out from a gap under the door in question constituted housebreaking. The more extreme decisions of this sort, however, have been put in doubt since the case of *Peter Alston and Alexander Forrest*.[137] There, by a narrow majority of four to three, the High Court decided that it was not housebreaking to obtain entry by turning a key left in a door-lock. As Lord Gillies put it[138]:

> "The object of the law is to protect the property of those who show due regard to their own property. The law cannot protect the careless and negligent."

Still less, then, can it be housebreaking to enter a building through an unlocked door or an open (or unfastened) window.[139]

10–33   Unusual routes of entry may also be described as housebreaking, even where the owner or occupier has taken no steps at all to make such routes secure. The view taken is that there is no need to secure chimney vents and sewer pipes since access to a building via them is hardly to be anticipated, or, in modern times, thought to be possible.[140]

Opening lockfast places

10–34   Once a thief has gained entry to a building, he may be confronted by further obstacles to his theftuous progress. Individual rooms may themselves be locked, and it is then moot whether "breaking" into them constitutes housebreaking[141] or the opening of lockfast places.[142] Since it will certainly constitute either one aggravation or the other, the issue is probably academic. But it is certainly not housebreaking to force open chests, safes, cupboards

---

133 Hume, *Commentaries*, i, 98 and the case of *Colin Fraser and Daniel Gunn* (1827) there at fn.a.
134 *John Maclean* (1828) Bell's Notes 36.
135 *Crown v Devin and Polin* (1829) 5 Deas & Anderson 145.
136 *John Dewar* (1777) Burnett 115; N.A.S. J.C. 13/21, loose papers Box 213.
137 *Peter Alston and Alexander Forrest* (1837) 1 Swin. 433.
138 *Peter Alston and Alexander Forrest* (1837) 1 Swin. 433 at 466.
139 Hume, *Commentaries*, i, 98; *Lafferty v Wilson*, 1990 S.C.C.R. 30.
140 But see *Rendal Courtney* (1743) Hume, *Commentaries*, i, 99 and *John Hunter* (1801) Hume, *Commentaries*, i, 99, fn.5.
141 Hume, *Commentaries*, i, 101.
142 See *Mary Young or Gilchrist and Cecilia Hislop* (undated) Bell's Notes 34.

or vehicles. These do not constitute "buildings" of any sort, and the appropriate aggravation will be the opening of lockfast places.[143]

Housebreaking with intent to steal

According to Hume[144] this was recognised as a crime separate **10–35** from, and of a lower order than theft in *Charles Macqueen and Alexander Baillie*.[145] This is still the case today.[146] The Appeal Court has determined that disconnecting a burglar-alarm system can amount to attempted housebreaking with intent to steal.[147] The view taken was that the alarm system was an integral part of the security of the building. It has also been decided that such an attempt could (depending upon the precise circumstances) be shown by smashing a security light.[148] Logically too, the separate crime of "opening lockfast places with intent to steal" might be anticipated; and it certainly exists.[149]

THEFT IN OTHER PARTS OF THE UNITED KINGDOM

If property is stolen in another part of the United Kingdom and **10–36** brought to Scotland by the thief, he may be dealt with as if the theft had been effected in Scotland.[150] This represents an extension of the normal, geographically limited jurisdiction of the Scottish courts (see above, para.2–38).

2. EMBEZZLEMENT

Introduction

The *Oxford English Dictionary*[151] gives the following as the only **10–37** modern definition of "embezzlement": "the fraudulent appropriation of entrusted property." This is not at all at odds with the meaning of "embezzlement" as a crime, despite the curious way in which nineteenth-century indictments were framed. In *John McLeod*,[152] for example, the accused was charged in terms that he

---

[143] See Hume, *Commentaries*, i, 98 and the statutory styles for theft in the Criminal Procedure (Scotland) Act 1995, Sch.2.
[144] Hume, *Commentaries*, i, 102.
[145] *Charles Macqueen and Alexander Baillie* (1810) Hume, i, 102, fn.2.
[146] See, e.g. *Mason v Jessop*, 1990 S.C.C.R. 387.
[147] *Burns v Allan*, 1987 S.C.C.R. 449.
[148] *Heywood v Reid*, 1996 S.L.T. 378.
[149] See, e.g. *Thompson v Carmichael*, 1990 S.C.C.R. 51.
[150] See the Criminal Procedure (Scotland) Act 1995 s.11(4)(a). This also appears to apply if the accused has simply received property stolen in any other part of the United Kingdom—s.11(4)(b); see also s.11(5), as inserted by the Postal Services Act 2000 Sch.8 para.24.
[151] *Oxford English Dictionary* (1989).
[152] *John McLeod* (1858) 3 Irv. 79.

did, "embezzle and fraudulently appropriate to [his] own uses and purposes" one pound sterling entrusted to him. Such tautology, however, was not unusual in the florid styles employed at that time, and does not imply that embezzlement had some meaning radically different from the accepted dictionary definition.

10–38   In the time of Hume and Alison, an important distinction lay bctwccn "thcft" on the one hand and "breach of trust and embezzlement" (as embezzlement was then known) on the other. Theft was a capital offence, whereas the other crime was not.[153] Because of this important practical difference, fine lines often required to be drawn and, "many nice cases require[d] to be distinguished."[154] This did not lead to a clear contrast being drawn between the two crimes. Today, neither offence being capital, it may seem unnecessary to distinguish between them at all; and the very real difficulty of attempting to do so is revealed in the Criminal Procedure (Scotland) Act 1995[155] which allows a conviction for theft to be returned on a breach of trust and embezzlement charge, and vice versa. From this point of view, then, it would not seem to matter which of the two was in fact charged. There are also very few modern, reported cases which comment on the essential features of embezzlement; and some modern texts on criminal law have omitted any reference to this crime at all.[156] But there is a definite role for it—separate from theft. Indeed, it covers dishonest appropriations where theft cannot operate, as where, say, a trustee or executor appropriates the trust or executry funds. He cannot steal these, since he stands as owner towards them[157]; but he can certainly embezzle them. It may also be possible to embezzle property which is incorporeal and, therefore, cannot be the subject of theft.[158]

General definition

10–39   A general definition in terms of Hume's[159] and Alison's[160] accounts is made difficult by their view that theft only applied to a dishonest taking-possession of goods from the owner, or other person legally entitled to such possession. For them, appropriation where there was no such taking was at best a breach of trust. Thus the appropriation by a servant of his uniform, by a watchmaker of the watch given him to repair, or by the finder of lost property was

[153] Hume, *Commentaries*, i, 61.
[154] Alison, *Principles*, i, 354.
[155] Criminal Procedure (Scotland) Act 1995 Sch.3 para.8(3),(4).
[156] See, e.g. J.R. Harper and P. Hamilton, *A Fingertip Guide to Criminal Law*, 3rd edn (Edinburgh: Law Society of Scotland/Butterworths, 1994).
[157] Gordon, *Criminal Law*, 3rd edn, paras 14.33, 17.28.
[158] *cf.* Gordon, *Criminal Law*, 3rd edn, para.17.01; see also *Grant v Allan*, 1988 S.L.T. 11; and *Guild v Lees*, 1995 S.L.T. 68 (Note).
[159] Hume, *Commentaries*, Ch.II.
[160] Alison, *Principles*, Ch.XII.

a breach of trust[161]; but such appropriations are now clearly thefts (see above, paras 10–05 and 10–06). In modern times, therefore, it would be better to regard embezzlement as the deliberate appropriation to one's own use and purpose of property entrusted to one by the owner (or person otherwise entitled) in such a way as to confer the status of a quasi-owner, for the purposes of dealing with that property and accounting for one's dealings with it to that owner (or person otherwise entitled). The various facets of this definition are developed below.

ACTUS REUS

Entrusted by the owner to the accused

The "owner" may be an individual, or the partners of a firm,[162] **10–40** or a co-executor or trustee[163]; and he (or they) must have given the accused authority to deal with the property in question on a quasi-owner basis.[164] Naturally, that authority must not have been rescinded before the act of appropriation. If it had been, then such appropriation would be theft (all other things being equal).[165] The range of persons entrusted with quasi-ownership status might include trustees, executors, factors, agents, managers, administrators, distributors and collectors, according to J.W. Angus[166]; but much depends on what persons answering to such descriptions are entitled to do with the property in question.[167] They should be authorised to avail themselves of some of the powers which an owner might have—such as the selling of the property, or its investment (speculatively or otherwise) or the using of it to raise money—all subject to an obligation to account to the owner for what has been done. A stock-broker, for example, may be given wide-ranging powers to "play the market" with a specific sum of money; in the course of his dealings with that money, he may in fact reduce the value of the capital sum to naught (since all investors are on notice that the value of investments may go down as well as up). And yet, provided he honestly discloses to the owner all that he has done (however incompetently) in the way of dealing,

---

[161] Alison, *Principles*, i, 354, 359, 360.
[162] See *Peter A. Sumner*, unreported, November 1983, Appeal Court, but see Gordon, *Criminal Law*, 3rd edn, paras 14.34 (at fn.25), 17.28.
[163] *John Lawrence* (1872) 2 Coup. 168.
[164] cf. *Kent v HM Advocate*, 1950 J.C. 38, where there was no evidence that such authority had ever been given and thus no prospect of a claimed appropriation being one of embezzlement.
[165] See *Alexander Mitchell* (1874) 3 Coup. 77.
[166] J.W. Angus and R.B. Shearer, *A Dictionary of Crimes and Offences According to the Law of Scotland* (Edinburgh: W. Green and Sons, 1895), under "Embezzlement."
[167] See, e.g. Hume's account of the powers of a farm steward at *Commentaries*, i, 60.

and has not pocketed any of the proceeds thereof without authority, there will be no question of embezzlement. Bad management or incompetence is not criminal; pocketing or otherwise appropriating the results of authorised dealings may well be.

10–41　If the accused lacked the powers which could be described as those of a quasi-owner, if he had been handed the property for a specific purpose and for a limited time (say, a broken watch to be repaired), then his appropriation of that property may well be theft rather than embezzlement.[168] If a painting or a book, for example, is loaned by its owner to another, it is plainly theft for that other person to sell it or destroy it or give it away.[169]

10–42　On the other hand, if an accused person had powers of dealing with the property, and had indeed dealt with it, the appropriation to his own use and purpose of any of the proceeds of that dealing would almost certainly identify him as an embezzler. The fact that his obligation was to account for those proceeds to the owner, and that he had failed to do so, might provide sufficient proof of his appropriation of them.[170] Were he to have had such "dealing" powers, but appropriated the property in the form in which it was received, or at least before any authorised "dealing" with it was entered into at all, there is precedent for the resulting crime being one of theft.[171] From this point of view also, the accused in *Catherine Crossgrove or Bradley*[172] should have been convicted of theft. Thus, if a stock-broker is given a sum of money by a client, with instructions to invest it as he sees fit for the best profit of that client, it would probably be theft for the broker to use the money to pay off his most pressing, personal creditors. It would certainly not amount to embezzlement since he had never begun the dealing he had been authorised to do.

THE MENS REA OF EMBEZZLEMENT

10–43　It is difficult to deduce from the case authorities what is the precise *mens rea* element of embezzlement. In *Edgar v Mackay*[173] what seemed to be looked for was evidence from which "the inference of dishonesty" might be drawn, so that it could be concluded "that the money in question was fraudulently appropriated." This is not very helpful; but what may have been meant is that a deliberate intent to appropriate has to be proved or inferred. This would involve forms of *mens rea* similar to those required in theft (see above, paras 10–21 to 10–27). Nevertheless, whereas

---

[168] cf. *William Keith* (1875) 3 Coup. 125, especially Lord Ardmillan at 133.
[169] See the statutory styles for theft in the Criminal Procedure (Scotland) Act 1995 Sch.5.
[170] See, e.g. *Edgar v Mackay*, 1926 J.C. 94.
[171] *J.D. Wormald* (1876) 3 Coup. 246.
[172] *Catherine Crossgrove or Bradley* (1850) J. Shaw 301; see above, para.10–11.
[173] *Edgar v Mackay*, 1926 J.C. 94, per Lord Justice-Clerk Alness at 97.

"dishonesty" may not be particularly relevant to theft, it was made almost the rationale of embezzlement in the decision in *Allenby v HM Advocate*.[174] There, a fish salesman sold the catches brought to port by several different trawler skippers, and placed the proceeds in one undivided account, as was his known, normal practice. He then advanced money from the pooled account to trawler skippers other than those entitled to it, and was charged with embezzlement. But since this was all done openly, and according to the custom pertaining at that port (Aberdeen), the Appeal Court felt that there was a basic lack of dishonesty and acquitted him. It is also noteworthy that in *HM Advocate v Wishart*[175] an intent to place clients' money at risk, or perhaps just a reckless course of action involving funds owing to them, was considered sufficient for conviction.[176]

DIFFICULT CASES

Since the Criminal Procedure (Scotland) Act 1995 (see above, **10–44** para.10–38) virtually allows charges of theft and embezzlement to be interchanged, it will be obvious that in some cases there is uncertainty as to which of the two would be the more appropriate. Indeed, some offences which clearly fit the definition of theft have been prosecuted to conviction as embezzlement—and vice versa. For example, in *Edgar v Mackay*[177] a solicitor was instructed to obtain payment of a debt for one of his clients. He apparently did succeed in obtaining the money; but did not forward it to the client or indeed communicate with him on the subject at all. After months of fruitless inquiries, that client instructed a second solicitor to pursue the matter. It was then discovered that the original solicitor had indeed secured possession of the moneys in question, but had unaccountably refused to hand them over. Eventually, the arrest of the first solicitor was effected on a charge of embezzlement. On appeal against conviction, it was held that conviction for embezzlement was justified in the circumstances. But since the lawyer in question had no authority to deal with the money, the conviction should probably have been one for theft. It may be said that a lawyer collecting such a debt is entitled to deduct his expenses and fees from the money received. But it is highly questionable whether such deductions would amount to "dealing by a quasi-owner". It may be, however, as Gordon aptly states, that professional persons embezzle rather than steal, theft being reserved for non-professional appropriators of property.[178]

---

[174] *Allenby v HM Advocate*, 1938 J.C. 55.
[175] *HM Advocate v Wishart* (1975) S.C.C.R. Supp. 78.
[176] It might also have involved an intent to deprive the true owners temporarily for a nefarious purpose—see above, paras 10–25 to 10–27.
[177] *Edgar v Mackay*, 1926 J.C. 94.
[178] See Gordon, *Criminal Law*, 3rd edn, paras 17.06, 17.16, 17.17.

3. ROBBERY

Introduction

10–45   This crime might loosely be described as "theft achieved by violence".[179] On that sort of description, robbery would appear to be no more than an aggravated theft. However, the tradition has always been to treat it as a crime separate from theft.[180] It is, however, often difficult to make such a distinction in an individual case.[181] Because of such difficulty, it is permissible to convict of theft on a robbery charge.[182] Nevertheless, one significant difference between the two offences is that a later appropriation of property already in one's possession can never be robbery (since a taking of possession is of the essence of robbery). It may also be true that violent efforts to retain what has already been snatched without force are not such as to convert a simple instance of theft to one of robbery.[183]

10–46   The force or violence involved in robbery tends to associate it with the crime of assault but the violence used need not amount to an assault at all and robbery is regarded as independent of it.[184] In *O'Neill v HM Advocate*,[185] where assault and robbery were both apparently charged, the accused was found guilty of robbery only, the assault having been found "not proven". The Appeal Court affirmed that that verdict had been competent and correct; but two of the appeal judges (Lords Hunter and Anderson) were of the persuasion that the "assault" mentioned in the indictment had been libelled as a mere aggravation of the robbery rather than as a separate crime.[186] Where specific acts of violence (or threats of violence) are narrated in the indictment or (less likely) complaint, and those acts (or threats) are not proved, there may be no other evidence from which it can be established that there was any violence associated with the taking of the property at all: and without violence, there can be no robbery.[187]

---

[179] Or as "forcible theft"—Hume, *Commentaries*, i, 104.

[180] See Alison, *Principles*, i, 227, 236.

[181] See *O'Neill v HM Advocate*, 1934 J.C. 98, per Lord Justice-Clerk Aitchison at 101.

[182] Criminal Procedure (Scotland) Act 1995 Sch.3 para.8(3).

[183] See *Thomas Innes and Ann Blair* (1834) Bell's Notes 42; *Daniel or Donald Stuart* (1829) Bell's Notes 42–43.

[184] See, e.g. *James Campbell* (1824) Hume, *Commentaries*, i, 107, fn.a; *James Fegen* (1838) 2 Swin. 25.

[185] *O'Neill v HM Advocate*, 1934 J.C. 98.

[186] *O'Neill v HM Advocate*, 1934 J.C. 98 at 102, 103.

[187] See, e.g. *Flynn v HM Advocate*, 1995 S.L.T. 1267; cf. *MacKay v HM Advocate*, 1997 S.C.C.R. 743.

DEFINITION OF ROBBERY

Robbery may be considered as the deliberate taking of moveable **10–47** and corporeal property from another by force and against his will. The "taking" referred to means the seizing of physical possession of the article in question. All other things being equal, "as soon as any article has fully passed into the hands of the invader,"[188] the crime is complete. It is even considered a "taking" for the purposes of this crime if the victim is so intimidated that he hands the things over himself, or stands passively by whilst the accused helps himself to what might be had.[189] Equally, if there is a struggle and the victim drops some article, there is a sufficient "taking" if the accused immediately picks it up.[190] There is little need to show that the things taken were then actually carried away; for even if the accused is arrested as soon as he has taken possession of them, or hands them back almost at once, the *actus reus* of the crime is still considered complete.[191]

It is probably popularly supposed that robbery involves the **10–48** taking of things which were about the victim's person or being carried by him at the time. Whilst that is often the case, it is not necessary that it should be so. As Hume puts it[192]:

> "[Robbery is applicable to] any thing which is under the immediate care and protection of the person invaded; so that unless by force or terror applied to him, it cannot be taken away."

A fair example of this point occurs in the case of *Thomas Kelly*[193] where a girl left in charge of a house was compelled to rush from it because of the accused's swearing and abusive, threatening words. Thus, the coast was left clear for the accused to take what he desired from the building. That, however, was no less a crime than robbery.[194]

The taking must be by force and against the victim's will

The important consideration is that the seizing or snatching **10–49** should be contrary to the wishes of the victim. This can be exhibited in various ways. There might, for example, have been the application of real, physical force. The accused might have struggled with the victim for mastery of some article that he had, or

---

[188] Hume, *Commentaries*, i, 105.
[189] Hume, *Commentaries*, i, 105.
[190] *Anderson, Paul and Bannatyne* (1791) Hume, *Commentaries*, i, 105.
[191] Hume, *Commentaries*, i, 105; Alison, *Principles*, i, 235.
[192] Hume, *Commentaries*, i, 106.
[193] *Thomas Kelly* (1837) Bell's Notes 44.
[194] Or "stouthrief", as that form of robbery was then known.

might have beaten him senseless in order to overcome his resistance.[195] Alternatively, "constructive" force or intimidation might be applied; and that would usually be quite sufficient. In *Samuel Riccards*,[196] for example, the accused made verbal threats of violence to a woman who at once handed over money and other goods. Again in *William Macmillan and Spence Gordon*,[197] repeatedly shaking a stick over a woman's head eventually achieved the desired result, i.e. she opened her lock-fast repositories from which the robbers could then help themselves. Even aggressive demands for money, coupled to "gripping" the victim, have been held sufficient.[198] Hume[199] is at pains to point out, however, that such intimidation has to make the victim fear reasonably for his immediate, personal safety and thus overcome his will to prevent the property being taken. What will reasonably achieve that is obviously a question of fact, but the number of persons involved, the weapons that they display, their demeanour and language are all of some significance. In one modern case, where two employees were told by an agent for an alleged creditor of their employer that they would not be allowed to leave their employer's premises until they had handed over the contents of the till (to help repay an alleged debt), their proven alarm was considered sufficient for robbery in relation to what they consequently handed over.[200] If the threat is other than one of immediate, personal violence, e.g. to set fire to a building, or to make false accusations of crime, Hume doubts its effectiveness to render the crime one of robbery; but Alison[201] is surely correct to point out that much will depend on the precise circumstances of each case. Who or what is liable to be consumed by a blazing building must obviously figure in the analysis. The evidential presumption applicable to theft and to reset that very recent possession of stolen property may, if there are other criminative circumstances, point to the possessor's being guilty of theft or reset (as the case may be),[202] would seem to be applicable also to robbery.[203] This is somewhat surprising, however, for the mere possession of property—no matter how recently taken from the owner or custodier—can raise no reasonable presumption as to the use or threat of violence, which is an essential feature of the crime of robbery.

---

[195] See, e.g. *William Adams or Reid* (1829) Bell's Notes 43.
[196] *Samuel Riccards* (1710) Hume, *Commentaries*, i, 107.
[197] *William Macmillan and Spence Gordon* (1829) Alison, *Principles*, i, 231.
[198] *Hugh Lundie* (1754) Hume, *Commentaries*, i, 107.
[199] Hume, *Commentaries*, i, 108.
[200] *Harrison v Jessop*, 1992 S.L.T. 465.
[201] Alison, *Principles*, i, 231–233.
[202] See, e.g. *Steele v HM Advocate*, 1992 J.C. 1.
[203] See *L v Wilson*, 1995 S.L.T. 673.

Moveable and corporeal property

Robbery probably extends to the same sort of property as can be **10–50** stolen (see above, paras 10–07 to 10–10), the value of what is taken being of little importance.[204] It is unclear if one can commit robbery in respect of property one owns but is not entitled at the material time to possess. The close links with theft would suggest, however, that a negative answer should be given.[205] It must be the case, however, that the property in question has to be owned by someone at the material time. This might pose problems if the accused intended to kill his victim, and only after he had succeeded in that purpose decided to make off with property from the body. Since no force would then have had to be applied, the subsequent taking would probably be theft rather than robbery; but to whom would the property then have belonged? Benjamin Bell, the author of the notes to the 1844 edition of Hume, points up this very problem and makes reference to the case of *James Blair*.[206] There no objection was apparently made to a charge of robbery from a dead body, where it was asserted that what was taken was "the property or in the lawful possession . . . of his [i.e. the deceased's] heirs and executors."

THE MENS REA OF ROBBERY

This is uncertain, but appears to encompass the intent to use force **10–51** and the intent to devote things taken by force to one's own uses and purposes. Hume unhelpfully refers to the *mens rea* as felonious intent, i.e. "a purpose to appropriate the thing."[207] Presumably, there must also be knowledge that the thing taken by force is not one's own. If that is so, then the position (apart from the matter of force) must be analogous to that which pertains in theft (see above, paras 10–21 to 10–28). It seems, however, that an assault, which in fact results in the accused's coming into possession of some property that the victim then had about his person, will raise the presumption that the *mens rea* for robbery exists—although that presumption may be rebutted.[208]

4. RESET

Introduction

The crime of reset in its traditional form is straightforward and **10–52** easy to understand. It exists to provide a strong disincentive to theft[209] by providing that those who knowingly receive stolen

---

[204] See *James Brodie* (1842) 1 Broun 341, where a conviction for robbery was obtained in respect of coin worth two pence.

[205] *cf.* Alison, *Principles,* i, 239.

[206] *James Blair* (1830) Bell's Notes 43, 44.

[207] Hume, *Commentaries*, i, 108.

[208] See Hume, *Commentaries*, i, 108 and the case of *Edgar Wright* (1788) mentioned there.

[209] Hume, *Commentaries*, i, 113.

property will themselves be guilty of an offence. Since reset applies to property obtained by robbery, fraud or embezzlement too,[210] it provides a disincentive to those crimes also. Unfortunately, the traditional form of the crime has been thrown into confusion by Lord Justice-Clerk Macdonald. As will be seen below, he added to its scope in a way which might be regarded as "unjustified" or even "unauthorised", but which certainly detracted from its clarity. For that reason, the text below discusses "traditional" and "Macdonald" resets separately.

Traditional reset

10–53   The definition of the traditional form is succinctly given out by Hume[211] as follows: "Reset of theft, is the receiving and keeping of stolen goods, knowing them to be such, and with an intention to conceal and withhold them from the owner." Alison[212] reproduces that formula, and indeed it admirably encapsulates the essence of the crime. The only addition is necessitated by the fact that reset is not now confined to the fruits of theft or robbery. It extends in modern times to property obtained by embezzlement and fraud as well.[213] The identification, let alone conviction, of the thief, robber, fraudster or embezzler is not a prerequisite for prosecution[214]; nor is it now necessary[215] to give details of the original theft, robbery, embezzlement or fraud in the complaint or indictment.[216] The crime, moreover, appears to apply to plagium.[217]

THE ACTUS REUS OF RESET

10–54   "It is the fundamental circumstance in the description of this crime, that the stolen goods are *received into the offender's possession* . . . [There must be] *a handling* of the things themselves, for the purpose of detention and concealment."[218] There is little doubt, then, that the traditional form of the crime requires the accused to have received possession of the property in question. It does not seem to matter greatly how that possession is acquired—Hume mentioning pledge, barter, safe-keeping (for the thief) and purchase (even for a fair price). It has to be noted, however, that the fairer the price, the more difficult it will be to show that the

---

[210] See Criminal Law (Consolidation) (Scotland) Act 1995 s.51; Criminal Procedure (Scotland) Act 1995 Sch.3 para.8(1).
[211] Hume, *Commentaries*, i, 113.
[212] Alison, *Principles*, i, 328.
[213] See above, para.10–52.
[214] Hume, *Commentaries*, i, 119, 120.
[215] *cf.* Alison, *Principles*, i, 335.
[216] Criminal Procedure (Scotland) Act 1995 Sch.3 para.8(1).
[217] See above, para.10–15 and *Margaret Cook* (1897) 2 Adam 471 at 474, which concerned an eight year old child.
[218] Hume, *Commentaries*, i, 113, emphasis added; see also Alison, *Principles*, i, 328.

accused possessed the required *mens rea*. Possession, of course, is not confined to personal handling. Goods delivered by others to one's house and placed somewhere within its rooms are as much possessed as if one had done the carrying and locating oneself— always provided that one knew they were to be so delivered and placed. It is within this context that Hume[219] refers to the "privity and connivance" of the house owner. If he permits the property to be so deposited, then he possesses it.[220] It is not, however, necessary for the accused to have received possession directly from the original thief, robber or whoever; but, naturally, the greater the number of hands through which it has passed en route to the accused, the greater will be his chances of casting doubt on his ever having known that it had been dishonestly come by in the first place.[221] It is, for example, clearly not unknown for stolen goods to find their way back eventually to legitimate retail outlets.

THE MENS REA OF RESET: KNOWLEDGE

There are two parts to the *mens rea* of reset. The first concerns **10–55** "knowledge of the vicious quality of the thing."[222] Presumably this should mean knowledge that the goods one receives were originally obtained from their true owner by theft, robbery, fraud or embezzlement. But strict adherence to that would often make the crime impossible to substantiate; and it is thought that knowledge that the goods were not honestly come by would suffice, provided that they were in fact stolen, or obtained by robbery, fraud or embezzlement. The requisite knowledge need not exist when possession is first taken. Macdonald[223] is surely correct to point out that knowledge can arise at a later point than that, and indeed this is borne out by case law, as in the case of *Latta v Herron*[224] where it was held that the accused, a lawyer, must have come to realise that two antique guns were stolen property when he reflected later on the suspicious circumstances of their sale to him.

Hume is adamant that anything less than "knowledge" will not **10–56** do. Thus, he rules out "bare suspicion" or "indiscretion."[225] Negligent inattention to the possibility that the goods are tainted by a dishonest mode of acquisition is, therefore, insufficient; but the Appeal Court has, in recent times, accepted that deliberately shutting one's eyes to the obvious is equivalent to knowing the true position.[226] It will be clear, then, that knowledge can be inferred

[219] Hume, *Commentaries*, i, 114.
[220] *cf. John and Elizabeth Bell* (1736) Hume, *Commentaries*, i, 114.
[221] See Alison, *Principles*, i, 329.
[222] Hume, *Commentaries*, i, 114.
[223] Macdonald, *Criminal Law*, 5th edn, p.68.
[224] *Latta v Herron* (1967) S.C.C.R. Supp. 18.
[225] Hume, *Commentaries*, i, 114.
[226] See, e.g. *Latta v Herron* (1967) S.C.C.R. Supp. 18 and *Friel v Docherty*, 1990 S.C.C.R. 351.

from the circumstances. If that were not so, then again it would be difficult to substantiate the offence in the absence of the theft, robbery, fraud or embezzlement having been observed by the accused, or the person from whom possession was obtained having confessed to the dishonest mode of acquisition. Such an inference will not, however, inevitably be drawn[227] since otherwise the whole notion of *mens rea* would be very substantially defeated.

10–57 Circumstances which Hume[228] considered valid in relation to the inference of knowledge are still in use today. They may be enumerated as follows (though most seem plain applications of common sense):

1. Concealment of the property in hidden places, which would include "under a seat"—e.g. see *MacLennan v Mackenzie*[229] where this was held not to be a usual place for the location of a car radio-cassette player—but not, in respect of carpet-laying tools, a bathroom cupboard[230];

2. False denial of having the goods at all[231];

3. Attempts to disguise or efface identification marks on the property, as, for example, the scraping-off of the serial number on a piece of electrical equipment[232];

4. Payment of a low price for the property—less than half the true value, for example, in *Latta v Herron*[233]—provided that the accused would or ought to have been aware of their true worth[234];

5. "Awkward" (as Hume puts it) stories of how the goods had been acquired, as in *MacLennan v Mackenzie*,[235] where the accused told the police that a stolen radio-cassette player had been taken by him from a car being repaired in his boss's premises, and that with the full permission of his boss; as in *Watt v Annan*,[236] where the accused claimed to have bought a valuable saw two and a half years earlier from one "Doddy Boyle" who had subsequently, and conveniently, died; as in *McKellar v Normand*,[237] where it seems that the accused

---

[227] See, e.g. *Shannon v HM Advocate*, 1985 S.C.C.R. 14.

[228] Hume, *Commentaries*, i, 114.

[229] *MacLennan v Mackenzie*, 1987 S.C.C.R. 473.

[230] See *Craigie v HM Advocate*, 1989 S.L.T. 631.

[231] See, e.g. *Davidson v Brown*, 1990 S.C.C.R. 304; *cf. Girdwood v Houston*, 1989 S.C.C.R. 578, where knowledge was more or less admitted.

[232] *MacLennan v Mackenzie*, 1987 S.C.C.R. 473.

[233] *Latta v Herron* (1967) S.C.C.R. Supp. 18.

[234] See *Latta v Herron* (1967) S.C.C.R. Supp. 18, where the accused was a knowledgeable collector of antique firearms; *cf. Murray v O'Brien*, 1993 S.C.C.R. 90.

[235] *MacLennan v Mackenzie*, 1987 S.C.C.R. 473.

[236] *Watt v Annan*, 1990 S.C.C.R. 55.

[237] *McKellar v Normand*, 1992 S.C.C.R. 393.

implied that it would be quite usual to buy a bed and a blanket at the door of one's house; or as in *Forbes v HM Advocate*,[238] where the accused, in respect of a substantial package partially concealing a valuable art-work, in an obvious position in the back of his vehicle, denied knowing that it was there at all, because he never checked the vehicle (which was normally left unlocked) for strange objects that might have been left there by persons unknown[239];

6. Where the quality of the property, in view of the circumstances and station in life of the accused, suggests that it could not have been come by honestly—a matter raised by the prosecutor, but not accepted by the Appeal Court, in *Craigie v HM Advocate*[240] in relation to two holdalls of expensive carpet fitter's tools found in the bathroom cupboard of a house where no one followed the profession of carpet-fitting, as was evident from the way in which the only carpet in that house had been laid; and

7. Where the pannel or his "author"[241] is a reputed thief or resetter.

To Hume's list, it may be prudent to add that it is a suspicious circumstance if the property found in the accused's possession has been very recently stolen, as in *Davidson v Brown*,[242] where garments and toiletries had been stolen just a few hours before they were found by the police in a plastic swing-bin balanced on the accused's knees as she sat in the back seat of a car.

Knowledge that the property in question was stolen or otherwise **10–58** dishonestly come by is, of course, insufficient by itself as the *mens rea* of reset. The second part of the mental element here is that the accused must have intended to detain the property from its true owner,[243] though he need not propose to do so by keeping it permanently himself.[244] If this second requirement were not to be insisted upon, then police and court clerks, who happened to have known stolen property in their possession for legitimate reasons connected with the administration of justice, would be guilty of reset. Such an intention to detain may be established by confession, or by inference from the same sorts of circumstances as figure in the establishing of knowledge. Where such an inference can be

---

[238] *Forbes v HM Advocate*, 1995 S.L.T. 627.
[239] See also *Mearns v McFadyen*, 2001 S.C.C.R. 25, where a series of "awkward", and inconsistent, stories was given out by the accused.
[240] *Craigie v HM Advocate*, 1989 S.L.T. 631.
[241] Or now, apparently, the company that he keeps—*Davidson v Brown*, 1990 S.C.C.R. 304.
[242] *Davidson v Brown*, 1990 S.C.C.R. 304.
[243] Hume, *Commentaries*, i, 115.
[244] Alison, *Principles*, i, 333.

drawn from the circumstances, the accused will have to provide some evidence to the contrary if it is not then to be drawn.[245] That does not imply, however, that some burden lies on the accused to show his innocence.[246]

TRADITIONAL RESET AND THEFT

10–59 Statute has permitted a conviction for reset to be returned on a theft charge.[247] This is because of the close connection that there can be between the two crimes. In *O'Brien v Strathern*,[248] for example, a serving soldier sold his regimental kilt (his uniform) to a shopkeeper who knew perfectly well that that amounted to theft on his customer's part. The shopkeeper was convicted of reset. But considering that the soldier's appropriation could be evidenced in no other way than by the sale itself, to which the shopkeeper was a party, the purchaser might as well have been convicted of theft, art and part, as of reset. (It would not be possible, of course, for the same person to be convicted of both theft *and* reset in respect of the same property.)[249] The instances which Hume[250] gives in illustration of the close connection between theft and reset tend to be ones where the "resetter" could well have been art and part guilty of theft in the circumstances. But conviction of reset on a theft charge does not require any suspicion of complicity in the original stealing.[251] It has also been held that although the original theft charge must specify with some precision when the alleged theft took place, this does not bind the Crown to establish that the implied alternative of reset occurred within the same stated time period (although, of course, no other time period will appear in the complaint or indictment).[252]

10–60   There is no provision, however, for a conviction for theft to be returned on a complaint or indictment which specifies reset.[253] This is probably because reset was seen historically as the lesser of the two crimes, and it would have been unfair to convict of an offence more serious than the one actually charged. Nevertheless, where the prosecutor has evidence which supports reset rather than theft, he may still charge theft, where there is evidence of possession of recently stolen property and of other "material" circumstances, and where the accused is reckoned as being unable to show a fair way

[245] Hume, *Commentaries*, i, 115.
[246] See *McDonald v HM Advocate*, 1989 S.C.C.R. 559.
[247] The Criminal Procedure (Scotland) Act 1995 Sch.3 para.8(2); see, e.g. *Gillespie v Brown*, 1999 S.L.T. 1115; and *Mearns v McFadyen*, 2001 S.C.C.R. 25.
[248] *O'Brien v Strathern*, 1922 J.C. 55.
[249] See, e.g. *Druce v Friel*, 1994 S.L.T. 1209.
[250] Hume, *Commentaries*, i, 115, 116.
[251] See, e.g. *MacLennan v Mackenzie*, 1987 S.C.C.R. 473; *Watt v Annan*, 1990 S.C.C.R. 55.
[252] *MacLennan v Mackenzie*, 1987 S.C.C.R. 473.
[253] *cf.* Criminal Procedure (Scotland) Act 1995 Sch.3 para.8(2)–(4).

of coming by that property.[254] It is impossible to be certain what will be acceptable as "recent" in this connection but possibly a matter of hours or days is the limit.[255]

Obviously, the shorter the time period involved, the more likely it is that the person found in possession of the property is also the person who stole it. But there must be more to it than that. There must be "other material circumstances" leading to the inference that the possessor is the thief. What are material circumstances or, as they now tend to be called, "criminative circumstances,"[256] will depend on the facts of the individual case. In *Cassidy v McLeod*,[257] for example, the accused were found in possession of beer (cans and bottles) and plastic crates in a house not far from an inn where a theft of such things had occurred the night before. The fact that the bottles and cans were similar to those stolen, and of such a mixed variety and type as to suggest that it was unlikely that they had been purchased, made it easy to infer that the accused were in possession of the very property that had been recently stolen, and indeed that was conceded when the case was argued before the Appeal Court. It was further established that the crates were not generally sold to the public, that one of the accused had telephoned the inn the previous evening and had asked for a "carry-out" on credit (which had been refused), and that a trail of cans and crates led across some waste-ground from the scene of the theft towards the very house occupied by the accused. The Appeal Court, therefore, considered that other criminative circumstances had indeed been established, that the accused had been unable to show an honest way of coming by the beer, and that therefore the charge of theft in the complaint had been fully substantiated.

MACDONALD RESET

Macdonald[258] narrates that there is another form of reset, namely: **10–61** "being privy to the retaining of property that has been dishonestly come by." No attempt, however, is made to explain what is meant by "being privy". The *Oxford English Dictionary*[259] definitions of "privy" suggest that it might mean, "participating in the knowledge of something secret"; or, "being an accessory to some secret transaction." If these suggestions are taken to be what Macdonald

---

[254] See, e.g. *Young v Webster*, 1993 S.L.T. 349; *Druce v Friel*, 1994 S.L.T. 1209.
[255] See *Watt v Annan*, 1990 S.C.C.R. 55—six months too long after the theft; *MacLennan v Mackenzie*, 1987 S.C.C.R. 473—two and a half months too long; *Craigie v HM Advocate*, 1989 S.L.T. 631—where a sheriff directed a jury that six weeks was too long; *Tudhope v Smellie* (1977) S.C.C.R. Supp. 186—where 19 to 20 days was held sufficient, although it was emphasised that it depends ultimately on the circumstances of each case.
[256] See, e.g. *Fox v Patterson*, 1948 J.C. 104.
[257] *Cassidy v McLeod*, 1981 S.C.C.R. 270.
[258] Macdonald, *Criminal Law*, 5th edn, p.67.
[259] *Oxford English Dictionary* (1931).

had in mind, then he surely refers to nothing more than a form of
art and part guilt in relation to traditional reset. There would be
nothing objectionable in that, save perhaps the undue widening of
the offence to property that had been "dishonestly come by".
Although that would include property obtained by theft, robbery,
embezzlement or fraud, it might also cover property acquired in
some non-criminal way which could nevertheless be stigmatised as
"dishonest".[260] But it is thought that there is no warrant for such an
extension to traditional reset. In any event, Macdonald gives out
this alternative form of the crime without reference to authority of
any kind. In 1968, however, the Appeal Court decided that it
represented a correct statement of the law,[261] although it remains
unclear what the alternative form is supposed to mean. It is plain,
however, from Macdonald's own example of its use, that it is by no
means confined to art and part guilt of traditional reset.

10–62   The example that is given in Macdonald's text runs as follows:

> "It is reset for a person to connive at a third party possessing
> or retaining the stolen goods, even if the person charged
> never laid a finger on the property stolen."

Again, this might refer to a form of art and part guilt. If so, it
would be wholly acceptable and unexceptionable. But the example
is derived, and obtains whatever authority it possesses, from a
direction to a jury made by Lord Justice-Clerk Macdonald himself
in 1903 in *HM Advocate v Browne*.[262] In the course of that
direction, he said:

> "If a man steals a bundle of notes out of a man's pocket, and
> after that informs another man that he has got these notes,
> that he has stolen them, or if the other man saw him stealing
> them and knew that they were stolen, then if the other man
> connived at it remaining in the possession of the thief or
> being put in any place for safe custody, such as hiding it in a
> cupboard, he is guilty of receiving feloniously even although
> he never puts his fingers on the notes at all. Reset consists of
> being privy to the retaining of property that has been
> dishonestly come by."

This must be taken along with a later passage in Macdonald's
textbook[263] which reads: "If the first offender with his knowledge
hide the property, even in a hole in a wall, and he connive at this,
he is guilty." There are a number of objections to this.

---

[260] *cf.* the situation in *Grant v Allan*, 1988 S.L.T. 11.
[261] See *McNeil v HM Advocate*, 1968 J.C. 29, following *McCawley v HM Advocate*
    (1959) S.C.C.R. Supp. 3.
[262] *HM Advocate v Browne* (1903) 6 F. (J.) 24 at 26.
[263] Macdonald, *Criminal Law*, 5th edn, p.68.

First, Macdonald thus makes dispensable what both Hume and **10–63** Alison[264] state is essential, that is, that the resetter should have received (handled, taken possession of) the property in question. This point was well taken by both Lord Justice-Clerk Grant and Lord Strachan in *Clark v HM Advocate*[265] and made them doubt that Macdonald could possibly have been correct. Their doubts were dismissed, however, by the Appeal Court in *McNeil v HM Advocate*,[266] apparently on the basis that the Macdonald alternative had appeared in his textbook without objection for a very long time. Secondly, it is clear from his examples that Macdonald did not have in mind any mere "art and part" form of guilt. The person who sees or knows of the thief's concealment of the property and "connives at" that is simply guilty of reset as actor. There is no other person, by hypothesis, who is guilty of reset and in respect of whose crime he might be art and part guilty; and Macdonald does not suggest that the accused might be art and part guilty of the theft itself. Thirdly, Macdonald makes no attempt to explain what is meant by "connive at", and this caused great difficulty to the trial judge and jury in *Clark v HM Advocate*.[267] The sheriff there, in fact, directed that the accused would be guilty if he knew that stolen property was being disposed of, yet did nothing to inform the police; but there had to be more to it than proof that the accused was merely in the company of the thief when the property happened to be disposed of. This somewhat inconsistent direction was clearly enough to confuse any jury, as the Appeal Court conceded when quashing the conviction for reset. But their Lordships did little to clarify the meaning of "connive at" other than to agree with both counsel that acts of a positive nature would have to be shown. No doubt this better accords with the philosophy that a person should not be convicted of a crime because of his mental attitude alone[268] but it gives little guidance as to the scope of Macdonald's examples. For these reasons alone, it can be suggested that the Macdonald form of reset should be abandoned by Scots law. His examples are also probably contrary to principle, in that they seem to require a person who knows of, or observes a crime to inform the authorities,[269] in the absence of any of the accepted legal duties discussed in Ch.3.

MISCELLANEOUS MATTERS

If property was stolen in any part of the United Kingdom other **10–64** than Scotland, receiving of that property in this country can still be dealt with by the Scottish courts.[270] This privilege does not extend,

---

[264] Hume, *Commentaries*, i, 113; Alison, *Principles*, i, 328.
[265] *Clark v HM Advocate*, 1965 S.L.T. 250 at 252, 253.
[266] *McNeil v HM Advocate*, 1968 J.C. 29.
[267] *Clark v HM Advocate*, 1965 S.L.T. 250.
[268] *cf. Girdwood v Houston*, 1989 S.C.C.R. 578.
[269] *Pace* the view taken in *McNeil v HM Advocate*, 1968 J.C. 29.
[270] Criminal Procedure (Scotland) Act 1995 s.11(4)(b); *cf.* the now replaced original wording in the Criminal Procedure (Scotland) Act 1975 ss.7(2), 292(2).

however, to property obtained outwith Scotland by fraud or embezzlement. It is also the case that a J.P. Court can deal with a case of reset, theft, fraud or embezzlement on complaint provided that the value of the property in question does not exceed level 4 on the standard scale.[271] Such a court cannot try cases of robbery at all, however. It may follow then that the reset of the proceeds of a robbery must be tried in a sheriff or High Court.

10–65　Any exposition of common law reset must acknowledge the existence of similar, but often wider, statutory offences which add somewhat to the complexity of the subject. For example, under the Proceeds of Crime Act 2002, a person commits an offence if he acquires, uses or has possession of criminal property.[272] "Property" for the purposes of this offence is construed very widely[273] and amounts to "criminal property" if it, "(a) constitutes a person's benefit[274] from criminal conduct or it represents such a benefit (in whole or part and whether directly or indirectly), and (b) the alleged offender knows or suspects that it constitutes such a benefit."[275] This in turn requires "criminal conduct" to be defined—as it is in s.340(2).[276]

5. FRAUD

Introduction

10–66　The common law crime of fraud helps protect persons from their own gullibility. Modern advertising techniques exploit the psychological fact that most persons can be imposed upon and influenced in ways they might hardly suspect. But the common law, knowing nothing of the advertising agent's skills, generally does not seek to prevent "bad bargains" or decisions taken on misleading information. Rather it seeks to proscribe deliberate falsehood, and not

---

[271] Criminal Procedure (Scotland) Act 1995 s.7(8)(b)(iii), as amended by the Criminal Proceedings etc. (Reform) (Scotland) Act 2007 (asp 6) Sch.1 para.9(4).

[272] Proceeds of Crime Act 2002 s.329(1). "Defences" are explained in s.329(2), and these include that the person in question "acquired, or used or had possession of the property for adequate consideration" (s.329(2)(c)); "inadequate consideration" is defined in s.329(3): see on this *Hogan v DPP* [2007] 1 W.L.R. 2944 DC.

[273] See the Proceeds of Crime Act 2002 s.340(9)—where "property" includes money, things heritable or moveable, and intangible or incorporeal property.

[274] Under the Proceeds of Crime Act 2002 s.340(5), a "person benefits from conduct if he obtains property as a result of or in connection with the conduct".

[275] Proceeds of Crime Act 2002 s.340(3).

[276] "Criminal conduct is conduct which—(a) constitutes an offence in any part of the United Kingdom, or (b) would constitute an offence in any part of the United Kingdom if it occurred there." (It should be noted that ss.329 and 340 of the Proceeds of Crime Act 2002 are amended by the Serious Organised Crime and Police Act 2005 s.102(4); s.103(4), (6); and Sch.4 para.174: s.340 is further amended by the Serious Crime Act 2007 Sch.8 para.130—"SOCA" there being defined by s.74(4) of the 2007 Act.)

"legitimate" persuasion techniques, in interpersonal and business dealings. Such protection as the law gives to consumers short of deliberate falsehood is a modern development under statutory law.[277] Fraud is archaically called, "falsehood, fraud and wilful imposition" in the Criminal Procedure (Scotland) Act 1995,[278] and "swindling" in Hume.[279] It is also an alternative verdict where theft has been charged,[280] presumably to cater for cases where consent to the appropriation is discovered in the course of the evidence.[281] It is further the case that a conviction for theft or reset can be returned on a fraud charge.[282]

Working definition

Currently, a working definition of the crime might run as follows: **10–67** that fraud consists of a false pretence made to another person in the knowledge of its falsity and with the intention that that other person should be deceived by it into acting in a way in which he would not otherwise have acted, provided that that other person *is* so deceived and *does* so act on account of it. It will be noted that the proviso reveals fraud to be a result crime (see above, para.2–36); a false pretence is of no avail for the completed crime unless it causes the specified result. More detailed consideration of this definition will be found in the following paragraphs.

ACTUS REUS: FALSE PRETENCE

What may be pretended falsely, and what may be the methods of **10–68** conveying falsehoods to another are matters difficult to generalise. As Hume puts it[283]:

> "It would be a vain, and a tedious attempt, to enumerate all the manifold shapes of cheating or fraud, in which falsehood is one of the chief ingredients of the guilt."

Yet, whatever it be that is expressed or implied, it has to be verifiably false there and then. If it happens to be true, then there can be no question of fraud. Of course, what is true or false is generally easy to establish. Whether a person is really who he says

---

[277] See, e.g. the Trade Descriptions Act 1968.
[278] e.g. Criminal Procedure (Scotland) Act 1995 Sch.3 para.8.
[279] Hume, *Commentaries*, i, 172.
[280] Criminal Procedure (Scotland) Act 1995 Sch.3 para.8(4).
[281] Consent obtained by falsehood is regularly taken at common law in Scotland to be a proper consent—*William Fraser* (1847) Ark. 280—although this would seem to be objectionable on moral grounds. In *Lord Advocate's Reference (No.1 of 2001)*, 2002 S.L.T. 466, opinion was reserved on this issue: see Lord Justice-General Cullen's opinion at 475B, para.36.
[282] Criminal Procedure (Scotland) Act 1995 Sch.3 para.8(2), (3).
[283] Hume, *Commentaries*, i, 177.

he is, whether the goods he has for sale are truly as he describes
them, or whether he is really entitled to claim what he presently
seeks, can be proved one way or the other with more or less
difficulty. But if a person is, for example, induced to buy or to sell
by reason of some future intention expressed by another, how can
fraud ever be a relevant charge? It stands to reason that a person's
future intentions relate to things that he would wish or hope to be
able to undertake. But the best-intentioned hopes or wishes may
never be fulfilled. They may turn out to have been over ambitious,
or to be frustrated by events; and it is their very uncertainty that
leads to the conclusion that future intentions cannot form part of
the province of fraud. A person's intentions cannot generally be
described as false when they are made. But it does not follow that
express or implied statements of intent can never be false.

10–69   Scots law takes the view that a statement of intention which its
maker *never* plans to fulfil is false when it is made. Thus, where
goods are obtained on credit by one who secretly plans not to pay
for them at all, and indeed does not pay for them, there is a false
pretence, since he has allowed the person delivering the goods to
believe that the normally implied intent to pay at a future date
applies in this case *comme toujours*.[284] In the same way, one who
orders a meal in a restaurant implies that his intention is to pay for
it after it has been consumed; but if he plans all along to walk out
without paying and eventually does so walk out, the impression he
creates in relation to his intentions is plainly false throughout.
Similarly, booking a room in a hotel for a few days' stay does not
normally involve payment in advance, but does involve the implied
undertaking that the guest in question will pay in the future when
his account is presented. If he plans from the moment of booking
onwards not to pay at all, then he impliedly makes a false pretence,
as has been recognised in the statutory styles of charge.[285]

10–70   In the case of *John Hall*[286] Lord Young rejected the view that
future intentions or promises could ever amount to false pretences
for the purposes of fraud. As he put it:

> "A purchaser without intention to pay may afterwards think
> better of it and pay, or his creditor may succeed in compel-
> ling payment. Again a purchaser intending to pay may
> subsequently change his mind and dishonestly refuse. Shall
> the former (who in fact pays) be punished as a criminal, and
> the latter (who does not) go free? A crime committed cannot
> thereafter be uncommitted."

This interesting dilemma ignores, however, the practicalities—and
Scots law is a very practical system. A crime cannot be committed

---

[284] See, e.g. charge 2 in the indictment in *Drew v HM Advocate*, 1995 S.C.C.R. 647.
[285] See the Criminal Procedure (Scotland) Act 1995 Sch.5, "You did obtain from
A.N. board and lodging to the value of L16 without paying and intending not to
pay therefor."
[286] *John Hall* (1881) 4 Coup. 438 at 447.

by intention alone; the person who initially intends not to pay, but thereafter does pay, will be guilty of nothing since his secret intentions are ultimately unfulfilled. The law does not usually concern itself with unfulfilled intentions. Although there may well be a theoretical fraud in such a case, it is unlikely to be discovered, there are no outward signs of criminality, and no harm or prejudice has been caused.[287] On the other hand, the person who initially intends to pay but ultimately changes his mind may well be charged with fraud, for it is impossible to see into a person's mind and detect such subtle changes in intent. If no payment is ever tendered, it may well be justifiably assumed that that person never intended to do so. That would not prevent, of course, the acceptance of some plausible excuse tendered on his part, for example, that he entered a restaurant and ordered a meal in good faith, thinking erroneously that he had his wallet or credit card in his pocket.

In any event, Lord Young's views were rejected in the more **10–71** modern case of *Richards v HM Advocate*[288] where the sale of a mansion house and ornamental grounds was induced by the accused's (or rather his nominee's) professed intention to live in it with his family and retain it entirely in its then current state. The seller's desire was that the property should not be built upon and should therefore not be bought by any entrepreneur attracted by the lure of its development potential. The prosecutor's case was that the professed intention of the purchaser was false from the beginning; and on that basis, the Appeal Court affirmed the correctness of the conviction for fraud. What matters then is a person's present intent as to his future conduct. It is his present intent which can be described as false for the purposes of fraud.

Examples of false pretences

Pretences may be express or implied. Under the "express" **10–72** banner, examples would include the written or spoken assumption of a false name or address, provided that gave the impression of wealth, status or just credit-worthiness[289]; assumption of a false status[290]; assertion that goods for sale were of much greater merit than was actually the case[291]; assertion that services rendered were

---

[287] Lord Young's example, where payment is compelled by civil process, may, however, be different.

[288] *Richards v HM Advocate*, 1971 J.C. 29.

[289] See, e.g. *Thomas Macgregor and George Inglis* (1846) Ark. 49, where the first-named accused passed himself off as "Captain" Macgregor and managed to obtain on credit, two gold watches, cattle and a grand piano.

[290] See, e.g. *Tapsell v Prentice* (1910) 6 Adam 354, where a woman gave a false name and address but also passed herself off as the manageress of a group of travelling people and thus able to purchase large quantities of groceries on the group's behalf.

[291] See, e.g. *Hood v Young* (1853) 1 Irv. 236, where two knackery-ready horses were glowingly described as "good workers" at an auction sale, the only reason for sale being given (falsely) that the seller was going abroad.

of much greater value than was in fact true (provided, of course, that their true value is also stated in the charge)[292]; assertion that a named person was guilty of a crime[293]; making of false claims to be owed money and raising court actions to recover what was said to be due[294]; or, making of false insurance claims.[295]

10–73   Pretences may be implied by what the accused does without any words being spoken or written at all. In *James Paton*,[296] for example, bulls to be displayed at a prize show were made more attractive for the judges by having their skins inflated with air and their horns enhanced with false extensions; and in the English case of *R. v Morris*[297] the accused switched price labels on goods displayed on a supermarket shelf so that the goods intended to be purchased then displayed a lower price than that originally attached by the store. Note might also be taken of *William Fraser*[298] where the accused was alleged to have tricked a married woman into believing that he was her husband. His behaviour towards her was said to have had that effect and, on that basis, she was said to have permitted him to have sexual intercourse with her. The majority of the court held that if the prosecutor's case could be substantiated, then the crime committed would be one of fraud rather than rape. Also, in *Strathern v Fogal*[299] the accused's failure to disclose on a rates return to the local assessor that he had obtained substantial premiums from tenants as a condition of his renewing their leases was considered to be sufficient for common law fraud. A failure to reveal what there is a legal duty to disclose can, therefore, be a sufficient false pretence.[300]

Cheque and "plastic money" transactions

10–74   It is probably clear (bearing in mind the relative dearth of Scottish authority) that false pretences can be involved in transactions where cheques or credit cards are tendered in payment for goods or services. Since no one generally makes any statement

---

[292] See, e.g. *HM Advocate v McAllister*, 1996 S.L.T. 220, where the accused pretended to an 87 year old woman that roof repairs (actually worth no more than £50—the cost of replacing one slate) had been done to the value of £2,000; *cf. Bennett v Houston*, 1993 S.L.T. 1182, where the actual value of the work done was omitted from the charges—which were, therefore, dismissed as irrelevant charges of fraud.

[293] See, e.g. *Elliot Millar* (1847) Ark. 355, where the accused misinformed the police that his wife was trying to murder him—even providing a cup of poisoned coffee and a bowl of his "own" vomit as real evidence.

[294] See, e.g. *George Kippen* (1849) J. Shaw 276; *McKenzie v HM Advocate*, 1988 S.L.T. 487.

[295] See, e.g. *Maciver and Macallum* (1784) Hume, *Commentaries*, i, 176.

[296] *James Paton* (1858) 3 Irv. 208.

[297] *R. v Morris* [1983] Q.B. 587.

[298] *William Fraser* (1847) Ark. 280 and 329.

[299] *Strathern v Fogal*, 1922 J.C. 73.

[300] *cf. Buchmann v Normand*, 1994 S.C.C.R. 929, where, although the charge was brought under s.7(4) of the Civic Government Act 1982, the failure to reveal previous convictions by leaving blank the space intended for them in a licence application form, had clear affinities with common law fraud.

concerning his relationship with the bank or credit card company where the account in question is held, what is in fact being asserted when a cheque or "plastic money" is tendered must be a matter of implication. In the nineteenth-century case of *Rae v Linton*[301] it was held that handing over a cheque in payment involves the following implied statements: that the person drawing the cheque has an account with the bank or other financial institution in question (which will not be true if, for example, that person has stolen the cheque book); that he has authority from that bank to draw a cheque for such an amount; and that there is good reason to believe that that cheque will be met when presented to that bank. It is not implied necessarily that the account holder has currently a credit balance in his account of at least the amount for which the cheque has been drawn; for it has to be accepted that in modern times, banks and similar institutions have a distinct interest in allowing customers to overdraw on their accounts—even where no special arrangements have been made. For that reason, it may be better to conclude that the important implied assertion is that, "the present state of affairs is such that, in the ordinary course of events, the cheque will on its future presentment be duly honoured."[302] This is better since it takes into account the normal delay in clearing a cheque which is presented for payment in the ordinary way. Special presentations apart, a person with no funds in his account may thus still draw a cheque without making any (implied) false pretence. The normal delay in clearance would provide a period of grace during which to make overdraft arrangements with his bank, or to pay money into his account.

Where a cheque card is also tendered along with one's cheque, it **10–75** would appear that, "the main implicit assertion"[303] will always be true. Provided that the conditions for the use of such a card are observed[304] then the bank or other issuing institution is obliged to honour the cheque in question, as a matter of commercial reality, if nothing else. However, it has been held in England that there is an extra implied assertion involved when such a card is used, namely, that the person tendering the card has authority from the issuing bank or other institution to use it and has not had that authority cancelled.[305] The rationale of this is that if the person accepting a cheque backed by such a card knew that the person tendering it was not authorised to use it, he would still be paid by the bank in question if he nevertheless proceeded with the transaction; but he would then be art and part guilty of that other person's fraudulent scheme. He cannot, therefore, be taken to have treated such a

---

[301] *Rae v Linton* (1874) 3 Coup. 67.
[302] *R. v Page* [1971] 2 Q.B. 330, per Phillimore L.J. at 333, quoting from an English textbook.
[303] See above, para.10–73.
[304] See *R. v Charles* [1977] A.C. 177.
[305] *R. v Charles* [1977] A.C. 177.

consideration as irrelevant. The same implied assertion of, "authority to use it" applies in England to credit card transactions[306]; and it is thought that the same sort of reasoning would find favour with Scottish courts in relation to the use of both sorts of cards.

Result of the false pretence

10–76   According to Macdonald[307]: "Fraud involves a false pretence made dishonestly in order to bring about some definite practical result." That the addressee of the pretence must be deceived by it in such a way that there is a, "definite practical result" has received support in the cases of *Adcock v Archibald*[308] and *HM Advocate v Wishart*;[309] but those words provide little guidance as to what is in fact a sufficient result. For that reason, the working definition proffered above (at para.10–67) draws on part of the opinion of Lord Hunter in *Adcock v Archibald*[310] to the extent that the person deceived must be induced to do what he otherwise would not have done. It is thought that this provides a reasonable guide to what is required, provided that it is borne in mind that, "doing what one otherwise would not have done" includes doing nothing at all, that is, "taking no steps to do what one otherwise would have done." It is also important to bear in mind that a conviction for fraud does not depend on the accused having gained anything as a result of his deception,[311] nor upon anyone having made any economic loss.[312] It is further important to note that where prejudice is suffered as a result of a false pretence, it may be so suffered by a person other than the very person deceived.[313]

Examples of results

10–77   Illustrations of "results" are numerous in the law reports and include a court ordering the arrestment of sums in the accused's hands and owing to his own creditors, the accused having initiated completely false actions for debt in fictitious names against those

---

[306] *R. v Lambie* [1982] A.C. 449. For a succinct explanation of the modern legal complexities in credit card transactions, see *OFT v Lloyds TSB Plc* [2007] 3 W.L.R. 733 HL, per Lord Mance at 740D–H, para.23.

[307] Macdonald, *Criminal Law*, 5th edn, p.52.

[308] *Adcock v Archibald*, 1925 J.C. 58, per Lord Justice-General Clyde at 61.

[309] *HM Advocate v Wishart* (1975) S.C.C.R. Supp.78, per Lord McDonald at 85.

[310] *Adcock v Archibald*, 1925 J.C. 58 at 61.

[311] *Alexander Bannatyne* (1847) Ark. 361, per Lord Justice-Clerk Hope (in his charge to the jury) at 380.

[312] See *Adcock v Archibald*, 1925 J.C. 58, where, because of a minimum wage agreement, neither the mining company nor any of its employees made any loss as a result of the accused's successful deceit.

[313] See, e.g. above, the subject matter of para.10–75; since there a retailer will be held to be deceived by any cheque or credit card fraud but only the bank or other institution will be prejudiced by having to pay out on the transaction.

creditors "to delay payment of a debt which was due from him"[314]; a mining company being induced to credit 1s 3d to a team of miners who had not worked the load of coal it represented at all[315]; police being forced to investigate a false accusation of murder[316]; a purchaser being induced to purchase, and thus come under an obligation to take and pay for, a misdescribed horse[317]; a woman refraining from preventing sexual intercourse since she had been induced to think her assailant was her husband[318]; a person sending a money order for £2, having been induced to do so by a forged letter, even though the accused never obtained possession of the order[319]; a prize being awarded to a bull, the meritorious condition of which being the result of cheating[320]; a firm of stock-brokers having been able to demonstrate substantial credit balances to the auditors appointed to inspect their accounts, after a solicitor had drawn cheques on his clients' account payable to the stock-brokers for that purpose alone—the understanding being that the stock-brokers would return the moneys to the solicitor as soon as the auditors had been deceived[321]; and solicitors being induced to raise actions for debt based on fabricated documents and false information.[322] Of course, the result must be caused by the false pretence, otherwise there can be no completed fraud.[323] If the person in receipt of the deception would have acted as he did in any event, then again there can be no fraud, although attempted fraud might then be considered.

THE MENS REA OF FRAUD

The accused must know that what he says or writes or implies is **10–78** false, and must intend thereby to deceive. It seems unlikely that recklessness as to the truth of statements made to another would be sufficient, as is apparently borne out by the decision of the Appeal Court in *Mackenzie v Skeen*.[324] There the accused showed the utmost carelessness in weighing offal intended to be sold to a pet-food manufacturer by weight, but was nevertheless acquitted of fraud. Of course, it could not be shown in the circumstances that

---

[314] *George Kippen* (1849) J. Shaw 276, per Lord Justice-Clerk Hope at 286.
[315] *Adcock v Archibald*, 1925 J.C. 58.
[316] *Elliot Millar* (1847) Ark. 355.
[317] *Hood v Young* (1853) 1 Irv. 236—see in particular the reply to counsel by Lord Justice-Clerk Hope at 239.
[318] *William Fraser* (1847) Ark. 280 (a decision made under common law).
[319] *Daniel Taylor* (1853) 1 Irv. 230.
[320] *James Paton* (1858) 3 Irv. 208.
[321] *HM Advocate v Wishart* (1975) S.C.C.R. Supp. 78.
[322] *McKenzie v HM Advocate*, 1988 S.L.T. 487—though charged as attempt to defraud the alleged debtors.
[323] See, e.g. *Mather v HM Advocate* (1914) 7 Adam 525; *Tapsell v Prentice* (1910) 6 Adam 354.
[324] *Mackenzie v Skeen*, 1971 J.C. 43.

he had any intention to deceive either his own employers or the pet-food company—obviously a matter of some importance to this crime.[325]

JURISDICTION

10–79 In a country as small as the United Kingdom, it is inevitable that fraudulent schemes will not always be respecters of borders. This may pose nice problems of jurisdiction. For example, if letters containing false pretences and orders for goods on credit are sent from Scotland to suppliers in England, as in *Thomas Macgregor and George Inglis*,[326] and these suppliers are induced to send the goods in question, there is an immediate problem. Fraud, as was stated at para.10–67, is a result crime and is not complete until someone is made to do what he otherwise would not have done (see above, para.10–76). No crime, therefore, would seem to have been completed in Scotland. Do Scottish courts, then, have jurisdiction over the whole crime? And what of the converse situation, as in *William Bradbury*[327] where goods were sent from Scotland in response to "false pretence" letters originating in England. If some definite rule was operated in Scots law, then one might be able to conclude that the Scottish courts had jurisdiction where, for example, the fraud was actually completed in Scotland, but not otherwise. In fact, in the two cases referred to above, the High Court affirmed that jurisdiction existed in Scotland over both situations as completed frauds; and it now seems clear that provided a material part of any fraudulent scheme can be said to have a Scottish domicile, the whole crime can competently be dealt with in Scotland, irrespective of whether the courts of any other country might also have had jurisdiction.[328] This is curious but is wholly in keeping with Scots law's intensely pragmatic approach to crime. If the courts of this country were to shackle themselves to a particular jurisdictional rule in such cases, then clear criminality might well go unpunished.

---

[325] See, e.g. *Paterson v Ritchie*, 1934 J.C. 42.
[326] *Thomas Macgregor and George Inglis* (1846) Ark. 49.
[327] *William Bradbury* (1872) 2 Coup. 311.
[328] *Laird v HM Advocate*, 1985 S.L.T. 298.

6. UTTERING AS GENUINE

DEFINITION OF THE CRIME

Uttering as genuine is a specialised type of fraud. It is closer to **10–80** attempted fraud than to fraud itself, since no result of the false pretence is required. The false pretence is also very specific. It has to amount to a forged document (or instrument, as the older authorities tend to call it). In the words of Lord Neaves in *Michael Hinchy*[329]:

> "Forgery, in order to satisfy the full meaning of the word as technically used, must be an overt act. The document must have gone forth to the world; the forgery is not committed unless this is done . . . [T]here is no doubt that the wicked and felonious using and uttering of a forged instrument is a completed crime. Whether the party succeeds is of no consequence; the essence of the crime is not the success but the perpetration of the act, of giving it forth from the party to another."

The *mens rea* element is probably very similar to that of fraud. Drawing the various facets of the crime together, an acceptable definition might read: a person is guilty of uttering as genuine if he deliberately exposes a forged document to another person, as if it was genuine, where he knows that it is forged and intends that that other person should be deceived by it.

A forged document

The classic example of such a document is one which bears a **10–81** forged signature. However, it is not necessary that the forgery should amount to a passable imitation of the signature of the person in question, nor is it necessary for the document even to purport to be signed by that person.[330] In *Daniel Taylor*,[331] the accused claimed to be the brother of the person to be deceived. He sent her a note in which he requested her to send money "poste restante" since he was in some kind of unexplained trouble. There was also an assertion that he had injured his hand. The note, he explained, had therefore been written at his request by another who had also had to adhibit his signature for him. It concluded with the words, "your afflicted brother Andrew Muir, signed for

---

[329] *Michael Hinchy* (1864) 4 Irv. 561 at 565–566.
[330] Compare with Hume's definition of this crime at *Commentaries*, i, 140, para.2.
[331] *Daniel Taylor* (1853) 1 Irv. 230.

me—I cannot." The note was nevertheless held to be a forgery, Lord Justice-General McNeill stating[332]:

> "I do not think it necessary that the signature of Muir should be there. It is enough that the letter professes to be signed by a person authorised to sign Muir's name."

It would, of course, have been monstrous if so crafty a ruse had been successful in removing the finished article from the ranks of forgeries.

10–82   A document with a genuine signature on it may, however, also be a forgery. The point here concerns the authority given or intended by the person who signed it. If one party gives a cheque to another in payment of an account for £6, careless drawing of that cheque might well give scope for the recipient to alter "six" to "sixty" and 6 to 60, as in the case of *William Mann*.[333] But the altered cheque then does not have the authority of the person who signed it, and must be regarded in total as a forgery. The same conclusion follows if a person, for example, were to sign a cheque in blank, leaving the recipient on trust to fill in the name of the payee and the amount. If the recipient, say a shop assistant, were to enter his own name on that cheque, instead of the store-name, as intended, or deliberately to double the agreed-on amount, there would certainly be a forgery.[334]

Deliberate exposure to another

10–83   The essence of this crime is not the forging of the document itself, but the deliberate communication of that document to another as if it was genuine. As Lord Neaves aptly put it in *Michael Hinchy*[335]:

> "A man may . . . fabricate a series of the most nefarious documents, but if he keeps them in his desk and never uses them, he has committed no crime . . .".

Were a thief, therefore, to break open such a desk and discover the forgeries, there would obviously be no crime of uttering as genuine; but if that thief were to take them and try to pass them off as genuine himself, the crime of uttering would then be committed thus far by him, and not by the original forger. It will be obvious, then, that the "utterer" need not himself be the manufacturer of

---

[332] *Daniel Taylor* (1853) 1 Irv. 230 at 234.
[333] *William Mann* (1877) 3 Coup. 376.
[334] cf. *Simon Fraser* (1859) 3 Irv. 467, where there could be no such forgery since the accused had written above a signature on an originally blank sheet of paper only that which the person signing it had expected would appear.
[335] *Michael Hinchy* (1864) 4 Irv. 561 at 564–565.

the forgery[336] but that the *actus reus* is complete when the document is deliberately placed in the hands of a third party as genuine.[337] If the forgery is sent by post to another, it seems that the uttering might be complete when the packet containing it is delivered to the postal authorities.[338] This would entail, however, completion of the crime before such a packet was ever opened and scrutinised by any third party. This odd rule, however, may simply represent a blurring of the edges of the crime to enable the Scottish courts to retain jurisdiction in cases where the addressee is domiciled outwith Scotland.[339] Such blurring is not unusual in fraud cases, however.[340] If a forged document were to be handed to another as forged, then the present crime cannot possibly be committed; but, depending on the facts, there might be evidence of attempted fraud or a criminal conspiracy.[341]

MENS REA

The accused must, of course, be aware that the document he **10–84** communicates to another is forged.[342] He must also intend to deceive that other person[343] and, possibly, to prejudice the person whose name was forged.[344] But he need have no success in his intentions:

> "It is sufficient, therefore, to complete the crime, if the forged instrument has been uttered . . . though it was challenged immediately as a forgery, and returned to the prisoner."[345]

In *John Smith*,[346] for example, a forged cheque crudely signed in the name of "Frankie Yewls" was sent by the accused to a "friend" to encash. The recipient, however, immediately reckoned it a forgery and handed to it the police. The fact that he was not himself deceived was held to be entirely irrelevant. A good or even understandable motive will also not suffice to acquit the accused. If, for example, goods were purchased and a receipt forgotten to be

---

[336] See *John Smith* (1871) 2 Coup. 1, per Lord Ardmillan at 12.
[337] *John Smith* (1871) 2 Coup. 1, per Lord Justice-General Inglis at 8.
[338] See *William Jeffrey* (1842) 1 Broun 337, in particular Lord Mackenzie at 341.
[339] As in *William Jeffrey* (1842) 1 Broun 337 itself.
[340] See above, para.10–79.
[341] Or even an entirely separate, common law crime—see *John Horne* (1814) Hume, *Commentaries*, i, 150, fn.1.
[342] See *John Smith* (1871) 2 Coup. 1, per Lord Justice-General Inglis at 9; *Barr v HM Advocate*, 1927 J.C. 51, per Lord Justice-General Clyde at 53.
[343] Hume, *Commentaries*, i, 154; *John Smith* (1871) 2 Coup. 1, per Lord Justice-General Inglis at 9–10.
[344] Hume, *Commentaries*, i, 154; *John Smith* (1871) 2 Coup. 1 at 10.
[345] Alison, *Principles*, i, 402.
[346] *John Smith* (1871) 2 Coup. 1.

obtained from the seller, it might be understandable for the purchaser to write out an appropriate receipt so as not to trouble the seller—but use of such a receipt would certainly amount to uttering as genuine according to Hume.[347] Whether such a case would ever actually be prosecuted would, of course, depend on the whole circumstances.

[347] Hume, *Commentaries*, i, 154–155.

CHAPTER 11

CRIMES AGAINST PROPERTY

The crimes in this chapter are mostly common law ones relating **11–01**
to the protection of property, other than incorporeal property,
from encroachment, damage or destruction.

1. TRESPASSING ON HERITABLE PROPERTY

Introduction

"Unless by virtue of some special statutory provision . . . pros- **11–02**
ecution does not lie under Scottish law merely for unauthorised
entry on another's land."[1] This is undoubtedly true; and as far as
the common law of crime is concerned, a trespasser "may indeed
jeer at the time-honoured placard, which threatens him with
rigorous prosecution, as *brutum fulmen* [a harmless thunderbolt]."[2]
As long as he does no harm to property,[3] no common law
accusation will lie. The status of "trespasser" in Scotland has,
however, been considerably affected by the provisions of the Land
Reform (Scotland) Act 2003 (asp 2). Under that Act, everyone is
entitled to exercise "access rights" in respect of land in general,
provided that this is done responsibly in relation to particular
purposes: the exercise of such rights does not of itself amount to
trespass. Existing statutory offences which give some protection
against "trespassers" have, therefore, had to be modified to take
account of such access rights.[4] A selection of these statutory
offences is dealt with below.

---

[1] T.B. Smith, *A Short Commentary on the Law of Scotland* (Edinburgh: W. Green,
1962), p.526.
[2] J. Rankine, *The Law of Land-Ownership in Scotland*, 4th edn (Edinburgh: W.
Green, 1909), p.140.
[3] *cf.* malicious mischief below at paras 11–08 *et seq.*
[4] See the Land Reform (Scotland) Act 2003 (asp 2) Pt 1 (for a detailed account of
"access rights"), and Sch.2 (for amendments to inter alia existing trespassory
offences).

(1) THE TRESPASS (SCOTLAND) ACT 1865

11–03 The offences contained in the Trespass (Scotland) Act 1865 as amended, most recently by the Roads (Scotland) Act 1984 and the Land Reform (Scotland) Act 2003, are contained in s.3(1) and currently stand as follows:

> "Every person who lodges in any premises [as defined—see below], or occupies or encamps on any land, being private property, without the consent and permission of the owner or legal occupier of such premises or land, and every person who encamps or lights a fire on or near any road [as defined in s.2] or enclosed or cultivated land, or in or near any plantation, without the consent and permission of the owner or legal occupier of such road, land or plantation, shall be . . . punishable as herein-after provided."[5]

According to Rankine[6] this Act, "was passed for the purpose chiefly of preventing strolling tinkers, gypsies, and others from squatting without permission on private property or private roads." But the offences are certainly not confined to such persons, the most significant limitation being concerned rather with the type of premises involved. In terms of s.2, premises, "shall mean and include any house, barn, stable, shed, loft, granary, outhouse, garden, stackyard, court, close, or inclosed space." It must, therefore, be doubted whether this Act can appropriately be invoked where strikers occupy their employer's factory or students stage a "sit-in" protest within the administration block of their college or university. This may be a matter for regret in some quarters, since those found committing an offence under the Act may be "apprehended and detained" by the police under s.4—patently a more rapid and effective way of restoring possession of the premises to the owner or legal occupier than can be provided by the civil law. On the other hand, it may be said that such powers of arrest are remarkable, given that the maximum penalty for those convicted of such offences is a mere fine of level 1 on the standard scale (see Appendix C).

11–04 Rankine[7] believed that the Trespass (Scotland) Act 1865 had been, "found very useful in putting a stop to much petty pilfering and wanton destruction of woods and fences in country districts." That may well be so; but there are very few reported cases on such offences. Indeed, searches in the usual repositories suggest that

---

[5] Under s.3(2), which is inserted by para.1 of Sch.2 of the Land Reform (Scotland) Act 2003 (asp 2), these offences do not apply to anything done by a person in the exercise of "access rights" as provided for under Pt 1 of the 2003 Act.

[6] Rankine, *Land-Ownership*, 4th edn, p.144.

[7] Rankine, *Land-Ownership*, 4th edn, p.145.

Paterson v Robertson[8] is probably the only reported case. There, subtenants of a furnished house had been given appropriate notice to quit. Whilst they were absent from the premises, the furniture was removed, the house securely locked, and the keys returned by the tenant to the house factors who acted as agents for the owners. Nevertheless, the subtenants returned to the property and gained access by obtaining a key from a neighbour. According to Lord Justice-General Normand, from that time on,

> "they were doing what they knew was wrong, and from that moment they were no better than squatters who had effected a lodgment in the house at their own hands."[9]

It would seem from this opinion that the *mens rea* of the crime might be knowledge on the accused's part that he had no entitlement whatsoever to lodge in the premises or encamp on the land; and, if that is so, then Gordon is possibly correct to say that a person who believed himself entitled, at least on reasonable grounds, would have a good defence.[10]

(2) THE CRIMINAL JUSTICE AND PUBLIC ORDER ACT 1994

1. Trespasser failing to obey a police direction to leave

The complex offence contained in s.61 of the Criminal Justice **11–05** and Public Order Act 1994 is applicable to Scotland.[11] In essence, it applies where at least two people "trespass" on land (where trespassing is defined[12] as entering or remaining upon land—which does not include buildings, other than agricultural ones or scheduled monuments, or roads, other than footpaths, cycle tracks and bridleways[13]—without lawful authority and without the occupier's[14] consent) and where they have the common purpose of residing[15] on that land for any period of time. That, however, is nowhere near sufficient for the offence to be committed. Not only must the occupier of the land have taken reasonable steps to ask them to leave, but he must also (apparently) have summoned the police. The senior police officer attending the *locus* must then reasonably believe that the people concerned are trespassers and that the

---

[8] *Paterson v Robertson*, 1944 J.C. 166.
[9] *Paterson v Robertson*, 1944 J.C. 166 at 170.
[10] Gordon, *Criminal Law*, 3rd edn, para.15.44.
[11] See the Criminal Justice and Public Order Act 1994 s.172(8).
[12] See s.61(9) of the 1994 Act, s.v. "trespass" at (b).
[13] See s.61(9).
[14] Occupier is defined in s.61(9) as the person in Scotland entitled to natural possession of the land.
[15] It is not a bar to being considered as having a purpose of "residing" there that one has a home elsewhere: s.61(9).

occupier has indeed taken reasonable steps to persuade them to depart from his land; he must also reasonably believe that one at least of the following is satisfied, viz: that the trespassers (or any of them) have caused damage to the land or to property (defined as heritable property other than land, or corporeal moveable property)[16] on it; that the trespassers (or any of them) have used threatening, abusive or insulting words or behaviour to the occupier, any member of his family, his employee or his agent; or, that the trespassers have brought six or more vehicles[17] on to the land. If he is so satisfied as to these points, the police officer may then direct the trespassers, all or some of them, to leave and to remove their vehicles and other property. The offence is committed where such a trespasser, in the knowledge of the police direction, fails to leave as soon as reasonably practicable, or, having once left in obedience to the direction, returns to the same land as a trespasser within a period of three months from the day when the direction was first given.[18] (Failure to remove vehicles or other property seems to be excluded from the offence; but the police may seize such property in terms of s.62.) There is also a statutory defence available. A person accused of a contravention of this section may try to show that he was not in fact trespassing at the relevant time, or, he may try to show that he had a reasonable excuse either for not leaving as soon as reasonably practicable or for returning as a trespasser within the specified period.[19] In the one case so far reported on the operation of this offence in Scotland,[20] it appeared that the land in question was subject to a dispute. There were two possible occupiers. That being so, the sheriff who heard the case took the view that it was necessary for the police to make enquiry as to which of the competing parties was the true occupier, since only that person could give instructions (or, possibly, have instructions given on his behalf) to the trespassers to depart. This might have been a question of some difficulty if only one of the two claimants had been prepared to ask the trespassers to leave: but that was not the case. The contending occupiers were entirely at one in wishing and instructing the departure of the persons in question, and consequently the Appeal Court had no difficulty in rejecting the sheriff's view. (This offence is obviously one of fairly limited scope, since it does not apply in general to buildings and is hedged about with qualifying conditions.)

---

[16] See s.61(9).
[17] Vehicles need not be roadworthy, and the term includes a chassis, a caravan, or a load carried in, by or attached to such a conveyance, s.61(9).
[18] See s.61(4). See also s.61(4A) and (4B) as inserted by the Land Reform (Scotland) Act 2003 (asp 2) Sch.2 para.11. (Note that s.61(5) was repealed by the Serious Organised Crime and Police Act 2005 Sch.17 Pt 2.)
[19] See s.61(6).
[20] *Neizer v Rhodes*, 1995 S.C.C.R. 799.

2. Aggravated trespass

The offence of "aggravated trespass"[21] requires that a person **11–06** should trespass[22] on land[23] in the open air, and deliberately conduct himself there so that those engaged (or about to be engaged) there (or on adjoining land) in "lawful activities"[24] will be intimidated and thus deterred from engaging in those lawful activities. It is also sufficient if he so conducts himself as to obstruct or disrupt those activities. This offence is aimed at those who set out to disrupt activities such as "field sports", and who do so (or attempt to do so) by trespassing on land. There is clearly a "public order" dimension to this offence; but the device of linking the crime to trespassing secures its place in this section of the text.[25]

3. Trespassory assembly offences

Equally, the "trespassory assemblies" offences[26] have public **11–07** order connotations; but they too entail the protection of land from trespass. For such offences to exist, there are a number of qualifying conditions. First, the chief officer of police must reasonably believe that an assembly of 20 or more persons[27] is intended to be held in a particular local authority area, at a place in the open air on land to which the public either has no right of access, or a very limited right of access.[28] He must also believe that that assembly is to be held there without the permission of the occupier,[29] or in excess of such permission as had been granted, or

---

[21] See s.68 of the 1994 Act, as that section is amended by the Anti-social Behaviour Act 2003 Sch.3. (Note that s.68(4) is repealed by the Serious Organised Crime and Police Act 2005 Sch.17 Pt 2.) For an example of a prosecution under s.68, see *McAdam v Urquhart*, 2004 S.C.C.R. 506.

[22] Under s.68(1A), as inserted by the Land Reform (Scotland) Act 2003 (asp 2) Sch.2 para.13, "trespassing" here includes the exercise of "access rights" (within the meaning of Pt 1 of the 2003 Act) up to the point when they cease to be exercisable by virtue of the commission of the offence under s.68(1).

[23] Land does not include highways or roads; see s.68(5)(a).

[24] As defined in s.68(2).

[25] Where a person is committing, intends to commit, or has committed an offence under s.68, or where two or more persons are trespassing with the common purpose of disrupting, etc. lawful activities there, it is also an offence for him or them to refuse to leave the land when directed to do so by a police officer—see s.69, as amended by the Anti-social Behaviour Act 2003 Sch.3. A statutory defence is provided at s.69(4). (Note that s.69(5) is repealed by the Serious Organised Crime and Police Act 2005 Sch.17 Pt 2.)

[26] Public Order Act 1986 ss.14A–14C, added thereto by ss.70 and 71 of the 1994 Act. (Note that s.14B(4) and s.14C(4) are repealed by the Serious Organised Crime and Police Act 2005 Sch.17 Pt 2.)

[27] See s.14A(9) of the Public Order Act 1986.

[28] The Public Order Act 1986 s.14A(9) suggests that a limited right of access would apply to a highway or a roadway. Under s.14A(9A), as inserted by the Land Reform (Scotland) Act 2003 (asp 2) Sch.2 para.9, the references in s.14A to the public's right (or limited right) of access does not include any right which the public or any member of the public may have by way of "access rights" within the meaning of Pt 1 of the 2003 Act.

[29] i.e. the person in Scotland lawfully entitled to natural possession of that land—s.14A(9), s.v. "occupier", at (b).

beyond the limited right of public access which exists. If he has such beliefs, he must also be of the reasonable persuasion that that assembly will effect, "serious disruption to the life of the community" or significant damage to the land itself or to a building (or monument) erected on it—where that land or building is of historical, architectural, archaeological or scientific importance.[30] Provided that he has been satisfied in these ways, he may then apply to the council of the relevant local authority for an order to prohibit the holding of all trespassory assemblies within a specified area for a specific period.[31] Provided further that the relevant council sees fit to make such an order, the holding of any such assembly will be forbidden, i.e. one which, "(a) is held on land to which the public has no right of access or only a limited right of access, and (b) takes place in the prohibited circumstances, that is to say, without the permission of the occupier of the land or so as to exceed the limits of any permission of his or the limits of the public's right of access."[32] Once such an order has been made, it will be an offence to organise or take part in an assembly which contravenes the terms of the order—provided the organiser or the participant is aware of that order.[33] It will also be an offence under certain conditions to disobey a direction from a police officer that a particular person, reasonably believed to be *en route* to such an assembly, should not continue in a direction which would lead him there.[34]

2. MALICIOUS MISCHIEF

Introduction

11–08   Malicious mischief might well be taken to be a result crime (see above, para.2–36) since the actions of the accused must normally be shown to have destroyed or damaged property belonging to another.[35] However, there are up to four different versions of the crime, and one of these appears to require no result at all (see below, para.11–23). Hume's account of malicious mischief[36] is particularly confusing and perplexing, and lends itself to misconstruction, as is evident in the case of *HM Advocate v Wilson*.[37] In an attempt to allay further confusion, four accounts of this crime

---

[30] See s.14A(1)(b).
[31] See s.14A(6) for the maximum area and time-period allowed to such an order.
[32] See s.14A(5)(a),(b).
[33] The offences are contained in s.14B.
[34] See s.14C.
[35] See, e.g. *Lord Advocate's Reference (No.1 of 2000)*, 2001 S.C.C.R. 296 at 309C, para.30.
[36] Hume, *Commentaries*, i, 122–125.
[37] *HM Advocate v Wilson*, 1984 S.L.T. 117; see particularly the opinions of Lord Justice-Clerk Wheatley and Lord McDonald.

are set out separately below, namely: riotous and wilful mischief; traditional malicious mischief; "Wilson"-type malicious mischief; and "Stewart" malicious mischief.

RIOTOUS AND WILFUL MISCHIEF

Hume[38] deals with a variety of cases which seem characterised by a **11–09** form of mobbing.[39] Certainly the essence of these appears to be, "violent or tumultuous molestation, intrusion, or invasion of property",[40] in the course of which damage may be very slight, or even non-existent as in *Mungo Grant*.[41] There, the rightful possessor was simply denied access to his house by the intrusion of the accused with an armed force. In other examples in this series, the damage that did occur was predicated upon the vindication of some alleged civil wrong, such as the raising of turf for a bowling green from a disputed piece of land[42] or the encroachment upon the accused's loft in the parish church.[43] Further in *Glass of Sauchie v Monro of Auchinbowie*,[44] although the accused was alleged to have broken down dam-dykes and thus stopped the machinery at a mill, it was claimed that he enjoyed at least the privilege of doing so in order to draw water for mills on his own property. That all of these cases were essentially civil matters is clearly admitted by Hume,[45] when he writes:

> "These judgments may serve as a specimen of the course of practice in former times, (for of late years the Civil Courts have more commonly been resorted to for the redress of such injuries)."

Their rationale as criminal causes was consequently not dependent on the damage done but rather on, "the due regard to the order and tranquillity of society." Of course, it is correct that Hume thought true (or "traditional") malicious mischief depended upon significant damage, in the absence of violence or tumult; but these strange, civil-dispute, insignificant-damage cases are really of their own kind, and Hume's "grounds of relevancy in such cases" must be employed with caution in other types of malicious mischief.[46]

That they have not been employed with caution[47] means that **11–10** Hume's "grounds of relevancy" and other comments cannot entirely be ignored. In particular he comments that:

---

[38] Hume, *Commentaries*, i, 122–123; see Alison, *Principles*, i, 448–449.
[39] See below, paras 12 02 *et seq.*
[40] Hume, *Commentaries*, i, 124.
[41] *Mungo Grant* (1712) Hume, *Commentaries*, i, 122.
[42] *Trotter of Mortonhall* (1714) Hume, *Commentaries*, i, 123.
[43] *Henry Trotter of Mortonhall* (1730) Hume, *Commentaries*, i, 123.
[44] *Glass of Sauchie v Monro of Auchinbowie* (1713) Hume, i, 122.
[45] Hume, *Commentaries*, i, 124.
[46] Hume, *Commentaries*, i, 124.
[47] See, e.g. *HM Advocate v Wilson*, 1984 S.L.T. 117.

"It does not serve to acquit the pannel . . . that he proceeded in the belief of a civil wrong, previously committed by the pursuer [sic] against him: He is not excusable when he forgets that the courts of law are open to his complaint."[48]

Further, he notes that in this type of case, "the pannel shall equally be convicted, whether he interferes with the property of another, or with his state only of peaceable and lawful possession."[49] But that his comments here are confined to a special form of the crime is revealed in his final remark, namely:

"That which the law chiefly regards in such debates, is not so much the patrimonial damage, which in most of these instances was but trifling, as the insult to the public and the individual, by the violence and tumult attending the execution."[50]

Actus reus and mens rea

11–11   So far as it can be determined, the *actus reus* of this type of the crime depends upon unauthorised interference with, and not necessarily physical damage to, the property of another, in circumstances of violence, tumult and public disturbance.[51] The *mens rea* appears to be "wilfulness"[52]; and it is not a defence that the accused acted out of a misapprehension of his civil law rights.[53]

TRADITIONAL MALICIOUS MISCHIEF

11–12   Traditional malicious mischief consists in the intentional or reckless damaging of property belonging to another, without that other's consent or permission.[54] Hume clearly recognised this form of the crime[55] but required the damage to be "great" or considerable if conviction was to follow in the absence of violence and tumult. The modern law, however, does not appear to insist on any such restriction, since even the "injury" done to grass by walking over it has been held sufficient for this form of the crime.[56]

---

[48] Hume, *Commentaries*, i, 124. In practice the courts have vacillated between giving effect to, and ignoring this remark in relation to examples of "traditional" malicious mischief; see below, paras 11–15 to 11–17.
[49] Reliance on these words has produced a novel type of malicious mischief in recent years; see above, *Wilson*, 1984 S.L.T. 117, per Lord Justice-Clerk Wheatley at 119 and Lord McDonald at 120–121.
[50] Hume, *Commentaries*, i, 124
[51] See, e.g. *Archibald Barr* (1834) Bell's Notes 47.
[52] Hume, *Commentaries*, i, 122.
[53] Hume, *Commentaries*, i, 124.
[54] Gordon, *Criminal Law*, 3rd edn, paras 22.01, 22.03.
[55] Hume, *Commentaries*,i, 122, 124.
[56] *Ward v Robertson*, 1938 J.C. 32.

Actus reus

It has been said that "an omission could never be an act of **11–13** malicious mischief"[57] and this is probably correct in this form of the crime. The accused must, therefore, bring about the damage or destruction by positive acts on his part. Certainly, all of the reported cases are of that description. In relation to inanimate things, these include the cutting of leather hosepipes[58]; or a horse's harness[59]; the breaking of window panes[60]; the burning of a "chariot" by pouring acid on it[61]; the tearing down of a fence[62]; the knocking away of pit-props such that the roof of a mine fell in[63]; the ruination of several thousand gallons of oil by opening containers and letting the liquid run to waste[64]; damaging a ship, its fittings and equipment[65]; and the setting fire to growing trees and plants.[66] The injury or killing of animals is also relevant. Thus in *Thomas Bellie*[67] poisoned feed-stuffs were thrown into a neighbour's yard where they killed some of her hens; and in *Archibald Thomson*[68] the accused killed a cow in calf by inserting the handle of a pitchfork into the animal's vagina. Likewise, trampling plants or pulling them out by the roots must be sufficient for this form of malicious mischief.[69] If, however, property is not destroyed or damaged where it is found, but first taken away from where the owner or legal possessor left it, that would normally be theft rather than the present crime.[70] It is, therefore, surprising that one of the three charges of malicious mischief in *Samuel Wallace and Thomas Ferguson*[71] referred to the removal of a gate and the dumping of it in a canal, unless, of course, the time interval involved had been so slight as to be considered irrelevant.[72]

Mens rea

The title of the crime here is, of course, malicious mischief, **11–14** which suggests that the *mens rea* required is "malice." Malice, indeed, was said by Lord Justice-Clerk Wheatley[73] to connote, "the

---

[57] *HM Advocate v Wilson*, 1984 S.L.T. 117, per Lord Stewart (dissenting) at 122, commenting on a Crown concession there.

[58] *Robert Hall* (1837) 1 Swin. 420.

[59] *Speid v Whyte* (1864) 4 Irv. 584; though this was later thought to be too trivial by Lord Justice-General Clyde in *Clark v Syme*, 1957 J.C. 1 at 6.

[60] *Ann Duthie* (1849) J. Shaw 227.

[61] *Colin Campbell* (1823) Alison, *Principles*, i, 450.

[62] *John and William Black v Laing* (1879) 4 Coup. 276.

[63] *Nicolson Muir* (1825) Alison, *Principles*, i, 450.

[64] *David Munro* (1831) Bell's Notes 48.

[65] *Lord Advocate's Reference (No.1 of 2000)*, 2001 S.C.C.R. 296.

[66] *Archibald Phaup* (1846) Ark. 176, although the charge there might more appropriately have been one of reckless fire-raising.

[67] *Thomas Bellie* (1600) Hume, *Commentaries*, i, 124.

[68] *Archibald Thomson* (1874) 2 Coup. 551.

[69] See, e.g. *Samuel Wallace and Thomas Ferguson* (1839) Bell's Notes 47.

[70] See Alison, *Principles*, i, 273–274.

[71] *Samuel Wallace and Thomas Ferguson* (1839) Bell's Notes 47.

[72] See Burnett, p. 116, fn.*.

[73] *HM Advocate v Wilson*, 1984 S.L.T. 117 at 119, column 2.

evil intent deliberately to do injury or damage to the property",
though no authority was advanced to justify such a view. Nevertheless, that interpretation allied to Hume's insistence[74] that the
damage or destruction be "wilful" suggests that the appropriate
mens rea is intention.[75] If intention to damage or destroy can be
shown or inferred from the circumstances, then that is certainly
sufficient for conviction, and there is no need to show any further
intent to spite the owner.[76] However, such intention is not necessary for conviction. As Lord Justice-Clerk Aitchison laid down in
Ward v Robertson[77]:

> "It is not essential to the offence of malicious mischief that
> there should be a deliberate wicked intent to injure another
> in his property. I am prepared to take the case upon the
> footing, although it may involve some departure from the law
> as laid down by Hume, that it is enough if the damage is done
> by a person who shows a deliberate disregard of, or even
> indifference to, the property or possessory rights of others."

This strongly suggests that simple recklessness is an alternative
form of *mens rea* for the crime[78]; and indeed Lord Justice-Clerk
Aitchison's above quoted remarks were specifically approved by
Lord Justice-General Clyde in *Clark v Syme*.[79] Consequently, if the
damage or destruction can be shown to have been the product of
the accused's recklessness (see above, paras 3–30 *et seq*), then
conviction must follow. Such recklessness cannot always be
inferred, however. Thus, in *Ward v Robertson*[80] *mens rea* could not
be inferred from the mere fact that the appellant had walked in a
straight line through a field of ordinary grass, causing some trivial
damage thereto. No reasonable person would have considered any
real or lasting harm to have been so caused. But the matter would
have been different, as Lord Justice-Clerk Aitchison emphasised,[81]
if a stroll had been taken through a more obvious crop (the grass
here having been intended merely for sheep grazing), or, as Lord

---

[74] Hume, *Commentaries*, i, 122.
[75] *cf.* Alison, *Principles*, i, 448, where mention is made of, "the wanton or reckless
destruction of property." See also *Lord Advocate's Reference (No.1 of 2000)*, 2001
S.C.C.R. 296, opinion of the court at 309C, para.30: "The *mens rea* of the crime
in the case of intentional damage ... consists in the knowledge that the
destructive conduct complained of was carried out with complete disregard for,
or indifference to the property or possessory rights of another." (The court there
then referred to *Ward*, 1938 J.C. 32.)
[76] *Archibald Thomson* (1874) 2 Coup. 551, per Lord Deas at 553; *Lord Advocate's
Reference (No.1 of 2000)*, 2001 S.C.C.R. 296, opinion of the court at 309E,
para.31.
[77] *Ward v Robertson*, 1938 J.C. 32 at 36.
[78] See Gordon, *Criminal Law*, 3rd edn, para.22.03.
[79] *Clark v Syme*, 1957 J.C. 1 at 5.
[80] *Ward v Robertson*, 1938 J.C. 32.
[81] *Ward v Robertson*, 1938 J.C. 32 at 36.

Mackay put it,[82] if the appellant had deliberately trampled the grass by taking many more steps than were necessary to traverse the field or by walking round and round in circles. It is also clear, however, that carelessness will not be sufficient, even apparently if gross.[83]

Vindication of rights

Hume appears to remark generally that if damage or destruction **11-15** is done under a, "misapprehension of right", that will not secure an acquittal.[84] This was undoubtedly upheld in *Clark v Syme*[85] where a farmer shot a sheep belonging to a neighbour on the basis that that neighbour had refused to prevent his animals straying into the farmer's fields and consuming turnips there. He shot the sheep in the belief that he was entitled to do so to protect his own property. His acquittal on a charge of malicious mischief was reversed on appeal, however, Lord Justice-General Clyde[86] holding:

> "The respondent in this case acted deliberately. He knew what he was doing and he displayed in his actings a complete disregard of the rights of others."

The fact that the respondent had acted under a mistake of law did not afford him a defence.[87] The approach of the courts to this defence in relation to malicious mischief has not, however, been entirely consistent.

In *Speid v Whyte*[88] the condition on which timber was to be **11-16** auctioned was that the price should be paid before removal. Because some of the timber was located too far from a road to make extraction of it economic, the auctioneer purported to sell it to a neighbouring farmer who insisted that he be allowed to remove it forthwith. When the owner of the timber realised that this particular lot of wood was being removed without the price having been first paid, he remonstrated with the farmer's men who were even then loading it up, and eventually he cut the harness securing a horse to a cart. For this he was convicted of malicious mischief—but acquitted on appeal. As Lord Neaves put the matter[89]:

> "[The appellant] was undoubtedly the proprietor of the wood till the conditions of sale were implemented, which they had

---

[82] *Ward v Robertson*, 1938 J.C. 32 at 37–38.
[83] See *Archibald Phaup* (1846) Ark. 176, per Lord Justice-Clerk Hope's charge to the jury at 177.
[84] Hume, *Commentaries*, i, 122.
[85] *Clark v Syme*, 1957 J.C. 1.
[86] *Clark v Syme*, 1957 J.C. 1 at 5.
[87] See *Lord Advocate's Reference (No.1 of 2000)* 2001 S.C.C.R. 296, opinion of the court at 335E, para.109. See also above, paras 8–40 *et seq.*
[88] *Speid v Whyte* (1864) 4 Irv. 584.
[89] *Speid v Whyte* (1864) 4 Irv. 584 at 586.

not been; and although he may not have acted judiciously, or even legally, in the course he adopted to vindicate his property, still he did act in vindication of his supposed rights, and not merely from a desire to injure or destroy the property of another."

Whether the essence of this case can be distinguished from that in *Clark v Syme* must be doubted[90] but Lord Neaves also said, "[the acts done] do not amount to that reckless and wilful destruction of property which is essential to the constitution of malicious mischief." These words can be construed such as to rest the acquittal on the *de minimis* principle (see above, para.2–51); and indeed Lord Justice-General Clyde in a much later case considered that the acquittal there had been right on that basis, namely, that the trivial nature of what had been done was not consistent with the correct degree of recklessness or wilfulness required by the crime.[91] Significantly, it was not considered to have been correct on the grounds that a proprietor is entitled to damage the property of another in order to safeguard his own.[92]

11–17   Again, in *John and William Black v Laing*[93] a father and son were eventually acquitted of malicious mischief on appeal. They had torn down a fence, recently erected by another along the boundary of a piece of land they possessed, on the basis that it had blocked the only access to their land. Although no formal opinion was delivered by the court, it does appear that the appellants were felt to be justified in destroying the fence in these circumstances.[94] In a later case with not dissimilar facts, however, the accused was convicted and his appeal dismissed.[95] Either, as Gordon suggests,[96] these cases cannot be relied upon and there is no defence of acting in vindication of supposed rights, or each such case must be dealt with individually and decided according to its own facts and circumstances, a not uncommon way for Scots criminal courts to deal with awkward issues. It seems, however, that the matter may have been placed beyond doubt by the *Lord Advocate's Reference (No.1 of 2000)*,[97] since in that case one of the questions specifically referred to the High Court was this: "(3) Does the belief of an accused person that his or her actions are justified in law constitute a defence to a charge of malicious mischief . . . ?"[98] The court's response was as follows:

---

[90] See Gordon, *Criminal Law*, 3rd edn, para.22.10.
[91] *Clark v Syme*, 1957 J.C. 1 at 6.
[92] *cf. Lord Advocate's Reference (No.1 of 2000)*, 2001 S.C.C.R. 296.
[93] *John and William Black v Laing* (1879) 4 Coup. 276.
[94] *John and William Black v Laing* (1879) 4 Coup. 276 at 278.
[95] See *Forbes v Ross* (1898) 2 Adam 513.
[96] Gordon, *Criminal Law*, 3rd edn, paras 22.09, 22.11.
[97] *Lord Advocate's Reference (No.1 of 2000)*, 2001 S.C.C.R. 296.
[98] *Lord Advocate's Reference (No.1 of 2000)*, 2001 S.C.C.R. 296, quoted at 297.

"The unequivocal answer to the question . . . is provided in the opinion of Lord Justice-General Clyde in *Clark v. Syme* at p.5. The mere fact that a person carried out acts which constituted a crime under a mistaken conception of legal rights is not a defence."[99]

Although the pre-*Clark v Syme* cases were not considered, it must be assumed that they are now of little or no authority. It is still possible, however, that vindication of supposed rights might be pled in mitigation of sentence.[100]

Provocation

It would seem on principle that provocation should be able to be **11–18** pled in mitigation in a malicious mischief case (involving damage to property) just as it may be in a case of assault (involving injury to the person). In practice, this appears to be true. In *Andrew Steuart*[101] the accused, who had had his gun with him for sporting purposes on the day in question, shot a horse belonging to a tenant farmer of his who had provoked him by removing most of the crops before the rent due for his property had been met. As Lord Deas remarked[102]:

"It is not in the least surprising that you were much offended and angry at what was going on. That, however, only goes to mitigate the offence. It does not take it away."

"WILSON"-TYPE MALICIOUS MISCHIEF

This type of malicious mischief was recognised in the case of *HM* **11–19** *Advocate v Wilson*[103] and may generally be described as the unauthorised interference with another's property such as to cause deliberate consequential loss to the owner or lawful possessor. In this form of the crime, no physical damage need be caused to existing property at all.

In *Wilson* the accused was charged with malicious mischief in **11–20** that he had pressed the emergency stop-button of a turbine at a power station, "whereby the full generation and feeding of electricity into the national electricity grid was brought to a halt for 28 hours or thereby and 12,113,800 kilowatt hour units of electricity . . . were lost and had to be replaced and fed into the national grid

---

[99] *Lord Advocate's Reference (No.1 of 2000)*, 2001 S.C.C.R. 296 at 335E, para.109.
[100] See *McDonald v Mackay* (1842) 1 Broun 435.
[101] *Andrew Steuart* (1874) 2 Coup. 554.
[102] *Andrew Steuart* (1874) 2 Coup. 554 at 555.
[103] *HM Advocate v Wilson*, 1984 S.L.T. 117.

from other sources at a cost of £147,000 or thereby."[104] The accused objected to the relevancy of this charge in that no physical damage had been caused either to the stop-button or to the turbine itself. This argument succeeded before Sheriff D.B. Smith but was rejected by a majority of the Appeal Court. Lord Justice-Clerk Wheatley[105] considered that physical damage was not essential to this type of charge, either because it accorded with Hume's views or because there was, "a wider cover to be given to the earlier view of the nature of the offence." However, his Lordship could only achieve congruity with Hume by importing from "riotous and wilful mischief" the conclusion that, "the pannel shall equally be convicted, whether he interfere with the property of another, or with his state only of peaceable and lawful possession."[106] It will be recalled, however, that mere interference with, as opposed to damage to, property was only to be considered criminal where there was also violence and tumult. As no violence or tumult was adverted to in the indictment, then it must follow that Lord Justice-Clerk Wheatley and Lord McDonald were really here extending the notion of traditional malicious mischief so as to create a novel form of the crime. It is thus criminal to interfere deliberately with the property of another with the intention of causing its owner or legal possessor financial loss, where such loss is actually incurred and where the property interfered with remains itself entirely undamaged. Loss, however, *must* be actual: in a case where the alleged conduct of the accused consisted in the redirecting of a surveillance camera so that it no longer cast its protective gaze over the front and entrance of bank premises, it was held that there was no loss since the running costs of the device would have been incurred in any event, and the "loss" of the security and deterrent effects normally provided by the camera were not quantifiable losses for the purposes of malicious mischief.[107]

11–21　　Extending the ambit of a crime by judicial decision is not, of course, entirely illegitimate or unknown in a common law based system; and there is indeed something illogical in concluding that had the stop-button in *Wilson* been operated by being hit with a hammer then malicious mischief would have been a relevant charge, whereas that would not have been so if an "undamaging" finger had been used to operate it instead. That type of illogicality clearly weighed heavily with Lord Justice-Clerk Wheatley[108] and Lord McDonald.[109] But, as Lord Stewart[110] pointed out in his dissenting judgment,

---

[104] *HM Advocate v Wilson*, 1984 S.L.T. 117, quoted in the opinion of Lord Justice-Clerk Weatley at 118.

[105] *HM Advocate v Wilson*, 1984 S.L.T. 117 at 120.

[106] Hume, *Commentaries*, i, 124; *HM Advocate v Wilson*, 1984 S.L.T. 117, per Lord McDonald at 120.

[107] *Bett v Hamilton*, 1997 S.C.C.R. 621.

[108] *HM Advocate v Wilson*, 1984 S.L.T. 117 at 119, column 2.

[109] *HM Advocate v Wilson*, 1984 S.L.T. 117 at 121, column 1.

[110] *HM Advocate v Wilson*, 1984 S.L.T. 117 at 122, column 1.

"if the infliction of damage is an essential element of the crime then the absence of such damage takes the actings, however reprehensible, out of the category of criminality . . . The distinction may seem narrow and artificial but it is nevertheless a distinction which in my opinion the law has made."

A dissenting judgment, however, can have no bearing on the outcome of the case—which is that a new form of malicious mischief has been conceived by the majority in *Wilson*. It differs from "riotous and wilful mischief" in that no violence or tumult need be shown; and it differs from "traditional malicious mischief" in that no physical damage to property need be caused.

Mens rea

It is as yet not entirely clear whether this new form of the crime **11–22** can be committed recklessly. Although the indictment certainly referred to "wilfully, recklessly and maliciously" activating the emergency stop-button, Lord Justice-Clerk Wheatley's opinion[111] refers to the deliberate nature of the initial act, and to the Crown's proper concession that, "consequential injury has to be intended", as also elsewhere to the libel's being, "habile to carry the inference that the initial positive, wilful, reckless and malicious act was intended to harm the employer by causing patrimonial injury." This is admittedly rather confusing[112] and scarcely settles the matter.

"STEWART" MALICIOUS MISCHIEF

Lord Stewart's interesting dissenting opinion in *HM Advocate v* **11–23** *Wilson*[113] contains the following passage:

"The term [i.e. malicious mischief] also includes maliciously placing any obstruction on a railway or wilfully and recklessly doing so in a manner calculated to obstruct [this being a quotation from Macdonald, *Criminal Law*, 5th edn, p.84] (see *Miller* and *Murdoch*). Actual damage to property may not be necessary if the malicious act is clearly intended to cause such damage."[114]

As stated above at para.11–21, the content of a dissenting judgment can hardly be taken as a statement of law; but since Lord

---

[111] *HM Advocate v Wilson*, 1984 S.L.T. 117 at 119, column 2.
[112] See also Lord McDonald's opinion at 120, column 2 to 121, column 1.
[113] *HM Advocate v Wilson*, 1984 S.L.T. 117 at 121–122.
[114] *HM Advocate v Wilson*, 1984 S.L.T. 117 at 122, column 1.

Stewart here envisages a form of malicious mischief without physical damage (apparently contrary to his own view of the crime) and refers for support to two nineteenth-century cases, his views merit some consideration.

11–24   Of the two cases to which Lord Stewart referred, only that of *David Miller*[115] is truly relevant. There the accused placed a stone on the rails of a railway line at a time when he knew a train carrying passengers was due. In fact, the danger of damage to the train and of injury to passengers was averted, since some unknown third party removed the stone before the train could make contact with it.[116] Miller pled guilty to a charge at common law of:

> "Wilfully, maliciously and unlawfully placing [that stone] . . . in a manner calculated and intended to obstruct such train and carriages and to endanger the lives and safety of the passengers and others travelling thereby."

If this was genuinely an instance of malicious mischief, then, since the case has never been overruled or questioned, it was understandable that Lord Stewart should wish to consider it along with his account of the crime. But the case contains no discussion of malicious mischief at all. Nor does the reporter (Arkley) refer to it, or index it as an example of such a crime. Indeed, it seems closer to the crime of endangering the lieges[117] than to malicious mischief.

11–25   In short, it is submitted that *Miller* does not disclose an exceptional form of malicious mischief at all. Rather at best it is, or would now be treated as, an example of attempted "traditional malicious mischief"—distinguishable from the completed crime by the very fact that no damage transpired. It seems to follow then that conduct which does not result in actual damage and which is not accompanied by violence and tumult or consequential loss cannot amount to the completed crime of malicious mischief, no matter how clear the intention to cause physical damage may appear to be. If this is correct, then the statutory form of charge in Sch.5 of the Criminal Procedure (Scotland) Act 1995—"You did maliciously place a block of wood on the railway line and attempt to obstruct a train"—may simply be an example of attempted malicious mischief, or, if not that, then an example of an attempt to commit a distinct crime of obstruction.

---

[115] *David Miller* (1848) Ark. 525.
[116] *cf. John E. Murdoch* (1849) J. Shaw 229, where a similarly placed stone was not removed and much actual damage ensued.
[117] See above, para.9–28.

3. VANDALISM

A statutory crime with a specification similar to that of "traditional **11–26** malicious mischief" was created in 1980,[118] but now appears in s.52 of the Criminal Law (Consolidation) (Scotland) Act 1995. In terms of that section:

> "any person who, without reasonable excuse, wilfully or recklessly destroys or damages any property belonging to another shall be guilty of the crime of vandalism."

This offence is plainly close to "traditional malicious mischief" in that it insists that there be actual damage caused to property and specifies that the *mens rea* required may be either wilfulness or recklessness. But there are some differences too. The Appeal Court, for example, in *Black v Allan*[119] emphasised that the statutory offence was not a mere echo of malicious mischief, but a separate crime in its own right. In particular, where recklessness is advanced as the appropriate form of *mens rea*, *Black v Allan* holds that part (at least) of the test for that in *Allan v Patterson*[120] is to be applied. Consequently, where one youth jumped on another's back in the course of horseplay in a public street and was somehow thrown or shrugged-off into a nearby glass windowpane (which broke), it was wrong for justices of the peace in a district court to conclude that there had been recklessness simply because there was always some danger of breakage when youths "fooled around" in such ways. What the justices should have asked themselves was whether the actions of the accused created such an obvious and material risk of damage to the window as to be considered reckless.[121]

Vandalism also differs from its common law equivalent in that **11–27** the damage or destruction must be, "without reasonable excuse." It will be necessary, therefore, for the Crown to show that what the accused did was without such excuse—not something which can be affirmatively stated in relation to traditional malicious mischief. What amounts to a reasonable excuse will depend on the facts and circumstances of each case.[122] In *MacDougall v Yuk-Sun Ho*,[123] for example, in immediate response to the breaking of a shop window by an unknown passer-by, the shop proprietor rushed into the street and damaged the windscreen of a car in which he erroneously supposed the culprit to be about to effect his escape:

---

[118] Criminal Justice (Scotland) Act 1980 s.78(1).
[119] *Black v Allan*, 1985 S.C.C.R. 11 at 12–13.
[120] *Allan v Patterson*, 1980 J.C. 57; see above, para.3–31.
[121] It has, of course, not been determined whether the *Allan v Patterson* notion of recklessness (or any part of it) is applicable to "traditional malicious mischief."
[122] See *John v Donnelly*, 1999 S.C.C.R. 802 at 805C.
[123] *MacDougall v Yuk-Sun Ho*, 1985 S.C.C.R. 199.

this was held to be a reasonable excuse in the given circumstances.[124] On the other hand, it has been decided that a sincerely held, "belief in the illegality of nuclear weapons" and anxiety, "at their potential appalling effects" did not amount to a reasonable excuse, where the accused had, "quite deliberately and without any immediate stimulus" damaged the perimeter fence at a naval depot where submarines capable of carrying such weapons were based.[125]

Maximum penalties, as between malicious mischief and vandalism, are also different. As usual, conviction of the common law crime exposes the accused to the maximum range which the trial court possesses (see Appendix D); but the statutory offence[126] carries a maximum fine of level 3 on the standard scale (see Appendix C) or a maximum prison sentence of 60 days, or both of these, in a district or J.P. court, and maxima of the "prescribed sum" (see Appendix C) and/or three months (six months for a second or subsequent conviction) in a sheriff court. In addition, summary procedure is mandatory for vandalism whereas malicious mischief in its common law manifestations can be, and often is, taken on indictment.

4. FIRE-RAISING

Introduction

11–28   In essence, the crime of fire-raising involves the intentional or reckless damaging or destroying of corporeal property belonging to another without his consent or permission. As such, it is simply a serious form of "traditional malicious mischief" where the damage or destruction is achieved in a specific way.[127] In modern times, therefore, there is probably little justification for treating fire-raising as a separate common law crime; but it does in fact continue to be so treated.[128] In fact, however, there are two *separate* fire-raising offences. These are referred to as "wilful fire-raising" and "culpable and reckless fire-raising",[129] and are distinguished by their differing *mens rea* requirements—of "intention" in the former and "recklessness" in the latter. As there is no statutory or common law rule permitting a conviction for culpable

---

[124] *cf. Murray v O'Brien*, 1994 S.L.T. 1051, where the court held that a district court had not been wrong to decide that there was no reasonable excuse in circumstances which *ex facie* were not too dissimilar to those in *MacDougall v Yuk-Sun Ho*, 1985 S.C.C.R. 199.
[125] *John v Donnelly*, 1999 S.C.C.R. 802 at 805B–D.
[126] See the Criminal Law (Consolidation) (Scotland) Act 1995 s.52(3).
[127] See *John Mackirdy* (1856) 2 Irv. 474, per Lord Justice-Clerk Hope at 475.
[128] See, e.g. *Carr v HM Advocate* 1995 S.L.T. 800; *Byrne v HM Advocate (No.2)*, 2000 S.C.C.R. 77.
[129] *Byrne v HM Advocate (No.2)*, 2000 S.C.C.R. 77 (court of five judges), opinion of the court, at 91G.

and reckless fire-raising to be returned on a charge which libelled only wilful fire-raising, it follows that prosecutors often charge both offences in the alternative, so that, in effect and depending on the evidence, both forms of *mens rea* can be considered by the court or jury.[130] The rationale advanced in *Byrne v HM Advocate (No.2)*[131] for having two separate offences is that, "the degree of blameworthiness will be relevant to penalty"—thus confirming that prima facie intentionally caused harm is more deserving of punishment than harm effected by recklessness. For the avoidance of doubt, it must be noted that, whatever may have been the law in the past, the two fire-raising offences apply to the setting of fire to *any* type of corporeal property.[132]

WILFUL FIRE-RAISING

This may be defined as the intentional setting fire to corporeal **11–29** property owned by another without his permission. Under s.5(4) of the Criminal Procedure (Scotland) Act 1995, it is competent to try wilful fire-raisings summarily—but not in a district or J.P. court.[133] Consequently, perhaps, under s.52(2) of the Criminal Law (Consolidation) (Scotland) Act 1995, it is declared incompetent, "to charge acts which constitute the offence of wilful fire-raising as vandalism."[134]

Actus reus

It is sufficient if the property has been burnt to any degree, no **11–30** matter how small.[135] Provided the fire has "taken effect", as nineteenth-century indictments put it,[136] then the *actus reus* of the crime is complete, even if the fire is extinguished by a "well disposed person" or of its own accord before any great damage has been done.[137] The property set on fire must, however, belong to

---

[130] *Byrne v HM Advocate (No.2)*, 2000 S.C.C.R. 77, opinion of the court at 92B–C; *cf.* malicious mischief, which is *one* offence with two alternative forms of *mens rea*.

[131] *Byrne v HM Advocate (No.2)*, 2000 S.C.C.R. 77 at 92B.

[132] *Byrne v HM Advocate (No.2)*, 2000 S.C.C.R. 77 at 92A, B. For an account of the complexities of the law prior to the decision in the leading case of *Byrne*, see, e.g. the second edition of this book (Edinburgh: W. Green, 1996), at paras 11–28 *et seq*. See also J. Chalmers, "Fireraising: From the Ashes?", 2000 S.L.T. (News) 57, which also contains a critique of *Byrne*.

[133] Criminal Procedure (Scotland) Act 1995 s.7(8)(b)(i), as modified by the Criminal Proceedings etc. (Reform) (Scotland) Act 2007 (asp 6) Sch.1 para.9(4). The exclusion extends to attempted wilful fire-raising.

[134] This rule also applies, however, to the sheriff court.

[135] Alison, *Principles*, i, 429; *John Arthur* (1836) 1 Swin. 124, per Lord Justice-Clerk Boyle at 152.

[136] See Hume, *Commentaries*, i, 127–128.

[137] See, e.g. *John Arthur* (1836) 1 Swin. 124, where due to the prompt action of a passer-by, a door was burnt only to the extent of one twentieth of an inch, according at least to the accused's counsel at 149; see also *Peter Grieve* (1866) 5 Irv. 263.

another[138]; and in one nineteenth-century case, it was declared that an indictment was defective in that it failed to state that the shop set on fire was the property of someone other than the accused, notwithstanding that he had been designed as a mere tenant of the premises.[139] It is clear, therefore, that a tenant who sets fire to premises let to him has fulfilled the *actus reus* of the crime.[140] Curiously, the older text-writers state that although it is generally not criminal for an owner of property to set fire to it, since, of course, it is his own, it may be "wilful fire-raising" for him to do so if that property has been let to a tenant or is subject to a liferent interest at the time.[141] It is, thus, not sufficiently his own, if subject to a tenancy; yet not sufficiently the tenant's own, if the tenant sets fire to it. According to Alison[142] it is not the existence of the tenancy or liferent right that matters, but rather whether the tenant or liferenter has taken occupancy or possession. This may be a just way of looking at these complex cases since it focuses attention on the danger to property or persons rather than on ownership; but there is no other warrant for it[143] and it strays rather far from the concept of "belonging to another."

Mens rea

11–31   The fire must be raised "wilfully", and Hume[144] leaves his reader in no doubt that that means, "with a purpose to destroy the thing to which it is applied." Provided that there is such a purpose, then setting fire to something other than the property meant to be burned, in the knowledge that the fire will naturally and inescapably spread to that property, is probably sufficient.[145] Thus, for example, to set fire to a pile of furnishings (moveable property) within a house, meaning and expecting it to take effect on the fabric of the house itself, will be enough for wilful fire-raising of that house (as well as of the original moveables) if the house or any of its fixtures is actually burnt to any degree. Even setting fire to one's own property will suffice if the fire spreads to a neighbour's property—provided that the spreading of fire to his property had been one's intention all along.

11–32   The *mens rea* of "wilful fire-raising" is thus intention—actual intention to damage or destroy the property burned.[146] Hume,[147] however, went further than that and considered a form of transferred *mens rea* to be applicable. If a person, for example, set fire

---

[138] Hume, *Commentaries*, i, 132–133.
[139] *John Mackirdy* (1856) 2 Irv. 474.
[140] Hume, *Commentaries*, i, 132; *Margaret Drysdale* (1826) Alison, *Principles*, i, 435.
[141] Hume, *Commentaries*, i, 133; Alison, *Principles*, i, 437; *Walter Buchanan* (1728) Hume, *Commentaries*, i, 133.
[142] Alison, *Principles*, i, 437.
[143] *cf*. Hume, *Commentaries*, i, 133.
[144] Hume, *Commentaries*, i, 128.
[145] Hume, *Commentaries*, i, 129–130.
[146] *Byrne v HM Advocate (No.2)*, 2000 S.C.C.R. 77, opinion of the court at 92A.
[147] Hume, *Commentaries*, i, 130.

to property A owned by another, intending to destroy or damage A only, but the fire spread to property B also owned by that other, then that person would be guilty of wilful fire-raising in respect of B, all other things being equal, provided that the spread of the fire to B was,

> "not of quite a fortuitous and extraordinary nature, but such as might naturally and not improbably ensue . . . What has ensued is a mischief, though higher, of the very same sort as that which he intended, and so likely to happen, that when he did the one, he must have been utterly indifferent whether this damage also should or should not ensue".[148]

Gordon[149] was of the opinion that Scots law did not accept the concept of transferred *mens rea*, at all; but, since the airing of that opinion in 1978, the Appeal Court accepted that that concept does apply to assault (see above, para.3–37). It was possible, therefore, that it might also apply to "wilful fire-raising". The Appeal Court has subsequently determined, however, that that is not so. In *Blane v HM Advocate*,[150] the accused set fire to a quilt in the room he occupied in a hostel. His intention was to create smoke so that he could inhale the same and thus commit suicide. He did not intend that flames should be caused, and did not intend, or apparently even foresee, that any fire so created should, or might, spread to the hostel building itself. In the event, fire did take hold on the building—some £15,000 worth of damage being caused. The accused was charged with wilful fire-raising in relation to the bedding *and* the premises and was convicted (the sheriff having directed the jury in accordance with Hume's notion of transferred intent). On appeal, the court considered that an intention, directly or indirectly, to set fire to the hostel building was essential for conviction in respect of the building itself, and that a fulfilled intention to set fire only to moveable property which just happened in turn to set fire to the building was insufficient.

Intention to set fire to the property described in the complaint or **11–33** indictment may, of course, be inferred from the evidence and in particular from the accused's conduct.[151] In *Blane v HM Advocate*,[152] however, it was suggested that the necessary intention for wilful fire-raising of a hostel building might be inferred if the accused had deliberately set fire to the furnishings in his room in such a way as to demonstrate his utter indifference whether the fire

---

[148] Hume, *Commentaries*, i, 130.

[149] Gordon, *Criminal Law*, 2nd edn, para.22–26.

[150] *Blane v HM Advocate*, 1991 S.C.C.R. 576; see also *Byrne v HM Advocate (No.2)*, 2000 S.C.C.R. 77, opinion of the court at 90A.

[151] *Byrne v HM Advocate (No.2)*, 2000 S.C.C.R. 77, opinion of the court at 90G–91A.

[152] *Blane v HM Advocate*, 1991 S.C.C.R. 576.

might spread to the building itself or not. This suggestion, that intention might be inferred from recklessness,[153] is unsound in principle and was emphatically rejected by a full bench in *Byrne v HM Advocate (No.2)*.[154] Consequently, the law is that no form of recklessness can be treated as equivalent to, or provide a basis for inferring, the necessary intent.[155]

11–34   Motive is, as usual, of no moment in ascertaining the *mens rea* for the crime.[156] If one intended to burn part of a house, such as a door, in order to obtain unauthorised entrance or exit, then the *mens rea* for wilful fire-raising would be present whatever was the ulterior reason for so intending. In *Jean Gordon or Bryan*[157] Lord Mackenzie expressed great doubt as to whether escapees from a prison at Banff could be guilty of wilful fire-raising by burning a hole in the prison door to gain their liberty. His view appears to have been that their intention was to escape and not to harm the prison itself. But if they could not effect their escape other than by burning the prison door, then surely they must have intended to damage that part of the prison by fire? In any event, Lord Mackenzie's views are obiter, since the charge was one of prison-breaking aggravated by setting fire to the doors and other parts of Banff Prison, and further are contrary to Hume's opinion, namely that, "it does not mend the case for the pannels, that this act [burning doors and other parts of a gaol] has been subservient to the other, and also felonious offence of mobbing, breaking gaol, and setting prisoners at large."[158]

CULPABLE AND RECKLESS FIRE-RAISING

11–35 Both Hume and Alison[159] clearly advert to such a crime. Alison in particular states[160] that,

> "if the burning the pannel's own house be attended with obvious risk to adjoining tenements, and one of them be actually burned in consequence, the guilty party, as for *culpable and reckless fire-raising*, is amenable to a severe punishment."

And the existence of this crime—as one separate from wilful fire-raising—has been affirmed by a full bench in *Byrne v HM Advocate*

---

[153] See also *Carr v HM Advocate*, 1995 S.L.T. 800.
[154] *Byrne v HM Advocate (No.2)*, 2000 S.C.C.R. 77, opinion of the court at 90C–91D.
[155] *Byrne v HM Advocate (No.2)*, 2000 S.C.C.R. 77 at 92A.
[156] See *Robert Smillie* (1883) 5 Coup. 287, per Lord Young at 290.
[157] *Jean Gordon or Bryan* (1841) 2 Swin. 545 at 546–547.
[158] Hume, *Commentaries*, i, 131.
[159] Hume, *Commentaries*, i, 128 and Alison, *Principles*, i, 433.
[160] Alison, *Principles*, i, 438.

(No.2).[161] The *actus reus* is similar to that of wilful fire-raising.[162] If fire in fact takes effect on the property of another, and it is causally related to an act on the part of the accused, then that is sufficient.

Mens rea

This offence is readily distinguishable from wilful fire-raising in **11–36** terms of the *mens rea* requirement. Wilful fire-raising cannot be committed recklessly; and the sole issue here is what recklessly means in this context. In *Robert Smillie*[163] Lord Young opined: "If a man, while engaged in some illegal act, raises a fire, he is guilty of the crime of wicked, culpable, and reckless fire-raisings." The truth of that statement was, however, questionable at the time of its utterance; if it had correctly reflected the law, it would have meant, for example, that a careless or unlucky thief would automatically have been guilty of reckless fire-raising if he had happened to cause a fire whilst engaged in the act of stealing property. That such automatic guilt was (and is) frowned upon in Scots law seemed apparent from the case of *James Stewart and John Walsh*.[164] There, the accused were stealing whisky from a cask on a railway waggon, and one of them "allowed" his lamp to come into contact with the spirit (or the fumes emanating from it), and thus caused a fire which destroyed the whisky, two casks, a chest of tea, six chairs and the railway waggon itself. There was no question of his having intentionally set fire to those items of property, of course; but because of grave doubts voiced by the court that he had scarcely done so recklessly either (in spite of having been engaged in an "illegal act" at the time) the Solicitor-General was compelled to withdraw the charge of reckless fire-raising. Any lingering doubts as to what was determined in that case have been resolved, however, by the more modern decision in *McCue v Currie*.[165] There, the appellant had been convicted of culpable and reckless fire-raising in circumstances where he had broken into a caravan in order to commit theft. He had been using a cigarette lighter to facilitate his search for goods to remove; that lighter had "burst in his hand", been dropped, and thus caused the caravan to catch fire. The appellant knew that a conflagration had been begun; nevertheless, he left the scene without making any attempt to extinguish the blaze or summon assistance to that end. His conviction was quashed by the High Court on appeal—the court's opinion including the observation that what Lord Young had said in *Smillie* (quoted above) had not been followed, had been subject to criticism, and (inferentially) should not be applied or taken to

[161] *Byrne v HM Advocate (No.2)*, 2000 S.C.C.R. 77.
[162] See above, para.11–30.
[163] *Robert Smillie* (1883) 5 Coup. 287 at 291.
[164] *James Stewart and John Walsh* (1856) 2 Irv. 359.
[165] *McCue v Currie*, 2004 S.C.C.R. 200.

represent the law.[166] The question remained, of course, whether, apart from that consideration, the appellant had shown the necessary "recklessness" to be convicted of the crime charged: but on the version of the facts accepted by the lower court, it was clear that the conflagration had occurred as a result of the accidental dropping of the lighter. The court was, therefore, of the opinion,

> "that fire raising which is merely accidental does not demonstrate the necessary mens rea and is not a crime, and cannot become so on account of subsequent behaviour on the part of the person concerned."[167]

11-37	There have, until recently, been few judicial pronouncements on the meaning of recklessness in this form of fire-raising. In *George MacBean*, Lord Justice-Clerk Hope said[168] that it would be sufficient if a person set a house on fire "in such a state of reckless excitement, as not to know or care what he was doing, but who had no deliberate intention of setting fire to the house." It now seems that that is the correct approach, and that, for example, directing a jury that the test for recklessness in such a crime can be taken from the road traffic case of *Allan v Patterson*[169] would be wrong. In *Thomson v HM Advocate*,[170] therefore, Lord Justice-Clerk Ross said this:

> "[I]n a case of fire raising it is not the manner of doing an act which would otherwise be lawful which is in issue [as in *reckless* driving], but the question whether the accused had the mens rea for the commission of the crime. It would have been appropriate for the sheriff therefore to confine his definition to the question whether the accused's actions showed a complete disregard for any dangers which might result from what he was doing and in particular of the fire taking effect on the premises."[171]

---

[166] *McCue v Currie*, 2004 S.C.C.R. 200 at 206F, para.22.

[167] *McCue v Currie*, 2004 S.C.C.R. 200 at 207D, para.25. The court did opine, however, at 207E, para.26, that there might be a case for "enacting a new crime . . . of culpably failing to take appropriate steps after a situation of danger to persons or property has arisen as a result of a person's actings."

[168] *George MacBean* (1847) Ark. 262 at 263.

[169] *Allan v Patterson*, 1980 J.C. 57 (a case of "reckless" driving in terms of the law then current).

[170] *Thomson v HM Advocate*, 1995 S.L.T. 827 at 829E (quoting from the opinion of the Lord Justice General in *Carr v HM Advocate*, 1995 S.L.T. 800).

[171] This accords (*mutatis mutandis*) only with the last part of the test for recklessness given in *Allan v Patterson*, 1980 J.C. 57, per Lord Justice-General Emslie at 60.

In so quoting, Lord Ross was agreeing entirely with the view expressed by Lord Justice-General Hope in *Carr v HM Advocate*[172]; and the correctness of these views has been underlined in the opinion of the full bench in *Byrne v HM Advocate (No.2)*.[173] It must be borne in mind, however, that the required recklessness must be, "determined by reference to the act of starting the fire and not by reference to something which took place thereafter."[174]

---

[172] *Carr v HM Advocate*, 1995 S.L.T. 800 at 803K–L. See also 803L–804A, where Lord Hope opined that it was wrong for the sheriff in that case to have told the jury that a *high degree* of recklessness was what was required. As in other crimes where recklessness was sufficient for the *mens rea* element, the true contrast was a simple one—between carelessness on the one hand and recklessness on the other.

[173] *Byrne v HM Advocate (No.2)*, 2000 S.C.C.R. 77 at 91B.

[174] *McCue v Currie*, 2004 S.C.C.R. 200, opinion of the court at 207A, para.23. It might be noted that the court observed at 206C, para.20, "that a distinction can be drawn between [the carrying of] a lit, scrunched up, roll of paper [as in *Carr v HM Advocate*, 1994 S.C.C.R. 521] which must be inherently dangerous and a lit cigarette lighter [as in *McCue*] which, barring an accident, is reasonably safe and easily extinguishable."

CHAPTER 12

CRIMES RELATING TO PUBLIC ORDER AND MORALITY

General introduction

12–01   This chapter introduces the best known crimes which attempt either to prevent disorder in the community or to uphold current notions of acceptability in individual behaviour. It must be noted at the outset that it has never been easy to justify all of the offences which presently fall within such parameters. Whilst public disorder can fairly easily be seen as a "harm" which requires discouragement (although it may sometimes be a somewhat vague "harm" against the community in general rather than particular individuals), it is much more difficult to justify the compelling of persons to behave, or not to behave, in specified ways because of the annoyance, nuisance or distress otherwise caused to other persons. One difficulty here is that individuals vary enormously in their sensitivity to the behaviour of others. It is far from easy, therefore, to establish what is acceptable and what is not acceptable, in the sense of being offensive, to the community in general. This is particularly so in sexual or quasi-sexual matters, where the identification of what is indecent or obscene is a difficult issue. In Scotland hitherto, such identification has usually been left to the good sense of the judge or jury, and little attempt has been made to specify in advance what is indecent or obscene as a matter of law. Arguably such appeal to good sense is the best method of resolving moral dilemmas affecting the common law, and of reflecting sufficient standards of acceptability. Also of importance, or course, is the extent to which some of the crimes dealt with below comply with the rights and fundamental freedoms under the European Convention on Human Rights as these have been brought into the law by the Human Rights Act 1998.[1] Breach of the peace, for example, has been found to comply with Art.7(1) of the Convention, provided that that offence is constrained in ways set out in certain authoritative dicta.[2]

---

[1] See Human Rights Act 1998 Sch.1.
[2] See below, para.12–11 *et seq*.

Where the moral issue at stake is a much more "public" one involving, for example, one's duty to tell the truth (perjury) or to refrain from betraying the security of one's country (treason), then some form of identifiable "harm" is more readily apparent.

1. Crimes Relative to Public Order

Mobbing

Definition of mobbing

The common law crime of mobbing is committed when persons **12–02** combine together to achieve a commonly-shared purpose by violence or intimidation (that is, by unlawful or criminal means), where their combined conduct causes alarm to the community and disturbance of the public peace. Everyone in a crowd or mob who, by his presence and behaviour, adopts and seeks to promote such a common purpose is guilty of this crime. In the very full indictments found in nineteenth-century case reports, accused persons (usually a mere fraction of the total mob) were always charged as having been part of a riotous and disorderly crowd which, acting of common purpose, did various alarming and disorderly things in implementation of that purpose. Thus was their guilt to be brought home; they had been part of a larger design—assisting, aiding and abetting it by their culpable presence.[3] This indeed is essentially still the way in which the crime is charged.[4] In addition to their being guilty of mobbing, the accused could also (and still can) be guilty of particular crimes, if such had been committed by individual members of the mob other than themselves—provided that such particular crimes were genuinely foreseeable, given the commonly-shared purpose and its method of implementation.[5] This, however, might be a very serious business if, say, someone had been killed as a result of the mob's conduct. Whereas mobbing in the nineteenth century was not itself a capital crime,[6] murder certainly was, even for one found guilty art and part.[7] Although murder is no longer, of course, a capital-punishment offence it is still today a serious matter for those accused of mobbing to face

---

[3] See, e.g. *James Cairns* (1837) 1 Swin. 597 at 597–600; *Daniel Blair* (1868) 1 Coup. 168 at 169–171.

[4] See the Criminal Procedure (Scotland) Act 1995 Sch.2 and below, para.12–06, fn.25; see also the indictments in (a) *Kilpatrick v HM Advocate*, 1992 J.C. 120, as quoted by Lord Justice-General Hope at 122, (b) *Coleman v HM Advocate*, 1999 S.C.C.R. 87, and *Weir v HM Advocate*, 2007 S.C.C.R. 59, as quoted by Lord Osborne at 62D–E, para.1.

[5] See, e.g. *Myles Martin* (1886) 1 White 297, per Lord Mure's charge to the jury at 304–306.

[6] Hume, *Commentaries*, i, 426.

[7] See, e.g. *William Gibson* (1842) 1 Broun 485.

the prospect of conviction for murder or other offences which they did not personally commit; but that is certainly still the law.[8] Modern charges tend to be so drawn that particular offences can be brought home to the accused either as members of the mob or as individuals (if evidence exists that they were individually responsible for committing them).[9]

Actus reus of mobbing

12–03   There must be a number of persons present before a "mob" can be constituted. It is uncertain, however, what the minimum acceptable number might be. Hume[10] unhelpfully refers to the necessity of there being "a great host or multitude", whereas Alison[11] adopts the number "12" from the Riot Act 1714.[12] In terms of reported cases, the size (often estimated) of a mob has varied from some 1,300[13] to eight[14]; and in *Sloan v MacMillan* Lord Salvesen hinted[15] that five might be too few. Clearly, however, the fewer the number involved, the more likely it is that all can be identified and charged directly with their individual offences, thus rendering resort to "mobbing" unnecessary.[16] It may be of interest here that the analogous English offence called "riot" requires a minimum of 12 persons.[17]

Commonly-shared purpose

12–04   There must be a common purpose. That, however, is hardly the most important issue in rendering a crowd's activities criminal, since a common purpose may well be a quite lawful one, as where persons gather to greet the return of a successful sporting team or to protest in a silent and peaceful manner over the imposition of some disliked fiscal measure. The crux of the matter is, therefore,

---

[8] See, e.g. *Hancock v HM Advocate*, 1981 J.C. 74; *Coleman v HM Advocate*, 1999 S.C.C.R. 87.
[9] See *Kilpatrick v HM Advocate*, 1992 J.C. 120, Lord Justice-General Hope at 125–126; *Coleman v HM Advocate*, 1999 S.C.C.R. 87.
[10] Hume, *Commentaries*, i, 416.
[11] Alison, *Principles*, i, 510.
[12] Now repealed; see the Statute Law (Repeals) Act 1973 s.1(1) and Sch.1 Pt V.
[13] *John G Robertson* (1842) 1 Broun 152.
[14] *Hancock v HM Advocate*, 1981 J.C. 74
[15] *Sloan v MacMillan*, 1922 J.C. 1 at 7.
[16] It has been held competent for the Crown, where there are large numbers involved, to raise separate indictments against groups of the accused: see *Weir v HM Advocate*, 2007 S.C.C.R. 59 (29 accused in all): it was also opined there (at 68F, para.21) that the court had no power to conjoin separate indictments.
[17] Public Order Act 1986 s.1.

that the common purpose itself should be a violent and mischievous one[18] or, if more peaceful in concept, should be implemented in a violent or intimidatory way.[19] It certainly does not
matter that the crowd considered that it was acting in vindication
of some supposed public or legal right in, say, preventing fish being
landed on a Sunday[20] or pulling down a wall thought to have been
erected over a public footpath.[21] If there is believed to be
infringement of a legal right, then the remedy of those disaffected
is clear. They must resort to the civil courts. If they choose not to
do so, but resort to main force and violence, that will certainly be
construed as an appropriate common purpose for mobbing.[22]

Although it is natural to think of a common purpose as **12–05**
something planned and known well in advance of the actual
incidents constituting mobbing, this need not be so. Provided that
such a purpose can be shown, then it is of no moment whether it
was conceived in advance or arose spontaneously at the relevant
time.[23] In *George Smith*,[24] for example, a large crowd assembled to
communicate to the magistrates of Glasgow their demands for
food, money and work. There seemed to be no pre-arranged plan
to do anything beyond that but, following dissatisfaction with the
magistrates' response to their demands, the crowd instantly became
a mob by forming, and implementing, there and then a purpose to
steal and rob.

Modern indictments and complaints are not, it seems, statutorily **12–06**
required to specify the exact common purpose.[25] But failure by the
Crown to show a specific common purpose or to prove facts from
which one might be inferred will inevitably spell the end of any
prosecution for mobbing.[26] Certainly, proof of a series of random

---

[18] See, e.g. the violent obstruction of officers of law in the execution of their duty in
Alexander McLean (1886) 1 White 232.

[19] e.g. the fraudulent intimidation used by the "mob" to persuade voluntary workers
in a coal mine to cease pumping operations during an industrial dispute—*Sloan v
MacMillan*, 1922 J.C. 1; the violence used by those intent on upholding the
Sabbath as a day of rest in *Alexander Gollan* (1883) 5 Coup. 317.

[20] *Alexander Gollan* (1883) 5 Coup. 317.

[21] *Alexander Macphie* (1823) Alison, *Principles*, i, 512, where the crowd's belief that
such a wall had been erected in obstruction of a public right of way was later
affirmed as correct by the jury court (civil) and the House of Lords.

[22] See, e.g. *Thomas Wild* (1854) 1 Irv. 552, per Lord Cowan's charge to the jury at
558.

[23] Alison, *Principles*, i, 513.

[24] *George Smith* (1848) Ark. 473.

[25] See the Criminal Procedure (Scotland) Act 1995, where the appropriate style in
Sch.2 is: "You formed part of a riotous mob, which, acting of common purpose,
obstructed A.B., C.D., and E.F., constables of the Northern constabulary on duty,
and assaulted them, and forcibly took two persons whom they had arrested from
their custody." It falls to be decided whether it accords with Convention rights
not to be more specific than the foregoing style requires: *cf. Smith (Pamela) v
Donnelly*, 2001 S.C.C.R. 800 at 808D, para.20—where the court commented on
the statutory style for breach of the peace.

[26] *Francis Docherty* (1841) 2 Swin. 635; *Hancock v HM Advocate*, 1981 J.C. 74;
Kilpatrick v HM Advocate, 1992 J.C. 120.

acts of violence and depredation, carried out by varying sets of persons who alighted from time to time from a transit van at different locations in a Scottish town, was held insufficient to raise an inference as to any common purpose at all.[27]

Alarm and disturbance

12–07   It also seems essential to this crime that the conduct of the mob should cause public alarm and disturbance.[28] Hume suggests too[29] that the level of such disturbance should be "significant", which, it is thought must be correct. In *John G. Robertson*, Lord Justice-Clerk Hope stated[30]:

> "If, as in this case, a crowd collect and act together, with intent to oppose the entrance of a Presbytery into a church where duty is to be performed, and oppose such entry by dense numbers, and by refusing to move, though there were no noise nor other acts,—that would be Mobbing . . .".

Were this dictum to be received as law, then peaceful protestors, who sit down in a road in order to block the entrance of traffic to some premises or other, would be guilty of mobbing for doing no more than that—which seems wholly inappropriate.[31] Indeed, in *Robertson*, there was substantial violence, damage and disturbance, such that Lord Justice-Clerk Hope's remarks are no more than obiter dicta. As such, they should not be followed. That is not to suggest, of course, that a crowd of persons could not cause alarm by intimidatory behaviour. But if that were claimed, much would depend on what was done or said.[32]

Mere presence in a mob

12–08   It is possible to find some judicial opinions which suggest that those who follow a crowd out of idle curiosity may be considered part of that crowd by their very presence there. Such persons might then become guilty of mobbing, and of anything else the crowd cares to do in pursuance of its common design, by presence alone, or rather by failing to remove themselves from that crowd once its

---

[27] *Hancock v HM Advocate*, 1981 J.C. 74.
[28] Hume, *Commentaries*, i, 416.
[29] Hume, *Commentaries*, i, 419–420.
[30] *John G. Robertson* (1842) 1 Broun 152 at 192.
[31] It may also conflict with the "Right of freedom of expression" and the "Right of freedom of assembly and association", as set out in Arts 10 and 11 of the European Convention on Human Rights. (See the Human Rights Act 1998 Sch.1.)
[32] See, e.g. *Sloan v MacMillan*, 1922 J.C. 1, where the mob claimed (falsely) that there were hundreds of disaffected, striking miners outside the pit, whose anger it would be difficult to contain if those working in the mine itself did not instantly cease their labours.

common purpose of violence or intimidation had become clear.[33] The overwhelming preponderance of authority, however, shows that such fears are groundless; and it is thought that Lord Young was correct in *John Nicolson*,[34] when he said to the jury:

> "If the prisoners, or any of them, were there from idle curiosity, that would not make him or them one of the mob. He would have to take the consequences, and when violence is used to disperse a mob, it frequently happens that those present out of curiosity suffer from that violence. But if in point of fact the prisoners were there not as participants in the conflict, not assenting to it, and not aiding it, they would not be guilty of mobbing . . . although they were physically present."[35]

Even where there is evidence that a person was present in a mob, his presence there has to be shown to be a "consenting or a supporting" one[36] (in the sense that he countenances and encourages the common purpose of the mob) before he can be eligible for conviction of mobbing. And, where it is proved that some specific crime (such as murder) was committed by the mob or specific members of it, it will have to be shown not only that that common purpose included a murderous purpose and that that particular purpose had been appreciated and espoused by a particular accused (who did not himself kill the deceased but was a member of the mob) but also that such an accused had remained a "subscribing" member of the mob whilst the killing was executed: if the Crown is unable to establish these matters in respect of any such accused, that accused may be convicted of mobbing, but not of murder via his membership of the mob.[37] He might be guilty of the murder if there was sufficient evidence that he had actually participated in the killing (with the necessary *mens rea*) as an individual or by art and part,[38] quite apart from his being a member of the mob in question.

---

[33] See *James Farquhar* (1861) 4 Irv. 28, per Lord Ardmillan at 40–41; *John G. Robertson* (1842) 1 Broun 152, per Lord Justice-Clerk Hope at 194–195.

[34] *John Nicolson* (1887) 1 White 307 at 314–315.

[35] See also Hume, *Commentaries*, i, 422; *John Urquhart* (1844) 2 Broun 13, per Lord Justice-Clerk Hope at 15; *Hancock v HM Advocate*, 1981 J.C. 74, per Lord Cameron at 83–84 and Lord Justice-General Emslie at 86; and the similar directions given to the jury by Lord McCluskey in a case of breach of the peace by a crowd of persons in *Boyle v HM Advocate*, 1993 S.L.T. 577 at 579I.

[36] See *Coleman v HM Advocate*, 1999 S.C.C.R. 87, Lord Coulsfield at 110D.

[37] This seems to be what was decided (or observed) in *Coleman v HM Advocate*, 1999 S.C.C.R. 87.

[38] See above, Ch.7, para.7–03 *et seq*.

Mens rea

12–09   None of the reported cases seems to deal with the issue of *mens rea* in mobbing; but the clear implication is that no one can be convicted of this crime unless he knew what the common purpose of the mob was, and intended to aid and abet it by whatever means he could.

Rioting

12–10   Many of the older cases refer to this crime as mobbing and rioting. But "rioting" was the general description of fighting between two or more persons[39] in breach of the public peace, and featured commonly before the inferior courts in Scotland from the seventeenth century onwards.[40] Although rioting was still being described as a viable offence in its own right as late as 1838,[41] it is now thought to be in desuetude. Particular examples of it today would be dealt with as assaults or breaches of the peace. In any event, it would be inaccurate to describe the crime currently being explored as mobbing and rioting, since fighting is very far from being an indispensable feature of it.

BREACH OF THE PEACE

Definition

12–11   The ambit of breach of the peace as a common law crime has been clarified and indeed somewhat narrowed by the decision of the Appeal Court in *Smith (Pamela) v Donnelly*.[42] Prior to that case, the offence had been very generally regarded as one applying to virtually any conduct which caused (or was reasonably likely to cause) alarm, annoyance, upset or embarrassment to another

---

[39] *Pace*, Alison, *Principles*, i, 510.
[40] See especially the Baron Court and Justice of the Peace Court records of the seventeenth and eighteenth centuries.
[41] See *John McCabe* (1838) 2 Swin. 20.
[42] *Smith v Donnelly*, 2001 S.C.C.R. 800. The essence of the offence, as clarified in *Smith*, was applied by a bench of five judges in *Jones v Carnegie; Tallents v Gallacher; Barrett v Carnegie; Carberry v Currie; Park v Frame*, 2004 S.C.C.R. 361 (see, especially, the opinion of the court at 366B–D, para.2), where one of the conjoined appeals had been concerned with an attempt (unsuccessful) to challenge the ruling in *Smith*—see the opinion of the court in *Jones* at 367C, para.5. That ruling has been upheld as compliant with Arts 5, 10 and 11 of the European Convention on Human Rights (on the matter of the admissibility of the application) by the European Court of Human Rights in *Lucas v United Kingdom* (2003) 37 E.C.H.R. CD 86, application no.39013/02 (the decision there being conveniently set out at 2004 S.C.C.R. 361, 377F–383C).

person or persons.[43] In *Smith v Donnelly*, however, the appellant argued that the offence had become so vaguely defined as to be in breach of Art.7(1) of the European Convention on Human Rights.[44] That Article, which *ex facie* makes it unlawful for a person, "to be held guilty of any criminal offence on account of an act or omission which did not constitute a criminal offence under national law . . . at the time when it was committed",[45] has been construed by the European Court of Human Rights to include the rule, "that an offence must be clearly defined in law." Further, that rule will be complied with,

> "where the individual can know from the wording of the relevant provision and, if need be, with the assistance of the courts' interpretation of it, what acts and omissions will make him liable."[46]

The Appeal Court in *Smith v Donnelly* determined that breach of the peace was capable of being defined so as to comply with Art.7(1), as so interpreted by the European Court of Human Rights. The decision of the Appeal Court concentrates, however, on the *actus reus* of the offence.

Actus reus

In *Smith v Donnelly*,[47] the Appeal Court agreed with counsel that **12–12** the essence of breach of the peace was to be discovered not from a, "close analysis of the facts of particular marginal decisions"[48] but from dicta in three authoritative cases.[49] When properly understood, these dicta generated a clear general test for conduct alleged to be sufficient for the offence: to suffice, that conduct had to be,

---

[43] See, e.g. *Dougall v Dykes* (1860) 4 Irv. 101; *Whitchurch v Millar* (1895) 2 Adam 9; *Turner v Kennedy* (1972) S.C.C.R. Supp. 30; *Montgomery v McLeod* (1977) S.C.C.R. Supp. 164; *Sinclair v Annan*, 1980 S.L.T. (Notes) 55; *Alexander v Smith*, 1984 S.L.T. 176; *Derrett v Lockhart*, 1991 S.C.C.R. 109; *Stewart v Lockhart*, 1991 S.L.T. 835; *MacDougall v Dochree*, 1992 J.C. 154; *Wyness v Lockhart*, 1992 S.C.C.R. 808; *Cameron v Normand*, 1992 S.C.C.R. 866: *cf.* now, *McMillan v Higson*, 2003 S.C.C.R. 125, where *Smith v Donnelly*, 2001 S.C.C.R. 800, was applied.

[44] See the Human Rights Act 1998 Sch.1.

[45] This is plainly not applicable to breach of the peace, which has been a known crime since at least the eighteenth century: see Hume, *Commentaries*, i, 439.

[46] *Kokkinakis v Greece* (1994) 17 E.H.R.R. 397 at 423, para.52.

[47] *Smith v Donnelly*, 2001 S.C.C.R. 800.

[48] *Smith v Donnelly*, 2001 S.C.C.R. 800 at 808B, para.19.

[49] These were, in order of priority, *Ferguson v Carnochan* (1889) 16 R (J.) 93, especially the opinion of Lord Justice-Clerk Macdonald at 94; *Young v Heatly*, 1959 J.C. 66, the opinion of Lord Justice-General Clyde at 70; and, *Raffaelli v Heatly*, 1949 J.C. 101, the opinion of Lord Justice-Clerk Thomson at 104.

"severe enough to cause alarm to ordinary people and threaten serious disturbance to the community."[50] It is plain from this case (and others)[51] that no evidence of actual alarm or disturbance is required; should there be such evidence, that will not in itself be conclusive, since the conduct in question must still meet the test set out above.[52] And that test is an objective one, since individual reactions to the behaviour of others can be highly subjective.[53] What seems to matter is the view the court takes of the ordinary (if not the reasonable) person's reaction to the conduct of the accused: should that estimated (or actual) reaction be one of annoyance, upset or mere irritation, or should the conduct be viewed as no more than inappropriate or a "breach of decorum",[54] it would be insufficient for breach of the peace.[55] The court in *Smith v Donnelly* realised that, of the many prior decisions relative to breach of the peace which existed, some would probably not have met the "conduct test" now represented as necessary for that offence to comply with Art.7(1) of the Convention; but no attempt was made to review these decisions,[56] and the impression is given that this case is intended to mark a new beginning for the offence. Hereafter, therefore: "[W]hat is required . . . is conduct which does

---

[50] *Smith v Donnelly*, 2001 S.C.C.R. 800 at 807A, para.17.

[51] See in particular *Jones v Carnegie*, 2004 S.C.C.R. 361 (court of five judges), at 368D–369E, paras 10–13, and *Dyer v Hutchison; Dyer v Bell; Dyer v Johnstone*, 2006 S.C.C.R. 377.

[52] See, e.g. *Farrell v Normand*, 1993 S.L.T. 793, where the accused's conduct, in beckoning a 10 year old girl and asking her if she would like a drink, was held not to be sufficient for breach of the peace, notwithstanding that the girl was alarmed and upset. It follows, of course, that even where there is evidence of actual alarm, that alarm must have been caused by the accused's conduct: *cf. Jones v Carnegie*, 2004 S.C.C.R. 361, opinion of the court at 376E–F, paras 47–48.

[53] See *Donaldson v Vannet*, 1998 S.C.C.R. 422 at 424B.

[54] See *Raffaelli v Heatly*, 1949 J.C. 101, Lord Justice-Clerk Thomson at 104; *cf. Allison v Higson*, 2004 S.C.C.R. 720, *HM Advocate v Greig*, 2005 S.C.C.R. 465 Sh. Ct., and *Dyer v Hutchison*, 2006 S.C.C.R. 377.

[55] In *Young v Heatly*, 1959 J.C. 66, Lord Justice-General Clyde (at 70) said that in the absence of evidence of actual alarm, the conduct would have to be of a "flagrant" character for the court to draw the necessary inference, i.e. that the objective test had been satisfied; but in *Dyer v Hutchison*, 2006 S.C.C.R. 377 at 387A, para.24, the Appeal Court took the view that "to concentrate on the word 'flagrant' . . . may risk narrowing the focus of attention too much", although, it seems, in a situation such as that encountered in *Young v Heatly* itself, reliance on that word was not necessarily incorrect (see 387B–D, para.25).

[56] As a court of three judges, it would not in any event have been possible for the Appeal Court in *Smith v Donnelly*, 2001 S.C.C.R. 800 to overrule prior decisions of the Appeal Court itself: 807F, para.19. The full bench in *Jones v Carnegie*, 2004 S.C.C.R. 361, did not attempt to review earlier decisions, although there is a hint of possible unsoundness as to the actual result in *Young v Heatly*, 1959 J.C. 66: see the opinion of the court at 369C–D, para.12 relative to conduct performed in private. (The court did, at 376A–B, para.43, overrule *Cochrane v HM Advocate*, 2002 S.C.C.R. 1051; but *Cochrane* was not concerned with breach of the peace.)

present as genuinely alarming and disturbing, in its context,[57] to any reasonable person."[58] Thus, if two men begin fighting in public, it might reasonably be supposed that such conduct is serious enough to cause alarm to others and threaten "severe disturbance" to the community.[59] At the opposite extreme, behaviour amounting to remarks addressed to a person which merely cause her embarrassment must fail the test.[60] Between these two extremes, however, lie many situations of a borderline nature. The court in *Smith v Donnelly* recognise this, and whilst they suggest that such borderline cases must simply be determined by the courts on their facts as such cases arise,[61] they do provide some general guidance.

The Appeal Court in *Smith v Donnelly*[62] clearly favour a "robust" **12–13** approach to be taken in cases of swearing, on the basis that for many individuals, swearing amounts to part of their normal mode of communication.[63] It follows that prior decisions which have upheld convictions for breach of the peace where complainers were merely "upset" by swearing—especially where the complainers were police constables—may have been wrongly decided.[64] The Court also notes that conduct which amounts to no more than a refusal to co-operate with the police, "even if forcefully or even truculently stated, is not likely to be sufficient in itself to justify a conviction."[65] Similarly, although breach of the peace can certainly be (and often is) committed in a private place,[66] the Court draws attention to things done or said in private, which have formerly

---

[57] The importance of "the context" of the conduct in question is stressed particularly by the court in *Dyer v Hutchison*, 2006 S.C.C.R. 377 at 387C–D, para.25—a case which also takes the view that any (even short lived) provocative (and/or racist) behaviour at a premier league football match (especially in sight of the opposing team's supporters) is likely to be taken as meeting the required test: see the opinion of the court at 387E–388D, paras 26–28; *cf. Owens v Donaldson*, unreported, 2005, but in respect of which the court's opinion is conveniently set out at 2006 S.C.C.R. 377 at 389G–390F—but see also the explanation for that decision offered by the court in *Dyer v Hutchison*, 2006 S.C.C.R. 377 at 389A–B, para.31.

[58] *Smith v Donnelly*, 2001 S.C.C.R. 800 at 807C, para.17.

[59] See, e.g. *Derrett v Lockhart*, 1991 S.C.C.R. 109, and *Butcher v Jessop*, 1989 S.L.T. 593; see also *Monson v Higson*, 2000 S.C.C.R. 751 (a case of "road rage"), and *McAlpine v Friel*, 1997 S.C.C.R. 453 (a case of "stalking" the complainer over an extended period, although the appeal is solely concerned with sentence).

[60] See *Sinclair v Annan*, 1980 S.L.T. (Notes) 55, and *Borwick v Urquhart*, 2003 S.C.C.R. 243 (insofar as concerns the charge of breach of the peace); *cf. Bryce v Normand*, 1997 S.L.T. 1351, and *Donaldson v Vannet*, 1998 S.C.C.R. 422.

[61] See, e.g. *Dyer v Brady*, 2006 S.C.C.R. 629 (low-key, peaceful protest held not to qualify as a breach of the peace).

[62] *Smith v Donnelly*, 2001 S.C.C.R. 800; see the opinion of the court at 808B–D, para.20.

[63] See, e.g. *Kinnaird v Higson*, 2001 S.C.C.R. 427; *Logan v Jessop*, 1987 S.C.C.R. 604: *cf. Grogan v Heywood*, 1999 S.C.C.R. 705.

[64] See, e.g. *Mackay v Heywood*, 1998 S.C.C.R. 210.

[65] *Smith v Donnelly*, 2001 S.C.C.R. 800, at 808B, para.20. As illustrations, see, e.g. *McDonald v Heywood*, 2002 S.C.C.R. 92; *Cardle v Murray*, 1993 S.L.T. 525.

[66] See, e.g. *Ferguson v Carnochan* (1889) 16 R (J.) 93.

been considered sufficient for the offence rather for their "unpleasant" or "disgusting" character than for their potential for any real disturbance.[67] On the other hand, the Court cautions the need to consider Art.10[68] of the European Convention on Human Rights relative to certain cases of alleged breach of the peace—although Art.10, of course, refers both to rights and responsibilities.[69] A situation such as was disclosed in *Alexander v Smith*[70] might be of particular concern here, since the accused was convicted of breach of the peace for insisting on attempting to sell right-wing newspapers to a crowd of persons, notwithstanding that some members of that crowd had announced their intention of stopping him from doing so—by force, if necessary.

12–14   The Appeal Court in *Smith v Donnelly*[71] notes that one of the statutory styles of charge for breach of the peace, viz: "You did conduct yourself in a disorderly manner and commit a breach of the peace"[72], is so lacking in specification that it probably falls foul of Art.6(3)(a) of the European Convention on Human Rights. That part of the Article narrates that:

> "Everyone charged with a criminal offence has the following minimum rights: (*a*) to be informed promptly, in a language which he understands *and in detail*, of the nature and cause of the accusation against him."[73]

Consequently, prior Scottish decisions,[74] which have upheld charges couched in the bare statutory style as adequate for the purposes of notice to the accused, may be considered to have been disapproved.[75]

Mens rea

12–15   The *mens rea* of breach of the peace has never been determined in any reported case. It is, therefore, uncertain what the *mens rea* might be. As breach of the peace is a common law crime, it must

---

[67] See, e.g. *Young v Heatly*, 1959 J.C. 66. See also *Jones v Carnegie*, 2004 S.C.C.R. 361, opinion of the court at 369C–D, para.12, where it is stated, "we would caution that where conduct complained of took place in private there requires to be evidence that there was a realistic risk of the conduct being discovered."

[68] Article 10 refers to the right of freedom of expression: see the Human Rights Act 1998 Sch.1. See, e.g. *Quinan v Carnegie*, 2005 S.C.C.R. 267.

[69] See Art.10(2). Since the issue of the effect of Art.10 was not debated in *Smith v Donnelly*, 2001 S.C.C.R. 800, the Court makes no more than the cautionary observation mentioned in the text above; *cf.* the facts in the case of *Smith v Donnelly* itself with those in *Colhoun v Friel*, 1996 S.C.C.R. 497.

[70] *Alexander v Smith*, 1984 S.L.T. 176. See also *Duffield v Skeen*, 1981 S.C.C.R. 66.

[71] *Smith v Donnelly*, 2001 S.C.C.R. 800 at 808D, para.20.

[72] Criminal Procedure (Scotland) Act 1995 Sch.5.

[73] See the Human Rights Act 1998 Sch.1 (emphasis added).

[74] See, e.g. *Butcher v Jessop*, 1989 S.C.C.R. 119; *Anderson v Allan*, 1985 S.C.C.R. 399.

[75] *cf. Jones v Carnegie*, 2004 S.C.C.R. 361, opinion of the court at 375B–376C, paras 39–45, and *McGraw v HM Advocate*, 2004 S.C.C.R. 637, opinion of the court at 639C–D.

be assumed that strict liability (see Ch.13) is not applicable, since, "[t]here is a presumption that all common law crimes require *mens rea*."[76] Probably if the accused's conduct, whatever it be, is deliberate or even reckless, and is causally connected, or reasonably could be so connected to the requisite alarm and disturbance, then that will suffice. It does not seem to be necessary for the accused to intend or even appreciate the effect (actual or likely) of his conduct on others. This seems to be borne out by *Hughes v Crowe*,[77] where the claim was made that the accused had had no *mens rea* at the relevant time. What had happened was that the occupants of the lower flat in a building were "entertained" to banging sounds and the playing of loud music from the flat above—all at 7.15 on a Saturday morning. The noises (all exceedingly loud) continued for about one hour, until put a stop to by the police. It was claimed that the accused had had no knowledge that there was anyone in the lower flat at the time, and that he had not been warned about his conduct before being charged. The Appeal Court, however, took the view that although *mens rea* was required for breach of the peace, it was to be inferred from the nature and quality of the actings. Here, it would have been obvious in a four-flatted building that persons were likely to be at home at that hour on a Saturday, and that the acts of the appellant, persisted in for a considerable period, thus showed a, "gross lack of consideration for others who might be present in the other flats in the block at the time."[78] This does not exactly settle what the precise *mens rea* element for the crime might be; but certainly a "good" or understandable motive for one's deliberate conduct seems to be of no moment at all, as in *Ralston v HM Advocate*[79] where a prisoner's deliberate roof-top protest caused complete disruption to the running of the prison, and was thus a breach of the peace—irrespective of the merits of his desire to publicise alleged poor prison conditions. On the other hand, in *MacDougall v Dochree*,[80] it appeared to be accepted by all three judges in the Appeal Court that it would not be breach of the peace for persons, who were suspicious that "peeping-tom" activities might be taking place in a locked toilet cubicle (which by exercise of ingenuity provided viewing access to a next-door solarium), to test their suspicions by peering under a gap at the bottom of the cubicle door whilst the toilet was occupied by the suspect. This suggests that a "good" motive, e.g. crime detection by persons other than the police, may provide a defence.

---

[76] Gordon, *Criminal Law*, 3rd edn, para.7.12.

[77] *Hughes v Crowe*, 1993 S.C.C.R. 320.

[78] *Hughes v Crowe*, 1993 S.C.C.R. 320, Lord Justice-General Hope at 323F.

[79] *Ralston v HM Advocate*, 1989 S.L.T. 474; and see above, para.3–21.

[80] *MacDougall v Dochree*, 1992 J.C. 154; *cf. Woods v Normand*, 1992 S.C.C.R. 805 (attempting to end what was mistakenly thought of as an assault on a friend by use of threatening words and behaviour, where the Appeal Court opined that even if there had been a "good motive", the tactics adopted went far beyond what was justified): the decision, however, could also be explained as an example of self-defence (see below, para.12–16).

Particular defences

12–16   It is apparently not a good defence that the accused committed a breach of the peace in order to bring to an end an existing breach, even one being committed outside his own house by some troublesome youths,[81] presumably on the basis that two wrongs do not make a right. But self-defence is definitely applicable to a "fighting" or assault type of the crime.[82] It may be a defence that only the police heard or saw the accused's conduct, unless the police, inured as they must be to reprehensible behaviour, were entitled to be (and, possibly, actually were) alarmed thereby.[83]

Analagous statutory offences

Failing to leave, etc. a "rave" after police direction

12–17   There are a number of statutory offences covering ground similar to some instances of breach of the peace.[84] One of the most complex of these is to be found in s.63 of the Criminal Justice and Public Order Act 1994. The marginal note to that section refers to a "rave"; but the substance of the offence explains that the crime relates to an actual or planned gathering of more than 100 persons (whether trespassers or not)[85] on land in the open air[86], where

---

[81] *Palazzo v Copeland*, 1976 J.C. 52.
[82] *Derret v Lockhart*, 1991 S.C.C.R. 109.
[83] See *Cavanagh v Wilson*, 1995 S.C.C.R. 693, applying the decision in *Logan v Jessop*, 1987 S.C.C.R. 604; but *cf. Norris v McLeod*, 1988 S.C.C.R. 572, *Saltman v Allan*, 1989 S.L.T. 262, and *Lochrie v Jessop*, 1992 S.L.T. 556, which all seemed to discredit *Logan v Jessop*, as having any value as a precedent.
[84] See, e.g. the Civic Government (Scotland) Act 1982 s.46 (inter alia, prostitute soliciting in a public place), s.49(1) (inter alia permitting any creature to give any other person reasonable cause for alarm or annoyance), s.54(1) (inter alia failing to desist from playing a musical instrument so as to give any other person reasonable cause for annoyance), and s.55(1) (touting for trade so as to give any other person reasonable cause for annoyance). See also the Criminal Law (Consolidation) (Scotland) Act 1995 s.50A, as inserted by the Crime and Disorder Act 1998 s.33 (racially aggravated harassment), the Antisocial Behaviour etc. (Scotland) Act 2004 (asp 8) s.45 (noise emitted from relevant property and exceeding the permitted level after service of a warning notice, etc.), and the Prostitution (Public Places) (Scotland) Act 2007 (asp 11) s.1 (soliciting in a relevant place for the purpose of obtaining the services of a person engaged in prostitution). In addition, if the Scottish Parliament were to enact in full the recommendations of the Scottish Law Commission (as realised in the draft "Sexual Offences (Scotland) Bill" annexed as Appendix A to the Commission's "Report on Rape and Other Sexual Offences", Scot. Law Com. No.209 (December 2007)), it may be that certain matters now prosecutable as breaches of the peace will be caught by the terms of cl.40(a),(b) of that Bill: see, e.g. cl.4, "Coercing a person into being present during a sexual activity" (and especially cl.4(2)(b)); cl.5, "Coercing a person into looking at an image of a sexual activity" (and especially cl.5(2)(b)); cl.6, "Communicating indecently" or, "Causing a person to see or hear an indecent communication" (and especially cl.6(3)(b)).
[85] This is not, therefore, predominantly a trespassory offence (see above, paras 11–05 *et seq.*). "Trespasser" is defined as in s.61(9); see s.63(10).
[86] This includes a place partly open to the air, such as a sports stadium (s.63(10)), but not in Scotland a place which has been licensed, under s.41 of the Civic Government (Scotland) Act 1982, as a place of public entertainment (s.63(9)(b)).

amplified music[87] is played at night (whether with intermissions or not) and is of such duration and loudness as to be likely to cause serious distress to inhabitants of the locality.[88] If a police officer of at least the rank of superintendent reasonably believes that two or more persons are on any land[89] making preparations for such a "rave", and/or that 10 or more persons are there attending it or waiting for it to begin, he can give direction that all such persons[90] are to leave the land and remove whatever vehicles or other property they may have brought to it. The offence is committed by failing to leave that land as soon as reasonably practicable, or returning to it within seven days of the direction's having been given[91]—both without reasonable excuse.[92] Before there can be a conviction, it must be shown that the accused was aware of the direction; but the direction is deemed to have been properly communicated if reasonable steps have been taken to bring it to the attention of those concerned.[93] Within a defined distance of such a "rave", a police officer can stop persons he reasonably believes are on their way to it and require that they should proceed in a "non-rave" direction; it is also an offence to fail to comply with such a requirement.[94]

2. CRIMES RELATIVE TO MORALITY

General introduction

The crimes dealt with under the above heading are those which **12–18** generally cannot be justified on the basis of direct harm done to another. Certainly no harm in any conventional sense need be caused by them. Rather the badge of criminality is borne because what is done offends against the currently accepted standards of moral behaviour or against the tenets of the "honour-code" which all upstanding citizens are presently expected to observe. Examples of the former kind consist of various sorts of "indecent conduct" (including incest, which is usually dealt with separately), and examples of the latter are the crimes of treason, sedition, perjury, giving false information to the criminal authorities, and various "attempts" to pervert or hinder the course of justice.

---

[87] This includes "sounds wholly or predominantly characterised by emission of a succession of repetitive beats", s.63(1)(b).

[88] See s.63(1).

[89] The land here need not be in the open air: see s.63(2), as amended by the Anti-social Behaviour Act 2003 Sch.3.

[90] Under s.63(2), this is not applicable to exempt persons, i.e. the occupier of the land, members of his family, or his employee or agent, as also those who have homes situated there (see s.63(6), (10)). "Occupier" is defined as in s.61(9), see s.63(10).

[91] See s.63(6). "Vehicle" is defined as in s.61(9)—see s.63(10).

[92] The onus of showing such an excuse is on the accused (s.63(7)).

[93] See s.63(4).

[94] See s.65.

PUBLIC INDECENCY

Introduction

12–19	From 1978 onwards,[95] the Scottish courts developed a crime of "shamelessly indecent conduct" which covered acts of indecent exposure,[96] the showing of indecent images (even to willing viewers in private),[97] selling or exposing for sale indecent things,[98] and various sorts of sexual behaviour.[99] The width of that crime and its amorphous nature made it very difficult to describe[100] or justify;[101] and in a case of 2003, Lord Justice-Clerk Gill concluded that that crime rested on an unsound theory, had an uncertain ambit of liability, and laid open to prosecution some forms of private conduct the legality of which should have been a matter for Parliament.[102] As a result of the decision of the Appeal Court in that 2003 case, "shamelessly indecent conduct" ceased to be an available criminal charge under Scots common law, and *Watt v Annan*,[103] the case which had begun its development, was overruled: also overruled was any case in which the ratio of *Watt v Annan* had been followed.[104] This did not necessarily mean that conduct formerly charged as "shamelessly indecent" would cease to be criminal at all[105]: what henceforward mattered (at common law) was whether such conduct could be brought within "lewd, indecent and libidinous practices"[106] or the crime (based on nineteenth-century authority[107]) now known as "public indecency".[108]

Public indecency

12–20	This should be seen as a crime which, "fulfills an appropriate role in the maintenance of public order."[109] The *actus reus* of this common law offence has two elements: (1) indecent conduct, and

---

[95] See *Watt v Annan*, 1978 J.C. 84.

[96] See, e.g. *Usai v Russell*, 2000 S.C.C.R. 57

[97] As in *Watt v Annan*, 1978 J.C. 84, itself.

[98] See, e.g. *Robertson v Smith*, 1980 J.C. 1.

[99] See, e.g. *R v HM Advocate*, 1988 S.L.T. 623; *HM Advocate v K*, 1994 S.C.C.R. 499.

[100] See earlier editions of this book, under the heading: "shamelessly indecent conduct".

[101] It was especially difficult to justify in terms of Art.7(1) of the European Convention on Human Rights: see the Human Rights Act 1998 Sch.1.

[102] *Webster v Dominick*, 2005 J.C. 65 (a five judge decision of 22 July, 2003), at 78, para.43.

[103] *Watt v Annan*, 1978 J.C. 84.

[104] *Webster v Dominick*, 2005 J.C. 65, Lord Justice-Clerk Gill at 78, para.46: the other four judges agreed with his opinion.

[105] See *Webster v Dominick*, 2005 J.C. 65, Lord Justice-Clerk Gill at 81, para.59.

[106] See above, para.9–20.

[107] See, in particular, dicta in *McKenzie v Whyte* (1864) 4 Irv. 570.

[108] *Webster v Dominick*, 2005 J.C. 65, Lord Justice-Clerk Gill at 79, para.51.

[109] *Webster v Dominick*, 2005 J.C. 65, Lord Justice-Clerk Gill (with whose opinion the other four judges agreed) at 80, para.58: see also 79, para.52.

(2) the effect of that conduct on the minds of the public.[110] As far as the first of these is concerned, the description certainly applies to sexual "improprieties" such as exposure of the "person" (usually the penis),[111] sexual intercourse in public view, and the making of sexual actions or gestures in a stage performance[112]: it is not yet decided whether "indecent conduct" can apply to non-sexual matters.[113] Whether or not relevant conduct can be described as "indecent" depends on the circumstances (including time and place) of each case, judged by the toleration standards of contemporary society—standards which will obviously be subject to change with the passage of time and alteration of tastes.[114] The "public" element is fulfilled if the indecent conduct occurs in public, or in private—if it is nevertheless visible to the public or takes place before unwilling witnesses[115]—and causes (on an objective basis, it seems)[116] public offence[117] or, "affronts public sensibility".[118] This offence is not committed if the conduct occurs in private but would cause offence to certain persons, were they to hear about it[119]; and it is not committed if there is a private showing of indecent images to willing viewers, or if indecent things are sold or exposed for sale. The one possible exception to such conduct which occurs in private before willing observers is said to be, "where the conduct is such as to offend even members of a consenting audience."[120] Whether or not an accused person indulged in the conduct for sexual gratification is irrelevant (since that is a matter of motive—relevant only to sentence)[121]; and questions as to the conduct's depraving or

---

[110] *Webster v Dominick*, 2005 J.C. 65 at 79–80, para.53.

[111] See, e.g. the charge in *Nelson v Barbour*, 2007 S.C.C.R. 283, as set out by Lord Johnston at 284B, para.1, and to which the appellant had pled guilty.

[112] *Webster v Dominick*, 2005 J.C. 65 Lord Justice-Clerk Gill at 80, para.53.

[113] *Webster v Dominick*, 2005 J.C. 65 at 80, para.54. Insofar as such conduct is "sexual", the Scottish Law Commission (in its "Report on Rape and Other Sexual Offences", Scot. Law Com. No.209 (December 2007)) has proposed that "public indecency" be partly subsumed by a series of new statutory offences contained in a draft "Sexual Offences (Scotland) Bill" which gives effect to the Commission's recommendations and appears as Appendix A to its Report: see, in particular paras 5–11 *et seq.* of the Report, and cll 4–7 (cl.7 especially, informing the new offence of "Sexual exposure"); 17–19; 24–26; 37 and 40 of the Bill. Notice too that the Commission has suggested that consideration be given to the creation of a distinct offence of necrophilia in Scotland: see the Report, paras 5–28 to 5–29 (and *cf.* the English "Sexual Offences Act 2003", s.70).

[114] *Webster v Dominick*, 2005 J.C. 65 at 80, para.58.

[115] *Webster v Dominick*, 2005 J.C. 65 at 80, para.55.

[116] *Webster v Dominick*, 2005 J.C. 65 at 79, para.52.

[117] *Webster v Dominick*, 2005 J.C. 65.

[118] *Webster v Dominick*, 2005 J.C. 65 at 79, para.50.

[119] *cf.* what was alleged in *Bott v MacLean*, 2005 J.C. 83.

[120] *Webster v Dominick*, 2005 J.C. 65 at 80, para.56: reference is made by Lord Justice-Clerk Gill to *Geddes v Dickson*, 2001 J.C. 69, as an example of conduct which could be offensive to "willing" observers: in that case, persons had been encouraged (by promise of reward) to expose their breasts or penises at a "fun" night held on licensed premises.

[121] *Webster v Dominick*, 2005 J.C. 65 at 80, para.53.

corrupting effects[122] are, "at most of indirect relevance".[123] The *mens rea* of the offence has not yet been discussed in a reported case; but it is clear that "shamelessness"[124] plays no part in the crime.[125]

Incest

12–21   The crime of incest has been largely statutory since the Reformation; but references in the standard texts[126] to the Incest Act 1567 must now be replaced by references to the Criminal Law (Consolidation) (Scotland) Act 1995. In terms of the modern law, it is incest for a person to have sexual intercourse with a close relative of the opposite sex, where he knew of the relationship at the time.[127] It is of no moment what age the closely related sexual partner is at the time (although sexual intercourse with girls under 16 is, of course, also penalised in other ways—see above, para.9–83). If the sexual partner consents to the intercourse, and he or she also knew of the close relationship, then both parties will be guilty.

12–22   The crime is confined to sexual intercourse, which, although not defined in the Act, must be taken to mean penetration of the vagina by the penis. It follows then that any lesser or different form of sexual behaviour cannot be incest. It may, however, amount (at common law) to lewd, indecent and libidinous practices,[128] or public indecency[129]; or it may constitute a statutory offence.[130] The close relatives of the opposite sex with whom one is not permitted to have sexual intercourse are clearly set out in a table in the Act.[131] Most are blood relatives, but it is to be noted that half-

---

[122] These were relevant considerations for the now discredited crime of "shamelessly indecent conduct".

[123] *Webster v Dominick*, 2005 J.C. 65, Lord Justice-Clerk Gill at 79, para.52, where it is emphasised that, as in the English offence of "outraging public decency" (see, e.g. *Rose v DPP* [2006] 1 W.L.R. 2626 QBD—oral sex in the foyer of a bank held to be insufficiently public, since witnessed only by one person), what really matters is whether the conduct objectively causes *public* offence; see also, however, *R. v Hamilton* [2008] 2 W.L.R. 107 CA) and the English authorities discussed there.

[124] Which featured prominently in the now discredited crime of "shamelessly indecent conduct".

[125] *Webster v Dominick*, 2005 J.C. 65, Lord Justice-Clerk Gill at 80, para.57. It remains to be seen how "public indecency" will be dealt with in practice—and to what extent it will be found useful by prosecutors: in *Webster*, at 79, para.51, Lord Gill describes the offence as having a place in the law of Scotland similar to that occupied by "public indecency" in the common law of South Africa—see Burchell and Milton, *Principles of Criminal Law*, 3rd edn, pp.876–877, where it is stated that the eponymous South African offence requires intention, and extends (in principle) to the publication of obscene matters.

[126] See, e.g. Hume, *Commentaries*, i, 447 *et seq.*; Alison, *Principles*, i, 563 *et seq.*

[127] Criminal Law (Consolidation) (Scotland) Act 1995 s.1.

[128] See above, para.9–20.

[129] See above, paras 12–18 to 12–20.

[130] See, e.g. the Criminal Law (Consolidation) (Scotland) Act 1995 s.6.

[131] Criminal Law (Consolidation) (Scotland) Act 1995 s.1(1), Table.

blood relationships are included. Thus, it would be incest for a brother to have sexual intercourse with his half-sister, e.g. where they were both born of the same mother but had been sired by different fathers. Legitimacy or illegitimacy is of no consequence in assessing relationships in the table. It is also to be noted that two adoptive relationships are within the ambit of the crime. It is, therefore, incest for a man to have sexual intercourse with his adoptive mother (or former adoptive mother) or with his adopted daughter (or former adopted daughter); and vice versa for a female, of course. Adoption is the process by which a person's ties with his natural parents are legally terminated. But for the purposes of incest, his relationship with his natural parents is deemed to continue.[132] It is a defence if the accused proves that he did not know of the close relationship and had no reason to suspect it, or that he did not consent to the sexual intercourse, or that he was married to the other person at the time.[133] Such a marriage would have had to have been contracted outwith Scotland, since the marriage and incest laws have been harmonised in this country, but be recognised as valid under Scots law.[134]

Rationale and related offences

The present formulation of incest is founded on a Scottish Law **12–23** Commission Report[135] which considered several reasons for maintaining it as a crime. These included protection and maintenance of the family unit,[136] genetic fault (in that the offspring of intercourse between persons closely related are more likely to suffer from mental or physical abnormalities than the children of non-closely related unions),[137] and moral repugnancy.[138] In modern society, however, where traditional family units are not as conspicuous as they once were, contraceptive measures are well understood and practised, techniques for the prediction and detection of foetal abnormalities are highly advanced, and abortions available widely, it is suggested that the only convincing rationale for the retention of incest in the criminal law is moral repugnancy. The crime is limited, however, in the sense that it does not extend to step-relationships, although moral repugnancy might well be thought to apply there also. If a man marries a woman who already

---

[132] Adoption (Scotland) Act 1978 s.41(1), as amended by the Incest and Related Offences (Scotland) Act 1986 Sch.1 para.5, and by the Civil Partnership Act 2004 s.86(10); Adoption and Children (Scotland) Act 2007 (asp 4) s.41(1)(b).

[133] Criminal Law (Consolidation) (Scotland) Act 1995 s.1(1)(a)–(c).

[134] On which, see A.E. Anton and P.R. Beaumont, *Private International Law*, 2nd edn (Edinburgh: W. Green, 1990), Ch.16.

[135] "Report on the Law of Incest in Scotland", Scot. Law Com. No. 69 (1981), Cmnd.8422.

[136] "Report on the Law of Incest in Scotland", paras 3–10 to 3–16.

[137] "Report on the Law of Incest in Scotland", paras 3–19 to 3–23.

[138] "Report on the Law of Incest in Scotland", paras 3–17 to 3–18.

has a daughter by a prior partner, it is not incest under the Act for him to have sexual intercourse with his wife's daughter—now his stepdaughter. For that reason, the 1995 Act contains the separate offence of "intercourse with step-child",[139] and also the crime of, "intercourse of person in position of trust with a child under 16", which amongst other things covers the case of a man who lives with, rather than marries, a woman who already has a young daughter from a prior relationship.[140] These provisions, however, are complex, and must be read carefully to appreciate their full impact.

"Honour-code" Offences

Introduction

12–24   The crimes, briefly dealt with below, can be classified as "honour-code" offences, meaning those where the accused was in breach of his plain duty to behave as an upright citizen of his country should. They can also, of course, be classified in other ways, e.g. as "offences against the state," "offences against public welfare," or "offences against the course of justice."[141] But none of these classifications has any official status; and, in the interests of economy, the one title which appears to cover all of those selected here has been preferred.

Treason

12–25   Since the Union with England, the Scots law of treason has been replaced by that which pertains in England.[142] There is consequently nothing particularly Scottish about it. Hume[143] and Gordon[144] both more than adequately describe the law; and reference to these standard texts should be made when details of the crime are needed. It must be seldom, however, that such details will be required. The crime of treason is of importance only in wartime, or in time of rebellion, when the aspect of it known as, "adhering to the Queen's enemies" may assume importance. At basis, as Hume narrates, treason includes,

> "all such offences as are more immediately directed against the person and Government of the [Queen]; and amount to a violation of that fidelity and allegiance which is due to [Her] Majesty from all [her] subjects . . .".[145]

---

[139] Criminal Law (Consolidation) (Scotland) Act 1995 s.2.
[140] Criminal Law (Consolidation) (Scotland) Act 1995 s.3.
[141] See Gordon, *Criminal Law*, 3rd edn, Vol.II, Pts VI, VII, VIII.
[142] See the Treason Act 1708.
[143] Hume, *Commentaries*, i, 512 *et seq.*
[144] Gordon, *Criminal Law*, 3rd edn, paras 37.01 to 37.25.
[145] Hume, *Commentaries*, i, 512.

Offences against state security in peace time are generally not regarded as treasons, but as specific statutory offences where the requirements of the statutes in question can be met.[146]

Sedition

Like treason, sedition is a crime of little importance in times of **12–26** peace and stable government, and, therefore, of little importance today. Certainly, Hume's account of the crime[147] suggests that almost any serious criticism of the monarchy, the government or the church might be appropriate for a charge of sedition, if,

> "suited and intended to disturb the tranquillity of the State,— for the purpose of producing public trouble or commotion, and moving [Her] Majesty's subjects to the dislike, resistance, or subversion of the established government and laws, or settled frame and order of things."[148]

The major part of Hume's text was, however, written during the period characterised by the French Revolution and the Napoleonic adventures in Europe, and is clearly coloured by contemporary fears for the stability of the British state. Further details of this crime, if required, may be found in the standard texts.[149]

Perjury

This common law crime consists of, "the judicial affirmation of **12–27** falsehood upon oath."[150] When a witness is called upon to give evidence under oath (or affirmation) in any judicial proceedings, then he promises to tell the truth, and clearly is on honour to do just that. If he gives evidence which he knows is not true, then he is in breach of the faith reposed in him and can be prosecuted for perjury if the evidence he gave was, "pertinent to the point at issue."[151] The *actus reus* of the offence is thus complete when the false evidence is uttered; and the *mens rea* is satisfied if the accused can be shown to have known that that evidence was false at the time he gave it. It has been held to be perjury where the accused gave evidence that he had been with A at the relevant time, when in truth he knew he could not recall whether he had been with A or with B.[152] As far as the "pertinence" of the evidence to the proceedings in which it was given is concerned, the following statements by Alison have been approved by the High Court:

---

[146] See, e.g. the "Official Secrets Acts 1911 to 1989" as they are now referred to under the Official Secrets Act 1989 s.16(2).
[147] Hume, *Commentaries*, i, Ch.XXVII, 553 *et seq.*
[148] Hume, *Commentaries*, i, 553.
[149] See, e.g. Gordon, *Criminal Law*, 3rd edn, paras 39.01 to 39.08.
[150] Hume, *Commentaries*, i, 366.
[151] Hume, *Commentaries*, i, 369.
[152] *Simpson v Tudhope*, 1988 S.L.T. 297.

"The falsehood must be in a matter pertinent to the issue, and competent to be asked of the witness; but if this be the case, it matters not in how trivial a matter the falsehood may consist, or how far from the original relevant matter the witness may have been led before he makes the false [statement]."[153]

It has also been held to be perjury for an accused person to give false evidence denying his guilt at his own trial.[154] There also exists the related offence of "subornation of perjury", which consists in the deliberate "seducing" of someone to commit perjury by, for example, promises of reward, actual bribery or threats of violence, provided that false evidence is eventually given by the "victim".[155]

Attempt to pervert or defeat or hinder the course of justice

12–28   It is thought that "attempt to pervert the course of justice" is not a distinct common law offence, but is either a general principle used to generate a variety of related, specific offences,[156] or a convenient description for a series of innominate crimes.[157] As a principle or a description, it can take a number of different formulations, such as, "attempt to defeat the course of justice",[158] "hindering the course of justice",[159] or "hinder and frustrate the course of justice and attempt to defeat the course of justice."[160] Where a complaint or indictment of such a nature uses a form which includes the word "attempt", this is generally not to be understood as a reference to an attempt to commit the crime. "Attempt" is used in this context as a mere word of style, as must be obvious from cases of "escaping from lawful custody" where the prisoner did indeed escape,[161] and of "hiding oneself away to avoid giving evidence for the Crown" where the accused did successfully spirit himself away.[162] These are completed crimes, and not attempts in the normal sense. Indeed it is equally common in such circumstances for the word "attempt" to be dropped altogether such that the charge simply narrates the perversion of the course of justice.[163] The course of justice must, of course, have been running

---

[153] Alison, *Principles*, i, 469 at "4"; approved in *Lord Advocate's Reference (No.1 of 1985)*, 1987 S.L.T. 187 at 192J.
[154] See *HM Advocate v Cairns*, 1967 J.C. 37, where Cairns had been acquitted of murder on a verdict of not proven, at a trial where he himself had given evidence denying that he had stabbed the victim; *cf. R. v Miell* [2008] 1 W.L.R. 627 C.A.
[155] See Hume, *Commentaries*, i, Ch.XII, 381 *et seq.*
[156] See *Bernard Greenhuff* (1838) 2 Swin. 236, per Lord Cockburn at 274.
[157] See *HM Advocate v Martin*, 1956 J.C. 1, per Lord Cameron at 3, where both views appear to have been advanced, the former ultimately being favoured.
[158] See, e.g. the charge in *HM Advocate v Martin*, 1956 J.C. 1.
[159] See, e.g. the charge in *Turnbull v HM Advocate*, 1953 J.C. 59.
[160] See *HM Advocate v Mannion*, 1961 J.C. 79.
[161] See, e.g. *HM Advocate v Martin*, 1956 J.C. 1.
[162] See *HM Advocate v Mannion*, 1961 J.C. 79.
[163] See, e.g. *McElhinney v Normand*, 1996 S.L.T. 238.

in order to have been perverted; but not much seems necessary to satisfy this element, since in one case it was held sufficient that police officers, having been shown an arrest warrant for a particular person, had set off to find him.[164] The *mens rea* element of these offences appears to be behaviour deliberately aimed at perverting the course of justice.[165] It is suggested that what unites cases classifiable under the heading of this paragraph is the accused's failure to obtemper his public, moral duty to allow the criminal justice system to run its appointed course, once set in motion. Witnesses should thus recognise their duty to give evidence when called upon to do so, or, at least, to make themselves available to give evidence when they suspect that that will be required of them; persons in lawful custody should seek only lawful methods of securing their liberty; witnesses should tell the truth when under oath to do so in judicial proceedings; and so on.[166] Where a specific named crime exists, however, it is customary to charge that rather than an "attempt to defeat the course of justice", as happens plainly in the case of perjury.[167]

Giving false information to the criminal authorities

The crime of giving false information to the criminal authorities **12–29** could be seen as an example of "attempting to defeat the ends of justice". But since the giving of such false information usually applies to the setting in motion of an investigation rather than contributing something negative to one already in train, the tendency is to charge it as a crime of its own kind. There are two distinct aspects. The first relates to the making of a false accusation of crime against a particular, named individual, where the accusation is, of course, known by its maker to be false. This is recognised as criminal by Hume[168]; and the case of *Simpkins v HM Advocate*[169] provides a modern example (although reported only on sentence). Hume[170] requires that there be special malice shown by the accused, although it is probably now sufficient that he plainly knew the story to be untrue when he uttered it. Negligence or perhaps even recklessness in assembling the facts on which such an

---

[164] *McElhinney v Normand*, 1996 S.L.T. 238, opinion of Lord Sutherland at 242D. The police had in fact spotted the person named in the warrant and were chasing him down the street when the accused in this case intervened by picking up the wanted man in a car and carrying him "safely" away.

[165] See, e.g. *Carney v HM Advocate*, 1995 S.L.T. 1208; *Johnstone v Lees*, 1995 S.L.T. 1174.

[166] It has been held insufficient, however, for an accused person to say that he will not co-operate with a warrant for him to be medically examined—unless his stated refusal is first put to the test: see *Vaughan v Griffiths*, 2004 S.C.C.R. 537.

[167] See above, para.12–27; but *cf. Waddell v MacPhail*, 1986 S.C.C.R. 593, where lies told to the police were dealt with under the present general principle.

[168] Hume, *Commentaries*, i, 341–343.

[169] *Simpkins v HM Advocate*, 1985 S.C.C.R. 30.

[170] Hume, *Commentaries*, i, 342.

accusation is based would probably not be enough, since there is clearly a public need not to discourage the reporting of crimes to the police or fiscal.

12–30　　The second aspect relates to the giving of false information to the police (or perhaps the local prosecutors) which makes them commence an investigation. This is certainly criminal, and is sometimes referred to as "wasting police time".[171] Whilst the information must be known to be false,[172] there is no need here for any person to be named as a culprit or for any suggestion to be made that a crime has been committed at all. In *Kerr v Hill*,[173] for example, the accused merely told the police that he had seen a collision between a bus and a cyclist, and left it entirely open as to whether a crime had been involved. As Lord Justice-General Normand put it[174]:

> "The point is that the criminal authorities were deliberately set in motion by a malicious person by means of an invented story. That is the essence of the crime . . .".

This plainly appears to be confirmed by the decision in *Bowers v Tudhope*[175] where a false allegation was made to the police that a giro cheque had been lost (not stolen). Once again, it seems sufficient that the accused knew that the information was false. In practice, malice on his part does not appear to be required.[176]

---

[171] See, e.g. Gane and Stoddart, *Casebook on Scottish Criminal Law*, 3rd edn, paras 17–02 *et seq.*

[172] See *Walkingshaw v Coid*, 1988 S.C.C.R. 454 Sh. Ct.

[173] *Kerr v Hill*, 1936 J.C. 71.

[174] *Kerr v Hill*, 1936 J.C. 71 at 75.

[175] *Bowers v Tudhope*, 1987 S.L.T. 748.

[176] See, e.g. *Gray v Morrison*, 1954 J.C. 31.

CHAPTER 13

STATUTORY OFFENCES

Introduction

The major part of this book has been concerned with non- **13–01** statutory offences, since Scotland still places considerable reliance upon the common law to generate and define its criminal law. But it is not possible, even in this country, to ignore or underestimate the considerable importance and impact of statutory crimes. Much of the time of the criminal courts is taken up, for example, in dealing with a wide range of particular offences set out in the Road Traffic Act 1988 and in the Misuse of Drugs Act 1971. It can hardly be expected, of course, that an introductory text on criminal law would deal in detail with all of the crimes to be found within those two Acts, let alone the many offences set out in literally hundreds of statutes currently in force.[1] Indeed, adequate consideration of road traffic and of drugs offences would require the construction of individual volumes of some length devoted entirely to those subjects. In any event, such volumes already exist—see below, Appendix A. It must also be borne in mind that there has never been a period since its inception when the United Kingdom Parliament has not been active in the promulgation of new crimes; and the Scottish Parliament now has similar powers in relation to non-reserved criminal matters.[2] The range of statutory offences is, therefore, likely to increase rapidly in relation to issues and matters which can hardly at this time be imagined. As far as the Scottish courts are concerned, the United Kingdom Parliament may do as it pleases. If a new offence has been created in an enactment which has passed both Houses and received the Royal Assent, then it is formally valid and cannot be questioned on the basis that it is otherwise unconstitutional.[3]

---

[1] Indeed, every piece of legislation should be closely examined for the presence of offences, e.g. even the innocuous sounding Christmas Day and New Year's Day Trading (Scotland) Act 2007 (asp 13) contains an offence which carries a maximum penalty on summary conviction of £50,000: see s.4.

[2] See above, para.2–11 *et seq.*

[3] For the position relative to the Scottish Parliament, see above, para.2–12.

INTERPRETATION I

13–02 Although a statutory crime cannot in general be struck down on the basis of its unconstitutionality[4] (unlike, say, the position in the United States), the criminal courts may still make a substantial contribution to the way in which that crime is received. This is achieved by the device of interpretation. A court has a duty to interpret the bare words used by Parliament.[5] In theory, anyone with a reasonable command of English should be able to understand the import of any statutory crime. It will after all have been laid out in a particular provision of the statute in question in plain English words. But initial appearances can be deceptive. A particular word may be found to have no plain, simple significance at all. Again, the plain meaning of a particular word may not have been intended. If that was not intended, then one would expect Parliament to have made that clear; and generally it does, by allocating a particular meaning in an "interpretation section"—which may be far removed from the very section which contains the word in focus. In s.28(1) of the Road Traffic Act 1988 (as substituted by the Road Traffic Act 1991 s.7), for example, it is stated: "A person who rides a cycle on a road dangerously is guilty of an offence." Relative to that, the United Kingdom Parliament has seen fit to give particular meanings to "dangerously" (in s.28(2) and (3)), and to "cycle" and "road" (both defined in s.192(1) of the Road Traffic Act 1988, as amended by the Road Traffic Act 1991 Sch.4 para.78(2)). It will be noted that with respect to "road", the inquirer is directed to a completely different Act—namely, the Roads (Scotland) Act 1984[6]—for part of the desired definition. Such definitions, however, may themselves require more particular interpretation when they are considered in relation to an actual case.[7] Where given, definitions require more particular interpretation, or where statutory words have not been defined at all, it is judges in courts, in actual criminal cases before them, who must so

---

[4] *cf.* above, paras 2–11, 2–12.

[5] This includes the correction of an obvious drafting error: *cf.*, e.g. the English case of *R. (on the application of CPS) v Bow Street Magistrates Court* [2007] 1 W.L.R. 291 QB, dealing with a provision of the Identity Cards Act 2006: that Act applies generally to Scotland, but s.5 of the Forgery and Counterfeiting Act 1981, which is referred to in the case, has never so applied.

[6] See, in particular, Roads (Scotland) Act 1984 s.151(1), as amended by the New Roads and Street Works Act 1991 Sch.8 para.94(b), and the Local Government (Scotland) Act 1994 s.146.

[7] See, e.g. *Beattie (John M.) v Scott*, 1990 S.C.C.R. 435; *Young v Carmichael*, 1991 S.C.C.R. 332; and *Aird v Vannet*, 1999 S.C.C.R. 322, in relation to the definition of "road" under the Roads (Scotland) Act 1984. See also *Dick v Walkingshaw*, 1995 S.L.T. 1254 (as to whether and in what circumstances the deck of a ferry can be considered as a "road"); and *Teale v MacLeod*, 2008 S.C.C.R. 12.

interpret or assign meanings.[8] When they do so, their decisions may be considered authoritative,[9] in which event the interpretations and assigned meanings become part of the statutory law itself. In relation to statutory road traffic offences, for example, what it means to "drive" a mechanically propelled vehicle is often crucial; but the Road Traffic Acts have never defined "driving" at all. The courts have, therefore, had to decide the meaning of that word, and its correlatives.[10] Clearly these interpretations and meanings do not appear in the bare text of the statutory crime. They will have to be searched for by the inquirer, using, for example, the *Current Law Statute and Legislation Citator* volumes.[11]

Decisions by English courts

When the precise meaning of a particular word or phrase in a **13–03** statutory crime is an issue in criminal proceedings, a court will look for interpretation sections within the Act itself, and also for interpretations laid down in authoritative decisions in the past. It is to be noted here that decisions by English criminal courts (or those elsewhere in the United Kingdom), no matter how eminent, are never more than "persuasive" in Scotland[12]; they are never required to be followed in this country, where judges may take an entirely different view. This certainly does happen—however regrettable it may be in relation to statutory offences which the United Kingdom Parliament intended to be applied uniformly on both sides of the border. In many offences under the Road Traffic Act 1988, for example, that the accused was "driving" a motor vehicle at the time is of some importance. But, where a person is standing outside a broken-down car, pushing it along a road by muscle power and making occasional adjustments to its direction by reaching for the steering-wheel, he is definitely "driving" that car under Scots law[13] but probably would not be doing so under

---

[8] *cf.* the English case of *R. v Da Silva* [2007] 1 W.L.R. 303, where the meaning of "suspecting" in the Criminal Justice Act 1988 s.93A(1)(a) (as inserted by the Criminal Justice Act 1993 s.29) was at issue: the modern equivalent of the now repealed s.93A(1)(a) is to be found in s.328(1) of the Proceeds of Crime Act 2002, which applies to Scotland: see the 2002 Act, s.461.

[9] See above, para.2–10.

[10] See, e.g. *Ames v MacLeod*, 1969 J.C. 1; *McArthur v Valentine*, 1990 S.L.T. 732; *Guthrie v Friel*, 1993 S.L.T. 899 (attempt to drive); and the unusual case of *Hoy v McFadyen*, 2000 S.C.C.R. 875. See also below, para.13–03.

[11] Covering 1948 to date: see the prefaces to each volume for full instructions on use.

[12] They may, of course, be regarded as "highly persuasive", usually meaning that they are well worth following—see, e.g. *Davies v Smith*, 1983 S.L.T. 644 (which adopts the reasoning given in *Federal Steam Navigation Co Ltd v Department of Trade and Industry* [1974] 1 W.L.R. 505); see also the general remarks of Lord Justice-General Hamilton (on the interpretation of the Human Rights Act 1998) in the full-bench decision of *Dickson v HM Advocate*, 2008 S.L.T. 12 at 18–19, para.27.

[13] *Ames v MacLeod*, 1969 J.C. 1; *McArthur v Valentine*, 1990 S.L.T. 732.

English law.[14] Again, in *Kelly v MacKinnon*[15] Lord Justice-General Emslie refused to entertain the view of the Lord Chief Justice of England in *Cafferata v Wilson*[16] that, for the purposes of s.57(1)(b) of the Firearms Act 1968, a starting-pistol or similar "gun" was a component part of a lethal weapon and thus a "firearm" since it could, by boring out the barrel and carrying out certain other operations, be made capable of firing live ammunition; and indeed the Lord Justice-General described the views expressed in the English case as "manifestly absurd" and "not only unsound but patently unsound."[17]

Repealed versions of the same crime

13–04   In *Kiely v Lunn*[18] a boy of 15 had had many absences from school. Consequently his father was charged with an offence under s.35(1) of the Education (Scotland) Act 1980,[19] namely: "Where a child of school age . . . fails without reasonable excuse to attend regularly at . . . school, his parent shall be guilty of an offence." The reason for the boy's protracted absence was that he was chronically addicted to glue sniffing, and showed no willingness to accept help in breaking the habit. In terms of s.42(1)(b) of the same Act, there would be deemed to be a reasonable excuse if, "the child had been prevented by sickness from attending school." The question which arose for decision was, therefore, whether a self-inflicted and self-perpetuated disability could be construed as "sickness." Since no interpretation was offered by the Act itself, and no previous cases could be found to shed light on the matter, the Appeal Court looked at previous versions of the same crime. In particular, they looked at the Education (Scotland) Act 1883, and at s.11, which held out as a reasonable excuse: that, "the child had been prevented from attending school by sickness or any other unavoidable cause." Although the last five words had been dropped from s.42(1)(b) of the 1980 Act, the Appeal Court took the view that these words still provided an excellent guide as to how "sickness" was to be interpreted, namely that it meant, "an unavoidable cause of absence, at least in the sense that it cannot be construed to include a state of ill health brought about by the deliberate actings of the child concerned."[20] The conclusion is,

---

[14] See, e.g. *R. v MacDonagh* [1974] Q.B. 448.
[15] *Kelly v MacKinnon*, 1982 J.C. 94 at 98, 99.
[16] *Cafferata v Wilson* [1936] 3 All E.R. 149.
[17] In one case it was said: "The result may be that different constructions are placed upon the Act of 1988 [Road Traffic Act] in Scotland and England, but this is the result of different police procedures in the two countries"—*Simpson v McClory*, 1993 J.C. 110, per Lord Justice-Clerk Ross at 119D.
[18] *Kiely v Lunn*, 1983 J.C. 4.
[19] Education (Scotland) Act 1980 (c.44), but given erroneously as (c.20) in the report.
[20] *Kiely v Lunn*, 1983 J.C. 4 at 7.

then, that it is legitimate to use the original wording of repealed but re-enacted statutory crimes as an aid to the construction of the latest re-enacted form, provided, of course, that it was not the legislature's clear intention to alter the substance of the original crime.

Use of dictionaries

Where all else fails, and the meaning to be assigned to a **13–05** particular word in a statutory offence is crucial to the determination of a case, the courts will often turn to dictionary definitions. If several meanings are proffered by a dictionary, the court will generally adopt the one that best accords with the word in its statutory context. In *Patchett v MacDougall*,[21] for example, the accused had shot a collie dog in the head and killed it. There was no evidence that it had survived the shooting for any significant length of time, or at all. Nevertheless, the accused was charged with causing, "unnecessary suffering to [the] animal" by wanton or unreasonable conduct, in terms of s.1(1)(a) of the Protection of Animals (Scotland) Act 1912. As he had shot the dog deliberately and without reason, his guilt or innocence plainly depended upon whether he had caused it to "suffer" or not. To determine this issue, Lord Justice-Clerk Wheatley examined the definition of "suffering" as given in the *Shorter Oxford English Dictionary* (a favoured work amongst the judiciary, presumably because of its convenient, two-volume size). He chose the second of the meanings offered there, namely, "the bearing or undergoing of pain", and concluded that there was no evidence that the unfortunate animal had undergone any such thing. The accused, therefore, had his conviction quashed, the Lord Justice-Clerk dismissing the argument that the dog had suffered by losing its life as metaphysical, and not what the Act envisaged at all.[22]

Similarly, in *White v Allan*[23] a woman was convicted of the **13–06** offence specified in s.46(1) of the Civic Government (Scotland) Act 1982, which states that: "A prostitute (whether male or female) who for the purposes of prostitution . . . (c) importunes any person who is in a public place, shall be guilty [of an offence] . . .". She was charged, then, as a person possessing a certain qualification, i.e. that she was a prostitute. She challenged the applicability of that special capacity to her.[24] It thus became necessary for the

---

[21] *Patchett v MacDougall*, 1983 J.C. 63.

[22] *Patchett v MacDougall*, 1983 J.C. 63 at 64. Most (and in particular s.1) of the Protection of Animals (Scotland) Act 1912 is now repealed by the Animal Health and Welfare (Scotland) Act 2006 (asp 11) Sch.2 para.5: s.19 of the 2006 Act now frames the appropriate offence of causing unnecessary suffering to a "protected animal" (as defined in s.17)—but "suffering" now receives a statutory definition in s.48 of that Act. (The 2006 Act in fact contains many interesting new offences which will repay close study.)

[23] *White v Allan*, 1985 S.C.C.R. 85.

[24] See now the Criminal Procedure (Scotland) Act 1995 s.255, as amended by the Criminal Procedure (Amendment) (Scotland) Act 2004 (asp 5) Sch.1 para.38.

Crown to demonstrate that she had possessed that qualification at the time of the alleged importuning. The main thrust of the argument was that this offence had originally been enacted in 1892[25] and was then committed only if the accused was a "common prostitute". Since Parliament had changed the wording of the offence in 1982 by dropping the adjective "common", this was claimed to have opened the way for a different interpretation, namely that if a person, such as the accused, behaved on the occasion in question as a prostitute might (as indeed the accused had), then she fell within the qualification and thus within the ambit of the offence. The Appeal Court, however, rejected that contention. It considered that the elision of the word "common" in the re-enacted offence made no difference, and that the standard meaning of "prostitute" in the *Concise Oxford Dictionary* ("a woman who offers her body to promiscuous sexual intercourse, especially for payment") still applied. Further, the court interpreted the statutory offence such that the accused had to possess the title of "prostitute", with that dictionary meaning, prior to the incidents which had led to the prosecution. Since the Crown had been quite unable to show that, then the conviction had to be quashed.[26]

Common law alternatives

13–07   If by way of interpretation (or otherwise) it is decided that the statutory offence charged cannot be established on the facts admitted or proved, all is not necessarily lost for the Crown. In terms of para.14(b) of Sch.3 to the Criminal Procedure (Scotland) Act 1995,

> "where the facts proved under the indictment or complaint do not amount to a contravention of the enactment but do amount to an offence at common law, it shall be lawful to convict of the common law offence."

This rather useful provision was taken advantage of by the sheriff in *Buchanan v Hamilton*[27] where he decided that vandalism had not been proved but that breach of the peace had. Although his decision to convict of the common law crime was overturned on appeal, this was simply on the basis that it was not for the sheriff to

---

[25] Burgh Police (Scotland) Act 1892 s.381(22).
[26] Where the meaning of legislation is ambiguous or obscure, it may be possible to use material from *Hansard*, or other reports of Parliamentary debates to assist in interpretation—*Pepper v Hart* [1993] A.C. 593 HL. It has been held in England that a court may correct obvious drafting errors in a statutory provision: see *R (on the application of CPS) v Bow Street Magistrates Court* [2007] 1 W.L.R. 291 QB.
[27] *Buchanan v Hamilton*, 1990 S.L.T. 244.

do so on his own, in the absence of a specific submission to invoke the provision from the Crown. The Appeal Court did not decide that it was incompetent to convict of breach of the peace in such circumstances.[28]

INTERPRETATION II

There is also a wider dimension to a court's interpretative powers. **13–08** This relates to a court's ability to decide whether *mens rea* will have to be proved, or facts from which it can be inferred will have to be established, by the Crown in relation to a particular statutory crime. It is usually taken that *mens rea* must be proved, or facts from which it can be inferred must be established in relation to all common law crimes as a matter of principle[29]; but it is accepted in modern criminal law that some statutory offences do not, and need not, conform to that principle. These form the class of "strict liability" crimes[30] within the general field of statutory offences. These "strict" offences and the courts' role in identifying them are considered in the paragraphs which follow.[31] Also briefly considered below is the subject of "vicarious liability". This sort of liability—where one person is deemed liable for the criminal act or omission of another—is again thought to be peculiar to statutory offences. It is peculiar to those Acts of Parliament which expressly allow it, or to those where the courts, by dint of interpretation, deem it to apply. Careful note must be taken, however, that in the totality of statutory offences, strict liability or vicarious liability is unusual, and certainly does not represent the norm.

How strict liability arises

Offences created by the United Kingdom or Scottish Parliament **13–09** have precisely worded definitions. Every word which appears in a statutory crime must, therefore, be taken to be meaningful. Equally, it can be argued that what does not appear is also meaningful (see below, para.13–10). As far as *mens rea* is concerned, many statutory offences expressly refer to some form of

---

[28] *cf. Anderson v Griffiths*, 2005 J.C. 169, where the Appeal Court considered it to be within its powers to substitute a "breach of the peace" verdict at an appeal, even though such a verdict had not been sought by the Crown at the original trial for a statutory offence. See also *Horsburgh v Russell*, 1994 S.L.T. 942.

[29] See, e.g. Gordon, *Criminal Law*, 3rd edn, para.7.12.

[30] For some comment on the justifications for the existence of these crimes, and an introduction to relevant (modern) academic literature on the subject, see John Stanton-Ife, "Strict Liability: Stigma and Regret" (2007) 27 O.J.L.S. 151.

[31] If a statutory offence expressly announces that it is to be taken as one of "strict liability", that must be accepted, and no "identification" criteria need then be applied: that would be rather unusual, but see, e.g. s.6 (relative to the offence created by s.4) of the Christmas Day and New Year's Day Trading (Scotland) Act 2007 (asp 13)—which nevertheless provides for a defence of "due diligence". Thus, s.6 of that Act provides an illustration of an offence which is of "strict", but not "absolute", liability: see below, para.13–13.

that concept. Thus, in the Criminal Law (Consolidation) (Scotland) Act 1995, it is stated in s.48(2)(a) that:

"Any person who intentionally obstructs a constable in the exercise of the constable's powers under sub-section (1) [i.e. powers to search suspects for offensive weapons] . . . shall be guilty of an offence . . .".

There, the central element of the *actus reus* of the offence is "obstruction", and clearly it will have to be shown by the Crown that the obstruction was "intentional" on the accused's part. A similar conclusion follows from the way in which the statutory offence of vandalism has been defined.[32] The central element of that crime relates to the destruction or damaging of property, and it is expressly stated that that must be shown to have been wilful or reckless on the part of the accused. The Misuse of Drugs Act 1971 also contains a further instance of the same idea. Section 8,[33] for example, indicates that:

"A person commits an offence if, being the occupier or concerned in the management of any premises, he knowingly permits or suffers any of the following activities to take place on those premises . . .".

It will there not be sufficient if any of the forbidden activities (which include producing or using a controlled drug) happens to take place on the premises concerned. To be convicted, an accused person must be shown to have *known* that they were taking place, and allowed them to do so in that state of knowledge.

13–10   Relative to crucial (or central) elements of the offences in question, the express use of words such as "intentionally", "recklessly", "wilfully", or "knowingly" demonstrates that these statutory crimes are to be treated similarly to common law ones—namely, that the specified form of *mens rea* must be proved by the Crown. If it cannot be proved, or if facts from which it might be inferred[34] cannot be established, then the prosecution's case will founder. But what is to be made of offences where Parliament has not made specific provision for any *mens rea* concepts? In s.47(1) of the Criminal Law (Consolidation) (Scotland) Act 1995, for example, it is laid down that:

---

[32] See above, para.11–26.
[33] As amended by the Criminal Justice and Police Act 2001 s.38.
[34] See, e.g. *Lees v Haig*, 1993 S.L.T. (Sh. Ct.) 76, where the inference was drawn that a concealed, rusty meat cleaver was intended by the accused for use by him for causing personal injury (relative to what is now s.47(4) of the Criminal Law (Consolidation) (Scotland) Act 1995—noting that s.47(4) is amended by the Offensive Weapons Act 1996 s.5; see also the terms of s.49B of the 1995 Act—offence of having an offensive weapon, etc. in a prison—as inserted by the Custodial Sentences and Weapons (Scotland) Act 2007 (asp 17) s.63).

"Any person who without lawful authority or reasonable
excuse, the proof whereof shall lie on him, has with him in
any public place any offensive weapon shall be guilty of an
offence . . .".

Quite apart from the difficulties of construing "public place"[35] and
"offensive weapon"[36] it would seem that conviction could follow on
mere proof that the accused *had* an offensive weapon about his
person, whether he knew it was there or not. That would appear to
be a fair reading of the subsection, taking the words used in a
completely literal sense; but whether it would be a fair interpretation in relation to an accused person, who had had an offensive
weapon slipped surreptitiously into his coat pocket by another, is a
different matter; and that is where the difficulty lies. It certainly
can be argued that if Parliament had wanted the courts to insist on
mens rea being shown, then it would have made appropriate
provision. It may, therefore, be meaningful that Parliament has
chosen here to exclude any reference to intention, recklessness,
knowledge or the like; and so the conclusion may well follow that
mens rea is not required to be shown by the Crown. Thus, on this
argument, if an offensive weapon had really been slipped into the
accused's pocket without his having been aware of it, then he
would still have "had it with him" as a matter of fact, and must be
convicted—his lack of knowledge being an irrelevant consideration,
since knowledge did not have to be shown. This is clearly a harsh,
but tenable, interpretative argument. On the other hand, if there is
some principle at work, even in statutory crimes, that *mens rea* is to
be presumed to be part of the definition of all offences, then *mens
rea* ought to be required even in the case of statutory offences
which are silent on the matter. Were the courts to adopt that
principle, then all statutory crimes would require some form of
mens rea, unless the United Kingdom or Scottish Parliament had
made it abundantly clear that that was exceptionally not to be so in
relation to a particular offence. The question faced by courts which
do espouse that view is, of course: "What form of *mens rea* is to be
required in the absence of the legislature's having given any plain
directions?"[37]

Presumption in favour of mens rea

It seems well established under English law that there is a **13–11**
presumption in favour of *mens rea* being required even in the kind
of statutory offences where the text is silent as to intention,

---

[35] See Criminal Law (Consolidation) (Scotland) Act 1995 s.47(4), as amended by
the Offensive Weapons Act 1996 s.5, and, e.g. *Normand v Donnelly*, 1994 S.L.T.
62.

[36] See again s.47(4), as amended by the Offensive Weapons Act 1996 s.5; and see
also, e.g. *McGlennan v Clark*, 1993 S.L.T. 1069; *McKee v MacDonald*, 1995 S.L.T.
1342; and *Lees v Haig*, 1993 S.L.T. (Sh. Ct.) 76.

[37] For the answer given by English courts in relation to what is now s.47(1) of the
Criminal Law (Consolidation) (Scotland) Act 1995 Act, see *R. v Cugullere* [1961]
1 W.L.R. 858, per Salmon J. at 860.

recklessness, knowledge, wilfulness or the like.[38] That presumption yields, however, where a court is satisfied that Parliament really did not wish *mens rea* to be considered. Since Parliament seldom[39] makes that plain, the courts must look for signs and hints within, or even outwith, the Act itself in order to deduce Parliament's intention. As can be imagined, this is a somewhat arbitrary process. But it does result in some such statutory offences being considered as of *mens rea* quality and others acquiring "strict liability" status,[40] where "strict liability" means that no *mens rea* need be proved or inferred in respect of an issue crucial for conviction.[41]

13–12   In Scotland, it seems to be the case that that presumption in favour of *mens rea* is fully accepted. Gordon[42] suggested that it was, although his authorities were mostly English; but acceptance of a sort can be shown in some twentieth-century dicta, especially in the opinions of Lord Justice-General Normand and Lords Wark, Moncrieff and Mackay in *Mitchell v Morrison*.[43] Lord Cameron, in *Swan v MacNab*,[44] was also moved to consider it as "a general proposition." Now, however, the position established in English law[45] seems to have been accepted as also forming part of Scots criminal law.[46] But it must be remembered that that presumption is a rebuttable one, and that a particular statutory offence may nevertheless be considered as one of "strict liability".[47] It must also be remembered that, in both Scotland and England, the threshold for the identification of "strict liability" is the existence of a statutory offence which omits any of the usual references to *mens rea*, at least in relation to the central element of the crime.[48] The question therefore lies as to the sort of criteria which might then

---

[38] See *Sweet v Parsley* [1970] A.C. 132 HL, per Lord Reid at 148G–H; *Gammon (Hong Kong) Ltd v Att-Gen of Hong Kong* [1985] A.C. 1 PC, per Lord Scarman at 14B–D; *B (A Child) v DPP* [2000] 2 A.C. 428 HL, Lord Nicholls of Birkenhead at 460F–G, Lord Steyn at 470H–471E, Lord Hutton at 478D–479E.

[39] Unusually, the Scottish Parliament has made this plain in s.6 of the Christmas Day and New Year's Day Trading (Scotland) Act 2007 (asp 13) relative to the offence created by s.4 of that Act.

[40] See, e.g. *Strowger v John* [1974] R.T.R. 124.

[41] *cf.* the Scottish Law Commission's "Report on Rape and Other Sexual Offences", Scot. Law Com. No.209 (December 2007), para.4–32 (meaning of "strict liability"): see also below, para.13–13.

[42] Gordon, *Criminal Law*, 3rd edn, paras 8.01, 8.02, fn.10.

[43] *Mitchell v Morrison*, 1938 J.C. 64 at 71, 87, 72–73 and 81–82, respectively.

[44] *Swan v McNab*, 1977 J.C. 57 at 61.

[45] See above, para.13–11.

[46] See *Smart v HM Advocate*, 2006 S.C.C.R. 120, opinion of the court at 127G–128E, para.22. It is to be noted that in considering what form the *mens rea* should take, after applying the presumption and concluding that the offence in question was not of strict liability, the court accepted that form favoured by the English Court of Appeal in *R. v Smith; R. v Jayson* [2003] 1 Cr.App.R. 212 (case 13) at 222, para.34, relative to the equivalent statutory offence under English law.

[47] See above, para.13–11.

[48] See *Wings Ltd v Ellis* [1985] A.C. 272, in relation to the Trade Descriptions Act 1968 s.14(1)(a).

be invoked to displace the presumption and mark the statutory offence under scrutiny as being one of strict liability. These criteria are considered below at para.13–14 *et seq.*

Strict or absolute liability

Two terms of art have been employed to denote criminal liability **13–13** which does not depend upon proof of *mens rea*. "Absolute liability" is the older, and now less fashionable of the two. It was certainly used extensively in Scotland during the first half of the twentieth century[49] and may indeed be not yet dead.[50] With its connotation of criminal liability not only without proof of *mens rea* but also without benefit of any form of defence, the term is probably much too sweeping, and is best reserved perhaps for those peculiar, "states of affairs" statutory offences which are sometimes encountered.[51] Better, probably, is the term "strict liability". It means criminal liability where the central element of the *actus reus* of the offence does not require proof of *mens rea* on the part of the accused, but does not exclude the possibility of there being some form of defence or indeed the possibility of some form of *mens rea* being required in relation to subsidiary elements. It sounds fairer, in other words, to assert that liability is "strict" rather than "absolute", and indeed may more accurately reflect the true situation.[52] In *Alphacell Ltd v Woodward*,[53] for example, Viscount Dilhorne pointed out that the statutory offence of "causing" polluting matter to enter a stream was not absolute. If it had been absolute, then mere accidental pollution of a stream might result in conviction, which he did not think to have been Parliament's intention at all. Rather, if the accused had been intentionally carrying on some industrial process, in such a way that the natural consequence would have been the pollution of a stream, and such pollution had in fact occurred, then he could be convicted—even though he had neither intended nor known about such pollution at all.[54] *Alphacell Ltd v Woodward* is, of course, an English case, but was specifically approved in *Lockhart v National Coal Board*.[55]

---

[49] See, e.g. *Gordon v Shaw* (1908) 5 Adam 469, where Lord McLaren refers to "absolute prohibition" at 478; *Howman v Russell*, 1923 J.C. 32, per Lord Cullen at 36; *Mitchell v Morrison*, 1938 J.C. 64, per Lord Justice-General Normand at 71.

[50] See, e.g. *MacNeill v Wilson*, 1981 J.C. 87, opinion of the court at 91.

[51] See above, para.3–15, and *Strowger v John* [1974] R.T.R. 124.

[52] See the use of the term "strict liability" in s.6 of the Christmas Day and New Year's Day Trading (Scotland) Act 2007 (asp 13)—clearly a correct use, since that section provides a defence to the offence created under s.4 of the Act; *cf.* the "Explanatory Notes" (prepared by the "Non-Executive Bills Unit")—which are not, of course, part of the Act and do not have the authority of the Scottish Parliament—where no attempt is made to explain what "strict liability" means, and where the relevant offence is erroneously attributed to s.5.

[53] *Alphacell Ltd v Woodward* [1972] A.C. 824.

[54] *Alphacell Ltd v Woodward* [1972] A.C. 824 at 839F, 839H–840C.

[55] *Lockhart v National Coal Board*, 1981 S.L.T. 161.

Criteria for identifying strict liability

13–14　　It is rare for Scottish courts to discuss, let alone follow, specific criteria for the identification of strict liability, statutory offences. The tendency in fact is to follow English precedents, if such exist[56] or to treat such problems of identification as meriting little more than the application of well-known interpretative techniques in a common-sense way.[57] There is the tendency also to treat each statute as a separate entity and to avoid laying down rules which might be generally applicable to other statutory offences. It would seem, therefore, fairly academic to attempt to consider what sort of criteria might carry weight with a Scottish court. But certain trends are discernible; and failure to consider these would make it impossible to predict when, in the case of new or untested statutory offences which made no express reference to *mens rea*, the accepted presumption in favour of *mens rea* could be displaced.[58] In any event, the sort of criteria to be borne in mind were hinted at by Lord McLaren in the early twentieth-century case of *Gordon v Shaw*.[59]

Gordon v Shaw

13–15　　In this case, the Sea Fisheries Regulation (Scotland) Act 1895,[60] by virtue of s.10(4) and associated byelaws,[61] made it an offence for any person to use certain trawl-fishing methods in the Moray Firth, i.e. within a line drawn between Duncansby Head in Caithness and Rattray Point near Peterhead. The accused was not the master of the vessel concerned, but an ordinary member of the crew. The court was prepared to accept that he might have been quite unaware of the exact location of the boat when the prohibited fishing took place; and the question lay whether his lack of such knowledge would be of any moment, given the non-*mens rea* wording of the offence. In deciding that it would not, and that the accused should be convicted, Lord McLaren mentioned four possible criteria which might be used to decide if such statutory offences were "absolute". These consist of the "policy of the statute", its "language", whether or not a requirement for *mens rea* might make it "very difficult to get a conviction against anyone", and "the duty of those who engage in the fishing industry to inform themselves, and to take care that they do not fish where they are not entitled to fish."[62] They are considered further in the paragraphs which follow.

---

[56] See, e.g. *Lockhart v National Coal Board*, 1981 S.L.T. 161.
[57] See, e.g. *Smith of Maddiston Ltd v MacNab*, 1975 J.C. 48, where nine judges sat.
[58] See above, paras 13–11, 13–12.
[59] *Gordon v Shaw* (1908) 5 Adam 469.
[60] Now repealed by the Inshore Fishing (Scotland) Act 1984, s.10, Sch.2.
[61] See above, para.2–15.
[62] *Gordon v Shaw* (1908) 5 Adam 469 at 477–478.

Policy of the statute

This criterion involves a court deciding that the aim which a **13–16** particular statutory offence sets out to achieve is of such importance that it ought to prevail over the maxim *actus non facit reum nisi mens sit rea*.[63] In other words, some statutory offences promote such things as the safety of the public[64] or the protection of the environment, and the securing of these aims may be considered to justify conviction without proof of *mens rea*. That this sort of thinking may figure in the deliberations of Scottish judges can be seen by considering such cases as *Mitchell v Morrison*,[65] where Lord Justice-General Normand referred to the "safety of the public" in the context of the statutory requirement to maintain records of truck-drivers' hours; *Anderson v Rose*,[66] where the prohibition against selling a heifer in calf for slaughter was clearly designed as a wartime measure to protect scarce food resources (as was hinted at by Lord Justice-Clerk Scott Dickson)[67]; *MacNeill v Wilson*,[68] where the prohibition against having an insecure load on a truck was obviously designed to prevent danger to the public; and *Lockhart v National Coal Board*,[69] where the protection of water supplies from pollution could be said to have taken precedence over the coal board's understandable claim to have done all that could reasonably have been expected of it in the circumstances.

Language used

Although it is unwise to rely too strongly on this, because of the **13–17** very varied nature of expression found in statutory offences, some words do appear to carry a similar significance relative to criminal liability, irrespective of the statute in which they appear. Thus, where liability depends on "possession" of some article, it is usual to regard the offence as requiring *mens rea* in the form of knowledge, whether the statute specifically mentions knowledge or not. One cannot "possess" what one does not know one has; and further, as Lord Justice-Clerk Ross said in *Gill v Lockhart*[70]:

> "Before there can be possession in terms of the Act [i.e. the Misuse of Drugs Act 1971 s.5(2)], it is well established that

---

[63] See above, para.3–01, for translation.
[64] See, e.g. *Gammon (Hong Kong) Ltd v Att-Gen of Hong Kong* [1985] A.C. 1.
[65] *Mitchell v Morrison*, 1938 J.C. 64 at 71.
[66] *Anderson v Rose*, 1919 J.C. 20.
[67] *Anderson v Rose*, 1919 J.C. 20 at 22.
[68] *MacNeill v Wilson*, 1981 J.C. 87.
[69] *Lockhart v National Coal Board*, 1981 S.L.T. 161.
[70] *Gill v Lockhart*, 1988 S.L.T. 189 at 190G.

there must be, on the part of an accused, both knowledge and control."[71]

The word "use", however, seems to be given a "strict" interpretation. Thus, where it is criminal to "use" on a road a motor vehicle which does not comply with prescribed regulations, it is not necessary to show that the user knew that his vehicle did not so comply at the relevant time.[72] On the other hand, where a statute forbids someone to "cause or permit" the "use" of something whilst it does not comply with prescribed regulations, both "causing" and "permitting" appear to require knowledge on the part of the accused that the thing was being so used in contravention of those regulations.[73] The "knowledge" need not be actual, however, where the court is satisfied that the accused deliberately avoided informing himself of the obvious.[74] But, where a statute forbade "causing or knowingly permitting" the entry of pollutants into a stream, the "causing" alternative was considered to be "strict".[75] In that case, however, English authority existed, which was accepted by both counsel and eventually the Appeal Court as being correct. Presumably also, the deliberate attachment of "knowingly" to the "permitting" was seen as significant. With reservations, then, it would seem worthwhile to argue by way of analogy that the interpretation given to a particular word in one statute ought to be decisive of its meaning in another.

Prosecution difficulties

13–18   That the insistence upon proof of *mens rea* would lead to the ineffectiveness of an offence is occasionally voiced as a reason for holding that offence to be of strict liability. The argument is that such insistence would make things just too difficult for the Crown, and that that would be disastrous given the aim which the statute seeks to achieve. Under the Road Traffic Regulation Act 1984 s.89(1), for example:

> "A person who drives a motor vehicle on a road at a speed exceeding a limit imposed by or under any [relevant] enactment . . . shall be guilty of an offence."

---

[71] See also *Black v HM Advocate*, 1974 J.C. 43 (relative to s.3—as amended by the Terrorism Act 2006 s.17(5), (6)—and s.4 of the Explosive Substances Act 1883) and *Smith v HM Advocate*, 1996 S.C.C.R. 49 (which confirms that a person possesses a firearm for the purposes of s.1 of the Firearms Act 1968 if he knows he has, and has control over, an object which happens to be a firearm).

[72] This is assumed in, e.g. *Swan v MacNab*, 1977 J.C. 57; see opinion of Lord Cameron at 58–63.

[73] See *Smith of Maddiston Ltd v MacNab*, 1975 J.C. 48; *cf. MacDonald v Howdle* 1995 S.L.T. 779.

[74] *Brown v W. Burns Tractors Ltd*, 1986 S.C.C.R. 146.

[75] *Lockhart v National Coal Board*, 1981 S.L.T. 161.

Clearly, if the prosecution were required to prove that a motorist knew he was exceeding a particular speed limit (the central element of the offence), there would be very few convictions and the purpose of the provision (presumably connected with road safety) would be substantially undermined. Similar thinking probably lies behind the view that offences of possessing or supplying controlled drugs do not require the Crown to show that the accused knew that some package or other actually contained controlled drugs. It is enough if an accused person can be shown to have had the knowledge (and control) necessary to establish his possession of the package—which happens to contain such drugs.[76] If he claims that he did not know what the contents of the package were, that is a matter for him to establish by way of defence.[77] "Prosecution difficulty" seems, however, to be a somewhat specious way of arguing for the imposition of strict liability. No doubt the Crown can experience similar difficulty in relation to the proof of some common law crimes; but few would suggest that those common law crimes should accordingly be treated as "strict".

Trade regulation

It is often argued too that statutory offences which bear no **13–19** express reference to *mens rea* and which are basically designed to impose standards for the carrying on of particular trades or activities should be prime candidates for strict liability. This is particularly so, apparently, where the offence can be regarded as dealing with acts which, "are not criminal in any real sense, but are acts which in the public interest are prohibited under a penalty."[78] Such *mala prohibita*,[79] it might be argued, are the price which has to be paid for participating in that trade or activity. Those who do so must simply observe strictly the standards imposed. If they fail to do so, even unknowingly, then they should be convicted.[80] Much the same might be said of motorists, of course, in relation to many offences found in the Road Traffic Act 1988.[81]

---

[76] See *Tudhope v McKee*, 1988 S.L.T. 153, in relation to the Misuse of Drugs Act 1971 s.4(3)(b). See also *Salmon v HM Advocate; Moore v HM Advocate*, 1998 S.C.C.R. 740; *Wali v HM Advocate*, 2007 S.C.C.R. 106.

[77] See Misuse of Drugs Act 1971 s.28, as interpreted in *Salmon v HM Advocate; Moore v HM Advocate*, 1998 S.C.C.R. 740 and *Henvey v HM Advocate*, 2005 S.C.C.R. 282.

[78] See Wright J. in *Sherras v De Rutzen* [1895] 1 Q.B. 918 at 922, quoted by Viscount Dilhorne in *Alphacell Ltd v Woodward* [1972] A.C. 824 at 839G, and by Lord Scarman in *Wings Ltd v Ellis* [1985] 1 A.C. 272 at 293D to 294E–F.

[79] See, e.g. *Beattie v Waugh*, 1920 J.C. 64, and the opinion of Lord Justice-Clerk Scott Dickson at 69 that the offence there was "a clear case of *malum prohibitum*"; see also above, para.2–37.

[80] See, e.g. *Dickson v Linton* (1888) 2 White 51; *Gordon v Shaw* (1908) 5 Adam 469, per Lord McLaren at 478.

[81] See, e.g. *Howman v Russell*, 1923 J.C. 32—the present law pertaining to the situation in that case now being found in the Road Traffic Act 1988 s.42 (as substituted by the Road Traffic Act 1991 s.8, and as amended by the Road Safety Act 2006 ss.18(3), 26(2)), and the Road Vehicles Lighting Regulations (SI 1989/1796) reg.24(1)(a).

Criteria in general

13–20   It would be wrong to imagine that the various criteria mentioned above form an exhaustive list or are applied on any consistent basis. It is also far from clear whether Scottish courts apply them at all.[82] Of far greater importance, probably, is the court's "feeling" for the particular offence in question; if it seems trivial, from the point of view of its maximum penalty,[83] and regulatory, as measured from the point of view of its content, it will probably be taken as "strict". Otherwise, it is much more difficult to predict how a court will react. It may be safest to conclude that the only strict liability offences are those which have already been recognised as such by a competent court in Scotland. Although that gives little insight into the likely treatment by the courts of new statutory offences, it should be borne in mind that most genuinely new offences, as opposed to re-enacted former ones,[84] do specify some form of *mens rea*.[85]

Defences to "strict" offences

13–21   If a particular statutory offence has been recognised as "strict", this does not preclude the possibility of a defence. This is obviously so in relation to statutes which themselves cater for such defences. In the Food Safety Act 1990, for example, s.8(1) narrates that "any person who (a) sells for human consumption . . . any food which fails to comply with food safety requirements shall be guilty of an offence." There is nothing to suggest that this would not be considered as a crime of strict liability.[86] But the Act provides specific defences to that crime. In s.21, for example, it is stated that it shall, "be a defence for the person charged to prove that he took all reasonable precautions and exercised all due diligence to avoid the commission of the offence by himself or by a person under his control."

13–22   Where no specific defences are provided by an Act to a strict liability offence, it was at one time thought that there might nevertheless be a defence of "excusable ignorance" in relation to matters central to that offence. In particular, a defence of that nature seemed to be recognised by Lord McLaren in *Gordon v Shaw*[87] when he said,

---

[82] *cf.* the approach of English courts, as in *R. v Bradish* [1990] 1 Q.B. 981.
[83] Although the matter of maximum punishment is very far from being decisive, in England, at least—see *Gammon (Hong Kong) Ltd v Att-Gen of Hong Kong* [1985] A.C. 1, Lord Scarman at 17F.
[84] See, e.g. the Food Safety Act 1990.
[85] See, e.g. the Computer Misuse Act 1990 s.1 (as amended by the Police and Justice Act 2006 s.35), s.2 (as amended by the 2006 Act Sch.14 para.17), s.3 (as substituted by the 2006 Act s.36) and s.3A (as inserted by the 2006 Act s.37).
[86] See, e.g. *Dickson v Linton* (1888) 2 White 51, per Lord McLaren at 58.
[87] *Gordon v Shaw* (1908) 5 Adam 469 at 479.

"where a person in the position of the respondent comes forward, and is able to satisfy the Sheriff that he was excusably ignorant of the position of the fishing vessel . . . his case will always receive indulgent consideration."

Lord Kinnear, however, reserved his opinion on the correctness of that view,[88] which was in turn doubted by Lord Justice-Clerk Scott Dickson in *Beattie v Waugh*,[89] and ignored in *Howman v Russell*.[90] On balance, it probably must be accepted that there is no such general defence to strict liability offences in this country; and that the concept of "excusable ignorance" can be given effect to, if at all, only as an aspect of prosecutorial discretion before commencement of proceedings[91] or in mitigation of sentence following conviction.

Vicarious liability

In the criminal law, vicarious liability means the responsibility **13–23** which A might be considered to have for the criminal conduct of B in the absence of any question of complicity (see above, Ch.7). This is bound to be unusual, since it involves imposing punishment on A where the *actus reus* of the crime in question was not committed by him and where he personally had no *mens rea*. For it to arise at all, therefore, there requires to be some relationship between A and B. In terms of the case law, that relationship is usually that of employer (A) and employee (B), or principal (A) and agent (B); but other relationships could be involved, if these were expressly catered for in a particular Act of Parliament.[92] The criminal conduct of B, however, must occur within the scope of the employment or agency agreement concerned.[93] If it does not, then only the actor (B) is criminally liable for what was done or omitted. The basis for this unusual form of responsibility is thought to be that those who employ others about a particular trade or business are responsible for the way in which those others conduct themselves in relation to the regulations which apply to that trade or business. The employer or principal will certainly avail himself of the rewards of that business; so it is not totally unfair to make him stand the risks—including vicarious criminal liability, where that is considered to exist. In any event, it may well make him more vigilant in relation to the law's requirements.

---

[88] *Gordon v Shaw* (1908) 5 Adam 469 at 481.
[89] *Beattie v Waugh*, 1920 J.C. 64 at 68; *cf.* Lord Salvesen (dissenting) at 69.
[90] *Howman v Russell*, 1923 J.C. 32.
[91] *Howman v Russell*, 1923 J.C. 32, per Lord Sands at 36.
[92] For a modern example of express imposition of vicarious liability, see the Breastfeeding etc. (Scotland) Act 2005 (asp 1) s.2; see also below, para.13–25.
[93] See, e.g. *City and Suburban Dairies v Mackenna*, 1918 J.C. 105, per Lord Justice-Clerk Scott Dickson at 110.

Presumption against

13–24   It seems to be well accepted that this form of liability does not
exist in relation to common law crimes.[94] Even in the field of
statutory offences, there is a presumption against it[95]; and it is
clearly for the Crown to show that it ought to exist in relation to a
particular crime.[96]

Ambit

13–25   Vicarious liability will certainly apply if the United Kingdom or
Scottish Parliament has expressly said that it should. In such cases,
the prosecutor will have no greater task than to point to the plain
words of the statute. Thus, in terms of the Breastfeeding etc.
(Scotland) Act 2005 (asp 1) s.2(1):

> "Anything done by a person in the course of that person's
> employment shall in any proceedings brought under this Act
> [i.e. for the commission of an offence under s.1(1)—
> deliberately preventing or stopping a person in charge of a
> child (under two years of age) from feeding milk to that child
> in a public place[97] or on licensed premises[98]] be treated for
> the purposes of this Act as done also by that person's
> employer, whether or not it was done with the employer's
> knowledge or approval."

The heading to the section actually reads "Vicarious liability"—
which puts the matter beyond any semblance of doubt. Express
imposition of that sort is, however, unusual; and indeed an
employer in such a situation is permitted a defence. He is invited
to prove that he, "took such steps as were reasonably practicable to
prevent the employee from committing such an offence in the
course of the employee's employment."[99]

---

[94] See, e.g. *Haig v Thompson*, 1931 J.C. 29, per Lord Ormidale at 33; *Dean v John
Menzies (Holdings) Ltd*, 1981 J.C. 23, per Lord Cameron (dissenting) at 33, 34,
Lord Stott at 36, and Lord Maxwell at 39; and *Transco Plc v HM Advocate (No.1)*,
2004 J.C. 29, per Lord Hamilton (with whom Lord MacLean agreed) at 54,
para.53.

[95] See, e.g. *Haig v Thompson*, 1931 J.C. 29, per Lord Anderson at 33, "the general
rule is that an employer cannot be made constructively or vicariously liable for
the criminal acts of an employee."

[96] See *City and Suburban Dairies v Mackenna*, 1918 J.C. 105, per Lord Dundas at
110; *Duguid v Fraser*, 1942 J.C. 1, per Lord Mackay at 6.

[97] See Breastfeeding etc. (Scotland) Act 2005 (asp 1) s.1(4).

[98] See Breastfeeding etc. (Scotland) Act 2005 (asp 1) s.1(4), noting that the
Licensing (Scotland) Act 1976 is repealed by the Licensing (Scotland) Act 2005
(asp 16) Sch.7: such premises are now defined in s.147(1) of the 2005 Act.

[99] See Breastfeeding etc. (Scotland) Act 2005 (asp 1) s.2(3); *cf.* the system to ensure
compliance set up by the employer in *Readers' Digest Association Ltd v Pirie*, 1973
J.C. 42, which was concerned with the Unsolicited Goods and Services Act 1971.

In the absence of express imposition, vicarious criminal liability **13–26** has been recognised in relation to regulatory offences concerned with various business transactions normally conducted by employees. Examples include selling things at prices beyond what the law permits,[100] using motor vehicles which do not comply with "construction and use" regulations,[101] and keeping records of hours worked by drivers.[102] In each of these cases, of course, it may be said that the selling, or the using or the keeping of records was something the employer could have done by himself as well as by the hands of his employees, and that that demonstrates that the employer was meant to "share" liability. It may be, therefore, that such liability will not be recognised where the wording of the offence makes it difficult to show that anyone other than the employee himself was intended to be responsible as, for example, where an offence is expressly aimed at those "driving" as opposed to "using" motor vehicles in contravention of regulations.[103]

Compared with corporate liability

Since employers may be not only sole traders but also public **13–27** limited companies or partnerships, which have separate legal personality yet are incapable of doing or intending anything save through their management and employees, the whole subject of vicarious liability is easily confused with "corporate criminal responsibility". The topic of such corporate responsibility concerns a direct criminal liability. It is not concerned with the vicarious liability of a company for crimes actually committed by its employees or agents, but rather with the criminal liability of the company itself. There, the actions and *mentes reae* of particular managers or senior employees are imputed to the company (according to the prevailing "controlling mind" theory)[104]; these become the actions and *mentes reae* of the company. In vicarious liability, on the other hand, the company becomes liable for what individual employees have done. The conduct remains that of the employees involved, the only question then being whether the company, as employer, should also be criminally liable on a vicarious basis.

---

[100] See *Duguid v Fraser*, 1942 J.C. 1.

[101] See *Swan v MacNab*, 1977 J.C. 57.

[102] See *Mitchell v Morrison*, 1938 J.C. 64.

[103] *cf. Swan v MacNab*, 1977 J.C. 57; see also *Docherty v Stakis Hotels Ltd; Stakis Hotels Ltd v Docherty*, 1991 S.C.C.R. 6, where the Appeal Court decided that certain food regulations were aimed only at those who actually had management and control of the premises in question, and, further, that a company could not have actual management and control.

[104] See *Purcell Meats (Scotland) Ltd v McLeod*, 1987 S.L.T. 528; *Transco Plc v HM Advocate (No.1)*, 2004 J.C. 29; *cf.* relative to homicide, the terms of the Corporate Manslaughter and Corporate Homicide Act 2007: see above, para.9–71.

13–28   The above distinction must be borne in mind where a statutory
offence imposes liability not only on the actor but also on any
person who "caused or permitted" the offence to occur. If an
employer, for example, is charged with "permitting" the contravention of a statutory rule by an employee, then that is a direct liability
attaching to the employer. As Lord Justice-Clerk Grant put it in
Mackay Brothers v Gibb[105]:

> "It is true that the general rule is that a person is not
> vicariously liable for the criminal acts of another. This,
> however, is not a case of vicarious liability and is not so
> charged. [It was in fact a "permitting" case.] The appellants,
> being a firm, act by the hands of their partners and
> employees. . . . Like a limited liability company, they are a
> separate legal *persona* and have no mind. The question
> accordingly is not whether they are vicariously liable for what
> their garage controller did [i.e. hire out a car which had an
> insufficient depth of tread on one of its tyres], but whether
> through him, knowledge of the defect is brought home to
> them."

Whether or not knowledge is required to be imputed to a company
or partnership in a true case of vicarious liability is a moot point. It
can certainly be argued that it is not so required, even where the
offence in question is not "strict". That, however, would tend to
suggest that all vicarious liability was a form of "strict" liability,
which probably goes further than present case law or thinking will
allow.

---

[105] *Mackay Brothers v Gibb*, 1969 J.C. 26 at 31.

CHAPTER 14

CONCLUSION

Introduction

It is not common practice to include a conclusion in a work **14–01** which aims to describe and analyse the criminal law. In many ways, however, Scotland is not quite like any other jurisdiction. It is felt that some general observations are appropriate. First, as the preceding chapters have detailed, the broad sweep of the criminal law, including both general principles and specific offences, is governed by the common law. It is true that there is a myriad of statutory offences and that much of the time of the criminal courts is spent dealing with these, specifically under road traffic legislation. Nevertheless, the articulation of the criminal law continues to be a significant function of the Scottish judiciary. Rather than a criminal code or a collection of statutes, it is a body of case law which defines most of the more serious crimes, as well as the fundamental concepts, including attempt and complicity. Moreover, many of the statutory offences are not strictly necessary, since the conduct in question is already punishable at common law. Nor does the fact that Parliament has chosen not to treat a given kind of behaviour as a statutory offence preclude it being regarded as a common law offence,[1] although the courts could well disapprove of an attempt to circumvent a statutory prescription by prosecuting at common law.[2]

Secondly, for the better part of three centuries, the legal system **14–02** in Scotland bore the heavy burden of serving as an expression of nationhood. Following the Union of 1707 with England and Wales, the fact that Scotland possessed its own indigenous legal institutions and law (particularly criminal law) served as a foundation of national identity. On occasion, this may have led to support for aspects of the Scottish system purely because they were different

---

[1] See *HM Advocate v K*, 1994 S.C.C.R. 499.
[2] See *Webster v Dominick*, 2003 S.C.C.R. 525 at 542G–543A, para.60, per Lord Justice-Clerk Gill. There may be an expectation that, where the common law crime also constitutes a statutory offence, the maximum sentence which can be imposed is that set by the statute: *Cartwright v HM Advocate*, 2001 S.C.C.R. 695.

from those elsewhere in the United Kingdom, and not because of a thorough examination of their appropriateness. It may also have led to a certain defensiveness and insularity in the face of the perceived threat of Anglicisation of the law. These might be seen as aspects of what has come to be known as "legal nationalism".[3] The unspoken counterpart must, of course, be "legal unionism". Writing from a unionist perspective, Dicey and Rait observed[4]:

> "Much less attempt than one would have expected has been made to assimilate the law of each country to one another, and even where the diversity has caused considerable evil."

Indeed, one of the more remarkable features of the Union has been the continuing existence of the divergent criminal justice system in Scotland. No doubt the absence of an appeal to the House of Lords in criminal cases has helped to preserve the native law. A further part of the explanation undoubtedly lies in the recognition in the Acts of Union that "a union of nations did not require a union of laws."[5] Scots law has long been dangerous territory for English trespassers to enter. Nevertheless, for almost 300 years, the two legal systems were the responsibility of the same (predominantly English) Parliament. Following the Scotland Act 1998, and the establishment of the Scottish Parliament, that is no longer the case. For the first time in the modern era, Scotland has its own legislature able to give attention to the criminal justice system. It is surely not coincidental that the post-devolution period has seen an (unofficial) *Draft Criminal Code for Scotland with Commentary*, produced by a group of legal academics.[6]

THE SCOTTISH ORTHODOXY

14–03   The onus is on those who would wish to change the current system to convince that reform is necessary. It might require rather more than asserting that codification, "is a useful thing to do", on the basis that, "[a]n organised set of legal rules is better than a

---

[3] See L. Farmer, "Under the Shadow over Parliament House: The Strange Case of Legal Nationalism" in L. Farmer and S. Veitch (eds), *The State of Scots Law* (Edinburgh: Butterworths, 2001), Ch.9.

[4] A.V. Dicey and R.S. Rait, *Thoughts on the Union Between England and Scotland* (London: Macmillan, 1920), p.329.

[5] B.P. Levack, "The Proposed Union of English and Scots Law in the Seventeenth Century", 1975 J.R. 97, 115.

[6] This was published under the auspices of the Scottish Law Commission in 2003. For differing views on the document, compare P.R. Ferguson, "Codifying Criminal Law (1): A Critique of Scots Common Law" [2004] Crim. L.R. 49 and "Codifying Criminal Law (2): The Scots and English Draft Codes Compared" [2004] Crim L.R. 105, with T.H. Jones, "Towards a Good and Complete Criminal Code for Scotland" (2005) 68 M.L.R. 448. For further, critical discussion, see L. Farmer, "Enigma: Unravelling the Draft Criminal Code" (2002) 7 S.L.P.Q. 68.

disorganised set."[7] This is the more so given the extent to which codification has in the past been regarded as distinctly counter to Scottish tradition.[8] From a historical perspective, there has been little evidence of any great pressure among Scots lawyers for more reliance on statute law or for codification. The orthodox view has been that the common law allows the courts a desirable flexibility in dealing with the cases that come before them. Lord Avonside commented in *Khaliq v HM Advocate*[9]: "The great strength of our common law in criminal matters is that it can be invoked to fill a need. It is not static." And indeed the law has on occasion been driven forward with considerable boldness in modern times. In particular, reference may be made to developments in the law of rape[10] and the recognition of a defence of necessity.[11] With only occasional (but perhaps more frequent) exceptions,[12] there has been no question of a court's waiting for a Parliamentary solution when novel problems have been set before it.

This tradition owes much to the continuing influence of Hume, **14–04** who was a strong advocate of a flexible, common law system. He recognised that the criminal law had, "to be bent and accommodated to the temper and exigencies of the times".[13] Hume saw this as a judicial function. Not all have shared this perspective. A century before Hume, Mackenzie was arguing: "It were to be wisht, that nothing were a Cryme which is not declared to be so, by a Statute; for this would . . . prevent the arbitrariness of Judges".[14] In a review of the 1844 edition of Hume, Lord Ardmillan commented[15]:

> "The proper function of judges is *jus dicere,* not *jus dare;* and nothing is more perilous to constitutional government and public liberty, than the confusion of the judicial and legislative departments of the State. The voice of the judge is but the voice of the existing law, statutory or common, which it is his part to declare and administer. New laws must proceed from the Legislature . . . in whom alone rests the power of enacting what all subjects are bound, as subjects, to obey."

---

[7] E. Clive, "Law-Making in Scotland from APS to ASP" (1999) 3 *Edin. Law Rev.* 131 at 149.
[8] See, e.g. J.A. Dixon, "The Codification of the Law" (1878) 18 *Jnl of Jurisprudence* 305.
[9] *Khaliq v HM Advocate*, 1984 J.C. 23 at 26.
[10] *S v HM Advocate*, 1989 S.L.T. 469 (abolition of marital rape exemption); *Lord Advocate's Reference (No.1 of 2001),* 2002 S.L.T. 466 (redefinition of the *actus reus* of rape as non-consensual sexual intercourse). For discussion of the latter decision, see P.W. Ferguson, "The Definition of Rape", 2002 S.L.T. (News) 163.
[11] *Moss v Howdle*, 1997 J.C. 123.
[12] See, e.g. *Quinn v Cunningham*, 1956 J.C. 22; *Grant v Allan*, 1987 J.C. 71; *HM Advocate v Forbes*, 1994 S.L.T. 861; *Paterson v Lees*, 1999 J.C. 159; *Transco Plc v HM Advocate (No.1)*, 2004 J.C. 29.
[13] Hume, *Commentaries*, i, 2.
[14] Mackenzie, *Laws and Customs of Scotland in Matters Criminal*, p.3.
[15] Lord Ardmillan, "Scottish Criminal Law" (1846) IV *North British Rev.* 313.

Thus whilst the Humean approach may have prevailed, there has long been a competing tradition in Scots law. There has continued to be voiced dissatisfaction with the expanded role accorded to the judiciary in the development of the criminal law under what remains predominantly a common law system.[16] The (unofficial) *Draft Criminal Code*, with its proposal, "to convert the common law to statutory form",[17] can be seen as a continuation of this alternative tradition.

IS RELIANCE ON THE COMMON LAW DESIRABLE?

14-05 In other jurisdictions, particularly in England and Wales, it has increasingly been felt that the defining of crimes is beyond the competence of the courts. In respect of English law, Ashworth identifies it as a, "constitutional principle . . . that the reach of the criminal law should be declared by the legislature".[18] On this view, it is not felt to be appropriate for the judiciary to play a leading role in formulating the criminal law. Such formulation is generally thought to be the prerogative of the legislature, in view of the policy considerations inevitably involved. As Lord Kilbrandon (an eminent Scottish judge elevated to the House of Lords) stated in *DPP for Northern Ireland v Lynch*[19]:

> "It will not do to claim that judges have the duty-call it the privilege-of seeing to it that the common law expands and contracts to meet what the judges conceive to be the requirements of modern society. Modern society rightly prefers to exercise that function for itself, and this it conveniently does through those who represent it in Parliament."

Lord Kilbrandon's brethren sitting in the High Court of Justiciary, however, have not consistently taken this view. Indeed, it has been known for a Scottish judge to take a position quite opposed to this. In *Watt v Annan*[20] Lord Cameron wished to place the responsibility on Parliament not to create a crime, but to restrict the extent of the common law crime of shameless indecency:

> "It would be impracticable as well as undesirable to attempt to define precisely the limits and ambit of this particular offence . . . If it were considered desirable or necessary that

---

[16] See, e.g. W.A. Elliott, *"Nulla Poena Sine Lege"*, 1956 J.R. 22; G.H. Gordon, "Crimes Without Laws", 1966 J.R. 214.
[17] E. Clive and P. Ferguson, "Unravelling the Enigma: A Reply to Professor Farmer" (2002) 7 S.L.P.Q. 81 at 82.
[18] Ashworth, *Principles of Criminal Law*, 3rd edn, p.62.
[19] *DPP for Northern Ireland v Lynch* [1975] A.C. 653 at 700.
[20] *Watt v Annan*, 1978 J.C. 84 at 89. This case was overruled in *Webster v Dominick*, 2003 S.C.C.R. 525.

this was a chapter of the criminal law in which precise boundaries or limits were to be set then the task is one which is more appropriate for the hand of the legislator."

It is perhaps just as well that contemporary Scottish judges have **14-06** tended not to apply an unalloyed version of Lord Cameron's philosophy. They recognise that there are limits to their powers and that there are some issues best left to Parliament.[21] There is also an appreciation that it is the duty of the judiciary to clarify the limits of common law crimes.[22] The Human Rights Act 1998, and the associated impact of the European Convention on Human Rights, have no doubt had some influence in this regard.[23] The important decision in *Webster v Dominick*,[24] effectively replacing the common law crime of shameless indecency with one of public indecency, indicates the modern approach of the High Court to reducing the scope of vague common law crimes.[25] It has become evident that there is no ratchet effect in the common law of crimes. A similar exercise in delimitation has been conducted in respect of breach of the peace. In *Smith v Donnelly*[26] there was a clear attempt to identify with sufficient certainty the core elements of the *actus reus* of the most flexible of common law crimes. The result of this process received the endorsement of the European Court of Human Rights in *Lucas v United Kingdom*.[27] It considered,

> "that the definition of the offence of breach of the peace as stipulated in *Smith v Donnelly* . . . is suffciently precise to provide reasonable foreseeability of the actions which may fall within the remit of the offence."[28]

Decisions such as *Webster v Dominick* and *Smith v Donnelly* demonstrate great sensitivity to the principle of *nullum crimen sine lege*[29] and to the approach required to ensure compliance with the

---

[21] See, e.g. *Transco Plc v HM Advocate (No.1)*, 2004 J.C. 29.

[22] As suggested in *Lindsay v HM Advocate*, 1997 J.C. 19 at 22A–B, it might be regarded as an occasion more appropriate for legislative reform, "[w]here the law has been stated so clearly and consistently by the judges."

[23] See T.H. Jones, "Common Law Crimes and the Human Rights Act 1998", 2000 S.L.T. (News) 95; Lord Reed and J. Murdoch, *A Guide to Human Rights Law in Scotland* (London; Edinburgh: Butterworths, 2001), paras 5–138 to 5–140.

[24] *Webster v Dominick*, 2003 S.C.C.R. 525.

[25] The approach typified by cases such as *Watt v Annan*, 1978 J.C. 84, and *McLaughlan v Boyd*, 1934 J.C. 19 (both now overruled), is a thing of the past.

[26] *Smith v Donnelly*, 2001 S.L.T. 1007; for detailed discussion, see above, paras 12–11 to 12–14.

[27] *Lucas v United Kingdom* (2003) 37 E.H.R.R. CD 86.

[28] *Lucas v United Kingdom* (2003) 37 E.H.R.R. CD 86 at CD89.

[29] See above, para.2–20; L. Loucaides, *Essays on the Developing Law of Human Rights* (Martinus Nijhoff, 1995), Ch.2. Compare the decision of the House of Lords in *R. v Rimmington; R. v Goldstein* [2006] 1 A.C. 459, where Lord Bingham said that conduct forbidden by law should be clearly indicated so that a person is capable of knowing that it is wrong before he does it and that no one should be punished for doing something which was not a criminal offence when it was done.

European Convention on Human Rights. The role of the High Court is to ensure that its decisions provide sufficient guidance as to the boundaries of conduct covered by the common law of crimes.

14–07 Between 1707 and 1999 there was no separate Scottish legislature; and, given its generally unenthusiastic attention to matters of Scottish law reform, the Westminster Parliament tended to be viewed with a somewhat jaundiced eye north of the border. In itself, of course, this state of affairs could not justify an extended role for the judiciary in the articulation of the criminal law. It could equally have led to an argument for a reform of the legislative process in respect of Scots law.[30] This saw fruition in the Scotland Act 1998. That said, the prevailing tradition in Scotland has been that judges are to be intimately involved in the shaping and defining of crimes. It would, therefore, be no argument at all to assert that the traditional Scottish position ought to be discontinued just because the traditions are different elsewhere. There is, nevertheless, a constitutional and democratic dimension to Scottish criminal law. Since the criminal law is society's most important form of sanction, it can be argued that decisions on its scope should be taken by elected representatives in Parliament, rather than by past and present judges. It should not be thought that this is a characteristically modern thesis. Writing extra-judicially a century-and-a-half ago, Lord Cockburn rejected with scorn the notion,

> "that on the question, whether any action is held to be indictable or not, the *community is safer under the absolute wisdom of two or three individuals,* no matter how great their wisdom and virtue, *than under the wisdom of Parliament!*"[31]

It is undeniable that there are policy considerations involved in formulating the criminal law. But a counter-argument to Lord Cockburn might have been that in a small, relatively homogeneous country such as Scotland, the judiciary is as much in touch with public opinion as the group of men and women elected to the Parliament. That argument, of course, might be thought to lack continuing validity in light of the existence of a distinctively Scottish Parliament. Nevertheless, the lack of public criticism of the inherent flexibility of Scots criminal law in the hands of the judiciary, and the apparent Parliamentary acquiescence in the role played by Scottish criminal judges, are not insignificant matters. The difficulty with this argument is that it is premised on the idea that judges are qualified to discern and represent societal values.

---

[30] See T.H. Jones, "Criminal Justice and Devolution", 1997 J.R. 201.
[31] Lord Cockburn, "Scottish Criminal Jurisprudence and Procedure" (1846) 83 *Edin. Rev.* 196 at 198.

Lord Cockburn was in no doubt that, on this issue, "Parliament is a better, and infinitely more extended representation of public sentiment."[32] The general principles of the criminal law, and almost all the crimes detailed in this book, come within the domain of the Scottish Parliament. The future will reveal whether the extended role assumed by the judiciary has been a response to legislative neglect, or whether it continues to be a supportable feature of the Scottish legal and political system.

JUDICIAL DEVELOPMENT OF THE LAW

It is well understood that the courts in any jurisdiction have an **14–08** important role in the development of the law through their decisions. It is generally recognised, however, that the opportunities for doing so are much greater in a common law system than in one based on a code or on statutes. Of course, judges can effectively develop law through their interpretation of a statutory or code provision. But there they simply consider the detailed meaning of what has already been given clear shape by a distinct policy-making body. Scottish judges of the High Court of Justiciary, of course, may go much further than that. They may, in relation to non-statutory matters, act as a policy maker and give shape to the law in the very case before them. Objections to this judicial role can be based not so much on the usurpation of a parliamentary function as on the principles of prospectivity and certainty.

Prospectivity

The principle of prospectivity stands for the proposition that **14–09** criminal liability should only attach to conduct which has previously been declared to be criminal. It is reflected in Art.7 of the European Convention on Human Rights, which sets out the fundamental freedom from retroactive criminal offences and punishment. The European Court of Human Rights has interpreted this provision as not being confined to prohibiting the retrospective application of the criminal law to an accused's disadvantage. It has been taken to embody the more general principles that only the law can define a crime and that the criminal law should not be extensively construed to an accused's detriment, for instance by analogy.[33] The freedom appears to have considerable significance for any common law system. The common law method appears to preclude the requisite degree of

---

[32] Lord Cockburn, "Scottish Criminal Jurisprudence and Procedure" (1846) 83 *Edin. Rev.* 196 at 215. These extra-judicial observations lend perspective to Lord Cockburn's opinion in *Bernard Greenhuff* (1838) 2 Swin. 236, discussed above in paras 2–28 to 2–33.
[33] *Kokkinakis v Greece* (1994) 17 E.H.R.R. 397 at para.52.

forewarning: a judicial decision will apply to the case immediately before the court, as well as forming a precedent for the future.[34] To some extent the same is true if the decision called for is the interpretation of a statutory provision; but the problem is raised in a crucial form by judicial creativity in the common law, where there is no legislative framework. The particular issue which will face a court is the fairness of deciding a case on the basis of a rule articulated after the conduct in question took place.

14–10   In a general sense all judicial decisions in the criminal law are retrospective, in that, "it is the subsequent decision which reaches back into time and places the authoritative stamp of criminality upon the prior conduct."[35] This is so whether the case is one of common law adjudication or statutory interpretation (although the task being attempted by the court will be different according to which category is involved). But, as Hall points out,[36] "the inevitability of a slight, 'normal' degree of retroactivity in judicial decisions provides no ground for tolerating it in its obvious manifestations." Thus, the issue is the "quality of the adjudication", rather than an absolute compliance with the principle of prospectivity. The crucial question to be asked is whether a particular decision is, "retroactive only in . . . [an] unavoidable way or is it also unexpected and indefensible by reference to the law which had been expressed prior to the conduct in issue?"[37] The European Court of Human Rights has adopted a similar approach. It has accepted that it is consistent with Art.7 of the Convention for a court to clarify the existing elements of a common law offence and to adapt it, "to new circumstances which can reasonably be brought under the original conception of the offence."[38] The key issue is whether the judicial development of the common law is, "consistent with the essence of the offence and could reasonably be foreseen".[39] The fundamental freedom from retroactive criminal offences should, "not be read as outlawing the gradual clarification of the rules of criminal liability through judicial interpretation from case to case".[40]

---

[34] This is not so if the law is developed in a Lord Advocate's Reference, where the decision of the court has no impact upon the immediate case. Compare the observations of Lord Maclean in *HM Advocate v H*, 2002 S.L.T. 1380 at 1381.

[35] Hall, *General Principles of Criminal Law*, 2nd edn, p.61.

[36] Hall, *General Principles of Criminal Law*, 2nd edn, p.61.

[37] Hall, *General Principles of Criminal Law*, 2nd edn, p.61.

[38] *X Ltd and Y v United Kingdom* (1982), case no. 8710/79, para.9. This was a decision of the now-defunct European Commission of Human Rights.

[39] *SW v United Kingdom; CR v United Kingdom* (1996) 21 E.H.R.R. 363 at para.36/34.

[40] *SW v United Kingdom; CR v United Kingdom* (1996) 21 E.H.R.R. 363 at para.36/34. See *HM Advocate v H*, 2002 S.L.T. 1380 at 1381. The essence of these principles is restated in *Streletz v Germany* (2001) 33 E.H.R.R. 31.

On the face of things, the decisions in *S v HM Advocate*[41] **14–11** (removal of the marital rape exemption) and *Khaliq v HM Advocate*[42] ("causing real injury" through supply of glue-sniffing kits) might appear to have been unexpected and thus indefensible in relation to the principle of prospectivity. On the law believed to have been current when each of the accused in these cases performed his deliberate actions, neither of them could have anticipated that his actions would have been criminal (according to the argument). That argument assumes that the prior law applicable to the case was itself precisely expressed. But the prior law applicable to marital rape, for example, was not in fact clearly expressed at all. It had been referred to obliquely by Hume[43] and eroded by the decisions in *HM Advocate v Duffy*[44] and *HM Advocate v Paxton*.[45] The European Court of Human Rights accepted an argument to this effect in deciding that the judicial abrogation of the exception in English law was compatible with Art.7.[46] It is not in the nature of the common law of crimes that its individual proscriptions are expressed with particular precision. Rather, the common law proceeds from a set of principles of a plain, moral nature. From that point of view, it rings hollow for the accused husband in *S v HM Advocate*,[47] for example, to claim that he forced sexual intercourse on his wife because he knew that the criminal law of rape granted immunity to husbands who behaved in that way; or for the accused in *Khaliq v HM Advocate*[48] to claim that he knowingly supplied children with vast quantities of life-threatening substances since he knew the criminal law could not touch him for that sort of thing at all. Naturally, if the accuseds' views of the pre-existing law had been correct, then one would have concluded that the criminal law was grossly defective. Indeed, the European Court of Human Rights has observed that the marital rape exemption was itself inconsistent with fundamental objectives of the Convention, the very essence of which was respect for human dignity and human freedom.[49] The only question then concerns the *method* by which such defects should be rectified. Scots law has to date chosen a method which has sometimes entailed conviction of the person whose conduct highlights the need for change, or, in the language appropriate to common law, clarification or correction[50]; and the persons so convicted, at least in the two cases cited, could hardly claim to be outraged on any moral considerations.

---

[41] *S v HM Advocate*, 1989 S.L.T. 469.
[42] *Khaliq v HM Advocate*, 1984 J.C. 23.
[43] Hume, *Commentaries*, i, 306.
[44] *HM Advocate v Duffy*, 1983 S.L.T. 7.
[45] *HM Advocate v Paxton*, 1984 J.C. 105; see above, para.9–78.
[46] *SW v United Kingdom; CR v United Kingdom* (1996) 21 E.H.R.R. 363.
[47] *S v HM Advocate*, 1989 S.L.T. 469.
[48] *Khaliq v HM Advocate*, 1984 J.C. 23.
[49] *SW v United Kingdom; CR v United Kingdom* (1996) 21 E.H.R.R. 363, para.44/42.
[50] See *HM Advocate v H*, 2002 S.L.T. 1380, per Lord Maclean at 1381.

Certainty

14–12 It would appear, then, that any failure on the part of Scots law to observe the principle of prospectivity is predicated on the basic uncertainty of common law rules. There can be no doubt that there is a degree of uncertainty in the common law. By definition, a common law system is less canonical and certain than one based on legislation. The courts have defined the *actus rei* of a number of offences, such as shameless indecency and breach of the peace, in very broad terms. The objection to uncertain rules of criminal law is, of course, the subsequent inability of persons to be wholly confident that their proposed conduct will not fall foul of the law; and that is an objection which a common law system may find it more difficult to meet. The European Court of Human Rights has held that the law has to be "adequately accessible", by which is meant that citizens, "must be able to have an indication that is adequate in the circumstances of the legal rules applicable to a given case".[51] They must also be able, "to foresee, to a degree that is reasonable in the circumstances, the consequences which a given action may entail".[52] The need to satisfy these requirements could lead one to the conclusion that a common law based system is fundamentally flawed and must be replaced by a code or a collection of statutes. But this conclusion is not inevitable: much depends on the degree of uncertainty, and whether that degree of uncertainty can be tolerated. Much depends also on the extent to which uncertainty is absent from codified or statutory regimes.[53] There are limits to how much uncertainty can be legislated away.[54]

14–13 The common law of crimes in Scotland is by no means uncertain. If it were, it would not have been possible for this book to be written, or for the courts to operate on a daily basis. But there may remain a degree of uncertainty as to the precise boundaries of rape, theft, malicious mischief and indeed any other such crime. It is the acceptability of that degree of uncertainty which is the true issue here. That is not to deny or ignore the very real problem posed in the past by the power of the High Court of Justiciary to declare new crimes[55]; but the exercise of that power would now be unlawful under the Human Rights Act 1998. The declaratory power will not therefore be used in modern circumstances, and it is, in any event, a separable issue. Certainly, in relation to crimes already recognised by the common law, there can be scant sympathy for those who attempt to exploit "blurred edges" for their own advantage—if that does, indeed, happen. In reality, it seems that

---

[51] *Sunday Times v United Kingdom* (1979) 2 E.H.R.R. 245 at para.49.
[52] *Sunday Times v United Kingdom* (1979) 2 E.H.R.R. 245 at para.49.
[53] See A. Cadoppi, "*Nulla Poena Sine Lege* and Scots Criminal Law", 1998 J.R. 73 at 81–85.
[54] See, generally, W. Brugger, "Concretization of Law and Statutory Interpretation" (1996) 11 *Tul. Eur. & Civ. L.F.* 207.
[55] See, further, the account of the declaratory power of the High Court in Ch.2.

few people ever take steps to ascertain whether or not their proposed conduct would definitely constitute a crime. Even if they did take such steps, they would still find a degree of uncertainty in a statute or code based system of criminal law. The argument that, because of its statutory basis, English criminal law is more predictable and stable than its Scottish counterpart would be difficult to sustain. The English Theft Act 1968, for example, has attracted a considerable body of interpretative case law, and, without access to those cases, the exact extent of what is forbidden cannot properly be appreciated. The English courts also seem on occasion to reach decisions which are difficult to reconcile with the intention of Parliament,[56] which rather undermines the claim of predictability of meaning for statute law. That body of case law is also constantly expanding. This is true also of offences found within the Road Traffic Acts, and indeed any other enactments which flow from Parliament. What matters to individuals, it seems, is that they should be able to have a fairly good outline of what the law is and what is expected of them; and it is on that sort of basis that most people are able to avoid criminality fairly successfully in the course of their daily business. From that argument of pragmatism, rather than principle, then, it does not greatly matter on what basis (judicial or legislative) the criminal law rests. A code may make the criminal law more accessible to those who work within the criminal justice system, but this is not the same thing as making the law available to the general public. To that end, a much more radical approach would be necessary, with a code drafted in everyday language and with simple proscriptions.[57] If there is a need to make the criminal law more understandable to the public, the solution may not lie in a document written by lawyers for other lawyers.[58] Codification is far from being a guarantor of an accessible criminal law.

Effectiveness and fairness

The effectiveness of the criminal law is only partly determined by **14–14** the way in which crimes are defined or brought into existence. It is rather a function of the whole of the criminal justice system in question. Thus, where flexible, common law methods define crimes and their extent, the system of criminal law can still be effective and fair provided that flexibility extends to the prosecutor and to the judge. In Scotland, prosecutors are trusted to proceed only

---

[56] See, e.g. the decisions of the House of Lords in *Lawrence v Metropolitan Police Commissioner* [1972] A.C. 626; *DPP v Gomez* [1993] A.C. 442; *R. v Hinks* [2001] 2 A.C. 241.

[57] See, generally, P.H. Robinson, *Structure and Function in Criminal Law* (Oxford: Clarendon Press, 1997).

[58] There is an argument that this is to make the law more accessible to the public, via the indirect route of consultation with a lawyer. See Austin, *Lectures on Jurisprudence or The Philosophy of Positive Law*, p.327.

where they perceive a need to do so in the public interest. Judges too are trusted in the same public interest to ensure that charges which come before them on complaint or indictment answer properly to the moral principles embedded in the common law. These public trusts reposed in prosecutors and judges amount to checks and balances to ensure that the Scottish criminal justice system operates fairly and effectively. That criminal justice system may not secure absolute compliance with all desirable principles of abstract criminal law, but, in the real world, compromises probably have to be made if the system is to function at all. And the Scottish system does seem to work, and to enjoy a high level of public confidence.

LAW REFORM

14–15 There is no system of criminal law, however, which could not benefit from frequent scrutiny and re-appraisal.[59] Whilst it is true that the Scottish system is gradually re-appraised by judges of the High Court, the weakness of that method lies in the random way in which that service is performed. It can only be done on a case by case basis, and is thus dependent to a large extent on matters of pure chance. Leaving to one side the judiciary's suitability to perform this function, an accusatorial criminal appeal court may not be the best forum in which to consider the wider policy issues involved in the development of the criminal law. The provision of a systematic re-appraisal programme would be better, such as has been mounted, in effect, by the Scottish Law Commission in relation to the civil law. Whilst it is true that matters affecting the criminal law have from time to time been referred to that Commission, these have been *ad hoc* and rather limited in scope. There is, therefore, a good case to be made for more active appraisal. The Scottish Parliament should be prepared to play a key role. The Commission's "Report on Rape and Other Sexual Offences",[60] which includes draft legislation, provides a good example of what a thorough review can achieve.

14–16 The desirability or otherwise of restating the common law in statutory form, as proposed by the authors of the (unofficial) Draft Criminal Code, remains an open question. There is no reason why the common law cannot reflect the values of prospectivity and certainty. Indeed, this is a requirement of the human rights regime prevailing under the Human Rights Act 1998 and the Scotland Act 1998. The European Court of Human Rights has accepted that, "rules of common law or other customary law may provide a

---

[59] See, generally, C.H.W. Gane, "Criminal Law Reform in Scotland" (1998) 3 S.L.P.Q. 101 (noting that this article is rather more "reformist" than the current text).

[60] Scottish Law Commission, "Report on Rape and Other Sexual Offences", Scot. Law Com. No.209 (December, 2007).

sufficient legal basis".[61] Provided that the common law meets the qualitative standards of accessibility and foreseeability,[62] it can be certain enough under the European Convention on Human Rights. What reliance upon the common law can never satisfy, of course, is the political argument that Parliament is the only legitimate institution to articulate and develop the criminal law. If the argument from the separation of powers is felt to be decisive, the judiciary should certainly be participating much less in the development of legal doctrine.[63] This does not, however, provide a conclusive argument for codification. There is no reason why the Scottish Parliament could not pass statutes to reform or consolidate aspects of the criminal law, without seeking codification. This would be incremental change, in contrast to the disruptive change represented by codification.[64] It may be that reform by instalments is more realistic than comprehensive codification (given the constraints on the time of parliamentarians).[65]

---

[61] *Gay News Ltd v United Kingdom* (1983) 5 E.H.R.R. 123 at para.6. See to the same effect *Wingrove v United Kingdom* (1997) 24 E.H.R.R. 1; *Steel v United Kingdom* (1999) 28 E.H.R.R. 603.

[62] See *Sunday Times v United Kingdom* (1979) 2 E.H.R.R. 245 at para.9.

[63] Compare the argument to this effect made by the accused in *HM Advocate v H*, 2002 S.L.T. 1380.

[64] These terms are used in a descriptive sense. The outcome of disruptive change can be beneficial.

[65] A. Eser, "Major Stages of Criminal Law Reform in Germany" (1996) 30 *Israel L.R.* 28 at p.33. An example may be provided by the Scottish Law Commission, "Report on Rape and Other Sexual Offences", Scot Law Com. No.209 (December, 2007), if legislative activity follows.

APPENDIX A

SELECT BIBLIOGRAPHY OF SCOTS CRIMINAL LAW

1. Works accorded authoritative status

Alison, Archibald J., *Principles and Practice of the Criminal Law of Scotland*, 2 Vols (Edinburgh: Wm Blackwood 1832–1833; Edinburgh: Law Society of Scotland/Butterworths, reprinted 1989).

Hume, D., *Commentaries on the Law of Scotland Respecting Crimes*, edited by B.R. Bell, 4th edn, 2 Vols (Edinburgh: Bell & Bradfute, 1844 (with Bell's Notes); Edinburgh: Law Society of Scotland, reprinted 1986).

Macdonald, J.H.A., *A Practical Treatise on the Criminal Law of Scotland*, edited by J. Walker and D.J. Stevenson, 5th edn (Edinburgh: W. Green, 1948, reprinted 1986).

2. General Texts

Anderson, A.M., *The Criminal Law of Scotland*, 2nd edn (Edinburgh: Bell & Bradfute, 1904).

Burnett, J., *A Treatise on Various Branches of the Criminal Law of Scotland* (Edinburgh: printed by George Ramsay and Co for Archibald Constable and Co, 1811).

Gordon, G.H., *The Criminal Law of Scotland*, 3rd edn, 2 Vols (Edinburgh: W. Green 2000–2001), together with the *Third Edition Supplement* (Edinburgh: W. Green, 2005).

Mackenzie, Sir George., *The Laws and Customs of Scotland in Matters Criminal*, 1st edn (Edinburgh: 1678; facs. ed., The Law Book Exchange Ltd: Clark, New Jersey, 2005), 2nd edn (Edinburgh: 1699).

Smith, T.B., *A Short Commentary on the Law of Scotland*, (Edinburgh, W. Green, 1962), particularly Chs 5–7.

Stair Memorial Encyclopaedia, *The Laws of Scotland* (Edinburgh: Butterworths, 1995; reissue, LexisNexis, 2005), Vol.7, s.v. "Criminal Law".

3. Texts on Particular Subjects

Chalmers, J. and Leverick, F., *Criminal Defences and Pleas in Bar of Trial* (Edinburgh: SULI/W. Green, 2006).

Davidson, F.P., *Evidence* (Edinburgh: SULI/W. Green, 2007)

Farmer, L., *Criminal Law, Tradition and Legal Order: Crime and the Genius of Scots Law, 1747 to the Present* (Cambridge: Cambridge University Press, 1997).

415

Ferguson, P.W., *Crimes Against the Person*, 2nd edn (Edinburgh: Butterworths,1998).

Gane, C.H.W., *Sexual Offences* (Edinburgh: Butterworths, 1992).

Sentencing Practice (Edinburgh: W. Green).

Raitt, F., *Evidence*, 3rd edn (Edinburgh: W. Green, 2001).

Renton and Brown's Criminal Procedure According to the Law of Scotland, 6th edn (Edinburgh: W. Green).

Renton and Brown's Statutory Offences (Edinburgh: W. Green).

Ross, M.L. with Chalmers, J., *Walker and Walker on Evidence*, 2nd edn (Edinburgh: T & T Clark, 2000).

Shiels, R.S., *Offensive Weapons*, 2nd edn (Edinburgh: W. Green, 1996).

Wheatley, J., *Road Traffic Law in Scotland*, 4th edn by Andrew Brown (Edinburgh: Tottel, 2007).

4. *Case Books* (Excluding standard case report volumes)

Gane, C.H.W., Stoddart, C.N. and Chalmers, J., *A Casebook on Scottish Criminal Law*, 3rd edn (Edinburgh: W. Green, 2001).

Sheldon, D., *Evidence: Cases and Materials*, 2nd edn (Edinburgh: W. Green, 2002).

CRIMINAL LAW CASE REPORTS

19th c. Advocates	*Scottish Law Reported* (part)	*Session Cases* (part)	*Scots Law Times* (part)	*Scottish Criminal Case Reports*	*Green's Weekly Digest* (part)
P. Shaw (1819–31)					
Syme (1826–29)					
1–2 Swinton (1835–41)					
1–2 Broun (1842–45)					
Arkley (1846–48)					
J. Shaw (1848–52)					
1–5 Irvine (1852–67)					
1–5 Couper (1868–85)	S.L.R. Vol 1 (1865)	1 Rettie (J.), 1873			
1–3 White (1885–93)					
1–7 Adam (1893–1916)		1 Fraser (J), 1898	S.L.T. Vol 1 (1893)		
		S.C.(J) 1907–16			
		J.C.— 1917			
	Vol 61 (1924)				
				S.C.C.R. Supplement (1950–1980)	
		(1950)	(1950)		
				S.C.C.R. 1981	
		(1981)	(1981)		
					G.W.D. –1986
		(1986)	(1986)	(1986)	
		to date	to date	to date	to date

417

Notes

1. *Session Cases* include (in the "P.C." section—from the year
   2000 onwards) relevant cases on "devolution issues" decided
   by the Judicial Committee of the Privy Council. *Scots Law
   Times Reports* and *Scottish Criminal Case Reports* carry such
   relevant Privy Council cases as part of their normal stock.
   (When the relevant provisions of the Constitutional Reform
   Act 2005 come into force, cases on "devolution issues" will be
   heard by the Supreme Court of the United Kingdom: see
   above, para.2–03, fn.4. An appropriate change will then have
   to be made to the way in which the standard reports are set out
   and, in relation to *Session Cases*, are referred to.)

2. From January 2008, *Scottish Criminal Law* has been published
   by W. Green. This monthly periodical contains inter alia
   articles on Scots criminal law and reports of Scots criminal
   cases (with commentaries). The general editor is Sheriff T.
   Welsh, Q.C.; a pilot issue was published in October 2007.

3. The same case may be found in more than one set of reports.
   It is traditional to regard a *Session Cases* version as superior;
   but in practice, modern sets of reports tend to be equally
   reliable. The S.C.C.R. series has the advantage of having
   commentaries written by Sir Gerald Gordon. *Green's Weekly
   Digest* contains short summaries of cases—not all of which will
   eventually be reported in full.

4. Reports of cases decided by the European Court of Human
   Rights may be found most conveniently in the series known as
   the *European Human Rights Reports* from 1979 to date: the
   bare reports, including the most modern ones, may be located
   at the following internet address:

   http://www.echr.coe.int/ECHR/ [accessed March 13, 2008].

5. Bare opinions in the most modern High Court of Justiciary
   cases may be located at the following internet address:

   http://www.scotcourts.gov.uk/opinionsApp/supreme.asp [accessed
   March 13, 2008].

APPENDIX C

THE STANDARD SCALE OF FINES

Almost all statutory criminal offences triable by summary procedure refer for their maximum fines to the standard scale. This was introduced by the Criminal Justice Act 1982 (c.48) which, by virtue of s.54, added s.289G to the now repealed Criminal Procedure (Scotland) Act 1975 (c.21). That Act of 1982, by s.53(a), also amended s.289D of the 1975 Act such that by new subss.289D(1) and (1A), the Secretary of State for Scotland might alter the various sums appearing on the standard scale if a change in the value of money seemed to necessitate this. In fact, the present scale values were set by Parliament itself, under s.17(1) of the Criminal Justice Act 1991 (c.53) but now appear in the Criminal Procedure (Scotland) Act 1995 (c.46) at s.225(2) for offences triable only by summary procedure, and, of course, remain alterable by the Secretary of State or Scottish Ministers (see the Scotland Act 1998 (c.46) s.53) in terms of the 1995 Act, s.225(4). Those current scale values are as follows:

Level 1	£200
Level 2	£500
Level 3	£1000
Level 4	£2500
Level 5	£5000

Where, however, a statutory offence is triable either on indictment or summary complaint, *and* the maximum fine on summary conviction is specified as one of level 5 on the standard scale, this is now to be read as a reference to the "statutory maximum" (see the Criminal Proceedings etc. (Reform) (Scotland) Act 2007 (asp 6) s.47, and below, the "statutory maximum").

THE PRESCRIBED SUM

Many statutory criminal offences refer to the "prescribed sum" as their maximum available fine. That term was introduced by the Criminal Law Act 1977 (c.45) s.63, Sch.11 para.5, which inserted s.289B into the Criminal Procedure (Scotland) Act 1975 (c.21). That provision is now repealed; and the present value of the prescribed sum can be found in s.225(8) of the Criminal Procedure (Scotland) Act 1995 (c.46), as amended by s.48 of the Criminal Proceedings etc. (Reform) (Scotland) Act 2007 (asp 6). The value, shown below, is alterable by the Secretary of State or Scottish

Ministers (see the Scotland Act 1998 (c.46) s.53) in the same way indicated above for levels on the standard scale.

Prescribed sum £10,000

THE STATUTORY MAXIMUM

The maximum fine for some statutory offences is expressed as "the statutory maximum". In Scotland this is to be taken as a reference to the "prescribed sum" (see above) by virtue of the Interpretation Act 1978 (c.30) Sch.1 (definition of inter alia the statutory maximum—as inserted by the Criminal Justice Act 1988 (c.33) Sch.15 para.58(b)), as amended by the Criminal Procedure (Consequential Provisions) (Scotland) Act 1995 (c.40) Sch.4 para.17(b).

APPENDIX D

SCOTTISH CRIMINAL COURTS

1. District or J.P. Courts

In 1975 (under the District Courts (Scotland) Act 1975 (c.20)) the older Burgh, Justice of the Peace and other minor courts were replaced by "District Courts": these are (as were the courts they replaced) local criminal courts with limited jurisdiction—both territorially and by crime. Under particular provisions of Pt 4 of the Criminal Proceedings etc. (Reform) (Scotland) Act 2007 (asp 6), existing district courts are eventually to be themselves replaced by "Justice of the Peace Courts" (to be known as "J.P. Courts") according to a timetable drawn up by the Scottish Ministers (see the 2007 Act ss.59, 64, and the explanatory notes relative thereto). It is intended that there will be a phased introduction of J.P. courts, and that both types of court will thus exist simultaneously, for a time at least (see the 2007 Act s.64). As the jurisdiction of the two courts will be similar, it is in general unnecessary to consider each separately here. The judges of these courts are (and will be) called "Justices of the Peace", or J.P.s for short (see the 1975 Act s.9, as amended by the Bail, Judicial Appointments etc. (Scotland) Act 2000 (asp 9) ss.8, 9(2) and Sch.1 para.2(1), and the 2007 Act ss.59(9), 67); they are usually, although not necessarily (see, e.g. the 2007 Act s.72), non-legally qualified but are (and will) always be assisted by legally qualified clerks (see the 1975 Act s.18; the 2007 Act s.63(3)–(5)). Procedure is always summary, i.e. on complaint, and non-jury if matters proceed to trial. In relation to such common law crimes as can be heard in these courts, maximum powers of punishment extend to imprisonment for 60 days or a fine not exceeding level 4 on the standard scale: see the Criminal Procedure (Scotland) Act 1995 s.7(4), (6), (8)–as amended by the 2007 Act Sch.1 para.9; see also above, Appendix C. Statutory offences, i.e. those which are triable by summary procedure, are punishable according to maxima similar to those which pertain to common law crimes, unless the enactment in question specifically allows a wider or different range (see the 1995 Act s.7(3),(7)—as also amended by the 2007 Act Sch.1 para.9).[1] J.P.s have important roles to perform in the granting of

---

[1] It should be noted that the Scottish Ministers may by SSI modify the maximum powers of J.P. courts relative to common law crimes or statutory offences, but not so as to exceed six months in prison or a fine of level 5 on the standard scale: 2007 Act s.46.

preliminary and incidental warrants. Where a stipendiary magistrate is appointed (see the 1975 Act s.5; the 2007 Act s.74) and he presides in a district court or a J.P. court, he has the enhanced jurisdiction and powers which a sheriff enjoys in a summary sheriff court (see below, "2"; and see the 1975 Act s.5 and the 1995 Act s.7(5), as amended by the 2007 Act Sch.1 para.9). The proceedings of district (or J.P.) courts are never reported (except sometimes in the press). Appeal lies only to the Scottish Court of Criminal Appeal.

2. Sheriff Courts

Founded probably in the twelfth century, these are local courts (with both civil and criminal law functions). They have limited territorial jurisdiction but extensive jurisdiction by crime. Of the commonly encountered common law crimes, only murders and rapes cannot be dealt with in these courts (see the Criminal Procedure (Scotland) Act 1995 (c.46) s.3(6)). Judges are called sheriffs of various descriptions, e.g. sheriff principal, floating sheriff, honorary sheriff, but all are of equal authority in criminal proceedings. With the exception of honorary sheriffs, they must be legally qualified and experienced in practice as either advocates or solicitors. Procedure may be either summary or on indictment, i.e. non-jury or jury if matters proceed to trial. In relation to common law crimes, Scottish prosecutors decide whether an offence merits jury trial or not. The choice exercised determines the maximum punishment available, i.e. in a solemn or indictment case, five years in prison (or more if the sheriff chooses to remit for sentence to the High Court: see the Criminal Procedure (Scotland) Act 1995 ss.3(3),[2] 195,[3] 219(8)[4]) and/or a fine of any amount; in a summary case, 12 months (see the Criminal Procedure (Scotland) Act 1995 s.5(2)(a), (d)[5]) *or* a fine not exceeding the prescribed sum: see above, Appendix C. Statutory offences (triable summarily, either way, or on indictment only) may be punished according to the maximum laid down by the enactment in question (but if the maximum laid down is more than five years in prison, a sheriff's powers are restricted to five years (the Criminal Procedure (Scotland) Act 1995 s.3(4), (4A),[6] (5))—though, once again, he might choose to remit for sentence to the High Court. Proceedings before sheriff courts are occasionally reported (in S.C.C.R. or in the Sh.Ct part of S.L.T.). Appeals of whatever nature may be taken only to the Scottish Court of Criminal Appeal.

---

[2] As amended by s.13(1)(a) of the Crime and Punishment (Scotland) Act 1997; this amending provision was brought into force on May 1, 2004 by virtue of the Crime and Punishment (Scotland) Act 1997 (Commencement No. 6 and Savings) Order 2004 (SSI 2004/176) art.2: *cf. McGhee v HM Advocate*, 2006 S.C.C.R. 712.

[3] As amended by the Crime and Punishment (Scotland) Act 1997 s. 13(3), and the Criminal Justice (Scotland) Act 2003 (asp 7) Sch.1 para.2(5)—noting that s.210E of the Criminal Procedure (Scotland) Act 1995, referred to in para.2(5), was inserted by s.1 of the 2003 Act.

[4] As amended by the Proceeds of Crime Act 2002 (c.29) Sched.11 para.29(4).

[5] Criminal Procedure (Scotland) Act 1995 s.5(2)(d) is amended by the Criminal Proceedings etc. (Reform) (Scotland) Act 2007 (asp 6) s.43.

[6] Criminal Procedure (Scotland) Act 1995 s.3(4) is amended, and s.3(4A) is inserted, by virtue of s.13(1)(b) and (c) of the Crime and Punishment (Scotland) Act 1997; and s.13(1)(b) and (c) came into force on May 1, 2004: see the Crime and Punishment (Scotland) Act 1997 (Commencement No. 6 and Savings) Order 2004 (SSI 2004/176) art.2.

3. High Courts of Justiciary

Founded as the court of the Justiciar in the twelfth century, a modern High Court consists (normally) of one judge. Such a court has territorial jurisdiction throughout Scotland, and can deal with all common law offences (and indeed is the only court competent to conduct rape and murder trials—see the Criminal Procedure (Scotland) Act 1995 (c. 46) s.3(6)) in addition to all statutory offences (other than those designated as "summary procedure" only). Judges (who are said to belong to the High Court, considered as a "college") are professional lawyers of great experience and are called "Lords Commissioners of Justiciary". (They are also the judges of the civil law court known as the Court of Session.) The effective president is titled "the Lord Justice-General", and the vice-president has the title of "Lord Justice-Clerk". Procedure is always solemn, i.e. involving a jury if matters proceed to trial. Maximum powers of punishment extend to life in prison and/or a fine of any amount (for common law crimes), or to the maximum laid down in the enactment in question (in the case of statutory crimes). Proceedings are quite regularly reported (in S.L.T., J.C., S.C.C.R. and G.W.D.: see above, Appendix B), and appeals of whatsoever nature lie to the Scottish Court of Criminal Appeal. Difficult matters arising during a trial may be referred (by a process called "certification") to a larger body of High Court judges.

4. The Appeal Court

The Scottish Court of Criminal Appeal (to give it a title which is increasingly in use) was founded in 1926 and consists of a minimum of two or three judges of the High Court (considered as a "college" of all High Court judges): see the Criminal Procedure (Scotland) Act 1995 (c.46) ss.103(1)–(4), 173.[7] All appeals from all lower courts are dealt with by such a bench of judges (which is called a "full bench" if more than three are present—although the exact number comprising such a full bench has always in modern times been an uneven one). Decisions are by a simple majority (where that is possible) of those present, and such decisions are final unless a bench of two judges cannot agree (see the Criminal Procedure (Scotland) Act 1995 (c.46) ss.103(3), 173(2)).[8] There is *no* further appeal to (say) the English House of Lords.[9] (Individual petition to the European Court of Human Rights is, however, recognised by the United Kingdom.)

---

[7] As amended by the Protection of Children (Scotland) Act 2003 (asp 5) s.16(6), and the Protection of Vulnerable Groups (Scotland) Act 2007 (asp 14) Sch.4 para.20.
[8] As amended by the Protection of Children (Scotland) Act 2003 (asp 5) s.16(6), and the Protection of Vulnerable Groups (Scotland) Act 2007 (asp 14) Sch.4 para.20.
[9] See above, para.2–13 of the main text for "Devolution Issues" and references or appeals to the Judicial Committee of the Privy Council.

5. *Nobile Officium Court*

This court consists of a minimum of three judges of the High Court (considered as a "college" of all High Court judges). It may provide a solution on an equitable basis where petitioned in relation to a matter of injustice which is truly unexpected and unforseeable and where the law provides no alternative remedy. See above, paras 2–64 and 2–65 of the main text for further information on the *nobile officium*.

INDEX

Abduction
generally, 9–02
Abortion
generally, 9–35
Absolute liability
and see **Strict liability**
generally, 13–13
Accident
introduction, 8–36
objective test, 8–37
recklessness, and, 8–38
self-defence, and, 8–39
Accusatorial procedure
generally, 2–52—2–53
Acquittal
actual offender, of
absence of mens rea, in,
7–31—7–35
generally, 7–28—7–29
joint principal, of, 7–30
Acting in concert
and see **Art and part guilt**
generally, 7–03
Acts of innocent agent
academic view, 4–03
generally, 4–15—4–16
Actual knowledge
art and part guilty, and, 7–08
Actus reus
assault, and, 9–05—9–11
attempts, and, 6–13—6–14
breach of the peace, and,
12–12—12–14
causation, 3–06
conduct crimes, 3–05
crimes against property, and
culpable and reckless fire-raising,
11–35
malicious mischief, 11–13
riotous and wilful mischief, 11–11
wilful fire-raising, 11–30
crimes against the person, and
assault, 9–05—9–11
culpable homicide, 9–52
murder, 9–43
crimes of dishonesty, and
embezzlement, 10–40—10–42
fraud, 10–68—10–77
reset, 10–54
robbery, 10–47—10–50
theft, 10–03
culpable homicide, and, 9–52

Actus reus—*cont.*
culpable and reckless fire-raising,
and, 11–35
embezzlement, and, 10–40—10–42
fraud, and, 10–68—10–77
introduction, 3–01—3–02
malicious mischief, and, 11–13
meaning, 3–03—3–04
mobbing, and, 12–03—12–08
murder, and, 9–43
omissions
duty to act, 3–10
generally, 3–13
introduction, 3–09
limiting harm caused by
dangerous act, 3–11—3–12
overt acts, 3–08
public indecency, and, 12–20
public order offences, and
breach of the peace,
12–12—12–14
mobbing, 12–03—12–08
reset, and, 10–54
result crimes, 3–05
riotous and wilful mischief, and,
11–11
robbery, and, 10–47—10–50
state of affairs, 3–15
theft, and, 10–03
types, 3–07—3–15
wilful fire-raising, and, 11–30
Administration of noxious substances
generally, 9–29
Adversarial procedure
generally, 2–54
Aggravated assault
generally, 9–17
Aggravated trespass
generally, 11–06
Aggravations
housebreaking, 10–31—10–33
housebreaking with intent to steal,
10–35
introduction, 10–30
opening lockfast places, 10–34
Aider
art and part guilt, and, 7–05
Alcohol
voluntary acts, and, 4–25
Alibi
special defences, and, 8–09

425

432   *Index*